# World Prehistory

## TWO MILLION YEARS OF HUMAN LIFE

PETER N. PEREGRINE
*Lawrence University*

Prentice Hall

*Upper Saddle River, New Jersey 07458*

*Library of Congress Cataloging-in-Publication Data*

Peregrine, Peter N. (Peter Neal)
    World prehistory: two million years of human life/Peter N. Peregrine.
        p. cm.
    Includes bibliographical references and index.
    ISBN 0-13-028172-7 (alk. paper)
    1. Prehistoric peoples. 2. Archaeology—Research. 3. Antiquities, Prehistoric. I. Title.

GN720 .P47 2003
930—dc21                                                    2002023990

*AVP/Publisher:* Nancy Roberts
*Managing Editor:* Sharon Chambliss
*VP, Director of Production and Manufacturing:* Barbara Kittle
*Editorial/Production Supervision:* Rob DeGeorge
*Copyeditor:* Sylvia Moore
*Prepress and Manufacturing Manager:* Nick Sklitsis
*Prepress and Manufacturing Buyer:* Ben Smith
*Creative Design Director:* Leslie Osher
*Interior Design:* Anne DeMarinis
*Cover Design:* Anne DeMarinis
*Electronic Art Creation:* Mirella Signoretto, Steve Mannion, Carto-Graphics (Maps)
*AVP/Director of Marketing:* Beth Mejia
*Senior Marketing Manager:* Amy Speckman
*Photo Researcher:* Sheila Norman
*Image Permission Coordinator:* Nancy Seise
*Cover Image Specialist:* Karen Sanatar
*Interior Image Specialist:* Beth Brenzel
*Manager, Rights and Permissions:* Zina Arabia
*Director, Image Resource Center:* Melinda Reo
*Cover Art:* Neil Beer/Getty Images

This book was set in 10/12 Garamond by Interactive Composition Corporation
and was printed and bound by Von Hoffmann Press, Inc.
The cover was printed by Phoenix Color Corp.

© 2003 by Pearson Education, Inc.
Upper Saddle River, New Jersey 07458

Printed in the United States of America
10  9  8  7  6  5  4  3  2  1

ISBN 0-13-028172-7

Pearson Education LTD., London
Pearson Education Australia PTY, Limited, Sydney
Pearson Education Singapore, Pte. Ltd
Pearson Education North Asia Ltd, Hong Kong
Pearson Education Canada, Ltd., Toronto
Pearson Educación de Mexico, S.A. de C.V.
Pearson Education—Japan, Tokyo
Pearson Education Malaysia, Pte. Ltd
Pearson Education, Upper Saddle River, New Jersey

## brief contents

# Contents

# Preface

The biggest challenge in writing a textbook for an introductory course in world prehistory is deciding what to cover. The ancient civilizations of Egypt, Mesopotamia, China, India, Mexico, and the Andes seem obvious choices, but they represent only a tiny portion of humanity's past. While we may know more about the urban civilizations who left behind massive pyramids and enduring works of art, most people did not live in these civilizations, and even among those who did only a small number had access to the impressive architecture and exotic goods upon which archaeologists often focus.

Without an understanding of the full range of variation in the way people lived in the past we can never hope to understand our past and ourselves. It would be as if we attempted to understand what it meant to be a person in the United States today by looking only at Beverly Hills. We need to study not only the wealthy and powerful, but also the ordinary and mundane. We need to recognize that over the two million years of humanity's existence most people have lived rather humble lives, just like most of us do. By focusing on the exotic we lose sight of the ordinary, and the ordinary is important. Prehistory, if we are true to the whole panorama of human life that has gone before us, has more to do with ordinary people living in ordinary places than with kings and priests living in Sumer or Thebes.

I wrote this book to provide a *complete* overview of world prehistory—not one focused purely on the "big" areas of research like Egypt, Peru, Mexico, and Mesopotamia, but one that provides balanced coverage of the entire world. I wanted not only to describe what prehistoric humans and their cultures were like but also to explain *why* they got to be that way, in all their variety. Doing so meant that I had to examine the whole range of cultures in the past, not just the high civilizations or the areas where the most field research has been done. I have been able to accomplish this in part because of the project I have been working on for the past six years—the nine volume *Encyclopedia of Prehistory* (Kluwer Academic/Plenum Publishers, 2001–2002). The *Encyclopedia of Prehistory* offers basic information on all the prehistoric cultures of the world. Its entries were written by over 200 scholars from more than 20 nations, and it has been a fundamental source of information for this textbook.

## HIGHLIGHTS OF THE SECTIONS

### Part I. Introduction

The first part of the book introduces the practice of archaeology. There are three chapters. In Chapter 1, Why Study the Past?, I discuss what is special and distinctive about archaeology and why it is an important discipline. In Chapter 2, The Archaeological Record, I explain the four types of materials that make up the archaeological record: artifacts, ecofacts, fossils, and features. Finally, in Chapter 3, The Process of Archaeological Research, I describe the five phases of the archaeological research process: Asking Questions, Building Models, Collecting Data, Analyzing Data, and Presenting Results.

### Part II. The Dawn of Humanity

The second part of the book explores the evolution of humans from our earliest ancestors to the Upper Paleolithic era, when regionally distinct cultures began to appear. There are four chapters in this section. In Chapter 4, The First Humans, I discuss our most ancient direct ancestors, the australopithecines and paranthropoids. In Chapter 5, The Origins of Culture, I discuss what culture is and how it may have evolved. I then discuss the first members of our genus, *Homo*, who are most likely responsible for the early signs of cultural behavior, stone tools. In Chapter 6, The Emergence of Modern Humans, I examine the transition between early *Homo* and modern-looking humans. I give special consideration to the Neandertals and the question of their relationship to modern humans. Finally, in Chapter 7, The Upper Paleolithic World, I consider the cultures of modern humans in the Upper Paleolithic period—roughly 40,000 to 10,000 years ago. I discuss their tools, their economies, and their art—the first art made by humans. I also discuss human colonization of North and South America.

### Part III. Regional Diversification

The eight chapters that comprise the third section of the book share a common focus: the archaeological record of a particular region of the globe. Each also shares a common framework. I begin each chapter with a brief overview of the geography and environment of the region. I then present the archaeological record for the region by considering settlements and other types of sites and their locations. I also examine the economic basis of the societies inhabiting the region and changes over time, with a focus on technology and food-getting. I consider the sociopolitical organization of the region's inhabitants as well, and changes over time. Each chapter ends with a summary that pulls together the information presented in the chapter. The eight chapters are: Chapter 8, The Arctic and Subarctic; Chapter 9, North America; Chapter 10, Middle America; Chapter 11, South America; Chapter 12, Africa; Chapter 13, Europe; Chapter 14, East Asia and Oceania; and Chapter 15, South and Southwest Asia.

## Part IV. Broad Patterns, Big Processes

The three chapters that comprise the fourth and final section of the book are intended to be synthetic. They each use information from the preceding chapters, mainly those in Part III, to test theories about major events and processes in cultural evolution. Chapter 16, The Evolution of Food Production, deals with the domestication of plants and animals. My discussion focuses mainly on the theories explaining why domestication evolved and the consequences of the shift from food collection to food production. Chapter 17, The Rise of Civilization, deals with the rise of centralized political systems, typically called state societies or civilizations. Again, my focus is on the theories that have been offered to explain the evolution of political centralization. Finally, Chapter 18, Trends in World Prehistory, poses a provocative question: Have there been underlying trends in world prehistory? In addressing that question I revisit much of the material covered in the text and provide an active example of why understanding our past is important.

## OTHER FEATURES

### Boxes in Each Chapter

The first fifteen chapters have two box features, each of which focuses on a particular archaeological site. They are intended to provide students with a fuller understanding of the archaeological record and the history of research at important locales. In the last three chapters single box features focus on important archaeologists. These are intended to familiarize students with some of the key figures in the history of archaeology.

### Media Lab

This feature brings to life topics that are related to each chapter. Each topic has been carefully chosen to pique students' interest and to further their knowledge of world prehistory. All of the necessary information is included at the end of each chapter; the static becomes dynamic once students access the *Companion Website*™ for animations or videos to illustrate the topic. As a summation, students are asked to communicate the results of their explorations.

### Summaries

In addition to an outline provided at the beginning of each chapter, I provide a synthesis at the end of each chapter that will help the student contextualize the major concepts and findings I discuss.

### Discussion Questions, Essay Questions, and Research Projects

I also provide seven questions at the end of each chapter. Discussion questions stimulate thinking about the implications of the chapter. Essay questions require students to critically examine the text or questions raised by it. Research projects require students to go beyond the text and find additional information to answer a question relevant to topics raised in the text.

### Glossary

In each chapter I identify new terms in boldface type and define them in the margin. A complete Glossary is provided at the back of the book to review all terms in the book and serve as a convenient reference for students.

### Archaeological Sites and Traditions

In each chapter, I also identify archaeological sites and traditions in boldface type and list them in the margin, along with their location and time period. This provides a convenient way for students to navigate through the book and to keep track of the places and periods being discussed.

### Bibliography

I believe firmly in the importance of documentation to tell readers what my descriptions and conclusion are based upon, and I have provided a list of sources at the end of each chapter. I also hope students will use this text as a resource both for research and essay questions and for pursuit of their own interests in world prehistory. For this reason I offer a comprehensive

Bibliography at the end of the book listing those sources I relied upon and found most useful.

## SUPPLEMENTS

**INSTRUCTOR'S RESOURCE AND TESTING MANUAL** For each chapter in the text, this manual provides a detailed chapter outline, discussion questions, classroom activities, and additional resources. The test bank includes multiple choice and essay questions for each chapter.

**PRENTICE HALL TEST MANAGER** This computerized software allows instructors to create their own personalized exams, to edit any or all test questions, and to add new questions. Other special features of this program, which is available for Windows and Macintosh, include random generation of an item set, creation of alternate versions of the same test, scrambling question sequence, and test preview before printing.

**COMPANION WEBSITE™** In tandem with the text, students can now take full advantage of the World Wide Web to enrich their study of world prehistory through the Peregrine *Companion Website*™. This resource correlates the text with related material available on the Internet. Features include chapter objectives, study questions, research projects, animations, and links to additional material that can reinforce and enhance the content of each chapter.
Address: www.prenhall.com/peregrine

**EVALUATING ONLINE RESOURCES, ANTHROPOLOGY, 2003** This guide provides a brief introduction to navigating the Internet and encourages students to be critical consumers of online resources. References related specifically to the discipline of anthropology are included. Free when packaged with any Prentice Hall textbook. Included with the Evaluating Online Resources guide is a free access code for Research Navigator™.

**RESEARCH NAVIGATOR™** Research Navigator™ is the easiest way for students to start a research assignment or research paper. Complete with extensive help on the research process and three exclusive databases of credible and reliable source material, including EBSCO's ContentSelect™ Academic Journal Database, *New York Times* Search by Subject Archive, and "Best of the Web" Link Library. Research Navigator™ helps students quickly and efficiently make the most of their research time.

## ACKNOWLEDGMENTS

I owe an enormous debt of gratitude to Carol R. and Melvin Ember, who trusted me to take on the *Encyclopedia of Prehistory* project and to join them in both revising their wonderful *Anthropology* textbook and in developing the *Physical Anthropology and Archaeology* textbooks, upon which Part II of this text is based. Their unwavering support and insightful advice have been indispensable, and their friendship treasured. I am also most grateful to Richard Blanton, whose instruction and mentoring have continued long after his obligations as professor ended.

I have to thank the people at Prentice Hall for all their help: Nancy Roberts, Publisher for the Social Sciences; Sharon Chambliss, Managing Editor; Rob DeGeorge, for seeing the manuscript through the production process; and Sheila Norman, for photo research.

I want to thank the following for reviewing the text and making suggestions: Charles Bolian, University of New Hampshire; Judith Habicht-Mauche, University of California; Melinda Leach, University of North Dakota; Randall McGuire, Binghamton University; Rachel Mason, University of Alaska, Anchorage; Gregory L. Possehl, University of Pennsylvania; Anne F. Rogers, Western Carolina University; Alan Simmons, University of Nevada, Las Vegas; and R.E. Taylor, University of California, Riverside. Thank you all, named and unnamed, who offered advice.

Finally, a loving thank you to my wife and children, who put up with many late nights and subsequent cranky days.

*—Peter N. Peregrine*

# About the Author

**Peter N. Peregrine** came to anthropology after completing an undergraduate degree in English. He found anthropology's social scientific approach to understanding humans more appealing than the humanistic approach he had learned as an English major. He undertook an ethnohistorical study of the relationship between Jesuit missionaries and Native American peoples for his master's degree, and realized that he needed to study archaeology to understand the cultural interactions that Native Americans had experienced prior to contact with the Jesuits.

While working on his Ph.D. at Purdue University, Peter Peregrine did research on the prehistoric Mississippian cultures of the eastern United States. He found that interactions between groups were common and had been shaping Native American cultures for centuries. Native Americans approached contact with the Jesuits simply as another in a long string of intercultural exchanges. He also found that relatively little research had been done on Native American interactions and decided that comparative research was a good place to begin examining the topic. In 1992, he began to participate in archaeological work in Syria, and has since extended his areas of interest to Africa and East Asia.

Peter Peregrine is currently chair of the anthropology department at Lawrence University in Appleton, Wisconsin. He serves as research associate for the HRAF Collection of Archaeology and is co-editor with Melvin Ember of the *Encyclopedia of Prehistory*. He has published more than fifty papers and is the author of seven books. He continues to do archaeological research and teaches a wide range of anthropology and archaeology courses to undergraduate students.

# The Study of World Prehistory

**Prehistory** refers to the time period in the past that is known to us primarily through the debris left by ancient peoples—the time before written history allows us to know ancient peoples through their own words. We know prehistory only by finding, recovering, and interpreting objects that ancient peoples discarded or lost. Prehistory, in this sense, exists only in the present, in the interpretations we make of the ancient items we find. But these items were left by real people, and prehistory must therefore also be a direct representation of the past, if only we can find the right tools to interpret these items. Prehistory, then, is something of a puzzle that we assemble from ancient material, which may be a large part of the fascination and the fun we have in studying prehistory.

But in being a puzzle, prehistory can also be confusing, even contentious. Indeed, there are some who suggest the word is insulting and implies that nothing happened before written history. To me this seems a serious misinterpretation of prehistory. Most of human life happened before written history, and calling the two million years during which humans spread across the globe and created the diversity of cultures we know today by the term **prehistory** does not imply that nothing was going on. The term *prehistory* simply indicates that we only know that lengthy time period through objects and not through written documents. It is an important distinction to make, because objects and written documents are collected, analyzed, and interpreted through very different means and by scholars trained in very different disciplines.

Scholars who study the physical items left behind by ancient peoples typically call themselves **archaeologists**. While many archaeologists also study physical items left behind by cultures that have also left behind written documents (the Maya, for example, or the peoples of Colonial Williamsburg, as in Figure 1.1), the opposite is not true for many historians or ethnographers. **Historians** are trained to identify and interpret written documents, but few historians are trained to work with other objects from the past. **Ethnographers** are trained to record the life of contemporary peoples, and while many have an interest in the material culture of the peoples they study, most are not trained, as archaeologists are, to systematically examine and discern behavior from them. Prehistory, then, can also be understood as the time period studied almost exclusively by archaeologists.

What makes prehistory difficult for historians or ethnographers to examine? The answer is: the source of information. Archaeological knowledge of the past is

**Prehistory:** the time in the past before written documents allow a good picture of life.

**Archaeologists:** scholars who practice archaeology.

**Historians:** scholars who use texts to describe and understand the past.

**Ethnographers:** scholars who record the behaviors, beliefs, and traditions of living peoples.

FIGURE **1.1**
Archaeologist Lucie Vinciquerra photographs the remains of an eighteenth century feature at Colonial Williamsburg.

FIGURE **1.2**
A student records information
about projectile points found
at the Hell Gap site in
Wyoming. Such information
provides the basis for the
archaeological study of
prehistory through material
culture.

based on the analysis of the relationships between and among the objects that make
up the physical record of the past—what archaeologists call artifacts, ecofacts, fossils, and features. This will be discussed in Chapter 2. These relationships are called
**context,** and archaeologists use the context of artifacts, ecofacts, fossils, and features to reconstruct what happened in the past. Historians use historical records and
sometimes archaeological materials, but their focus is on the analysis of textual data
(that is, written documents), not contextual data (that is, the relationships between
and among objects from the past). And, except for the fairly recent past, textual
data does not supply much information. Similarly, ethnographers use the knowledge
and memory of living peoples, and their focus is on behavior today and memory of
past behaviors, not the physical record of behavior. Again, except for the fairly
recent past, memory (even oral tradition or oral history) does not supply a full
account of life and culture. The methods used by archaeologists are designed to
allow for the study of prehistory—the time period before texts or memory allow
much to be known about life and culture (see Figure 1.2).

## WHY STUDY WORLD PREHISTORY?

Why is world prehistory worthy of study? Why do we want to know about the past?
The most basic answer is that world prehistory is interesting and entertaining. We
share a fascination about the past. Who lived before us? What were they like? What
happened to them? Those questions intrigue us, and it's a worthwhile activity to try
to answer them, if only to satisfy our own interest. In the United States today there
are over 100 archaeological societies, many with several thousand members. Some
200,000 people subscribe to *Archaeology* magazine. We regularly see television

**Context:** the relationships
between and among ancient
objects.

documentaries on prehistory, and there are even several television series devoted to it. The study of world prehistory provides engaging entertainment and is a serious pastime for many thousands of people. But there are, I think, some more important reasons than amusement for studying world prehistory.

"Man . . . hangs on the past: however far or fast he runs, that chain runs with him."
—Friedrich Nietzsche, *The Use and Abuse of History* (1874)

One important reason to study world prehistory is to recognize the contributions and achievements of our predecessors. All of us have inherited the legacy of our ancestors—both the good and the bad—and it is important for us to understand our ancestors' contributions, for several reasons. The first is simply to honor our ancestors. We exist because they did, and it is right to acknowledge that. For those of us whose ancestors colonized the places we now live, we must also reckon with the fact that our homes and schools are built on lands once occupied by indigenous peoples. The study of prehistory helps us understand the contributions and achievements of those indigenous peoples whom our ancestors dispatched or displaced.

World prehistory also provides precedents for the way we do things today. I think Karl Marx put this idea best when he wrote: "Men make their own history, but they do not make it just as they please; they do not make it under circumstances chosen by themselves, but under circumstances directly found, given and transmitted from the past." What we do today is in part based on what we did yesterday. There is very little that is really "new" in any society, just things transformed. It is valuable for us to understand where the things we do today started (i.e., in prehistory), if only to return to that starting place and try again if our transformations have failed or have created unanticipated problems.

Our ties to the past can also be used for political purposes, and it is important for us to understand how the past can be used in political maneuvering. When we re-elect a representative we are using the past, sending a person back to office based on what they did previously. We often use the past conservatively, to argue against change since "that's the way we've always done it." We can use the past to promote change, arguing for a transformation of past practices or for the prevention of previous mistakes. But prehistory can be used for more far-reaching political purposes. A clear example can be found in the Gulf War (1991). Part of Saddam Hussein's claim to Kuwait was that Iraq was the direct inheritor of the Assyrian Empire, an empire that flourished almost 3,000 years ago and which had the area now known as Kuwait within its borders. Many less extreme, yet still politically powerful, claims are made on the basis of archaeological evidence. In the United States, for example, Native American groups have made extensive use of archaeological evidence in pursuing Federal recognition and treaty rights. So, prehistory is also important because it is used as a political tool, and this is why the way in which the past is represented and who gets to represent it can become a contested issue (see the box titled "Nazi Archaeology").

"Those who cannot remember the past are condemned to repeat it."
—George Santayana, *Life of Reason* (1905)

A second reason to study world prehistory is because it offers vital information about experiments in technology, economics, society, and political organization; experiments that more often than not were failures and thus only survive in the archaeological record. If you think about the great civilizations of the past—Pharaonic Egypt, Sumeria, the Inca Empire, to name a few—you'll notice one important commonality: They are all gone. Indeed, most civilizations that have ever existed ultimately collapsed or were conquered. Why? That's a very important question because it seems likely that our civilization will ultimately collapse too if the established pattern continues. One way to hedge against our civilization's downfall

# Nazi Archaeology

It may be difficult to envision how an activity as seemingly apolitical as the study of the ancient past could have a political impact on the present, but one need only look to the most infamous polity of the twentieth century—Nazi Germany— to understand how potent prehistory can be if used (or misused) by those in power. The Nazis had more than simply their authority to promote when they took power in 1933; they also needed to pull together a nation shattered by war, depression, and the punitive Treaty of Versailles. One way they sought to accomplish this feat was to create a mythical German culture (one has to remember that Germany was not unified into a nation until 1898) complete with its own prehistory. The prehistory that the Nazis sought to develop and promote was that northern Europeans—Aryans—established the first European civilizations, spread throughout the continent (in some versions even founding Classical Greece), but were pushed back into the territory of modern Germany by aggressive non-Aryans.

If this sounds far-fetched, it is, but it didn't stop the Nazis from creating eight new chairs in German prehistory in their first two years of power and four major research institutes, as well as providing unprecedented levels of funding for archaeological research. It also didn't stop established archaeologists from climbing aboard and accepting chairs and funding, despite the clear political aims of the Nazi interest in prehistory. Indeed, archaeological research was so important to the Nazis that the infamous SS (an elite branch of the military) had their own

is to understand how and why previous civilizations fell. That answer has to include conquest, because it is always a question why a conqueror succeeds in overthrowing an established civilization—the conqueror's success points either to overwhelming strength or, more likely, to some preexisting weakness in the conquered civilization.

In addition, conquerors or those remaining in a given area following a civilization's collapse often alter or neglect established patterns of life that may offer unique adaptations to that area. For example, the potato was exported to Europe following the Spanish conquest of the Andes in the sixteenth century; unfortunately, the rich diversity of potatoes, each variety adapted to specific environmental conditions, were not exported. Three centuries later Irish civilization nearly collapsed through a potato famine caused by a blight that spread rapidly because of the uniformity of potato varieties being grown in Ireland. Understanding the past adaptation, the diversity of potatoes that helped prevent such a catastrophic crop failure, has taught us how valuable it is to preserve plant varieties, just as the Inca had done five hundred years ago. It's those kinds of lessons a knowledge of world prehistory can provide (see the box on raised field agriculture and Figure 1.3).

"The past is never dead. It's not even past."
—William Faulkner, *Requiem for a Nun* (1951)

A third and perhaps more important reason for studying world prehistory is that it helps us to better understand ourselves. Prehistory, in all honesty, is a rather archaeological research projects. Not only were the SS double lightning bolt insignia taken from an ancient Germanic rune, but the swastika emblem of the Nazis themselves was taken from an ancient Indo-European sun symbol. Under the Nazis the entire prehistory of Europe was rewritten: the Bronze and Pre-Roman Iron Ages became the "Early Germanic Period"; the Roman Iron Age became the "Climax Germanic Period"; even the historic eleventh to thirteenth centuries became the "Germanic Middle Ages."

Why is this important to know? Isn't this all just a myth made up by the Nazis that only lasted as long as they were in power? Well, yes, but while the Nazis were in power the myth had tremendous influence. Consider Poland, created as a modern nation-state in the aftermath of World War I. Poland, under the Nazi myth of prehistory, was an intrusion of aggressive, barbaric Slavs into traditional Aryan country. With a nation believing this myth, it would be easy to promote aggression against Poland or even its conquest, citing as justification the "fact" that Poland was traditional Aryan land and should be part of the new, united Germany. And this, of course, is precisely what happened. Not only did the Nazi version of prehistory promote Germany's attempted conquest of Europe, but it also promoted the Nazi's racist doctrines. Germany, after all, was Aryan under the myth. Slavs, Jews, Gypsies, and others had been "traditional enemies" of the Aryans and should be expelled from Germany or outright killed. Hence prehistory, used as a political tool, can even feed genocide.

SOURCES: Arnold, Bettina, 1990, "The past as propaganda: Totalitarian archaeology in Nazi Germany," *Antiquity* 64:464–478; 1992, "The past as propaganda," *Archaeology* 45(4):30–38.

strange thing. We can never go back to the past (at least until someone creates a time machine), so the past only exists in the present, in our own minds. This does not mean, as some archaeologists have suggested, that a real past doesn't exist, nor does it mean that we can never accurately reconstruct the past. What it does mean is that our reconstructions of the past are always subject to question and revision. One can never go back and examine an event as it occurred. One can only view the results and try to understand them. That's the nature of prehistory.

Since our understanding of prehistory is based on our thoughts, assumptions, insights, and hypotheses in the present, prehistory is as much a product of the present as it is of the past. As Immanuel Wallerstein elegantly explains: "recounting the past is a social act of the present done by men of the present and affecting the social system of the present." This is something we cannot ignore. We can never know prehistory as it truly was, but only the way it exists today in our imagination, given the information we have about it. As Marc Bloch explains: "The past is, by definition, a datum which nothing in the future will change. But the knowledge of the past is something progressive which is constantly transforming and perfecting itself." Our understanding of prehistory, then, is a product both of our knowledge of the past and how we interpret it.

So, why study world prehistory? Because it provides important insights about our society and ourselves. It is a powerful, and sometimes misused, political tool. It offers ideas about how to, and how not to, organize our society, technology, and economy. In addition to all that, world prehistory is inherently interesting. I hope

# Raised Field Agriculture: A Lesson from the Past

Although examples are still, unfortunately, rare, some governments are starting to learn lessons from their prehistoric past. In the region around Lake Titicaca on the Peru-Bolivian border, for example, archaeologists have determined that in pre-Incan and Incan times farmers used "raised" fields for their crops. They dug ditches for irrigation and piled the soil from those ditches into linear mounds on top of which they planted their crops. Wetland plants grew wild in the irrigation ditches, and these were collected annually and spread on top of the raised fields too, acting as fertilizer. The whole system worked beautifully—the irrigation system provided both water and fertilizer, and the raised fields surrounded by water helped to prevent animals and other pests from gaining access to the crops and also provided a hedge against frost damage. When the Spanish took over the region they transformed indigenous agriculture into a Spanish open-field model, and the ancient raised-field systems stopped being used.

Archaeologist Clark Ericson started researching these raised-field systems in 1981, and in 1982 he rebuilt one of the ancient raised fields to see how it worked (see Figure 1.3). It was a remarkable success, and soon the local farmers, with the aid of the Peruvian government, were rebuilding many more raised fields, gaining two to three times greater crop production for their effort. On the Bolivian side of Lake Titicaca, archaeologist Alan Kolata encouraged a local farmer to rebuild a raised-field system in 1987. Again, within a few years more than fifty villages had

FIGURE **1.3**
Modern raised fields in the Bolivian highlands built using ancient techniques rediscovered by archaeologists.

rebuilt ancient raised fields with the assistance of the Bolivian government. Both the Peruvian and Bolivian governments learned that lessons from the past can be of great value today. The ancient peoples of the Titicaca basin developed a highly successful agricultural regime, one that had been lost with the Spanish conquest. With the help of archaeologists, this unique agricultural system is being put back into place.

The Andes is not the only place in South America where ancient agricultural systems are being restored. In the region of the Bolivian Amazon known as the Llanos de Mojos, Clark Ericson has discovered a similar raised-field system. Throughout the historic period the region has been sparsely inhabited and marginal for agriculture—half the year it is a near desert, the other half it is inundated by rainfall and snowmelt from the Andes. But Ericson has shown that until roughly 500 years ago the region had a dense population that supported itself on raised-field agriculture and aquaculture—farming fish in the canals between the fields. Ericson has rebuilt some of these raised fields and canals, just as he did in the Titicaca basin, and has demonstrated that highly productive agriculture and aquaculture are possible in the region. The Bolivian government became interested, and by 1993 several communities were collaborating on a project to rebuild these ancient raised fields. Once again, the lessons of the past are starting to be learned.

SOURCES: Erickson, Clark L., 1988, "Raised field agriculture in the Lake Titicaca Basin," *Expedition* 30 (3):8–16; Mann, Charles C., 2000, "Earthmovers of the Amazon," *Science* 287 (4 February):786–789; Straughan, Baird, 1991, "The secrets of ancient Tiwanaku are benefiting today's Bolivia," *Smithsonian* 21 (February): 38–49.

that answer is good enough to get you interested in learning more about world prehistory, because that's what the rest of this book is all about.

## A BRIEF HISTORY OF PREHISTORY

How did the study of world prehistory begin? Who was the first archaeologist? One common answer is Nabonidus, the last ruler of Babylon. Nabonidus inherited an empire on the brink of collapse and, according to both legend and history, did his very best to push it over the edge. As the empire fell apart around him, Nabonidus apparently sent work parties out to excavate ancient Babylonian sites, in the hope of discovering how his predecessors had managed to hold the empire together. The undertaking was a failure, but it is interesting to note that, if the story of Nabonidus is true, then the study of prehistory was a political act from the very start.

Another individual who is commonly credited with being the first archaeologist is Cyriacus of Ancona, an Italian merchant who lived in the early fifteenth century. He traveled widely in Greece and the eastern Mediterranean, drawing buildings, sculptures, and inscriptions from ancient sites, and, of course, collecting artifacts. As Renaissance scholars began to look toward classical Greece as the fountainhead of Western culture, collecting classical artifacts became a popular pastime, especially for the nobility. By the eighteenth century classical art was the subject of scholarly study, and excavations were undertaken throughout the classical world in order to discover ancient works of art and literature.

FIGURE **1.4**
Drawing of a Hallstatt burials
by Johann Georg Ramsauer
illustrates the wonderful
descriptive detail achieved by
antiquarians.

FIGURE **1.4**
Drawing of a Hallstatt burials by Johann Georg Ramsauer illustrates the wonderful descriptive detail achieved by antiquarians.

The eighteenth century also saw the birth of what is commonly called anti-quarianism—the forerunner of archaeology. **Antiquarians** were scholars who went beyond the simple collection of ancient artifacts and attempted to systematically record and describe ancient monuments and objects, primarily from northern Europe (see Figure 1.4). They also attempted to understand how these ancient monuments and objects may have been used, and to reconstruct ancient cultures. What antiquarians lacked was a good sense of time. They could not easily determine how old an object was because they had few ways to date the object, and most scholars still believed the earth was relatively young—perhaps only 6,000 years old.

By the twentieth century scholars knew that the earth, as well as many ancient monuments and objects, was much older than 6,000 years, but they still had no empirical way to determine precisely how old. Antiquarians, who by this time had begun to develop the methods that we today call **archaeology,** had to rely on texts, artifact similarities, and the relative depth of archaeological deposits to provide estimated dates. Indeed, it was not until the 1950s that techniques were developed that could provide true dates in years before the present for either the age of the earth or for archaeological materials. To be sure, some of the techniques used by antiquarians to estimate age have proven to be uncannily accurate, and many are still used today, but without the ability to check them against more precise methods, antiquarians could only guess at the age of archaeological materials.

The antiquarians also lacked information and theory. They found and were able to describe ancient objects, but they lacked an accepted body of theory to tie those objects to human behavior. It may seem difficult to understand from today's standpoint, but when antiquarians were faced with objects never before encountered, they had a difficult time making sense of what they found. Antiquarians lacked the rich ethnographic and material record that helps archaeologists today interpret their finds. The information and theory the antiquarians needed to link the archaeological record to human behavior had to await the birth of anthropology. **Anthropology** is the comparative and evolutionary study of humans and their cultures. With anthropology to provide both ethnographic information about other cultures and theory to explain how human behaviors leave physical traces, antiquarians were able to move beyond simply cataloguing the record of the past and begin to explain how and why it exists and what it means.

## ARCHAEOLOGY AS ANTHROPOLOGY

In the United States today one can obtain a degree in archaeology at only a handful of universities. To be sure, one can obtain a degree in **classical archaeology,** focusing

**Antiquarians:** eighteenth- and nineteenth-century scholars who were the first to systematically record and describe ancient monuments and objects.

**Archaeology:** a method or set of techniques for collecting and analyzing ancient objects and their contexts.

**Anthropology:** the comparative and evolutionary study of humans and their cultures.

**Classical archaeology:** archaeology focused on the "classical" civilizations of Greece and Rome.

on the "classical" civilizations of Greece and Rome, at a number of universities, and one can also earn degrees that provide sound archaeological training in subjects like Near Eastern languages and civilizations. However, these courses of study tend to focus on areas where there are ancient texts to help interpret the archaeological record. Otherwise, if you are interested in archaeology, your degree will come from an anthropology department, at least in the United States. Why? There are two main reasons. One is the historical situation within which archaeology first developed in the United States; the other is that anthropological archaeology is effective, so even after the historical situation that established archaeology as part of anthropology changed, many archaeologists preferred to remain with and train new students among other anthropologists.

The historical situation in which archaeology developed in the United States reflects the development of anthropology in the United States as a whole, and both were tied closely to the conquest of the continent and the "problem" of Native Americans. It may seem amazing to us today, but some of the first comprehensive scientific excavations in the United States were carried out to determine who built the many mounds that are found throughout eastern North America. Scholars of the day simply did not believe that "Indians" were capable of building the carefully constructed and often astronomically aligned earthen mounds, pyramids, and enclosures that dotted the eastern United States. Of course we know today that Native Americans were (and are) capable of building such "civilized" monuments, and it was Bureau of American Ethnology archaeologist Cyrus Thomas who demonstrated that fact in 1894 through the systematic excavation and analysis of a diverse group of these earthworks. Thomas's work stands as the first example of systematic archaeological research undertaken in the United States (see Figure 1.5), and the first time that the scientific establishment came out with a strong statement that "Indians" were indeed capable of "civilization."

If the atmosphere at this time sounds racist to you, it was, and it was not only Native Americas whom many scholars believed were incapable of "civilization," but also African Americans, Irish Americans, immigrants from Eastern Europe, and others. Anthropology in the United States began within this context, and its first tasks were to counter the widespread racism of the day by demonstrating its flaws and fallacies. The chief architect of that mission was Franz Boas, considered the father of American anthropology. Boasian anthropology had two basic agendas. The

FIGURE **1.5**
A rather fanciful image of a Louisiana mound being excavated in the mid-nineteenth century.

first was to "salvage" as much information about Native American cultures as possible before the onrush of settlers changed them forever. The second was to promote the idea that Native American cultures could only be understood through the framework of historical particularism, and not through the universal evolutionary theory that was often used as a justification for racist thinking.

**Universal evolutionary theory** was developed to explain why cultures differ and how they change over time. The suggestion was that there is an underlying, universal path along which all cultures progress. Progress is the operative term here—cultures always move toward something better, and that "better" thing is "civilization." What constitutes civilization? Western European culture, of course! Within this framework, cultures like those of most Native American groups had not progressed very far. They were "stuck" in the stages of "barbarism" or even "savagery." The task of Western European cultures was to "civilize" these people, to help move them along the universal evolutionary path toward civilization. Clearly this was a theory that helped to justify colonization and conquest, as well as to further racist thought.

**Historical particularism** was developed as an alternative explanation for why cultures differ and how they change over time. The basic idea was that each culture was the product of a particular set of historical circumstances. The historical circumstances in which each culture develops are unique; hence all cultures differ. None are more or less "evolved" and there is no underlying universal progression going on. Each culture is unique and can only be understood through a detailed understanding of its particular history. It should be obvious how historical particularism counters universal evolutionism, and it should also be clear where archaeology fits in. Archaeology provides the evidence for the particular historical circumstances through which a culture seen today evolved.

Through historical particularism Americanist archaeology developed what is today the most basic way that archaeologists interpret the archaeological record—**culture history.** The idea behind culture history is that one can reconstruct the history of the cultures that inhabited a particular location by examining the relative depth of archaeological materials in the ground. Materials near the surface are more recent than materials underlying them, and if those materials show differences, that allows one to create a simple chronology of cultures, a culture history. Culture history was essentially the only school of thought in Americanist archaeology until the 1940s, and other schools of thought (which are discussed in the next chapter) did not become widespread until the 1970s. That is not to downplay the importance of culture history. Culture history still underlies virtually all archaeological research, since it is the basic tool archaeologists use to identify change through time.

That might explain why archaeology's roots in the United States were classified within anthropology, but why stay with anthropology now? That is a question being asked by many archaeologists today, particularly those who see anthropology's movement away from "traditional" ethnography and toward what have been called more "literary" approaches to culture (ones that focus more on what daily life means to a person rather than on what that person physically does all day, for example) as having little connection with archaeology. While such a perspective is certainly valid, I argue that anthropology still offers archaeologists unique information and insights. Anthropology provides the ethnographic record; it provides the methods and insights of over a century of research on variation in human behavior; and it provides a rich body of theory about cultural stability and change.

How does anthropology provide all this? The answer is in what is called the **four-field approach,** which combines information and methods from four major subdisciplines to focus on the study of humans and their behavior. Figure 1.6 illustrates these four subdisciplines and how they inter-relate. Ethnographers, as I've already discussed, examine the beliefs and practices of living peoples. Linguistic anthropologists study humans' unique capacity for language. Archaeologists study the peoples and cultures of the past. Finally, biological anthropologists study humans in terms

**Universal evolutionary theory:** posits that there is an underlying, universal path along which all cultures progress.

**Historical particularism:** the theoretical framework that viewed each culture as the product of a particular set of historical circumstances and not as the product of a universal evolutionary process.

**Culture history:** a descriptive chronology of the cultures that inhabited a given location.

**Four-field approach:** refers to anthropology's combined use of four distinct subdisciplines—ethnography, linguistic anthropology, archaeology, and biological anthropology—to address questions about human behavior and culture.

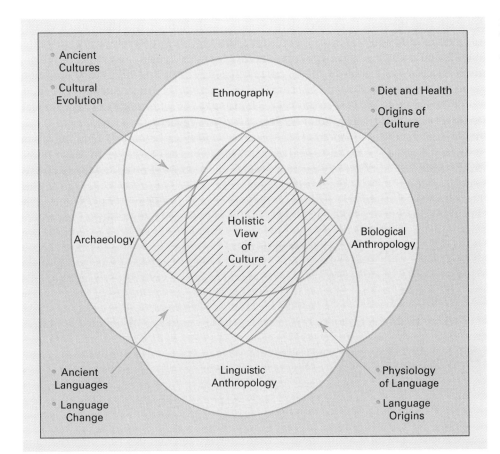

FIGURE **1.6**
The four-field approach in anthropology.

of anatomy, physiology, evolution, and the like. What is unique about anthropology is that, while distinct, each subdiscipline relies on the others for at least some of their methods and information. For example, ethnographers may rely on anthropological linguists to help them understand and learn the language of a group of people they wish to study; they may rely on biological anthropologists to understand the group's health and diet; they may rely on archaeologists to understand the group's past. Thus, each subdiscipline uses the others, and together the understandings they develop are better than if each subdiscipline acted independently.

Perhaps more important, however, anthropology offers archaeology access to "the big question": What does it mean to be human? While archaeology alone can do a great job of honoring our ancestors, learning from past successes and mistakes, and even gaining insights into ourselves today, archaeology needs anthropology to address the question of what it means to be human. Archaeologists need the knowledge gained from living people, both about their culture and their biology. Archaeologists also need the insights of paleoanthropology to help understand how humans differ from primates and other mammals, and how humans evolved. Archaeologists need the insights of anthropological linguistics to understand the unique human capacity for language. In return, anthropologists need archaeology to look through time and directly examine evolutionary trends in human culture and behavior. Only through such a broad anthropological perspective (often called *holistic*) can archaeologists address what it means to be human. And what is the answer to that "big question"? Let's leave that to the end of the book.

## ⚙ SUMMARY

Prehistory refers to the time period before written records were kept, a time period studied exclusively by archaeologists, who gain information about the past by analyzing the material objects left by individuals in the past. There are a variety of reasons for studying world prehistory, among them entertainment; to better understand ourselves, our ancestors, and our political world; and to learn lessons from successes and failures in the past. The study of world prehistory has roots going back perhaps as far as the Babylonian Empire. The direct ancestors of modern archaeologists are nineteenth-century antiquarians who made the first detailed records of ancient sites and monuments. Modern archaeology in the United States has its roots in the anthropology of Franz Boas and the school of thought known as historical particularism. Historical particularists used archaeology to learn about the historical circumstances in which a particular culture evolved. Modern archaeologists still use some of the historical particularist methods to construct the culture histories that provide an overview of the cultures that inhabited a particular area. The central chapters of this book are an example of such culture histories.

## ⬢ DISCUSSION QUESTIONS

1. How does the work of an historian differ from the work of an archaeologist?
2. What are three reasons for studying world prehistory?
3. Why is archaeology considered a part of anthropology in the United States?

## ⬢ ESSAY QUESTIONS

1. Using the text and any other resources you wish, explain how archaeology, a discipline that focuses on the past, can help us today and in the future. What utility does archaeology have for the world's people?
2. Choose a question about the past that interests you and describe how the four-field approach might provide a more complete answer to that question than archaeology alone. What does the four-field approach offer to archaeology?
3. Current international and ethnic conflicts are often rooted in earlier conflicts. Choose a conflict that is currently making headlines and examine how the past is used by both sides. How is the past used in conflicts today?

## ⬈ RESEARCH PROJECT

Pay a visit to your local historical society or museum and examine how the past is portrayed. What elements of the past are emphasized? What elements seem to be missing? What "story" about the past seems to be told? How might local politics be playing into the presentation of the past? (If you don't have a local historical society or museum, you can do the same project using one or more books on local history and prehistory).

## ⬢ KEY SOURCES

### Why Study World Prehistory?

Bloch, 1953; Braudel, 1980; Crabtree and Campana, 2001; Fagan, 2001; Marx, 1913; Price and Feinman, 2001; Wallerstein, 1974; Wenke, 1999.

### A Brief History of Prehistory

Bahn, 1996; Christenson, 1989; Daniel, 1950, 1981; Meltzer, Fowler, and Sabloff, 1986; Trigger, 1989; Willey, and Sabloff, 1980.

### Archaeology as Anthropology

Gibbon, 1981, 1989; Gosden, 1999; Taylor, 1948; Wiseman, 1998, 2001.

# CAREERS IN ARCHAEOLOGY

Archaeology in the United States is part of the discipline of anthropology. In order to begin a career in archaeology, you must have a bachelor's degree in anthropology as well as a graduate degree in anthropology, with a focus in archaeology. Either a Master's degree or a Ph.D. in anthropology will give you the training to work as an archaeologist. In this Web Activity, you will view an interview with an archaeologist who describes the various career pathways available to the student of archaeology.

## WEB ACTIVITY

Archaeology has evolved in the last four decades into a science related directly to the research goals of anthropology. The new student of anthropology and archaeology must decide just what specialization to pursue during his or her studies. Today, archaeology is divided into four major career areas, each being a technical specialization. In this activity you will hear descriptions of how archaeologists work in today's modern discipline of archaeology.

## Activity

1. View the video. What are the four major career areas of archaeology? Which ones involve fieldwork?

2. What type of work do curators do? What is survey work? How does field excavation differ from survey?

3. Why is the area of Cultural Resource Management (CRM) so important? What contributions can it make to the field of anthropology?

**The Media Lab can be found in Chapter 1 on the** *Companion Website*™ http://www.prenhall.com/peregrine

# The Archaeological Record

I'll never forget my first experience doing archaeology. I worked for eight dirty, sweat-seasoned weeks in the Illinois River valley excavating an ancient village—the C. W. Cooper site—that had three prehistoric occupations. Between nights filled with cheap beer and days filled with the slow *chuck, chuck, chuck* sound of my shovel scraping thin layers of soil from the floor of an excavation unit, I realized how much a trained eye could learn from the archaeological record. The record of the past—the accumulation of meals and homes discarded in sorrow or neglect and covered in centuries of dirt—paints a detailed picture of ancient

life for those trained to see it. In this chapter and the next I'll introduce you to some of the methods archaeologists and **paleoanthropologists** (archaeologists who study our early human ancestors) use to create a picture of the past, and I'll start by focusing on the archaeological record itself.

## ARTIFACTS, ECOFACTS, FOSSILS, AND FEATURES

Archaeologists and paleoanthropologists divide the vast realm of discarded things that make up the archaeological record into four major categories: artifacts, ecofacts, fossils, and features.

### Artifacts

**Artifacts** are objects made or modified by humans—this book, the chair you are sitting in, the lamp on the desk, the pen you are using to underline this sentence—all are artifacts. We are surrounded by artifacts, and we will lose or throw away most of them, which is how things enter the archaeological record. Think about how much garbage you produce in a day. You throw away things all the time—paper, wood (from the ice cream bar you had at lunch), plastic (like the pen that ran out of ink last night), and even metal (the soda can you opened after class). They go into the garbage and out to the landfill. Under the right conditions many of those items will survive for future archaeologists to find. Most of the artifacts that make up the archaeological record are just this kind of mundane waste—the accumulated garbage of daily life that archaeologists may recover and examine to reconstruct what daily life was like long ago.

By far the most plentiful artifacts from the past are stone tools, which archaeologists call **lithics** (see Figure 2.1). Indeed, lithics are the only artifact available for 99 percent of human history. Humans first started using stone tools more than two and a half million years ago (see Chapter 5), and some tools of stone (grinding and polishing stones, for example) are still used today. Stone has been used for almost any purpose you can think of, from cutting tools to oil lamps, although their most common use has probably been as hunting, butchering, and hide-processing tools. At the C. W. Cooper site where I had my first field experience, for example, we found all sorts of stone tools. We found scrapers of various kinds that had been used to clean hides, knives used to cut and carve meat and wood, drills used for working wood and hides, and projectile points used for hunting. This kind of diversity in stone tools is common on archaeological sites, and stone tools can tell the archaeologist or paleoanthropologist a lot about the kinds of daily activities in which people were engaged.

Another common kind of artifact is **ceramics** (pots and other things made from baked clay—see Figure 2.2). Humans first started making ceramics about 10,000 to 15,000 years ago, and ceramic objects such as storage and cooking vessels came to be used all over the world in a relatively short period of time (see Chapter 16). Because ceramics are fragile, easy to make, and slow to decay, they show up in quantity in the archaeological record. Ceramics were by far the most plentiful artifacts we found at

**Paleoanthropologist:** a scholar who studies ancient humans and human evolution.

**Artifact:** any object of human manufacture.

**Lithic:** a stone tool made or used by humans.

**Ceramic:** an artifact made from clay (paste) that has been heated (fired) to give it strength.

FIGURE **2.1**
Flaked stone bifaces from
Rock Island, Wisconsin.

the C. W. Cooper site—dozens of pieces a day. Cooking vessels and storage jars were the most common type, and most of these were broken into many pieces, which is probably why they were discarded. Even when broken, ceramics can tell the archaeologist a lot about what people were doing in the past—ceramic forms can indicate how items were used, damage can indicate use as well, and residue trapped within the ceramic can even indicate what an object held.

Wood and bone artifacts are common too, and they were used to make hide-working, cooking, hunting, and even butchering tools (see Figure 2.3). Wood and bone tools have been used by humans at least as long as stone tools, but unlike stone tools, they tend not to survive well in the archaeological record. At the C. W. Cooper site, for example, preservation of bone was fairly poor, but even so, we found hundreds of bone tools, suggesting bone was being used quite extensively by the site's prehistoric inhabitants. They used deer long bones as awls and knives, scapula as hoes, and antler tips as projectile points.

FIGURE **2.2**
A reconstructed Huron pot
from Rock Island, Wisconsin.

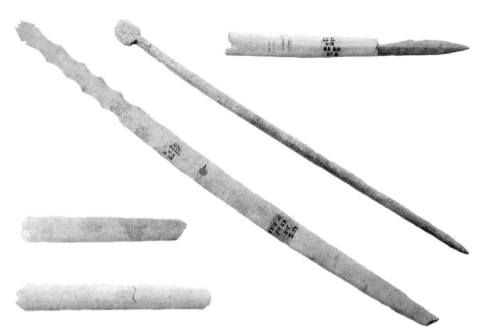

FIGURE **2.3**
Bone tools from Rock Island, Wisconsin.

In some places metals and glass are common artifacts (see Figure 2.4). These survive well in the archaeological record, and hence they are often found where they were used. Since the C. W. Cooper site was completely prehistoric, we didn't find any glass or metal there. (Native Americans didn't use glass and in only a few regions used metal before European contact.) On nearby sites dating to the historic period, however, European trade goods such as steel knives and glass beads are found routinely.

## Ecofacts

**Ecofacts** are natural materials that have been used by humans. Typical ecofacts include the remains of plants and animals that were eaten by a group of people. A good example are the bones of animals that people have eaten. These bones are somewhat like artifacts, but they haven't been made or modified by humans, just used and discarded by them. At the C. W. Cooper site, we found literally thousands of bones. These came from animals, birds, and fish that the people living at the site had eaten. By studying these bones, the archaeologist or paleoanthropologist can discern how people used the environment around them.

Because humans also bring plants back to their houses to use, pollens from many plants commonly are found in archaeological deposits. These pollens may not all have come from the same location or environment—pollens from swamp and grassland plants might be found together in archaeological deposits. The only reason they are together is that they have been brought together by human use. Yet another example of ecofacts are the remains of insect and animal pests that associate with humans, such as cockroaches and mice. Their remains are found in archaeological deposits because they associate with humans and survive by taking advantage of the conditions that humans create. Their presence is in part caused by the human presence, and thus they are considered ecofacts too. We took soil samples at the C. W. Cooper site so that we could extract seeds, shells, pollens, and other small ecofacts to reconstruct what sorts of plants the inhabitants of the site were using.

Among the most important ecofacts are the remains of humans themselves—their bones, tissues, and chemical residues of their bodies (see Figure 2.5). At the C. W. Cooper site we also found human remains, and like many other experiences that summer, the discovery of prehistoric burials was thought provoking for me.

**Ecofact:** a natural object that has been used or modified by humans.

FIGURE **2.4**
Glass trade beads from Rock
Island, Wisconsin.

Why should we disturb these people? Why can't we let them rest? Many others have
been similarly troubled by excavating human remains, and today, twenty years after
my experience, archaeologists are beginning to take seriously their own and others'
misgivings. Burials today are typically excavated only when they are threatened with
destruction, and in many cases excavated remains are reburied after analysis (see the
box feature titled "Whose Bones Are They?"). However, from an archaeological
point of view, burials are perhaps the most important find that can be made. Not
only do burials offer archaeologists their only chance to actually "meet" the people
they are trying to understand, but a person's bones provide a record of their diet,
health, and lifestyle. The way individuals are buried can also provide a window on
ancient beliefs about life and death. And, since individuals in many cultures are
buried in ways that reflect their social status and the social roles they played in society when alive, burials can offer insight into ancient social systems as well. Burials
and the human remains they contain are among the best sources of information we
have about the past.

## Fossils

**Fossil:** the remains of an
ancient plant or animal
that has turned to stone
through a complex process
of mineralization.

The bodies of very ancient humans and the plants and animals they used are often
found as fossils. **Fossils** are the remains of living things that have been turned into
stone (see Figure 2.6). Through a complex chemical process taking place over thousands of years, the molecules that comprise the bones of humans and animals are

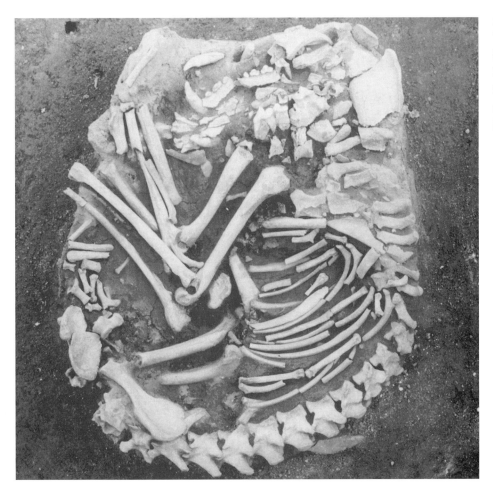

FIGURE **2.5**
This dog was buried at a site in Tennessee, and, like a human skeleton, can provide information about the animal's diet, health, and lifestyle.

FIGURE **2.6**
A fossil trilobite from the Cambrian period, 500 million years ago.

# Whose Bones Are They?

On July 28, 1996, two men watching a hydroplane race on the Columbia River near Kennewick, Washington, discovered a skeleton washing out of the river bank. Police contacted archaeologist James Chatters to recover the skeleton and investigate its origins. Chatters initially thought the skeleton was that of a late-nineteenth or early-twentieth-century settler, so he was surprised to find what appeared to be an ancient stone projectile point embedded in the pelvis. He was more surprised when he received the initial radiocarbon date from the skeleton—8410±60 B.P. This was not a recent pioneer, but an ancient one, perhaps a member of one of the first populations to colonize the Kennewick area. A few days after its antiquity was established, the skeleton became the centerpiece of one of the most contentious questions facing contemporary archaeologists—Whose bones are they?

The question arises because indigenous peoples around the world are asking governments to give them responsibility for caretaking or disposing of the remains of their ancestors. Many indigenous people feel that the bones of their ancestors have been treated as curiosities by museums and collectors and that even archaeologists treat human remains as artifacts rather than with the respect and dignity they deserve. Some people's religious beliefs imbue skeletal remains with a soul that is trapped until the bones decay. For these people, museum collections of human remains are essentially prisons of the dead. On the other hand, human remains are the single most valuable and important source of information about the past, and as DNA techniques and our understanding of human genetics improves, they will only become more important sources of information. The question, then, is one of balance. Do the bones of the dead belong to the public as a source of information about the past, or do they belong to the descendents of the dead? Which is more important?

In 1990 the U.S. Congress passed the Native American Graves Protection and Repatriation Act (NAGPRA), which attempted to provide a balanced answer. The law made it a felony to collect, possess, or transfer human remains of known affinity to an existing Native American culture, except by the members of that culture. The law also mandated institutions receiving federal money and which had such remains or objects to notify representatives of the affiliated culture and to establish a process to "repatriate" those remains and objects; that is, to transfer them to the affiliated Native American group for curation. In some ways NAGPRA is much like the historic preservation laws that preceded it, laws which are rooted in the idea that antiquities are part of the public record claimed for all citizens and made the responsibility of the federal government to find and protect. Federally recognized Native American groups are legally sovereign nations, and thus, antiquities relating to those groups are part of *their* public record and should be held in trust by the sovereign groups themselves for their citizens. NAGPRA turns the responsibility of managing the archaeological record of another sovereign nation (a federally recognized Native American group) over to that nation. The sovereign nation can choose to accept the responsibility or not, but if they accept it, then NAGPRA requires that all pieces of their archaeological record held in federal agencies or agencies receiving federal funds must be turned over to that nation.

In other ways NAGPRA seems to contradict the history of U.S. historic preservation, at least in the way it has been implemented. One of the major problems with the law stems from identifying to which Native American group archaeological materials belong. Once we go back into prehistory, it is often impossible to follow ancestry. Yet some Native American groups have claimed that *all* prehistoric materials are part of their public record, and should be repatriated. Indeed, conflicting claims have led to arguments between Native American groups over the deposition of archaeological materials. A second problem with NAGPRA is that some Native American groups having rather strong claims to particular aspects of the archaeological record are not federally recognized, and thus don't fall under the law. Provisions for nonrecognized groups have been developed because of this problem, but in practice these provisions have opened up the contention for who gets what materials to all kinds of political and religious interest groups rather than to sovereign nations.

Many of these problems are evident in the Kennewick case. The skeleton is ancient and has characteristics that suggest it may not be related to any existing Native American group. The archaeological record for the area in which the skeleton was found has several gaps, and thus tracing ancestry back through time archaeologically is not currently possible. There are five Native American groups sharing a claim to the skeleton, yet it is not clear under NAGPRA whether such shared claims are allowed. There have also been conflicting claims from other groups (though these have since been dropped). The more significant problem in the Kennewick Man case is the ultimate fate of the skeleton itself. The Umatilla Tribe has stated the skeleton will be reburied in an undisclosed location. But should that be the fate of a skeleton this old and rare? Should a find with such potential value to understanding the origins of *all* Native Americans be subject to reburial (and hence destruction) because that is the desire of the group upon whose land the skeleton was found? Should other Native American groups, who may also be descended from this individual or his group, also have a say in what happens? If this is an individual who appears not to be related to contemporary Native Americans, then should the U.S. government decide what happens to his remains? There are no easy answers, and these questions will remain at the forefront of archaeological scholarship for years to come.

SOURCES: Downey, Roger, *Riddle of the bones: Politics, science, race, and the story of the Kennewick Man* (New York: Copernicus, 2000); Mihesuah, Devon, ed., *Repatriation reader: Who owns American Indian remains?* (Lincoln: University of Nebraska Press, 2000); Thomas, David Hurst, *Skull wars: Kennewick Man, archaeology, and the battle for Native American identity* (New York: Basic Books, 2000).

FIGURE **2.7**
Remains of a hearth
uncovered on Rock Island,
Wisconsin. It is simply an
area of soil that has been
baked and is surrounded with
charcoal and ash, and hence,
cannot easily be removed
from the site like an artifact.

FIGURE **2.7**
Remains of a hearth
uncovered on Rock Island,
Wisconsin. It is simply an
area of soil that has been
baked and is surrounded with
charcoal and ash, and hence,
cannot easily be removed
from the site like an artifact.

replaced by minerals, turning the bones into rock. The impressions of the bodies (often called soft tissue) of animals and plants in mud or volcanic ash can also harden and be turned to stone, later to be recovered by archaeologists or paleoanthropologists. I will describe one of the most famous examples in the human fossil record—a trail of footprints preserved in volcanic ash at Laetoli, Tanzania, dating to some 3.6 million years ago—in the next chapter (also see Color Plate 1).

## Features

The footprints preserved at Laetoli might also be considered features of the Laetoli site. **Features** are artifacts, ecofacts, or fossils that cannot be removed from an archaeological site. They are things like the remains of houses, buildings or monuments, storage and garbage pits, hearths and ovens, and even human footprints. We found, for example, numerous hearths at the C. W. Cooper site. When humans build a fire on bare ground the soil becomes heated and is changed—all the water is driven out of it and its crystalline structure is broken down and reformed. When we found a hearth at the C. W. Cooper site, what we actually found was an area of hard, reddish-orange soil, often surrounded by charcoal and ash. It was an artifact—an object of human manufacture, but it would have been very difficult, if not impossible, to dig out the hearth and take it back to the lab for study like we did with the lithics and ceramics we found. A hearth is really an intrinsic feature of a site—hence the name "feature" (see Figure 2.7).

Several less obvious, but no less important, types of features are pits, activity areas, living floors, and middens. *Pits* are simply holes dug by humans that are later filled with garbage or eroded soil. They are usually fairly easy to distinguish because the garbage or soil they are filled with is often different in color and texture from the soil into which the pit was dug. *Activity areas* are locations on a site where a group of artifacts associated with a particular activity (e.g., stone working, pottery making, food processing) are found together. Often the artifacts found are the refuse

**Feature:** human creations and disturbances that have become intrinsic parts of archaeological sites.

from the activity. *Living floors* are locations on a site where artifacts associated with a household are found. Living floors are basically the floors of houses, encampments, and the like. Frequently living floors will be compacted and will be quite noticeable. Materials found on living floors tend to be small refuse from daily life. *Middens* are substantial and well-defined accumulations of artifacts and ecofacts. Middens can be the product of natural processes; for example, rainwater can collect materials in low spots; however, middens are often created by humans dumping refuse in one location over a long period of time. Middens are one of the most informative deposits an archaeologist can find. Almost everything a group of people use will be thrown away eventually, and most of what is discarded ends up in a midden. Middens typically contain everything from broken tools to kitchen refuse to human remains.

Artifacts, ecofacts, fossils, and features are the basic building blocks of archaeological data, but they are not themselves archaeological data. Archaeological data consist of the relationships between and among artifacts, ecofacts, fossils, and features; that is, archaeological data are archaeological materials in *context*.

## CONTEXT

What is context? Here's an example: What if we found a set of artifacts something like this set of letters: A E G I M N N. They are arranged here in alphabetical order, the way a set of beautiful artifacts might be arranged in a museum display in order of size. But do these arrangements tell us anything? Not really. What if we knew something about the relationships between and among these letters—their context? What if, for example, we knew that the M was the first letter found, and that the A and E were found next to the M, but in reverse order, that one N was found between the E and I, and that the other N was found between the I and the G? Knowing in what context the letters were found would tell us that the letters should be arranged like this: M E A N I N G. And meaning is exactly what context gives to artifacts, ecofacts, fossils, and features. Context allows them to be "read" by the archaeologist or paleoanthropologist, just as it allows us to read the letters that make up the words in this sentence.

Archaeological context, however, has two dimensions. One is spatial, like the relationships between letters in the example above. The other is temporal. The archaeological record is created over time, and artifacts, ecofacts, fossils, and features need to be associated with one another both spatially and temporally. Identifying spatial association is pretty easy—either the archaeological materials are found together or they are not. But how do archaeologists and paleoanthropologists determine temporal context? One way is by using spatial context, through what is known as *stratigraphy*. The other is by using various dating methods to determine the age of an archaeological deposit.

As I noted in the previous chapter, it was in the 1950s that archaeologists first gained access to methods that could date archaeological deposits to an absolute age in years before the present. Before those "absolute" methods were developed, archaeologists relied on what are commonly called "relative" methods for dating archaeological deposits.

**Relative dating:** techniques used to assign a date to an object or deposit based on its relative context with other objects or deposits.

### Relative Dating Methods

**Relative dating** methods provide chronological context by establishing the position of an archaeological or fossil deposit relative to a deposit of a known age.

The earliest and still the most commonly used method of relative dating is based on **stratigraphy,** the study of how archaeological deposits or rock formations

**Stratigraphy:** the analysis and interpretation of stratified deposits.

FIGURE **2.8**

Stratigraphic profile from Operation 1 at Tell es-Sweyhat.

SOURCE: From *Subsistence and Settlement in a Marginal Environment*, ed. by Richard Zettler, MASCA vol. 14, 1997, pg. 14. Reprinted by permission of The University of Pennsylvania Museum of Archaeology and Anthropology.

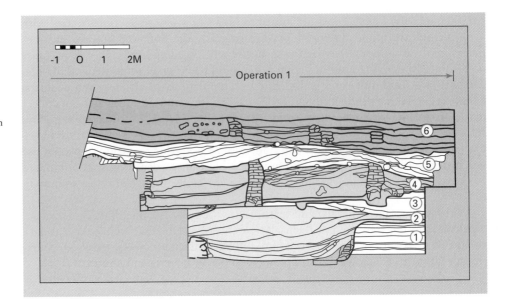

containing fossils are laid down in successive layers or *strata*. Older layers are generally deeper or lower than more recent layers. Archaeologists and paleoanthropologists use **indicator fossils** for establishing a stratigraphic sequence for the relative dating of new finds. Indicator fossils can be artifacts (such as projectile points), ecofacts (such as a particular species of snail), or even features (such as a particular type of burial chamber) that spread widely over a short period of time, or that developed or disappeared fairly rapidly. Different artifacts, ecofacts, fossils, or features are used as indicators of relative age in different areas of the world. On human fossil sites in Africa, for example, elephants, pigs, and horses have been particularly important in establishing stratigraphic sequences, while at Tell es-Sweyhat in Syria James Armstrong and Richard Zettler identified six distinct phases of occupation based on the excavated ceramics.

In the stratigraphic profile shown in Figure 2.8, the lowest occupation, phase 1, contained well-made buff to pink-colored ceramics that are very similar to those found at other sites in the area dating to around 5000 B.P. Based on this, Armstrong and Zettler argued that the site was first occupied during that time period, perhaps as early as 4900 B.P. The next two phases (two and three) contain pieces of distinctive "metallic ware" ceramics (so-called because they ring like metal when tapped) that are known to date from around 4500 B.P., meaning that those strata must date to about that time. Phase four has several radiocarbon dates (see the next section) which average about 4150 B.P., and give a solid anchor to the site's stratigraphy. Finally, phases five and six have ceramics that are similar to those found on sites dating to around 4000 B.P. By combining indicator fossils (in the form of distinctive ceramics) with radiocarbon dates, Armstrong and Zettler were able to determine when each strata was occupied, and thus, to provide dates covering nearly a thousand years of human habitation at Tell es-Sweyhat.

Once the stratigraphy of an area is established, the relative ages of two different archaeological or fossil deposits in the same or different sites can be determined by their associated indicator fossils. For example, now that the stratigraphy at Tell es-Sweyhat has been established, other researchers in the area can use it as the basis for establishing the occupational periods at their sites by comparing what they find to what was found at Tell es-Sweyhat. But while stratigraphy is quite useful, it is never a completely satisfactory means of dating an archaeological or fossil deposit because it only provides relative dates. One knows a deposit dates to the same general period as another deposit sharing the same indicator fossils, but one cannot,

**Indicator fossil:** any artifact, ecofact, fossil, or feature that is unique to a particular time period and by its presence can be used to indicate the date of an archaeological deposit.

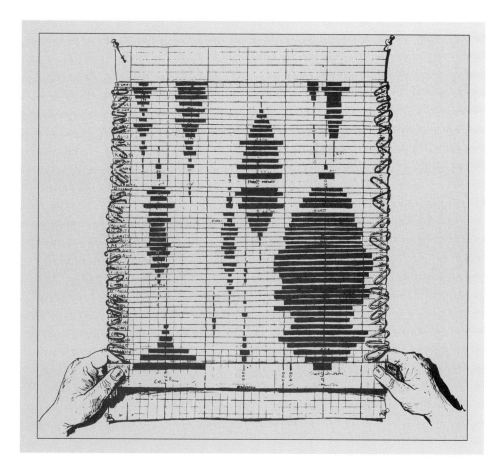

FIGURE **2.9**
Method of constructing a
seriation graph. Frequencies
of the types in each collection
are drawn as bars along the
top of graph-paper strips.
These are arranged to discover
the type–frequency pattern
and are fastened to a paper
backing with paper clips.
When the final arrangement
has been determined, a
finished drawing may be
prepared.

SOURCE: James A. Ford, *A Quantitative
Method for Deriving Cultural
Chronology* (1962). Courtesy of the
General Secretariat of the Organization
of American States.

based on that information alone, know chronologically the time to which the deposit dates. Such chronological dates are estimated by absolute dating methods, which I will describe in the next section.

If a site has been disturbed, stratigraphy will not be a satisfactory way to determine even relative age because the disturbance may have moved indicator fossils into other strata. However, one can use the artifacts that have been found to create a relative dating scheme through a technique known as seriation. **Seriation** uses artifact typologies to create a time series that is purely relative, although it can be tied into an absolute chronology if one or more of the artifacts can be associated with dated materials. The basic premise of seriation is that artifact types come into use and go out of use slowly. Thus, if one were to look at the whole range of ceramic types on a site, for example, at any given point some types will be more popular than others. The less popular ones will either be coming into use or going out of use. By charting the percentages of each type, one should be able to create a logical series showing the types coming into and going out of use. The traditional way of doing this is to create "battleship" diagrams as shown in Figure 2.9, although more sophisticated statistical and graphical methods have also been developed.

## Absolute Dating Methods

**Absolute dating** methods are preferred over relative dating methods because they provide a true, or absolute, chronological date for an archaeological or fossil deposit. Many of the absolute dating methods are based on the decay of a radioactive isotope. When the rate of radioactive decay is steady over time (as is the case with many isotopes), the age of the specimen can be estimated by measuring how much of the isotope is left in the specimen.

**Seriation:** a method of relative dating that uses the percentages of particular artifact styles to assign relative dates.

**Absolute dating:** techniques that provide absolute dates in years before the present.

FIGURE **2.10**

The carbon-14 cycle.

SOURCE: Figure 3.1, "Radiocarbon dating model: Production, distribution, and decay of 14C," from "Radiocarbon Dating" by R. E. Taylor in *Chronometric Dating in Archaeology* by R. E. Taylor and M. J. Aitken, eds., Plenum Publishing, pg. 67, 1997. Reprinted by permission of the publisher and author.

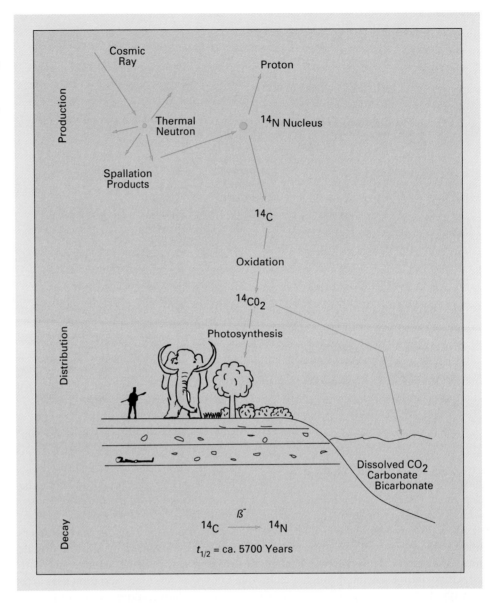

**Radiocarbon dating:** a method of absolute dating that uses the decay of carbon-14 to assign a date to an object.

**Radiocarbon dating,** sometimes called carbon-14 (14C) dating, is perhaps the best-known method of determining the absolute age of a specimen. It is based on the principle that all things living at the same time possess the same ratio of radioactive carbon (carbon-14, or 14C) to nonradioactive carbon (carbon-12, or 12C) in their tissues (see Figure 2.10). Radioactive carbon, produced when nitrogen-14 is bombarded by neutrons derived from the breakup of air molecules by cosmic rays, is absorbed from the air by plants and then ingested by animals that eat the plants. After an organism dies, it no longer takes in any of the radioactive carbon. Carbon-14 decays at a slow but steady pace and reverts to nitrogen-14. The rate at which the carbon decays (its half-life) is 5,730 years; that is, half of the original amount of 14C in an organism's tissue will have disintegrated 5,730 years after the organism's death; half of the remaining 14C will have disintegrated after another 5,730 years; and so on. To discover how long an organism has been dead, one needs to determine the ratio of 14C to 12C in the organism. One way to measure the ratio of 14C to 12C is simply to count the number of radioactive particles being released by a sample to estimate the amount of 14C in the sample. A newer and more efficient method is to use a particle accelerator to separate by weight 14C from 12C and measure the amount of each in a sample. After about 50,000 years, the amount of

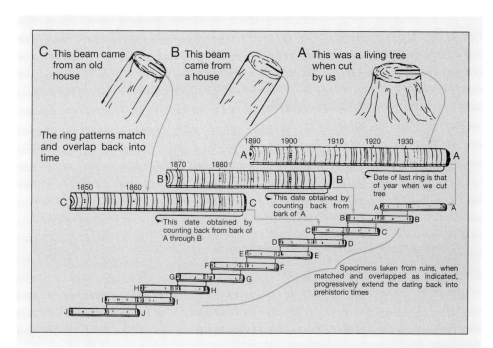

FIGURE **2.11**

The basic principles of dendrochronology.

SOURCE: Bannister, Bryant, and Smiley, Terah L., 1955. "Dendrochronology." In *Geochronology, Physical Science Bulletin No. 2:* ed. T.L. Smiley. Tucson: University of Arizona.

14C remaining in the organic matter is too small to permit reliable dating, limiting the use of radiocarbon dating to the last 50,000 years or so.

Another accurate and widely used absolute dating technique in some areas of the world is dendrochronology. **Dendrochronology** is based on the fact that all trees of the same species in a given region add annual growth rings at the same rate, and that rate varies by temperature and rainfall. In a drought year, all the trees of the same species will add a thin growth ring, while in a wet year they will all add a thicker ring. The pattern of rings in a tree, then, allows one to determine the year in which the tree died—that will be the last growth ring. With the help of radiocarbon dating, an absolute chronology for the growth patterns of various species of trees have been developed. In the southwestern United States, for example, the growth of the bristlecone pine has been charted for the last 9,000 years. When a southwestern archaeologist comes across a piece of bristlecone pine they may well be able to determine a range of years during which the tree lived, and perhaps the date the tree died (Figure 2.11).

Radiocarbon dating is also limited to the remains of living things. But there are several absolute dating techniques that have been developed to date nonorganic artifacts such as ceramics.

*Thermoluminescence dating,* for example, is based on the fact that many minerals emit light when they are heated (thermoluminescence), even before they become red hot. This cold light comes from the release under heat of "outside" electrons trapped in the crystal structure. Thermoluminescence dating makes use of the principle that if an object is heated at some point to a high temperature, as when clay is baked to form a pot, it will release all the trapped electrons it held previously. Over time, the object will continue to trap electrons from radioactive elements (potassium, thorium, uranium) around it. The amount of thermoluminescence emitted when the object is heated during testing allows researchers to calculate the age of the object, if it is known what kind of radiation the object has been exposed to in its surroundings (for example, the surrounding soil in which a clay pot is found).

*Electron spin resonance (ESR) dating* is a technique related to thermoluminescence. Like thermoluminescence dating, ESR dating measures trapped electrons from surrounding radioactive material. But the method in this case is different. The material to be dated is exposed to varying magnetic fields, and a spectrum of the microwaves absorbed by the tested material is obtained. Because no heating is

**Dendrochronology:** an absolute dating method that uses the annual growth rings of trees to determine the year in which a tree died.

required for this technique, electron spin resonance is especially useful for dating organic material such as bone and shell, which decompose if heated. ESR dating, like thermoluminescence, is well suited to samples of ancient pottery, brick, tile, or terra cotta that were originally heated to a high temperature when they were made. This method can also be applied to burnt flint tools, hearth stones, lava or lava-covered objects, meteorites, and meteor craters.

*Paleomagnetic dating* is based on the fact that when rock, soil, or metal is liquefied, as in a volcanic event, the molecules within these substances align themselves with the earth's magnetic field. If the material is then quickly solidified, it will create a record of the earth's magnetic field at that moment in time. When this knowledge is put together with the fact that the earth's magnetic poles wander and the earth's magnetic field has reversed itself many times, the geomagnetic patterns in rocks, soils, or metals can be used to date artifacts or fossils found within those materials. When an archaeologist finds a hearth, pottery kiln, metal workshop, or something else in which earth, rock, or metal was heated to its melting point and cooled in place, the archaeologist can take a sample of that material, carefully recording its location in terms of the earth's present-day magnetic field, and then measure the material's magnetic field in the laboratory. The difference between the polarity and direction of the earth's present-day magnetic field and that recorded in the material can be used to date when the material was melted and cooled. Strictly speaking, paleomagnetic dating is not an absolute dating method, but changes in the polarity and direction of the earth's magnetic field over time have been dated absolutely in conjunction with potassium-argon (see next paragraph) and radiocarbon dating.

Of the absolute dating methods just discussed only paleomagnetic dating allows absolute dates for sites older than about 50,000 years (see Figure 2.12). How do paleoanthropologists date fossil deposits? One common method uses the ratio of potassium to argon in a sample of igneous rock. Potassium-40 (40K), a radioactive form of potassium, decays at an established rate and forms argon-40 (40Ar). The half-life of 40K is known, so the age of a material containing potassium can be measured by the amount of 40K compared with the amount of 40Ar it contains. Radioactive potassium's (40K's) half-life is very long—1,330 million years. This means that *potassium-argon (K-Ar)* dating may be used to date samples from 50,000 years old up to 3 billion years old.

Another absolute dating method used on very old sites is called *uranium series dating*. The decay of two kinds of uranium, 235U and 238U, into other isotopes (such as 230Th, thorium) has proved useful for dating sites where stalagmites and other calcite formations grow. Because water that seeps into caves usually contains uranium but not thorium, the calcite formations trap uranium. Uranium starts decaying at a known rate into other isotopes (such as thorium-230, or 230Th ), and the ratio of those isotopes to uranium isotopes can be used to estimate the time elapsed. The thorium-uranium ratio is useful for dating cave sites less than 300,000 years old where there are no volcanic rocks suitable for the potassium-argon method. There are different varieties of uranium-series dating, depending on the specific isotope ratios used.

Uranium can also be used to determine the date of a high-temperature event, such as a volcanic eruption. Scientists know that 238U, the most common uranium isotope, decays at a slow, steady rate. This decay takes the form of spontaneous fission, and each separate fission leaves a scar or track on an appropriate sample of material, such as crystal, glass, and many uranium-rich minerals, which can be seen when chemically treated through a microscope. To find out how old a sample is, one counts the tracks, then measures their ratio to the uranium content of the sample.

There are many other absolute dating techniques that have been applied to archaeological and paleoanthropological sites, but those described here are among the most commonly employed. The important thing to note is that there are many different techniques, each useful on different types of materials and different time ranges (Figure 2.12). In most cases several of these techniques are used together to

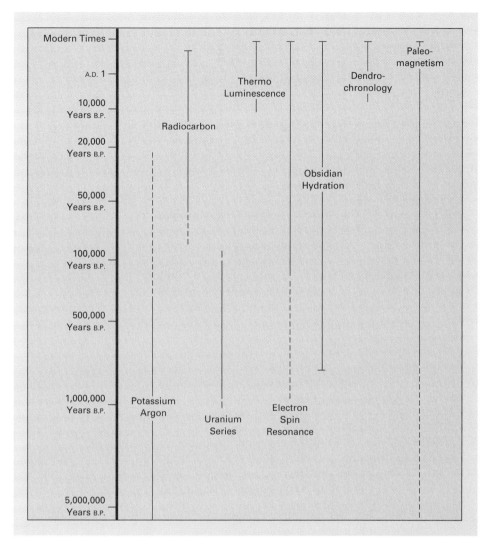

FIGURE **2.12**

Useful time ranges for various dating techniques.

SOURCE: Brian M. Fagan, *In the Beginning: An Introduction to Archaeology, 10/E* (Upper Saddle River, NJ: Prentice Hall, 2001), p. 136. Reprinted by permission of Pearson Education, Inc.

ensure that problems of contamination, measurement error, and the like are identified and eliminated.

## ARCHAEOLOGICAL SITES

When we find a location where archaeological materials (artifacts, ecofacts, fossils, and features) exist in spatial and temporal context, we call that location an **archaeological site.** Archaeological sites exist everywhere, and we are creating them all the time. However, sites containing the data archaeologists need to answer questions about the past are quite rare. Why? Because most archaeological materials decay over time and literally disappear. Those that do survive often lose context. Natural processes like erosion or freezing and thawing move archaeological materials out of their original locations. Humans are good at disturbing archaeological materials too. We dig new storage pits where old ones were located, we cover old house foundations with new ones, we drag plows across ancient fields and farmsteads. At the C. W. Cooper site, for example, people living around 1800 B.P. built a burial mound; later people, living around 1000 B.P., built houses on the mound, cutting right through the earlier burials; even later people, living around 500 B.P., built another settlement on top of the mound, disturbing both burials and the earlier settlement. Because of poor preservation and destruction of context, it is the rare exception when an undisturbed record of ancient human behavior is preserved in an

**Archaeological site:** a location where artifacts, ecofacts, fossils, and features are found in context.

# Preserving the Past

Archaeological sites that preserve a clear record of the past are rare and are constantly decaying, some by natural processes, others by human intervention. While we cannot often stop natural processes from destroying archaeological sites, we can influence human activity and promote means to help preserve the past. In the United States the archaeological community has taken two basic paths to influencing human activities in order to help preserve the past: legislation and education.

Archaeological legislation in the United States begins with the Antiquities Act of 1906, which made it a felony to damage or remove archaeological or historical sites on government property. A basic idea behind the law is that the archaeological record is part of the public record, just as are marriage licenses, death certificates, real estate titles, and the like. Just as one cannot go around throwing away or burning titles to real estate, one cannot destroy the archaeological record—it too is a public document. A second basic idea in the law is that the federal government assumes the responsibility for protecting the archaeological record. In essence, they "claim" the archaeological record for all U.S. citizens.

A federal government laying claim to all antiquities found within its borders is not unusual in the world; in fact, many countries today have such laws, basically outlawing the personal ownership of antiquities. Obviously, this is not the case in the United States, for while the law establishes the principle that the archaeological record is part of the public record, it only formally protects that part of the archaeological record found on federal land or in the course of an activity where federal funds are involved. This is a third important principle in archaeological legislation that has its roots in the Antiquities Act of 1906.

The Historic Sites Act of 1935 is a logical extension of the Antiquities Act since it declared a national policy to identify and protect important archaeological and historical sites on federal land. If you think about it, this is necessary to enforce the Antiquities Act, but it also goes farther. It makes it part of federal policy to actually go out and find sites in order to preserve and protect them. This policy was further developed and strengthened through the Historic Preservation Act of 1966, which established the National Register of Historic Places and the National Trust for Historic Preservation.

The National Register of Historic Places is a list of historic properties and archaeological sites that have been nominated, evaluated, and approved as a

archaeological site (see the box feature on "Preserving the Past"). And ancient human behavior is what we are really talking about when we speak of archaeological data, for that is what archaeologists assume is preserved in the context of artifacts, ecofacts, fossils, and features.

Sites are created when the remnants of human activity are covered or buried by some natural process. The most dramatic one is volcanic activity; the record of significant part of U.S. history. Sites on the National Register are protected to the extent that they cannot be wantonly altered or destroyed (although they can be with approval from a state or federal historic preservation officer). The establishment of the National Register, however, has had much broader impact than simply creating a list of important sites. Part of the act which created the National Register also created a fund of money, the National Trust for Historic Preservation, to be used in evaluating sites for the National Register. In order to locate and evaluate National Register-eligible sites, and to disperse funds from the National Trust, the Historic Preservation Act also required each state to create a liaison officer for historic preservation. It is from this requirement that the current network of state archaeologists emerged.

Finally, the Archaeological Resources Protection Act of 1979 made it necessary to obtain a permit to excavate or remove archaeological materials from federal land. It also encouraged federal agencies to work together in the granting permits. Both have allowed the government to carefully monitor archaeological work on public lands. The Act also provided a clear statement of activities that are not allowed—excavating or removing artifacts without a permit. Such activities became subject to strong civil and legal penalties. And since these activities are illegal, artifacts recovered through such activities are essentially stolen goods, and can be confiscated if found.

Together, these laws have been very effective in promoting archaeology and historic preservation, but the archaeological community has also attempted to promote preservation through education. Many states have an archaeology week during which the state's archaeological resources are presented to the public through lectures, tours, and press releases. Most museums and universities with archaeological facilities have public education programs that bring in speakers, provide workshops or training sessions in archaeology and preservation, support local amateur archaeological groups, and sponsor public outreach events such as artifact identification days or tours of archaeological sites. These activities may do more than legislation to promote historic preservation because they are proactive and help the public understand why legislation is necessary, why it is important to preserve the past.

SOURCES: King, Thomas, *Cultural resource laws and practice: An introductory guide* (Walnut Creek, CA: AltaMira Press, 1998); Smith, George, and John E. Ehrenhard, eds., *Protecting the past* (Boca Raton: CRC Press, 1991).

human behavior (and even the humans themselves) can be totally buried within seconds. The most impressive example of this must be Pompeii, an entire city that was buried in the eruption of Mount Vesuvius in 1921 B.P. Today archaeologists are digging out the city and finding the remains of ancient life just as it was left in the moments before the eruption. Less dramatic means of burying the record of human behavior are the natural processes of dirt accumulation and erosion. Wind- or water-borne soil and debris can cover a site either quickly (as in a flood) or over a long period of time, preserving intact the artifacts, ecofacts, fossils, and features left by humans. Finally, the processes through which soils are built up can also bury artifacts, ecofacts, fossils, and features in a way that allows archaeologists to uncover them later. In forests, for example, falling leaves cover the locations where humans camped. Over time the leaves decay and build up soil, covering the remains of the human encampment slowly but completely over many years.

Since good locations to live and work in are often re-used by humans, many sites contain the remains of numerous human occupations. As I noted earlier, at least three groups of people used the area that became the C. W. Cooper site, each depositing artifacts and ecofacts and creating features that were disturbed by later peoples, including the farmer who found the site while plowing and archaeologists like myself who excavated the site. The most valuable sites to archaeologists and paleoanthropologists are those in which the burial processes worked quickly enough that each re-use of the site is clearly separated from the previous one. Such sites are called **stratified**; each layer, or stratum, of human occupation is separate like a layer in a layer cake. Not only do stratified sites allow the archaeologist or paleoanthropologist to easily distinguish the sequence of site occupations, but the strata themselves provide a way to know the relative ages of the occupations since earlier occupations will always be below later ones.

It is important to note that the very processes that create sites can often damage or destroy them. The study of the processes of site disturbance and destruction is called **taphonomy**. Some archaeologists and paleoanthropologists argue that natural processes such as wind and water erosion not only bury the materials left by humans but may affect them so significantly that one needs to be very cautious when interpreting what is found in an archaeological site. There were all kinds of disturbances at the C. W. Cooper site. Plowing had moved much of the surface material around, but thankfully deep plowing had never been done. Plant roots, however, had reached deep into the soil and had moved small artifacts and ecofacts with them. More significantly, burrowing animals and snakes had dug holes deep into the site over the centuries, and some of these created significant disturbances to the archaeological deposits. Despite all this, much of the archaeological record remained in place. What we, as archaeologists, had to be mindful of was the possibility that disturbances may have created or destroyed patterns, and we needed to be cautious in making interpretations.

## INTERPRETING THE ARCHAEOLOGICAL RECORD

The way archaeologists interpret the archaeological record is rooted in two fundamental assumptions: (1) that the archaeological record accurately preserves the material remains of human behavior and (2) that human behavior can be accurately reconstructed from its material remains. The truth is actually much more complex, and there are a variety of schools of thought on the nature of the archaeological record. All of them, at some level, come back to one idea: that we can know the past from the material record of human behavior, if only quite imperfectly. If archaeologists didn't believe that, they couldn't be archaeologists—there would be no point at all to it. So, while some of these schools of thought may seem to suggest a knowable past is unattainable, no one can actually believe that and still be an archaeologist.

*Behaviorist theories*, as I call them, suggest that the archaeological record is really a snapshot of ancient behavior. The archaeologist's job, in behaviorist theory, is twofold. First, the archaeologist must determine how human behavior affects or is transmitted to the archaeological record. Second, the archaeologist must determine how to apply that knowledge to reconstructing the behavior that is manifested in the archaeological record.

**Stratified:** archaeological sites that have clear separation between deposits dating to different times.

**Taphonomy:** the study of site formation and disturbance.

One of the most influential behaviorist theorists is Lewis Binford. In *Nunamuit Ethnoarchaeology,* for example, Binford examined how contemporary Inuit hunters created a material record of their behavior as they waited for game at a small hunting camp. Binford compared the patterns of material remains he saw the hunters create to those he excavated at an ancient hunting camp nearby. Through this comparison, Binford was able to reconstruct the behavior of those ancient hunters—hunters who, not surprisingly, behaved quite similarly to the way contemporary ones did.

What I call *interpretive theories* are in many ways parallel to behaviorist theories in suggesting that the archaeological record is a record of human behavior, but they go beyond that to suggest that from the archaeological record archaeologists can sometimes recover ancient thoughts, beliefs, motivations, and even feelings. I call these interpretive theories because the thoughts of ancient peoples are not as clearly manifest in the material record as most think human behaviors are, but must be teased out of the archaeological data through an interpretive (often called a *hermeneutic*) process. In fact, one of the most influential proponents of interpretive theories, Ian Hodder, has suggested that the archaeological record can be understood as a text that, like a book, can be read to understand the characters and action or can be interpreted to get at the underlying meanings, motivations, and feelings of those characters.

Hodder's work has been diverse, but perhaps his most influential work has focused on the Neolithic period in Europe. The Neolithic was a time of transition from a mobile hunting and gathering lifestyle to a sedentary agricultural one. In works like *The Domestication of Europe,* Hodder attempted to move beyond behavioral understandings of how this transition took place to more interpretive understandings of what the transition meant to the people who took part in it. For example, Hodder interpreted an increase in contrasting patterns on ceramics in southern Scandinavia as reflecting the increasing differentiation in society. He argued that the transition to farming must have led to an undercurrent of social conflict and unease that was represented, perhaps unconsciously, by individuals decorating their pottery. Similarly, ceramic decorations in northern Europe during the same period show a different pattern—one of sharply segregated but repeating patterns (Figure 2.13). Hodder interpreted this as reflecting a marked territorialization of once fluid social groups as agricultural land came to be a valued resource. Again, Hodder suggested that these underlying social conditions were transferred to pottery decorations, and such decorations can be "read" and interpreted to disclose their underlying meaning.

While interpretive theories might be seen as a step forward into teasing more information from the archaeological record, what I call *taphonomic theories* represent a step back, questioning how much information is actually there. The basic position taken by taphonomic theories is that while the archaeological record may manifest a record of human behavior and even thought when it is deposited, the natural world steps in after deposition and, through a variety of processes from frost heave to burrowing rodents, mixes those materials to the point where archaeologists often can't be certain what they reflect. Most taphonomic theorists are not completely nihilistic in their view; that is, they don't go so far as to suggest that the past can never be understood through the archaeological record. They do, however, caution that even the most apparently well-preserved archaeological site might in reality be significantly disturbed.

The primary work of taphonomic theorists has been to identify the processes that can disturb the archaeological record. For example, Michael Schiffer's *Formation Processes of the Archaeological Record* describes dozens of natural and cultural processes that affect the context, patterning, and characteristics of artifacts and sites. Through several case studies he demonstrates that "evidence of the cultural past is created by a variety of cultural and noncultural processes that have varied and ubiquitous effects, introduce variability into the historical and archaeological records, and must be taken into account in [archaeological] inference." Indeed, Schiffer ends his book on a rather incendiary note: "A large task looms

FIGURE **2.13**

Stylistic changes on Neolithic Ceramics from southern Scandinavia and northern Europe. Bottom row shows the earliest vessels, top row the latest.

SOURCE: Figure "Stylistic changes on Neolithic ceramics from southern Scandinavia and northern Europe" by Louwe Kooijmans, 1976, in *Symbolic and Structural Archaeology* by Ian Hodder, ed., copyright © 1982, Cambridge University Press, p. 173. Reprinted by permission of Cambridge University Press.

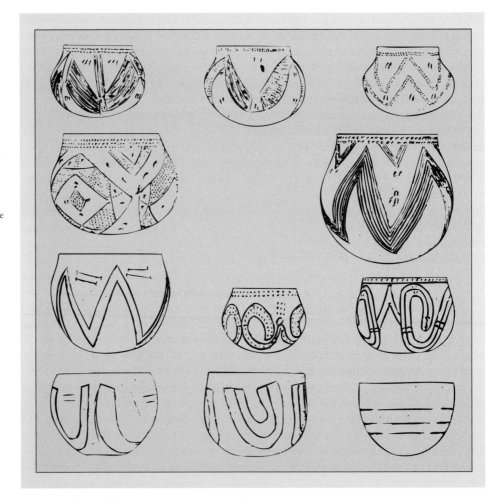

ahead, that of reevaluating all previous [archaeological] inferences with respect to how well formation processes have been understood and taken into account." The implication is that if formation processes have not been understood, the inferences may well be wrong. While this is a valid and important point, if archaeologists took this view to its logical extreme they would have to toss out almost everything they thought they knew about the past—an extreme that I am certain even Schiffer doesn't really think is necessary.

In the 1980s, as part of a larger reaction against empirical and scientific forms of knowledge which has come to be known as poststructuralism, postmodernism, or postprocessualism, a group of archaeologists began to develop a set of what I call *reactionary theories* against the established schools of archaeological thought. These theories tend to promote two interconnected positions: (1) that we can never describe or understand a real past because (2) our knowledge of the past is filtered through our own, uniquely individual interpretations of the archaeological record and of the reports, books, and articles written by archaeologists about the archaeological record. In a sense, reactionary theories suggest that sites and artifacts are nothing more than mirrors of ourselves. Archaeologists look at them and see only their own thoughts, beliefs, motivations, and biases, not those of ancient peoples.

The work of Michael Shanks and Christopher Tilley perhaps best captures the work of reactionary theorists. In their controversial book *Re-Constructing Archaeology,* Shanks and Tilley argue that "there can be no *objective* link between patterning perceived in material culture and processes which produced that patterning." By this they mean that archaeological knowledge is the product of the archaeologist's mind and, in turn, of their education, life history, and social world. As Shanks and Tilley put it, "While real, objects of archaeological knowledge are nevertheless meaningless in themselves. They are raw matter which require completion to turn them into discursive objects. It is at this point they become meaningful, can be discussed, be known." From what I have already told you about archaeology, I hope you can understand that most archaeologists would readily agree. Archaeological knowledge is created in the minds of archaeologists and in the act of collecting, analyzing, and evaluating data. As I explained in the last chapter, the past is a product of the present and tells us as much about ourselves as about the past. More significantly, the past is political, and it is used to promote and justify political agendas. The past is powerful, and therefore the act of creating the past through archaeology can be a powerful act.

But for Shanks and Tilley, recognizing the inherent subjectivity and political nature of archaeological research leads to a stifling subjectivity: "There is no *independently definable* reality or past as far as we are all concerned," and they yield archaeological knowledge to the vagaries of the powers-that-be: "archaeology . . . [is] a passive function of the present, producing pasts relevant to and/or in support of particular interest groups." Yet is it really subjective of me to say that people lived, worked, and died at the C. W. Cooper site five hundred years ago? Are the features I've excavated only meaningful in my own subjective presentation of them? I don't think so, and when pushed, I don't think Shanks and Tilley would think so either. There is a past. Things really happed before us and left real, observable material traces. The job of archaeologists is to figure out what those traces can tell us. Surely how archaeologists do that will be effected by their education, opinions, theories, and social world. But just as surely the burials I excavated at the C. W. Cooper site held the remains of real people who had once lived there. It is the archaeologist's job to help those ancient people tell us how they lived.

## ⚙ SUMMARY

The archaeological record consists of artifacts, ecofacts, fossils, and features. Artifacts are movable objects of human use or manufacture. Ecofacts are natural objects that have been used or altered by humans. Fossils are the remains of ancient plants and animals that have turned into stone through a complex chemical process over a long period of time. Features are objects of human manufacture that cannot be moved from a site—they are a part of or embedded in the context of the site. While the archaeological record consists of these material objects, it is the context between and among artifacts, ecofacts, fossils, and features which makes up archaeological data. Archaeological sites are locations where artifacts, ecofacts, fossils, and features are preserved in context and can be recovered by a trained archaeologist or paleoanthropologist.

An important part of recovering context is determining the age of an object or deposit. Archaeologists have developed two sets of techniques for determining age: relative dating techniques and absolute dating techniques. Relative techniques determine the age of an object or deposit through its relationship with other objects or deposits of known age. Common relative dating techniques include stratigraphy, the use of indicator fossils, and artifact seriation. Absolute dating techniques determine the age of an object or deposit itself by analyzing some characteristic of the object or deposit that changes over time in a known way. Major absolute dating techniques include radiocarbon, dendrochronology thermoluminescence, electron spin resonance, paleomagnetics, potassium-argon, and uranium series dating.

Archaeologists use a variety of theories to interpret and bring meaning to the archaeological record. Behaviorist theories suggest the archaeological record can be used to reconstruct ancient behaviors. Interpretive theories suggest we can use the archaeological record to understand the thoughts, motivations, and beliefs of ancient peoples. Taphonomic theories caution that the archaeological record is more a record of natural processes affecting artifacts, ecofacts, fossils, and features than it is a record of human history, behavior, or thought. Finally, reactionary theories suggest the archaeological record is a mirror that reflects only ourselves, not a real past.

## DISCUSSION QUESTIONS

1. What is context and why is it so important in archaeology?
2. What are the differences between relative dating and absolute dating?
3. What conditions are necessary to create an archaeological site?

## ESSAY QUESTIONS

1. Use one or more archaeological site reports or journal articles to illustrate how archaeologists use context to discern patterns and interpret the archaeological record. How is context used by archaeologists?
2. Describe some of the natural processes that might disturb archaeological deposits in the area where you now live. How destructive might these processes be to archaeological sites in your area? How might an archaeologist working in your area account for these processes when interpreting an archaeological site?
3. If the building you now live in were suddenly to collapse and was never rebuilt, what artifacts, ecofacts, or features might be left in a thousand years? What might a future archaeologist find? How might they interpret the site?

## RESEARCH PROJECT

Examine the context of artifacts in your desk or room. List the artifacts that are present, and describe the context of each to the other artifacts around them. Map the artifacts. Now, examine the list and map for patterns. What patterns do you see? Can you associate these patterns with particular behaviors? How would you interpret the "site" of your desk or room?

## KEY SOURCES

### Artifacts, Ecofacts, Fossils, and Features

Binford, 1964; Davies, 1987; Ehrenreich, 1991; Frank, 1982; Glumac, 1991; Gremillion, 1997; Hastorf and Popper, 1988; MacGregor, 1985; O'Connor, 2000; Pearsall, 1989; Sinopoli, 1991; Unger, Schniewind, and Unger, 2001; Whittaker, 1994.

### Context

Aitken, 1990; Baillie, 1995; Fleming, 1976; Harris, 1989; Taylor and Aitken, 1997.

### Archaeological Sites

Goldberg, Nash, and Petraglia, 1993; Holliday, 1992; Lyman, 1994; Schiffer, 1987; Vita-Finzi, 1978.

### Interpreting the Archaeological Record

Binford, 1977; Binford and Binford, 1968; Clarke, 1972; Gibbon, 1989; Hodder, 1991; McGuire, 1992; Preucel, 1991; Schiffer, 1976, 2000; Shanks and Tilley, 1992; Thomas, 2001; Ucko, 1995; Watson, LeBlanc, and Redman, 1984; Yoffee and Sheratt, 1993.

# THE PROCESS OF FOSSILIZATION

The bodies of very ancient humans and the plants and animals they used are often found as fossils. Fossils are the remains of living things that have been turned into stone. Through a complex chemical process taking place over thousands of years, the molecules that comprise the bones of humans and animals are replaced by minerals, turning these bones into rock. Impressions of the bodies of animals and plants cast in mud or volcanic ash can also harden into soft tissue casts. In this Web Activity, you will view the fossilization process, sped up millions of times. The text of Chapter 2 describes the process of fossilization and the importance of fossils to anthropologists.

The Media Lab can be found in Chapter 2 on the *Companion Website*™ http://www.prenhall.com/peregrine

## WEB ACTIVITY

Fossils impart an important body of knowledge in the field of anthropology. Fossil finds are just one part of how archaeologists interpret the archaeological record. Both plants and animals are fossilized, giving us some hint as to the past environment. Besides fossils, features are sometimes cast into the ancient surface. This chapter details one such discovery: the footprints preserved at Laetoli. In this activity you will view the process of fossilization and discuss the importance of fossils in anthropology.

## Activity

1. View the video. What are the five stages of fossilization? Is any stage more important than others? Explain. Are shapes and details always preserved? Why?
2. Explain how soft tissues are hardened into fossils.
3. What is the value of the footprints discovered at Laetoli? How did they form?

# The Process of Archaeological Research

When I look back over my journal for the period when I did my

first fieldwork in Syria, I can see that I had two primary fears: (1) dying;

and (2) not knowing how archaeologists do research in Syria. The first may have

been justified given the remote village I lived in and the hazardous conditions I faced,

but the second was wholly unjustified. Why? Because regardless of where archaeologists

work they follow a standard process for conducting research, and that process is trans-

ferable to any area of the world. The process consists of five separate phases: asking

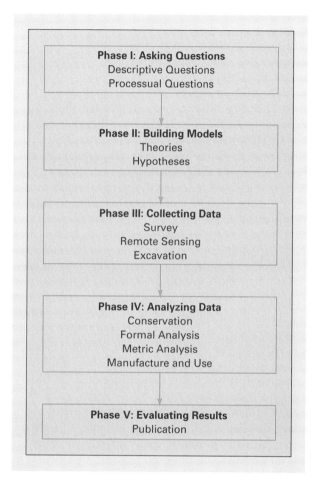

FIGURE **3.1**
The archaeological research
process.

questions, building models, collecting data, analyzing data, and evaluating results
(Figure 3.1). Each phase takes different amounts of effort and money (asking questions, for example, may only take a moment of free thought, while analyzing data
may take years and cost tens of thousands of dollars), but all are vital to understanding the archaeological record. In this chapter I'll introduce you to each phase
of the archaeological research process.

## PHASE I: ASKING QUESTIONS

All archaeological research begins with questions, and there are two basic types of
questions asked by archaeologists: descriptive and processual. **Descriptive questions**
ask about the nature of the archaeological record and can be thought of as questions
that start with who, what, when, or where. They ask what material is present, what
the state of preservation is, when the material was deposited, and, ultimately, who
made the material. **Processual questions** ask how and why the archaeological record

**Descriptive questions:** ask
about the nature of the
archaeological record and
can be thought of as
questions that start with
who, what, when, or where.

**Processual questions:**
ask how and why the
archaeological record takes
the form it does, and about
the processes of cultural
stability and change over
time.

takes the form it does, and about the processes of cultural stability and change over time (the focus on processes is what makes these *processual* questions). Most archaeologists find processual questions the most interesting to pursue, but it is important to note that descriptive questions have to be asked and answered before processual ones can be addressed.

In the previous chapter I mentioned a set of ancient hominid footprints that were discovered at the Laetoli site in Tanzania (see Color Plate 1). These were discovered while answering a set of descriptive questions about the site. The famous paleoanthropologist Louis Leakey and his wife Mary had visited the site on two occasions to look for fossils (the site is only a short distance from Olduvai Gorge, where the Leakeys worked for decades) but did not find much of interest. After work at Olduvai Gorge was completed, Mary decided to look again at Laetoli. A friend had found some interesting fossils there, and a geologist determined that the exposed fossil-bearing rocks were older than those in Olduvai Gorge.

In 1974 Mary Leakey began work at Laetoli seeking answers to basic descriptive questions: Who lived here? What materials did they leave? When did they live here? Where are their remains located? In her 1976 season of work at the site, the remarkable fossil footprints were discovered by accident by two of Leakey's field crew walking back to camp from excavations (and, according to legend, flinging elephant dung at one another). The find answered a number of the questions fairly quickly—clearly hominids were present, and since their footprints were located in volcanic ash that was dated to roughly 3.2 million years ago, Leakey knew they had been at the site at the same time. Like most projects, the find also opened up new questions—Who were these hominids? What were they doing? How did they live?—that are still being worked on today.

A good example of a project undertaken to answer a set of processual questions is the Valley of Oaxaca (pronounced wa-ha-ka) Settlement Pattern Project. A powerful state evolved in the Valley of Oaxaca, Mexico, centered at a site called Monte Albán (see Color Plate 2), and the Valley of Oaxaca Settlement Pattern Project was designed to answer the question: Why did the Monte Albán state evolve? That question really had three parts, all of which required answers: (1) Why did the state evolve? (2) Why did it evolve at Monte Albán and not elsewhere? and (3) Why did it evolve when it did, not earlier or later? As I discuss in a later chapter, the question of state origins is one of great interest to many archaeologists, and the Valley of Oaxaca project was designed to focus a particular technique—the analysis of settlement patterns—on this question.

Notice that the questions addressed through the Valley of Oaxaca project were all based on a substantial understanding of the existing archaeological record. Indeed, the Valley of Oaxaca was chosen specifically as a research locale because (1) it was a place where a state evolved that (2) had a reasonably well-understood archaeological record that (3) was easily accessible through archaeological survey, allowing the technique of settlement pattern analysis to be used. Thus, the general question of state origins started the whole project and was, from the start, linked to a particular archaeological method. Once the question was framed, a location where answers could be found was sought, and that location turned out to be the Valley of Oaxaca.

## PHASE II: BUILDING MODELS

Once a question has been posed, an archaeologist begins to devise model answers to the question, or more simply, models. Model answers for descriptive questions are based on the two fundamental assumptions discussed in the last chapter: (1) that the archaeological record accurately preserves the material remains of human behavior and (2) that human behavior can be accurately reconstructed from its material remains.

Model answers for processual questions are based on theories of human culture. These are different from the theories described in the last chapter—theories for interpreting the archaeological record. Those theories posited a relationship between human behavior and the archaeological record; that is, how human behavior is recorded through artifacts, ecofacts, fossils, and features. Theories about human culture attempt to predict specific aspects of cultures and how they vary under a given set of conditions.

In archaeology two schools of cultural theory predominate: materialist and ecological. **Materialist theories** posit that the way humans organize labor and technology to get resources out of the material world is the primary force shaping culture. Major forces promoting change are innovations in technology, environmental changes or catastrophes, and internal conflicts over labor organization and access to resources. **Ecological theories** posit that human culture is an adaptation to the environment, and thus culture functions to maintain humans and the environment in a sustainable balance. The major force promoting change, then, is the environment itself—as the environment changes, so do human cultures. However, a basic assumption in many ecological theories is that human population has an overall tendency to grow, and this often puts pressure on resources and the environment as a whole—pressure that leads to change. I hope it is obvious that these two schools of theory are closely related and that both share a common focus on the environment and how humans use it.

While some model answers for processual questions aim at broad processes like those previously mentioned—human use of or interaction with the environment—most are aimed at evaluating very specific theories within those larger schools. The Valley of Oaxaca project was directed toward evaluating an ecological theory proposed by the agricultural economist Esther Boserup. Boserup suggested that as population grows in societies that practice agriculture, the society will find ways to intensify agricultural production to support the growing population. In this way, cultural change is seen to stem from population growth—as population increases the society will have to innovate to continue to support the growing population. The archaeologist William Sanders applied this idea to the rise of the Teotihuacan state in the Valley of Mexico, arguing that the state evolved there as a way to centrally control the agricultural economy and intensify production to support a growing population. The Valley of Oaxaca project was designed to test this idea in a different location; in other words, to *replicate* the findings from the Valley of Mexico.

The basic model used in the Valley of Oaxaca project was a population growth model, based on Boserup's theory. The model answer to the question Why did the state evolve? was that population grew to the point where a state was required to control the agricultural economy. The model answer to Why did it evolve at Monte Albán and not elsewhere? was that Monte Albán was located on prime agricultural land where production could easily be centralized and intensified. The model answer to Why did it evolve when it did, not earlier or later? was that it evolved when population reached a point where it could no longer be intensified without centralized control. Based on these model answers, the project team developed a series of *hypotheses* or predictions for how the archaeological record should look. Most fundamentally, they suggested, was that there should be evidence of population growth through time, particularly right before the founding of the Monte Albán state. Once that primary hypothesis was established, a clear set of variables that needed data became obvious, most obvious being data on changes in population density through time in the Valley. Thus, the question led to a model answer that told the archaeologists precisely what data needed to be collected. This is how the archaeological research process is supposed to work (see the box feature titled "Why Archaeology Is a Science").

Of course, many projects are not so clearly directed at answering a particular descriptive or processual question or have such a specific model answer. For example, I have been working since 1990 on a project with colleagues at the University of Pennsyvania Museum and the Semitic Museum at Harvard University trying to

**Materialist theories:** posit that the way humans organize labor and technology to get resources out of the material world is the primary force shaping culture.

**Ecological theories:** posit that human culture is an adaptation to the environment, and thus culture functions to maintain humans and the environment in a sustainable balance.

## Why Archaeology Is a Science

In Chapter 1 I noted that some archaeologists think archaeology should be divorced from anthropology and stand on its own. Many archaeologists believe that anthropology itself is heading for divorce between those who see the discipline as a branch of social science and those who see it as a branch of the humanities. Where does archaeology fit in all this? In my mind archaeology is unquestionably a science, but one so closely tied to anthropology that it cannot be easily separated.

What is a science? The anthropologist Leslie White gave what I think is the best answer to that question in a chapter title: "Science Is Sciencing." In other words, science is what scientists do. It is an activity, a process, and not a thing. What is the activity then? Well, it involves empirical observation of the world, measurement of the things observed, and the discovery of patterns or regularities within the observations through mathematics and logical reasoning.

If we accept this definition of science, then archaeology must be considered a science, since the process I am describing in this chapter is clearly a scientific process. What do archaeologists do? First they ask a question about the past and build a model to guide their exploration. So far, that's not necessarily scientific. Next they collect data. Here is where science enters in—in collecting data archaeologists are making empirical observations of the world and recording and measuring the things they have observed. What follows is analysis, and this too is a scientific activity—archaeologists continue making measurements and begin the search for patterns or regularities. When finished, archaeologists ask more questions. But so what? Why am I making a point of saying that archaeology is a science? The answer is that being a science profoundly affects the types of questions archaeologists ask and the types of research that archaeologists undertake.

Archaeological questions have to able to be examined and evaluated through empirical observations of the archaeological record. Answers have to be developed

understand settlement in part of a large, Early Bronze Age (ca. 4150 B.P.) city in northern Mesopotamia called Tell es-Sweyhat (pronounced sway-hot)(Figure 3.2). The city is divided, as are virtually all northern Mesopotamian cities, into an inner town or acropolis containing a palace-and-temple complex and elite residences and an outer town containing workshops and common residences. Unfortunately, little work has been done in the outer towns of northern Mesopotamian cities. We know, in general, what to expect in the outer town of Tell es-Sweyhat, but many descriptive questions remain. Our primary question, however, is a processual one, concerning the political and economic relationship between residents in the inner and outer towns. Clearly the residents of the inner town were supported by the craftspeople and agricultural workers who lived in the outer town, but what was the nature of their relationship? How did the residents of the inner town "earn" support? Why did residents of the outer town support elites in the inner town?

and evaluated using logic and reason, and those answers have to be based on empirical observations. Archaeologists cannot ask questions about supernatural forces or effects, because they are, by definition, not part of the natural world, and hence not observable. If archaeologists develop answers that do not lend themselves to direct observation, for example, about advanced civilizations that have left no trace in the archaeological record or about ancient visitors from outer space that one cannot now observe, then one must question or even ignore those answers until clear, direct, and reasonable empirical supporting evidence is presented.

Logic and reason are important here too. Empirical evidence that requires a leap of logic or reasoning, or that contradicts a well-established body of existing empirical evidence, must be suspect. When Graham Hancock, for example, argues that the Andean site of Tiawanaku is some 12,000 years old based on his empirical observations of the site's celestial alignments, those claims must be suspect because they violate a large body of evidence—radiocarbon dates, stratigraphy, ceramic sequences, and the like—that demonstrate a clear development of the site over several thousand years, and beginning about 4,000 years ago (not 12,000). One must question whether Hancock's observations are accurate, whether he is imposing a set of alignments on a site (and culture) for which those alignments are meaningless, and thus are simply accidental, or whether he is misreading the alignments that are there.

Recognizing that archaeology is a science is important because it keeps us from accepting all claims about the past as equally true. We only have to worry about those that are based on clear empirical evidence examined through logic and reason. The many others we can disregard.

SOURCES: Gibbon, Guy, *Explanation in archaeology* (Oxford: Basil Blackwell, 1989); Hancock, Graham, *Fingerprints of the gods* (New York: Three Rivers Press, 1995); Kelley, Jane, and Marsha Hanen, *Archaeology and the methodology of science* (Albuquerque: University of New Mexico Press, 1988).

Our model answers for both the descriptive and processual questions are based on prior research and theory. We know something about the archaeological record in outer towns from other excavations, and we also know something about it from ancient texts dating to the Early Bronze Age. We have several bodies of theory on the relationship between elites and commoners in early cities like Tell es-Sweyhat, and the basic model we have taken from them is that elites provided military and religious services to the commoners, who were basically coerced to support them, but who also willingly gave support for the military defense provided by the city and by the supernatural support provided through the temple complex. Our main hypothesis is that clear distinctions will be present in the activities taking place in the inner versus the outer town, with the inner town focused on military and religious activities and the outer town on craft and agricultural production. We need to gather a variety of data, then, on the organization of the settlement and on the

FIGURE **3.2**
Ongoing excavations at Tell es-Sweyhat.

differences in activities taking place in the town in order to answer both our descriptive and processual questions.

## PHASE III: COLLECTING DATA

The outer town of Tell es-Sweyhat covers roughly 40 hectares. How do we go about collecting a variety of data on settlement organization and residential activities over such a large area? We can't possibly excavate that whole area, and indeed, since all of the information is buried, we can't even tell where the most informative data are buried—we don't know where to dig. The Valley of Oaxaca researchers faced an even larger problem: how to gather information on changes in population density over an area of more than 2,000 square kilometers! How do archaeologists collect data over such large areas? There are three basic methods used, and which one is employed by the archaeologist on a given project depends on the data required to answer their particular question. The three methods are pedestrian survey, test excavation, and remote sensing.

**Pedestrian survey** is the primary way archaeologists find archaeological deposits. Pedestrian survey is what the name suggests—walking around and looking for sites (see Figure 3.3). Usually a group of archaeologists will line up about five meters apart and walk in straight lines across an area looking for artifacts, ecofacts, fossils, or features that would indicate the presence of a buried site. It is a low-tech yet highly effective method. However, there are a number of techniques that archaeologists and paleoanthropologists use to make pedestrian survey more efficient. These include the use of sampling and systematic surveying methods to reduce the area to be covered on foot. Another way archaeologists reduce the area to be examined is by focusing their search on places humans are likely to have occupied—in the eastern United States such locations are often flat, well-drained river terraces.

**Pedestrian survey:** a method of finding archaeological sites by walking along while scanning the ground surface for artifacts.

FIGURE **3.3**
Pedestrian survey in progress.

Paleoanthropologists typically focus their surveys only on those locations where there are exposed fossil beds dating to the time period of the species they are interested in finding.

Archaeologists recognize that pedestrian survey is problematic because much of the archaeological record is deeply buried and there may not be artifacts, ecofacts, fossils, or features visible on the ground surface. In most cases, then, pedestrian survey is used only to find general locations where sites are located, and not as a primary means of data collection. There are rare situations where pedestrian survey can, however, be used to collect the data needed to answer an archaeologist's questions. The Valley of Oaxaca project, for example, was based almost entirely on pedestrian survey. The location had been chosen specifically because most of the Valley was under cultivation and thus subsurface deposits were regularly brought to the surface. Also, ancient houses had been built on raised platforms that were still visible throughout the Valley. If you'll recall, the main data the researchers needed concerned population change through time. Because population can be estimated both by community size and house size, pedestrian survey provided all the information needed. This is an unusual case, however. Most archaeological projects use survey only to locate sites, not to collect primary data.

Often archaeologists combine pedestrian survey with small **test excavations** to determine how much of the archaeological record is actually visible on the surface. Test excavation is more difficult and time consuming than pedestrian survey, but it offers a much better knowledge of the actual archaeological deposits, and it is the only technique available when artifacts cannot be seen on the ground surface or when suspected archaeological deposits are thought to be deeply buried. At Laetoli, for example, Mary Leakey and her team combined survey of exposed rock with excavations in locations where fossils had been found.

The term **remote sensing** covers a variety of techniques that provide the ability to locate archaeological deposits below the ground without digging (see Figure 3.4). Most remote sensing techniques are borrowed from exploration geology and are the same ones geologists use to find buried mineral or oil deposits. They typically involve the measurement of minute variations in things like the earth's magnetic or gravitational field, or changes in an electric current or pulse of energy directed into the ground. When these subtle changes, called *anomalies,* are located, more detailed remote sensing, pedestrian survey, or test excavations can be done to map the extent and depth of the buried archaeological deposits.

**Test excavation:** small excavations used to test whether important archaeological deposits are located in a given area.

**Remote sensing:** a variety of techniques that provide the ability to locate archaeological deposits below the ground without digging.

FIGURE **3.4**
Remote sensing techniques used in archaeology. Each technique provides the capability of "seeing" different types of buried materials, or of seeing those materials in different ways, and thus are often used in combination.

|  | PASSIVE | ACTIVE |
|---|---|---|
| **POTENTIAL FIELD** | Magnetic Surveying<br><br>Gravity Surveying | Electrical Surveying<br><br>Electro-Magnetic Surveying |
| **WAVE** | Photographs<br><br>Multi-Spectral Scanners | Radar<br><br>Seismic Surveying |

One of the most common remote sensing techniques used in archaeology is geomagnetics. Geomagnetic sensing is based on the fact that the earth has a strong magnetic field that varies locally depending on what is beneath the ground. Features such as hearths, stone walls, and pits filled with organic material can alter the earth's magnetic field, as can metal and ceramic artifacts. By carefully measuring the earth's magnetic field an archaeologist can often locate these features and artifacts. The archaeologist uses a highly sensitive instrument called a magnetometer to map the earth's magnetic field over a large area. When the map is complete, areas with anomalously high or low readings point to locations where buried features or artifacts may be present.

I used geomagnetics to help map the outer town at Tell es-Sweyhat. If you'll remember, the outer town is roughly 40 hectares in size, and most of the archaeological deposits are buried under about a meter of soil, so pedestrian survey is only of marginal utility. And pedestrian survey couldn't really provide the information we needed to plan our excavations, as we were interested in locating and excavating a representative variety of residences, workshops, and the like. What the geomagnetic maps provided, in combination with pedestrian survey and test excavations, was a detailed map of the outer town, one which offered both a good idea of how the outer town is laid out and where the best places to excavate should be.

Geomagnetic sensing is called a "passive" technique because the archaeologist simply measures the existing magnetic field. There are also "active" remote sensing techniques which involve sending a pulse of energy into the ground and recording how it is affected by whatever is buried (see Figure 3.4). One of the most commonly used active techniques is soil interface radar (SIR), sometimes also called ground penetrating radar (GPR). This technique is based on the fact that different soils reflect radar energy differently. By sending a radar pulse into the ground and recording how the soils reflect it, the archaeologist can map the various soils below the ground. More important, if there are features such as walls and pits below the ground, those can be mapped as well. To conduct a radar survey, the archaeologist pulls an antenna along the ground—the size varies depending on the depth of penetration the archaeologist wants and the features expected. The antenna both sends and receives the radar pulses, and the received radar reflections are recorded on a paper strip or in a computer file. These recordings give the archaeologist a picture of what is below the ground.

FIGURE **3.5**
A small excavation unit at Tell es-Sweyhat.

Excavation, the careful recovery of buried archaeological data in context, is the primary data collection method used by archaeologists, and probably the one that comes to mind when one thinks of an archaeologist at work (Figure 3.5). Excavation itself is a complex process with two goals: (1) to find every scrap of evidence (or a statistically representative sample) about the past that a given site holds, and (2) to record the horizontal and vertical location of that evidence with precision. Archaeologists and paleoanthropologists have developed many excavation strategies and techniques to accomplish these goals, but all of them involve the careful removal of the archaeological deposits; the recovery of artifacts, ecofacts, fossils, and features from the soil those deposits have been buried in; and the detailed recording of where each artifact, ecofact, fossil, and feature was located on the site.

Excavation does not mean simply digging holes—not even neat square ones. Because few sites can ever be fully excavated (the cost involved would be tremendous, and most archaeologists feel it is important to leave some archaeological deposits undisturbed in case new techniques are developed that might be employed later on the site), archaeological excavations must be carefully planned, usually using some method of sampling. **Sampling** allows archaeologists to recover a full range of artifacts, ecofacts, fossils, and features while only excavating a small portion of a site. Sampling, however, requires that the archaeologist carefully plan where excavations will be conducted so that all areas of the site have an equal likelihood of being examined.

To date, no one has figured out a way to recover artifacts, ecofacts, fossils, and features from a site without destroying the site in the process, and this is one of the strange ironies of archaeological research. Again I emphasize: It is context—the relationships between and among artifacts, ecofacts, fossils, and features—that are of most interest to archaeologists, and it is precisely these relationships that are destroyed when archaeologists remove artifacts and other materials from a site. For this reason most excavation by professional archaeologists today is done only when a site is threatened with destruction, and then only by highly trained personnel using rigorous techniques.

**Excavation:** the recovery of buried archaeological data in context.

**Sampling:** the process of selecting a small number of representative cases from a larger group of cases.

Archaeologists and paleoanthropologists collect data in basically the same ways, with one important difference. Archaeologists tend to be most concerned with recovering intact features, while paleoanthropologists tend to be most concerned with recovering intact fossils. This leads to some differences in approaches to collecting data, particularly in where to look. Archaeologists tend to seek out undisturbed sites where intact features can be found. Paleoanthropologists, on the other hand, seek sites dating to the time period when the species of interest lived and might have been fossilized. In many cases, disturbances are a plus for paleoanthropologists, because disturbed sites may make finding fossils easier—they may be eroding out of the surface of the ground and be easily visible without digging. This doesn't mean archaeologists never excavate disturbed sites, because they do. And paleoanthropologists have sometimes made important discoveries by excavating undisturbed sites.

Excavation is also not a uniform process; rather, it is designed to recover the specific information needed to answer the question the archaeologist is pursuing. In the outer town at Tell es-Sweyhat, for example, we have a carefully planned schedule of excavation that will likely take the careers of several scholars to complete. So far we have excavated a segment of the external fortifications, a residence built against the fortification wall, several additional residences, and two workshops. This has taken about five years, and we only have achieved a first glimpse of how the outer town was structured, but five years is really not long for an archaeological project. The Valley of Oaxaca project took about fifteen years from beginning to end, and that was without excavation. Louis and Mary Leakey spent more than thirty years working at Olduvai Gorge. Why do archaeological projects take so long to complete? Largely because data collection must be meticulous. Once artifacts are collected during survey or archaeological deposits removed during excavation they can never be put back—they have to be collected properly the first time.

## PHASE IV: ANALYZING DATA

Excavation, while itself a long and sometimes tedious process, only supplies data. Data analysis is an even longer and more tedious process. In fact, it has been estimated that an archaeologist will spend a week doing data analysis for every hour spent collecting data. That may seem extreme, but there is a lot that goes into data analysis. All materials collected have to first be cleaned, stabilized (if they are decaying or breaking), and preserved. They then need to be catalogued—numbered, photographed, and described. That alone can take hours for any given piece of material, and that's before analysis can even begin!

It should be obvious from the last chapter that much of the archaeological record never survives. It is also the case that much of what does survive comes to us in fragments and in a fragile, deteriorated state. Before doing analysis, then, archaeologists and paleoanthropologists must first conserve and reconstruct the materials they have found.

**Conservation** is the process of treating artifacts, ecofacts, fossils, and in some cases features, to stop decay and, if possible, even reverse the deterioration process. Some conservation is very simple, involving only cleaning and drying the item. Other conservation is highly complex, involving long-term chemical treatments and, in some cases, long-term storage under controlled conditions. The so-called "Ice Man," for example, the 5,000-year-old individual found in 1993 in the Italian Alps (see Color Plate 3), is kept in permanently glacial-like conditions after investigators found to their dismay that warming the remains for study induced the growth of mold. The archaeologists studying him removed the mold, but they decided that his remains would have to be kept under the same conditions that preserved them in the first place. A complex storage facility had to be built to recreate the glacial environment in which he was originally found.

**Conservation:** the process of treating artifacts, ecofacts, fossils, and in some cases features, to stop decay and, if possible, even reverse the deterioration process.

FIGURE **3.6**
Archaeologist assembling a large ceramic jar from an excavation in Russia.

Reconstruction is like putting together a jigsaw puzzle—but a three-dimensional puzzle where you're not sure which pieces belong and you know not all of the pieces are there (see Figure 3.6). First, materials have to be sorted into similar types. For example, to reconstruct ceramics from a site, all the ceramics have to be sorted into types with similar color, decoration, and shapes. Then the similar pieces are compared to see if any seem to come from the same vessel. Once all the pieces thought to be from the same vessel are located, they can be assembled. Reconstruction is clearly a long, difficult process—in some cases taking years!

Once conservation and reconstruction are complete, the archaeologist or paleo-anthropologist can begin to analyze the artifacts they have found. As I noted in Chapter 2, archaeologists consider everything used or affected by humans to be part of the archaeological record, but many of our analyses are focused on only two types of materials: lithics and ceramics. Why are lithics and ceramics primary forms of archaeological data? Largely because they preserve well and are readily recoverable in the archaeological record. They are found all over the world, literally every-where humans have lived, and so archaeologists in all world areas learn how to analyze them. Also, lithic and ceramic styles of manufacture and decoration change regularly through time, and that makes them good time markers and excellent tools for developing culture histories. Finally, since both lithics and ceramics are important in the economies of the peoples who use them (particularly lithics), their analysis can tell archaeologists a lot about how a group of people used their environment, and that (like floral and faunal data) is important in both materialist and ecological theory.

Archaeologists have developed specific and often unique ways to analyze the many different types of artifacts, but there are some commonalities in the way artifacts are analyzed. First, archaeologists typically examine the *form* of an artifact—how it is shaped. For most common artifacts, such as lithics and ceramics, forms are known well enough so that they have been grouped into typologies. Placing artifacts into a **typology** is often the primary purpose of *formal analysis* (that is, the analysis of an artifact's form), because typologies allow archaeologists to place a par-ticular artifact into context with other artifacts found at the site or even at other sites. Typologies often provide a lot of information about an artifact, including its age, the species or culture with which it is affiliated, and in some cases even how it was made, used, or exchanged in the past. Figure 3.7 shows a projectile point typology for a site

**Typology:** a set of categories (or types) that represent the range of known variation in a given object.

FIGURE **3.7**

A projectile point chronology from the Icehouse Bottom site in Tennessee.

in Tennessee and the time period between about 7,300 years ago and 5,000 years ago. Over time the forms of the projectile points changed. The bases of points (f) and (g) are very different in their form from those of (c), (d), and (e), and all of them are different from (a). With this sort of typology, an archaeologist can estimate the age of a projectile point they find just by looking at the form of its base.

Second, archaeologists often measure artifacts, recording their size in various, often strictly defined, dimensions. Such *metric analyses,* as this activity is called, is used much like formal analysis to group artifacts into a typology. With these measurements one can create a typology similar to that in Figure 3.7. Instead of looking at the form of the projectile points, one looks at their sizes. Clearly the base widths of points (a), (d), and (f) in Figure 3.7 are going to differ in a manner similar to the way their base forms differ. The value of metric analysis, however, is that the typology created is less subjective than a typology using forms. In addition, many measurements can be taken from broken or partial artifact that might not be able to be classifiable by formal analysis.

Third, archaeologists often attempt to understand how an artifact was made. By examining the material the artifact is made from and how that material was manipulated, archaeologists can learn about the technology, economy, and exchange systems of the peoples who made the artifact. For example, if the material is not locally available, that means the people traded for it. Archaeologists can also study living people and how they make similar artifacts to understand how ancient artifacts were made. Anne Underhill was interested in understanding how ceramics were produced during the Longshan period in China—a period known for its elegant thin-walled pottery. In addition to studying the Longshan ceramics and the sites they came from, Underhill also visited living potters who make similar vessels today. She found that both full-time and part-time potters produce ceramics today, but was this the case in the past? Underhill measured ceramics being produced by these potters and performed a metric analysis. She found, to her surprise, that both full-time and part-time potters produce high-quality and highly uniform ceramics, difficult to tell apart from one another.

Finally, archaeologists attempt to understand how an artifact was used. Knowing how an artifact was used allows the archaeologist a direct window into ancient life. Because this information is so important, a number of sophisticated techniques have been developed to determine how artifacts were used. For stone, bone, and

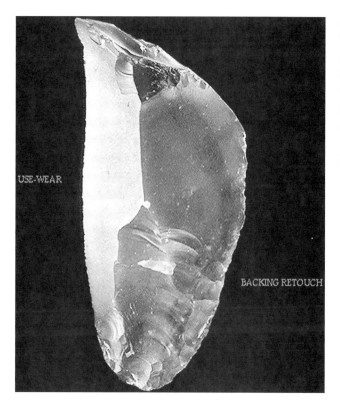

USE-WEAR

BACKING RETOUCH

FIGURE **3.8**
The jagged edge on the left side of this flake are an indication of damage caused by use wear. The edge can be examined microscopically to determine what material was being cut when the damage was caused.

wood tools, a technique called *use-wear analysis* has been developed, which can determine how a tool was used by the careful examination of the wear on its edges (see Figure 3.8). For ceramics vessels, techniques have been developed to extract residues trapped in the clay and determine what the vessel held. Archaeologist Patrick McGovern and chemist Rudolf Michel, for example, took samples of a pale yellow residue found in grooves inside ceramic vessels from Grodin Tepe in Turkey. Their analysis determined that the residue was from barley beer, providing the earliest evidence of brewing in the world (the ceramics date from 5500 to 5100 B.P.).

But what can archaeologists really learn by placing artifacts in typologies through formal and metric analysis, or by learning how an artifact was manufactured and used? A lot. Typologies allow archaeologists to use relative dating to determine the age of an artifact or site by locating it in a sequence involving other artifacts and sites with known ages. Typologies thus allow archaeologists to determine which groups were related to one another in the distant past, how information was shared among those groups, and in some cases even what social behavior was like (how labor was organized, who traded with whom). For example Carla Sinopoli examined the ceramics from the Iron Age site of Vijayanagara in southern India (Figure 3.9). Previous excavations had identified distinct residential areas of the site, including a "Noblemen's Quarter" composed of elite residences of high-caste Hindus, and the "East Valley," which was thought to contain residences of lower-caste Hindus. When Sinopoli compared ceramics across the three areas, she found distinct differences: The "Islamic Quarter" had significantly more eating vessels than either of the two other areas, a difference which Sinopoli interpreted as being related to Hindu restrictions on the use of ceramics for holding food (some Hindus will not re-use food containers, so they are often made of disposable materials, such as leaves). So ceramics not only can inform the archaeologist about the social organization of a site, they can also reveal religious beliefs.

Knowing how an artifact was manufactured allows the archaeologist to understand the technology and technical abilities of peoples in the past. For example, Thomas Wynn analyzed both the final forms and the methods used by earlier

FIGURE **3.9**

Vijayanagara city plan, showing the three major residential areas of the site.

SOURCE: Peter N. Peregrine, Carol R. Ember, and Melvin Ember, *Archaeology: Original Readings in Method and Practice* (Upper Saddle River, NJ: Prentice Hall, 2002), p. 63. Reprinted by permission of Pearson Education, Inc.

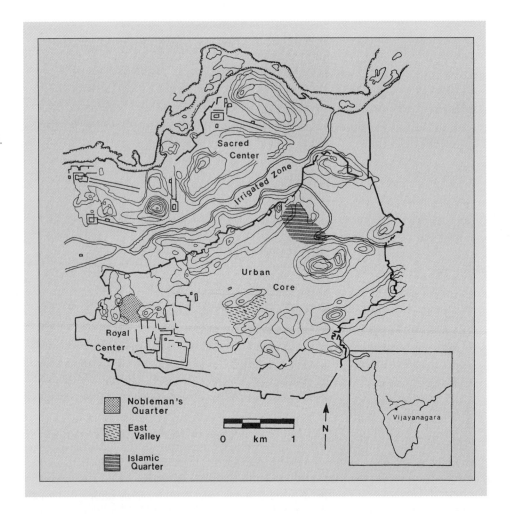

humans—*Homo erectus*—to manufacture stone tools roughly 300,000 years ago. He found that manufacturing these tools was a multistage process, involving several distinct steps and several distinct stone-working techniques to arrive at the finished product. He then evaluated this information in terms of a measure of human cognitive ability developed by Jean Piaget. He concluded that the people who made these tools probably had organizational abilities similar to those of modern humans.

Finally, knowing how an artifact was used allows the archaeologist to know something of people's behavior and activities in the past. Lawrence Keeley conducted detailed use-wear analyses on a type of stone tool called a hand axe made by *Homo erectus* peoples and found that they displayed a wide variety of uses. Some were apparently used to cut meat, others to cut wood, and still others to dig in the ground (probably for edible roots). On some hand axes, one edge was apparently used for one activity while the other was used for a different activity. Thus hand axes appear to have been multipurpose tools for our *Homo erectus* ancestors— something of a Swiss Army knife that they carried along with them. This knowledge gives us a rather interesting picture of the behavior of our ancient ancestors that is unavailable from any other source of information.

The analysis of artifacts, then, can give archaeologists insight into past behaviors, societies, and even thoughts. But they are not the only elements of the archaeological record that provide insights into the past. Archaeologists use ecofacts to reconstruct ancient environments, to determine what plants and animals people were using for food or tools, to reconstruct how plants and animals were domesticated, and, through fossils, to study ancient plants and animals themselves.

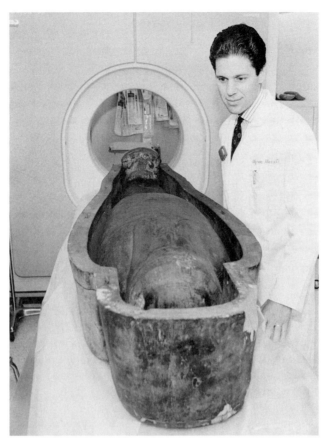

FIGURE **3.10**
A mummy from the Boston
Museum of Fine Arts being
CAT-scanned so that its
skeleton can be examined
without unwrapping.

Paleoanthropologists can tell a great deal about an extinct animal from its fossilized bones or teeth, but that knowledge is based on much more than just the fossil record itself. Paleoanthropologists rely on comparative anatomy to help reconstruct missing skeletal pieces as well as the soft tissues attached to bone. New techniques such as electron microscopy, CAT scans, and computer-assisted biomechanical modeling, provide much information about how the organism may have moved, the microstructure of bone and teeth, and how the organism developed (Figure 3.10). Chemical analysis of fossilized bone can suggest what the animal typically ate. Paleoanthropologists are also interested in the surroundings of the fossil finds. With methods developed in geology, chemistry, and physics, paleoanthropologists use the surrounding rocks to identify the time period in which the organism died. In addition, the study of associated fauna and flora can suggest what the ancient climate and habitat were like.

Much of the evidence for human evolution comes from teeth, which are the most common animal parts (along with jaws) to be preserved as fossils. Animals vary in dentition—the number and kinds of teeth they have, their size, and their arrangement in the mouth. Dentition provides clues to evolutionary relationships because animals with similar evolutionary histories often have similar teeth. For example, no primate, living or extinct, has more than two incisors in each quarter of the jaw. That feature, along with others, distinguishes the primates from earlier mammals, which had three incisors in each quarter. Dentition also suggests the relative size of an animal and often offers clues about its diet. For example, comparisons of living primates suggest that fruit eaters have flattened, rounded tooth cusps, unlike leaf and insect eaters, which have more pointed cusps. CAT scan methodology has helped paleoanthropologists image the internal parts of teeth, such as the thickness of enamel, which can also suggest the diet (seed and nut eaters have thicker enamel). Electron microscopy has revealed different patterns of growth in bones and teeth; different species have different patterns.

Paleoanthropologists can tell much about an animal's posture and locomotion from fragments of its skeleton. Animals that live in trees often have front and back limbs of about the same length; because their limbs tend to be short, their center of gravity is close to the supports on which they move. They also tend to have long grasping fingers and toes. Animals that live in open lands are often more adapted for speed, so they have longer limbs and shorter fingers and toes. Disproportionate limbs are more characteristic of brachiators (species that swing through the branches), as they have longer forelimbs. Even though soft tissues are not preserved, much can be inferred from the fossils themselves. For example, the form and size of muscles can be estimated by marks found on the bones to which the muscles were attached. The underside of the cranium may provide information about the proportions of the brain devoted to vision, smell, or memory. The skull also reveals information about characteristics of smell and vision. For example, animals that rely more on smell than on vision tend to have large snouts. Nocturnal animals tend to have large eye sockets.

Archaeologists and paleoanthropologists also learn about the past by analyzing features. The analysis of features is a little bit different from the analysis of artifacts, ecofacts, and fossils. Because features cannot be removed to the lab, they cannot be subjected to the same range of analyses as artifacts, ecofacts, and fossils. However, archaeologists have developed a number of powerful tools to analyze features in the field. The primary one is detailed mapping, usually using a surveyor's transit (Figure 3.11). Extensive records are made about each feature, explaining not only what the feature is but also what archaeological materials were found associated with it. This information can be brought together using a geographic information system (GIS). A GIS allows the archaeologist to produce a map of the features on a site and combine that map with information about the archaeological materials that were also found. Combining these kinds of information can reveal patterns in the archaeological record that tell us about human behaviors in the past.

A good example of how patterns of features can reveal past human behavior comes from the Range Site in west-central Illinois. Humans lived on the Range Site for over a thousand years, and during that time the way they organized their settlement changed. About 2,300 years ago the people at the Range Site lived in small houses

FIGURE **3.11**
An archaeologist using a surveyor's transit.

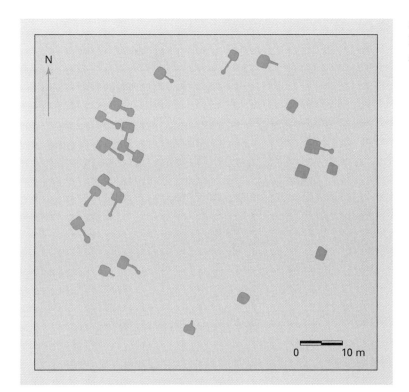

FIGURE **3.12a**
Range site community plan at
about 2300 B.P.

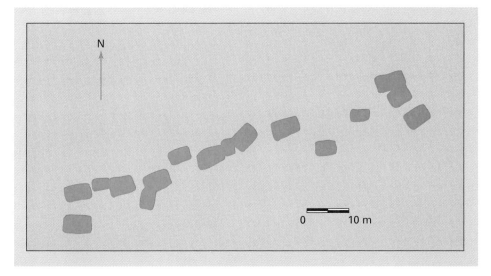

FIGURE **3.12b**
Range site community plan at
about 1000 B.P.

arranged around a circular courtyard (Figure 3.12a). This pattern continued and was
elaborated upon for almost 700 years: The courtyard area was a focus of activity and
perhaps ritual. About 1,000 years ago the pattern changed. Houses became more substantial and were arranged linearly in rows (Figure 3.12b). This change suggests a radical change in social organization. From cross-cultural research (comparative studies
using ethnographic data) we know that where circular communities are found, the
communities commonly function as a single political and economic unit, while communities arranged linearly often do not function as one political and economic unit.
What the changes in the Range Site seem to show is an attenuation of the basic social
and economic unit, from the community to the individual household. This change
seems to be related to the evolution of a large, centralized polity located at Cahokia,
only 15 kilometers from the Range Site, whose impact on surrounding communities
like the one at the Range Site may have been dramatic, transforming a socioeconomic
structure that had persisted for almost a millennium.

## Archaeology's Dirty Secret

I was brought up to believe that publishing one's research was a sacred principle of archaeology, a task to be completed before new excavations were begun. The great British Egyptologist Flinders Petrie was an early advocate of prompt and full publication. His reports are verbose and far from complete by modern standards, but at least they provide a body of basic information with which to work. Mortimer Wheeler was also careful to publish his excavations in full. My mentors did not always practice what they preached, but they taught us that prompt and full publication was a fundamental responsibility for any archaeologist who ventures into the field. The archaeological world has changed since Wheeler's day. A generation ago, most site reports were the work of a single scholar. Today, even a modest dig can involve a team of specialists and a quantity of data that may take years to study and write up. Ironically, in an academic culture that considers publication the most desirable of all scholarly activities, most archaeologists prefer to keep on digging.

The common forum for presenting field data is the academic conference, where twenty-minute papers summarize new work. In recent years, publishers have printed volume after volume of such papers, often grouped under a general title, with little editorial coherence. Invariably, conference papers give a nod to current theoretical debates, present some limited original data, and end with a brief synthesis noting how the new work advances research in a particular subject area. Often, the same paper appears in several places, recast slightly to reflect a different audience or academic emphasis. In an academic world where jobs are scarce and publication of any kind is seen as the road to employment, such bibliography padding has become commonplace, if not endemic. In one's later career the pressure to publish such papers to obtain tenure and regular promotions continues unabated. Too often definitive reports on sites, artifacts, or survey work never appear.

Clearly an overwhelming case can be made for less excavation and more analysis of previous work. Unfortunately, our scholarly culture rewards people for new and original research, sometimes defined in the narrowest terms as participation in an active fieldwork program. Grant-giving agencies contribute to the problem by funding field research while rarely giving monies for laboratory analysis or publication. Neither is a terribly sexy pursuit in a world in which museums and

## PHASE V: EVALUATING RESULTS

Once data have been collected and analyzed, the process of evaluating them in terms of the original question and model answers can begin. This might seem to be a fairly straightforward phase of the research process, but it isn't. Usually the data answer only part of the original question, or the data are contradictory. Sometimes they even contradict the originally proposed model. In the Valley of Oaxaca, for example, not only did the researchers find that population was never high enough to put pressure on resources, they actually fell dramatically in some areas over time. In

universities thrive on headline-catching discoveries, and, to quote a recent University of California staff document, "productive faculty publishing in refereed journals." The problem is further compounded by the exigencies of cultural resources management, or salvage archaeology, whose requirements for prompt reporting result for the most part in factual accounts with limited, if not restricted, distribution. A researcher can spend days, sometimes months, tracking down what is technically published information. Meanwhile definitive archaeological monographs, such as those on the Maya city of Tikal, which appear at regular intervals, are becoming a rarity. Few outlets remain for such valuable studies. Economic realities make it ever harder for even the best endowed academic presses to produce such monographs.

Surprisingly, there is little, if any, academic discussion of these issues. Perusing the programs of several major conferences, I see no panel sessions on this issue, nor on alternative means of disseminating archaeological data. Hershel Shanks, editor of *Biblical Archaeology Review,* calls the crisis "archaeology's dirty secret." In a recent editorial, he recommended the creation of a new profession: archaeology editor/writer, "specialists who know how to publish reports."

Archaeologists have a clear obligation to publish their research promptly and in full. After all, ours is the only science that "murders its informants," as American archaeologist Kent Flannery once put it. If we were to devote as much time to publishing as we do to excavating, we would not be accused, with some justification, of being a self-serving, special-interest group that keeps its finds to itself. Some of those who make such accusations are now picking up on the publishing problem and arguing that by not producing final reports we are effectively looters ourselves. Writing final reports and monographs is far from glamorous work. But as Mortimer Wheeler and others pointed out many years ago, only the archaeologist who did the work and led the research team can write the final and definitive report that records exactly what was found and what it means. We are witnessing a sea change in the way archaeologists go about their business. I do not agree with Hershel Shanks that the solution lies in specialist report writers. It lies in archaeologists living up to their fundamental responsibilities. Fortunately, creative solutions await those bold enough to seize them.

Adopted from "Archaeology's dirty secret" by Brian Fagan, 1995, *Archaeology* 48(4):14–17.

fact, the researchers found that the population fluctuated a great deal, and this fluctuation may have had more impact on cultural change in the Valley of Oaxaca than population growth. These kinds of problems are found all the time in archaeological research, and are really part of the whole evaluation process, and one reason why evaluation is really an ongoing part of any archaeological project.

While formal evaluation of the original question happens only at the end of the research process, more informal evaluation goes on all the time. As data are recovered and analyzed it often becomes clear that they won't be sufficient to answer the question posed. Sometimes, as in the case of Oaxaca, they confuse or

FIGURE **3.13**
An artist's rendering of a Tell es-Sweyhat tomb.

even contradict original models or assumptions, and the entire research process itself has to be called into question. Indeed, surprises are part of the game in archaeology, a part of the research process that keeps it from being too highly formalized or procedural. We can never know what the ground is going to hold until we dig it up, and what we dig up is often a surprise. So while I have outlined here a rather formal process, recognize that it is a process built to be flexible, to allow for change midstream, and, most important, a process that allows new questions to arise.

A few years ago my colleagues at the University of Pennsylvania visited Tell es-Sweyhat to check on things between seasons. The farmer who owns the southern part of the outer town complained to them that our excavation holes were draining all his irrigation water. This sounded a bit strange, since our excavations in that part of the site were rather shallow, so they went out to look at the holes the farmer was complaining about. It turned out that the irrigation water had percolated through the soil and eaten through limestone caps that covered Early Bronze Age shaft tombs, and several were now open and filling with water. This is the kind of surprise that often occurs in archaeology. We now think there may be as many as 120 tombs on the western side of the site, and we have spent two seasons with part of the crew excavating the disturbed ones (Figure 3.13). So, while formal, the archaeological research process has to be flexible enough to allow us to pursue surprises like these. Indeed, this surprise should lead to very interesting questions about the relationship between the inner and outer towns, since these tombs precede architecture in the outer town and are covered up by it, yet the people building houses some two centuries after these tombs were capped apparently didn't know they were there!

New questions not only arise from surprises, but are an important aspect of the evaluation phase for any project; indeed, most archaeological projects end in new questions, not in answers to old ones. My dissertation research and much of the research I have done since has focused on questions arising from the Valley of Oaxaca project. Imagine the researcher's surprise when they found that their population pressure model could not alone explain the rise of the state. What could? Well, one thing the researchers noticed was that the Monte Albán state had attempted to take control of the economy. For example, the state mass-produced ceramics that were used by everyone, and it does not appear that there were any independent ceramic producers. How would emergent leaders gain this type of economic control? Under what conditions could this happen? Warfare seems to have been endemic in the Valley of Oaxaca before the rise of Monte Albán. Could conquest and pacification by a single group have led to this state? Could it have led to economic control too? These were the sort of questions the researchers in Oaxaca were left with, and are the sort of questions I was directed toward by my mentors and colleagues who were part of the Oaxaca project. The archaeological research process, then, never really ends. It leads to new questions that are, in turn, addressed, sometimes by a new generation of archaeologists.

In order for the archaeological research process to be a continuing one, however, archaeologists must disseminate their findings. An essential aspect of any archaeological project, therefore, is **publishing** the results. In fact, a conscientious archaeologist will produce a report during each phase of the research process, and often several for the data collection and analysis phases. Unfortunately, not all do. The bulk of contemporary archaeological literature consists of data analysis reports. Altogether too few archaeologists produce final reports for the evaluation phase, which is a continuing problem in archaeology today (see the box feature titled "Archaeology's Dirty Little Secret"). It is an understandable problem, however, since projects always end in new questions, and it can be difficult to stop the research process to take the time to answer the questions already asked. Also, as projects evolve, sometimes those old questions turn out to be unanswerable, or at least the wrong ones to ask, and writing a report about them is almost impossible. Still, archaeologists are required to disseminate the results of their research. If they don't, they are no better than looters who take artifacts from sites for personal collections or monetary gain. Indeed, the thing that most clearly separates an archaeologist from an artifact collector is the research process I've just outlined and the responsibility of reporting the results of research to the larger community of archaeologists and to the public as a whole. Publication is the only thing that can give "life" to the archaeological research process—that can give it the ability to continue through new questions and new archaeologists pursuing answers.

## ⚙ SUMMARY

All archaeological research begins with questions. Archaeologists go about answering those questions through the research process—it begins with questions and ends with answers (and usually more questions). The first step in answering questions is to propose a possible answer or a set of answers. These possible answers are called models, and are based on particular bodies of theory that provide a set of assumptions for how humans behave. Once models are developed, the archaeologist decides what specific information is necessary to evaluate them.

Field research—survey and excavation—is initiated only after questions have been asked and models built. Why? Because an archaeologist can't possibly collect everything, and so they have to determine beforehand what specific information is needed in order to test their model. Sampling also helps archaeologists determine precisely what data to collect. Once collected, data must be interpreted to determine what they mean. Archaeologists have developed a powerful set of analytical tools to recover meaning from the archaeological record. Once data have been analyzed and interpreted they can be evaluated in relation to the theoretical model under which they were collected. The outcome of most evaluations are a new set of questions, and that, in essence, starts the process of archaeological research all over again.

## ⚙ DISCUSSION QUESTIONS

1. Describe each of the five phases of the archaeological research process.
2. Describe some of the types of information archaeologists can obtain through the analysis of recovered artifacts, ecofacts, fossils, and features.
3. Why is publishing findings and results an essential part of archaeological research?

**Publishing:** an important part of archaeological research, since archaeologists are required to disseminate the results of their research to others.

## ⬡ESSAY QUESTIONS

1. Examine an archaeological report from a book or journal and outline the research process used. How does it differ from the one presented here? In what ways is it similar? To what extent does the archaeological report you read support the idea that there is a standard research process in archaeology?

2. Archaeological excavation is intended to be a method that allows artifacts, ecofacts, fossils, and features to be recovered in context. Explain how excavation allows context to be recovered. How are the relationships between artifacts, ecofacts, fossils, and features maintained once they are taken out of the ground?

3. In the first chapter I made the point that the past is political because it can be used today to set goals and justify actions based on the precedent of the past. Given this idea, is the archaeological research process presented here also political? In what ways might politics interrupt, alter, or extend the research process presented here?

## ✒ RESEARCH PROJECT

Use your local library to find books or videos on "fantastic" or "mysterious" archaeological topics such as ancient visits by aliens, the lost world of Atlantis, or channeling ancient spirits to learn about the past. Examine at least two or three of these types of works, and then consider them in the light of the archaeological research process described in this chapter. In what ways do they attempt to model that process? How do they violate it? What makes these types of research into the past nonarchaeological and nonscientific?

## ⬡KEY SOURCES

### Phase I: Asking Questions

Gibbon, 1984; Hodder, 1999; Peregrine, 2001.

### Phase II: Building Models

Bell, 1994; Binford, 1983, Clarke, 1972; Ingersoll, Yellen, and Macdonald, 1977; Ramenofsky and Steffen, 1998; South, 1977.

### Phase III: Collecting Data

Barker, 1993; Clark, 1996; Dillon, 1993; Hester, Shafer, and Feder, 1997; Neumann and Stanford, 2001; Webster, 1974.

### Phase IV: Analyzing Data

Banning, 2000; Brothwell, 1981; Brothwell and Pollard, 2001; Cronyn, 1990; Davies, 1987; Henderson, 2000; Hesse, 1985; Hodder and Orton, 1976; Keeley, 1980; Knecht, 1997; Lambert, 1997; O'Connor, 2000; Odell, 1996; Orton, Tyers, and Vince, 1993; Pearsall, 1989; Rice, 1987; Sease, 1994; Shepard, 1963; Silva, 1997; Sutton and Arkush, 1996; Ubelaker, 1989.

### Phase V: Evaluating Results

Peregrine, 2001; Peregrine, Ember, and Ember, 2002.

# WHAT ARCHAEOLOGISTS ARE TRYING TO UNDERSTAND

The process of archaeological research proceeds in stages or phases. These phases are what help define archaeology as a science—science being a process rather than a thing. Science is an activity, a process which involves empirical observations of the world, measurement of the things being observed, and the discovery of patterns or regularities within these observations through mathematics and logical reasoning. In this Web Activity, you will view an archaeologist on a southwest American pueblo site, describing how he uses the scientific process to discover the chronology of the pueblo. The text of Chapter 3 describes the scientific process used by archaeologists and explains how archaeologists are scientists.

The Media Lab can be found in Chapter 3 on the *Companion Website*™ http://www.prenhall.com/peregrine

## WEB ACTIVITY

The southwestern United States is a seemingly dry, nearly barren terrain. Yet over many centuries numerous peoples have flourished there, some building great pueblos and then disappearing forever. The significance of the southwest in archaeology has been manifold. Many anthropologists claim that scientific archaeology began here. The American southwest (Colorado, Arizona, New Mexico, and Utah) is mostly desert and as such has preserved much of the archaeological record. The prehistoric people of the southwest built their homes out of rock and made many different types of pottery, both of which preserve virtually forever. In this activity, you will view modern footage of the archaeological process as a backdrop to one southwest archaeologist describing the questions which archaeologists often ask.

## Activity

1. View the video. What do the various pottery styles found in this site tell us? How do the questions and answers fit into the author's five stages of the process of archaeological research?

2. What has the southwest archaeologist in this video determined to be the origins of the people that make up this pueblo? How did he arrive at this determination? Where do these conclusions fit into the author's description of the process of archaeological research?

3. How can an archaeologist determine when particular sections of a pueblo were built, at least in a relative sense?

# The First Humans

Where should I begin the discussion of world prehistory? I could go back to the beginnings of life on earth, some 3.5 billion years ago (Figure 4.1). Or I might start with the physical structure of our cells, which have an ancestry going back more than a billion years, to the time of the first eukaryotic cells (which have a membrane-bound nucleus). Each of our cells contains structures called mitochondria, which manufacture enzymes our cells use to produce

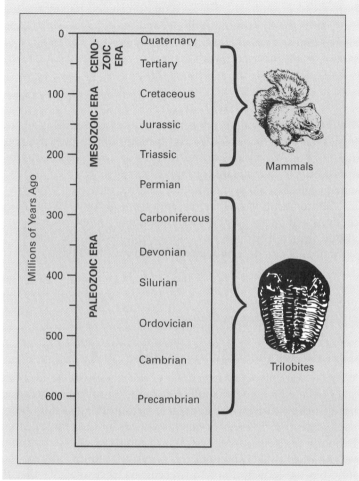

FIGURE **4.1**
A time-line of life on earth.
All animal life has genetic
roots going back to the
Precambrian era. Complex
animals can trace roots back
to more primitive ones, like
Trilobites, living in the
Paleozoic era. And mammals
can trace roots back to the
Mesozoic era, more than
100 million years ago.

SOURCE: Adapted from Bernard G.
Campbell & James D. Loy,
*Humankind Emerging, 8/e.* Published
by Allyn and Bacon, Boston, MA.
Copyright © 2000 by Pearson
Education. Reprinted by permission
of the publisher.

energy, and these structures can be traced back to ancient bacteria that joined in a symbiotic relationship with early eukaryotic cells perhaps a billion years ago. We carry traces of the first mammals as well. These traces are more obvious and more visible than mitochondria. We share hairy bodies, mammary glands, a four-chambered heart, and warm-blooded metabolism with mammals living as much as 100 million years ago.

We also carry traces of our primate heritage, stretching back more than 60 million years to when mammalian insect eaters took to the trees and adapted to life in the branches of ancient forests. Over time, basic primate features such as a generalized limb structure in which arms and legs are similar, grasping hands and feet with nails instead of claws, mobile digits and excellent hand–eye coordination, increased reliance on sight over smell, improved color vision and depth perception, and an enlarged brain capable of rapidly processing visual input and translating it into precise movement evolved as adaptations to arboreal life.

But humans don't ordinarily live in trees and are certainly not habitually arboreal. We live on the ground, and we are unique among the other primates (even those that live on the ground) in being habitually **bipedal.** For most paleoanthropologists, the evolution of habitual bipedalism marks the beginning of our human family—the **hominids.** Why does bipedalism mark the beginning of humanity? Most scholars think that habitual bipedalism was the catalyst for other changes, both physical and behavioral, that fundamentally transformed our ancient ancestors from apes into humans. These changes included freeing the hands for tool use, an increase in brain size and complexity, and changes in the pelvis that may have altered human reproductive and social behavior. For this reason I begin the discussion of world prehistory with the evolution of bipedal locomotion.

## THE EVOLUTION OF BIPEDAL LOCOMOTION

We do not know whether bipedalism developed quickly or gradually because the fossil record for the period when bipedalism first appeared, roughly 5 million years ago, is poor. We do know, on the basis of their skeletal anatomy, that many fossil apes dating to the time before bipedalism appeared were probably capable of standing upright. Bipedal hominids emerged first in Africa, during a time when the physical environment was changing from tropical forest to more discontinuous patches of forest and open country. Beginning about 16 million years ago, a drying trend set in that deprived African rain forests of humidity and rainfall, and caused areas of savanna (grasslands) and scattered deciduous woodlands to become more common. The tree-dwelling apes did not completely lose their customary habitats, because some tropical forests remained in wetter regions. But the new, more open country probably favored adaptations to ground living in some apes, and one of these adaptations was probably bipedalism.

### Theories for the Evolution of Bipedalism

What in particular may have favored bipedalism? One idea is that bipedalism was adaptive for life amid the tall grasses of the savannas because standing erect may have made it easier to spot ground predators as well as potential prey. Unfortunately, this theory does not adequately account for the development of bipedalism. Baboons and some other Old World monkeys also live in savanna environments, yet, although they can stand erect and occasionally do so, they have not evolved fully bipedal locomotion. And recent evidence suggests that the area where early hominids lived in East Africa was not predominantly savanna; rather, it seems to have had a mix of woodland and open country.

Other theories stress the importance of freeing the hands. If some hand activity is critical while an animal is moving, bipedalism may be favored because it frees the hands to perform other activities at the same time. What hand activities might have been so critical?

Gordon Hewes suggested that carrying food in the hands was the critical activity; if it were necessary to carry food from one locale to another, moving about only on the hind limbs would have been adaptive. In particular, the ability to carry any food to a place safe from predators may have been one of the more important advantages of bipedalism. C. Owen Lovejoy suggested that food carrying might have been important for reproduction. If males provisioned females and their babies by carrying food back to a home base, the females would have been able to conserve energy by not traveling and therefore might have been able to produce and care for more babies. Thus, whatever the advantages of carrying food, the more bipedal a protohominid was, the more it might reproduce.

But carrying food or provisioning families might not have been the only benefit of freeing the hands—bipedalism may have made feeding itself more efficient.

**Bipedal:** locomotion in which an animal walks on its two hind legs.

**Hominids:** the group of primates consisting of humans and their direct ancestors, the australopithecines and the paranthropoids.

FIGURE **4.2**
Artist's reconstruction of a
*Homo habilis* individual
making a stone tool.

Clifford Jolly argued that bipedalism would have allowed protohominids to efficiently harvest small seeds and nuts because both hands could be used to pick up food and move it directly to the mouth. In the changing environments of eastern Africa, where forests were giving way to more open woodlands and savannahs, an advantage in foraging for small seeds and nuts might well have proven important for survival.

Bipedalism might also have freed the hands of protohominids to use, and perhaps even make, tools that they could carry with them as they moved about (Figure 4.2). Consider how advantageous such tool use might have been. Sherwood Washburn noted that some contemporary ground-living primates dig for roots to eat, "and if they could use a stone or a stick they might easily double their food supply." David Pilbeam suggested that, in order to be eaten, many of the plant foods in the grassy areas inhabited by protohominids probably had to be chopped, crushed, or otherwise prepared with the aid of tools. Tools may also have been used to kill and butcher animals for food. Without tools, primates in general are not well equipped physically for regular hunting or even scavenging. Their teeth and jaws are not sharp and strong enough, and their speed afoot is not fast enough. So the use of tools to kill and butcher game or prepare foraged food might have enlarged even further protohominids' ability to exploit the available food supply.

Finally, tools may have been used as weapons against predators, which would have been a great threat to the relatively defenseless ground-dwelling protohominids. In Milford Wolpoff's opinion, it was the advantage of carrying weapons continuously that was responsible for transforming occasional bipedalism to completely bipedal locomotion. But some anthropologists question the idea that tool use and toolmaking favored bipedalism. They point out that our first clear evidence of stone tools appears more than two million years after the emergence of bipedalism. So how could toolmaking be responsible for bipedalism? Wolpoff suggests an answer. Even though bipedalism appears to be at least two million years older than stone tools, it is not unlikely that protohominids used tools made of wood and bone, neither of which would be as likely as stone to survive in the archaeological record.

Some researchers have taken a closer look at the mechanics of bipedal locomotion to see if it might be a more efficient form of locomotion in the savanna–woodland environment, where resources are likely to be scattered. Compared with the quadrapedal locomotion of primates such as chimpanzees, bipedalism appears to be more efficient for long-distance travel. But why travel long distances? If protohominids had the manipulative ability and tool-using capability of modern chimpanzees (who can, for example, use stones to crack nuts and twigs to "fish" for termites) and those ancestors had to move around in a more open environment, then those individuals who could more efficiently travel longer distances to exploit scattered resources might do better.

Finally, bipedalism might have helped protohominids regulate body temperature in the increasingly hot and dry environments of eastern Africa during the time when bipedalism evolved. Peter Wheeler argued that a bipedal posture limits the area of the body directly exposed to the sun, especially when the sun is at its hottest, midday. Bipedal posture would also facilitate convective heat loss by allowing heat to rise up and away from the body rather than being trapped underneath it. (We radiate a lot of our body heat through the head.) Cooling through the evaporation of sweat would also be facilitated by a bipedal posture, as more skin area would be exposed to cooling winds. Thus bipedalism may have developed because it reduced heat stress in the warming environments of eastern Africa.

We must remember that there are also "costs" to bipedal walking. Bipedalism makes it harder to overcome gravity to supply the brain with sufficient blood, and the weight of the body above the pelvis and lower limbs puts greater stress on the hips, lower back, knees, and feet. As Adrienne Zihlman pointed out, the stresses on the lower body are even greater for females. Females have to support extra weight during pregnancy, and as mothers they usually are responsible for carrying nursing infants. So whatever the advantages of bipedalism, they must be greater than the disadvantages—or our ancestors never would have become bipedal.

## The "Costs" of Bipedalism

The evolution of bipedalism required some dramatic changes in the ancestral ape skeleton. While apes today can and do walk bipedally, they cannot do so efficiently or for long periods of time. To be habitually bipedal the ancestral ape skeleton had to be modified, and the major changes that allowed the protohominids to become fully bipedal occurred primarily in the skull, pelvis, knees, and feet (Figure 4.3).

In both ancient and modern apes the spinal column enters the skull toward the back, which makes sense because apes generally walk on all fours, with the spine roughly parallel to the ground. In bipedal hominids, the spinal column enters the skull through the bottom. Thus, when hominids became bipedal, the skull ended up on top of the spinal column.

The shape of ancient and modern ape pelvises is considerably different from that of a bipedal hominid. Ape pelvises are long and flat, forming a bony plate in the lower back to which the leg muscles attach. In bipedal hominids the pelvis is bowl-shaped, which supports the internal organs and also lowers the body's center of gravity, allowing better balance on the legs. The hominid pelvis also provides a different set of muscle attachments and shifts the orientation of the femurs (the upper leg bones) from the side of the pelvis to the front. These changes allow hominids to move their legs forward in a bipedal stride (and do things like kick a ball). Apes, in comparison, move their legs forward (when they walk bipedally) by shifting their pelvis from side to side, not by kicking each leg forward alternately as we do.

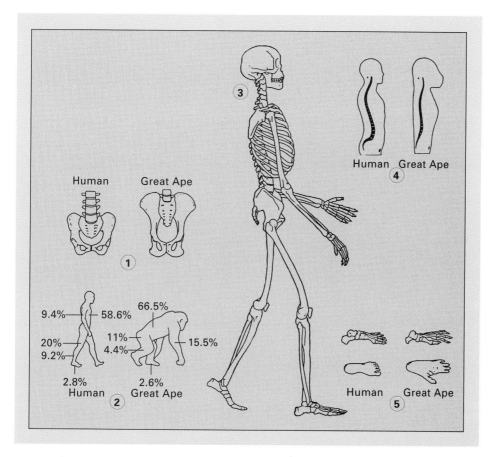

FIGURE **4.3**

Skeletal evidence of bipedalism.

Because humans move about on their legs only, the human skeleton differs from the skeleton of the great ape. The human head is more or less balanced on the backbone (*see* the feature marked 3 in the figure). There is no need for powerful muscles at the back of the neck, as in the great ape. The human vertebral column (*see* 4 in the figure) has a forward curvature in the neck and lower back regions. These two extra curves, along with the curvature in the middle back region, allow the backbone to act more like a spring, which is advantageous given that the legs have to bear all the weight and given the need to balance on one leg with each stride. Bipedal locomotion has favored a human pelvis (*see* 1 in the figure) that is lower and broader than the ape pelvis. In contrast to the apes, the legs in humans are longer than the arms and represent a larger proportion of the body weight (*see* 2 in the figure); this change lowers the body's center of gravity and is advantageous with bipedalism. The most obvious adaptation to bipedalism is the human foot (*see* 5 in the figure). The big toe is not opposed to the other toes, as in the other primates, and the foot can no longer grasp. When we walk, the big toe is the last point of contact with the ground before the leg swings forward, which explains why the big toe has become aligned with the other toes.

SOURCE: From Stephen Jones, Robert Martin, and David Pilbeam, eds., *The Cambridge Encyclopedia of Human Evolution* (New York: Cambridge University Press, 1992), p. 8. Copyright © by Cambridge University Press. Reprinted by permission of Cambridge University Press.

Another change associated with the hominid ability to kick the leg forward is our "knock-kneed" posture. Ape legs hang straight down from the pelvis. Bipedal hominid legs, on the other hand, angle inward toward one another. This not only helps us move our legs forward, but also helps us maintain a center of gravity in the midline of our bodies, so that our center of gravity does not shift from side to side when we walk or run.

FIGURE **4.4**

Sites discussed in Chapter 4.

SOURCE: From *Human Evolution Source Book* by Clochon/Pleagle, © 1993. Reprinted by permission of Pearson Education, Inc., Upper Saddle River, NJ.

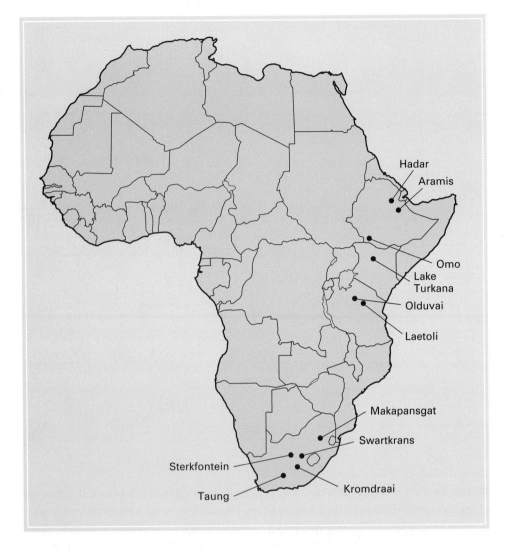

***Ardipithecus ramidus:***
perhaps the first hominid, dating to some 4.4 million years ago. Its dentition combines ape-like and australopithecine-like features, and its skeleton suggest it was bipedal.

Finally, hominid feet have two major changes compared to those of apes. First, hominid feet have an enlarged group of ankle bones forming a robust heel that can withstand the substantial forces placed on them as a result of habitual bipedalism. Second, hominid feet have an arch which also aids in absorbing the forces endured by the feet during bipedal locomotion. We know this arch is vital to our ability to be habitually bipedal because "flat-footed" people who lack it have chronic problems in their feet, ankles, knees, and back.

When did these changes take place? We don't know for sure, but fossils from East Africa—Ethiopia, Tanzania, and Kenya—clearly show that bipedal hominids lived there between 4 million and 3 million years ago, perhaps even earlier (Figure 4.4). In fact, there is some evidence that *A. ramidus,* perhaps a hominid ancestor, walked bipedally as early as 4.4 million years ago.

## ARDIPITHECUS: THE FIRST BIPEDAL APE?

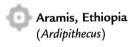
**Aramis, Ethiopia**
(*Ardipithecus*)

In 1992 a team of researchers led by anthropologist Tim White began surveying a 4.4-million-year-old fossil deposit at **Aramis** in the Middle Awash region of Ethiopia. There they discovered a remarkable find—seventeen fossils of what may be the earliest hominid (and some ninety more have been found since). At first White

FIGURE **4.5**
Paleoanthropologist Tim
White with *A. ramidus*.

and his colleagues thought that the remains were from an early australopithecine (a group of early hominids), but after re-examining the fossils, they decided the fossils were different enough from the australopithecines to warrant their own **genus** (a taxonomic category given to a distinct group of species).

What makes *A. ramidus* unique is the combination of ape-like dentition along with evidence of bipedal locomotion (Figure 4.5). Like apes, *A. ramidus* has relatively small cheek teeth with thin enamel and relatively large canines. However, the base of its skull shows that the spinal column is positioned directly underneath the skull, just like in definitely bipedal hominids. While more evidence is needed to be sure, *A. ramidus* appears to be the earliest direct human ancestor yet found.

**Genus:** a group of related species.

**Australopithecine:** a general term referring to members of the genus *Australopithecus*.

**Australopithecus:** the genus associated with the first well-established bipedal hominids.

## *AUSTRALOPITHECUS:* THE FIRST DEFINITE HOMINID

While some doubt remains about the status of *Ardipithecus* as a direct human ancestor, there is no doubt that the **australopithecines** (members of the genus *Australopithecus*) were hominids. Their teeth share the basic hominid characteristics of small canines, flat and thickly enameled molars, and a parabolic shape to the palate (see Figure 4.6), and there is unambiguous evidence that even the earliest australopithecines were fully bipedal. Not only do their skeletons reflect bipedal locomotion, but there is other evidence. As I discussed in earlier chapters, Mary Leakey found more than fifty hardened humanlike footprints dating to about 3.6 million years ago at **Laetoli, Tanzania** (see Color Plate 1). These fossilized footprints give striking confirmation that the hominids there were fully bipedal. The bipedalism of the australopithecines does not mean that these earliest definite hominids were terrestrial all of the time. All of the australopithecines, including the later ones, seem to have

**Laetoli, Tanzania**
(*Australopithecus afarensis*)

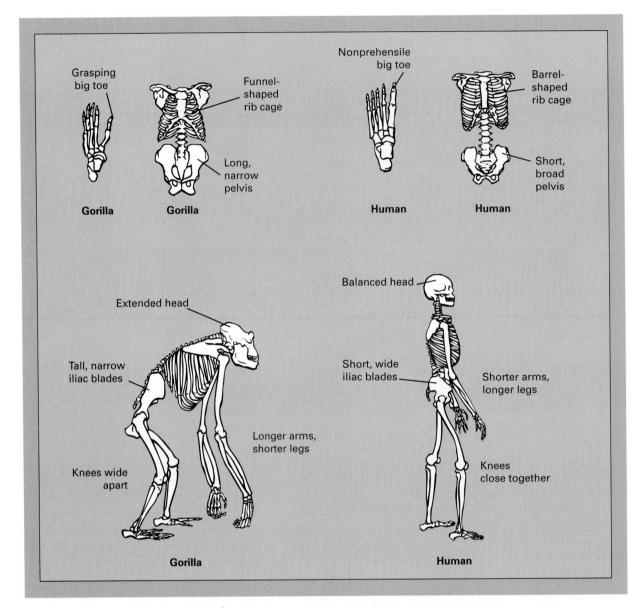

FIGURE **4.6**

Key skeletal differences between bipedal hominids and quadrupedal apes (*see also* Figure 4.3).

SOURCE: From Bernard G. Campbell & James D. Loy, *Humankind Emerging, 8/e.* Published by Allyn and Bacon, Boston, MA. Copyright © 2000 by Pearson Education. Reprinted by permission of the publisher.

*Australopithecus anamensis:* an australopithecine that lived perhaps 4.2 million years ago.

*Australopithecus afarensis:* an australopithecine that lived 4 to 3 million years ago in East Africa and was definitely bipedal.

been capable of climbing and moving in trees because their arms are about the same length as their legs (in contrast with later hominids, whose arms are shorter than their legs), and they have long, muscular fingers that would have allowed them to climb and grasp branches well.

The australopithecines show considerable variability, and paleoanthropologists divide the genus *Australopithecus* into at least three species: *A. anamensis, A. afarensis,* and *A. africanus* (Figure 4.7). *Australopithecus anamensis,* which may be 4.2 million years old, is the earliest australopithecine, and has been found only in northern Kenya. Other hominids found in East Africa from 4 million to 3 million years ago are classified by most paleoanthropologists as belonging to the species *Australopithecus afarensis.* A few paleoanthropologists do not think that these hominids should be placed in a separate species, because they resemble the later

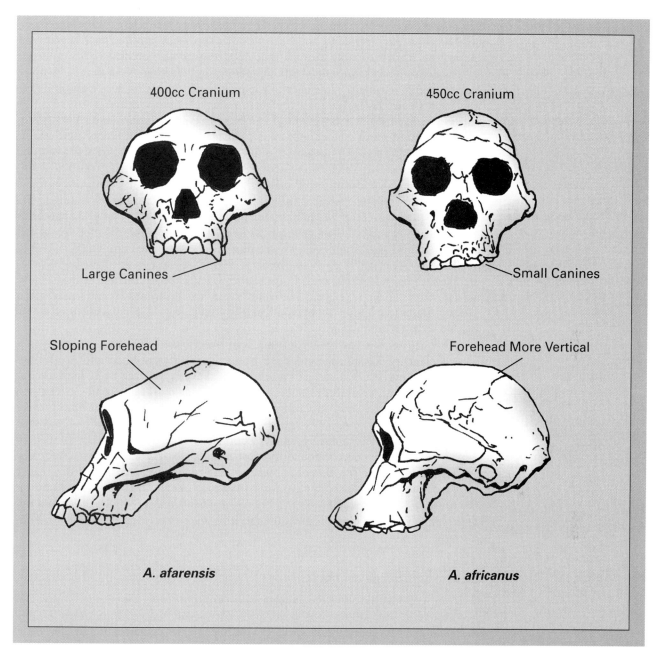

FIGURE **4·7**

Comparison of skulls of *A. afarensis* and *A. africanus*, illustrating key differences.

hominid species *Australopithecus africanus*, which lived between about 3 million and 2 million years ago, primarily in southern Africa. But the temporal and spatial separation of these australopithecines leads many paleoanthropologists to argue that they must have been different species.

Within the past several years, two additional australopithecine species have been proposed. In 1996 Ethiopian paleoanthropologist Berhane Asfaw and his team discovered *Australopithecus garhi* in rock dating to approximately 2.5 million years ago. Asfaw and his colleagues expected the new find to resemble one of the previously known australopithecine species, but it did not. The teeth and jaws were not like *A. afarensis* or any of the other australopithecines, despite having limb bones

*Australopithecus africanus:* an australopithecine that lived between about 3 and 2 million years ago, and is known primarily from southern Africa.

*Australopithecus garhi:* an australopithecine from East Africa dating from about 2.5 million years ago.

*Australopithecus bahrelghazali:* an australopithecine that lived in what is today Chad about 3 million years ago. It is the first early hominid found outside of the African Rift Valley system.

*Kenyanthropus platyops:* a newly discovered hominid from East Africa dating to about 3.5 million years ago. Many scholars believe it to be a new species of australopithecine and not a new genus as currently designated.

very like them. The remains of butchered animals were also found in the same rock layer as the *A. garhi* remains, and since no other species of hominid have been found in the area, it is reasonable to think that *A. garhi* was the butcher.

*Australopithecus bahrelghazali* was discovered farther west than any other early hominid, in what is now central Chad. *A. bahrelghazali* dates to about 3 million years ago and is very similar to contemporary *A. afarensis* fossils from the Rift Valley of East Africa. It differs from *A. afarensis* in having thinner enamel on its premolar teeth and more well-defined roots, but the important difference is where *A. bahrelghazali* lived. Most scholars assume the early hominids represent a specific adaptation to the Rift Valley. The discovery of an early australopithecine some 2,500 kilometers west of the Rift Valley calls this assumption into question.

In addition to these two australopithecines, a new hominid genus dating to the same time period as *Australopithecus afarensis*—roughly 3.5 million years ago—has recently been proposed. This new genus, *Kenyanthropus*, is represented by several dozen teeth and skull fragments, as well as a nearly complete cranium, all found in northern Kenya in 1999. *Kenyanthropus platyops* (as these fossils have been classified) shares many features with *A. afarensis* but has enough differences that Maeve Leakey, who led the team that discovered these fossils, argues it warrants its own genus designation. Other scholars argue the fossils should be classified as a new species of australopithecine.

The picture that emerges from this brief overview of the australopithecines is one of diversity. There seem to have been many different species of australopithecine, and even within species there seems to have been a relatively high level of variation. All the australopithecines shared similar environments in eastern and southern Africa, but those environments were diverse and changing. Forests were giving way to open woodlands and grasslands. Large lakes were formed and then broken apart through uplifting and volcanic activity in the rift valley of eastern Africa. And the climate continued to warm until at least 2 million years ago. The apparent diversity of the australopithecines may reflect a dispersal and divergence of bipedal hominids caused by these dynamic environmental conditions. Whatever the cause, diversity seems to be the key word when thinking about the australopithecines. Let's take a closer look at the three most well-known species of *Australopithecus.*

## *Australopithecus anamensis*

The earliest australopithecine species is *Australopithecus anamensis,* which has been found in several locations in northern Kenya and is dated to between 3.9 and 4.2 million years ago. While there is controversy about some of the specimens included in *A. anamensis,* the general picture is that it was a small (probably chimpanzee-sized) bipedal hominid with teeth similar to those of the later *A. afarensis.* The more controversial specimens have long bones suggesting well-developed bipedalism, but their elbow and knee joints look more like later *Homo* genus than any other species of *Australopithecus.*

## *Australopithecus afarensis*

*Australopithecus afarensis* is the most well-represented australopithecine species to date. Mary Leakey unearthed remains from at least two dozen individuals at Laetoli, and the remains of at least thirty-five individuals have been found at another site, Hadar, in Ethiopia (see the box on Hadar). The Hadar finds are remarkable for their completeness. Whereas paleoanthropologists often just find parts of the cranium and jaws, many parts of the skeleton were also found at Hadar, including the famous 40 percent complete skeleton of a female hominid named Lucy by its discoverer, Donald Johanson (see Color Plate 4). Although Lucy and the other

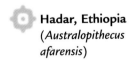
**Hadar, Ethiopia**
(*Australopithecus afarensis*)

# Hadar

Hadar today is as barren and arid a place as any on earth. It is a geologically active area, part of the great East African rift valley, and has an extemely rugged topography due to faulting and erosion. Three million years ago, however, the region was on the shores of a lake, and was lush with grasses and trees.

It was in 1973 that the potential of the Hadar region as an early hominid fossil site first became apparent. In that year an international team led by Maurice Taieb, Yves Coppens, and Donald Johanson discovered a 3-million-year-old hominid knee, giving clear evidence of bipedalism perhaps a million years earlier than many scholars at the time expected to find it. The team returned the following year, and discovered the famous Lucy skeleton—a 40 percent complete female australopithecine that was to become the clearest example of the species *Australopithecus afarensis*.

In 1975 the team discovered in a single location (known as locality 333) a collection of some 200 fossil fragments representing at least thirteen individuals. Since males, females, and infants were all present, the researchers termed the collection the "first family" and suggested that they may have died and been buried together in a sudden catastrophe (others suggest the remains were brought together by a predator who over time dragged its hominid kills back to a favorite spot to devour). All the finds discovered during this three-year period date from between 2.8 and 3.3 million years ago, making the collection a remarkably large one for such an early date.

Government interference and later civil war kept Johanson and other Western researchers out of Hadar for more than a decade. In 1992 Johanson returned and was immediately taken to spots where hominid fossils had been found by locals who were members of Johanson's field crew years earlier. One of these turned out to be the most complete *Australopithecus afarensis* skull yet discovered, another was a location with a wealth of fossil materials. In the three years that followed almost fifty new hominid fossils were discovered. Hadar continues to be one of the richest and most important places for early hominid research.

SOURCES: Johanson, Donald, and Maitlin Edey, *Lucy: The Beginning of Humankind* (New York: Simon and Schuster, 1981); Johanson, Donald, 1996, "Face to face with Lucy's family," *National Geographic* 189: 96–118.

hominids at Hadar were once thought to be about as old as those at Laetoli (roughly 3.6 million years old), recent dating suggests that they are somewhat younger—less than 3.2 million years old. Lucy probably lived 2.9 million years ago. The environment Lucy lived in was semiarid, upland savanna with rainy and dry seasons.

The existence of such extensive fossil collections has allowed paleoanthropologists like Donald Johanson and Tim White to develop a portrait of this ancient

**Sexually dimorphic:**
marked differences in size and appearance between males and females of a species.

hominid species. *A. afarensis* was a small hominid, and, like most of the living great apes (but unlike modern humans), was **sexually dimorphic,** meaning that males and females had significantly different body sizes. Females were smaller, weighing around 65 pounds and standing a little more than 3 feet tall. Males were much larger, weighing more than 90 pounds and standing about 5 feet tall (see Color Plate 5).

*A. afarensis* teeth were large compared to their body size, and they had thick molar enamel. They also had large ape-like canines which, on some specimens, projected beyond the adjacent teeth. The thick enamel on the molars and wear patterns on the molar crowns suggest that small, hard materials like nuts and fruit with hard pits made up a significant part of the diet of *A. afarensis.* The cranium of *A. afarensis* reflects its dentition. The face juts forward because of the large teeth and jaws, and the base of the skull flares out to provide attachment areas for large neck muscles to support the heavy face. The brain is small, about 400 cc, but relatively large for an animal this size.

The arms and legs of *A. afarensis* were about the same length, and the fingers and toe bones are curved, suggesting they were heavily muscled. Most scholars believe these limb proportions and strong hands and feet point to a partially arboreal lifestyle. In other words, it appears that *A. afarensis* spent a lot of time in the trees, probably feeding, sleeping, and avoiding terrestrial predators. The pelvis and leg bones of *A. afarensis,* however, demonstrate that it moved bipedally when on the ground. The pelvis is wide and flaring, but has the bowl-like shape of all later hominids. The legs angle inward, and the feet have an arch and an ankle much like later hominids. Detailed analyses of the Laetoli footprints suggest that *A. afarensis* may have had a shorter and less efficient stride than modern humans.

## *Australopithecus africanus*

*A. africanus* holds the distinction of being the first australopithecine species to be indentified. In 1925, Raymond Dart presented the first evidence that an erect bipedal hominid existed millions of years ago through the fossil of a child he called **Taung,** after the name of the South African cave in which the fossil was found. Since Dart's discovery of the Taung child more than 75 years ago, the remains of hundreds of other similar australopithecines have been unearthed from the caves at **Sterkfontein** and **Makapansgat** in South Africa (see the box feature on Sterkfontein later in this chapter). From this abundant evidence a fairly complete picture of *A. africanus* can be drawn (Figure 4.8).

Like *A. afarensis, A. africanus* was very small; the adults were 3.5 to 4.5 feet tall, weighed 60 to 90 pounds, and were also sexually dimorphic. Their skeletons show remarkable similaritiy to *A. afarensis* as well, and, like *afarensis, africanus* may have routinely spent time in trees. *A. africanus* had a brain averaging about 450 cc. It also had a large, chinless jaw and a forward-projecting face like that of *A. afarensis,* but some of the dental features of *A. africanus* are more similar to those of later hominids—broad incisors and small, short canines. And, although its premolars and molars are quite large compared to the size of *africanus's* skull, their form is also similar to those of later hominids. Presumably, function and use were also similar, perhaps meaning they had a broader diet than *A. afarensis.*

Dating of the australopithecine finds from the South African limestone caves is somewhat difficult because the stratigraphy is very complex and the types of volcanic materials typically needed for absolute dating techniques are very rare. But relative dating is possible. Comparisons of the fauna found associated with *A. africanus* with fauna found elsewhere suggest that the South African *A. africanus* lived between 3 million and 2 million years ago. The climate was probably semiarid, not too different from the climate of today.

**Taung, South Africa** (*Australopithecus africanus*)

**Sterkfontein, South Africa** (*Australopithecus africanus, Homo habilis*)

**Makapansgat, South Africa** (*Australopithecus africanus*)

FIGURE **4.8**
Skull of *Australopithecus africanus* from Sterkfontein.

*Paranthropus:* a genus of early hominids with extremely large faces and teeth.

**Paranthropoids:** members of the genus *Paranthropus*.

**Sagittal crest:** a ridge of bone running along the top of the skull in apes and early hominids.

*Paranthropus robustus:* a paranthropoid found in South Africa dating from about 1.8 to 1 million years ago.

*Paranthropus boisei:* the largest of the paranthropoids, this East African species dates from about 2.2 to 1.3 million years ago.

*Paranthropus aethiopicus:* the earliest paranthropoid, dating to about 2.5 million years ago, and found in East Africa.

**Kromdraai, South Africa** (*Paranthropus robustus*)

**Swartkrans, South Africa** (*Paranthropus robustus*)

**Omo Basin, Ethiopia** (*Paranthropus boisei, Homo habilis*)

**Lake Turkana, Kenya** (*Paranthropus aethiopicus, Paranthoropus boisei, Homo habilis*)

**Olduvai Gorge, Tanzania** (*Paranthoropus boisei, Homo habilis*)

## PARANTHROPUS

Living alongside the australopithecines in East Africa and in South Africa from about 2.5 million to 1 million years ago were a distinct group of hominids, members of the genus *Paranthropus*, literally "beside humans"(see Figure 4.9). These **paranthropoids** resemble australopithecines in many ways, but have much larger faces, jaws, and teeth. Some individuals had a ridge of bone called a **sagittal crest** on the top of their heads that anchored the heavy musculature needed for their huge teeth and jaws. In addition, two paranthropoid species, *P. robustus* and *P. boisei*, have somewhat larger cranial capacities (about 490 to 530 cc) than any of the australopithecine species. In other ways, however, *Paranthropus* is so close to *Australopithecus* that many paleoanthropologists don't use the *Paranthropus* genus, but apply *Australopithecus* to all paranthropoids. I consider the differences between the paranthropoids and australopithecines to be fairly clear and warrant a clear distinction. Thus I use *Paranthropus* throughout this text.

The paranthropoids were found first in South African caves, in **Kromdraai** and in **Swartkrans,** and later in East Africa, in the **Omo Basin** in Ethiopia, on the east and west sides of **Lake Turkana** in Kenya, and **Olduvai Gorge** in Tanzania. Most paleoanthropologists classify the South African paranthropoids from about 1.8 million to 1 million years ago as *Paranthropus robustus* and the East African paranthropoids from 2.2 million to 1.3 million years ago as *Paranthropus boisei.* The third robust species, *Paranthropus aethiopicus,* is even earlier, dating back more than 2.5 million years ago, and may have been ancestral to *P. boisei.*

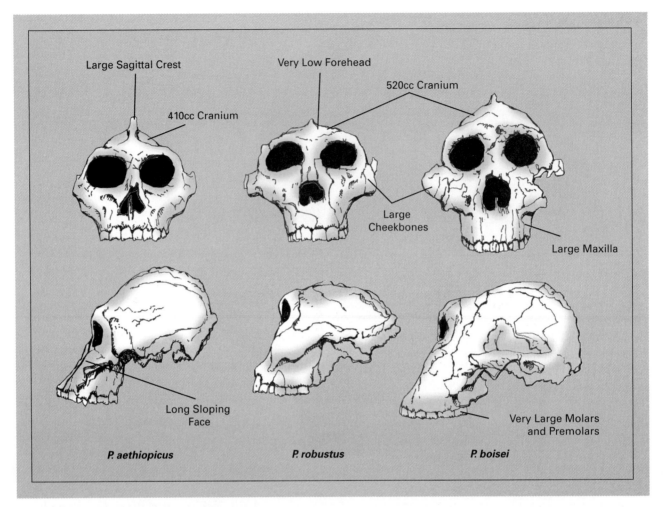

FIGURE **4.9**

Comparison of skulls of *P. aethiopicus,* *P. robustus,* and *P. boisei,* illustrating key differences.

It used to be thought that the paranthropoids were substantially bigger than the other australopithecines. But recent calculations suggest that the paranthropoids were not substantially different in body weight or height as compared with the australopithecines. The differences are primarily in the skull and jaw, most strikingly in the teeth. If the paranthropoids were larger in body size, their slightly bigger brain capacity would not be surprising, since larger animals generally have larger brains. However, because the bodies of the paranthropoids appear to be similar to that of *A. africanus,* the brains of the paranthropoids were relatively larger than the brain of *A. africanus.*

## Paranthropus aethiopicus

*Paranthropus aethiopicus* is the earliest and also the least well known of the paranthropoids. *P. aethiopicus* is represented by a small group of fossils found in northern Kenya and southern Ethiopia dating to between 2.3 and 2.7 million years ago, including one spectacular find—a nearly complete skull (known as the "Black Skull" because of its dark color) found in 1985. It seems clear that *P. aethiopicus* was quite different from the australopithecines living in the same area at about the same time. *P. aethiopicus* differs from *A. afarensis* specimens from roughly the same region and perhaps even the same time period by having much larger dentition, particularly molars, huge cheek bones, projecting and dish-shaped (round and flat) faces, and large sagittal crests, but they are similar to *A. afarensis* in most other ways. Overall, *P. aethiopicus* resembles *A. afarensis* but has a much larger face and teeth.

### *Paranthropus robustus*

In 1936 Robert Broom, then curator of vertebrate paleontology at the Transvaal Museum in South Africa, discovered the first paranthropoid—*Paranthropus robustus*. Broom had initiated his search for fossil hominids in order to find evidence supporting the idea that *Australopithecus* represented an early human ancestor, and he was quite successful finding new fossils (see the box feature on Sterkfontein). But unlike another example of *A. africanus*, which Broom had expected to find, the skull of *P. robustus* was larger. It had larger teeth and a massive jaw, and it had a sagittal crest. It also had a larger brain than *A. africanus*—around 500 cc. While the jaw was larger and thicker than *A. africanus*, the face of *P. robustus* was flatter and very broad, with huge cheek bones. After considering these differences, Broom decided that the fossil represented an entirely new hominid genus—*Paranthropus*.

### *Paranthropus boisei*

Legendary paleoanthropologist Louis Leakey began his search for a human ancestor in 1931 at Olduvai Gorge in western Tanzania. It was not until 1959 that his efforts paid off with the discovery of *Paranthropus boisei* (named after a benefactor, Charles Boise). How did *P. boisei* differ from *P. robustus*? Compared with *P. robustus*, *P. boisei* had even more extreme features that reflected a huge chewing apparatus—enormous molar teeth and expanded premolars that look like molars, a massive thick and deep jaw, thick cheek bones, and a more pronounced sagittal crest. Indeed, *P. boisei* has been called "hyper-robust"—a name that definitely captures the species (see Figure 4.10 on page 82).

*P. boisei* lived between about 2.3 and 1.3 million years ago. Like *P. robustus* it appears to have lived in a dry, open environment and to have eaten a lot of coarse seeds, nuts, and roots. Living in East Africa at the same time as the *P. boisei* was also the first member of our genus, ***Homo.***

## EARLY *HOMO*

The first members of our genus were not dramatically different from the australopithecines and paranthropoids. They lived in the same areas and, as I discuss in the next chapter, probably had a similar lifestyle. The major difference between early *Homo* and the earlier hominids is the size of the brain. The australopithecines had relatively small cranial capacities, averaging about 450 cc—not much larger than that of chimpanzees. The paranthropoid brain was not much larger, averaging about 530 cc. But around 2.3 million years ago some hominids showed evidence of enlarged brain capacity. These hominids, early *Homo*, had cranial capacities averaging about 640 cc, which is about 50 percent of the brain capacity of modern humans (average slightly more than 1,300 cc).

What might have favored the increase in brain size? Many anthropologists think that the increase is linked to the emergence of stone toolmaking about 2.5 million

***Homo:*** the genus to which modern humans and their ancestors belong.

## Sterkfontein

In 1936 Robert Broom, the curator of vertebrate paleontology at the Transvaal Museum in Pretoria, South Africa, was searching for additional australopithecine fossils to support Raymond Dart's assertions that *Australopithecus* was a human ancestor. On August 7 Broom visited the Sterkfontein quarry near Pretoria and was handed what looked like a fossilized brain—an endocranial cast (a natural cast of the inside of the skull formed by sediment filling the cranium after the animal died) of an ancient ape. The cast had been blasted from the limestone only that morning, and Broom quickly began searching through the rest of the blast debris. By the end of the next day he had most of the skull of an adult *Australopithecus africanus*. In the years that have followed, dozens of additional finds have been made at Sterkfontein, including an australopithecine pelvis, spine, ribs, femur, foot, and several partial skulls.

As with most South African cave sites, Sterkfontein was formed as silt and sand washed into a subsurface limestone cavern. The region at the time of the australopithecines was cooler and dryer than it is today and was covered in a mosaic of savannas and woodlands. The australopithecine deposits were revealed as the limestone eroded and exposed the ancient cave deposits. These cave deposits were quarried beginning in the late 1800s, and many were blasted away before the site became recognized as one with fossil hominids. Who knows how many hominid remains are now parts of Pretoria streets and buildings. In this way, Sterkfontein is like most of the South African fossil hominid sites. There is little clear stratigraphy, and many of the remains have been found through quarrying and are, thus, out of context and difficult to date.

years ago. The reasoning is that stone toolmaking was important for the survival of our ancestors, and therefore bigger-brained individuals would have been favored because they had motor and conceptual skills that enabled them to be better toolmakers. According to this view, the enlargement of the brain and more sophisticated toolmaking would have developed together. Other anthropologists think that the enlargement of the brain might have been favored by other factors, such as hunting and language.

For example, Grover Krantz argued that "persistence hunting" might have been the driving force behind the enlargement of the brain. He posited that early hominids would not usually have been able to kill prey outright, but rather would have wounded and tracked their prey for long periods of time—perhaps days—before the wounded animal finally succumbed and could be dispatched. In this scenario, a bigger brain would have improved memory and concentration, and hunters with bigger brains would have been more successful. Gordon Hewes also suggested hunting might have been the driving force behind brain enlargement, but because hunting would have required cooperation among early hominids and cooperation

Sterkfontein has been the subject of careful excavation, and some recognizable stratigraphy has been discerned at the site. The australopithecine materials come from strata that date about 3.5 to 2 million years ago, while later material is limited to what is known as Member 5—a stratigraphic feature dating to roughly 1.8 to 1.5 million years ago. The remains of three hominids (assigned to *Homo habilis* or, possibly, *Paranthropus*) have been found in Member 5, along with more than 1,200 other bones and bone fragments, representing a diversity of large animals, mainly bovids. In addition, more than 200 stone tools were recovered in association with these bones. These are mostly simple pebble tools—round pieces of rock with several flakes knocked off to form a crude cutting edge, but there are also flake tools present.

The subsurface cavern that formed the Sterkfontein site may have been used as a shelter or home base by ancient peoples. Robert Brain suggested that the cave may have been occupied seasonally, when local resources were most productive. When living at Sterkfontein, these peoples hunted or scavenged a variety of bovid species, and probably ate a wide variety of gathered plant foods as well. There has long been debate about how substantial a role meat played in the diet of ancient South African hominids. Some have suggested meat played an important role, others that it was only supplemental to a primarily herbivorous diet. Aside from meat, it is likely that hominids living at Sterkfontein had a highly varied diet that included grasses, fruits, and roots.

SOURCES: Brain, C.K., *The Hunters or the Hunted? An Introduction to African Cave Taphonomy*. (Chicago: University of Chicago Press, 1981); Partridge, T.C., 1978, "Re-appraisal of lithostratigraphy of Sterkfontein hominid site," *Nature* 275: 282–287; Robinson, J.T., 1957, "Occurrence of stone artefacts with *Australopithecus* at Sterkfontein," *Nature* 180: 521–524.

would have required language. In Hewes's perspective, hunting fostered language, and language fostered the increase in brain size.

Dean Falk has also argued that it was language that fostered an increase in hominid brain size. She points to evidence from endocranial casts that australopithecine and early *Homo* brains had larger temporal lobes than apes, and argues that this suggests their ability to identify, remember, and name unique items in their environment was significantly better than apes. She further argues that language would have been beneficial to early hominids in many ways—hunting, defense, social interactions, and the like—and would have been equally beneficial to all ages and sexes. Thus Falk suggests that the development of language may be the single best candidate for an underlying cause of hominid brain enlargement. Most paleoanthropologists, however, see little evidence of language in either the fossil or archaeological record until long after the brain had enlarged. As I discuss in the next chapter, many scholars think that language may be unique to our species, *Homo sapiens*.

We may never know the specific factors which led to a significant increase in the brain size of early hominids, but we do know that it is a primary feature

FIGURE **4.10**
Skull of *Parathropus boisei* from Olduvai Gorge.

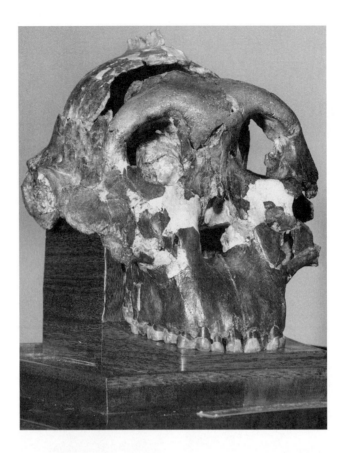

distinguishing between the australopithecines, paranthropoids, and early *Homo*. In addition to a larger brain, early *Homo* also showed some changes in the face, teeth, and jaws. The australopithecines and paranthropoids all have cheek teeth that are very large relative to their estimated body weight, and thick jawbones. This is probably because their diet was especially high in small, tough plant foods such as seeds, nuts, and tubers. One reason that early *Homo* had smaller dentition might be that members of the *Homo* genus ate foods that were easier to chew. Such foods might have included roots, fruits, and meat.

## Early *Homo* Fossils

The first members of the genus *Homo* appeared about two and a half million years ago. Early *Homo* fossils are generally divided into two species: **Homo habilis** and **Homo rudolfensis**. Both are known primarily from the western parts of Kenya and Tanzania, but remains have been found elsewhere in eastern and southern Africa, including the Omo Basin of Ethiopia and Sterkfontein Cave in South Africa.

Homo habilis appears to be the earlier of these two species, appearing around 2.3 million years ago (Figure 4.11). In addition to its larger brain, *Homo habilis* had reduced molars and premolars when compared with the australopithecines and paranthropoids. The rest of its skeleton is reminiscent of the australopithecines and paranthropoids, including the presence of powerful hands and relatively long arms, suggesting *H. habilis* was at least partially arboreal. *H. habilis* may also have been sexually dimorphic like the australopithecines and paranthropoids, as individuals seem to have greatly differed in size according to their sex.

Homo rudolfensis is roughly contemporary with *Homo habilis*, and shares many of its features. Indeed, many paleoanthropologists make no distinction

**Homo habilis:** an early species belonging to our genus, *Homo*, found in East Africa, and dating from about 2 million years ago.

**Homo rudolfensis:** an early species belonging to our genus, *Homo*, that is similar enough to *Homo habilis* that some paleoanthropologists make no distinction between the two.

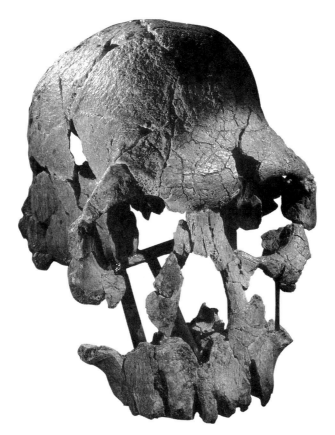

FIGURE **4.11**
Skull of *Homo habilis/rudolfensis* from Kenya.

between the two species, lumping *H. rudolfensis* into *H. habilis*. Those who do see them as distinct species point to the larger and more thickly enameled cheek teeth of *H. rudolfensis*, its flatter and broader face, and its more modern limb proportions. Even with its larger teeth and broader face, the dentition of *H. rudolfensis* is considerably reduced over the australopithecines and paranthropoids and, like *H. habilis*, its brain is at least a third larger.

We have little postcranial skeletal material for either early *Homo* species, so it is impossible to tell whether or in what ways the skeleton had changed. But, with brains averaging a third larger than the australopithecines and paranthropoids, it seems likely that some modifications to the female pelvis must have appeared in order to allow these bigger-brained, and thus bigger-headed, babies to be born. We do know that changes in the female pelvis to accommodate bigger-brained babies can be seen in *Homo erectus*, and I'll discuss that species in the next chapter.

## ONE MODEL OF HUMAN EVOLUTION

At this point you may well be wondering how all these species fit together. Figure 4.12 shows one model entertained by paleoanthropologists about how the known fossils may be related. The main disagreement among paleoanthropologists concerns which species of *Australopithecus* were ancestral to the line leading to modern humans. For example, the model shown in Figure 4.12 suggests that *A. afarensis* is ancestral to both *Homo* and *Paranthropus*, as well as to *A. africanus*. *A. bahrelghazali* and *A. garhi* are not ancestral to either the *Paranthropus* or *Homo* lines. Those who think that *A. afarensis* was the last common ancestor of all the hominid think the split to *Homo* occurred about 3 million years ago, as shown in

FIGURE **4.12**

One model of the relationships between the species discussed in this chapter.

SOURCE: Kenneth L. Feder and Michael Alan Park, *Human Antiquity: An Introduction to Physical Anthropology and Archaeology, 4/E* (Mountain View, CA: Mayfield Publishing Company, 2002), p. 241.

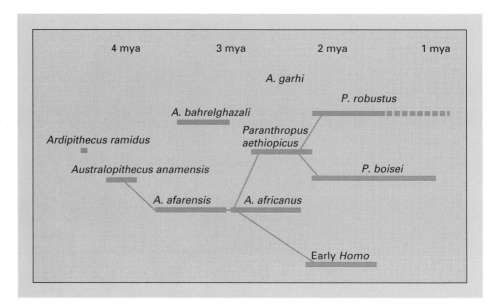

Figure 4.12. Despite the uncertainty and disagreements about what species was ancestral to the *Homo* line, there is widespread agreement among paleoanthropologists about other aspects of early hominid evolution: (1) There were at least three separate hominid lines between 3 million and 1 million years ago (*Australopithecus, Paranthropus,* and *Homo*); (2) the paranthropoids were not likely ancestral to modern humans but became extinct about a million years ago; and (3) early *Homo* were in the direct ancestral line to modern humans.

## ✿ SUMMARY

World prehistory begins with the evolution of the first humans, and the human family—the hominids—are defined primarily by our being habitually bipedal. Although many monkeys and apes can and do walk bipedally sometimes, habitual bipedalism is a uniquely human form of locomotion among the primates. Bipedalism requires a number of significant changes in the primate skeleton, especially in the pelvis, legs, and feet. While there are many theories for why bipedalism may have developed, it must have conveyed a distinct advantage to our earliest ancestors.

A. *ramidus* is the earliest known hominid, dating to about 4.4 million years ago. Two major groups of hominids followed, the australopithecines and the paranthropoids. The australopithecines lived between about 3.5 million years ago and 2 million years ago, primarily in eastern and southern Africa. They were small, partially arboreal, and lived on a mixed diet of fruit, seeds, nuts, and perhaps meat. The paranthropoids lived between about 2.5 and 1 million years ago in eastern and southern Africa. They had larger faces, teeth, and jaws than the australopithecines, and somewhat larger brains. It is thought that their larger dentition evolved because they had a diet of coarser and harder food than the australopithecines, perhaps a diet focused primarily on seeds and nuts.

The first members of our genus, *Homo*, evolved about 2.5 million years ago in eastern Africa. They were similar to the australopithecines in body size, but had much larger brains—about a third larger than the australopithecines and paranthropids who were living at the same early *Homo* evolved. Early members of the

*Homo* genus also had somewhat smaller teeth than the australopithecines and paranthropoids, perhaps pointing to a diet consisting of foods easier to chew, such as roots, fruits, and meat.

## ⚙ DISCUSSION QUESTIONS

1. What changes had to be made in the primate skeleton to accomodate bipedal locomotion?
2. Describe the major differences between *Australopithecus, Paranthropus*, and early *Homo*.
3. Describe the major trends in hominid evolution from *Ardipithecus* to *Homo*.

## ⚙ ESSAY QUESTIONS

1. The transition to bipedalism had obvious costs in terms of the major reorganization of the ancestral hominid skeleton it required. Given the various models for the origins of bipedalism discussed in this chapter, and the information you have gained from this or other resources about the changing environments of East Africa at the time when bipedalism was evolving, discuss the relationship between bipedalism and environmental change. What advantages did bipedalism offer early hominids?
2. Compare and contrast a scientific report of a newly identified fossil species (often published in the journals *Nature* and *Science*) with the report of fossil species presented in this text. How are they similar? Different? What is lost in the translation from a scientific publication to a textbook? What is gained?
3. Consider the situation in East Africa two million years ago when early *Homo* and *Paranthropus boisei* were both living in the same environment. How might these species have interacted? Would they have been in competition for the same resources? What characteristics did *Homo* possess that allowed members of that genus to survive while the paranthropoids went extinct?

## ➶ RESEARCH PROJECT

Visit a local or regional zoo that houses primates. Spend at least two hours observing one or more primate species. Pay particular attention to locomotion and the use of hands and feet. How do these primates move? How do they manipulate objects in their environment? How do they use their hands and feet in social interactions? How do they carry and care for infants? Next visit a local park or recreation center, and spend two hours watching humans. Consider the same questions you did for primates, and then answer the following question: How does bipedalism change the way humans behave in comparison with other primates?

## ⚙ KEY SOURCES

### The Evolution of Bipedal Locomotion

Hewes, 1961; Jolly, 1970; Lovejoy, 1988; Rose, 1984; Wheeler, 1984, 1991; Zihlman, 1992.

### *Ardipithecus:* The First Bipedal Ape?

White, Suwa, and Asfaw, 1994, 1995.

### *Australopithecus:* The First Definite Hominid

Aiello and Dean, 1990; Conroy, 1990; Dart, 1925; Fleagle, 1999; Johanson and White, 1979; Leakey, Feibel, McDougall, and Walker, 1995; Shipman, 1986; Simpson, 2002; Washburn, 1960; Wood, 1992.

### *Paranthropus*

Broom, 1950; Grine, 1986, 1988, 1993.

### Early *Homo*

Falk, 1980; Leakey, 1979; McHenry, 1982.

# FINDING LUCY

The *Australopithecus afarensis* skeleton known as Lucy is probably the most famous early hominid in the world. Recently dated to approximately 3.2 million years ago, Lucy was only 1.2 meters (4 feet) tall and 19 to 21 years old. Nearby the remains of at least thirteen other females, males, and children of the same species were found. *A. afarensis* was a hardy species that survived for over a million years in harsh and changing environments.

In this Media Lab, you will view an interview with Dr. Donald Johanson, in which he describes the discovery of Lucy, and then you will see footage of East African digs. The text of Chapter 4 describes the Hadar locality where Lucy was found and explains its importance in human paleontology.

Dr. Donald Johanson
Institute of Human Origins

**The Media Lab can be found in Chapter 4 on the** *Companion Website*™ <u>http://www.prenhall.com/peregrine</u>

## WEB ACTIVITY

Hadar, part of the Afar Triangle in northeastern Ethiopia, is one of the most important eastern African areas for early australopithecines. The significance of the Afar region of Ethiopia was first brought to light in the 1960s. Explorations in the 1970s focused on the Hadar locality in the central Afar. In 1981, a multidisciplinary team surveyed the Middle Awash region south of Hadar. Work in the area continues today and discoveries are far from complete. In this Media Lab, you will view contemporary footage of ongoing work.

## Activity

1. View the video. How was the discovery of Lucy made? Why was it extraordinary?

2. What specific research methods was Dr. Johanson using when he and his colleagues discovered Lucy?

3. Observe the shots of Dr. Johanson and his colleagues in the field. Who makes up the research team? What facilities are available for the team's working and living arrangements? Describe the site and the camp.

# The Origins of Culture

In Chapter 4 I explained that the evolution of bipedalism among our ancestors, occurring about 5 million years ago, marked the beginning of world prehistory because it marked the beginning of our group of primates—the hominids. I also explained that the enlargement of the brain, beginning about 2.5 million years ago, marked the beginning of our genus, *Homo*. In this chapter I discuss the evolution of what I think is the most important characteristic that distinguishes us as humans—our capacity for culture.

**Culture,** as I use it here, refers to the learned behaviors shared by a group of people that aid them in the ongoing process of survival. Culture is an integral part of the survival process for humans, and thus it changes regularly as new threats to survival emerge and as new opportunities to aid survival appear. This chapter will describe how our unique capacity for culture evolved.

When did culture first appear? The earliest evidence of culture seems to be stone tools that were made in East Africa beginning about 2.5 million years ago. Because stone tools are found at various sites in East Africa around the time early *Homo* appeared (see Figure 5.1), most anthropologists surmise that members of these early *Homo* species, rather than the australopithecines and paranthropoids, made those tools. But in fact none of the earliest stone tools are clearly associated with early *Homo* so it is impossible as yet to know who made them. What were these tools like and why might they (and the other cultural behaviors likely associated with them) have evolved where and when they did?

Before answering that question, I will explain how I have organized the cultural information in this book. Two million years ago or so, humans first developed culture, and the rest of this chapter, and indeed the rest of this book, examines how culture evolved and changed over time. In order to look at change we need to have some unit of culture that we can compare across time, and for the purposes of this book that unit will be the **archaeological tradition.** Archaeological traditions form the basic framework through which I describe and attempt to explain how culture evolved and expanded over the last two million years.

**Culture:** the learned behaviors shared by a group of people that aid them in the ongoing process of survival.

**Archaeological tradition:** a group of populations sharing similar subsistence practices, technology, and forms of sociopolitical organization, which are spatially contiguous over a relatively large area and which endure temporally for a relatively long period.

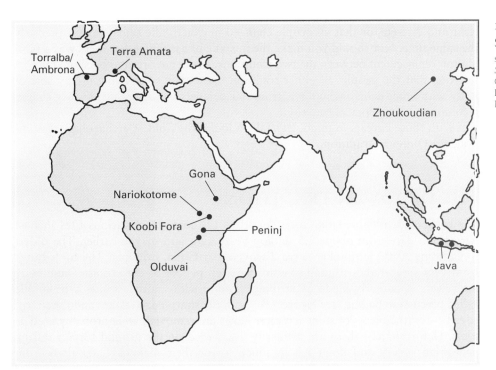

FIGURE **5.1**

Sites discussed in Chapter 5.

SOURCE: From *Human Evolution Source Book* by Clochon/Fleagle, © 1993. Reprinted by permission of Pearson Education, Inc., Upper Saddle River, NJ.

**Cultural evolution:**
changes in the scale, complexity, or integration of cultural behaviors among a group of people.

**Percussion flaking:** a toolmaking technique in which one stone is struck with a stone or other object to remove a flake.

What is an archaeological tradition? An archaeological tradition is defined as *a group of populations sharing similar subsistence practices, technology, and forms of sociopolitical organization, which are spatially contiguous over a relatively large area and which endure temporally for a relatively long period.* The idea is that groups of people who share similar lifestyles can be identified and used as a unit of comparison for examining cultural evolution. Similar lifestyles, at least as they can be identified archaeologically, usually can only be defined through technology and perhaps subsistence, since evidence of those aspects of culture are what survives best in the archaeological record.

What is cultural evolution? I use the term **cultural evolution** to refer to changes in the scale (the size of a population or geographical area), complexity (the number of distinct roles or statuses), or integration (the number of connections between people or roles) of cultural behavior among a particular group of people. For example, an early *Homo* group might consist of only a few individuals (small scale); there might be a simple division of work between men and women and between old and young, but otherwise all individuals have the same status and role within the group (low complexity); and the connections between people are simple face-to-face interactions (low integration). The group of people who live, as I do, in Wisconsin numbers in the millions (large scale); there is a complex division between the many different jobs and social roles within the state (high complexity); and there is a hierarchical bureaucracy, a myriad of marketplaces, and a variety of communication systems that connect individual jobs and roles with one another (high integration). Seeing these changes I can state emphatically that cultural evolution has taken place over the last 2 million years.

Using archaeological traditions as the basis for examining cultural evolution may make it seem like world prehistory can be easily cut up into discrete chunks. It cannot. Archaeological traditions are to some extent arbitrary, and they are most certainly meaningless in the context of the lives of the prehistoric peoples themselves. They are a device I've created, in the present day, to make it possible to comparatively examine cultures of the past. So when I say that one tradition was followed by another, you should not assume that the break between the two was clear and discrete, or that all people changed in exactly the same ways at precisely the same time. Nor should you make the mistake of assuming that there was a population replacement between the two traditions. More important, you should not be thinking that the peoples of either tradition knew they were living in any sort of unity with other people whom we, from our perspective today, suggest they shared a common archaeological tradition.

With those caveats in mind, let's take a look at the oldest archaeological tradition, the **Oldowan tradition.**

**Oldowan Tradition** (ca. 2.5 million to 1.0 million B.P.). Associated with *Homo habilis* and early *Homo erectus* in Africa. Characterized by simple flaked pebble stone tools and the use of unmodified stone flakes as tools.

**Gona, Ethiopia** (Oldowan)

**Olduvai Gorge, Tanzania** (Oldowan)

**Koobi Fora, Kenya** (Oldowan)

## THE OLDOWAN TRADITION

The earliest identifiable stone tools found so far come from various sites in East Africa and date from about 2.5 million years ago, and maybe earlier. The oldest tools, some 3,000 in number, were discovered at **Gona**, Ethiopia. The tools range from very small flakes (thumb-size) to fist-sized pebble or core tools. These early tools were apparently made by striking a stone with another stone, a technique called **percussion flaking** (see Figure 5.3). Both the sharp-edged flakes and the sharp-edged cores (the pieces of stone left after flakes are removed) were probably used as tools. Unfortunately, these are primarily discovered on the ground surface during pedestrian survey and don't tell us much about their makers. Later finds from archaeological deposits in East Africa, particularly **Olduvai Gorge** and **Koobi Fora** (see Box Feature titled "Koobi Fora Site 50") have provided a much better picture of the Oldowan tradition.

# Koobi Fora Site 50

Koobi Fora Site 50 is one of several important early *Homo* occupation sites located in the Koobi Fora region on the east side of Lake Turkana in Northwest Kenya. The region has been subject to extensive volcanic activity since well before early *Homo* occupied the area. At times the lake inundated the region and buried the surface under alluvium, at other times volcanic activity raised the ground surface or buried it under layers of volcanic ash, called *tuffs*. During the Oldowan period the area was a broad river floodplain teaming with plant and animal life. Koobi Fora Site 50 was excavated between 1977 and 1979 by a team from Harvard University led by the late Glynn Isaac. During that period some 200 square meters of the site were exposed.

Koobi Fora Site 50 has provided some of the most well-preserved archaeological deposits for the Oldowan tradition. Indeed Isaac has suggested that the site was a home base for a small group of people, a place where they brought stones to work and animals to butcher and eat, and where they probably socialized and slept. More than 2,000 bones and bone fragments, many of which show evidence of butchering, have been found at the site. This suggested to Isaac that early *Homo* peoples were bringing food to the site and butchering and eating it there. These bones were found in a very good state of preservation, suggesting the site had been rapidly buried by river alluvium after its inhabitants left. Thus, the site may have been the record of a single occupation in the distant past.

Numerous stone tools were recovered from Site 50, and many were found in what appear to be areas where early *Homo* individuals made stone tools. The presence of these stone working areas allowed Nicholas Toth to undertake a number of detailed studies of the flake debris. He determined that flakes were more important to early *Homo* than core tools, and some of the so-called core tool forms may be nothing more than the result of knappers knocking flakes off of nodules with similar sizes and shapes. Toth also found that early *Homo* curated stone—finding quality raw materials in local riverbeds, removing unwanted cortex, and bringing the resultant nodules back to base camps to create flakes and core tools. Toth and colleague Lawrence Keeley also performed use-wear studies on the stone tools found at Site 50, and they determined that Oldowan peoples used their stone tools on a variety of materials, including wood. This suggests that wooden tools were likely also a part of the Oldowan tool kit and were perhaps used for digging up plant roots and tubers.

SOURCES: Harris, J.W.K., and G. Isaac, 1976, "The Karai Industry: Early pleistocene archaeologial evidence from the terrain east of Lake Turkana, Kenya," *Nature* 262 (1976): 102-107. Isaac, Glynn, 1984, "The archaeology of human origins: Studies of the lower pleistocene in east Africa, 1971–1981," *Advances in World Archaeology* 3 (1984): 1–87. Isaac, Glynn, *Plio-pleistocene Archaeology* (Oxford: Clarendon Press, 1997). Keeley, Lawrence, and N. Toth, 1981, "Microwear polishes on early stone tools from Koobi Fora, Kenya," *Nature* 237: 464-465. Toth, Nicholas, 1985, "The Oldowan reassessed: A close look at early stone artifacts," *Journal of Archaeological Science* 12: 101–120.

FIGURE **5.2**
Archaeologists working at
Koobi Fora Site 50.

Olduvai Gorge is located in northwestern Tanzania in a location that was once surrounded with lakes and marshes. Over time water-borne silt and ash from local volcanoes built up a series of stratigraphic layers, which were exposed through geological uplifting beginning about 200,000 years ago. The oldest cultural materials from the lowest stratigraphic layer, called Bed I, date from about 1.8 to 1.6 million years ago. The stone artifacts include core tools and sharp-edged flakes. Flake tools predominate. Among the core tools, so-called *choppers* are common (see Figure 5.3). Choppers are cores that have been partially flaked and have a side that might have been used for chopping. Other core tools, with flaking along one side and a flat edge, are called scrapers. Whenever a stone has facets removed from only one side of the cutting edge, it is called a **unifacial tool.** If the stone has facets removed from both sides, it is called a **bifacial tool.** Although there are some bifacial tools in the early stone tool assemblages, they are not as plentiful or as elaborated as in later traditions.

Archaeologists have speculated about the lifestyles of early hominids from Olduvai and other sites. Some of these speculations come from analysis of what can be done with the tools, microscopic analysis of wear on the tools, and examination of the marks the tools make on bones; other speculations are based on what is found with the tools.

Oldowan flakes appear to be very versatile; they can be used for slitting the hides of animals, dismembering animals, and whittling wood into sharp-pointed sticks (wooden spears or digging sticks). Larger Oldowan tools (choppers and scrapers) can be used to hack off branches or cut and chop tough animal joints. Those who have made and tried to use stone tools for various purposes are so impressed by the sharpness and versatility of flakes that they wonder whether most of the core tools were really used as tools. The cores could mainly be what remained after wanted flakes were struck off. Archaeologists surmise that many early tools were also made of wood and bone, but these do not survive in the archaeological record. For example, present-day populations use sharp-pointed digging sticks for extracting roots and tubers from the ground; stone flakes are very effective for sharpening wood to a very fine point.

None of the early flaked stone tools can plausibly be thought of as weapons. So, if the toolmaking hominids were hunting or defending themselves with weapons,

**Unifacial tool:** a tool worked or flaked on one side only.

**Bifacial tool:** a tool worked or flaked on two sides.

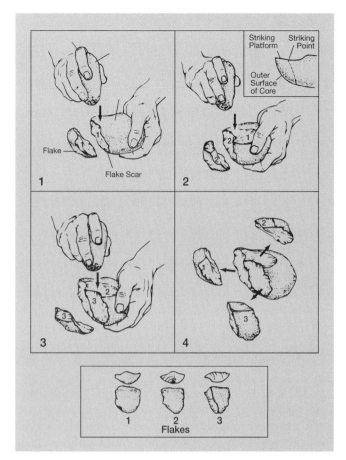

FIGURE **5.3**

The production of a simple Odowan chopper core and the resultant flakes.

SOURCE: From "The First Technology" by R. Freyman in *Scientific American*, April 1987. Reprinted by permission of the artist, Ed Hanson.

they had to have used wooden spears, clubs, or unmodified stones as missiles. Later Oldowan tool assemblages also include stones that were flaked and battered into a rounded shape. The unmodified stones and the shaped stones might have been lethal projectiles.

It seems clear that people of the Oldowan tradition were cutting up animal carcasses for meat. Microscopic analyses show that cut marks on animal bones were unambiguously created by stone flake tools, and use-wear analyses of stone tools indicate that they were used for cutting meat. We still do not know for sure whether these hominids were just scavenging meat (taking meat from the kills of other animals) or hunting the animals. On the basis of her analysis of cut marks on bone from Bed I in Olduvai Gorge, Pat Shipman suggested that scavenging, not hunting, was the major meat-getting activity. For example, the cut marks made by the stone tools usually (but not always) overlie teeth marks made by carnivores. This suggests that the hominids were often scavenging the meat of animals killed and partially eaten by nonhominid predators. The fact that the cut marks were sometimes made first, however, suggested to Shipman that the hominids were also sometimes the hunters. On the other hand, prior cut marks may indicate only that the hominids scavenged before carnivores had a chance to consume their prey.

The artifact and animal remains from Bed I and the lower part of Bed II at Olduvai suggest a few other things about life in the Oldowan tradition. First, it seems that the hominids moved around during the year; most of the sites in what is now Olduvai Gorge appear to have been used only in the dry season, as indicated by an analysis of the kinds of animal bones found there. Second, whether the early Olduvai hominids were hunters or scavengers, they apparently exploited a wide range of animals. Although most of the bones are from medium-sized antelopes and

FIGURE **5.4**

Olduvai "hut." A ring of stones and bones found in Bed I of Olduvai Gorge that Mary Leakey interpreted as the remains of an ancient hut.

SOURCE: Carol R. Ember, Melvin Ember, and Peter N. Peregrine, *Physical Anthropology and Archaeology* (Upper Saddle River, NJ: Prentice Hall, 2002), p. 108. Reprinted by permission of Pearson Education, Inc., Upper Saddle River, NJ.

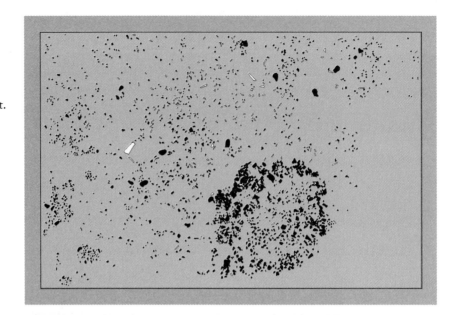

wild pigs, even large animals such as elephants and giraffes seem to have been eaten. It is clear, then, that the Olduvai hominids scavenged or hunted for meat, but we cannot tell yet how important meat was in their diet.

There is also no consensus yet about how to characterize the Olduvai sites that contain concentrations of stone tools and animal bones. In the 1970s, there was a tendency to think of them as home bases to which hominids (presumably male) brought meat to share with others (presumably nursing mothers and young children). Indeed, Mary Leakey identified two locations where she thought early hominids had built simple structures (Figure 5.4). One was a stone circle that she suggested formed the base of a small brush windbreak. The other was a circular area of dense debris surrounded by an area virtually lacking debris. Leakey suggested that the area lacking debris may represent the location of a ring of thorny brush with which early hominids surrounded their campsite in order to keep out predators—much like pastoralists living in the region do today. But archaeologists today are not so sure these sites were home bases. For one thing, carnivores also frequented the sites. Places with meaty bones lying around may not have been so safe for hominids to use as home bases. Second, the animal remains at the sites had not been completely dismembered and butchered. If the sites had been hominid home bases, we would expect more complete processing of carcasses. Third, natural processes as simple as trees growing through a site can create circular areas of debris such as the ones Leakey identified as structures, and without better evidence that early hominids made them, one cannot be sure that the circles of debris were indeed structures.

If these sites were not home bases, what were they? Some archaeologists are beginning to think that these early sites with many animal bones and tools may have been just places where hominids processed food but did not live. Why would the hominids return repeatedly to a particular site? Richard Potts suggested one possible reason—that hominids left caches of stone tools and stones for toolmaking at various locations to facilitate recurrent food-collecting and processing activities. Future research may tell us more about early hominid life. Did they have home bases, or did they just move from one processing site to another? How did they protect themselves from predators? They apparently did not have fire to keep the predators away. Did they climb trees to get away or to sleep?

## STONE TOOLS AND CULTURE

I stated earlier that the presence of stone tools means that these early hominids had probably developed culture. Toolmaking certainly does not imply that early humans had anything like the complex cultures of humans today. Indeed, chimpanzees use tools, even simple stone tools, but they do not have much in the way of cultural behavior.

What, exactly, makes human *culture* so different from other forms of animal behavior? Anthropologists have spent more than a century trying to answer this question, and there is still no widely accepted answer. One thing is clear, however—culture must be understood as a set of interrelated processes, not as a thing. What are the processes that make up culture? Let's consider some of the more important ones.

First, culture is *learned* and *shared*. This is the fundamental difference between culture and most other forms of animal behavior. Culture is not a set of innate behaviors, but rather a set of learned ones. Culture is something individuals acquire during their lifetimes as they grow up and interact with others. Interaction is key here, because not only are cultural behaviors learned, they are learned through interaction with others, through education, through shared experiences. Culture, then, is a social process, not an individual one.

Second, culture is generally *adaptive*. What this means is that most of the learned and shared behaviors that make up a culture are thought to have developed and spread through a group of people because they help that group of people survive in a given environment. Thus, cultural behaviors may be favored by natural selection just as genes are. The extent to which human culture is a product of natural selection is hotly debated, but few anthropologists would argue that culture is not a key aspect of human adaptation. What makes culture quite different from the behavioral systems of other animals is that, because culture is learned and shared rather than innate, humans can develop new behaviors quickly and adapt to diverse and changing conditions with relative ease. Adaptation, then, is perhaps the most significant process of culture.

Change is the third major process of culture, for culture is always *changing*. Culture change regularly occurs as new and beneficial means of adaptation are developed and shared. But anthropologists also assume that when new behaviors are developed they tend to become integrated with existing behaviors. That is to say new behaviors that conflict with established ones may lead to one or the other changing. A group of early humans could not have, for example, both scavenged meat and at the same time had a prohibition against eating meat that they did not themselves kill. Such a situation would create a contradiction, and something would have to change. Working out contradictions between new, highly beneficial behaviors and established but less beneficial ones may be one of the reasons that cultures are so dynamic.

So, culture is a dynamic system of learned and shared behavior that helps humans adapt to their environments. But how did this dynamic set of interrelated processes we call culture shape the behavior of early humans?

It seems clear that the early hominids, like other primates, were social beings. It also seems clear from the archaeological record that early hominids were making and using stone tools on a regular basis. As I have mentioned earlier, tools are frequently found in discrete concentrations, often in association with animal bones and other debris from human activity. And, as I have already noted, a number of paleoanthropologists have argued that such concentrations of debris may represent campsites or even small shelters. Home bases of some sort may have been a part of early hominid culture.

Whether they reflect home bases or not, large numbers of animal bones and tools are found in discrete locations, and these accumulations suggest that the areas were being used by groups of individuals over periods of time. In such a situation

FIGURE **5.5**
Artist's reconstruction of a group of early humans making tools and sharing meat. Such activities mark the beginnings of culture.

sharing of food is very likely. It seems counterintuitive to think that individuals would have purposely brought food to a common location only to keep it to themselves. And although we must move into the realm of pure speculation, it does seem reasonable to think that closely related individuals, like parents, children, and siblings, would be more likely to associate and share food with one another than more distantly related individuals. This speculation is supported by the fact that when food sharing takes place among chimpanzees it is usually among closely related individuals. Thus, the ancient locations of early hominid social activity may be evidence of family groups (Figure 5.5).

It is interesting that the archaeological record of early hominids may represent some of the essential features of modern human cultures. These include home bases, sharing, and families. If we think of culture as a process, such a combination of features seems quite likely to form a foundation to human culture. Culture is learned and shared, so a common place where learning and sharing occur—a home base— is something we should expect in early hominid cultures. Culture is adaptive, and adaptation has two important facets—reproduction and survival. Thus, we would expect families and the sharing of food at the base of human culture. How would such a system of social behavior—the creation of a common meeting, resting, and living place for a group of related individuals to share food—have evolved? Let's consider one model.

## One Model for the Evolution of Culture

As I've already noted, early *Homo* had a large brain. One of the possible consequences of brain expansion was the lessening of maturity at birth. That babies were born more immature may at least partly explain the lengthening of the period of infant and child dependency in hominids. Compared with other animals, we spend not only a longer proportion of our life span but also the longest absolute period in a dependent state. For example, a month-old human infant is completely dependent upon its mother—it cannot move itself and is only beginning to have the hand–eye coordination to reach for and grasp objects. A month-old chimpanzee, on the other hand, can move by itself (though not well), hold onto its mother even when she is

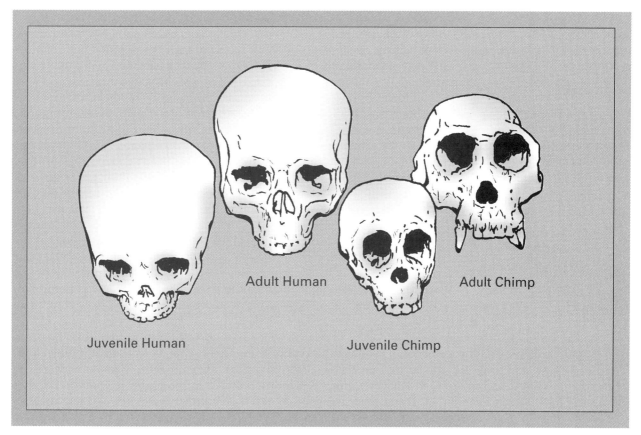

FIGURE **5.6**

Comparison of skulls of juvenile and adult humans and chimpanzees. The juvenile human has a much larger brain than the juvenile chimp, and also more closely resembles the adult form. Maturation brings significant morphological changes to other primates, but not to humans. In a sense, we retain juvenile characteristics our whole lives.

moving swiftly, and reach for and grasp objects (Figure 5.6). Prolonged infant dependency has probably been of great significance in human cultural evolution. It used to be thought that the australopithecines had a long period of infant dependency, but more recent analyses of australopithecine teeth suggests that the early australopithecines followed an apelike pattern of tooth emergence during infancy, and thus may have matured rapidly like apes. Thus, prolonged infant dependency may be relatively recent, but just how recent is not yet known.

Prolonged infant dependency is probably a result of the size of the brain in *Homo* species. A large brain needs a large head, and a large head requires a large birth canal in order to be born. In the *Homo* genus the juvenile brain and head are so large that the mother's birth canal could not possibly accommodate them. The solution to this problem is that *Homo* infants are born at a very juvenile state—a state in which the brain has not yet fully developed. But with undeveloped brains, *Homo* infants lack full control over their bodies and their senses—they are unable to control muscles and unable to respond to stimuli well. Thus, *Homo* infants are incapable of surviving without parental care until their brains have developed to the point where they can control their bodies and senses, and in modern humans this takes several years. Indeed, in the first month of life modern human infants can choke on the weight of their own heads and smother under something as light as a pillow, since they cannot control movements well enough to shift their position or purposely move even a very light item.

*Homo erectus:* the first hominid species to be widely distributed in the Old World. The earliest finds are possibly 1.8 million years old. The brain (averaging 895–1,040 cc) was larger than that found in any of the australopithecines or *H. habilis* but smaller than the average brain of a modern human.

Bipedalism would have exacerbated this problem, for both the newborn and for the mother. Walking bipedally requires sophisticated coordination and balance, and in modern humans most infants are not capable of such coordination until they are at least a year old. For mothers, this means that infants have to be carried for at least the first year of life, and probably for several years. The changes in the pelvis that were required for bipedalism would have also caused problems for mothers, as the shift of the femur heads toward the front would have narrowed the width of the birth canal. Thus, childbirth, even without an increase in brain size, is more difficult for a bipedal hominid than for a quadrupedal ape. Add to this the larger brain size in the *Homo* genus and childbirth becomes a physically demanding and even dangerous process.

With the challenges of infant dependency and childbirth in mind, let's get back to our model for the evolution of culture. Although some use of tools for digging, defense, or scavenging may have influenced the development of bipedalism, full bipedalism may have made possible more efficient toolmaking and consequently more efficient foraging and scavenging. As I have noted, there is archaeological evidence that early hominids were butchering and presumably eating big game some 2 million years ago.

Whenever it was that hominids began to scavenge for game and perhaps hunt regularly, the development of scavenging would require individuals to travel long distances frequently in search of suitable carcasses. Among groups of early *Homo,* longer infant and child dependency may have fostered the creation of home bases. The demands of childbirth and caring for a newborn might have made it difficult for early *Homo* mothers to travel for some time after the birth. Because early *Homo* males (and females without newborns) would have been able to roam freely, they probably became the scavengers or hunters. While they were away seeking carcasses or small game, women with newborn children may have gathered wild plants within a small area that could be covered without traveling far from the home base.

The creation of home bases among early *Homo* groups may have increased the likelihood of food sharing. If mothers with newborns were limited to gathered plant foods near a home base, the only way to ensure that they could obtain a complete diet would have been to share the other foods obtained elsewhere. With whom would such sharing take place? Most likely with close relatives. Sharing with them would have made it more likely that the mother and newborn child would survive. Thus early *Homo* groups located at a home base and connected by bonds of family and sharing could have encouraged the development of the learned and shared behaviors that we call culture.

Obviously this is a "just-so" story—a tale that we never may be able to prove really happened. However, it is a tale that is consistent with the archaeological record. Stone tools did not appear until early *Homo* came on the scene. And with early *Homo* we see the start of several trends in hominid evolution that appear to be related to the manufacture and use of stone tools—the expansion of the brain, the modification of the female pelvis to accommodate bigger-brained babies, and a general reduction in the size of teeth, face, and jaws. While these trends are present in early *Homo,* they are more apparent in *Homo erectus.*

## HOMO ERECTUS

*Homo erectus* may be our closest human ancestor and follows *Homo habilis* almost immediately, appearing in Africa about 1.6 to 1.8 million years ago and spreading rapidly to Asia (see Figure 5.1). Examples of *H. erectus* were found first in **Java** in the late nineteenth century, later in China in the early twentieth century, and still later in Africa. Because *H. erectus* appears almost simultaneously in Asia and Africa (indeed, some dates for Asia are earlier than Africa), there are a few scholars who suggest *H. erectus* may have evolved in Asia and either became a side-branch of the

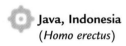
**Java, Indonesia**
(*Homo erectus*)

human tree (with African *H. ergaster,* which I discuss in the next section, being ancestral to later *Homo* species), or even that *H. erectus* moved westward to Europe and Africa. Indeed, the discoverer of *H. erectus,* Eugene Dubois, argued that the species evolved in Southeast Asia, and recent findings there have demonstrated that some *H. erectus* fossils from Asia are as old (and perhaps older) than the oldest *H. erectus* fossils in Africa. Most scholars think these overlapping dates are the result of a rapid migration out of Africa and the inherent error range of the dating techniques used, but others are not so sure. Carl Swisher and his colleagues, who performed careful redating of *H. erectus* fossils from Java, suggest that the dates do overlap, and *H. erectus* most likely evolved in Asia. Recent finds from Longgupo cave in China, dating perhaps as old as two million years ago, may even point to an earlier hominid in Asia.

Most of the arguments about *H. erectus* in Asia revolves around the issue of whether there is only one species of *H. erectus* or whether *H. erectus* contains several distinct species. Some scholars see enough differences between Asian and African populations of *H. erectus* to argue that they should be separated into two distinct species, *Homo erectus* for the Asian populations and *Homo ergaster* for the African ones. Furthermore, *Homo erectus* (or *Homo ergaster*) fossils are also found in Europe; but some paleoanthropologists think that the finds in Europe typically classified as *H. erectus* are actually early examples of our species, *H. sapiens.* Others think these European fossils and similar ones found in southern Africa and the Near East should be grouped into a distinct species, *Homo heidelbergensis.* It is all a bit confusing. Later in this chapter and in the next chapter I will help you sort it all out.

## Physical Characteristics of *Homo erectus*

The *Homo erectus* skull generally is long, low, and thickly walled, with a flat frontal area and prominent brow ridges (see Color Plate 6). It has a unique pentagonal shape when looked at from the back, formed in part by a rounded ridge, called a **sagittal keel,** running along the crest of the skull. There is also a ridge of bone running horizontally along the back of the skull, called an **occipital torus,** which adds to the skull's overall long shape.

Compared with early *Homo, H. erectus* had relatively small teeth. *H. erectus* was the first hominid to have third molars that are smaller than the second or first molars, as in modern humans. The molars also had an enlarged pulp cavity, called **taurodontism,** which may have allowed the teeth to withstand harder use and wear than the teeth of modern humans. But the jaw is lighter and thinner than early *Homo,* and the face is less **prognathic** or forward-thrusting in the upper and lower jaw (see Figure 5.7).

The brain, averaging 895 to 1,040 cc, was larger than that found in any of the australopithecines, paranthropoids, or early *Homo* species, but smaller than the average brain of a modern human. Endocasts, which provide a picture of the surface of the brain, suggest that it was organized more like the brain of modern humans than australopithecines or paranthropoids.

*Homo erectus* had a prominent, projecting nose, in contrast to the australopithecines' and paranthropoids' flat, nonprojecting nose. From the neck down, *H. erectus* was practically indistinguishable from modern humans. In contrast to the smaller australopithecines and early *Homo* species who lived in East Africa around the same time the first *H. erectus* did, *H. erectus* was comparable to modern humans in size. The almost complete skeleton of a boy found at **Nariokotome,** Kenya, suggests that he was about 5.5 feet tall when he died at about 11 years of age; the researchers estimate that he would have been well over 6 feet had he lived to maturity (Figure 5.8). About 1.6 million years ago, the Nariokotome region was probably open grassland, with trees mostly along rivers. *Homo erectus* in East Africa was

**Sagittal keel:** an inverted v-shaped ridge running along the top of the skull in *Homo erectus.*

**Occipital torus:** a ridge of bone running horizontally across the back of the skull in apes and some hominids.

**Taurodontism:** having teeth with an enlarged pulp cavity.

**Prognathic:** a physical feature that is sticking out or pushed forward, such as the jaws in apes and some hominid species.

**Nariokotome, Kenya**
(*Homo erectus*)

FIGURE **5.7**

Typical features of the *Homo erectus* cranium.

SOURCE: Carol R. Ember, Melvin Ember, and Peter N. Peregrine, *Physical Anthropology and Archaeology* (Upper Saddle River, NJ: Prentice Hall, 2002), p. 122. Reprinted by permission of Pearson Education, Inc., Upper Saddle River, NJ.

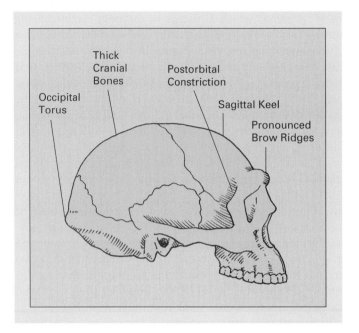

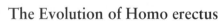

similar in size to Africans today who live in a similarly open, dry environment. *H. erectus* was also less sexually dimorphic than the australopithecines, paranthropoids, or early *Homo*. The degree of sexual dimorphism in *H. erectus* was comparable to that in modern humans.

Those scholars who distinguish African populations as a distinct species—*Homo ergaster*—point to several differences between them and other *Homo erectus* populations: The cranial proportions differ in *Homo ergaster*; the brow ridge is thinner and is arched above each of the eye sockets; the eye sockets are more rounded; and the face is oriented more vertically below the skull, among other differences. On the other hand, some scholars believe the differences between *Homo erectus* and modern humans are not large enough to call us different species, and these scholars argue that *Homo erectus* populations should be lumped into *Homo sapiens*. These arguments will not be settled anytime soon, and for the purposes of this book I will stick with the single name, *Homo erectus*.

## The Evolution of Homo erectus

The evolution of *Homo erectus* reflects a continuation of the general evolutionary trends I noted for early *Homo*. The brain continued to expand, increasing more than a third over early *Homo* (just as early *Homo* had increased more than a third over the australopithecines and paranthropoids). The face, teeth, and jaws continued to shrink, taking on an almost modern form (see Figure 5.9). The reasons for these changes are also likely a continuation of those I discussed earlier. For example, an increasing use and variety of tools may have led to a further development of the brain. Similarly, there is good evidence that *Homo erectus* was eating and probably cooking meat, and this may have furthered a reduction in the teeth and jaws.

One additional change in *Homo erectus* is an apparent reduction in the extent of sexual dimorphism to almost modern levels. Recall that the australopithecines, paranthropoids, and early *Homo* were quite sexually dimorphic—males were larger and females smaller. *Homo erectus* does not appear to be as sexually dimorphic as these earlier hominids. What might have caused this change? In other primates sexual dimorphism appears to be linked to social systems in which males are at the top of dominance hierarchies, and dominant males control sexual access to multiple

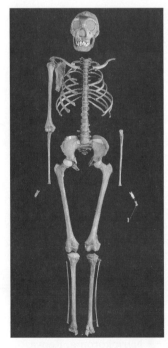

FIGURE **5.8**

The *Homo erectus/ergaster* skeleton from Narikotome, Kenya.

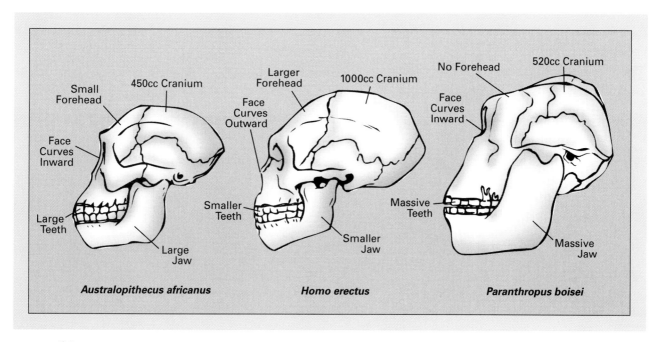

FIGURE **5.9**

Comparison of the skulls of *A. africanus*, *H. erectus*, and *P. boisei*, illustrating key differences.

SOURCE: Estimated cranial capacities from Ian Tattersall, Eric Delson, and John van Couvering (eds.), *Encyclopedia of Human Evolution and Prehistory*. Copyright © 2002. Reproduced by permission of Routledge, Inc., part of the Taylor & Francis Group.

females. In contrast, lack of sexual dimorphism seems most pronounced in both primates and other animals where pair-bonding exists, that is, where one male and one female form a long-lasting breeding pair. Could pair-bonding have developed in *Homo erectus?*

Early *Homo* seems to have established some of the basic elements of human culture, including home bases, family groups, and sharing. Another basic element of recent human culture, one that is present in all known cultures, is marriage. Marriage is a socially recognized sexual and economic bond between two individuals that is intended to continue throughout the lifetimes of the individuals, and which can produce socially accepted children. It is essentially a pair bond which is formalized through human culture into a set of behaviors, expectations, and obligations that extend beyond the pair to those individuals' families. With marriage, the competition between males for access to females may have diminished, lessening the importance of sexual dimorphism. But why might marriage have developed in *Homo erectus?*

In animal species where females can feed themselves and their babies after birth, pair-bonding is rare. But in species where females cannot feed both themselves and their babies, pair-bonding is common. Why? Perhaps because a pair bond provides the best solution to the problem of providing food to the mother—a male can obtain food and bring it back to his female partner and children. Most primates lack pair-bonding. This may be because primate infants are able to cling to their mother's fur soon after birth, so that mother's hands are free to forage (interestingly, human infants demonstrate a residual form of this innate ability to cling during their first few weeks of life, called the Moro reflex—if a human infant feels they are falling backward they will automatically stretch out their arms and clench their fists). We have no way of knowing if *Homo erectus* had fur like other primates, but they may not have because they may have worn clothing. The brain in *Homo erectus* may also have already expanded enough that *Homo erectus* infants, like modern human infants, could not adequately support their heads even if they could hold

FIGURE **5.10**
The environments of Africa and East Asia 1.5 million years ago.

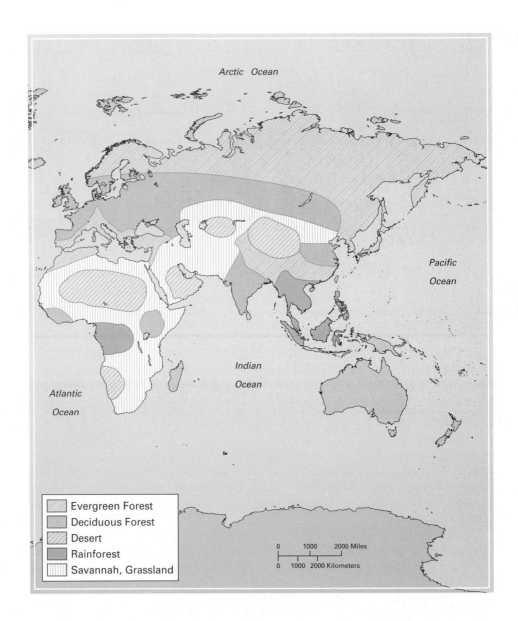

Arctic Ocean

Pacific Ocean

Indian Ocean

Atlantic Ocean

Evergreen Forest
Deciduous Forest
Desert
Rainforest
Savannah, Grassland

0   1000   2000 Miles
0   1000   2000 Kilometers

on to their mother's fur. In any case, when early hominids began to depend on scavenging and hunting for food (and skins for clothing), it would have been difficult and hazardous for mothers with infants to engage in these activities with their infants along. Marriage would have been an effective solution to this problem (see Color Plate 7).

Another important aspect of the evolution of *Homo erectus* was the movement of populations out of eastern and southern Africa. As with the lessening of sexual dimorphism, it seems likely that cultural innovations were key to allowing *Homo erectus* to move into new environments (see Figure 5.10). Why? Because upon entering new environments *Homo erectus* would have been faced with new (and generally colder) climatic conditions, new and different sources of raw material for stone and other tools, and new plants and animals they needed to rely on for food. All animals adapt to such changes through natural selection, but natural selection typically takes a relatively long time and requires physical changes in the adapting organisms. *Homo erectus* was able to adapt to new environments very quickly and without apparent physical changes. This suggests that the primary mechanisms of adaptation for *Homo erectus* were cultural rather than biological.

FIGURE **5.11**
Artist's reconstruction of *Homo erectus* individuals wearing animal skins. *Homo erectus* would have had to hunt, rather than scavenge, animals to obtain intact skins.

What cultural adaptations might *Homo erectus* have made? Fire might have been one cultural adaptation to colder climates. As I will discuss later, there is tantalizing evidence that *Homo erectus* used fire. But fire can only warm people when they are stationary—it doesn't help when people are out collecting food. To be mobile in colder climates, *Homo erectus* may have begun wearing animal furs for warmth. Some *Homo erectus* tools look like hide-processing tools used by more recent human groups, and it seems unlikely that *Homo erectus* could have survived in some of colder locations where they have been found in eastern Europe and Asia without some form of clothing. And if *Homo erectus* was wearing furs for warmth, it seems likely they must have been hunting. *Homo erectus* could not have depended on scavenging to acquire skins—the skin is the first thing predators destroy when they dismember a carcass. *Homo erectus* would have had to go out and kill fur-bearing animals themselves if they wanted intact skins for clothing (Figure 5.11).

It is interesting to consider that in eastern Africa *Homo erectus* coexisted with at least one other species of hominid (*P. boisei*), and possibly with as many as three (*P. boisei*, *A. africanus*, and *H. habilis/rudolfensis*). Why did *Homo erectus* survive and flourish while these other species went extinct? Again, culture may be the answer. *P. boisei* seems to have been a specialized grasslands species. Their large molars and powerful dental architecture allowed them to eat hard grass seeds and other coarse materials that other hominids could not chew. However, they had to compete against the many other grassland animals who also relied on these plants, but who also reproduced faster and had speed to help them escape from predators. Early *Homo* was apparently a tool user and relied at least in part on scavenging and hunting, but compared to *Homo erectus* early *Homo* technology was crude and their social organization was not as complex. *Homo erectus* appears to have been better organized to scavenge and hunt and to defend themselves against predators. These differences in culture may have provided enough of an advantage to *Homo erectus* that they drove early *Homo* to extinction.

The above scenario, just like the one I suggested for the evolution of early *Homo*, is a just-so story that may or may not be true. But it does fit the facts we know about *Homo erectus* and the area in which it evolved. Regardless of this particular story's accuracy, there seems no doubt that the development of a more complex culture was vital to the evolution of *Homo erectus*.

# ARCHAEOLOGICAL TRADITIONS ASSOCIATED WITH *HOMO ERECTUS*

**Acheulean Tradition** (1.8 million to 200,000 B.P.). Associated with *Homo erectus* in Africa and Europe and characterized by a unique stone tool kit that included hand axes.

**Zhoukoudian Tradition** (600,000 to 200,000 B.P.). Associated with *Homo erectus* in Asia, and characterized by stone tools similar to Acheulean, but lacking hand axes.

**Peninj River, Tanzania** (Acheulian)

**Lower Paleolithic:** the time period encompassing the Oldowan and Acheulean traditions.

**Soft hammer:** a technique of stone tool manufacture in which a bone or wood hammer is used to strike flakes from a stone.

**Hard hammer:** a technique of stone tool manufacture where one stone is used to knock flakes from another stone. Flakes produced through hard hammer percussion are usually large and crude.

Two distinct archaeological traditions are associated with *Homo erectus*. The first is the **Acheulean tradition,** dating between about 1.8 million and 200,000 years ago, and named after the site in France where stone tools that are diagnostic of the tradition were first found. The second is the **Zhoukoudian tradition,** dating between about 600,000 and 200,000 years ago, and named after a site in China that contains the most extensive record of *Homo erectus* in East Asia. The stone tools made by *Homo erectus* are traditionally called **Lower Paleolithic.**

Although all archaeological finds of tools and other cultural artifacts dating from the time of the Acheulean and Zhoukoudian traditions are assumed to have been produced by *Homo erectus,* fossils are not usually associated with these materials. Therefore it is possible that some of the tools and other archaeological remains during this period were produced by hominids other than *H. erectus,* such as paranthropoids earlier and *H. sapiens* later. Acheulian tool assemblages dating from 1.5 million years ago to more than a million years later are very similar to each other, and *H. erectus* is the only hominid that spans the entire period, so it is conventionally assumed that *H. erectus* was responsible for most if not all of the assemblages I describe next.

## The Acheulian Tradition

The Acheulian tradition, like the Oldowan before it, is defined primarily by stone tools. The oldest Acheulian tools recovered are from East Africa, on the **Peninj River,** Tanzania, dating back about 1.5 million years. In contrast to Oldowan, Acheulian assemblages have more large tools created according to standardized designs or shapes. Oldowan tools have sharp edges made by a few blows. Acheulian toolmakers shaped the stone by knocking more flakes off most of the edges. Many of these tools were made from very large flakes that had been struck from very large cores or boulders. One of the most characteristic and prevalent tools in the Acheulian tool kit is the so-called hand axe, which is a teardrop-shaped bifacially flaked tool with a thinned sharp tip (see Figure 5.12). Other large tools resemble cleavers and picks. There were also many other kinds of flake tools, such as scrapers with a wide edge.

Early Acheulian tools appear to have been made by blows with a hard stone, but later tools are wider and flatter and may have been made with a soft "hammer" of bone or antler (Figure 5.13). This **"soft hammer"** technique of making stone tools was an important innovation. Tools made by a **"hard hammer"** technique, rock against rock, have limits in terms of their sharpness and form because only large and thick flakes can be made with a hard hammer technique (unless the flintknapper is very skillful and the stone being used has unique qualities). Flakes created by soft hammer flaking are much thinner and longer than hard hammer flakes, and the flintknapper generally has better control over their size and shape. This means that thinner and sharper tools can be made, as well as tools with complex shapes. Hand axes can be made with either technique since their shape is simple, but those made using a soft hammer have much thinner and sharper edges.

We cannot be sure what hand axes were used for, but experiments with them suggest that they are not good for cutting trees (as the name might suggest); they seem more suited for butchering large animals. Lawrence Keeley microscopically examined some Acheulian hand axes, and the wear on them is consistent with animal butchery. They may have been used for woodworking, particularly hollowing and shaping wood, and they are also good for digging. William Calvin has even suggested that hand axes could be used as projectiles thrown like a discus into herds of animals in the hope of injuring or killing an animal.

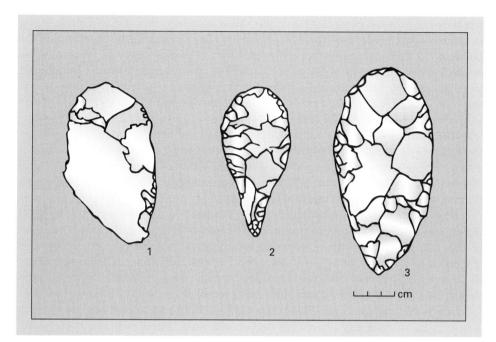

FIGURE **5.12**
Two handaxes (*center* and *right*) and a cleaver (*left*) illustrate typical Acheulean stone tools.

SOURCE: David W. Phillipson, *African Archaeology* (New York, NY: Cambridge University Press, 1985), p. 50. Reprinted with the permission of Cambridge University Press.

BIG-GAME EATING Some of the Acheulian sites have produced evidence of big-game eating. F. Clark Howell, who excavated sites at **Torralba and Ambrona**, Spain, found a substantial number of elephant remains and unmistakable evidence of human presence in the form of tools. Howell suggests that the humans at those sites used fire to frighten elephants into muddy bogs, from which they would be unable to escape. To hunt elephants in this way, the humans would have had to plan and work cooperatively in fairly large groups.

But do these finds of bones of large and medium-sized animals, in association with tools, tell us that the humans definitely were big-game hunters? Some archaeologists who have reanalyzed the evidence from Torralba think that the big game may have been scavenged. Because the Torralba and Ambrona sites are near ancient

 **Torralba and Ambrona, Spain** (Acheulian)

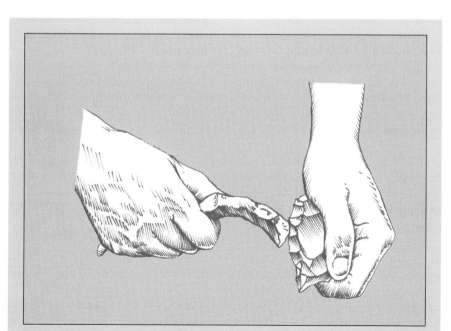

FIGURE **5.13**
Soft hammer flaking using an antler, as illustrated here, produces thinner and longer flakes than hard hammer flaking, and provides better control. Thinner, sharper, and more complex tools can be made using the soft hammer technique.

streams, many of the elephants could have died naturally, their bones accumulating in certain spots because of the flow of water. What seems fairly clear is that the humans did deliberately butcher different kinds of game—different types of tools are found with different types of animal. Thus, whether the humans hunted big game at Torralba and Ambrona is debatable; all we can be sure of, as of now, is that they consumed big game and probably hunted smaller game.

CONTROL OF FIRE    One way in which *H. erectus* is thought to have hunted is by using fire drives—a technique still used by hunting and gathering peoples in recent times. It is highly effective—animals are driven out of their hiding places and "homes" by fire and dispatched by hunters positioned downwind of the oncoming flames. Most peoples who use this technique today set fires deliberately, but fires caused by lightning strikes also may have been utilized. Did *H. erectus* set these fires? Because *H. erectus* was the first hominid to be found throughout the Old World and in areas with freezing winters, most anthropologists presume that *H. erectus* had learned to control fire, at least for warmth. There is archaeological evidence of fire in some early sites, but fires can be natural events. Thus, whether fire was under deliberate control by *H. erectus* is difficult to establish.

Suggestive but not conclusive evidence of the deliberate use of fire comes from Kenya in East Africa and is over 1.4 million years old. Better evidence of the deliberate use of fire comes from Europe somewhat later. Unfortunately, the evidence of control of fire at these European sites is not associated with *H. erectus* fossils either, so the link between deliberate use of fire and *H. erectus* cannot be definitely established yet. The lack of clear evidence does not, of course, mean that *H. erectus* did not use fire. After all, *H. erectus* did move into cold areas of the world, and it is hard to imagine how that could have happened without the deliberate use of fire. Cooking also would have been possible if *Homo erectus* was able to control fire. Cooking made all kinds of food (not just meat) more safely digestible and therefore more usable. Fires also would have kept predators away, a not inconsiderable advantage given that there were a lot of them around.

CAMPSITES    Acheulian sites were usually located close to water sources, lush vegetation, and large herds of grass-eating animals. Some camps have been found in caves, but most were in open areas surrounded by rudimentary fortifications or windbreaks (see Figure 5.14). Several African sites are marked by stony rubble brought there by *H. erectus,* possibly for the dual purpose of securing the windbreaks and providing ammunition in case of a sudden attack.

The presumed base campsites display a wide variety of tools, indicating that the camp was the center of many group functions. More specialized sites away from camp have also been found. These are marked by the predominance of a particular type of tool. For example, a butchering site in Tanzania contained dismembered hippopotamus carcasses and rare heavy-duty smashing and cutting tools. Workshops are another kind of specialized site encountered with some regularity. They are characterized by tool debris and are located close to a source of natural stone suitable

**Terra Amata, France** (Acheulian)

for toolmaking. A camp has been excavated at the **Terra Amata** site near Nice, on the French Riviera (see box feature titled "Terra Amata"), which produced evidence of several huts or windbreaks and areas where tool manufacture was apparently going on (Figure 5.14).

RELIGION AND RITUAL    Thus far I have described the technology, settlement, and subsistence of the Acheulean peoples, but I have not discussed the less material aspects of life, such as religion and ritual. What beliefs did *Homo erectus* hold about the world around them? Did they take part in rituals? Did *H. erectus* have religion? So far the answer seems to be no. But the data we have to examine these questions are limited, and there are, in fact, some hints that ritual and religion may have been a part of the Acheulean tradition.

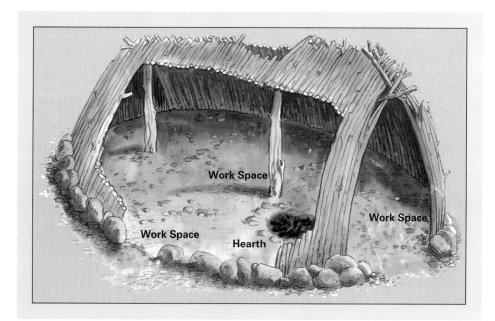

FIGURE **5.14**

A reconstruction of the oval huts built at Terra Amata. These huts were approximately 4 meters by 10 meters.

SOURCE: Copyright © 1969 by Eric Mose. Reprinted by permission of Eric Mose, Jr.

Remains of red ochre (oxidized clay) have been found on a number of Acheulean sites. This may be significant because in many later cultures, even modern ones, red ochre has been used to represent blood or, more generally, life in rituals of various types. Ochre seems to be particularly important in burial rituals, and human remains sprinkled with red ochre have been found in many parts of the world and dating back as far as 200,000 years ago. However, there is no evidence that *Homo erectus* buried their dead, nor any evidence that ochre was being used in rituals. It may have been used for body decoration, or simply for protection against insects or sunburn.

## The Zhoukoudian Tradition

While there is little evidence for religion or ritual in the Acheulean tradition, some interesting, although controversial, evidence comes from the Zhoukoudian tradition. The excavators of **Zhoukoudian cave** (in north China) suggested that some of the *H. erectus* remains there showed evidence of ritual cannibalism. The foramen magnum (the hole through which the spear enters the skull) of some specimens had been deliberately enlarged and the facial bones had been deliberately broken away from the cranium on others (Figure 5.15 on page 110). Some scholars have argued that the reason was to remove the brain for ritual consumption. Ritual cannibalism has been widely reported among living peoples, so its presence among ancient peoples is not impossible. But in the absence of formal burial rituals, cannibalism seems improbable. In addition, scholars point out that the parts of the skull that seem to have been purposely enlarged (to remove the brain) are those that are also the weakest points on the skull, and may have broken away because of decay or disturbance over the millennia.

Acheulian tools are found widely in Africa, Europe, and western Asia, but bifacial hand axes, cleavers, and picks are not found as commonly in eastern and southeastern Asia—the region of the Zhoukoudian tradition. This difference in tool technology is one of the primary differences between the two traditions. Why might this difference exist? Some archaeologists have suggested that large bifacial tools may be lacking in Zhoukoudian tradition because *H. erectus* in Asia had a better material to make tools out of—bamboo. Bamboo is used today in Southeast Asia for many purposes, including incredibly sharp arrows and sticks for digging and cutting. Geoffrey Pope showed that bamboo was present in those areas of Asia where hand axes and other large bifacial tools are missing.

**Zhoukoudian Cave, China** (Zhoukoudian)

## Terra Amata

Terra Amata must rank among the sites with the best locations in the world. Today it sits under an upscale apartment block on the French Riviera near Nice. When inhabited some 400,000 years ago, the site was in a sheltered cove on the sandy shore of the Mediterranean Sea, surrounded by fir, oak, and pine forests growing on the slopes of Mount Chauve and the hills of Mont Boron, which rise behind the site.

The site was excavated in a hurry, literally ahead of bulldozers digging the foundations for the apartment building which shares the site's name (when the importance of the site was realized a section of the building's basement was converted into a museum housing collections and a portion of the site itself). Excavation director Henry de Lumley supervised more than 300 workers in the excavation of more than 100 square meters of the site. Many artifacts were found, and stone artifacts were the most common. These were primarily scrapers and other flake tools, but some hand axes and cleavers were also recovered during the excavations. Many animal bones were also found, including bird, turtle, rabbits, stag, elephant, wild boar, ibex, rhino, and wild ox. Large game animals are by far the most common, as are juveniles, suggesting that the peoples living at Terra Amata were fairly selective hunters. A few shells of oyster, mussels, and limpets as well as fish bones show that the residents of Terra Amata also used resources from the sea. The presence of so many bones attests to the excellent preservation at the site, but they are not the most interesting materials found there.

Like Acheulian peoples, the peoples of the Zhoukoudian tradition hunted big game and lived in small, mobile groups. They also seem to have controlled fire. Good evidence of human control of fire, dating from nearly 500,000 years ago, comes from the cave at Zhoukoudian in China where *H. erectus* fossils have been found. In that cave are thousands of splintered and charred animal bones, apparently the remains of meals. There are also layers of ash, suggesting human control of fire. But recent analysis raises questions about these finds. The most serious problem is that human remains, tools, and ash rarely occur together in the same layers. In addition, there are no hearths at the Zhoukoudian site. Fires can spontaneously occur with heavy accumulation of organic matter, so clear evidence of human control of fire is still not definitely attested. Even the inference that humans brought the animals to the cave for butchering is only possibly a correct guess. Throughout the cave there is evidence of hyenas and wolves, and they, not the humans, may have brought many of the animal parts to the cave.

## DID *HOMO ERECTUS* HAVE LANGUAGE?

We know that language is a universal human capacity that is, at least in part, "hard-wired" into our brains. Dean Falk has shown that some of the structures of the brain that are important for language are present on endocasts from the earliest

THE ORIGINS OF CULTURE    **109**

More remarkable than anything else at Terra Amata are human coprolites (fossilized feces) discovered near the remains of what appear to be small windbreaks or huts. The coprolites contained pollen from plants that flower in the late spring or early summer, giving a good idea of when the site was occupied. At least eleven distinct occupations can be discerned, suggesting that the site was used annually for at least a decade, probably by the same group of people. The remains of several structures were also found. These consisted of hut poles and blocks of stone surrounding an oval floor some 7 to 15 meters long and 4 to 6 meters wide. Each hut had a hearth at the center, and some of the hearths had small windbreaks on one side of them, suggesting the huts were rather drafty and flimsy. In some of the huts there are obvious stoneworking areas, some even containing the impression of animal skins the knapper sat on.

What does this remarkable site tell us about life 400,000 years ago? First, it suggests that people moved seasonally in an annual round of hunting and gathering, stopping at particularly good locations year after year. Second, it suggests that big game was the focus of subsistence, but that a wide variety of other resources were also used. The excellent preservation on the site makes it clear that our picture of *Homo erectus* material culture is highly skewed. While stone tools are present, wood and bone are also present in abundance. Indeed, one enigmatic feature may be the remains of a wooden bowl. Finally, the Terra Amata site gives us a picture of a highly social group, sharing shelters, hearths, and food. The site gives us a picture of life from the distant past that in many ways we find hauntingly familiar today.

SOURCES: de Lumley, Henry, 1969, "A Paleolithic camp at Nice" *Scientific American* 220: 42–50. Villa, Paola, 1983, *Terra Amata and the Middle Pleistocene Archaeological Record of Southern France.* Berkeley, University of California Press–Publications in Anthropology, No. 13.

members of our genus (Figure 5.16). Modern apes have the ability to acquire rudimentary forms of language in specific settings, and all humans acquire language in an apparently universal manner. Does this mean that *Homo erectus* had language? Or were they only beginning to develop what would later become this distinctive human capacity?

One of the most striking things about language is its diversity—there are some 2,000 languages currently spoken and perhaps an equal number that have recently gone extinct. Language and culture are intimately linked, and we know that the diversity of languages in the world is paralleled by a similar diversity of cultures. *Homo erectus* culture lacks apparent diversity (or at least the diversity of modern culture). The Acheulean and Zhoukoudian traditions are strikingly similar, and within these traditions there is little diversity. For example, hand axes from different parts of the world show some divergence, but the basic form and technique of manufacture are much the same. Similarly, language, like culture, is constantly changing and innovating, and we might expect peoples with language to have constant change in their material culture such as we find among modern humans. But the Acheulean and Zhoukoudian traditions remained remarkably unchanged for more than a million years.

Perhaps more significantly, language is a complex system of symbolic communication, and in modern cultures complex symbolic communication is not restricted

FIGURE **5.15**

The base of a *Homo erectus* skull from Zhoukoudian Cave. The lighter colored areas are where bone was missing. Some have suggested the base of the skull was opened to extract the brain for ritual consumption.

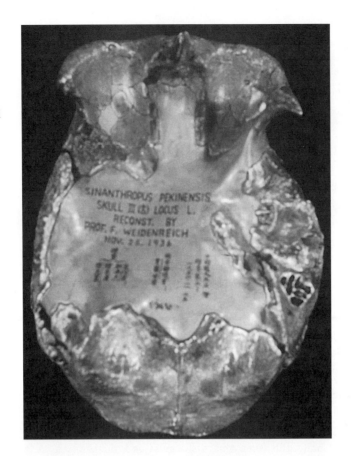

FIGURE **5.16**

The arrows shown on the left frontal lobe of a chimpanzee (left) and human (right) points to Broca's area, which is associated with language. Broca's area is much larger in humans. *Homo habilis* also had an enlarged Broca's area, which may indicate it had a greater capacity for language than the australopithecines.

SOURCE: From Dean Falk, *Primate Diversity* (New York, NY: W. W. Norton and Company, 2000), p. 338.

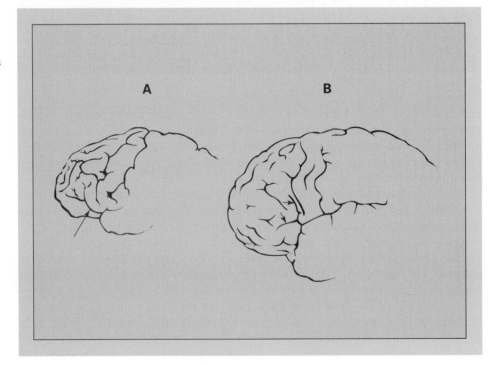

to spoken language but is represented in the entire range of material culture. We find stylistic variation, artistic expression, and experimentation widely represented in the material culture of modern peoples. People today use material culture to convey ideas and beliefs, along with status, wealth, and identity. Neither the Acheulean nor the Zhoukoudian traditions have presented evidence of art or of meaningful stylistic variation or experimentation. Those materials that do exist do not appear to have been used to convey meaning to others.

Thus, the material record of *Homo erectus* suggests that complex symbolic communication was not present, and it therefore seems likely that *Homo erectus* did not have language, at least not language as we know it today. Their social behavior and ability to move into new and challenging environments suggest that they must have had a complex system of communication, but it does not appear to have the productive and highly symbolic elements of human language. Most scholars today believe that language is a more recent development—perhaps as recent as the last 50,000 years, a time when human culture began to display the kinds of complex symbolic communication (such as art) that *Homo erectus* seems to lack. We consider the evolution of modern humans and their cultures in the next chapter.

## ◉ SUMMARY

Culture is a shared and learned process of adaptation and change. Human culture first appears in the Oldowan tradition as early *Homo* developed a distinctive assemblage of stone tools, began to eat big-game animals, and perhaps created home bases. Culture may have developed as an adaptation to brain growth. As the hominid brain enlarged it became impossible for females to give birth to offspring with fully developed brains. Thus infants had to be born at a relatively early stage of development, and were almost completely dependent on adult caretakers for a long period of time. Infant dependency caused problems for caretakers as well, since they were unable to easily forage while taking care of dependent infants. Culture, in the creation of home bases and families, may have been the answer to this problem. Home bases would have allowed individuals to bring food back to a common location to share with the rest of their families.

*Homo erectus* evolved in east Africa about 1.8 million years ago. Compared to early *Homo, Homo erectus* had a larger brain, smaller face and dentition, and an essentially modern body. *Homo erectus* was clearly a cultural animal, and not only created home bases, but also began using fire, hunting for food, and perhaps taking part in rituals. *Homo erectus* was the first hominid to leave Africa, reaching Europe by 1.7 million years ago and Indonesia by at least 1.6 million years ago and perhaps earlier. Two distinct archaeological traditions are associated with *Homo erectus*—Acheulean and Zhoukoudian. The Acheulean tradition is characterized by a distinctive stone tool kit that included hand axes and tools made by the soft-hammer flaking technique. Acheulean-type tools are rare in the Zhoukoudian tradition, and hand axes are not present. The lack of these tools in the Zhoukoudian tradition may be due to the use of bamboo for tools rather than stone.

## ◉ DISCUSSION QUESTIONS

1. Describe the way in which Oldowan and Acheulean tools were made. How do these techniques differ?
2. What are the main differences between *Homo erectus* and early *Homo*.
3. What cultural practices allowed *Homo erectus* to leave Africa?

## ⬡ ESSAY QUESTIONS

1. Use library and web resources on parenting to explore problems faced by parents today. With this information explain why a long period of infant dependency might have had significance in the evolution of human culture. How would culture have helped infants to survive?

2. Use library resources to examine a single archaeological site associated with *Homo erectus*. What evidence is left after such a long period of time? What evidence seems to be lacking? How do the researchers use the archaeological techniques discussed in the beginning chapters of this book to reconstruct the lives of these ancient humans?

3. Using the information in this chapter and any other information you can find about the culture of early humans, explore the following question: How could *Homo erectus* have spread across the world and developed the cultural features noted in this chapter without having spoken language?

## ✒ RESEARCH PROJECT

Visit a local or regional zoo that houses primates. Spend at least two hours watching the social interactions of a single primate species. You may want to employ a formal method used in animal behavior studies such as focal follow, time allocation, or spot observation (you will need to research these methods or ask your instructor to provide information about them). Next go to an area in the zoo where humans are interacting with one another, such as a cafeteria or gift shop, and spend two hours watching the social interactions of humans. How do social interactions among humans differ from those among the primate species you watched? Could you recognize cultural behaviors among humans? Among the other primate species? What role did vocal communication play in human interactions? In the other primate species?

## ⬡ KEY SOURCES

### The Oldowan Tradition

Clark, 1970; Isaac, 1984; Leakey, L., 1960; Schick and Toth, 1993; Susman, 1994.

### Stone Tools and Culture

Dobzhansky, 1962; Isaac, 1971; Leakey, M., 1971; Potts, 1988; Shipman, 1986; Whittaker, 1994.

### *Homo erectus*

Balter and Gibbons, 2000; Day, 1986; Fleagle, 1999; Gabunia et al., 2000; Jones, Martin, and Pilbeam, 1992; Kramer, 2002; Rightmire, 1990, 2000; Swisher et al., 1994; Wolpoff and Nkini, 1985.

### Archaeological Traditions Associated with *Homo erectus*

Binford and Ho, 1985; de Lumley, 1969; Freeman, 1994; Klein, 1989; Yamei et al., 2000.

### Did *Homo erectus* Have Language?

Deacon, 1997; Dickson, 1990; Falk, 1983; Lieberman, 1991; Noble and Davidson, 1996; Savage-Rubaugh, 1992.

# WHAT CAN WE LEARN ABOUT THE PAST?

This chapter covers the Miocene Epoch, the time of a large-scale radiation of apes. This is a confusing period for those who study human origins because of the large number of hominoid species, the paucity of links between these species and the living apes, and much disagreement over taxonomy and nomenclature. Many of these hominoids lived in dense tropical forests, where acidic forest floors and abundant bacteria tend to chemically degrade their skeletal remains. Equally important, modern forests still cover most of the forest areas of the past, making investigations of these important areas difficult.

So why attempt to put together a fossil record of this difficult period? In this Media Lab, you will hear Dr. Ruben G. Mendoza from California State University discuss some of the reasons for studying the past.

## WEB ACTIVITY

Hominoids first appeared in dense lowland forests of Africa about 20 million years ago. Throughout the Miocene, many genera and species evolved. Subsequently, four major changes led to the evolution of the hominids: separation of the gibbon and its relatives from the line leading to the great apes and hominids (about 12–15 million years ago); divergence of the orangutan from the lineage leading to the African apes and hominids (10–12 million years ago); the split of the gorilla from hominids and chimpanzees (about 8 million years ago); and, finally, the split of the hominid and chimpanzee lineages (between 5 and 8 million years ago). Working on the identification and taxonomy of early hominoids is the key to confirming and refining these dates.

The Media Lab can be found in Chapter 5 on the *Companion Website*™ http://www.prenhall.com/peregrine

## Activity

1. View the video. Based on the interview, what are biological anthropologists ultimately trying to discover?
2. What adaptations led to the evolution of the hominoids and the modern apes.
3. Based on the chapter and the video, can you think of reasons why it is more difficult to find hominoid remains than human remains?

# The Emergence of Modern Humans

In this chapter I discuss the fossil evidence as well as the controversies about the transition from *H. erectus* to modern humans, *Homo sapiens,* a transition which may have begun 500,000 years ago. I also explain what we know about the archaeological traditions of the people who lived during this transition—people of the East Asian Middle Paleolithic, Middle Stone Age, and Mousterian traditions.

## THE TRANSITION FROM *HOMO ERECTUS* TO *HOMO SAPIENS*

Most paleoanthropologists agree that *H. erectus* evolved into *H. sapiens*, but they disagree about how and where the transition occurred. As I noted in the last chapter, there is also disagreement about how to classify some fossils from 500,000 to about 200,000 years ago that have a mix of *H. erectus* and *H. sapiens* traits. A particular fossil might be called *H. erectus* by some anthropologists and "archaic" *Homo sapiens* by others. Still other anthropologists see so much continuity between *H. erectus* and *H. sapiens* that they think it is completely arbitrary to call them different species. According to these anthropologists, *H. erectus* and *H. sapiens* may just be earlier and later varieties of the same species, and therefore all should be called *H. sapiens*. (*H. erectus* would then be *H. sapiens erectus*.)

### Homo heidelbergensis

In recent years scholars have suggested that the "transitional" fossils share common traits and may actually represent a separate species—***Homo heidelbergenesis,*** named after a jaw found in 1907 in the village of **Mauer** near Heidelberg, Germany. Other specimens that have been suggested as members of this species have been found in many parts of the world: Bodo, Hopefield, Ndutu, Elandsfontein, and Rabat in Africa; Bilzingsleben, Petralona, Arago, Steinheim, and Swanscombe in Europe; and Dali and Solo in Asia (see Figure 6.1).

    *Homo heidelbergensis* differs from *Homo erectus* in having smaller teeth and jaws, a much larger brain (on the order of 1,300 cc), a skull that lacks a sagittal keel and occipital torus, a brow ridge that divides into separate arches above each eye, and an overall robusticity in its skeleton. *Homo heidelbergensis* differs from modern *Homo sapiens* in retaining a large and prognathic face with relatively large teeth and jaws, a brow ridge, a long, low cranial vault with a sloping forehead, and in its overall robusticity (Figure 6.2). Many scholars question whether *Homo heidelbergensis* represents one or several species, or whether it represents a separate species at all. Many would argue that *Homo heidelbergensis* should be considered an archaic *Homo sapien*.

### Neandertals: *Homo sapiens* or *Homo neandertalensis?*

There may be disagreement about how to classify the mixed-trait fossils from 500,000 to 200,000 years ago, but recently an outright battle has emerged about many of the fossils that are less than 200,000 years old. Some anthropologists argue that they were definitely *Homo sapiens*. Others, that they were part of a distinct species, ***Homo neandertalensis,*** more commonly referred to as the **Neandertals.** The Neandertals have been a confusing hominid fossil group since the first specimen was found in 1856. Somehow, through the years the Neandertals have been misrepresented as burly ape-men, incapable of complex thought or culture. Actually, they might go unnoticed in a cross-section of the world's population today. Does that mean they were part of our species? For a while the answer seemed to be yes. But

**Mauer, Germany** (*Homo heidelbergensis*)

**Homo sapiens:** the technical name for modern humans.

**Homo heidelbergensis:** a transitional species between *Homo erectus* and *Homo sapiens.*

**Homo neandertalensis:** the technical name for the Neandertals.

**Neandertals:** a group of robust and otherwise anatomically distict hominids that are close relatives of modern humans.

FIGURE **6.1**
Sites discussed in Chapter 6.

SOURCE: From *Human Evolution
Source Book* by Clochon/Fleagle,
© 1993. Reprinted by permission of
Pearson Education, Inc., Upper Saddle
River, NJ.

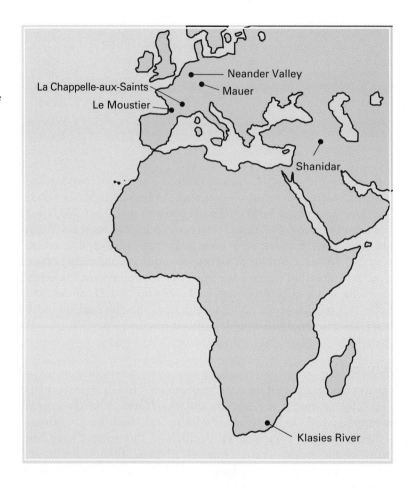

 **Neander Valley,
Germany (***Homo
neadertalensis***)**

recent archaeological and genetic evidence has led many to question the relationship between Neandertals and modern humans, and today the tide seems to be turning against those who would group them together. Let's take a look at some of the history of research on the Neandertals.

In 1856, three years before Darwin's publication of *The Origin of Species*, a skullcap and other fossilized bones were discovered in a cave in the **Neander Valley** (tal is the German word for "valley"), near Düsseldorf, Germany (Figure 6.1). The fossils in the Neander Valley were the first that scholars could tentatively consider as an early hominid. (The fossils classified as *Homo erectus* were not found until later in the nineteenth century, and the fossils belonging to the genus *Australopithecus* not until the twentieth century.) After Darwin's revolutionary work was published, the Neandertal find aroused considerable controversy. A few evolutionist scholars, such as Thomas Huxley, thought that the Neandertal was not that different from modern humans. Others dismissed the Neandertal as irrelevant to human evolution; they saw it as a pathological freak, a peculiar, disease-ridden individual. However, similar fossils turned up later in Belgium, Yugoslavia, France, and elsewhere in Europe, which meant that the original Neandertal find could not be dismissed as an oddity.

The predominant reaction to the original and subsequent Neandertal-like finds was that the Neandertals were too "brutish" and "primitive" to have been ancestral to modern humans. This view prevailed in the scholarly community until well into the 1950s. A major proponent of this view was Marcellin Boule, who claimed between 1908 and 1913 that the Neandertals would not have been capable of a fully erect posture (see box feature titled "Boule's Reconstruction and Its Legacy"). Since the 1950s, however, a number of studies have disputed Boule's claim, and it is now generally agreed that the skeletal traits of the Neandertals are very similar to

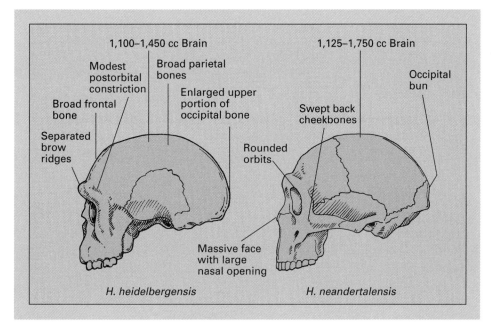

FIGURE **6.2**

Comparison of the crania of *Homo heidelbergensis* and *Homo neadertalensis,* showing important differences.

SOURCE: Carol R. Ember, Melvin Ember, and Peter N. Peregrine, *Physical Anthropology and Archaeology* (Upper Saddle River, NJ: Prentice Hall, 2002), p. 138. Reprinted by permission of Pearson Education, Inc., Upper Saddle River, NJ.

modern humans. Perhaps more important, when the much more ancient australopithecine and *H. erectus* fossils were accepted as hominids in the 1940s and 1950s, anthropologists realized that the Neandertals did not look so different from modern humans—despite their sloping foreheads, large brow ridges, flattened braincases, large jaws, and nearly absent chins (Figure 6.2). After all, they did have larger brains (averaging more than 1,450 cc) than modern humans (slightly more than 1,300 cc). Some scholars believe that the large brain capacity of Neandertals suggests that they were capable of the full range of behavior characteristic of modern humans. Their skeletons did, however, attest to one behavioral trait markedly different from behaviors of most modern humans: Neandertals apparently made very strenuous use of their bodies.

It took almost 100 years for scholars to accept the idea that Neandertals were not so different from modern humans and therefore should be classified as *Homo sapiens neanderthalensis.* But in the last few years there has been a growing debate over whether the Neandertals in western Europe were ancestral to modern-looking people who lived later in western Europe, after about 40,000 years ago. Neandertals lived in other places besides western Europe. A large number of fossils from central Europe strongly resemble those from western Europe, although some features, such as a projecting midface, are less pronounced. Neandertals have also been found in southwestern Asia (Israel, Iraq) and Central Asia (Uzbekistan). One of the largest collections of Neandertal fossils comes from **Shanidar Cave** in the mountains of northeastern Iraq, where Ralph Solecki unearthed the skeletons of nine individuals (see the box feature on Shanidar Cave on pages 128 and 129). What has changed scholars' opinions of the Neandertals so that they are now most commonly seen as not belonging to the *Homo sapiens* group?

In 1997 a group of researchers from the United States and Germany published findings that forced a reconsideration of the Neandertals and their relationship to modern humans. These scholars reported that they had been able to extract DNA from the original Neandertal specimen found in 1856. The DNA they extracted was not nuclear DNA—the material which makes up the human genome. Rather, the DNA came from a tiny structure found in all eukaryotic cells (that is, cells with a membrane-bound nucleus) called *mitochondria.* The mitochondria produce enzymes needed for energy production, and they have their own DNA, which replicates when a cell replicates but is not thought to be under any pressure from natural selection.

**Shanidar Cave, Iraq**
(*Homo neadertalensis*)

## Boule's Reconstruction and Its Legacy

In 1908 the respected French paleontologist and anatomist Marcellin Boule was given an enviable assignment—to reconstruct the nearly complete skeleton of a recently discovered adult Neandertal. Boule was apparently eager to take on the task, and he reported initial results within months. Shortly thereafter a popular account of the reconstruction appeared in the French periodical *L'Illustration* and included a striking image (see Figure 6.3). It depicts the Neandertal as an ape-like brute, standing bent-kneed and hunched over, covered in long hair, and scowling, with a club and a rock in either hand. Boule's official reconstruction, published between 1911 and 1913, is not much different. Boule argued that Neandertals had divergent big toes like the great apes, could not fully straighten their knees

FIGURE **6.3**
This 1909 image of Neandertal as a monstrous beast was influenced by Boule's inaccurate reconstruction.

or backs, and that their brains, while as large as modern humans, were "rudi-mentary" and incapable of higher thought. It is from Boule that we get the pop-ular image of the Neandertal as a simple-minded brute—the image we use when we call someone a Neandertal because of something awkward or stupid they have done.

The problem is that Boule was wrong. The skeleton he reconstructed, that of a 50-year-old man, had a number of pathologies that Boule apparently ignored. He had severe arthritis, and, indeed, could not fully straighten his knees. Several of his vertebrae had been effected by the disease and were essentially fused, making his back arched. He was indeed robust and muscular, but those characteristics were extreme even for Neadertals, who were more muscular than modern humans. In addition to ignoring these facts, Boule also took some creative liber-ties in his reconstruction. The divergent toe Boule seems to have simply made up, misaligning the foot bones to create what looked like divergence. The skull and brain, while indeed having a low forehead, was larger than most modern humans and shows all the areas of higher thought that modern human brains have. There is simply no reason to believe that this individual was any less intelligent than modern humans.

Boule created a caricature, one that has been corrected by modern scholars, so why discuss it here? Because the caricature remains in the popular imagination and in our language. Why? One answer may be the images themselves that were created by Boule and by artists using his reconstruction. They are still striking today, displaying a beast the likes of which we find in fairy tales and science fiction—a powerful monster seeking to smash our heads and drag us into its cave. But more important, perhaps, is what the images say about us. Making the most recent premodern hominid a brutish monster makes us feel all the more human—we are not animals or brutes like Neandertals, we are compassionate, thoughtful humans.

The legacy of Boule's reconstruction, then, is a lesson to us about the power of representation and myth. Archaeology is an act we do in the present and is thus as much a statement about us, today, as it is a reconstruction of the past. We need to be aware of the fictional aspects of the stories we tell about the past, and we need to be willing to change our stories as we gain new information about the past. In short, the legacy of Boule's reconstruction is one of caution and modesty. We should never have the hubris to think we actually know, with certainty, what happened in the past. Nor should we ever be so blind as to think that the present is not affecting our understanding of the past. We will never know the past the way it truly was, but only the way it truly is today, based on our current knowledge and theory.

SOURCES: Moser, Stephanie, 1992, "The visual language of archaeology: A case study of the Neanderthals," *Antiquity* 66: 831–844; Shreeve, James, Sept. 1994, "In our images of Neanderthals, we haven't always let the facts get in the way of what makes us feel best," *Smithsonian* 25: 17–20.

**La Chappelle-aux-Saints, France**
(*Homo neadertalensis*)

FIGURE **6.4**

Differences in mtDNA sequences among humans, the Neandertal, and chimpanzees. The x-axis shows the number of sequence differences; the y-axis shows the percent of individuals that share that number of sequence differences.

SOURCE: Reprinted from "Neandertal DNA Sequences and the Origin of Modern Humans," by M. Krings, A. Stone, R.W. Schmitz, H. Krainitzkl, M. Stoneking, and S. Paabo in *Cell*, 90. Copyright 1997 with permission from Elsevier Science.

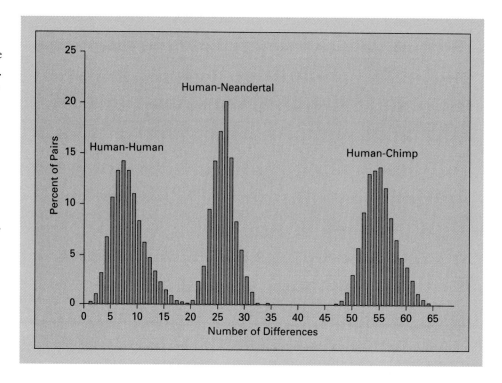

The only source of change in mitochondrial DNA (usually referred to as mtDNA) is random mutation. Mitochondrial DNA are inherited only from mothers in animals; it is not carried into an egg cell by sperm, but left with the sperm's tail on the outside of the egg. These unique characteristics make it possible to use mtDNA to measure the degree of relatedness between two species, and even how long ago those species diverged. The longer two species have been separated, the more differences there will be in their mtDNA, which is thought to mutate at a fairly constant rate of about 2 percent per million years. Thus the number of differences between the mtDNA of two organisms can be converted into an estimated date in the past when those organisms stopped being part of the same breeding population. While there is still controversy over many details of how and why mtDNA mutates and its accuracy for determining absolute dates of divergence, most scholars agree that it is a powerful tool for examining relative degrees of relatedness between species.

How similar is Neandertal mtDNA to modern human DNA? Not as similar as many scholars expected. Between individuals who are modern humans, there are usually five to ten differences in the sequence of mtDNA examined by the U.S. and German researchers. Between modern humans and the Neandertal specimen, there tends to be about 25 differences—more than three times that between modern humans (Figure 6.4). This suggested to the researchers that the ancestors of modern humans and the Neandertal must have diverged about 600,000 years ago. If the last common ancestor of ours and the Neandertal lived that long ago in the past, the Neandertal would be a much more distant relative than previously thought. Similar results have since been obtained from two other Neandertal skeletons, and all three reinforce recent archaeological findings from Europe and the Near East that are relevant to the issues.

It has been known for decades that both modern human and Neandertal fossils are found in the same locations in parts of the Levant, but recent improvements in dating and newly discovered fossils have even more clearly demonstrated that the two kinds of hominid coexisted (see Color Plate 7). In fact, several caves in the Mt. Carmel region of Israel contain both modern human and Neandertal occupations. The fact that these two groups of hominids coinhabited the Near East for perhaps as much as 30,000 years strongly suggests that the two are different species. Finds in Europe seem to corroborate that assessment. As early modern humans began moving into Europe they appear to have displaced populations of Neandertals already living there. Sites with tools thought to be associated with Neandertals disappear throughout Europe as sites with tools thought to be associated with modern humans expand their range (there are, unfortunately, very few fossils from this time period—roughly 40,000 years ago—to make certain who made the tools). Significantly, the area of Europe (Iberia) last colonized by modern humans contains the very latest Neandertal fossils yet found, dating to some 30,000 years ago.

## ARCHAEOLOGICAL TRADITIONS ASSOCIATED WITH NEANDERTALS

The archaeological tradition associated with the Neandertals in Europe and the Near East is called the **Mousterian** tradition and dates from about 200,000 years ago to about 40,000 years ago. In Africa, the **Middle Stone Age** tradition seems to be associated with Neandertals, while in East Asia the **East Asian Middle Paleolithic** tradition dates from the same time period. All three traditions are primarily defined by stone tool assemblages.

### Mousterian

The Mousterian tradition is named after the tool assemblage found in a rock shelter at **Le Moustier** in the Dordogne region of southwestern France. Compared with an Acheulian assemblage, a Mousterian tool assemblage has a smaller proportion of large core tools such as hand axes and cleavers and a bigger proportion of small flake tools such as scrapers (Figure 6.5). Although many flakes struck off from a core were used "as is," the Mousterian is also characterized by flakes that were often altered

**Mousterian**
(ca. 200,000 to 40,000 B.P.). Associated with Neandertals in Europe, North Africa, and the Middle East, and characterized by a tool kit including many flake tools, especially manufactured using the Levallois technique.

**Middle Stone Age**
(ca. 150,000 to 40,000 B.P.). Associated with Neandertals and early modern humans in Africa, and characterized by a tool kit including numerous Levallois flake tools.

**East Asian Middle Paleolithic**
(ca. 200,000 to 40,000 B.P.). Associated with Neandertals and early modern humans in East Asia, and characterized by a tool kit similar to the Zhoukoudian tradition, with many pebble tools and unmodified flakes.

**Le Moustier, France** (Mousterian)

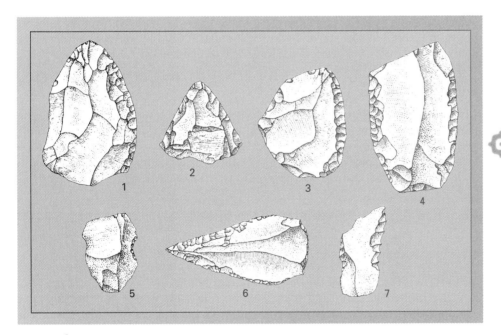

FIGURE **6.5**
A typical Mousterian tool kit.
A Mousterian tool kit emphasized sidescrapers (1–4), notches (5), points (6), and saw-toothed denticulates (7). How these stone artifacts were actually used is not known, but the points may have been joined to wood shafts, and denticulates could have been used to work wood. The tools illustrated here are from Mousterian sites in western Europe.
SOURCE: From Richard G. Klein, "Ice-Age Hunters of the Ukraine." Reprinted with permission of Nelson H. Prentiss.

or "retouched" by striking small flakes or chips from one or more edges. Studies of the wear on scrapers suggest that many were used for scraping hides or working wood. The fact that some of the tools, particularly points, were thinned or shaped on one side suggests that they were hafted, attached to a shaft or handle.

Toward the end of the Acheulian tradition, a technique developed that enabled the toolmaker to produce flake tools of a predetermined size instead of simply chipping flakes away from the core at random. In this **Levallois method,** the toolmaker first shaped the core and prepared a "striking platform" at one end. Flakes of predetermined and standard sizes could then be knocked off (see Figure 6.6). Although some Levallois flakes date as far back as 400,000 years ago, they are found more frequently in Mousterian tool kits.

The tool assemblages in particular sites may be characterized as Mousterian, but one site may have more or fewer scrapers, points, and so forth than another site. A number of archaeologists have suggested possible reasons for this variation. For example, Sally Binford and Lewis Binford suggested that different activities may have occurred in different sites. Some sites may have been used for butchering and other sites may have been base camps; hence the kinds of tools found in different sites should vary. And Paul Fish has suggested that some sites may have more tools produced by the Levalloisian technique because larger pieces of flint were available.

## Middle Stone Age

**Klasies River, South Africa** (Middle Stone Age)

Like Mousterian tools, many of the Middle Stone Age tradition tools were struck off prepared cores in the Levalloisian way. The assemblages consist mostly of various types of flake tools (Figure 6.7). A well-described sequence of such tools comes from the area around the mouth of the **Klasies River** on the southern coast of South Africa. This area contains rock shelters and small caves in which *Homo heidelbergensis*, Neandertals, and *Homo sapiens* lived. The oldest cultural remains in one of the caves may date back 120,000 years. These earliest tools include parallel-sided flake blades (probably used as knives), pointed flakes (possibly spearpoints), burins or gravers (chisel-like tools), and scrapers. Similar tools discovered at Border Cave, South Africa, may have been used almost 200,000 years ago.

## East Asian Middle Paleolithic

Unlike the Mousterian and Middle Stone Age traditions, East Asian Middle Paleolithic tools show only modest development from earlier Zhoukoudian tools. Prepared core technology was not used, and tool forms were fairly limited. Tools included choppers, picks, scrapers, and, of course, flakes. Unfortunately, there is little skeletal material associated with these tools, so it is not clear who was making them.

## Common Aspects of Neandertal Traditions

Despite the differences in locations and tool assemblages, archaeological traditions associated with Neandertals share some common elements.

HOMESITES Most of the excavated Mousterian homesites in Europe and the Near East are located in caves and rock shelters. The same is true for the excavated Middle Stone Age homesites in sub-Saharan Africa and many of the East Asian Middle Paleolithic sites from Southeast Asia. We might conclude, therefore, that Neandertals lived mostly in caves or rock shelters. But that conclusion could be incorrect. Caves and rock shelters may be overrepresented in the archaeological record because they are more likely to be found than are sites that originally were in the open but now are hidden by thousands of years, and many feet, of sediment. Sediment is the dust, debris, and decay that accumulates over time; when we dust the furniture and vacuum the floor, we are removing sediment.

**Levallois method:** a method of making stone tools that allowed flake tools of a predetermined size to be produced from a shaped core.

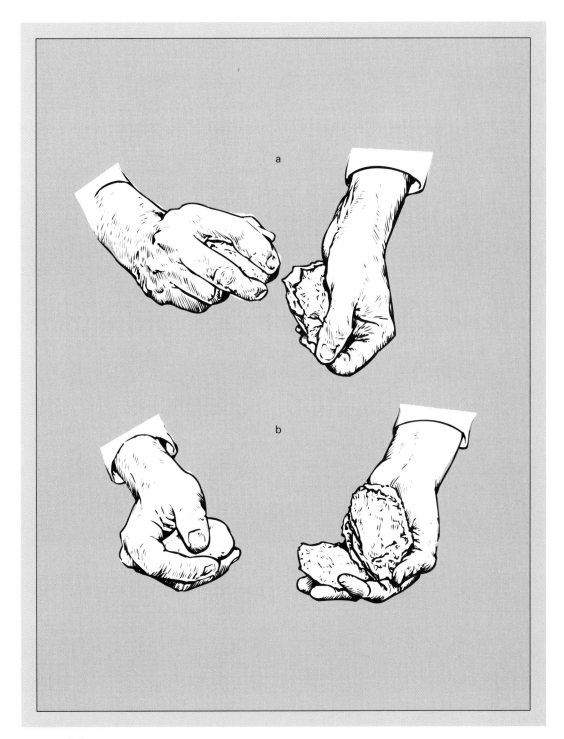

FIGURE **6.6**
In the Levallois method, a core is prepared (a) so that a single blow will produce a flake of
predetermined size and shape (b).

Still, we know that many Neandertals lived at least part of the year in caves.
This was true, for example, along the Dordogne River in France. The river gouged
deep valleys in the limestone of that area. Below the cliffs are rock shelters with over-
hanging roofs and deep caves, many of which were occupied during the Mousterian
era. Even if the inhabitants did not stay all year, the sites do seem to have been

FIGURE **6.7**

Some Middle Stone Age tools, including scrapers (1 & 2), a handaxe (3), and knives or projectile points (4 & 5)

SOURCE: David W. Phillipson, *African Archaeology* (New York, NY: Cambridge University Press, 1985), p. 79. Reprinted with the permission of Cambridge University Press.

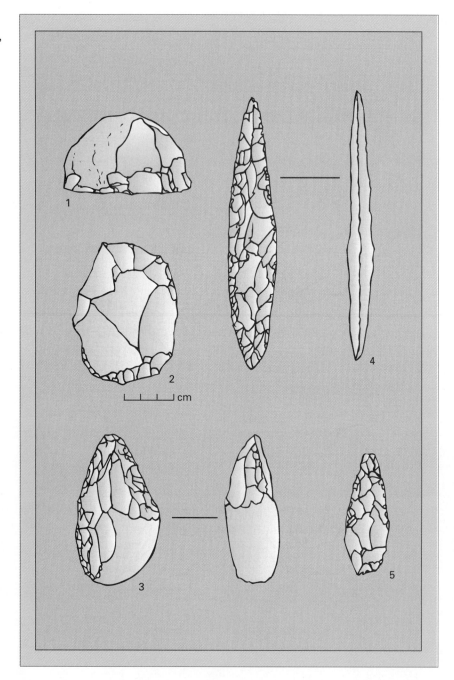

occupied year after year. Although there is evidence of some use of fire in earlier cultures, Neandertals seem to have relied more on fire. There are thick layers of ash in many rock shelters and caves and evidence that hearths were used to increase the efficiency of the fires.

Quite a few Neandertal homesites were in the open. In Africa, open-air sites were located on floodplains, at the edges of lakes, and near springs. In Asia, sites dating to the Middle Paleolithic period were often on river terraces. Many open-air sites have been found in Europe, particularly eastern Europe. The occupants of the well-known site at Moldova in western Russia lived in river-valley houses framed with wood and covered with animal skins. Bones of mammoths, huge elephants now extinct, surround the remains of hearths and were apparently used to help hold the animal skins in place. Even though the winter climate near the edge of the glacier nearby was cold at that time, there would still have been animals to hunt because the plant food for the game was not buried under deep snow.

The hunters probably moved away in the summer to higher land between the river valleys. In all likelihood, the higher ground was grazing land for the large herds of animals the Moldova hunters depended on for meat. In the winter river-valley sites archaeologists have found skeletons of wolf, arctic fox, and hare with their paws missing. These animals probably were skinned for pelts that were made into clothing.

SUBSISTENCE How Neandertals got their food varied with their environment (see Figure 6.8). In Africa, they lived in savanna and semiarid desert. In Asia, they lived in a variety of environments, from forests to steppelands (though, again, we don't have enough skeletal evidence to know that sites dating to the Middle Stone Age were associated with Neandertals). In western and eastern Europe, they had to adapt to cold; during periods of increased glaciation, much of the environment was steppe grassland and tundra. Neandertals were good at exploiting a wide range of resources no matter where they lived. However, in all areas Neandertals were hunters, and they focused their hunting on large game where it was present.

The European environment during this time was much richer in animal resources than the tundra of northern countries is today. Indeed, the European environment inhabited by Neandertals abounded in game, both big and small. The tundra and alpine animals included reindeer, bison, wild oxen, horses, mammoths, rhinoceroses, and deer, as well as bears, wolves, and foxes. Some European sites have also yielded bird and fish remains. For example, people in a summer camp in northern Germany apparently hunted swans and ducks and fished for perch and pike. Little, however, is known about the particular plant foods the European Neandertals may have consumed; the remains of plants are unlikely to survive thousands of years in a nonarid environment.

In Africa, too, early *Homo sapiens* varied in how they got food. For example, we know that the people living at the mouth of the Klasies River in South Africa ate shellfish as well as meat from small grazers such as antelopes and large grazers such as eland and buffalo. But archaeologists disagree about how the Klasies River people got their meat when they began to occupy the caves in the area.

Richard Klein thinks they hunted large as well as small game. Klein speculates that because the remains of eland of all ages have been found in Cave 1 at this site, the people there probably hunted the eland by driving them into corrals or other traps, where animals of all ages could be killed. Klein thinks that buffalo were hunted differently. Buffalo tend to charge attackers, which would make it difficult to drive them into traps. Klein believes that because bones from mostly very young and very old buffalo are found in the cave, the hunters were able to stalk and kill only the most vulnerable animals.

Lewis Binford thinks the Klasies River people hunted only small grazers and scavenged the eland and buffalo meat from the kills of large carnivores. He argues that sites should contain all or almost all of the bones from animals that were hunted. According to Binford, since more or less complete skeletons are found only from small animals, the Klasies River people were not at first hunting all the animals they used for food.

But there is new evidence suggesting that people were hunting big game as much as 400,000 years ago. Wooden spears that old were recently found in Germany in association with stone tools and the butchered remains of more than ten wild horses (Figure 6.9). The heavy spears resemble modern aerodynamic javelins, which suggests they would have been thrown at large animals such as horses, not at small animals. This new evidence strongly suggests that hunting, not just scavenging, may be older than archaeologists used to think.

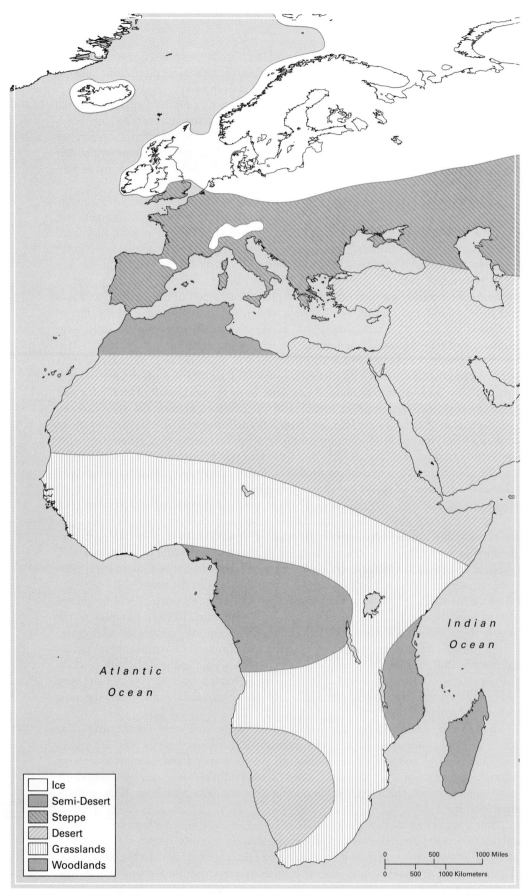

FIGURE **6.8**

The environments of Europe and Africa during the Neandertal era.

FIGURE **6.9**
Wooden spear point from Germany dating to about 400,000 years ago.

In East Asia subsistence was similarly varied. People hunted or scavenged large game animals such as horse, rhinocerous, and tapir. Interestingly, there seems to be no evidence that people ate fish or shellfish, even in coastal areas. Preserved seeds from Zhoukoudian and several other sites provides evidence that people of the East Asian Middle Paleolithic tradition also gathered a variety of wild plant foods.

**FUNERAL RITUALS?** Some Neandertals were deliberately buried. At Le Moustier, the skeleton of a boy fifteen or sixteen years old was found with a beautifully fashioned stone ax near his hand. Near Le Moustier, graves of five other children and two adults, apparently interred together in a family plot, were discovered. These finds, along with one at Shanidar Cave in Iraq, have aroused speculation about the possibility of Neandertal funeral rituals (see box feature titled "Shanidar Cave").

## THE EMERGENCE OF MODERN HUMANS

**Cro-Magnon** humans, who appear in western Europe about 35,000 years ago, were once thought to be the earliest specimens of modern humans, or *Homo sapiens*. (The Cro-Magnons are named after the rock shelter in France where they were first found in 1868.) But we now know that modern-looking humans appeared earlier outside of Europe. As of now, the oldest known fossils unambiguously classified as *H. sapiens* come from Africa. Some of these fossils, discovered in one of the Klasies River Mouth caves, are possibly as old as 100,000 years. Other modern-looking fossils of about the same age have been found in Border Cave in South Africa, and a find at Omo in Ethiopia may be an early *H. sapien*. Remains of anatomically modern humans found at two sites in Israel, at Skhul and Qafzeh, which used to be thought to date back 40,000 to 50,000 years, may be 90,000 years old (see Color Plate 8). There are also anatomically modern human finds in Borneo, at Niah, from about 40,000 years ago, and in Australia, at Lake Mungo, from about 30,000 years ago.

These modern-looking humans differed from the Neandertals, *Homo heidelbergensis,* and *Homo erectus* in that they had higher, more bulging foreheads, thinner and lighter bones, smaller faces and jaws, chins (the bony protuberances that remain after projecting faces recede), and only slight brow ridges or no ridges at all (see Figure 6.10 on page 130).

**Cro-Magnon:** modern humans who lived in western Europe about 35,000 years ago.

## Shanidar Cave

Shanidar Cave may be one of the longest occupied sites in the world. It is located in a valley of the Zagros mountains in the Ruwanduz district of northeastern Iraq, and it has been occupied on and off for some 80,000 years. Kurdish goatherders still lived in the cave at the time it was being excavated. The Mousterian tradition occupation of the cave dates to about 80,000 to 40,000 years before the present. During the time of the Mousterian occupation the environment appears to have been milder than today. The area was covered in oak forests, and wild goat and pig were abundant.

The cave itself is large, about 25 meters wide and 110 meters long. It has a large south-facing opening that would have provided abundant light and warmth to the cave's inhabitants. The site was excavated by Ralph Solecki in four seasons from 1951 to 1960, and because of its long occupation and abundant hominid fossil remains it has become one of the most significant Paleolithic sites excavated during the last century.

The Mousterian layers of the cave were found nearly 9 meters below the current ground surface. Although the remains of nine Neandertals were found, few artifacts were discovered, and most of these were stone scrapers. On the other hand, the nine Neandertals, including two infants, provide a remarkable cross-sample of Neandertals. Both men and women, old and young are represented. Several of the individuals were apparently killed by rock falls from the cave roof and were left in

## Theories about the Origins of Modern Humans

Two theories about the origins of modern humans continue to be debated among paleoanthropologists. One, which can be called the single-origin or "Out of Africa" theory, suggests that modern humans emerged in just one part of the Old World (most likely Africa) and then spread to other parts, replacing other *Homo* species. The second theory, which has been called the multiregional theory, suggests that modern humans evolved in various parts of the Old World after *Homo erectus* spread out of Africa.

SINGLE-ORIGIN THEORY According to the single-origin theory, most of the premodern *Homo* populations did not evolve into modern humans. Rather, according to this view, all the premodern *Homo* species became extinct because they were replaced by modern humans by about 35,000 years ago. The presumed place of origin of the first modern humans has varied over the years as new fossils have been discovered. In the 1950s the source population was presumed to be the Neandertals in the Near East, who were referred to as "generalized" or "progressive" Neandertals. Later, when earlier *Homo sapiens* were found in Africa, paleoanthropologists postulated that modern humans emerged first in Africa and then moved to the Near East and from there to Europe and Asia. Single-origin theorists place after death (although additional rocks may have been added to the place where one individual was killed, perhaps as a memorial of some kind), while others were purposely buried in the cave floor (see Color Plate 9). Eric Trinkaus, who studied the skeletons, has argued that they show a remarkably high incidence of disease and trauma, including fractures. One individual, Shanidar 1, appeared to have suffered from, among other things, a paralyzed right arm, and Shanidar 3 had evidence of having received a spear wound between his ribs. Whether this latter injury was due to interpersonal violence or accident is unknown. Also intriguing is the discovery of pollen grains accompanying the burial of Shanidar 4 and evidence for artificial cranial deformation in Shanidar 1 and 5.

All together, Shanidar Cave gives a fascinating glimpse of Neandertal life. Life appears to have been unchanging for thousands, perhaps tens of thousands, of years. People hunted and gathered in the area around the cave. They kept a continual fire going in the cave itself, both for warmth and to ward off wild animals, but perhaps also as a signal of their own presence and life. Individuals, even infants, died in the cave and were buried. Some individuals met sudden, violent deaths, and most were scarred by accidents during life. Life for the residents of Shanidar Cave seems to have been one of routine, almost monotony, punctuated by traumatic events. All understood those events, cared for those who suffered them, and mourned those who did not survive.

SOURCES: Solecki, Ralph S., *Shanidar: The First Flower People* (New York: Knopf, 1971); Trinkaus, Erik, *The Shanidar Neandertals* (New York: Academic Press, 1983).

think that the originally small population of *H. sapiens* had some biological or cultural advantage, or both, that allowed them to spread and replace other *Homo* species.

The main evidence for the single-origin theory comes from the mtDNA of living peoples. In 1987 Rebecca Cann and her colleagues presented evidence that the mtDNA from a sample of people from the United States, New Guinea, Africa, and East Asia showed differences suggesting that their common ancestor lived only 200,000 years ago. They further claimed that, since the amount of variation between individuals was greatest in African populations, the common ancestor of all modern humans lived in Africa. (It is generally the case that people living in a homeland exhibit more variation than any emigrant descendent population.) Thus was born what the media called the "mitochondrial Eve" and the "Eve hypothesis" for the origins of modern humans. There were many problems with this initial study, but over the years those problems have been addressed, and new and better mtDNA analyses have been performed. Most scholars now agree that the mtDNA of modern humans shows a remarkably small degree of variation (in fact, less than half the variation found in most chimpanzee populations), which strongly suggests that we all share a very recent common ancestry.

The recent mtDNA analyses of Neandertals, and the archaeological evidence suggesting that Neandertals and modern humans lived separately in Europe and the

FIGURE **6.10**

Important characteristics of the modern human cranium.

SOURCE: Carol R. Ember, Melvin Ember, and Peter N. Peregrine, *Physical Anthropology and Archaeology* (Upper Saddle River, NJ: Prentice Hall, 2002), p. 147. Reprinted by permission of Pearson Education, Inc., Upper Saddle River, NJ.

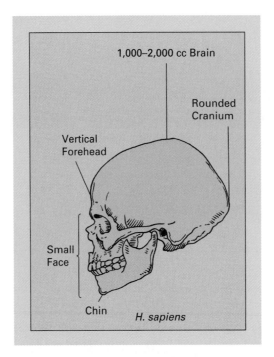

Near East also tends to support the single-origin theory. However, the lack of unambiguous *Homo sapiens* skeletal material from Africa in the 150,000 to 200,000 year ago time range makes it impossible as yet to support the single-origin theory through the fossil record. Even if we had such evidence, it would not necessarily question the validity of the multiregional theory of human origins.

MULTIREGIONAL THEORY According to the multiregional theory, *Homo erectus* populations in various parts of the Old World gradually evolved into anatomically modern-looking humans. The theorists espousing this view believe that premodern *Homo* species (such as the Neandertals and *Homo heidelbergensis*) represent phases in the gradual development of more modern anatomical features. Indeed, as I have noted, some of these theorists see so much continuity between *Homo erectus* and modern humans that they classify *Homo erectus* as "archaic" *Homo sapiens*.

Continuity is the main evidence used by the multiregional theorists to support their position. In several parts of the world there seem to be clear continuities in distinct skeletal features between *Homo erectus* and *Homo sapiens*. For example, *Homo erectus* fossils from China tend to have broader faces with more horizontal cheek bones than specimens from elsewhere in the world, and these traits also appear in modern Chinese populations. Southeast Asia provides more compelling evidence, according to multiregional theorists. There, a number of traits—including relatively thick cranial bones, a receding forehead, an unbroken browridge, facial prognathism, relatively large cheekbones, and relatively large molars—appear to persist from *Homo erectus* through modern populations (Figure 6.11). But others suggest that these traits cannot be used to establish a unique continuation from *Homo erectus* in Southeast Asia because these traits are found in modern humans all over the world. Still others argue that the traits are not as similar as the multiregional theorists claim.

In support of their position, multiregional theorists argue that the mtDNA evidence supports multiregional evolution rather than a single origin of modern humans, that the mtDNA evidence may reflect the emigration of *Homo erectus* out of Africa rather than the emigration of *Homo sapiens*. This interpretation would mean that the accepted rate of mutation in mtDNA is wrong, that mtDNA actually mutates much more slowly than currently thought. However, this interpretation is

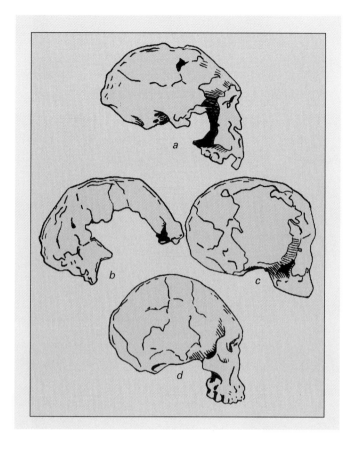

FIGURE **6.11**

Fossil evidence for regional continuity

Continuity in southeast Asian and Australian populations: Skulls of (a) *Homo erectus,* (b) early *Homo sapiens,* and (d) modern *Homo sapiens,* all from southeast Asia and Australia, have similar foreheads, brow ridges, and occipital and facial shapes, while skulls from Africa, represented here by (c), an early *Homo sapiens,* have different forms. The similarity in Southeast Asian and Australian populations over more than 500,000 years argues for regional continuity rather than replacement.

SOURCE: Carol R. Ember, Melvin Ember, and Peter N. Peregrine, *Physical Anthropology and Archaeology* (Upper Saddle River, NJ: Prentice Hall, 2002), p. 138. Reprinted by permission of Pearson Education, Inc., Upper Saddle River, NJ.

contradicted by established correlations between differences in mtDNA among human groups known to have colonized New Guinea and Australia at particular points in time which seem to fit the accepted rate of mutation, and with the divergence between humans and apes, the date of which also seems to accord with the accepted faster rate of mtDNA mutation.

To explain why human evolution would proceed gradually and in the same direction in various parts of the Old World, multiregional theorists point to cultural improvements in cutting-tool and cooking technology that occurred all over the Old World. These cultural improvements may have relaxed the need for heavy bones and musculature in the skull. The argument is that unless many plant and animal foods were cut into small pieces and thoroughly cooked in hearths or pits that were efficient thermally, they would be hard to chew and digest. Thus people previously would have needed robust jaws and thick skull bones to support the large muscles that enabled them to cut and chew their food. But robust bone and muscle would no longer be needed after people began to cut and cook more effectively.

Most paleoanthropologists today cautiously favor the single-origin theory over the multiregional theory, but that may not hold true forever. New fossils, new or revised dates, and new findings in genetics may sway opinion one way or the other. For now, both theories seem reasonable explanations for the origins of modern humans.

## WHAT HAPPENED TO THE NEANDERTALS?

Regardless of which theory (single-origin or multiregional) is correct, it seems clear that Neandertals and modern humans coexisted in Europe and the Near East for at least 20,000 years, and maybe as long as 60,000 years. What happened to the Neandertals? Three answers have generally been considered. First, they interbred

FIGURE **6.12**

This striking image of a Neandertal child reminds us that, while a different species, Neandertals were similar to modern humans in many ways.

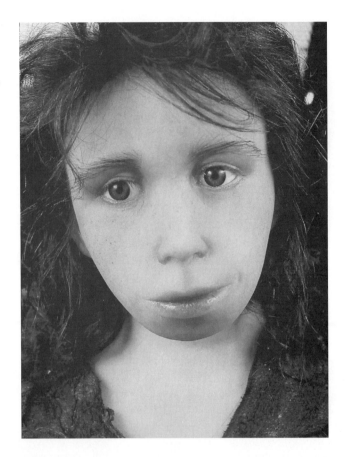

with modern humans, and the unique Neandertal characteristics slowly disappeared from the interbreeding population. Second, they were killed off by modern humans. Third, they were driven to extinction due to competition with modern humans. Let's take a look at each of these scenarios in turn.

The interbreeding scenario seems the most probable, yet evidence supporting it is weak. If modern humans and Neandertals interbred, we should be able to find "hybrid" individuals in the fossil record. In fact, a group of scholars has recently argued that an Upper Paleolithic child burial from Portugal demonstrates a combination of modern human and Neandertal features (Figure 6.12). The finding remains controversial, however, because it is based on a child's skeleton (approximately four years old) and its Neandertal-like features have not been corroborated by other scholars. More significantly, if the inbreeding hypothesis is correct, then the mtDNA analysis I have mentioned must be wrong. On the other hand, recent research on Neandertal tools suggests they adopted new techniques of tool manufacture that are thought to be uniquely associated with modern humans. If Neandertals were learning from modern humans, then the idea that they could have interbred and perhaps absorbed within the modern human population gains credibility.

The genocide scenario, that modern humans killed off Neandertals, has appeal as a sensational story, but there is little evidence. Not a single "murdered" Neandertal has ever been found, and one might wonder whether, in a fight between the powerful Neandertals and the more lightly built modern humans, who might get the better of whom.

Finally, the extinction scenario, that Neandertals simply could not compete with modern humans, seems to have the best archaeological support. As I noted earlier, there appear to be "refugee" populations of Neandertals in Iberia as recently as perhaps 30,000 years ago. The "retreat" of Neandertals from the Near East, Eastern

Europe, and finally Western Europe following the movement of modern humans into the region seems to support the "refugee" interpretation. More important, physical anthropologist Erik Trinkaus has argued, based on both physical characteristics of the Neandertal skeleton and their apparent patterns of behavior, that Neandertals were less efficient hunters and gatherers than modern humans. If this is true, a modern human group would have been able to live and reproduce more easily than a Neandertal group in the same territory, and this would likely drive the Neandertals away. When there were no new territories to run to, the Neandertals would go extinct—precisely what the archaeological record seems to suggest.

But were modern humans and their cultures really that much more efficient than premodern *Homo* cultures? As we will see in the next chapter, the Upper Paleolithic does seem to mark a watershed in the evolution of human culture, allowing humans to expand their physical horizons across the globe and their intellectual horizons into the realms of art and ritual.

## ◉ SUMMARY

*Homo erectus* evolved into modern humans beginning about 500,000 years ago. Several transitional species are known, including *Homo heidelbergensis* and *Homo neandertalensis*. Both these species have larger brains than *Homo erectus*, and more modern-like dentition. They also have more sophisticated cultures than *Homo erectus*. Neandertals developed the Levallois technique of tool manufacture, which used prepared cores to create flakes of predetermined size and shape. These allowed Neandertals to develop a more sophisticated tool kit than *Homo erectus*. Neandertals relied on a wide variety of plants and animals, but hunted large game when it was present. Neandertals were the first humans to purposely bury their dead.

There are two major theories for the origins of modern humans, the Out of Africa theory and the Multiregional theory. The Out of Africa theory posits that the first modern humans evolved within a small, isolated population in Africa about 200,000 years ago and spread across the world from there. The Multiregional theory posits that modern humans evolved slowly around the world out of indigenous populations of earlier *Homo* species. There is evidence supporting both theories, although most paleoanthropologists today support the Out of Africa theory.

## ◉ DISCUSSION QUESTIONS

1. How do *Homo heidelbergensis*, *Homo neandertalensis*, and *Homo sapiens* differ from one another? How do they differ from *Homo erectus*?

2. In what ways does Neandertal culture differ from the culture of *Homo erectus*?

3. What are the two main theories for the origins of modern humans, and how do they differ?

## ◉ ESSAY QUESTIONS

1. Compare and contrast the archaeological traditions described in this chapter with the archaeological traditions described in the last chapter. How are they similar? How do they differ? In what directions does cultural evolution seem to have been moving between these time periods?

2. Neandertals appear to have been a species located primarily in Europe and the Near East. Using the information in this chapter and any other resources you can find, explain why this might have been the case. How might their apparently limited distribution help to explain their extinction?

3. In the first chapter of this book the idea was presented that the past is political, and even the distant past of our protohuman ancestors has been used for political purposes. Consider the two major models of modern human origins. What might be some of the political ramifications associated with each model? Is it a political act to say modern humans evolved in Africa? To say they evolved simultaneously all over the world?

## ⟋ RESEARCH PROJECT

Use the library, the Internet, and visits to local or regional museums if available to gather as many images of Neandertals as possible. Compare and contrast these images to explore how they have changed over time. If possible, compare and contrast images of Neandertals from different nations as well, to explore variation over space. What do these images tell you about the changing perspective on the Neandertals' relationship to modern humans? In what ways might these images reflect social or political concerns in a given time or place?

## ⊙ KEY SOURCES

### The Transition from *Homo erectus* to *Homo sapiens*

Krings et al., 1997; Rightmire, 1997; Smith, 1984; Spencer, 1984; Stringer, 1985, 2000; Trinkaus, 1984, 1985; Trinkaus and Shipman, 1993.

### Archaeological Traditions Associated with Neandertals

Binford, 1984; Binford and Binford, 1969; Bordes, 1961; Fish, 1981; Klein, 1974, 1977, 1983, 1989; Phillipson, 1993; Schick and Toth, 1993; Strauss, 1989; Whittaker, 1994; Wilford, 1997.

### The Emergence of Modern Humans

Ayala, 1995; Bräuer, 1984; Cann, 1988; Cann, Stoneking, and Wilson, 1987; Frayer et al., 1993; Lieberman, 1995; Stringer, Hublin, and Vandermeersch, 1984; Templeton, 1993, 1996; Valladas et al., 1988; Vigilant et al., 1991; Wolpoff, 1999.

### What Happened to the Neandertals?

Bahn, 1998; Duarte et al., 1999; Mellars, 1996, 1998; Tattersall, 1999; Trinkaus, 1986; Trinkaus and Howells, 1979.

# TOOL MAKING

This chapter covers the archaeological traditions associated with Neandertals in Europe and the Near East called the Mousterian tradition; it dates from about 200,000 years ago to about 40,000 years ago. In Africa, the Middle Stone Age tradition seems to be associated with Neandertals, while in East Asia, the East Asian Middle Paleolithic tradition dates from the same time period. All three traditions are primarily defined by stone tool assemblages.

The Mousterian tradition is named after the tool assemblage found in a rock shelter at Le Moustier in the Dordogne region of southwestern France. The Middle Stone Age tools were struck off prepared cores in the Levalloisian way. Unlike the Mousterian and Middle Stone Age traditions, East Asian Middle Paleolithic tools show only modest development from earlier Zhoukoudian tools.

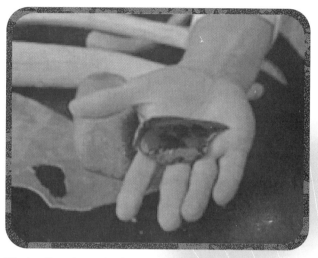

The Media Lab can be found in Chapter 6 on the *Companion Website*™ http://www.prenhall.com/peregrine

## WEB ACTIVITY

When modern peoples appeared in Europe, so did stone tools made from blades; these were elongated pieces of stone, parallel-sided and at least twice as long as they were wide, and deftly struck off a specifically prepared core. From these blades a wide variety of specialized tools could be made, such as the burin, a chisel-like tool that had many uses. In addition to this new technology, other materials, such as bone, antler, and ivory, were also artfully shaped into useful items.

This Media Lab shows how simple but highly effective tools were made. There is significant regional variation, however, in tool industries of the Upper Paleolithic, suggesting cultural differences among groups.

## Activity

1. Summarize how tool-making ability would reveal cultural differences between groups that lived thousands of years before the written word.
2. Were you surprised by the "sharpness" of cutting tools made in the video? What types of evolutionary advantages would be derived from making and developing such tools?
3. After seeing this video, how different do you think you (and all the people around you) are from the first modern humans who developed these tools? What are the most important differences?

# The Upper Paleolithic World

Beginning about 40,000 years ago a way of life developed in Europe, Africa, the Near East, and Asia known as the Upper Paleolithic. In many respects, lifestyles during the Upper Paleolithic were similar to lifestyles before. People were still mainly hunters and gatherers who lived in small mobile bands. They made their camps out in the open in skin-covered huts and in caves and rock

shelters. But the Upper Paleolithic is also characterized by a variety of new developments. One of the most striking is the emergence of art—painting on cave walls, decorative objects, and personal ornaments out of bone, antler, shell, and stone. Perhaps for this as well as other purposes, people began to obtain materials from distant sources. Because more archaeological sites date from the Upper Paleolithic than from any previous period and some Upper Paleolithic sites seem larger than any before, many archaeologists think that the human population increased considerably during the Upper Paleolithic. And new inventions, such as the bow and arrow, the spear-thrower, and tiny replaceable blades called **microliths,** that could be fitted into handles appear for the first time. Such inventions may have been crucial in the expansion of Upper Paleolithic peoples across all environments of the Old World, including the Arctic, and into the New World.

## THE LAST ICE AGE

The environment of the Upper Paleolithic was very different from that of today. The earth was gripped by the last ice age, with glaciers covering Europe as far south as Berlin and Warsaw, and North America as far south as Chicago. To the south of these glacial fronts was a tundra zone extending in Europe to the Alps and in North America to the Ozarks, Appalachians, and well out onto the Great Plains. Both Europe and North America probably resembled contemporary Siberia and northern Canada. Elsewhere in the world, conditions were not as extreme but were still different from conditions today (see Figure 7.1).

For one thing, the climate was different. Annual temperatures were as much as 10 degrees Celsius below today's temperatures, and changes in ocean currents would have made temperature contrasts (that is, the differences between summer and winter months) more extreme as well. The changing ocean currents also changed weather patterns, and Europe experienced heavy annual snowfall. Not all the world was cold, however, but the presence of huge ice sheets in the north changed the climate throughout the world—North Africa, for example, appears to have been much wetter than today, while South Asia was apparently drier. And everywhere the climate seems to have been highly variable.

The plants and animals of the Upper Paleolithic world were adapted to these extreme conditions. Among the most important, and dramatic, were the large game animals collectively known as **Pleistocene megafauna.** These animals, as their name suggests, were huge compared to their contemporary descendants. In North America, for example, giant ground sloths stood some 2 or 3 meters tall and weighed several thousand kilograms. Siberian mammoths were the largest elephants ever to live—some standing more than 4 meters tall. In East Asia, species such as wooly rhinoceros and giant deer were present.

Let's take a look at some of the archaeological traditions associated with Upper Paleolithic peoples, in order to gain a better idea of their lives and cultures (see Figure 7.2).

**Microliths:** small, razorlike blade fragments that were attached to wooden or bone handles to form cutting tools and projectile points.

**Pleistocene megafauna:** giant species of animals that lived during the last ice age.

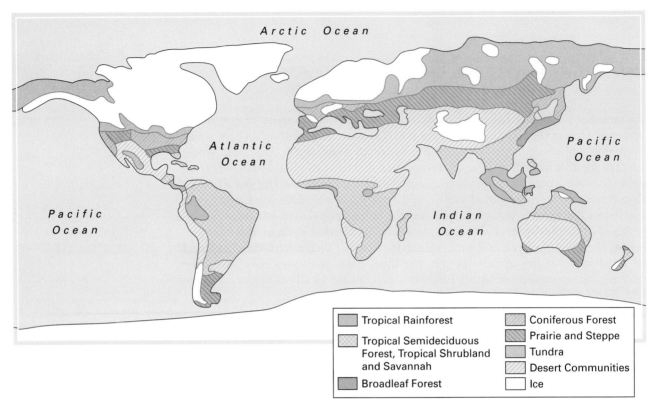

FIGURE **7.1**

General environments of the world during the last ice age.

SOURCE: M.A.J. Williams, D.L. Dunkerley, P. De Dekker, A.P. Kershaw, and T. Stokes, *Quarternary Environments, 2/E* (London: Edward Arnold, 1998), p. 214.

# AFRICA

**Hunting and gathering:**
a way of life where subsistence is based exclusively on wild foods.

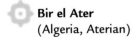 **Aterian**
(70,000–20,000 B.P.)

**Iberomaurusian**
(20,000–7500 B.P.)

**Bir el Ater**
(Algeria, Aterian)

**Dar es Soltan**
(Morocco, Aterian)

The **Aterian** (70,000 to 20,000 B.P.) tradition marks the beginning of the Upper Paleolithic in northern Africa. The Aterians lived in what would become the lush Mediterranean coast and arid Sahara regions of contemporary Africa. With the vast supplies of meat available from megafauna, it is not surprising that many Upper Paleolithic cultures relied on hunting, and this was certainly true of the Aterians. The Aterian peoples were followed by peoples of the **Iberomaurusian** (20,000 to 7500 B.P.) tradition who continued a nomadic hunting and gathering way of life, but appear to have significantly expanded the range of food sources used. Both these traditions are good representatives of what might be called the "typical" features of Upper Paleolithic life and represent a common pattern throughout the Old World.

## Hunting and Gathering

Perhaps the most basic feature of Upper Paleolithic life was that subsistence was based on **hunting and gathering**. At the Aterian site of **Bir el Ater** in Algeria, for example, the remains of horse, buffalo, auroch, and wildebeest were found. At **Dar es Soltan** in Morocco, bones of rhinocerous, hippo, boar, gazelle, and antelope were found. Findings like these suggest that the Aterian people hunted a wide variety of game, but focused primarily on big game that provided lots of meat from each animal killed. Peoples of the Iberomaurusian tradition appear to have hunted a

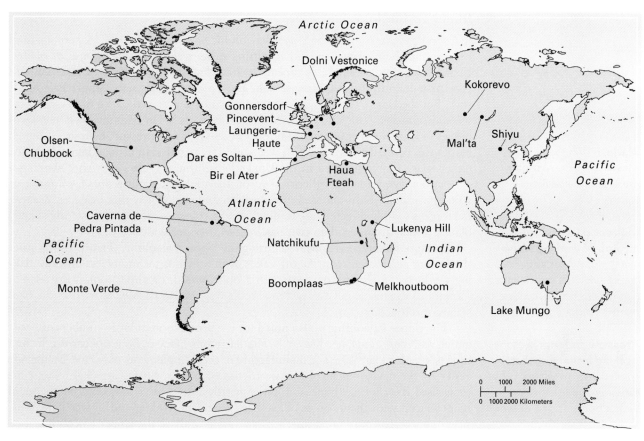

FIGURE **7.2**
Sites discussed in Chapter 7.

somewhat greater range of game than their Aterian predecessors. For example, **Haua Fteah,** on the Libyan coast, contains remains of both large game animals like Barbary sheep, hartebeest, and auroch, but also extensive evidence of marine mollusk and land snail shells, suggesting both were eaten in large numbers. Such finds are common on Iberomaurusian sites.

Evidence for gathering is, unfortunately, quite slim. In fact there is virtually no archaeological evidence for the plant species used by either the Aterian or Ibero-maurusian peoples. This is likely due to poor preservation, but may reflect a near absence of such foods in their diet. Elsewhere in Africa, where preservation is bet-ter, a variety of plant remains have been found. For example, at **Natchikufu Cave** in Zambia, peoples of the **Nachikufan** (ca. 16,000 to 2000 B.P.) tradition lived sea-sonally in the cave to exploit locally available resources. These resources included a wide range of animals such as eland, hartebeest, and wildebeest. Also found in the cave were the remains of nut shells, fruit seeds, and stones used to process these foods. Stones with a hole through the center were also found at Natchikufu, and these are thought to be weights for digging sticks, which would have been used to dig edible roots out of the ground. Similarly, there is good evidence that peoples of the **Wilton** (10,000 to 4000 B.P.) tradition of South Africa developed a broad-spectrum hunting-fishing-gathering way of life. Wilton cave sites such as **Melkhoutboom** have preserved an abundant record of edible roots and tubers, a variety of nuts, fruits, and seeds. Both Nachikufan and Wilton peoples appear to have settled in these locations seasonally while plants in the area were producing nuts or fruits, then moved to other locations as plants in those areas came into season.

**Haua Fteah**
(Libya, Iberomaurusian)

**Natchikufu Cave**
(Zambia, Natchikufan)

**Nachikufan**
(ca. 16,000–2000 B.P.)

**Wilton**
(10,000–4000 B.P.)

**Melkhoutboom**
(South Africa, Wilton)

## Blade Technology

A second basic feature of the Upper Paleolithic world was that the technology used for hunting, butchering, and other cutting tasks was based on the use of **blades.** Upper Paleolithic toolmaking appears to have had its roots in the Mousterian and post-Acheulian traditions, because flake tools are found in many Upper Paleolithic sites. But the Upper Paleolithic is characterized by a preponderance of blades; there were also burins, bone and antler tools, and microliths. In addition, two new techniques of toolmaking appeared—indirect percussion and pressure flaking. Although blades can be made in a variety of ways, **indirect percussion** using a hammer-struck punch was commonly used in the Upper Paleolithic (Figure 7.3). After shaping a core into a pyramidal or cylindrical form, the toolmaker put a punch of antler or wood or another hard material into position and struck it with a hammer. Because the force is readily directed, the toolmaker was able to strike off consistently shaped blades, which are more than twice as long as they are wide.

**Pressure flaking** also appeared during the Upper Paleolithic (Figure 7.4). Rather than using percussion to strike off flakes as in previous technologies, pressure flaking works by employing pressure with a bone, wood, or antler tool at the edge of the tool to remove small flakes. Pressure flaking would usually be used in the final stages of retouching a tool.

The Upper Paleolithic is also noted for the production of large numbers of bone, antler, and ivory tools; needles, awls, and harpoons made of bone appear for the first time (see Color Plate 10). The manufacture of these implements may have been made easier by the development of many varieties of burins. Burins are chisel-like stone tools used for carving; bone and antler needles, awls, and projectile points could be produced with them. Burins have been found in Middle and Lower Paleolithic sites but are present in great number and variety only in the Upper Paleolithic.

**Blades:** thin stone flakes whose lengths are usually more than twice their widths.

**Indirect percussion:** a method of working stone using a punch of antler or wood, which is struck with a hammer to produce stone blades from a core.

**Pressure flaking:** a stone-working technique whereby small flakes are struck off by pressing against the core with a bone, antler, or wood tool.

FIGURE **7.3**

One way to remove blades from a core is to hit them with a punch using indirect percussion. The object being struck is the punch, which is made of bone or horn.

SOURCE: From Brian M. Fagan, *In the Beginning,* 10/E (Upper Saddle River, NJ: Prentice Hall, 2001), p. 254.

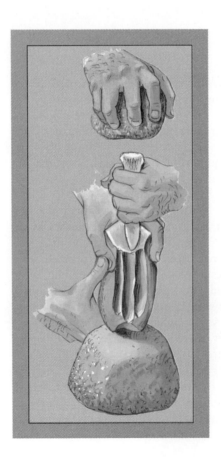

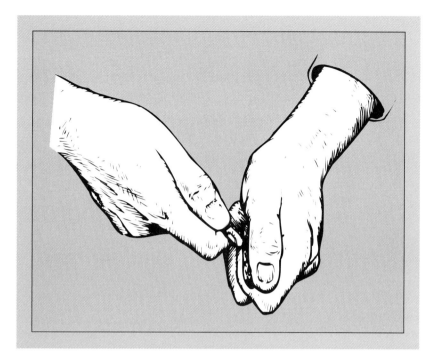

FIGURE **7.4**
Pressure flaking, as illustrated here, allows very small flakes to be removed from a stone tool with great precision.

The tools made by Upper Paleolithic peoples suggest that they were much more effective hunters and fishers than their predecessors. During the Upper Paleolithic, and probably for the first time, spears were shot from a **spear-thrower** or *atlatl* (the Aztec word for "spear-thrower") rather than thrown with the arm. We know this because bone and antler atlatls have been found in some sites. A spear propelled off a grooved board could be sent through the air with increased force, causing it to travel farther and hit harder, and with less effort by the thrower (Figure 7.5). The bow and arrow was also used in various places during the Upper Paleolithic, and harpoons, used for fishing and perhaps for hunting reindeer, were invented at this time.

**Spear-thrower:** a stick or board used to help propel a spear, giving the thrower greater force and accuracy.

FIGURE **7.5**
How an atl-atl is used to propel a spear. Note the weight attached to the shaft.
SOURCE: Courtesy of the William S. Webb Museum of Anthropology. University of Kentucky.

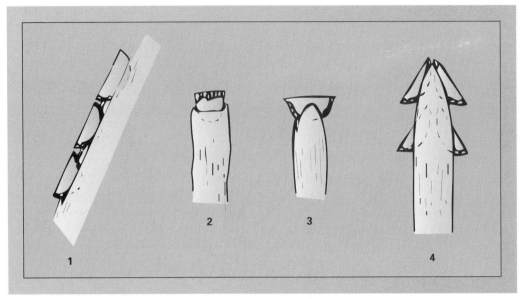

FIGURE **7.6**

Some of the many ways microliths could be used: (1) as a knife or sickle, (2) as a scraper or adze, (3) as a transverse projectile point; (4) as a barbed projectile point.

SOURCE: David W. Phillipson, *African Archaeology* (New York, NY: Cambridge University Press, 1985), p. 59. Reprinted with permission of Cambridge University Press.

Of course, not all Upper Paleolithic peoples used exactly the same kinds of tools. Indeed, some peoples developed an entirely separate toolmaking tradition using small blades called microliths. These microliths were often hafted or fitted into handles, one blade at a time or several blades together, to serve as spears, adzes, knives, and sickles (Figure 7.6). The hafting required inventing a way to trim the blade's back edge so that it would be blunt rather than sharp. In this way the blades would not split the handles into which they might be inserted; the blunting would also prevent the users of an unhafted blade from cutting themselves. Peoples of the **East African Microlithic** (20,000 to 5000 B.P.) tradition of western Kenya, Tanzania, and Uganda, for example, used microliths as a way to create light points for arrows. Similarly, peoples of the **West African Late Stone Age** (ca. 40,000 to 5000 B.P.) tradition had a tool kit that included both large flake tools and microliths. Large tools were used as axes, adzes, picks, and the like, employed for rough working of wood, for digging, and even for mining stone, while microliths appear to have been used for general cutting and scraping. The use of different technologies, however, also might have been related to raw materials. Where local materials were poor, larger and more expedient technologies might have been necessary, while in locations where obsidian and other good stone was available, microlithic and other blade technologies might have been preferred.

Some archaeologists think that the blade technique was adopted because it made for more economical use of flint. André Leroi-Gourhan of the Musée de l'Homme in Paris calculated that with the old Acheulian technique, a 2-pound lump of flint yielded 40 centimeters of working edge and produced only two hand axes. If the more advanced Mousterian technique were used, a lump of equal size would yield 2 meters of working edge. The indirect percussion method of the Upper Paleolithic would yield as much as 20 meters of working edge. And microlithic technology allowed even small stone cores to yield useful blades. With the same amount of material, a significantly greater number of tools could be produced using a blade technology. Getting the most out of a valuable resource may have been particularly important in areas lacking large flint deposits.

**East African Microlithic** (20,000–5000 B.P.)

**West African Late Stone Age** (ca. 40,000–5000 B.P.)

Jacques Bordaz suggested that the evolution of toolmaking techniques, which continually increased the amount of usable edge that could be gotten out of a lump of flint, was significant because people could then spend more time in regions where flint was unavailable. Another reason for adopting the blade toolmaking technique may have been that it made for easy repair of tools. For example, the cutting edge of a tool might consist of a line of razorlike microliths set into a piece of wood. The tool would not be usable if just one of the cutting edge's microliths broke off or was chipped. But if the user carried a small prepared core of flint from which an identical-sized microlith could be struck off, the tool could be repaired easily by replacing the lost or broken microlith. A spear whose point was lost could be repaired similarly. Thus, the main purpose of the blade toolmaking technique may not have been to make more economical use of flint, but rather to allow easy replacement of damaged blades.

## Band Organization

A third basic feature of Upper Paleolithic life is social organization rooted in small, nomadic groups called **bands.** In sub-Saharan Africa, peoples of the **Southern and Eastern Africa Later Stone Age** (40,000 to 2000 B.P.) tradition followed the Middle Stone Age peoples, and since some of their ways of life are not much different from contemporary hunters and gatherers living in the area, the cultures of these contemporary people can help us understand something about Upper Paleolithic life.

Band organization is fundamental among the present-day San of Namibia (Figure 7.7), peoples who appear to be direct descendants of the peoples of the Later Stone Age. San bands are groups of fifteen to thirty people, often related, who work together as a single social and economic unit. Men of the band hunt in small groups, while women gather plant foods, trap small animals, and care for children. All food, both hunted and collected, is brought back to a campsite where it is prepared and shared by all members of the band. San bands tend to be highly mobile, moving to a new campsite every few days. San bands also tend to be highly fluid in their membership. Individuals and families (a married couple and their dependent children) will sometimes leave one band to join another with which they have come into

**Southern and Eastern Africa Later Stone Age** (40,000–2000 B.P.)

**Bands:** groups of fifteen to thirty people who live and work together as a single social and economic unit.

FIGURE **7.7**
Two San hunters examining animal tracks near Kalahari National Park, South Africa.

contact. The reasons for movement are varied—sometimes individuals meet friends or relatives and want to spend time with them; in other cases personality conflicts encourage individuals to leave a particular band. Leadership in San bands is informal and is often based on consensus, and society itself is egalitarian, with little or no status differences between individuals except those based on age and sex.

Band organization seems to be illustrated in the archaeological record of many Upper Paleolithic peoples. At **Lukenya Hill** in Kenya, for example, excavations of a small rockshelter demonstrated that a small group of people repeatedly occupied the site, probably after annual heavy rains when herds of hartebeest, wildebeest, and zebra frequented the area. Similarly, at **Boomplaas** Cave in South Africa, more than sixty pits dug into the cave floor by Upper Paleolithic peoples were identified and excavated. Some of these pits had been lined with grass and used to store plant foods. Such storage suggests a relatively long-term occupation of the site, at least during those periods where local plants were in season. Both sites suggest that Upper Paleolithic peoples in eastern and southern Africa were living in relatively small groups that moved seasonally between well-established base camps located to exploit nearby resources.

## SOUTH AND SOUTHWEST ASIA

On the Indian subcontinent, peoples of the **South Asian Upper Paleolithic** (30,000 to 7000 B.P.) tradition were hunters and gatherers who appear to have slowly expanded in both population and range. Early in the period there are few sites and these appear to be located mainly in places where earlier Middle Paleolithic peoples lived. As time went on habitations were established across the subcontinent. Most sites are small lithic workshops near outcrops of workable stone or campsites near desired resources. Houses were small, oval huts, and communities themselves were small—probably consisting of no more than twenty or thirty people. Hunters sought a wide variety of game, from elephants and rhinoceros to rodents and reptiles. Fish were important resources in many areas. Roots and fruits appear to have been the primary gathered foods. There is tantalizing evidence of a religion involving a female deity, and complex burial rituals have been identified at several sites, but there is little more known about the belief system of these people.

In what is today Iran, Pakistan, and Afghanistan peoples of the **Iranian Upper Paleolithic** (40,000 to 12,000 B.P.) tradition followed a way of life very similar to those in India. The region was generally hot during the Upper Paleolithic, and forests covered much of the region. Peoples of the Iranian Upper Paleolithic lived in rockshelters and caves and exploited the animals and plants of the area, hunting deer, boar, and small game in the forests and gazelle, auroch, and sheep in the uplands. Collected foods probably included nuts and cereals, since grinding stones are found on some sites, but direct evidence of these plant foods is lacking. The Iranian Upper Paleolithic toolkit was based on retouched blades and included scrapers, burins, backed knives, and projectile points.

On the Arabian peninsula, peoples of the **Arabian Upper Paleolithic** (40,000 to 11,000 B.P.) tradition faced what appear to be harsh climatic conditions like those that prevail in the region today. However, small lakes created by runoff from stabilized dunes provided regular sources of water for animals and humans, and a great diversity of arid-adapted animal species were present, including oryx, gazelle, ostrich, and camel. Peoples of the Arabian Upper Paleolithic exploited these animals in what must have been very small, highly mobile groups. No formal campsites or habitations of these people have yet been found, although areas that appear to have been lithic workshops near sources of flint have been identified. It seems likely that the population of the region was very small, and perhaps only seasonal.

Finally, in the Levant and Mesopotamia, peoples of the **Epipaleolithic** (40,000 to 10,500 B.P.) tradition lived in the myriad environments of the region. Most people

**Lukenya Hill** (Kenya, Eastern and Southern Africa Later Stone Age)

**Boomplaas** (South Africa, Eastern and Southern Africa Later Stone Age)

**South Asian Upper Paleolithic** (30,000–7000 B.P.)

**Iranian Upper Paleolithic** (40,000–12,000 B.P.)

**Arabian Upper Paleolithic** (40,000–11,000 B.P.)

**Epipaleolithic** (40,000–10,500 B.P.)

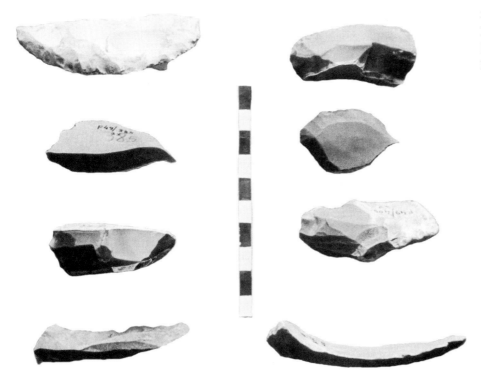

FIGURE **7.8**
Epipaleolithic scrapers and blades from Mount Carmel, Israel.

inhabited small, open-air campsites and occasionally rockshelters and caves, almost all of which are located in the Mediterranean zone. Occupations commonly contain hearths but few other features apart from the rare evidence of lightly constructed circular huts. People lived in small, egalitarians bands of ten to twenty-five individuals, comprising a few nuclear families. Some large "megasites" have been found in eastern Jordan, and these may indicate larger periodic or seasonal aggregations of people, perhaps for rituals or to trade, or both.

The basic toolkit of the Epipaleolithic peoples were blade, bladelet, and flake chipped stone tools (Figure 7.8). These were made into projectile points, scrapers, burins, and microliths used in composite tools such as sickles. Grinding and pounding equipment on limestone and basalt increased in quantity and diversity during the course of the Epipalaeolithic tradition, perhaps as cereals and nuts grew in dietary importance. Plant foods exploited by Epipaleolithic peoples included nuts, fruits, seeds, lentils, and tubers. Animal foods included gazelle, deer, onager, ibex, and fish. There is no evidence of domesticated foods.

Around 12,000 B.P. a period of significant warming occurred in the Levant. The climate became more moderate and wet, and forests and grasslands spread. During this time period, and perhaps as a direct result of these climatic changes, the **Natufian** (12,000 to 10,500 B.P.) tradition developed. The peoples of the Natufian tradition are distinct from their Epipaleolithic predecessors and neighbors in being more sedentary and perhaps more socially complex. They appear to have developed a reliance on the intensive harvesting of stands of wild grain and on the annual production of fruits and nuts. The Natufian peoples developed small but relatively permanent villages, ranging in size from perhaps 45 to perhaps more than 200 people. Trade emerged among these communities, and shell from the Mediterranean and Red Sea, obsidian from Anatolia, and greenstone and malachite from a yet unknown source moved between these communities. People also began to bury their dead in formal cemeteries, and some have argued that the goods placed with the dead and the overall arrangement of the cemeteries suggests emergent social stratification

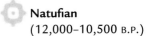 **Natufian**
(12,000–10,500 B.P.)

among the Natufian peoples. The Natufians expanded the range of decorative art as well, and began to engrave tools and utensils such as stone bowls with geometric designs and even human and animal figures. These ventures into artistic expression, however, were minor compared to those undertaken by some of the Upper Paleolithic peoples of Europe.

The Epipaleolithic and Natufian traditions illustrate another general trend among Upper Paleolithic peoples around the world—increasing sedentism. Increased sedentism, in turn, seems to be linked to an increasingly sophisticated exploitation of locally available resources. With sedentism there is also a trend for more complex cultural features to develop, including social differentiation, religious ritual, and art. Nowhere is the development of the latter in the Upper Paleolithic more dramatic than in Europe.

## EUROPE

**Aurignacian**
**(40,000–25,000 B.P.)**

The earliest Upper Paleolithic peoples of Europe are those of the **Aurignacian** (40,000 to 25,000 B.P.) tradition. The Aurignacian peoples, like other Upper Paleolithic groups I have already discussed, were hunters of large game animals who wandered seasonally through large territories in small groups. They lived during a period when glacial ice sheets retreated across Europe and forests and grasslands moved northward. The Aurignacian peoples apparently followed the forests northward and spread across the European continent. In their dissemination across Europe, the Aurignacians appear to have displaced the European Neandertals, who went extinct during the time period of the Aurignacian tradition.

Technologically, the Aurignacians were much like other Upper Paleolithic peoples. They had a distinctive blade tool technology and made extensive use of bone and wood for such items as needles, awls, and even projectile points (see Color Plate 10). The Aurignacians were among the first peoples on earth to create works of expressive art. Aurignacian art includes both personal ornaments, such as shell beads, and more enigmatic items such as engraved antler "batons" and engraved bone that may have been record-keeping or mnemonic devices.

**Perigordian**
**(30,000–22,000 B.P.)**

**Dolni Vestonice** (Czech
Republic, Perigordian)

The Aurignacian peoples were followed by peoples of the **Perigordian** (30,000 to 22,000 B.P.) tradition. Like the Aurignacians, the Perigordians were nomadic or seminomadic hunters of large game animals. Individual bands may have congregated in some highly productive locations during part of the year. The site at **Dolni Vestonice** in what is now the Czech Republic, dated to around 25,000 years ago, is one of the first for which there is an entire settlement plan. The settlement seems to have consisted of four tentlike huts, probably made from animal skins, with a large open hearth in the center (Figure 7.9). Around the outside were mammoth bones,

FIGURE **7.9**
A reconstruction of Upper Paleolithic dwellings at the site of Dolni Vestonice. They were constructed using mammoth bones to form walls and roof supports, which were covered with mammoth skins.

some rammed into the ground, which suggests that the huts were surrounded by a wall. All told, there were bone heaps from about 100 mammoths. Each hut probably housed a group of related families—about twenty to twenty-five people. (One hut was approximately 9 by 15 meters and had five hearths distributed inside it, presumably one for each family.) Assuming that all four huts were occupied at the same time, the population of the settlement would have been 100 to 125.

Up a hill from the settlement was a fifth and different kind of hut. It was dug into the ground and contained an oven and more than 2,300 small, fired fragments of animal figurines. There were also some hollow bones that may have been musical instruments. Another interesting feature of the settlement was a burial of a woman with a disfigured face. She may have been a particularly important personage, because her face was found engraved on an ivory plaque near the central hearth of the settlement.

The Perigordians developed several refinements in blade tool technology and began using antler, bone, and ivory extensively for tools. They also created works of art, including some three-dimensional carvings. Some of the most famous works of cave art were created by the Perigordians, as were many of the famous "Venus" figurines, which I discuss in the next section.

The **Solutrean** (22,000 to 18,000 B.P.) tradition followed the Perigordian. The Solutreans also hunted large game in small and apparently widely separated groups. Solutrean stone tool technology is marked by the development of sophisticated flaked projectile points and knives. Solutreans apparently invented both the eyed needle and the spear-thrower. The Solutrean tradition is followed by the **Magdalenian** (18,000 to 11,000 B.P.) tradition, the last Upper Paleolithic tradition in Europe. The Magdalenian peoples developed an extensive bone tool industry in addition to their own unique styles of stone blade tools. Like the other Upper Paleolithic Europeans, they lived in small mobile groups and subsisted by hunting large game.

As with the other European Upper Paleolithic traditions, most of the Solutrean and Magdalenian sites that have been excavated were situated in caves and rockshelters. **Laugerie-Haute** in southwestern France is a good example of a Solutrean cave site. It was occupied for at least 1,000 years, and it may have served as a central overwintering site for bands living in the region. Many changes were made to the cave to make it more habitable: Numerous stone-lined hearths were created, there is evidence of stone-paved floors, and tents were apparently built to keep out the cold. Reindeer was the primary food source for people living in the cave, and there is a wide variety of stone manufacturing debris, suggesting that the site also served as a central place for the manufacture of stone tools and other craft goods. Some open-air sites have also been excavated. **Gonnersdorf**, for example, is an open-air Magdalenian site in western Germany. Numerous habitations are evident from rock-lined hearths surrounded by stone slabs, which probably formed the floor of tents, and dense occupational debris. Another example is Pincevent, described in the box feature.

**Solutrean**
(22,000–18,000 B.P.)

**Magdalenian**
(18,000–11,000 B.P.)

**Laugerie-Haute**
(France, Solutrean)

**Gonnersdorf** (Germany, Magdalenian)

## Upper Paleolithic Art

The earliest discovered traces of art are beads and carvings, and then paintings, from Upper Paleolithic sites. We might expect that early artistic efforts were crude, but the cave paintings of western Europe show a marked degree of skill. So do the naturalistic paintings on slabs of stone excavated in southern Africa. Some of those slabs appear to have been painted as much as 28,000 years ago, which suggests that painting in Africa is as old as painting in Europe. But painting may be even older than that. The early Australians may have painted on the walls of rock shelters and cliff faces at least 30,000 years ago and maybe as much as 60,000 years ago.

The subjects of the paintings are mostly animals (see Color Plate 11). The paintings rest on bare walls, with no backdrops or environmental trappings.

# Pincevent

Pincevent is an important European Upper Paleolithic site. It is located on the left bank of the Seine, about 100 kilometers from Paris, and was occupied by people of the Magdalenian tradition about 12,000 years ago. It consists of a number of open-air occupations and contains an assemblage of remarkably well-preserved artifacts and faunal remains. It is also one of the most carefully excavated Upper Paleolithic sites in the world. Its excavator, André Leroi-Gourhan, used the site to develop a method of broad horizontal exposure rather than deep stratigraphic excavation in order to observe patterns in artifact distributions across a single occupation. Almost 5,000 square meters of a single occupation level have been excavated at Pincevent, an enormous scale in Upper Paleolithic archaeology. The data produced by the excavations at Pincevent have undergone sophisticated analyses and have been used in the development and testing of new methods of spatial analysis.

At the time Pincevent was occupied it was located on a narrow portion of the Seine River that was used frequently by reindeer during their fall migration, and activities at the site focused on reindeer hunting. The vast majority of faunal remains from the site are of reindeer. Stone tools were made at the site from local materials. Blades dominate the assemblage, which includes both modified and unmodified blade knives, scrapers, and points. Bone and antler tools include awls, needles, scrapers, and points. The site contains numerous concentrations of debris from tool manufacture as well, so that it is clear these items were both made and used at the site. From the tool assemblage it seems clear that hunting, butchering, and hide processing were the major activities taking place at the site.

Pincevent contains remains of multiple concentrations of features that appear to have similar characteristics. At the center of each concentration is a hearth.

Perhaps, like many contemporary peoples, Upper Paleolithic men and women believed that the drawing of a human image could cause death or injury. If that were indeed their belief, it might explain why human figures are rarely depicted in cave art. Another explanation for the focus on animals might be that these people sought to improve their luck at hunting. This theory is suggested by evidence of chips in the painted figures, perhaps made by spears thrown at the drawings. But if hunting magic was the chief motivation for the paintings, it is difficult to explain why only a few show signs of having been speared. Perhaps the paintings were inspired by the need to increase the supply of animals. Cave art seems to have reached a peak toward the end of the Upper Paleolithic period, when the herds of game were decreasing.

The particular symbolic significance of the cave paintings in southwestern France is more explicitly revealed, perhaps, by the results of Patricia Rice and Ann Paterson's statistical study. The data suggest that the animals portrayed in the cave paintings were mostly the ones that the painters preferred for meat and for materials

Near the hearth (within 2 meters or so) are one or more areas containing small pieces of debris, such as stone flakes and small bone fragments. Farther from the hearth is an area with a more uniform distribution of debris, often large pieces of bone. It has been suggested that the concentrations of small debris are within what were small (1 to 2 meters in diameter) skin tents or windbreaks, where the site's inhabitants sat while they worked, while less dense scatters of small debris around the hearths are the remains of work being done by people sitting by the fires. The scatter of larger debris was material discarded randomly by people simply tossing waste material away from their living areas.

Several such hearth areas were occupied simultaneously at Pincevent, and these probably reflect the individual households of several families making up a single band. The households show little difference in kinds or amounts of material goods, suggesting egalitarian social structure. More significantly, scholars have been able to refit the bones from individual reindeer carcasses to show that meat was shared between households, which seems to reflect the kinds of sharing that are typical in egalitarian hunting and gathering societies. What we see at Pincevent, then, is a classic picture of a hunting and gathering band. A small group of people, perhaps fifteen to twenty in all, visited the site annually during fall reindeer migrations to hunt the vulnerable reindeer herds as they crossed the Seine. Each family maintained its own hearth and shelter, and each produced the tools it needed to survive. But, just as is the case with modern hunter-gatherers like the San, each family was also linked to the others through bonds of reciprocal sharing.

SOURCES: James G. Enloe, Francine David, and Timothy S. Hare, 1994, "Patterns of faunal processing at Section 27 of Pincevent: The use of spatial analysis and ethnoarchaeological data in the interpretation of archaeological site structure," *Journal of Anthropological Archaeology* 13: 105–124; André Leroi-Gourhan, and Michel Brézillon, *Fouilles de Pincevent: Essai d'analyse ethnographique d'un habitat magdalénien* (Paris: VIIe Supplément à Gallia Préhistoire, 1972).

such as hides. For example, wild cattle (bovines) and horses are portrayed more often than we would expect by chance, probably because they were larger and heavier (meatier) than the other animals in the environment. In addition, the paintings mostly portray animals that the painters may have feared the most because of their size, speed, natural weapons such as tusks and horns, and unpredictability of behavior. That is, mammoths, aurochs, and horses are portrayed more often than deer and reindeer. Thus, the paintings are consistent with the idea that "the art is related to the importance of hunting in the economy of Upper Paleolithic people." Consistent with this idea, according to the investigators, is the fact that the art of the cultural period that followed the Upper Paleolithic also seems to reflect how people got their food. But in that period, when getting food no longer depended on hunting large game (because they were becoming extinct), the art ceased to focus on portrayals of animals.

Upper Paleolithic art was not confined to cave paintings. Many shafts of spears and similar objects were decorated with figures of animals. Alexander Marshack

FIGURE **7.10**

The Venus of Willendorf, one of the most famous Venus figurines.

**Venus figurines:** small sculptures of women with exaggerated hips and breasts, made by Upper Paleolithic peoples.

has an interesting interpretation of some of the engravings made during the Upper Paleolithic. He believes that as far back as 30,000 years ago, hunters may have used a system of notation, engraved on bone and stone, to mark the phases of the moon. If this is true, it would mean that Upper Paleolithic people were capable of complex thought and were consciously aware of their environment. In addition, figurines representing the human female in exaggerated form have been found at Upper Paleolithic sites. Called Venuses, these figurines portray women with broad hips and large breasts and abdomens (Figure 7.10).

What the **Venus figurines** symbolized is still controversial. Most scholars believe these figurines represented a goddess or fertility symbol, but that belief is not universally held. For example, LeRoy McDermott has argued that Venus figurines are not symbolic representations at all, but rather accurate self-portraits made by pregnant women. Their exaggerated breasts, hips, and stomachs are distortions that can be attributed to the perspective gained by a person looking down at themselves, as is the lack of facial details on many of the figurines. Others have argued that the figurines are examples of early erotica made by males for their sexual gratification or education. Still others suggest they were made by females to instruct young women in pregnancy and childbirth.

The controversies surrounding Venus figurines provide insight into a basic problem in the study of world prehistory—there is often little or no evidence available that allow archaeologists to accept or reject a particular interpretation. Rather, in most cases archaeologists have to balance data and interpretation to come to an informed judgment, recognizing that their current judgments will likely change as new data are uncovered.

## EAST ASIA

In East Asia there are a number of regionally distinctive Upper Paleolithic traditions. The glacial epochs that characterize the Upper Paleolithic world had varying effects across East Asia. Open steppelands and forests appear to have dominated the eastern portions of Central Asia throughout the Pleistocene and Holocene, and peoples of the **Eastern Central Asian Paleolithic** (40,000 to 6000 B.P.) hunted large game on the vast open plains and lush alluvial valleys of the region. They left little material debris behind, and almost nothing is known about their ways of life.

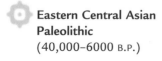

**Eastern Central Asian Paleolithic** (40,000–6000 B.P.)

More is known about the peoples of the **Southeast Asia Upper Paleolithic** (40,000 to 10,000 B.P.), but, interestingly, their stone tools lack evidence of blade technology. Most tools are crude choppers and flakes. One reason for this may be a lack of suitable stone. Another might be the presence of bamboo which grew throughout the region even during the Pleistocene, and can be used to make sharp cutting tools. The region appears to have been much dryer than today, with parklands and grasslands common. Herds of large mammals lived in these environments, and became the predominant prey for Upper Paleolithic hunters. In coastal areas marine resources were also important, and since the islands of Indonesia, New Guinea, and Australia were populated during this time, Southeast Asian Upper Paleolithic peoples must have had boats.

Australia was colonized by Upper Paleolithic peoples from Southeast Asia sometime before 40,000 years ago. These people of the **Early Australian** (ca. 40,000 to 7000 B.P.) tradition discovered a continental-sized landmass dominated by grasslands and savanna woodlands teeming with marsupials, birds, and reptiles. Some of the marsupials and birds were very large, similar in size to the megafauna found in Southeast Asia, and went extinct rapidly after human colonization, perhaps due to human hunting. The Early Australian peoples were hunters and gatherers, and they appear to have focused on locally available resources. Coastal groups, for example, made extensive use of the sea, while groups in the southeast intensively fished the many local lakes. At **Lake Mungo,** for example, fish remains are plentiful. Lake Mungo peoples also hunted wallabies and kangaroo, and likely collected a wide variety of plant food from the marshy lakeshores. Rockshelters seem to have been preferred locations for settlements, although many open air sites are also known (like Lake Mungo). No evidence for housing has been found, suggesting simple brush huts or skin tents were all that were used. Groups seem to have been small and mobile, much like Upper Paleolithic peoples elsewhere in Southeast Asia.

Japan was also colonized during this period, and there a regionally distinctive tradition, the **Japanese Upper Paleolithic** (20,000 to 12,000 B.P.) tradition developed. Little is known about the lifeways of these Upper Paleolithic peoples because the acidic soils of the Japanese archipelago have destroyed most of their remains, but they had a distinctive stone tool kit and must have made extensive use of marine resources. They may be descended from peoples of the northern China **Ordosian** (40,000 to 8500 B.P.) tradition, whose culture is better known. Ordosian peoples lived in small, mobile groups hunting and gathering in the relatively cold grasslands and forests of the region.

One well-studied Ordosian site is **Shiyu,** located on a broad alluvial plain in Shanxi province, China. The site covers an area of roughly 1,000 square meters and consists of a series of deposits sealed by fine, wind-blown soil. About 70 square meters of the site have been excavated. So far, no evidence of structures or living floors have been identified, and it seems clear that the site was a short-term camping station for a small group of people. There are abundant remains of stone tools and tool manufacture, including both blade tools and bifacially flaked projectile points (see Figure 7.11 on page 154). There are also hide-working tools such as borers and backed blades. The peoples living at Shiyu appear to have focused their hunting on horses since the remains of horses predominate in the faunal assemblage. The site may have been a location where horses watered and where Ordosian hunters could easily ambush a herd and dispatch several animals. These were then butchered and their hides cleaned and prepared while the group lived off the meat for several days before moving on.

## Arctic and Subarctic

Arctic regions of the globe did not change as dramatically as other areas during the late Pleistocene and early Holocene since glacial conditions were always the norm

**Southeast Asia Upper Paleolithic**
(40,000–10,000 B.P.)

**Early Australian**
(ca. 40,000–7000 B.P.)

**Lake Mungo** (Australia, Early Australian)

**Japanese Upper Paleolithic**
(20,000–12,000 B.P.)

**Ordosian**
(40,000–8500 B.P.)

**Shiyu** (China, Ordosian)

# Mal'ta

The Mal'ta site is located on the Belaia River in southeast Siberia, and is one of the most well-known Upper Paleolithic sites in Central Asia. Mal'ta contains the remains of an open-air campsite inhabited by Upper Paleolithic hunters between roughly 22,000 B.P. and 20,000 B.P. in what was at the time a tundra-steppe environment along the shore of a large lake that filled this portion of the Belaia River valley.

The Mal'ta site was discovered in 1928 and excavated intermittently through the 1930s, again in the 1950s, and finally during the 1990s. Over 1,500 square meters of the site have been excavated, yielding an assemblage of well over 45,000 artifacts and ecofacts. There is a large and interesting stone tool assemblage, which is dominated by blade tools and includes retouched blades, blade points, a variety of scrapers and burins based on blades, as well as fist-sized pebble choppers. Bone, antler, and ivory tools were also found in relative abundance, and include both tools—such as projectile points, awls, needles, and chisels—and ornaments such as beads and pendants. Bone and antler were also used as handles for blades. In addition, some thirty ivory "Venus" figurines of various styles, a number of small statues of birds and other animals, and several engraved ivory pieces were discovered at the site.

Reindeer antlers and bones are the most numerous items in the faunal remains from Mal'ta, and probably reflect the primary subsistence focus of the people who lived there. A wide array of other animals are also represented, including mammoth, woolly rhinoceros, horse, bison, sheep, cave lion, wolf, fox, wolverine, rabbit, and various birds (goose, silver gull, and crow). These faunal remains suggest that while the inhabitants of Mal'ta were primarily reindeer hunters, they hunted a wide variety of animals, including small mammals and birds, and frequently had to defend themselves against large predators such as cave lions and wolves.

A large number of features of various types—hearths, pits, middens, post-holes, and the like—have been discovered at Mal'ta, and three distinct types of structures have been identified. One type probably reflects simple skin tents, which are numerous and found all across the site. A second reflects circular, semisubterranean structures that appear much more substantial than tents. They have stone-lined walls and post-holes for roof supports, and they are surrounded by

in those regions. The glaciers did extend arctic conditions southward, so areas that are today called the arctic and subarctic extended farther to the south than they do today. Within those regions peoples practiced a nomadic big-game-hunting lifestyle, much like Upper Paleolithic peoples elsewere in the world.

The peoples of the **Siberian Upper Paleolithic** (42,000 to 11,000 B.P.) were all nomadic big-game hunters adapted to the changing environmental conditions of the late Pleistocene and early Holocene. They lived in both open sites and caves, and primarily hunted caribou and moose in what were probably dense boreal forests that covered much of southern Siberia during this time period. Tents were the

## Siberian Upper Paleolithic
(42,000–11,000 B.P.)

antlers and stones, which probably served to hold down a skin roof. There is a central, stone-lined hearth and storage pits in the floor of these structures. The third type of structure is cut into the sloping bank that fronts the Belaia River. These structures are oval, with one long side open toward the river and the other dug into the slope a half-meter or more deep. The walls are lined with stone slabs, and there are post-holes reflecting roof supports. These structures each have several hearths and are thought to have been covered by a single mammoth skin. They may represent structures built to resemble rockshelters.

The excavators of Mal'ta argue that these structures demonstrate a clear division of men's and women's roles. Artifacts found on the right side of the structures typically include stone working debris and items such as antler tine projectile points, which the excavators argue reflect men's activities. Artifacts found on the left side of the structures typically include hide-working tools such as scrapers and needles, which the excavators suggest reflect women's activities. Interestingly, almost all of the Venus figurines were found in what were interpreted as women's areas of the structures, while the animal figurines were found in men's areas. Perhaps this pattern provides a glimpse of family organization and sexual division of labor within the Upper Paleolithic world. If so, it seems not unlike that among contemporary hunters and gatherers.

The remains of two children were also found at Mal'ta, and these represent some of the only human remains from the Upper Paleolithic in the region. One child was apparently three or four years old, the other only about one year old. They were buried under the floor of a dwelling, perhaps on top of one another, or perhaps one was an earlier burial and the second placed in the same location later. The grave pit was topped by a large stone slab. The burials were covered in red ochre and contained a variety of grave goods, including a bead necklace, a braclet, a mammoth tusk "diadem," and a number of stone and bone tools. These Upper Paleolithic peoples, then, not only mourned and buried their dead, but may have provided tools for their use in the afterlife.

SOURCES: V. Alekseev, "The physical specificities of Paleolithic hominids in Siberia," in *The Paleolithic of Siberia: New Discoveries and Interpretations,* edited by A.P. Derev'anko, pp. 329-335 (Urbana: University of Illinois Press, 1998); M.M. Gerasimov, "The Paleolithic site Mal'ta: Excavations of 1956-1957," in *The Archaeology and Geomorphology of Northern Asia: Selected Works,* edited by H.N. Michael, pp. 3-32. (Toronto: University of Toronto Press, 1964); G. Medvedev, "Upper Paleolithic sites in south-central Siberia," in *The Paleolithic of Siberia: New Discoveries and Interpretations,* edited by A.P. Derev'anko, pp. 122-132. (Urbana: University of Illinois Press, 1998).

primary residence, and at sites such as **Kokorevo** many remains of tents, defined by rings of stone, an ash and debris-laden circular floor, and a central stone-lined hearth, have been recovered. There are also areas on the site where stone tools were made and where animals were butchered. During the middle of this period there was a return to very harsh glacial conditions throughout Siberia, and Pleistocene megafauna such as wooly mammoth and steppe bison came to dominate the region's fauna. During this time the Upper Paleolithic peoples in some areas moved into large settlements with substantial structures that were perhaps inhabited for many years. The most famous of these sites is **Mal'ta,** described in the box feature.

**Kokorevo** (Siberia, Siberian Upper Paleolithic)

**Mal'ta** (Siberia, Siberian Upper Paleolithic)

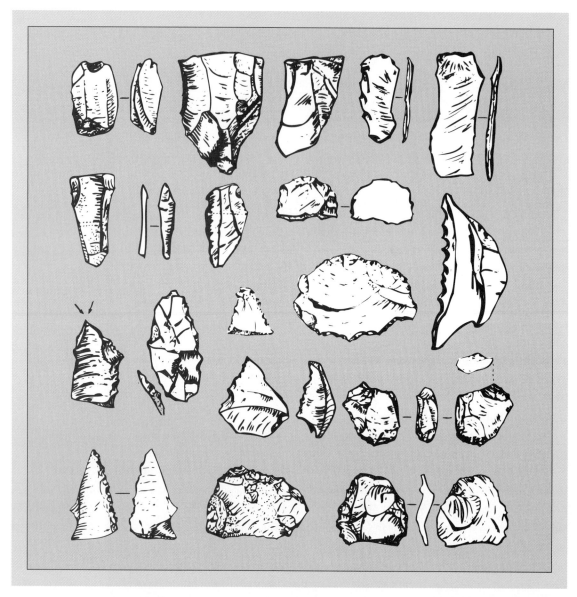

**FIGURE 7.11**

Stone tools from the site of Shiyu include both blades and flakes which were worked into a wide variety of forms. This great diversity in tool forms is characteristic of many Upper Paleolithic tool kits.

SOURCE: From L.P. Chia et al., *KKHP* 1972, no. I, p. 49.

## THE AMERICAS

Most archaeologists believe that at least one place that peoples of the Siberian Upper Paleolithic tradition moved to was into the New World. Because no remains of early humans have been found in the Americas despite over a century of active research on the peopling of the New World, it seems clear that humans first came to the New World sometime in the Upper Paleolithic. But exactly when these migrations occurred is subject to debate, particularly about when people got to areas south of Alaska. On the basis of similarities in biological traits such as tooth forms and blood types, and on possible linguistic relationships, anthropologists agree that Native Americans originally came from Asia. The traditional assumption is that they came

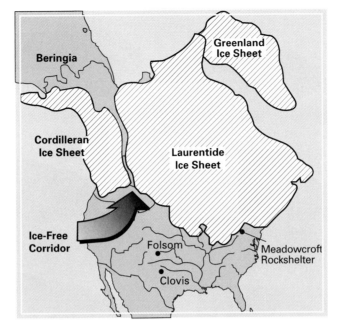

FIGURE **7.12**

Beringia and the ice sheets.

SOURCE: David K. Meltzer, "Pleistocene Peopling of the Americas," in *Evolutionary Anthropology, Vol. 1,* 1993. Copyright © 1993. Reprinted by permission of Wiley-Liss, Inc., a subsidiary of John Wiley & Sons, Inc.

to North America from Siberia, walking across a land bridge (Beringia) that is now under water (the Bering Strait) between Siberia and Alaska. The ice sheets or glaciers that periodically covered most of the high latitudes of the world contained so much of the world's water (the ice sheets were thousands of feet thick in some places) that **Beringia** was dry land in various periods, some lasting for thousands of years (Figure 7.12). Since then, the glaciers have mostly melted, and the Bering "bridge" has been completely covered by a higher sea level.

Until recently, the prevailing view was that humans were not present south of Alaska until after 11,500 years ago. Now evidence from several archaeological sites indicate that modern humans got to southern South America by at least 12,500 years ago, and to eastern North America maybe as early as 18,000 years ago. Most scholars today believe that even when the glaciers were at their fullest extent, there was a small ice-free corridor through which people could have walked to North America from Asia. And there was always the possibility of using boats to follow the coast down into North and even South America.

Parts of Beringia were exposed from about 60,000 to 25,000 years ago. It wasn't until between 20,000 and 18,000 years ago that the land bridge was at its maximum. It was widely believed that Beringia was flooded around 14,000 years ago, but recent evidence suggests that walking across the land brigde was still possible until about 10,000 years ago. Even if an ice-free corridor allowing movement from Beringia into North America were present after 25,000 years ago, that corridor is not likely to have supported big game and permitted humans to hunt enough food to survive until after about 14,000 years ago. So some investigators suggest that moving through the ice-free corridor to what is now south of Canada was not likely until after that time.

**Beringia:** a landmass, located in what today is the Bering Sea, that linked Asia and North America during the last ice age.

## North America

We are not yet sure when or how humans first entered the New World, but we do know that by about 12,000 B.P. humans were well established in both North and South America. These first clear inhabitants of the North America were members of the **Paleoindian** (12,200 to 6000 B.P.) tradition. These people were nomadic hunters and gatherers who relied heavily on large game animals. Paleoindian sites are found

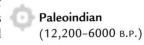

**Paleoindian**
(12,200–6000 B.P.)

FIGURE **7.13**
Clovis points (*right*) and
Folsom points (*left*)

throughout the United States, Mexico, and in unglaciated parts of Canada. For example, just south of the farthest reaches of the last glaciation, the area east of the Rockies known as the High Plains abounded with mammoths, bison, wild camels, and wild horses. The tools found with mammoth kills are known as the Clovis complex, which includes the Clovis projectile point as well as stone scrapers and knives and bone tools. The Clovis projectile point is large and leaf shaped, flaked on both sides. It has a broad groove in the middle, presumably so that the point could be attached to a wooden spear shaft (Figure 7.13). Because one mammoth was found with eight Clovis points in it, there is little dispute that Clovis people hunted large game such as the mammoth. Recent dating places most Clovis sites in the range of 11,200 to 10,900 years ago.

The mammoth disappeared about 10,000 years ago, and the largest game animal became the now-extinct large, straight-horned bison. The hunters of that bison used a projectile point called the Folsom point (Figure 7.13), which was much smaller than the Clovis point. Tools are also found with many other kinds of animal remains, including wolf, turtle, rabbit, horse, fox, deer, and camel, so the bison hunters obviously depended on other animals as well. In the Rio Grande valley, the Folsom toolmakers characteristically established a base camp on low dune ridges overlooking both a large pond and broad, open grazing areas. If we assume that the pond provided water for the grazing herds, the people in the camp would have been in an excellent position to watch the herds.

As the climate of what is now the American Southwest became drier, the animals and the cultural adaptations changed somewhat. About 9,000 years ago the smaller modern bison replaced the earlier straight-horned variety. Base camps began to be located farther from ponds and grazing areas and closer to streams. If the ponds were no longer reliable sources of water during these drier times, the animals probably no longer frequented them, which would explain why the hunters had to change the sites of their base camps. Not much is known about the plant foods these Paleoindian people may have exploited, but on the desert fringes plant gathering

FIGURE **7.14**
Remains of stampeded bison at the Olsen-Chubbuck site.

may have been vital. In Nevada and Utah, archaeologists have found milling stones and other artifacts for processing plant food.

The **Olsen-Chubbuck** site, a kill site excavated in Colorado, shows the organization that may have been involved in hunting bison. In a dry gulch dated to 8500 B.P. were the remains of 200 bison (Figure 7.14). At the bottom were complete skeletons and at the top, completely butchered animals. This find clearly suggests that Paleoindian hunters deliberately stampeded the animals into a natural trap—an arroyo, or steep-sided dry gully. The animals in front were probably pushed by the ones behind into the arroyo. Joe Wheat estimated that the hunters may have obtained 55,000 pounds of meat from this one kill. If we judge from nineteenth century Plains Indians, who could prepare bison meat to last a month, and estimate that each person would eat a pound a day, the kill at the Olsen-Chubbuck site could have fed more than 1,800 people for a month (they probably did not all live together throughout the year). The hunters must have been highly organized not only for the stampede itself but also for butchering. It seems that the enormous carcasses had to be carried to flat ground for that job. In addition, the 55,000 pounds of meat and hides had to be carried back to camp.

Although big game may have been most important on the High Plains, other areas show different adaptations. For example, Paleoindian people in woodland regions of what is now the United States seem to have depended more heavily on plant food and smaller game. In some woodland areas, fish and shellfish may have been a vital part of the diet. On the Pacific coast, some Paleoindian people developed food-getting strategies more dependent on fish. And in other areas, the lower Illinois River valley being one example, Paleoindian people who depended on game

**Olsen-Chubbock**
(U.S., Paleoindian)

FIGURE **7.15**
Archaeologists examining the
site of Monte Verde, Chile.

and wild vegetable foods managed to get enough food to live in permanent villages
of perhaps 100 to 150 people.

## South America

**Old South American
Hunting-Collecting**
(ca. 13,000–10,000
B.P.)

**Monte Verde** (Chile,
Old South American
Hunting-Collecting)

The earliest archaeological tradition in the Andes is the **Old South American
Hunting-Collecting** (ca. 13,000 to 10,000 B.P.) tradition, and it may be the oldest
established archaeological tradition in the New World, currently predating all other
recognized traditions. Peoples of the Old South American Hunting-Collecting tradition were, as the name implies, nomadic hunters and gatherers of Pleistocene
megafauna and plant species. The most important site of the Old South American
Hunting-Collecting tradition is Monte Verde, located in southern Chile (Figure 7.15).

The **Monte Verde** site has two cultural layers. The first (called Monte Verde II)
is dated around 12,500 years ago while the second (called Monte Verde I) is dated
around 33,000 years ago. Only the Monte Verde II layer is clearly associated
with human occupation, and the earlier Monte Verde I layer has only tantalizing evidence of human presence at the site. The Monte Verde II layer, however, contains
remarkably well-preserved archaeological deposits, including remains of a long tent-
like structure associated with impressions of human footprints, hearths, clusters of
animal and plant foods, and a wide variety of stone, bone, and wood tools.

The frame of the tent-like structure was constructed of logs and planks
anchored by stakes, and the walls were of poles covered with animal hides. Rope
made of junco weed was found wrapped around wooden posts and wooden stakes
recovered among the remains of the structure. Inside the structure were what
appeared to be individual living spaces divided by planks and poles. On the floors
of each living space were fire pits lined with clay, stone tools, and the remains of
edible seeds, nuts, and berries. Outside the structure were two large communal
hearths, a store of firewood, wooden mortars with their grinding stones, and even
three human footprints in the clay near a large hearth.

A second structure was made of wooden uprights set into a foundation of sand
and gravel hardened with animal fat. Mastodon carcasses had been butchered in this
structure, hides prepared, and tools manufactured. There may even have been

healing carried out with the aid of medicinal plants. These combined activities suggest this structure was a public or nonresidential one, unlike the long tent.

The remains of a wide variety of edible plants, along with mastodon, paleo-llama, small animals, and freshwater mollusks were recovered from the site, and it appears that aquatic plants from marshes, bogs, and lagoons provided the greatest variety and, along with meat, the bulk of the diet. Most of these wetlands were located far away from the site, suggesting that the people living at Monte Verde regularly traveled to distant locations to gather or that they acquired food and other items from distant locations through trade.

Many of the artifacts excavated at Monte Verde are of wood, and bone artifacts are also present. Three different stone tool technologies have been described: chipped bifaces, ground bola stones, and pebble tools. Analysis of the stone tools, bone, plant, and other artifact collections suggests a mixed hunting and gathering economy focused on many different ecological zones.

Until recently it was thought that the Amazon basin was the last area of South America to be inhabited by humans. Today we know that the Amazon was inhabited from the time the first humans entered the continent. Peoples of the **Old Amazonian Collecting-Hunting** (11,000 to 7000 B.P.) tradition entered the region as nomadic collectors of forest nuts and fruits, fishers, and hunters of small game. Only one Old Amazonian Collecting-Hunting site has been carefully excavated, **Caverna da Pedra Pintada** in the Para state of Brazil. The site is located in a cave, and consists of a 30-cm layer of black soil containing food remains, stone tools, and chipping debris. The stone tools include projectile points, scrapers, gravers, and blades (Figure 7.16). There were several hearths found as well, but no structures or pits. The depth of the deposit and lack of structures suggests that the site was used repeatedly over a long period of time but only for short intervals.

The people living at Caverna da Pedra Pintada appear to have practiced broad-spectrum gathering and hunting. The most common food remains were cracked and burned nutshells and fruit pits of tropical rain-forest trees. There were also numerous carbonized fragmentary bones of small fish and small fauna, such as turtles, lizards, and rodents. Remains of large game animals were rare.

**Old Amazonian Collecting-Hunting** (11,000–7000 B.P.)

**Caverna de Pedra Pintada** (Brazil, Old Amazonian Hunting-Collecting)

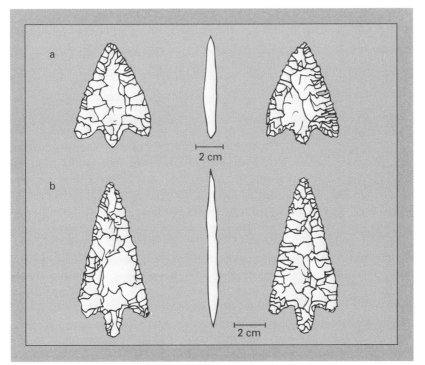

FIGURE **7.16**

These projectile points from Caverna da Pedra Pintada, Brazil, date to perhaps 11,000 years ago.

SOURCE: Reprinted with permission from *Science* Vol. 272 (April 19, 1996): 373. Copyright 1996 American Association for the Advancement of Science.

One of the more interesting features of Caverna da Pedra Pintada is the presence of paintings on the cave ceiling. These paintings, as well as those at other locations that appear to be associated with the Old Amazonian Collecting-Hunting tradition, include images of possible suns, moons, stars, comets, and eclipses, all of which suggest the cave's inhabitants had an interest in and knowledge of astronomy. Both human and animal figures are also depicted. The humans are typically not painted as well as the animals, but are often larger. There are also images of mythical animals with human hands and feet but animal or insect torsos and heads. Thus, even in South America the Upper Paleolithic saw the emergence of art depicting both the natural and, apparently, the supernatural world.

## THE END OF THE UPPER PALEOLITHIC

After about 10,000 years ago the glaciers began to disappear. With their disappearance came major environmental changes. The melting of the glacial ice caused the oceans to rise, and, as the seas moved inland, the waters inundated some of the richest fodder-producing coastal plains, creating islands, inlets, and bays. Other areas were opened up for human occupation as the glaciers retreated and the temperatures rose. The cold, treeless plains, tundras, and grasslands of Eurasia and North America eventually gave way to dense mixed forests, mostly birch, oak, and pine, and the large Pleistocene megafauna became extinct. The warming waterways began to be filled with fish and other aquatic resources.

Archaeologists believe that these environmental changes induced some populations to alter their food-getting strategies. When the tundras and grasslands disappeared, hunters could no longer obtain large quantities of meat simply by remaining close to large migratory herds of animals, as they probably did during Upper Paleolithic times. Even though deer and other game were available, the number of animals per square mile (density) had decreased, and it became difficult to stalk and kill animals sheltered in the thick woods. Thus, in many areas of the world people turned from a reliance on big-game hunting to the intensive collecting of wild plants, mollusks, fish, and small game to make up for the extinction of the large game animals they had once relied upon.

Environmental change also seems to have hastened the process of settling down that had begun in many areas of the world. As people began to know and exploit the varied resources in local areas, they moved less, and developed new, regionally distinctive cultures. It is to these distinct regional traditions of culture history that we now turn.

## ⬡ SUMMARY

The Upper Paleolithic world was one in which the first modern humans began to develop regionally distinctive cultures. While all Upper Paleolithic peoples based their livelihoods on hunting, fishing, and gathering, and all lived in small bands, peoples in each area of the world began to adapt their ways of life to the local environment in ways that appear much more sophisticated than their predecessors. Upper Paleolithic peoples also colonized the New World, opening up vast new areas for settlement and cultural adaptation. In their quest to adapt to local environments, the Upper Paleolithic peoples also broadened the range of plants and animals they ate. By drawing on a broader range of resources, Upper Paleolithic peoples created a more stable food supply, and in some areas were able to settle into seasonal villages.

Upper Paleolithic peoples also developed new technologies that helped them to broaden the range of resources they used. The most fundamental is blade production, which allowed more efficient use of stone, and also allowed for a wider range of tools than bifacial stoneworking. Bone, antler, and wood were used more widely as well, perhaps due to the development of burins used to work these raw materials. Along with technology, Upper Paleolithic peoples also developed art. In Europe, art took the form of magnificent cave paintings. Elsewhere art was carved on rock and sculpted into stone and bone pieces. Utensils were sometimes decorated, and individuals began adorning themselves with beads, pendants, and other ornaments. Art, perhaps more than anything else, illustrates the evolution of culture in the Upper Paleolithic world. Not only did humans expand the range of environments they lived in, the range of resources they used, and the range of tools they produced, but they also appear to have expanded the human mind into the realm of the abstract and the beautiful.

## ● DISCUSSION QUESTIONS

1. How do microliths differ from other types of blade tools? What are the advantages of using microliths? What are the disadvantages?

2. Several ideas about the significance of cave paintings within the Upper Paleolithic world have been presented in this chapter. Can you think of other ways to understand the significance of cave art?

3. Describe the physical environment of the Upper Paleolithic. How might this have affected people who lived in glacial areas? In temperate areas?

## ● ESSAY QUESTIONS

1. Author Jared Diamond has described the Upper Paleolithic as a "great leap forward" for humanity. Using the information in this chapter, describe the most significant cultural developments that appeared in the Upper Paleolithic. In what ways is the Upper Paleolithic a "great leap forward" when compared to the Middle and Lower Paleolithic periods?

2. Among the most significant human accomplishments in the Upper Paleolithic were the colonization of Australia and the New World. What factors might have led humans to colonize these areas? What does the ability of Upper Paleolithic peoples to colonize these areas tell us about their cultures? What social and technological innovations were needed to accomplish these colonizations?

3. Compare and contrast the Middle Paleolithic tools discussed in the last chapter with the Upper Paleolithic tools discussed here. How do they differ? What might be the significance of these differences in terms of human intellect and culture?

## ✦ RESEARCH PROJECT

This chapter has focused on similarities among Upper Paleolithic archaeological traditions. Use library or Internet resources to research at least two of the archaeological traditions discussed in the chapter. Compare and contrast these archaeological traditions, looking specifically for differences. How do these archaeological traditions differ?

## ● KEY SOURCES

### The Last Ice Age
COHMAP, 1988; Dawson, 1992; Martin and Wright, 1967; Mellars, 1994; White, 1982.

## Africa

Bordaz, 1970; Clark, 1982; Deacon, H., 1976; Deacon, J., 1984; Hawkins and Kleindeinst, 2001; Keeley, 1980; Klein, 1994; Lubell, 1984, 2001; McIntosh, 2001a; Miller, 2001a; Mitchell, 1997; Peregrine, 2001; Phillipson, 1993; Sampson, 1974; Schick and Toth, 1993; Semenov, 1970; Van Noten, 1982; Wadley, 1993, 2001; Wendorf, 1968, 2001; Wendorf, Schild, and Close, 1989; Whittaker, 1994.

## South and Southwest Asia

Goring-Morris, 2002a, 2002b; Jayaswal, 2002; Peregrine, 2002.

## Europe

Barton et al., 1991; Dobres, 1998; Enloe, 2001; Gamble, 1986; Knecht, Pike-Tay, and White, 1993; McDermott, 1996; Marshack, 1972; Mellars, 1989; Mellars and Stringer, 1989; Morell, 1995; Peregrine, 2001; Peterkin, Bricker, and Mellars, 1993; Pike-Tay, 2001; Rice and Paterson, 1985, 1986; Straus, 2001; Soffer, 1987, 1993; Ucko and Rosenfeld, 1967; Zvelevbil, 1986.

## East Asia

Aikens and Higuchi, 1982; Chang, 1986; Derevyanko and Zun-E, 1992; Hiscock, 2001a; Miller-Antonio, 2001; O'Connell and Allen, 1998; Okladnikov, 1990; Peregrine, 2001; Peregrine and Bellwood, 2001; White and O'Connell, 1982; Wu and Olsen, 1985; Yamanaka and Peregrine, 2001.

## Arctic and Subarctic

Anderson, 1970; Derevyanko, 1998; Dumond, 1987; Goebel, 2001; Larichev, Kholushkin and Laricheva, 1988, 1990; Peregrine, 2001.

## The Americas

Dillehay, 2000; Gibbons, 1995; Greenberg and Ruhlen, 1992; Hoffecker, Powers, and Goebel, 1993; Judge and Dawson, 1972; McDonald, 1998; Parry, 2002; Roosevelt, 1996, 2002; Soffer and Praslov, 1993; Szathmary, 1993; Tankersley, 2001; Tankersley and Issac, 1990; Turner, 1989; Wheat, 1967.

# CAVE PAINTINGS OF LASCAUX

The Upper Paleolithic began approximately 40,000 years ago. The earth was gripped by the last ice age, the Wurm, in Europe, and ice sheets covered much of the northern regions of North America, Europe, and Asia. Along the margins of these ice sheets and to their south was a new culture, the Upper Paleolithic, which populated Europe with modern humans. Africa, while not covered in ice sheets, was much wetter, the Sahara being a forest rather than the desert it is today. In both of these parts of the world, hunting and gathering were the ways of life. Art may have flourished for thousands of years before the major cave paintings of the Upper Paleolithic. We will probably never know, as it apparently was impermanent. But maybe as early as 60,000 years ago, Australians were painting the walls of rock shelters, Africans were painting slabs of stones 28,000 years ago, and in Europe, caves were painted with many animals, mostly megafauna. The caves of Lascaux were painted 17,000 years ago, in the south of France.

The Media Lab can be found in Chapter 7 on the *Companion Website*™ http://www.prenhall.com/peregrine

## WEB ACTIVITY

Modern humans entered the caves of Lascaux 17,000 years ago, carrying small oil lamps. These humans created wonderful artworks of animals, including cows, bulls, horses, and reindeer, but rarely recorded an image of themselves. These paintings are remote and hard to view without modern lighting, so many archaeologists question the meaning of these paintings. Could these paintings be spiritual or religious? Could they be omens for hunting success? Why did the humans who lived here throw spears at some of these paintings and why were almost all of the animals painted also those that they ate? In this activity, you will view images from Lascaux and share in the wonder that these images produce in people today.

## Activity

1. View the video. What do these pictures tell us about the climate of Europe during that time period? What food supply did the people of this region utilize?
2. What forms may social organization have taken to facilitate hunting some of the megafauna? Could this hunting activity have some impact on political organization?
3. What types of weapons and tools were necessary for living and hunting in this cold environment? What materials did the animals provide to humans, other than meat?

# Arctic and Subarctic

**o v e r v i e w**

**North Asia**

**North America**

**BOXES**

**Onion Portage**

**Yuquot**

The Arctic and Subarctic form a common environmental zone that crosses through a number of different nations, each with individual histories of archaeological method and practice. Indeed, the Cold War separated the two major areas of Arctic and Subarctic research—Canada and Siberia—from one another for more than forty years, and language differences perpetuate that divide. At the same time, it is clear that both regions underwent cultural evolution in relative isolation from one another despite regular contact across the Bering Sea. Thus it is reasonable to talk about two major regions of the Arctic and Subarctic—North American and North Asian—and to discuss the prehistory of these two regions separately (see Figure 8.1).

FIGURE **8.1**

Sites discussed in Chapter 8.

## NORTH ASIA

Humans first entered the North Asian Arctic during the Mousterian era, roughly 130,000 years ago. These Neandertal hunters were replaced by anatomically modern humans of the Siberian Upper Paleolithic tradition sometime around 42,000 years ago. As I discussed in the chapter on the Upper Paleolithic world, these Upper

Paleolithic peoples were hunters of big game, and, indeed, of some of the Pleistocene megafauna that are the most closely identified with the Upper Paleolithic world—wooly mammoth, wooly rhinocerous, mastodon, and the like. While Holocene climatic changes did not effect the Arctic and Subarctic as dramatically as they did some other parts of the world, the retreat of the glaciers opened up large areas of tundra, and boreal forests moved far northward into lands that were once arctic deserts.

The North Asian Arctic today is dominated by three environmental zones (Figure 8.2). In the far north are areas of **high arctic**—lands largely barren of vegetation except during the brief summer months, dark and frozen for four long winter months, covered in glaciers, snowpack, and frozen sea ice much of the year. While birds, small mammals, and their predators live in small numbers in these regions, the principal biotic community is the sea, rich in fish and sea mammals. To the south of the high arctic is the **tundra**. Like the high arctic, tundra lands are dark nearly half the year, and only lichens, mosses, and grasses have the chance to grow. Permafrost takes hold of the ground perhaps a foot beneath the ground surface, and

**High arctic:** arctic lands largely barren of vegetation and covered in snow or ice much of the year.

**Tundra:** arctic lands where lichens, mosses, and grasses grow.

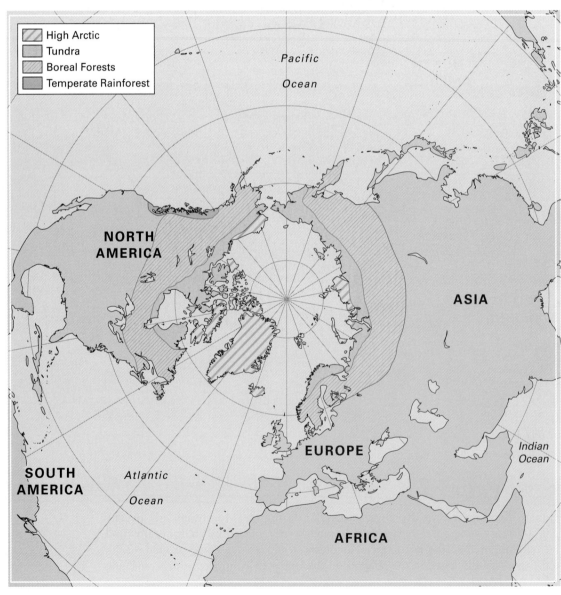

FIGURE **8.2**
Environments of the Arctic and Subarctic.

as the surface melts in the summer sun the tundra becomes a wet quagmire of buzzing insects. This is the land of caribou and musk oxen—large herding animals who live off the meager plant foods they can obtain easily in summer but must dig for through snow and ice in winter. While musk oxen spend the whole year on the tundra, caribou migrate annually from the tundra to the **boreal forests** to the south. These forests are often dense, marshy, and teeming with fish, birds, elk, moose, deer, small mammals and predators, and, of course, caribou.

It was in these forests and forested river valleys running through tundra lands that peoples of the **Siberian Neolithic and Bronze Age** (8000–2100 B.P.) tradition significantly broadened the range of animals hunted by Upper Paleolithic peoples, developed fishing techniques and technology, and began to collect plant foods of various kinds. They also incorporated microlithic technology and ceramics into their tool kits and, later, metal. Stone tools other than microliths include projectile points and scrapers made from blades. Polished stone axes and adzes were used to work wood. Ceramics tended to be poorly fired and were usually simple bowl shapes. Only a few bronze tools have been found, and these appear to have been traded up from the south, as there is no evidence of indigenous metal working. Villages tended to be small, consisting of five to fifteen dwellings located on river terraces. Houses were semisubterranean pit houses ranging in size from 10 to 25 square meters in floor area, only large enough to house a single nuclear family. Thus most communities housed no more than thirty or forty people.

In the region surrounding and north of Lake Baikal, peoples of the **Baikal Neolithic and Bronze Age** (8000–3000 B.P.) developed a unique way of life. These people lived in small, nomadic bands that wandered among the many rivers and lakes in the region spearing fish and hunting both large and small game. Their basic tool kit included microliths, blades, chipped stone points and scrapers, and small projectile points that suggest use of the bow and arrow. Bone was used extensively, particularly for projectile points and harpoon heads. The Baikal Neolithic and Bronze Age peoples also made ceramics, typically oval in shape and with net impressions. While a few bronze tools have been found, these were obtained through trade and not manufactured locally. No Baikal Neolithic and Bronze Age dwellings have been excavated, suggesting they were probably no more substantial than skin tents or simple brush structures. Sites tend to be small clusters of debris, perhaps surrounding a stone-lined hearth. Some sites show evidence of multiple habitations, perhaps by groups returning to the same place several years in a row.

In the tundra of northern Siberia, the Neolithic and Bronze Age peoples were ultimately replaced by nomadic reindeer herders of the **Siberian Protohistoric** (2000–500 B.P.) tradition, peoples who likely migrated north from the Lake Baikal region some 2,000 years ago. Reindeer were used for milk and blood as well as slaughtered for meat. During the summer, groups of ten or more families would share a settlement near a prime fishing location and work together caring for herds, socializing, and performing ceremonies. Fish were caught using nets and spears and were taken in large numbers. In this situation, the large labor pool available in summer camps allowed the fish to be processed by smoking or drying before they spoiled. In the winter, families would separate and wander in search of fodder for their reindeer. Housing during both the summer and winter were large conical skin tents (see Figure 8.3 on page 168). The tool kit of the Siberian protohistoric peoples was simple, consisting of metal, stone, bone, and ceramic items, many of which were obtained through trade.

## Kamchatka and the Sea of Okhotsk

The Kamchatka peninsula is a huge landmass connected at the north by a narrow strip of land to the Asian mainland. Between Asia and Kamchatka lies the Sea of Okhotsk. The peninsula itself is largely volcanic in origin and is both mountainous and rich in mineral resources. The environment of Kamchatka is harsh, with

**Siberian Neolithic and Bronze Age** (8000–2100 B.P.)

**Baikal Neolithic and Bronze Age** (8000–3000 B.P.)

**Siberian Protohistoric** (2000–500 B.P.)

**Boreal forests:** dense subarctic conifer forests located south of tundra zones.

FIGURE **8.3**
A modern Saami stands with one of his reindeer. In the back is a traditional conical tent and wooden sled, both similar to those used by peoples of the Siberian Protohistoric tradition.

**Kamchatka Mesolithic**
(8000–4000 B.P.)

**Tarya Neolithic**
(4000–2500 B.P.)

**Old Itel'man**
(2500–500 B.P.)

**Semisubterranean:** a structure built partially below ground.

temperatures below freezing most of the year and having abundant snowfall (see Figure 8.2). Separated as it is from the mainland, the peoples of Kamchatka have developed unique ways of life since Upper Paleolithic times.

Peoples of the **Kamchatka Mesolithic** (8000–4000 B.P.) tradition were big-game hunters like their Upper Paleolithic predecessors. However, they also began to draw significant resources from the sea—a pattern that would be followed by all the later peoples of Kamchatka. As the glaciers retreated, new species of fish and sea mammals began to move north, and it was these that the peoples of the Kamchatka Mesolithic began to rely upon, particularly seal. Unfortunately, Kamchatka Mesolithic coastal sites were inundated as glacial meltwaters raised sea levels. Inland sites are small, ephemeral camps consisting of only several conical tents and perhaps ten to fifteen people. Lithics were simple and included microlithic, blade, and chipped items made from locally available stone (see Figure 8.4). Wood and bone tools were also used.

This combination of fishing and hunting continued in the **Tarya Neolithic** (4000–2500 B.P.) and **Old Itel'man** (2500–500 B.P.) traditions. The first ceramics in Kamchatka were apparently made during the Tarya Neolithic tradition, but only a few fragments have been found. Later Old Itel'man ceramics are round-bottomed and relatively thick. Peoples in both traditions fished extensively, often using weirs, but during the Old Itel'man tradition certain technological innovations developed suggesting that hunting of sea mammals became more important. The primary innovation was the toggling harpoon, which in turn suggests that Old Itel'man peoples used boats to hunt mammals in the open sea. Both Tarya Neolithic and Old Itel'man peoples hunted land mammals using bows and arrows armed with small, triangular projectile points. Projectile points and other cutting and scraping tools were made with locally available stone during both traditions, but Old Itel'man peoples began using metal as well. Both chipped stone and polished stone tools were used, and various bone tools and ornaments were present.

Tarya Neolithic settlements are found in both coastal and inland locations. Summer settlements are found along the coasts, often near the mouths of rivers. Winter settlements were inland, often near freshwater sources such as rivers and lakes. Summer houses were light frame structures, while winter houses were semisubterranean sod structures (**semisubterranean** means that the floors of these structures were dug into the earth a meter or so, forming a deep basin for the structure). Sod was layered

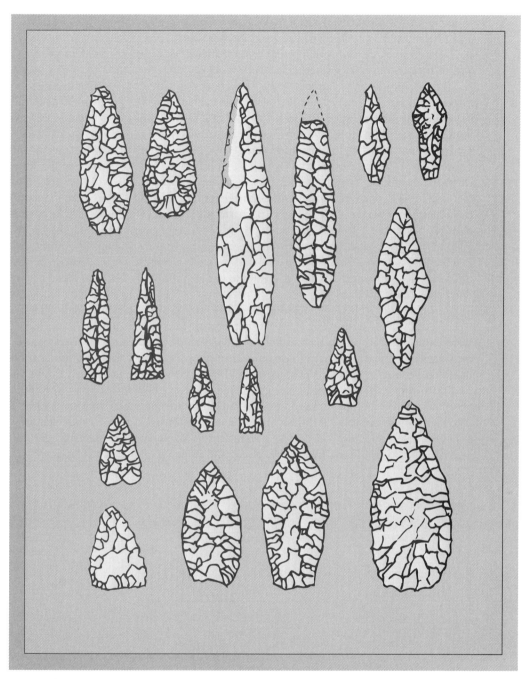

FIGURE **8.4**

A variety of bifacial flaked tools of the Kamchatka tradition, including knives, spear points, and arrow points.

SOURCE: Henry N. Michael (ed.), *The Archaeology and Geomorphology of Northern Asia: Selected Works* (Toronto: University of Toronto Press, 1964), p. 276. Reprinted with permission of University of Toronto Press.

across a wooden support frame to form a solid and well-insulated structure. Neither summer nor winter settlements were very large, consisting of at most forty or fifty people. The general pattern of seasonal settlements continued in the Old Itel'man tradition, but with some interesting changes. First, many Old Itel'man winter communities had a group of semisubterranean sod houses surrounding a single, large sod structure, which was likely used for community gatherings and celebrations. Second, some larger, perhaps semisedentary communities developed in central

Kamchatka. On the central Kamchatka River, for example, communities were large and fortified with a system of walls and ditches. Such changes suggest some degree of community leadership was present to coordinate the creation of defensive works and to host community gatherings or ceremonies.

Across the Sea of Okhotsk from Kamchatka is a region of coastlines, dense forests, and rich alluvial plains. People living in this area, the peoples of the **Amur Neolithic and Bronze Age** (12,000–1500 B.P.) tradition, established a broad-spectrum hunting-gathering-fishing economy based in large, sedentary villages, particularly along the seacoast. Communities consisted of twenty or thirty semisubterranean sod houses. These houses were often over 100 square meters in size, suggesting a large extended family or several families lived in them. Thus it is likely that many Amur Neolithic and Bronze Age communities had several hundred residents. The main animals hunted were deer, bear, and boar that resided in the dense forests. The forests also provided nuts, fruits, and other plant foods that were gathered seasonally. Fishing, however, was the primary subsistence activity of most Amur Neolithic and Bronze Age communities. Late in the tradition the domestic pig was incorporated into the diet, and perhaps some domestic crops, although no clear evidence of domestic plants has been found.

The tool kit of the Amur Neolithic and Bronze Age peoples included ceramics (see Figure 8.5). These were typically flat-bottomed and grit-tempered, and they were manufactured using the paddle and anvil technique. Ceramics were decorated in a variety of ways including cord-marking, incising, and stamping. Stone tools included both chipped and polished types. Blade tools were particularly common, and slate was used extensively as well. Antler and bone were used for harpoons, arrowheads, needles, and other items. Late in the tradition metal was incorporated into the tool kit, but there is no evidence of local metalworking. The Amur Neolithic and Bronze Age peoples also made a wide variety of personal ornaments, particularly beads and pendants, from shell, ivory, and bone.

**Amur Neolithic and Bronze Age**
(12,000–1500 B.P.)

FIGURE **8.5**

Examples of Amur Neolithic and Bronze Age ceramic forms.

SOURCE: Henry N. Michael (ed.), *The Archaeology and Geomorphology of Northern Asia: Selected Works* (Toronto: University of Toronto Press, 1964), p. 251. Reprinted by permission of University of Toronto Press.

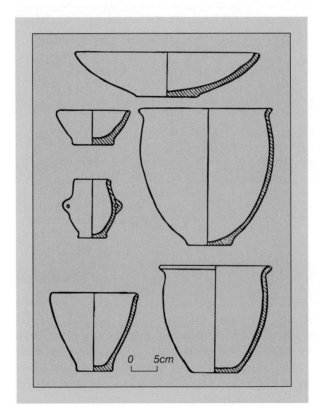

## Asian High Arctic

While the Neolithic and Bronze Age peoples of Siberia began diversifying subsistence, focused hunting populations remained in the far northeast of Asia and the far northwest of North America. These peoples of the **Paleo-Arctic** (11,000–6000 B.P.) tradition continued to hunt large game in the arctic regions of the retreating glacial ice sheets. Primary game animals included elk, moose, bison, and mammoth, which the Paleo-Arctic peoples followed along their migration routes. Needless to say, Paleo-Arctic peoples were nomadic and lived in small bands or individual family groups. Their settlements were short-term and ephemeral, often located near freshwater sources or on high promontories where game could be seen from far away. No evidence of housing has been found and was likely simple skin tents. The Paleo-Arctic tool kit was based on microblades which were fitted into bone and wood handles to make composite tools such as knives and spears.

**Paleo-Arctic**
(11,000–6000 B.P.)

The Paleo-Arctic peoples were followed in the Asian high arctic by peoples of the **Holocene Stone Age** (10,500–3000 B.P.) tradition. These peoples were specialized hunters of the elk and reindeer that became the dominant big-game animals during the Holocene. They lived in small, nomadic groups that followed reindeer herds or moved through the boreal forests hunting elk. Housing was apparently in simple skin tents, and technology was relatively simple, based on blades and bifaces, polished stone, and bone and ivory tools. Ceramics were also made, and these include some with unique pastes tempered with reindeer hair.

**Holocene Stone Age**
(10,500–3000 B.P.)

One well-documented site from the Holocene Stone Age is **Zhokhov**, located on the New Siberian island of the same name just below 76 degrees north latitude. Zhokhov is a remarkably large site, covering more than 8,000 square meters, some 148 square meters of which have been excavated to date. Those excavations have recovered a wide range of stone, bone, and ivory tools and toolmaking debris, along with a large faunal assemblage. Most of the tools appear to have been composite, made of microblades inset into bone or antler handles or shafts. No evidence of housing was found. Perhaps the most interesting aspect of the Zhokhov site is the faunal assemblage. Roughly half of the game animals represented were reindeer, but the other half were mostly polar bear. The implication is that polar bear was a primary subsistence food for the Zhokhov peoples.

**Zhokhov** (Siberia, Holocene Stone Age)

## NORTH AMERICA

The North American Arctic is similar to the Asian Arctic in terms of its environment, although more of the landmass is located in high arctic environmental zones (see Figure 8.2). The first peoples to penetrate the North American Arctic were members of the Paleo-Arctic tradition, who first inhabited the area sometime before 10,000 B.P. Their way of life was the same as their cousins in Asia, but they spread farther and persisted considerably longer than their Asian cousins. By 8000 B.P. the Paleo-Arctic peoples had spread eastward, apparently following the front of the retreating glacial ice sheets and living as nomadic hunters. Although nomadic and having a simple technology, the Paleo-Arctic peoples did leave a clear record of their presence at sites like **Onion Portage,** described in the box feature.

**Onion Portage**
(Alaska, Paleo-Arctic)

## North American High Arctic

In the high arctic, the peoples of the Eastern Arctic Small Tool and Western Arctic Small Tool traditions, descendents of the Paleo-Arctic peoples, continued a subsistence regime focused on nomadic hunting. As their names suggest, both had tool kits based on microlithics. The peoples of the **Eastern Arctic Small Tool** (4000–2700 B.P.) tradition were oriented to the arctic coasts; they based their economy on hunting sea mammals and polar bear. They also hunted musk ox and caribou, and small game

**Eastern Arctic Small Tool**
(4000–2700 B.P.)

## Onion Portage

The Onion Portage site is among the rare examples of a deep, stratified site in the arctic. The site is located on the bank of the Kobuk River in northwestern Alaska at a spot where the river runs between two steeply cut banks. Soil washing down from these banks has covered the site over the last 8,500 years to a depth of more than 5 meters in places. Such deep deposits are almost unknown in the arctic, where soils build up exceedingly slowly, if at all.

The site is located in a prime environment for arctic hunters. It is situated near the edge of the forest zone, and from the tops of the surrounding river banks one can see well onto the tundra to the north. To the south, the taiga stretches as far as one can see, broken here and there with small woodlands. The location was a spot caribou often used to cross the Kobuk River during their seasonal migrations, and caribou herds could be spotted well in the distance whether moving from the north or the south. The Kobuk River provides fish, and the area itself has plentiful wild game. It is no wonder that peoples of northwestern Alaska would have returned to occupy the site over such a long period of time.

The Onion Portage site was discovered in 1941 by archaeologist J.L. Giddings, but he did not begin excavations at the site until 1964—the year he died. In 1966 excavations were taken over by his student, Douglas Anderson, and a team from the University of Pennsylvania under the direction of Froelich Rainey. Anderson and Rainey excavated several areas of the Onion Portage site, uncovering nine major periods of occupation spanning 8,500 years.

such as arctic hare and birds. There is evidence that Eastern Arctic groups followed a seasonal pattern of camping on the sea ice during the winter hunting seal and polar bear, spending the summer and fall on the mainland and islands hunting musk ox and caribou. Settlements varied in size from those of family campsites to villages with ten or twenty structures. Structures themselves were simple skin tents, often with the sides held down by rocks. There was usually a central stone-lined hearth in the tent, and sometimes the floor was divided by a paired line of vertically arranged flat slabs of rock, creating two "rooms" within the tent.

**Umingmak** (Northwest Territories, Eastern Arctic Small Tool)

The **Umingmak** site is a good example of an Eastern Arctic Small Tool summer village. It is located on Banks Island in the Northwest Territories. Three stone-lined hearths were found at the site, one surrounded by a circle of rocks and musk ox skulls, suggesting the hearths were covered with skin tents. Over 80 percent of the faunal remains on the site were from musk ox—73 musk ox skulls were recovered from the surface alone! Most of the bones showed cut marks and other signs of heavy processing, and most of the long bones were broken open to extract the marrow. The excavators suggest the site was a summer camp where musk oxen were hunted, butchered, and their meat dried and preserved for winter use. Another village site is **Port Refuge** on Devon Island. Over fifty round, shallow depressions, sometimes surrounded by a ring of stones or containing a central hearth, have been interpreted as the remains of Eastern Arctic Small Tool tent dwellings. They are situated

**Port Refuge** (Northwest Territories, Eastern Arctic Small Tool)

The earliest remains at Onion Portage date to the Paleo-Arctic tradition, and they represent one of the most complete archaeological assemblages for any Paleo-Arctic site. Anderson refers to the Onion Portage Paleo-Arctic materials as Akmak, after the northern-Alaskan Eskimo word for chert. Chert tools dominate the archaeological assemblage and include both large blades, microblades, and bifaces. The bifaces are unique. They are carefully prepared disks with one edge that has been sharpened into a cutting edge. Microblades, rectangular in form, were used in a variety of composite tools from knives to projectile points. Blades were used primarily as cutting and scraping tools and to produce burins for woodworking.

In addition to these tools, the remains of several hearths and perhaps dwellings were recovered from Onion Portage. These are represented by hearths, often containing burnt reindeer bone, surrounded by a circular area of extensive habitation debris. It is thought this area of debris was the floor of a skin tent with a central hearth. Activities that apparently went on within these dwellings included butchering and cooking animals, carving wooden and ivory tools and perhaps personal ornaments, stone working, and preparing hunting equipment. Taken together, the materials preserved at the Onion Portage site have given us an unprecedented view of what life was like for prehistoric peoples of the arctic.

SOURCES: Anderson, Douglas D., 1968, "A Stone Age Campsite at the Gateway to America," *Scientific American* 218(6): 24–33; 1970, "Microblade Traditions in Northwestern Alaska," *Arctic Anthropology* 7(2): 2–16.

in clusters of two to five, which may each reflect repeated annual encampments by one group over a period of perhaps a dozen or more years. The faunal remains suggest heavy reliance on seal, which may reflect either a summer or winter habitation.

The peoples of the **Western Arctic Small Tool** (4700–2500 B.P.) tradition, while sharing with the Eastern Arctic Small Tool tradition the extensive use of microliths, had an entirely different economy, one focused on inland resources, particularly salmon and caribou. The Western Arctic peoples also had some more permanent communities that may have been winter villages. In winter villages a group of several small pithouses were constructed, perhaps covered with a skin roof. Other sites are small and ephemeral, consisting of simple scatters of debris and food refuse. On some campsites the refuse is found in roughly circular areas, suggesting skin tents were used. Most of these small campsites are along inland lakes and streams, at caribou passages, and on the seacoast. It seems likely that these habitations reflect an annual round of movement from inland winter villages to the coast and back again.

A representative campsite of the Western Arctic Small Tool tradition is **Cape Krusenstern,** located on Kotzebue Sound in northwestern Alaska. Here on a series of beach ridges a large number of what are inferred to be Western Arctic Small Tool tent sites have been found. Each of these apparent tent sites consists of a hearth and scatter of lithic debris, including microblades, microblade cores, macroblades, and

**Western Arctic Small Tool** (4700–2500 B.P.)

**Cape Krusenstern** (Alaska, Western Arctic Small Tool)

FIGURE **8.6**
A caribou surrounded by typical taiga vegetation.

**Punyik Point** (Alaska, Western Arctic Small Tool)

**Norton** (3000–1000 B.P.)

**Brooks River** (Alaska, Norton)

**Labret:** an ornamental lip plug.

bifacially flaked knives. The site is located near prime spring seal hunting locations and was probably a spring or early summer encampment used by several families soon after the winter ice broke up. An example of a winter village is the **Punyik Point** site on Itivlik Lake in western Alaska. The site sits near a divide in the Brooks range through which migrating caribou often cross during their seasonal migrations. Thus, the site is in a prime location for hunting caribou and processing their meat for later use. Houses at the site were semisubterranean structures covered with sod, and hence were likely occupied in the winter, perhaps to hunt caribou in the fall and live off the processed meat during the winter.

The Western Arctic Small Tool tradition was followed by the **Norton** (3000–1000 B.P.) tradition. The Norton peoples were the first in the region to make ceramics, and they appear to have made more extensive use of ocean resources than their predecessors. Norton ceramics were coil made and pit fired, were tempered with fiber, and were often decorated with linear or check stamping (see Figure 8.7). Norton peoples also developed the ornamental lip plug or **labret,** which spread throughout the arctic and is still a common personal ornament today. Beyond ceramics and personal ornaments, the Norton peoples had a tool kit that employed ivory and bone for items such as harpoon heads and arrow points, bows, and handles to which chipped stone points or blades would be attached. The Norton peoples subsisted primarily on seal, fish, and caribou. Seal were hunted on the coasts, while fish and caribou were taken from locations around inland lakes and streams. It seems likely that a seasonal pattern developed with winter habitation on the coasts and summer habitation inland.

Some Norton settlements were quite large and appear semipermanent. For example, the **Brooks River** site, located near Brooks Lake in northern Alaska,

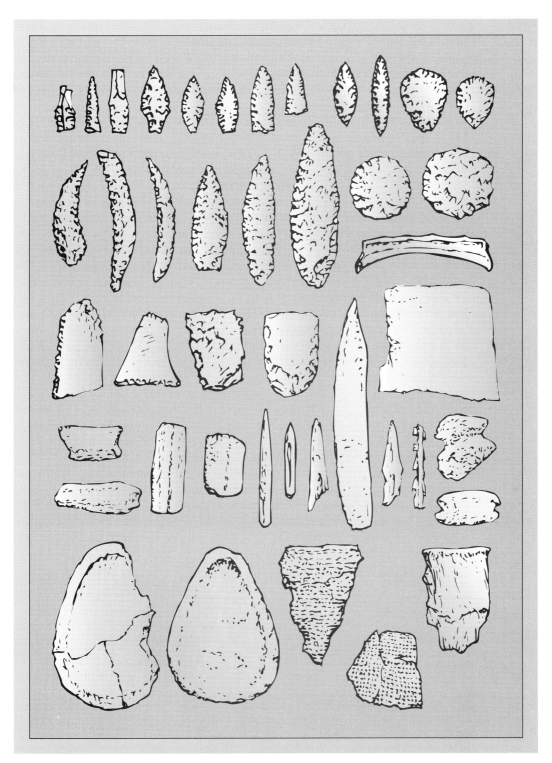

FIGURE **8.7**

Artifacts of the Norton tradition, including stamped ceramic fragments. These are earliest ceramics in the North American arctic.

SOURCE: Jesse D. Jennings (ed.), *Ancient Native Americans* (New York, NY: W.H. Freeman & Company, 1978), p. 251.

contains the remains of square, semisubterranean houses, roughly 4 meters on a side. These had a central fireplace and sloping entry and were likely covered with sod. It is unlikely that the houses were contemporary since they are widely separated, but more likely they represent repeat seasonal visits to the Brooks River, perhaps during annual salmon runs. The salmon captured during these runs and the other fish and game surrounding Brooks Lake may have allowed the residents at the Brooks River site to remain there for a long period of time—perhaps six months or more. Similarly, at the **Cape Nome** site, located on the western Alaska coast, the remains of more than 320 houses have been found, many of which date to the Norton tradition. Typical houses were square and semisubterranean and varied between 4 and 6 meters on a side. The site was used for centuries, so it is not clear how many houses were present at any one time, but several concentrations suggest that as many as ten or twelve may have been occupied at a given time. The faunal remains from the site suggest a mixed economy of hunting sea mammals and caribou.

Peoples of the **Thule** (2100–100 B.P.) tradition, which is associated with the direct ancestors of contemporary Inuit peoples, followed the Norton tradition. The Thule peoples continued the Norton emphasis on hunting both marine and terrestrial mammals, and furthered the practice of populations congregating in large seasonal villages during part of the year. These large seasonal villages were occupied during the winter and were composed of a dozen or more square semisubterranean sod houses located on beaches providing boat lauches (see Figure 8.8). Houses had entry passageways that prevented cold from entering, and central hearths for warmth. Stone lamps provided both light and heat. Sitting or sleeping benches were built against the walls. Houses were often arranged around a larger central "men's house," and in some areas villages were surrounded by a **palisade,** a defensive wall built of vertical posts, suggesting intervillage conflict (also suggested by burials of individuals killed by arrows). In both cases it appears that some kind of village-level authority must have been active, perhaps a village or military council.

The Thule peoples hunted sea mammals while living in these large winter villages, including walrus and whale, which must have required coordinated hunting using boats. In the summer, individual families hunted and gathered on their own, taking caribou, musk oxen, and small game, as well as fishing. Berries and other plant foods were gathered seasonally. The tool kit employed by the Thule peoples was

**Cape Nome**
(Alaska, Norton)

**Thule**
(2100–100 B.P.)

**Palisade:** a defensive wall built of vertical posts.

FIGURE **8.8**
Remains of a Thule house built using whale skulls and mandibles as wall supports.

simple but sophisticated. Toggling harpoons were the primary weapon used to take sea mammals, while the bow and arrow were used on land. Knives were made from chipped stone and hide and woodworking tools from polished slate. Ceramics and stone bowls were used for storage, cooking, and as oil lamps. Some of the raw materials used in tools and ornaments were obtained through trade, including small amounts of iron from Asia. Both trade and seasonal movements suggest that while maintaining large villages the Thule peoples were also highly mobile, and by 1000 B.P. they began to spread across the arctic, displacing the Dorset peoples to the east.

The peoples of the **Dorset** (2800–700 B.P.) tradition followed the people of the Eastern Arctic Small Tool tradition. They lived in small, nomadic groups subsisting on arctic land and marine mammals, employing an elegant microlithic technology before being either displaced or incorporated into the Thule tradition. Dorset settlements are typically located along coastlines in protected coves. They were composed of several structures, each housing a nuclear family within a skin tent or a larger, semisubterranean sod house. Seal and walrus were primary game species, and were hunted with unique nontoggling harpoons, often with decorated foreshafts (see Figure 8.9 on page 178). Microblades were used to arm harpoon heads and for a variety of composite cutting tools, while chipped stone points armed spears used to hunt caribou and musk oxen. Bone, antler, and wood were used extensively for such items as handles, barbed harpoon points, awls, needles, and small sculptures that are found on many Dorset sites. Slate was also used extensively, particularly for wood and hide working tools. Stone bowls were used as lamps for heat and light.

**Dorset**
(2800–700 B.P.)

## Gulf of Alaska and Aleutians

Along the coast and among the islands of what is today the Gulf of Alaska two unique traditions developed following the Paleo-Arctic tradition—**Ocean Bay** (8000–4000 B.P.) and **Kodiak** (4000–700 B.P.). Peoples of both traditions were strongly oriented to the sea and subsisted primarily off of marine mammals and fish. They lived in sedentary coastal villages, which consisted of ten or more houses arranged along the coastline. Each house was a circular or oval structure, perhaps a tent, although no clear structural remains have been found. A typical village likely housed 100 or so people. The major difference between these traditions is in their tool kits. Peoples of the Ocean Bay tradition employed microlithic technology, while peoples of the Kodiak tradition developed toggling harpoons and an extensive slate industry. In this way, the two traditions parallel the development of technology elsewhere in the Arctic, but are unusual in their ability to maintain a sedentary way of life. Sedentism was probably achieved because of the abundance of fish and sea mammals in the Gulf of Alaska (similar to the Northwest Coast, which also produced early sedentary villages of hunter-fishers).

**Ocean Bay**
(8000–4000 B.P.)

**Kodiak**
(4000–700 B.P.)

In what is today the Aleutian Islands a similarly unique tradition developed— the **Aleutian** (5500–250 B.P.) tradition. Like the Ocean Bay and Kodiak peoples, peoples of the Aleutian tradition focused subsistence on the sea. They lived in sedentary coastal villages, made up of several dozen semisubterranean sod houses. Some of these houses were very large, had multiple side rooms, and housed several families. In some areas a local hierarchy of villages suggests some degree of political hierarchy, and ethnographic accounts of Aleut peoples suggests social ranking was an important feature of sociopolitical organization. High-ranking individuals held some political authority and were expected to coordinate regional groups of villages.

**Aleutian**
(5500–250 B.P.)

A good example of an Aleutian village is the site of **Korovinski**, located on the north coast of Atka Island in the central Aleutians. The site contains thirty-three Aleutian house depressions and several small burial mounds. The houses are located near the shore on a small spit of land. Each house was oval, semisubterranean, and probably housed a single nuclear family. Within the village and its associated midden were found chipped stone projectile points, knives, scrapers, bone harpoons, spears,

**Korovinski**
(Aleutian Islands, Aleutian)

FIGURE **8.9**

Dorset bone and ivory tools, illustrating the wide range of forms and the decorations found on many Dorset tradition items.

SOURCE: Moreau S. Maxwell, *Prehistory of the Eastern Arctic*, copyright 1985, Elsevier Science (USA), reproduced with permission from the publisher.

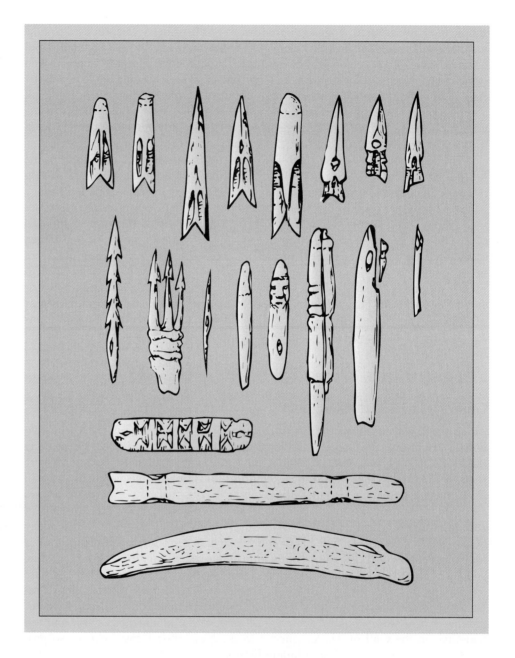

fishhooks, polished stone lamps, and a number of bone and ivory ornaments. Together these offer a fairly clear picture of the simple and utilitarian material culture of the Aleutian peoples. Faunal remains included those of sea mammals, fish, maritime birds, and marine invertebrates. Together with local plant foods such as wild celery, the peoples living at Korovinski were able to maintain a stable, adequate diet.

## North American Subarctic

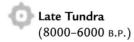

**Late Tundra**
(8000–6000 B.P.)

**Northern Archaic**
(6000–4500 B.P.)

In the interior of the North American Arctic the peoples of the **Late Tundra** (8000–6000 B.P.) and **Northern Archaic** (6000–4500 B.P.) traditions developed an economy focused on exploiting the large herds of caribou that ranged across the tundra. The primary differences between the two traditions are in their technology—Late Tundra peoples used a microlithic technology, while the Northern Archaic peoples did not. The most well-studied sites for both traditions consist of artifact scatters on promontories overlooking caribou migration routes. At these locations small groups would have camped during the summer and fall waiting for the annual

FIGURE **8.10**

A harp seal, one of the many sea mammals hunted by peoples of the North American arctic.

caribou migration, hunting other game in the area, and perhaps collecting berries in season. There also appear to have been winter villages with round, semisubterranean houses, usually referred to as **pit houses,** though only a few have been excavated. These villages consisted of several oval or circular semisubterranean dwellings, probably covered with sod. The few that are known are located near good fishing locales, perhaps in areas where seasonal salmon runs would have provided an abundance of food or in coastal areas where sea mammals could be hunted (see Figure 8.10).

In the western Subarctic, peoples of the **Northwest Microblade** (7000–2000 B.P.) tradition were neighbors of the Northern Archaic peoples. While their name suggests the use of microblades, the Northwest Microblade peoples also used bifacially flaked spearpoints and knives, and a variety of larger blade and flake tools. Bone and wood were almost certainly used for spear shafts, composite tools, and other utensils, but these have not survived. Northwest Microblade settlements tended to be located on lakes, which provided both a source of water and fish. Evidence of extensive obsidian trade among Northwest Microblade peoples suggests that lakes and rivers may also have served as "highways" for movement across the western Subarctic, probably in skin or bark canoes. Northwest Microblade sites are small and suggest occupation by only a few people—perhaps no more than one or two families. There has been no evidence of housing found, suggesting that dwellings may have been simple tents or above-ground wood and brush structures. Peoples of the Northwest Microblade tradition practiced what appears to be a broad-spectrum regime of hunting, fishing, and gathering.

The Northwest Microblade people were followed by the peoples of the **Proto-Athapaskan** (2000–150 B.P.) tradition, whose patterns of life survived into the historic period. Proto-Athapaskan sites are found throughout the western subarctic, in all kinds of environments and locations. This broad settlement pattern reflects the broad-spectrum hunting-fishing-gathering lifestyle that the Proto-Athapaskan peoples followed. Most habitations were short-term and in a location where local resources were plentiful—for example, a prime fishing stream, an area where cranberries or blueberries were in season, a caribou migration crossing, or the like. Housing was simple and mobile—skin tents were used and simple brush shelters were constructed (see Figure 8.11). In winter a more substantial semisubterranean sod house might be built in an area rich with game and fish, in which several families

**Pit houses:** round, semisubterranean dwellings, often covered with a thatch or sod roof.

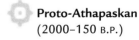 **Northwest Microblade** (7000–2000 B.P.)

**Proto-Athapaskan** (2000–150 B.P.)

FIGURE **8.11**

Tents used by these historic Sarcee peoples are probably similar to those used by peoples of the Proto-Athapaskan tradition.

might live and hunt together until spring. In the summer large groups of Proto-Athapaskan people would come together at prime fishing spots to socialize, trade, and perform ceremonies.

While Proto-Athapaskan peoples did hunt, gather, and fish broadly, caribou remained the primary source of food—at most sites representing 90 percent or more of the faunal remains. To hunt caribou, Proto-Athapaskan peoples watched seasonal migration routes and worked cooperatively to surround and dispatch the animals. In some locations they built corrals into which caribou would be driven and held until ready to butcher. Of course, hunting of single or small groups of caribou also went on during nonmigration periods. During these times small game such as hare, beaver, muskrat, and wildfowl were important, as were the more rarely encountered large game such as bear and moose. Fish were important year-round. Proto-Athapaskan technology was simple. Flaked stone knives, projectile points, scrapers, and the like were common. Polished stone axes and adzes were used to cut and work wood. Wood, bone, and antler were used for spear and arrow shafts, handles, barbed fish spears, snowshoes, needles, and many other items. Some groups made ceramics, but containers were more commonly made from hide or birch bark.

Like other subarctic groups, the peoples of the **Shield Archaic** (6000–3000 B.P.) tradition in the eastern Subarctic developed a broad-spectrum hunting and gathering lifeway, with a focus on caribou and fish. They hunted using flaked stone projectile points, butchered and worked hide with flaked stone knives and scrapers. The Shield Archaic peoples also made use of local copper to make tools. Tools fashioned from copper include spear points, knives, and fishhooks. Interestingly, there is a lack of polished stone tools, suggesting woodworking was not important in Shield Archaic life. The Shield Archaic peoples lived in small nomadic groups of one or two nuclear families and moved seasonally to exploit locally abundant resources such as berries when in season, fish when spawning, and caribou during migrations. Settlements were small and short-term, although relatively deep deposits on some sites suggest they were reoccupied annually over a long period of time. House floors on these sites suggest the use of simple brush and bark shelters or skin tents.

The Shield Archaic peoples were followed by peoples of the **Initial Shield Woodland** (2160–600 B.P.) tradition, who emphasized a broad-spectrum subsistence strategy similar to the Shield Archaic peoples, but who also manufactured ceramics. These ceramics are grit tempered and thin walled and appear to be very well made,

**Shield Archaic**
(6000–3000 B.P.)

**Initial Shield Woodland**
(2160–600 B.P.)

considering they are the first ceramics in the region. They typically have a conical base and a smooth finish, perhaps with some rim or lip decoration. In addition to ceramics, Initial Shield Woodland peoples also made chipped stone projectile points, knives, and scrapers. Small, triangular points are common, suggesting the bow and arrow was used. Cold-hammered copper was used for awls, gouges, and fishhooks. Bone and antler were used for items such as awls, scrapers, barbed fish spears, and harpoons, including toggling harpoons. These tools were used in an economy focused on fishing and hunting deer, elk, and moose in the dense boreal forests of the region. Wild rice may have been harvested by groups in the south, and berries and nuts were probably collected when available.

Initial Shield Woodland sites tend to be small and short-term, consisting of a thin scatter of artifacts and the remains of one or two oval house floors. Sites tend to be located close to lakes or rivers with abundant fish. Houses were apparently built on a wooden frame covered by skins or bark. They had a central hearth and usually one or more storage pits dug near the hearth. At the **Ballynacree** site on the Winnipeg River in southwest Ontario, for example, the remains of three such houses were found. Each was approximately 4 by 8 meters in size, had an entrance facing east, and had a bench built along the western wall, perhaps for sleeping. Floor stains suggest either pine boughs or woven mats were used as carpeting. There is also evidence for racks located outside of the structures, perhaps for drying meat and fish or for working hides.

**Ballynacree**
(Ontario, Initial Shield Woodland)

## Northwest Coast

The northwest coast of North America forms a unique environment, in many ways similar to the Asian coast of the Sea of Okhotsk (see Figure 8.2). On the Northwest Coast a range of high, rugged mountains come directly down to the sea, leaving only a narrow shoreline. The effect of the mountains and the warm waters flowing northward with the Japanese current create a unique climate along the coast—one where temperatures are moderated and rainfall is abundant. Dense boreal rainforest dominates the slopes of the mountains, and large rivers run from their tops carrying runoff to the sea. Each year huge numbers of anadromous fish return to these rivers to spawn. A wide array of fish live in the moderate waters of the coast and Gulf of Alaska, and the many islands are used as colonies for sea mammals and maritime birds. In short, the environment is remarkably rich, and the peoples that lived along the Northwest Coast took full use of these riches.

The peoples of the **Early Northwest Coast** (9500–5500 B.P.) tradition developed an economy based on the exploitation of sea mammals and fish. They used crude pebble tools and the flakes struck from them, along with well-made leaf-shaped projectile points. A few bone and antler harpoons have been found, and it is likely the Early Northwest Coast peoples also used nets and boats to fish in the ocean, but these have not survived. Sites are located on the coast or along major inland waterways such as the Columbia and Frasier Rivers, allowing easy access to fish and marine resources. Few features and no houses have been recovered, which suggests houses were either tents or brush structures that left no remains.

**Early Northwest Coast**
(9500–5500 B.P.)

The Early Northwest Coast tradition developed into the **Middle Northwest Coast** (5500–1500 B.P.) tradition, which is characterized by the emergence of sedentary villages along the coast. Like the Early Northwest Coast peoples, those of the Middle Northwest Coast tradition relied heavily on fish and sea mammals, but the presence of large shell middens also suggests an increased importance of shellfish. By about 3000 B.P. large winter villages began to develop along the coasts. These were inhabited by several to several dozen households, each resident in a large, rectangular post-and-plank structure (see Figure 8.12). Households consisted of ten to twelve people forming a single extended family. During the spring and summer these families would split up to hunt, fish, and gather independently, but would return in the fall and live off stored resources during the winter. Winter was a time of community ceremonies, storytelling, and craft work. Remains of woven

**Middle Northwest Coast** (5500–1500 B.P.)

FIGURE **8.12**
An historic Haida house
similar to those first
constructed by peoples of
the Middle Northwest Coast
tradition.

FIGURE **8.12**
An historic Haida house
similar to those first
constructed by peoples of
the Middle Northwest Coast
tradition.

capes, baskets, cedar plank boxes, and carved wood and horn suggest some of the craft items that might have been made during the winter.

## Chiefs and Chiefdoms

Middle Northwest Coast winter villages were relatively large, with several hundred residents being common. In such large villages some authority to keep order is typically found, and it is likely that something like the **chiefs** that were present in the historic period developed by this time. Chiefs are typically defined as individuals who base political authority on their high status rather than on ability or the use of force. A **chiefdom,** then, is a society having a central political figure whose authority rests on status rather than force. A chief is typically born into the position, although there are cases where chiefs are elected or appointed. Even in these cases, however, chiefs typically come from a high-status social group, such as a particular **descent group.** Indeed, chiefs are often the heads of a high-status descent group, and being head of that group automatically conveys the position of chief.

Descent is a concept that we all understand, but we don't often comprehend how powerful a tool descent can be for organizing people and resources. In North America and Europe, most people inherit their surname from their father. All the people who share a last name can be thought of as a descent group, with membership defined by sharing the same last name. In anthropology one would call this a **patrilineal** descent group, because membership is inherited through the father (if we normally obtained our last names from our mothers, then descent would be **matrilineal**). In societies where descent groups are used to organize people and resources, members of the same descent group recognize one another as a single social, economic, and political unit—sort of like a single large family. If we had patrilineal descent groups in our society, I would consider all people with the last name Peregrine as my close relatives—my brothers and sisters, even as my parents

**Chiefs:** political leaders who base authority on high status rather than on the use of force.

**Chiefdom:** a polity having a central political figure whose authority rests on status rather than force.

**Descent group:** a group of people who share descent from a common ancestor.

**Patrilineal:** descent traced through fathers.

**Matrilineal:** descent traced through mothers.

if they were in my parent's generation. My position in society would be defined by the position of the Peregrine descent group. The Peregrine descent group would control a set of resources, such as land, boats, or fishing rights to particular rivers, and I would gain access to those resources through my birth into the Peregrine patrilineage. Similarly, the Peregrine descent group would play a particular role in society—perhaps coordinating ritual or warfare—and I would therefore take on the responsibilities of that role simply through my birth into the Peregrine patrilineage.

How do chiefs emerge out of descent groups? First consider a family of five in a society where men are typically the rulers—father and mother and three children. Who is the "ruler" of the family? Probably the father. Who is the "ruler" among the children? Probably the oldest son. If a descent group grew out of this family, which group would have the responsibility of providing leadership for the society? The group that traces its ancestry to the oldest son, and that's how chiefs emerge out of descent groups—they are the oldest son of the oldest son of the oldest son. After a few generations, the actual links to ancestors become unclear, and most descent groups have a status affixed to them as being "elder" or "younger" based on links to the past that are assumed or even mythical (some descent groups, such as **clans**, trace ancestry back to mythical founders of the society). So, chiefs are leaders of high-status descent groups.

Being the leader of a high-status descent group is often not sufficient to be recognized as a chief. Chiefs often need to demonstrate that they are chiefs through their behavior as well as through descent, and in many descent groups the position of chief is not entirely clear—there may be rivals who share equivalent or nearly equivalent positions in the descent group, and hence they are equally qualified by descent to be chief. What kinds of behaviors or duties do chiefs have to perform? Often chiefs are expected to have supernatural power to cause or cure illness, or to ensure safety and prosperity for the group. If a chief cannot demonstrate such power, a rival may take the position. Sometimes chiefs are expected to excel in warfare or food production and, again, if they cannot demonstrate such excellence, they may lose their position. Most often chiefs are expected to be generous and to give away vast amounts of wealth on a regular basis. If chiefs are not competent and savvy enough to regularly acquire wealth to give away, again they will lose their position.

In the historic period, chiefs along the Northwest Coast gave away wealth in a competitive event called the **potlatch.** During a potlatch, chiefs would attempt to embarrass or overwhelm rivals through the sheer volume of material they gave away or even destroyed. The potlatch was meant to be an overt display of wealth and generosity that demonstrated a chief's ability to be chief. Evidence of copper and obsidian obtained through long-distance trade during the Middle Northwest Coast tradition suggests that perhaps something like the historic potlatch may have started during this tradition. The size of individual dwellings increased dramatically over time, and several more specific changes such as the emergence of labrets, found only with women, suggest that matrilineal descent groups may have developed during the Middle Northwest Coast tradition. Since the ethnographic record demonstrates that matrilineal descent and generosity were the foundations upon which the authority of Northwest Coast chiefs were based in the historic period, it seems reasonable to argue that chiefs first developed during the Middle Northwest Coast tradition, when evidence for these two foundations are first found.

By 1500 B.P. the **Late Northwest Coast** (1500–200 B.P.) tradition had developed, which is associated with the historic peoples of the Northwest Coast. These peoples lived in large, sedentary villages composed of numerous multifamily houses. Houses were large, rectangular post-and-beam constructions covered with wood planks. Some houses were as much as several hundred square meters in area and contained numerous interior walls separating individual family spaces. A low platform was often built along the walls for sleeping. At the center of the houses was a large hearth and common area. Houses were arranged linearly along the coast, with their

**Clan:** a descent group that traces ancestry back to mythical founders of the society.

**Potlatch:** an event among Northwest Coast peoples in which chiefs gave away vast amounts of wealth in order to demonstrate power and embarrass other chiefs.

**Late Northwest Coast** (1500–200 B.P.)

# Yuquot

The Yuquot site, located on the southeastern end of Nootka Island off the west coast of Vancouver Island, British Columbia, represents the remains of a Late Northwest Coast village. Although the Late Northwest Coast village is perhaps the most important aspect of the archaeological deposits at Yuquot, the area was occupied continuously for more than 4,000 years, and there was a permanent village at the site from roughly 1200 B.P. to the present day. Thus, Yuquot also represents a prime Northwest Coast village location on a protected inlet with abundant fresh water sources from mountain streams. Both marine mammals and fish were easily obtainable from the ocean, and the inland hemlock forests provided roots, berries, deer, bear, and small game.

Excavations at Yuquot were begun in 1966 by archaeologists John Dewhirst and Bill Folan. The site consisted of a linear midden stretching parallel to the beach some 200 meters, and from 30 to over 60 meters wide and up to 5 meters high. The contemporary village was built atop the site, so Dewhirst and Folan had to limit their excavation to a single 5-meter trench through the midden. Despite the limited excavation area, Dewhirst and Folan located over 7,400 artifacts, 240,000 ecofacts, and 9 human burials. These represent one of the largest and most well-documented collections of Late Northwest Coast material in existence.

The materials collected at Yuquot showed that the site's residents engaged in a wide variety of activities. Tools were manufactured and repaired at the site, fishing was extensive, hunting for both inland and sea mammals, including whales, took place, and personal ornaments were created. It is likely that Yuquot was inhabited during the winter and through to the late summer—a time when the ocean would have provided the most resources to the Yuquot peoples. During the fall, people would move inland to harvest salmon, which were dried and returned to the village to be stored for the winter. Fall was also a time to hunt and collect berries inland. Once winter approached, people would return to the village and again focus on ocean resources.

SOURCE: Folan, William, and John Dewhirst, *The Yuquot Project,* Volumes 1–3 (Ottawa: Canadian National Historic Parks and Sites Branch, 1980–1981).

entrances facing the ocean. Villages ranged in size from perhaps 100 to more than 1,000 residents. Each matrilineal house had a chief, and these house chiefs together formed the core of village leadership. The chief of the highest-ranked matrilineal house served as village chief, although his powers were limited and for most activities the house chief was the preeminent leader. There are a number of well-studied villages dating to the Late Northwest Coast tradition, one of which, the **Yuquot** site on Nootka Island, is described in the box feature.

As in earlier traditions, subsistence was based on fish, sea mammals, and sea invertebrates. Fishing and hunting of sea mammals was done from large plank

**Yuquot**
**(British Columbia,**
**Late Northwest**
**Coast)**

boats, from which animals as large as whales were hunted. Salmon were important to most groups because of their large numbers and predictability. Plant foods of various kinds were also collected on the mountain slopes and in river valleys, and hunting of deer and small game was also done. Meat and plant foods were dried, smoked, or kept in oil to preserve them for use during the winter, when hunting and collecting virtually ceased. The technology used by the Late Northwest Coast peoples was simple. Flaked and polished stone tools were used for cutting, hide processing, and woodworking. Bone and antler were used for harpoons and handles, as well as for awls and scrapers. Wood was used for items ranging from bowls to boxes to spear and arrow shafts. Ceramics were not manufactured, but woven and skin bags, as well as wooden boxes and bowls, served well for storage.

Art was abundant among the Late Northwest Coast peoples. While small ornaments such as labrets and beads, made of stone, copper, and ivory, were common, the Late Northwest Coast is best known for its extensive woodcarving. The range of items that received decoration is staggering—roof beams, doorways, pillars, house fronts, boats, and other large surfaces were sometimes covered completely with carved anthropomorphic designs. Small items such as boxes and other wooden utensils received similar decorations. In some areas woven textiles were made, while in others copper was fashioned into large, decorated sheets. Masks used in winter ceremonies range widely in design and style, and rank among the world's greatest works of art (see Color Plate 12). Finally, the famed totem poles placed before houses to indicate the lineage membership of its inhabitants are well recognized as significant works of art.

## ❧ SUMMARY

The Arctic and Subarctic were colonized by big-game hunters during the Upper Paleolithic, and many aspects of their cultures appear to have continued throughout prehistory. Hunting-fishing-gathering economies dominated the region in prehistory, and life in small, nomadic or seminomadic groups was typical. With this in mind it is interesting that coastal populations on both sides of the Bering Sea developed sedentary and apparently more socially and politically complex cultures than other groups in the region. A major factor may have been their heavy reliance on marine resources, an emphasis which allowed a degree of sedentism that was not possible elsewhere in the region. While it is true that over time inland populations in both North America and northern Asia tended to become more efficient at exploiting a broad range of plant and animal resources, allowing them to remain sedentary at least seasonally, inland populations never achieved the range of material culture or sociopolitical complexity found among peoples on both coastlines. Finally, the populations of the high arctic developed sophisticated adaptations to the harsh environment very early in prehistory, adaptations that have in many ways continued to today. These include a focus on caribou or reindeer (ultimately domesticated in northern Asia) and marine mammals, and a sociopolitical organization that combines a highly nomadic lifestyle with seasonal communal gatherings.

## ❧ DISCUSSION QUESTIONS

1. What is a chiefdom, and how do chiefs obtain political authority?
2. The Arctic and Subarctic seem marginal environments for human habitation. Why did humans begin living there, and why did they persist?
3. The North Asian and North American Arctic have been connected to a greater or lesser extent for at least the past 12,000 years. In what ways are the prehistory of the two areas similar? In what ways are they different? What effect has the connection had on the prehistory of each area?

## ✿ ESSAY QUESTIONS

1. This is the first of the "culture history" chapters in the book, and it presents a strongly materialist picture of prehistory; that is, it focuses largely on the material record of the past—technology, housing, economy, and the like. Why this materialist perspective? How does the chapter's materialist focus shape the way prehistory is seen or understood? What is missing from the chapter because of its materialist focus?

2. It is interesting that sedentary societies developed both the Northwest coast and the Asian coast of the Sea of Okhotsh. Use library and Internet resources to explore the environments of these two areas and the specific ways the peoples living there have used them. In what ways are the two areas similar? In what ways do they differ? Why did sedentary societies develop in these locations and not in other parts of the Arctic and Subarctic?

3. Reindeer or caribou were basic to subsistence in both the Asian and North American Arctic and Subarctic, yet in Asia these animals became domesticated, while in North America they did not. Use library and Internet resources to examine the use of reindeer and caribou in the two areas, both historically and prehistorically. Why were reindeer domesticated in Asia and caribou not domesticated in North America?

## ✒ RESEARCH PROJECT

The Arctic is an energy-poor environment, and yet for humans to live in the Arctic they must obtain more energy than those living in warm climates in order to survive the cold. How do humans accomplish this? Research the animals hunted and the fish and other food collected by arctic peoples, and reconstruct the food chain from its base in plants and ocean microorganisms to humans. Where do the animals, fish, and other foods that humans rely on in the Arctic obtain energy to grow? How important is movement from warmer climates (where there is more solar energy) to the Arctic for the survival of these animals? Do arctic peoples obtain energy from warmer climates by relying on migratory animals and fish?

## ✿ KEY SOURCES

### North Asia

Ackerman, 1982; Chernetsov and Moszynska, 1974; Chernykh, 1992; Derevianko, 1990, 1998; Goebel, 2001a, 2001b, 2001c, 2001d; Goebel and Peregrine, 2001; Larichev, Khol'ushkin, and Laricheva, 1988, 1990; Link and Weber, 2001; Mochanov, 1969; Okladnikov, 1959, 1965, 1970, 1990; Pitul'ko, 1993, 2001; Pitul'ko and Kasparov, 1996; Powers, 1973; Slobodin, 1999, 2001a, 2001b, 2001c; Sulimurski, 1970; Vasil'ev, 1993; Weber, 1994, 1995.

### North America

Ackerman, 1992, 2001a, 2001b; Ames, 1994; Ames and Maschner, 1999; Anderson, 1968, 1970, 1988; Bockstoce, 1979; Borden, 1975; Carlson and Bona, 1996; Clark, D.W., 1979, 1991, 1992, 1997, 2001a, 2001b, 2001c; Clark, G.H., 1977; Coupland, 1998, 2001; DeLaguna, 1975; Dumond, 1981, 1987, 2001a, 2001b; Erlandson, Tveskov, and Byram, 1998; Fitzhugh and Crowell, 1988; Fladmark, 1990; Giddings, 1964; Giddings and Anderson, 1986; Helmer, VanDyke, and Kense, 1977; Henn, 1978; Laughlin, 1980; Linname, 1975; Martindale, 2001; Mason, 1981, 2001; Matson and Coupland, 1995; Maxwell, 1976, 1985; McCartney and Veltre, 2001; McGhee, 1990, 1996; Moss and Erlandson, 1998; Park, 2001; Schledermann, 1990; Stoltman, 1973; West, 1981, 1996; Workman, 1992; Wright, 1967, 1972, 1995.

## THE INUKIAK ESKIMOS

In Chapter 7, we saw how Upper Paleolithic peoples adapted to a full range of environments and learned how to exploit native species of animals and plants almost everywhere on earth. This chapter discusses the adaptations necessary to survive in possibly the harshest environments of all: the Arctic. The Arctic is a region of almost perpetual ice covering both land and sea. The sea contains almost all of the life in this region. Adaptations to the Arctic involve living on the ice and exploiting sea life—both fish and mammals. The tundra environment, just south of the Arctic ice, is also very cold and covered with ice for much of the year. But during the cold summers, plants—including grasses—take hold on the tundra. Caribou live here during the summer months, along with musk oxen. Thus hunting turns to land mammals in tundra areas of the Arctic.

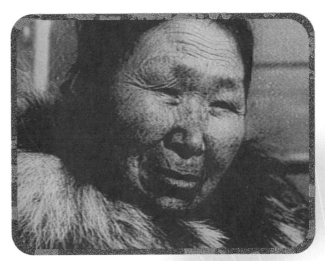

**The Media Lab can be found in Chapter 8 on the** *Companion Website*™ http://www.prenhall.com/peregrine

### WEB ACTIVITY

The Inukiak Eskimos who live along the Arctic coast of Alaska have adapted to one of the harshest climates on earth. The video "The Story of Nanukalaq" displays many of the cultural adaptations these people have made to the Arctic environment.

### Activity

1. View the video. Based on what you see of the Inukiak material culture and what you have read in Chapter 8, describe the cultural adaptations made by these people to their environment. Speculate on how these adaptations were invented.

2. What skills must a young Inukiak learn in order to be a successful whale hunter? Whom would a young Inukiak child turn to for knowledge?

3. What are the dangers of new ice? How does an Inukiak determine that ice is new? Do the Inukiak have to be more knowledgeable about their physical environment than we do? Why?

# North America

**o v e r v i e w**

North America was first populated by Upper Paleolithic peoples, but as we saw in the chapter on the Upper Paleolithic world, there is no clear consensus about when or how people came to North America. Most archaeologists agree that one way humans came to North America was across Beringia, a landmass joining Asia and North America that was exposed by the lowering of sea levels during the last ice age. Most archaeologists also agree that people were in North America by 11,000 B.P., and many archaeologists believe there is good evidence of earlier inhabitants. Beyond that, there is much debate.

The environments of North America changed rapidly at the end of the Upper Paleolithic. Glacial ice sheets that covered the midcontinent as far south as Chicago retreated and opened large areas of land. The Great Lakes, formed by the action of the glaciers, filled with glacial meltwaters and became the largest expanse of fresh water on the planet. The Great Plains were formed from glacial outwash, and, later, the major river valleys cut their way through them. As the glaciers retreated, forests moved northward and covered most of eastern North America, while grasslands became well-established on the glacial outwash plains. The environment changed less dramatically to the west of the Rocky Mountains, but those areas experienced the same general warming trend as the rest of the continent. And all areas of North America witnessed a dramatic decline in large animal species.

By around 8000 B.P., five major environmental zones had developed in North America (Figure 9.1). These environmental zones are: the Eastern Woodlands, the Great Plains, the Southwest, the Plateau, and California. While there is great diversity (both cultural and environmental) in each of these zones and none of them has clear boundaries, each does represent a rather distinct group of archaeological traditions. Thus North American archaeologists have often found that a five "culture area" division provides a useful framework for looking at the prehistory of North America (Figure 9.2).

## EASTERN WOODLANDS

The Eastern Woodlands of North America are dominated by **deciduous forests** (Figure 9.1). In the far south, mangrove swamps line the coast, and southern pine forests are present farther inland. Oak-hickory forests dominate the central regions of the Eastern Woodlands, blending into birch-maple forests as one moves farther north. A wide range of birds and mammals call the Eastern Woodlands home, particularly deer, squirrel, fox, bear, turkey, and duck. Fish, shellfish, and reptiles are plentiful in the many rivers and lakes that wander through the region. The forests themselves produce an abundance of nuts and seeds. The region as a whole is characterized by a mild climate, with warm summers and cool winters.

As glaciers retreated and broadleaf forests spread northward, people living in the Eastern Woodlands began to rely more on smaller, forest-dwelling game species and resources. The peoples of the **Early Eastern Archaic** (10,000–8000 B.P.) tradition began settling in small residential "base camps" that moved seasonally and sometimes combined into larger "macroband" camps. A single band consisting of several families and perhaps ten to fifteen people occupied most base camps, while several bands probably resided together at macroband camps. No evidence of housing has been found, but archaeologists have speculated that simple brush shelters or skin tents were used.

Like other groups at the end of the Upper Paleolithic, the Early Eastern Archaic peoples appear to have adapted to changing conditions by significantly broadening the range of plants and animals they subsisted upon. Deer became the primary game species, and were hunted with spears armed with large, bifacially flaked projectile points and propelled with the aid of a spear thrower. Smaller game such as squirrels,

**Early Eastern Archaic**
(10,000–8000 B.P.)

**Deciduous forests:**
forests comprised of trees that lose their leaves in the winter.

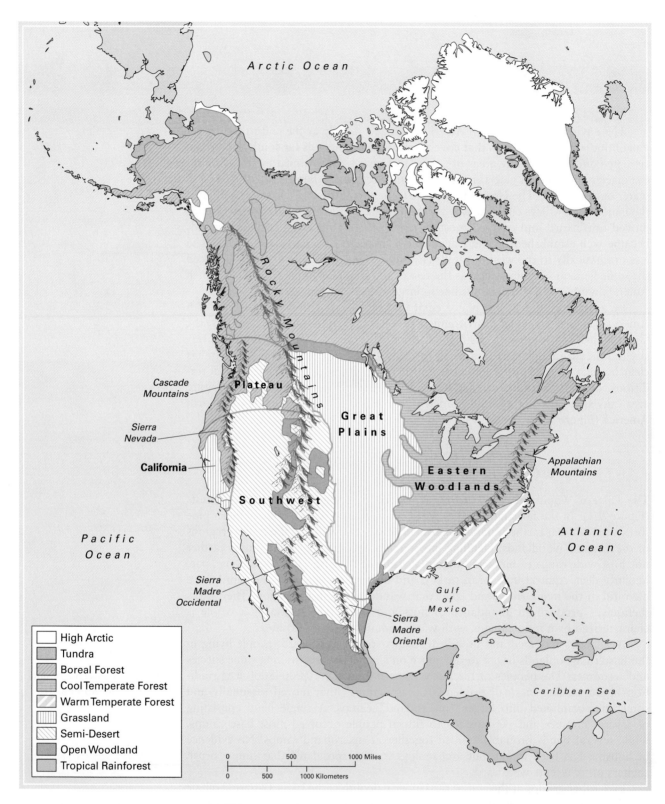

FIGURE **9.1**
Environments of North America.

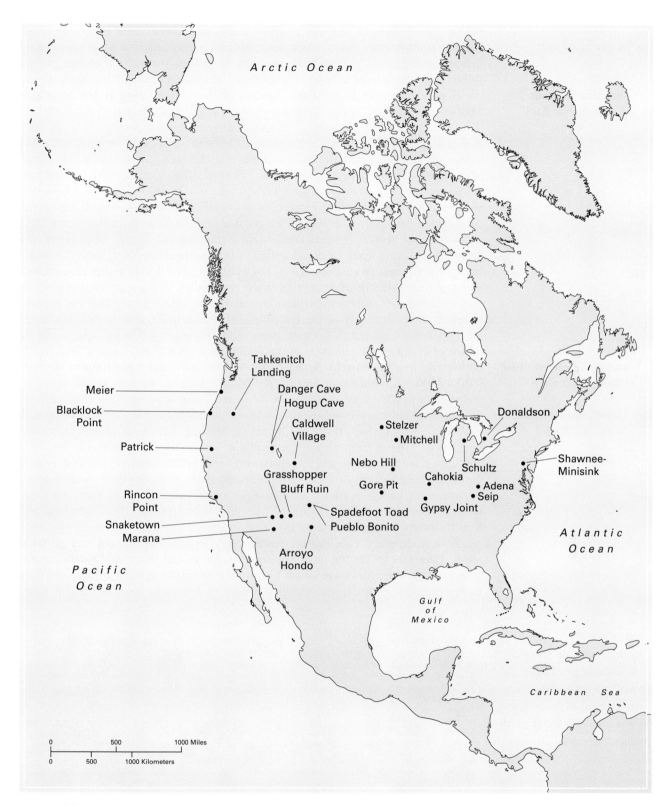

FIGURE **9.2**
Sites discussed in Chapter 9.

rabbits, and fish were also taken. Nuts, including acorns, were important plant foods, but many other seeds, fruits, and roots were also collected using woven baskets and netted bags. A key addition to the Early Eastern Archaic tool kit was ground stone tools, which were used to process nuts and seeds, and to cut and work wood.

A good example of an Early Eastern Archaic base camp is the **Shawnee-Minisink** site in the upper Delaware River valley of northeastern Pennsylvania (Figure 9.2). There were two distinct Early Eastern Archaic occupations of the site, both dating around 9000 B.P. Stone tools were the most frequent artifact, and some sixty tools and cores were found. Tool types included side- and corner-notched projectile points, knives, scrapers, blades, and worked flakes, among others. About half of these were made from locally available stone. Two hearths were found, and surrounding these hearths were large "living floors" with abundant and compacted debris from daily life. The picture we get from the Shawnee-Minisink site is of a small group of people, living at the site for a short period of time on perhaps two different occasions. They worked locally available stone while there, as well as stone brought with them from elsewhere. They collected plant foods and perhaps fished and captured turtles or other reptiles in the river valley. In the surrounding uplands they collected nuts and firewood, and hunted deer and small game. This site appears to reflect the typical way of life for people of the Early Eastern Archaic tradition.

Populations started to become more sedentary and to develop more efficient means of hunting and collecting in the deciduous forests of the Eastern Woodlands during the **Middle Eastern Archaic** (8000–6000 B.P.) and **Late Eastern Archaic** (6000–3000 B.P.) traditions. During the Middle Eastern Archaic tradition settlements seem to have been seasonal, in many areas switching between riverine locations during the summer and upland locations during the winter. Most communities were small, with perhaps thirty to fifty people residing together in several individual households. Houses themselves were circular structures roughly 4 meters in diameter, and were relatively simple and impermanent. Some permanent settlements appeared during the Late Eastern Archaic tradition, particularly along the Gulf coast, but also in some river valley locations. Communities remained small, even the permanent ones. Houses remained simple domed huts, and were typically circular to oval and 4 to 10 meters in length (Figure 9.3).

Both Middle and Late Eastern Archaic peoples relied on hunted and gathered foods. Deer was by far the most important game animal, but many smaller mammals, birds, and reptiles were taken. Fish were important for many Middle and Late Eastern Archaic peoples, and shellfish became a dominant food source for some

◆ **Shawnee-Minisink** (Pennsylvania, Early Eastern Archaic)

◆ **Middle Eastern Archaic** (8000–6000 B.P.)

◆ **Late Eastern Archaic** (6000–3000 B.P.)

FIGURE **9.3**
This drawing of an historic Native American village shows bark-covered domed houses similar to those used by peoples of the Late Eastern Archaic tradition.

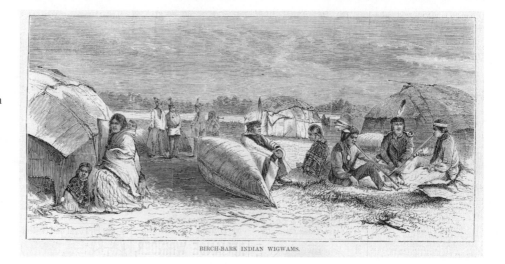

BIRCH-BARK INDIAN WIGWAMS.

groups in the Midwest and Midsouth. Nuts, particularly acorn, walnut, and hickory, were important plant foods and were gathered in great quantities in the fall. Fruits such as grape and blackberry were also important. Many other regionally available plants and roots were used as well, among the more important were goosefoot, sumpweed, and sunflower, all of which produce edible seeds, and both squash and bottle gourd. Interestingly, these plant species began to be domesticated by Middle Eastern Archaic peoples starting around 7000 B.P., and were fully domesticated during the Late Eastern Archaic tradition.

**Domestication:**
process through which humans manipulate plant or animals species to enhance desirable features and eliminate undesirable ones.

## Domestication

**Domestication** refers to a process through which humans manipulate plant or animals species to enhance desirable features and eliminate undesirable ones. For example, both squash and bottle gourd developed thinner rinds and larger seeds between about 7000 and 4000 B.P. Why? It seems likely that Eastern Archaic peoples ate the seeds of these plants, and so encouraged the growth of plants with larger seeds. People also dried the rind of these plants and used them for containers. A thinner rind would dry more quickly than a thick one, and therefore plants with thinner rinds may have been encouraged to grow.

For seed plants such as goosefoot, sumpweed, and sunflower, the seeds themselves became larger between about 4000 B.P. and 3000 B.P., and the seed coats thinner and more brittle, allowing them to be broken more easily. How might these changes have been brought about? One theory is that they occurred by chance, as peoples selectively harvested plants with desirable characteristics. These plants would have been carried back to base camps, and new plants with the desired characteristics would have grown from discarded seeds at these locations. Hence, with human help, plants with desired characteristics would have been more widely distributed than others, and over time would have become the most prevalent variations of the species. Another theory for domestication is that people actively sowed seeds from plants with desired characteristics near their base camps or in other suitable locations to ensure there were plenty of those plants around, and that one would not have to go far to harvest them. The truth is probably a combination of these two theories. The selective harvesting of plants with desired characteristics would have given the plants a greater distribution, and active sowing would have only increased the distribution of these plants. Thus, over time, domesticated varieties of plants would come to be prevalent in the environment, and certainly in the archaeological record.

Domesticated plants were only one of the technological innovations made by the Middle and Late Eastern Archaic peoples. In the region around the Great Lakes copper became an important raw material for making tools such as spear points and knives, as well as for personal ornaments such as beads and bracelets (Figure 9.4). Copper was worked cold, by pounding raw ingots into a desired shape. Even where copper was used, however, stone remained the primary raw material for tools. Both the Middle and Late Eastern Archaic peoples made distinctive stemmed projectile points and used chipped stone for knives, scrapers, drills, and the like. Ground and polished stone tools became widely used, and new styles of axes, adzes, and celts appeared. Some polished stone items, particularly knives, spear-thrower weights, and gorgets, were of great artistry and were made from stone clearly selected because of its color or grain. Some of this stone was apparently traded over long distances. Soapstone, carved into bowls used for cooking, was also traded widely. Woven baskets and netted bags were used for storage.

Ceramics were first introduced into the Eastern Woodlands by peoples of the **Early Eastern Woodland** (3000–2100 B.P.) tradition. These early ceramics were often crude and thick, and tempered with grit. Over time the ceramics became thinner and

**Early Eastern Woodland** (3000–2100 B.P.)

FIGURE **9.4**
Archaic copper tools from Wisconsin, including a large gaff hook (*top*), a tanged knife (*middle*), and a socketed spear point (*bottom*).

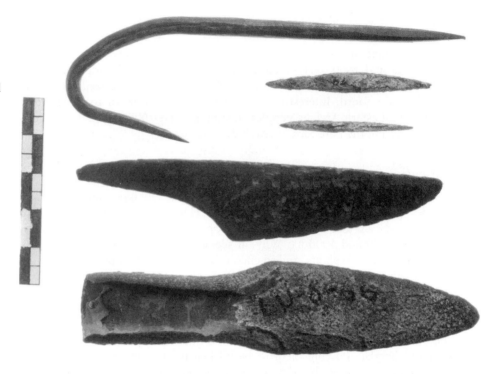

were sometimes decorated with stamping or cord marking. Chipped and ground stone tools were in many ways similar to those used by Eastern Archaic peoples. Chipped stone projectile points and knives were often large and lanceolate in shape, and ground stone axes and celts were common. Bone, shell, and antler were used for a variety of tools and personal ornaments, and trade in marine shell had become important. Other materials traded by Early Eastern Woodland peoples included copper, galena, mica, pipestone, rhyolite, and other exotic stones. It seems clear that formal trade networks cutting across the Eastern Woodlands were established during the Early Eastern Woodland tradition.

Early Eastern Woodland communities were semisedentary, with large base camps housing a dozen or more families for months at a time and with smaller groups leaving the base camp for shorter periods of time to hunt or procure special resources. These base camps were located near floodplain soils where desired plants grew and could be cultivated, and within short distance of both uplands, where wood was obtained and most hunting and collecting was done, and fresh water. These communities consisted of five or six circular structures made of posts supporting bark walls, roughly 5 meters in diameter, each probably housing a single family of five to ten people. Thus communities typically ranged in size from thirty to fifty inhabitants. Smaller sites, often upland hunting camps, housed only single families, and usually consisted of a single domed "wigwam"-like structure.

**Schultz** (Michigan, Early Eastern Woodland)

A good example of an Early Eastern Woodland base camp is the **Schultz** site, located at the junction of the Tittawbawassee and Saginaw rivers in east-central Michigan. The site was situated on the floodplain of the Tittawbawassee river, and was surrounded by mixed hardwood forests and swamplands where both forest and riverine resources were within easy reach. The site itself consists of scattered artifacts covering an area of about 370 square meters. A total of thirty hearths have been located, which probably represent the locations of dwellings. A number of postholes, pits, and other features have been found on the site, but no clear remains of structures. It is thought that at any given time the site probably had two to four structures and associated work areas, with perhaps twenty-five people in residence.

Floral and faunal remains from the site suggest it was a seasonal base camp occupied in the early summer and again in the fall. Shellfish were collected in the early summer, and domesticated plants were sown. In the fall, plants were harvested and nuts from the surrounding forests were collected and processed. Hunting took place during both seasons.

Early Eastern Woodland peoples continued experimentation with domesticated plants that had begun during the preceding Late Eastern Archaic tradition, and these plants became an important part of the subsistence regime in some areas. The primary domesticates were squash and gourd, sumpweed, goosefoot, sunflower, and maygrass. Nuts continued to be important collected foods, as were a variety of non-domesticated plants. Deer and elk were the primary big game animals hunted, but a wide variety of smaller mammals, such as woodchuck, beaver, and raccoon, as well as birds, especially turkey and waterfowl, were also hunted. Fish contributed to the diet of most Early Eastern Woodland peoples and was a staple in some areas, particularly coastal areas. Shellfish were also important to some coastal people and to many other groups as well.

By 2000 B.P. several distinct traditions had developed in the Eastern Woodlands. The **Adena** (2600–1900 B.P.) tradition was the earliest, and was focused in a relatively discrete area around the central and upper Ohio River valley. The Adena peoples lived in settlements dispersed along major river valleys. Settlements were small, containing perhaps twenty-five or thirty people. Houses were round and up to 10 meters in diameter. They were constructed with walls of bark or woven reeds held between two rows of posts, and likely had a conical roof. Adena subsistence was essentially the same as that of the Early Eastern Woodlands peoples—hunting and gathering of woodland and riverine resources supplemented by some domesticated plants. Adena technology was also similar to that of the Early Eastern Woodlands peoples. However, trade seems to have expanded, and raw materials from distant sources are relatively common on Adena sites. These include materials such as copper from the western Great Lakes and marine shell from the Gulf coast. Many of these "exotic" raw materials were fashioned into personal ornaments such as beads, rings, bracelets, and gorgets.

Most Adena communities were associated with particular burial mounds located in the uplands. The separation of residential and burial areas continued among many groups in the Eastern Woodlands until the historic period. Adena mounds were conical and range from a meter to over 20 meters in height. Within these mounds several to several dozen individuals might be buried over a period of several years. For example, the **Adena Mound** (after which the tradition was named), located on the Scioto river in south-central Ohio, was built in two stages. The first included some twenty-three individuals who were buried in several different ways. Seven individuals were buried in log-lined tombs (two individuals were place in one of the tombs) with abundant grave goods, including both personal ornaments and tools. Four individuals were buried in a large central pit tomb, two of whom were cremated. Grave goods were abundant in this central pit as well. The other twelve individuals were buried in the mound itself, and most had some grave goods. The second construction stage included twelve individuals buried in the mound fill, most with grave goods including both personal ornaments and tools. When completed, the mound stood some 8 meters tall and 135 meters in diameter.

Most archaeologists believe Adena mounds represent cemeteries for individual descent groups. The mounds both symbolized the unity of the group, and physically served as a marker of the group's territory, which, it is thought, is why the mounds are often located on ridge tops or other highly visible locations. Analysis of the grave goods in these mounds has suggested to some scholars that Adena society had formal leaders, and perhaps even chiefs. For example, the log-lined tombs and large central pit tomb in the Adena mound suggest that the individuals buried in those

**Adena**
(2600–1900 B.P.)

**Adena Mound**
(Ohio, Adena)

locations held a special status in society. The most likely explanation is that these individuals were descent group leaders who received special treatment when they died.

Peoples of the **Hopewell** (2100–1700 B.P.) tradition continued this basic pattern of separate settlement and burial sites, but expanded the territory in which it was found throughout the Ohio River valley and into southern Michigan and Wisconsin. Analysis of mound and community location has established a picture of a territorially organized settlement system. Mound groups appear to be located with fairly regular spacing along major river systems. Near these mound groups are scattered agricultural hamlets located adjacent to fertile soils. Most hamlets contain only five or six houses and probably fewer than thirty residents. Houses were varied in form; they appear to range from domed **wigwam**-like structures (see Figure 9.3) to more substantial rectangular **wattle-and-daub** structures. Wattle refers to a woven mat of small branches or reeds while daub is mud; thus, wattle-and-daub structures have mat walls covered with mud to form a solid and relatively substantial enclosure.

Mound groups also varied. Some contained only one or two mounds, while others contained multiple mounds which, in some cases, were enclosed by geometric earthworks. One of the most famous of these is the **Seip Mound** State Memorial near Chilicothe, Ohio. The site consists of three geometric earthwork enclosures, about a meter in height, representing two circles and a square (Figure 9.5). These earthworks touch one another, and there are small passages between them. Together, the three enclosures cover an area of roughly 50 hectares. Within the enclosures are a number of small mounds, a larger group of three joined mounds, and a large, rectangular central mound. The mounds were used for burials and rituals. The main mound at Seip, for example, was built over a large public or ritual structure that was purposely burned and capped. Other mounds were built above central crypts. Additional burials and layers of soil were added to the mounds over time.

It is thought that these mound groups and their associated hamlets formed a single territorial unit integrated through an overarching social and political structure. Analyses of mound internments from Seip and other sites suggests that mound groups represented local descent groups. These local groups were likely headed by elders or other formal descent group heads. **Biodistance** studies, which examine the

---

**Hopewell**
(2100–1700 B.P.)

**Seip Mound**
(Ohio, Hopewell)

**Wigwam:** a structure constructed of poles bent to form a dome and covered with bark or woven reeds.

**Wattle-and-daub:** building using mat walls covered with mud to form a solid and relatively substantial structure.

**Biodistance:** studies which use genetic markers to determine the biological relationships among populations.

FIGURE **9.5**
The geometric earthworks at the Seip site.

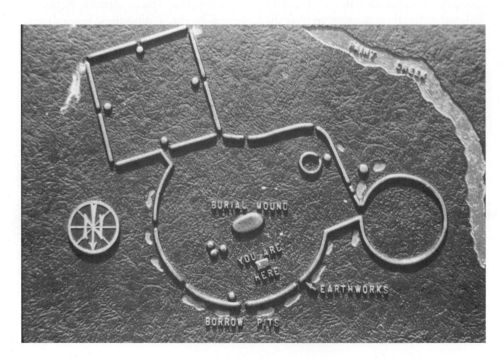

biological relationships among populations, suggest that local descent groups regularly intermarried with descent groups in neighboring territories. Intermarriage may have fostered regional alliances and trade networks, probably headed by descent group leaders. Trade was clearly an integrating force in Hopewell societies. Networks of long-distance trade were developed by the Hopewell people, allowing materials from the Atlantic and Gulf coasts, the Rocky mountains, and the Canadian shield all to find their way into the Ohio River valley.

From these exotic raw materials the Hopewell peoples created some remarkable works of art (see Color Plate 13). Obsidian was chipped into large knives of outstanding craftsmanship. Copper was hammered into elegant rings, braclets, beads, and earspools, as well as into remarkable masks and headdresses. Mica was cut into masks and effigies. Effigy pipes were developed into a particularly expressive medium by Hopewell peoples and include figures representing birds, frogs, beavers, fish, and even humans. Human and animal effigies were also sculpted in clay and cut from mica and copper sheets. In other ways, however, Hopewell technology was much like that of earlier peoples in the Eastern Woodlands (Figure 9.6). Chipped stone projectile points, knives, scrapers, and the like were basic to the tool kit. Ground stone axes, adzes, celts, as well as grinding stones and mortars and pestles were used extensively. There was a rich bone and antler industry that included bone awls, hoes, needles, and antler projectile points and flaking tools. Hopewell ceramics were grit tempered and usually cord marked, although incised and stamped designs were used as well, especially for burial ceramics.

In addition to raw materials, maize (corn) was apparently also traded into the Hopewell world, probably from the Southwest, and became an important part of

FIGURE **9.6**
Hopewell tradition stone tools (*top row*) and ceramic fragments, showing the wide range of decorative styles Hopewell peoples used.

the diet by about 1800 B.P. Indeed, maize replaced other domesticates, such as goosefoot and sumpweed, which had been important to earlier traditions in eastern North America. The reasons for this are unclear, but may have to do with maize being easier to harvest and prepare than indigenous domesticates. Even with the addition of maize, collected plant foods and other domesticated plants remained important. Squash and gourds were still planted, as was sunflower and other seed plants. Nuts also remained important, and were gathered in great quantities in the fall. Deer remained the primary game animal, although, like earlier peoples of the Eastern Woodlands, small mammals, waterfowl, turkey, and reptiles were hunted. Fish and shellfish were eaten in large quantities by many Hopewell groups.

**Northeast Middle Woodland** (2400–1000 B.P.)

**Donaldson** (Ontario, Northeast Middle Woodland)

To the northeast of the Hopewell people, peoples of the **Northeast Middle Woodland** (2400–1000 B.P.) tradition continued to rely primarily on foods obtained through seasonal rounds of hunting and gathering. Groups would come together at prime fishing or collecting sites in the spring and summer, and disperse into individual hunting bands or families during the fall and winter. The **Donaldson** site on the Saugeen River in southern Ontario appears to represent such a macroband encampment. The site is located in a prime fishing area and is surrounded by forests providing wood and small game. The site itself covers an area of about 1.2 hectares, mainly along the river bank. A number of rectangular, wattle-and-daub houses, roughly 4 meters by 6 meters in size, have been uncovered, and are interpreted as single-family dwellings. At any given time there were probably ten to twelve such houses, and perhaps fifty to sixty people. The site was probably occupied during the spring, when fish spawning in the Saugeen River could have been harvested in large numbers, and through the summer until local resources were exhausted. The people living at the site would then split up to hunt and gather as small bands or independent families throughout the fall and winter, returning to the site again in the spring.

**Middle Eastern Woodland** (2200–1400 B.P.)

The Hopewell peoples' neighbors to the southeast, those of the **Middle Eastern Woodland** (2200–1400 B.P.) tradition became sedentary and began to increase their reliance on domesticated plant foods. Middle Eastern Woodland peoples also built mounds, and Middle Eastern Woodland mounds include both flat, platform-like constructions and conical mounds. Not all mounds have burials, and many of the platform mounds contain a unique array of artifacts and ecofacts that suggest they were used for ritual feasting. Mounds are found in both special mound sites, some of which have surrounding earthworks like Hopewell sites, but are also found associated with habitation communities. And while large mound centers are located along major trade routes, there is no evidence of an organized settlement system like that among Hopewell peoples.

Middle Eastern Woodland residential communities vary in size, but tend to be relatively small, with some half-dozen houses. Houses, round to oval, are often constructed with a single large central post, suggesting they were conical or domed in shape. Each structure probably housed a single family of five to ten people, suggesting that typical villages rarely exceeded thirty to fifty residents. Middle Eastern Woodland peoples had a mixed economy that combined hunting, fishing, and gathering with domesticated plants. Indeed, the extent to which some communities relied on domesticated plants suggests that they had become fully agricultural.

## Agriculture

**Agricultural:** societies that rely primarily on domesticates and use land intensively.

What is the difference between **agricultural** subsistence and the use of domesticated plants? Archaeologists usually consider two elements important in the distinction. First, agricultural societies rely primarily on domesticates; that is, domesticates do not simply supplement the diet, they are the most significant element of the diet. Second, agricultural societies use land intensively; that is, they alter the land so that

FIGURE **9.7**
Artist's reconstruction of how Cahokia may have looked about 900 B.P. In the background is the massive Monk's Mound, the largest pre-Columbian structure in North America. In the foreground are typical Mississippian tradition houses.

crops can be grown for a number of years. Sometimes this is by the simple means of cutting brush and trees, letting them dry, and burning the debris, a technique called **slash and burn** or **swidden** agriculture. In other cases it means preparing and maintaining formal agricultural fields through terracing, canal building, fertilizing, and the like.

Domesticates became increasingly important across the Eastern Woodlands in the period between about 1500 B.P and 1000 B.P., and by 1000 B.P. there were many agricultural societies in eastern North America. In some of these societies chiefdoms emerged; the earliest were probably among peoples of the Mississippian tradition. These **Mississippian** (1100–500 B.P.) polities developed large civic-ceremonial centers with multiple flat-topped pyramidal mounds and adopted corn-bean-squash agriculture as the primary subsistence base. Perhaps the most important was **Cahokia,** which is described in the box feature (Figure 9.7). But there were many other important Mississippian sites, ranging from small farming hamlets to large agricultural villages to cities like Cahokia.

One of the most thoroughly examined small Mississippian sites is the **Gypsy Joint** site located in southeastern Missouri. The site is a hamlet consisting of two roughly square houses, each about 5 meters on a side, and of wattle-and-daub construction. The materials in and around these two houses were carefully collected and analyzed, and they provide a good picture of life in a Mississippian hamlet. The site was occupied for only about 3 years by a nuclear family of five to seven people. One of the houses was probably a summer house, and the other, with its floor cut deeper into the ground and with a central hearth, was probably a winter house. The family subsisted on a combination of maize agriculture and hunting. Maize was raised on nearby floodplain soils and stored in an above-ground crib. Nuts were also collected in large numbers and were processed by boiling to extract oil. Deer, turkey, turtle, squirrel, and beaver remains were found, with deer dominating the faunal assemblage. Stone tool manufacturing and animal butchering areas were identifiable by their debris. The family made all of its own tools, prepared its own food and clothing, and was basically self-sufficient. The only nonlocal items were galena and ocher, both used as pigments, which were probably obtained at the nearby Mississippian center of Powers Fort.

In the Northeast, people of the **Proto-Iroquois** (950–350 B.P.) and **Northeast Late Woodland** (1000–500 B.P.) traditions also developed sedentary chiefdoms based on corn-bean-squash agriculture. Large villages containing hundreds of residents and often surrounded by strong defensive palisades were built by peoples of both traditions. Most scholars see this concentration of population and construction of defensive works as evidence of increased warfare in the region during this time period. Certainly historical records report endemic warfare in the area from the time of European contact (ca. 500 B.P.) onwards. Historical records also document

**Mississippian**
(1100–500 B.P.)

**Cahokia** (Illinois, Mississippian)

**Gypsy Joint** (Missouri, Mississippian)

**Proto-Iroquois**
(950–350 B.P.)

**Northeast Late Woodland**
(1000–500 B.P.)

**Slash-and-burn:** a way of preparing agricultural fields by cutting brush and trees, letting them dry, and burning the debris.

**Swidden:** a form of agriculture where fields shift from location to location every few years. The slash-and-burn method is often used to prepare swidden fields.

# Cahokia

Cahokia, located near the confluence of the Mississippi and Missouri Rivers in East St. Louis, Illinois, is the largest pre-Columbian settlement in North America. The site covers an area of some 13 kilometers and contains at least 104 earthen mounds, including Monks Mound, the largest pre-Columbian structure in North America. It has been estimated that between 10,000 and 40,000 people lived at Cahokia at the height of its power, around 1000 B.P., but that number may be somewhat misleading since the Cahokia region is dotted with large sites, including a major center that was destroyed during the construction of the modern city of St. Louis, Missouri. While no clear estimate of the region's population is available, it is safe to say that at 1000 B.P. the Cahokia area had more residents than any other region in pre-Columbian North America.

Cahokia developed beginning around 1100 B.P. and quickly grew into a large center. Within a few decades the most important features of the site—the central mound complex and grand plaza, later enclosed within a palisade, the outer defensive palisade, enclosing an area of some 83 hectares, and several celestial observatories called "woodhenges"—were put into place. Within a century the site and its environs grew to its maximum size, and came to dominate the Mississippi River valley and much of central North America. By 800 B.P., however, the site had declined, and it basically disappeared from the map of important communities.

Cahokia's rapid rise and fall, and its dominance during the height of its power, have made it a focus of research since the early nineteenth century. A number of important excavations were undertaken in the 1920s and 1930s, but sustained research at Cahokia did not begin until the 1960s, when highway construction in the area threatened the site. The Illinois Department of Transportation supported the development of an integrated research plan and large-scale excavations at the site. These continued through the early 1970s, when work shifted to areas around the site soon to be impacted by additional highway construction. In 1983 the site was registered on the UNESCO World Register of Historic Places.

powerful chiefs both on the Atlantic coast and along the St. Lawrence River (Figure 9.8). Indeed, Proto-Iroquois groups were organized into a hierarchical polity typically referred to as the "League of the Iroquois." Villages each had a chief who represented the most important descent group and who led a village council composed of the adult men of the village. Village chiefs themselves formed a council for one of five Iroquois nations, and the five nations comprised the League.

The reasons for political centralization and increased conflict is a question of great interest. The development of powerful Mississippian chiefdoms must have had some effect on populations in the Northeast, but the extent to which Mississippians influenced political development is unclear. The adoption of agriculture had an

The nature of the Cahokian polity has also been a focus of research. Most archaeologists assume that Cahokia was the center of a chiefdom. The argument is based largely on ethnographic documents describing early historic chiefdoms in eastern North America—chiefdoms that were clearly related to later Mississippian polities—and on the combined archaeological record of other Mississippian tradition polities, all of whom share classic features of chiefdoms. Cahokia, however, seems different. It is larger in scale than any other Mississippian polity, and its influence stretched across a wider area. Cahokia's leaders were able to amass huge amounts of labor to build and maintain the palisade and the numerous mounds, and the mounds themselves tell an interesting tale. Within Mound 72, for example, was a central burial with the individual laid atop a platform of shell beads. Associated with this individual were a number of sacrificial victims interpreted as retainers offered as part of the central burial rituals. Elsewhere in the mound was a pit containing the remains of over fifty young women between the ages of 18 and 25, four males buried together but without heads or hands, and a group of ten individuals buried upon litters. All these suggest complex burial rituals involving human sacrifice, and this has suggested to some archaeologists that Cahokia's leaders had considerable power.

Cahokia's influence was felt as far away as central Minnesota, Wisconsin, Iowa, and Kansas. Indeed, refugees or delegates from Cahokia lived in communities near St. Paul, Minnesota; Milwaukee, Wisconsin; and Kansas City, Missouri. Raw materials from as far away as Lake Superior, the Rocky Mountains, and the Gulf of Mexico flowed through Cahokia, and at Cahokia some of these were changed into finished goods that were traded to other locations. In particular, a significant shell-working industry was present at Cahokia, with literally dozens of shell bead workshops present at the site. Whether these were controlled by the Cahokian polity or not has been a point of debate, but it is clear that Cahokia was not only a political center, but also an economic center.

SOURCES: Emerson, Thomas, and R. Barry Lewis, *Cahokia and the Hinterlands* (Urbana: University of Illinois Press, 1991); Fowler, Melvin, *The Cahokia Atlas* (Springfield: Illinois Historic Preservation Agency, 1989); Milner, George, *The Cahokia Chiefdom* (Washington, DC: Smithsonian Institution Press, 1998); Stoltman, James, *New Perspectives on Cahokia* (Madison: Prehistory Press, 1991).

effect as well, as once mobile populations began to settle into permanent communities with surrounding agricultural fields. Agricultural fields and nearby resources would have had to be defended, and some of the centralization that went on within both these traditions may have been in part fostered by conflict over prime agricultural lands and access to trade routes and hunting and gathering territories in areas near agricultural villages. Finally, there has been a long-standing argument that Proto-Iroquois people were migrants into the Northeast from the Southeast, and their acquisition of territory created conflict and sparked political centralization. Each of these models has some support, and the truth of the situation may be a combination of these factors.

FIGURE **9.8**

This 1585 drawing of the town of Pomeiock represents a typical Northeast Late Woodland palisaded village.

For a typical person in a Proto-Iroquois or Northeast Late Woodland village, life consisted of a seasonal round of activities. In the spring, fields were prepared with shell or stone hoes, and maize, beans, and squash were planted. Men traveled for trade or warfare during the summer, while women tended the fields. Fall was harvest time and a time for the collection of nuts and fruits. Trees might be felled and brush cleared for new fields to be cultivated in the spring. Village defenses were repaired at this time as well, and intervillage and national councils were held. Hunting and fishing were the primary activities during the winter, but were also undertaken during the regular course of the year. Utensils were made by each family, and these too were fashioned year-round. Ceramics were thin walled and shell tempered, manufactured using the paddle-and-anvil technique and fired in open pits. Chipped stone was used for small, triangular projectile points and larger lanceolate knives, as well as for scrapers, drills, and hoes. Bone and antler were used extensively for hide-working tools such as awls and needles, and for projectile points and harpoons. Shell was used for hoes, spoons, and cups, as well as for personal ornaments such as beads, pendants, and gorgets.

**Late Eastern Woodland**
(1300–500 B.P.)

**Oneota**
(1000–230 B.P.)

**Fort Ancient**
(1000–200 B.P.)

People of the **Late Eastern Woodland** (1300–500 B.P.), **Oneota** (1000–230 B.P.), and **Fort Ancient** (1000–200 B.P.) traditions lived as neighbors to the chiefdoms of the Northeast, but maintained more diverse ways of life. Late Eastern Woodland and Oneota peoples living in northern Minnesota, Wisconsin, Michigan, and southern Canada retained a reliance on hunting and gathering and lived in relatively mobile bands, while domestic plants were important and communities were more sedentary among populations living farther south. The primary differences between these traditions have to do with location and technology. In particular, ceramic forms and decorations differ between the traditions. Late Eastern Woodland ceramics are often grit tempered and decorated with cord marking. Oneota ceramics are shell tempered and have distinctive chevron and "stab and drag" decorations (Figure 9.9). Fort Ancient ceramics are usually grit tempered, and have their own distinctive incised decorations.

FIGURE **9.9**
Oneota tradition ceramics from Wisconsin. Note the flaring rims and stab-and-drag decorations that are characteristic of Oneota pottery.

It is interesting that none of these traditions appear to have developed central-ized polities like the traditions in the Northeast and Southeast. Two factors may have played a role. First, resources may have been abundant and populations smaller than elsewhere, although there seems no clear evidence that this was the case. Environments varied throughout the Eastern Woodlands, and there were loca-tions of abundance in all regions. Similarly, there seems no evidence that population was higher in the Northeast or Southeast; but rather, populations in those areas chose to centralize, creating locally dense populations. Second, agriculture may not have played as significant a role in these societies. There is some evidence that maize, for example, did not produce well in the short growing season of the Upper Midwest where many peoples of the Oneota and Late Eastern Woodland traditions lived. However, some Late Eastern Woodland and Fort Ancient populations dwelled in a climate well-suited to maize, so this cannot be the sole factor.

Village life was similar among the three traditions. Communities were typically moderate in size, containing perhaps a dozen houses arranged around a central work area or plaza. Over time it became common for villages to have one or more defensive palisades surrounding them. Houses varied from oval to rectangular, and were typically constructed of wattle and daub walls supported by posts set into the ground. A single family resided in each house, although over time some larger multi-family houses appeared. Communities were probably organized through descent groups, with descent group leaders acting as community leaders who organized peo-ple for community work and defense. On a daily basis, however, most families were largely autonomous. A typical community of this kind probably housed some fifty to one hundred people. Among groups still practicing hunting and gathering, com-munities were smaller and more mobile, with large summer villages in which a num-ber of families came together and smaller winter camps comprised of only one or two families.

## GREAT PLAINS

The North American Great Plains are a unique ecosystem, and it is not surprising that a unique way of life would develop there (Figure 9.1). The dominant features of the Great Plains are vast expanses of tallgrass prairies and shortgrass plains, and the dominant animal is the bison (Figure 9.10). The Great Plains have a modest climate, with warm, humid summers and cool winters. Precipitation is adequate for horticulture, averaging some 500 mm a year. The landscape of the Central and Southern Plains is relatively flat to rolling, but large rivers such as the Arkansas, Platte, Republican, and Red cut east-west across the region creating deep valleys with high bluffs. The floodplains of these rivers are often quite wide, and provide rich alluvial soils for agriculture. While grasses are the dominant flora, cottonwood and willow trees also grow throughout the region, and small forests of elm, ash, and elder are present in river valleys. Literally millions of Bison were present, and pronghorn antelope, deer, elk, and a wide variety of smaller animals such as rabbit, fox, and coyote also thrived in the region. The rivers themselves were home to fish, shellfish, and turtles, as well as water fowl.

**Plains Archaic**
**(9000–2500 B.P.)**

The first peoples of the Great Plains were members of the **Plains Archaic (9000–2500 B.P.)** tradition. They established a basic way of life that would remain the core of all archaeological traditions to follow on the Great Plains. The basis of this way of life was bison, which were hunted in large numbers, particularly in the western portions of the Great Plains. Deer and small game, fish, shellfish, and many plants were also used by Plains Archaic peoples. Hunting was done with chipped stone projectile points, and butchering with chipped stone knives and scrapers. Hides were worked with bone and both chipped and ground stone tools. Ground stone tools were used to process plants and for woodworking.

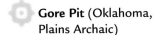

**Gore Pit** (Oklahoma, Plains Archaic)

Plains Archaic communities tended to be small (often only one or two families), mobile, and egalitarian. At the **Gore Pit** site in southwestern Oklahoma, for example,

FIGURE **9.10**

A bison being pursued on the vast shortgrass region of the Great Plains.

some thirty concentrations of fire-cracked rock were uncovered in addition to several middens containing burned rock and shell. These were interpreted as earth ovens for cooking shellfish, meat, and plants. A variety of chipped and ground stone tools were also found, along with abundant faunal remains, suggesting animals were butchered on the site before being cooked. There were no remains of structures, but because of the many ovens and diversity of tools, the site has been interpreted as a seasonal camp for a small group. At the **Nebo Hill** site in northwestern Missouri, the remains of several ovens, refuse pits, and two possible house floors were uncovered. A wide range of chipped and ground stone tools, including projectile points and knives, hoes, axes, celts, as well as faunal and floral remains (black walnut shells in some abundance) suggest the site was a seasonal fall residence for a small group of Plains Archaic peoples.

The basic way of life of the Plains Archaic peoples, then, a way of life characteristic of much of Great Plains prehistory, was that of nomadic hunting in small, egalitarian communities. Bison was the focus of hunting, although many other animals were taken. Grassland seed and root plants were collected as well as fish and shellfish. Daily life involved the constant movement needed to stay near herds of bison as well as to maintain access to water, wood fuel, and grassland plants.

Peoples of the **Plains Woodland** (2500–200 B.P.) tradition continued the way of life established by the Plains Archaic peoples, but added ceramics and the bow and arrow to the tool kit. Ceramics were sand or grit tempered and cord marked, while evidence for the bow and arrow comes in the form of small, triangular chipped stone points. Spears were also still used for hunting, as large chipped points are also found. Indeed, subsistence seems relatively unchanged from the Plains Archaic tradition across most of the region. Bison still formed the basis of subsistence, with deer, small mammals, fish and shellfish, and plants all contributing to the diet. However, some Plains Woodland peoples on the eastern edges of the Great Plains also added domesticated plants to the diet. These included maize, sunflower, and squash, all of which were grown in river valley alluvium.

Sedentary or semisedentary villages began to appear among those Plains Woodlands people who had adopted agriculture. Elsewhere, habitations tended to be small and impermanent. However, semisedentary villages may also have developed at some prime bison hunting locations. For example, the **Stelzer** site located in northern South Dakota contains a large number of fire and roasting pits, trash pits, and large quantities of bison bones. A large number of butchering and hide working tools were also found, along with domestic refuse such as ceramics, personal ornaments, and plant processing tools such as grinding stones. In addition, five burial mounds are associated with the site, suggesting that much more was going on there than simple bison butchering. Archaeologists have interpreted the Stelzer site as being a location where bands coalesced each summer for communal bison hunts, to interact socially, and to perform ceremonies, including death rituals.

In the major river valleys that cut across the Great Plains, agriculture was possible, and larger and more sedentary communities developed. Peoples of both the **Central Plains Village** (1050–150 B.P.) and **Northern Plains Village** (950–150 B.P.) traditions built communities of earth lodges near prime agricultural soils where they raised maize, beans, and squash. An **earth lodge** is a semisubterranean structure constructed with wattle and daub or sod walls and a thatched or sod roof (Figure 9.11). Earth lodges were organized around a central village work area or plaza, and in some cases were even formally laid out in rows. Many villages were palisaded or had other defensive works. Northern Plains Village communities were quite large, often consisting of more than 100 earth lodges, each housing an extended family or, in some cases, several related families. Central Plains Village communities typically consisted of five to ten large earth lodges, each containing several families, probably related through descent.

**Nebo Hill** (Missouri, Plains Archaic)

**Plains Woodland** (2500–200 B.P.)

**Stelzer** (South Dakota, Plains Woodland)

**Central Plains Village** (1050–150 B.P.)

**Northern Plains Village** (950–150 B.P.)

**Earth lodge:** semisubterranean structure constructed with wattle and daub or sod walls and a thatched or sod roof.

FIGURE **9.11**
A Pawnee earth lodge, the typically dwelling of the Central Plains Village and Northern Plains Village peoples.

Villages were located near fresh water and firewood and adjacent to good agricultural lands. Such locations were often in large river valleys. Subsistence was based on maize-beans-squash agriculture supplemented by meat provided through communal bison hunts. Communal hunts took place after crops were planted in the spring, and perhaps again after the fall harvest. The technology used by both the Central Plains and Northern Plains Village people was similar to that used by earlier peoples of the Great Plains. Chipped and ground stone tools were basic utensils, and bone and wood were used. Ceramics were grit tempered, often globular in form, and typically finished with cord marking. Although villages in both traditions had 100 or more residents, there is no evidence of formal political offices in either tradition. Villages probably had recognized leaders who achieved authority through their abilities in hunting and perhaps war, but these were probably not formal or inherited positions. In both traditions descent groups probably formed the basic organizing structure of society

**Mitchell** (South Dakota, Northern Plains Village)

The **Mitchell** site on the James River in southeastern South Dakota is an excellent example of a Northern Plains Village community. The site contains some forty-five earth lodges, each a rectangular semisubterranean structure with thick wattle-and-daub walls and a thatched roof. The lodges were situated around an open plaza, and the community itself was surrounded by a double palisade wall. Outside the defensive wall were four burial mounds. It is likely that about 200 to 300 people lived at the Mitchell site. They farmed the valley bottomlands and hunted and gathered in the surrounding grasslands and woodlands. Large numbers of bison bones suggest communal bison hunts contributed significantly to the diet. Thus, one can trace a continuum on the Great Plains from the earliest prehistoric inhabitants to the latest. Families lived in largely egalitarian societies that came together regularly to hunt bison. Communal hunting continued its importance even when families settled together in agricultural villages, where egalitarian lifeways were maintained despite population concentration.

## High Plains

The High Plains form a distinct subregion of the Great Plains (Figure 9.1). They are a region of flat to rolling topography extending from the foothills of the Rocky Mountains to the tall grass prairies of the Great Plains. The area is dominated by short grass prairies that supported large herds of bison, antelope, and deer. The higher elevations of the Black Hills contained deciduous forests, while the badlands and other regions of low elevation were semidesert. The Rocky Mountain foothills were primarily sagebrush steppe moving into spruce and juniper forests as elevation increased. Thus elevation created marked differences in environment and provided for a great diversity of animal species and plants.

Peoples of the **High Plains Archaic** (8000–1500 B.P.) and the **High Plains Late Prehistoric** (1500–150 B.P.) traditions shared similar ways of life, differing primarily in their technology. High Plains Late Prehistoric peoples used the bow and arrow and ceramics, while High Plains Archaic peoples did not. This difference, however, reflects some differences in subsistence as well. For High Plains Archaic peoples communal bison hunts were an annual (and perhaps biannual) event that brought the otherwise dispersed population together. For the High Plains Late Prehistoric peoples, communal bison hunts appear to have been less important, perhaps because the introduction of the bow and arrow allowed individual bands to successfully hunt bison without the need for large numbers of people.

People in both traditions, however, were nomadic, moving between the diverse environments of the High Plains to hunt and collect seasonally abundant resources. Deer, elk, antelope, and a wide variety of smaller game were hunted in addition to bison. Sunflower, choke cherries, grapes, acorns, turnips, onions, and many other seasonally abundant foods were collected. Chipped and ground stone tools were the primary utensils, which included projectile points, knives, scrapers, drills, grinding stones, and abraders. Bone was used for awls, needles, scrapers, and other tools. High Plains Late Prehistoric peoples made ceramics, while High Plains Archaic peoples relied on woven or skin bags. Organization in both traditions was egalitarian, and the family was the fundamental structure of social life.

**High Plains Archaic**
(8000–1500 B.P.)

**High Plains Late Prehistoric**
(1500–150 B.P.)

## SOUTHWEST

Many areas of the southwestern United States appear arid and inhospitable today, yet the region holds a rich prehistory that includes some of the most socially and politically complex societies in North America. Three major environments dominate the region: deserts, piñon-juniper woodlands, and montane forests (Figure 9.1). The deserts range from being very hot in Arizona and New Mexico to being mild to cool in Utah, but all are arid and have plants and animals adapted to these arid conditions such as succulents, sagebrush, and burrowing animals. Piñon-juniper woodlands are typically at a higher altitude than deserts and are both cooler and less arid. As the name suggests, they are dominated by piñon and juniper trees that grow in discontinuous groves separated by grasslands. These grasslands support antelope, deer, and other small animals, and the seeds of the piñon and juniper attract birds and small mammals as well. Finally, the montane forests of the southern Rocky Mountains exist at higher altitudes and are generally cooler and moister than either the deserts or piñon-juniper woodlands. Conifers such as ponderosa pine dominate the flora, while deer and elk are the major large mammals.

In terms of its topography, four major areas are subsumed within the Southwest: the Great Basin, the Basin and Range, the Colorado Plateau, and the Rocky Mountains (Figure 9.1). The Great Basin, as the name suggests, is a vast flatland extending across western Utah, southern Idaho, Nevada, and eastern California. To the east of the Great Basin is a large, relatively flat upland called the Colorado Plateau. The area is drained by the Colorado River and its tributaries, which have cut deep canyons, making parts of the area quite rugged. To the south of the Great Basin and Colorado Plateau is the Basin and Range. This is a region with parallel mountain ranges separated by broad alluvial basins. Finally, the southern Rocky Mountains cut through the eastern side of the Basin and Range and Colorado Plateau.

FIGURE **9.12**

Deerskin moccasins preserved in the dry conditions of Hogup Cave in Utah.

**Early Desert Archaic**
(10,000–8000 B.P.)

**San Dieguito**
(10,000–8000 B.P.)

**Danger Cave** (Utah, Early Desert Archaic)

**Hogup Cave** (Utah, Early Desert Archaic)

**Middle Desert Archaic**
(8000–1600 B.P.)

**Late Desert Archaic**
(1600–500 B.P.)

The earliest distinct Southwestern traditions are the **Early Desert Archaic** (10,000–8000 B.P.) and **San Dieguito** (10,000–8000 B.P.) traditions. Peoples of both traditions lived during a time when the Southwest was cooler and moister than today, and large Pleistocene marshes and lakes still dotted the region. Peoples of both traditions were mobile hunters and gatherers who exploited a wide variety of plant and animal resources. Settlements were limited to short-term campsites, and dwellings were simple brush huts or skin tents. Caves and rockshelters were favored campsites, as were locations near seasonal lakes. A wide variety of game was hunted, including deer, antelope, bighorn sheep, and, in some areas, bison. Seed-bearing plants and nuts were collected in well-made baskets and processed with grinding stones and mortars. Chipped stone tools were used to hunt and butcher game.

Dry caves in the area have provided remarkably well-preserved organic materials from these traditions. From **Danger Cave** in west-central Utah, for example, have come well-preserved fragments of twined baskets, rope, and the wooden shaft of a spear thrower. From **Hogup Cave** in northwest Utah have come fragments of rabbit fur robes, coiled willow baskets, rope, and wooden items (Figure 9.12). Both these caves also contained preserved human feces, which demonstrated that their inhabitants had a broad diet that included pickleweed, prickly pear, hackberry, and bulrush, suggesting that plant foods formed a significant part of the diet for Early Desert Archaic and San Dieguito peoples. Faunal remains also demonstrated the continuing importance of meat, including antelope, deer, bighorn sheep, bison, small mammals, and waterfowl. The preserved organic tools demonstrated that technology was simple and made by individuals who used the items, and the small size of these sites suggests that small bands consisting of a single or, at most, several families formed the basis of social organization.

This general way of life continued through the **Middle Desert Archaic** (8000–1600 B.P.) and **Late Desert Archaic** (1600–500 B.P.) traditions. Despite climatic changes that saw the Southwest transformed into the hot, arid region we know today, Middle Desert Archaic peoples maintained a mobile hunting and gathering way of life by intensifying the use of seed plants and small animals such as rabbits, creating a way of life that continued through the Late Desert Archaic tradition and into the historic period. It has been suggested, based on an increased frequency of grinding stones, that the Late Desert Archaic peoples relied more heavily on seeds and perhaps nuts than their predecessors. They differed little from the Middle Desert Archaic peoples in their focus on rabbits and deer.

The tools used by the Middle and Late Desert Archaic peoples were simple and could easily have been made by the individuals employing them. The primary hunting tool was the bow and arrow, the arrows armed with small triangular projectile points, commonly side notched and sometimes with an additional basal notch. Chipped stone was also used for knives, scrapers, and the like. Ground stone was used for food processing tools such as manos and metates. Wood was used for bows and arrows, as well as for digging sticks. Woven baskets have been recovered, and were likely used both for storage and for winnowing seeds. Late Desert Archaic peoples made simple brown-ware ceramics in jar forms with pointed to round bases made by coiling and in most cases finished with a paddle and anvil.

Middle and Late Desert Archaic communities were small and mobile, consisting of a few families and less than thirty or so people. Communities were located in all environments, and it is likely that they shifted regularly as local resources were consumed. The remains of houses are scarce, but what have been found appear similar to the ethnographically described *wickiups* used by the Shoshone. These are small, circular structures made of brush and used primarily for storage by a single nuclear family (Figure 9.13). Sociopolitical organization was likely also similar to ethnographically known hunter-gatherers in the region. These were composed of small, mobile family groups who would join into larger groups several times during the year to perform rituals and take part in communal hunts.

Domesticated plants appeared in the Southwest by 2000 B.P., and while peoples of the of the **Patayan** (1600–500 B.P.) tradition used them to supplement an otherwise mobile hunting and gathering lifestyle, peoples of the **Basketmaker** (2300–1300 B.P) and **Fremont** (1600–500 B.P.) traditions developed a more sedentary existence with a higher reliance on domesticated plants. Basketmaker peoples appear to have been largely nomadic until about 2000 B.P., when they began to settle in small villages of a few pit houses. Basketmaker pit houses were circular, semisubterranean structures roughly 3 to 4 meters in diameter, with a central hearth and storage pits in the floor, and roofed with logs or earth. These villages were located in a variety of areas and may have been seasonally occupied rather than permanent. They may have been located to take advantage of seasonally abundant

**Patayan**
(1600–500 B.P.)

**Basketmaker**
(2300–1300 B.P.)

**Fremont**
(1600–500 B.P.)

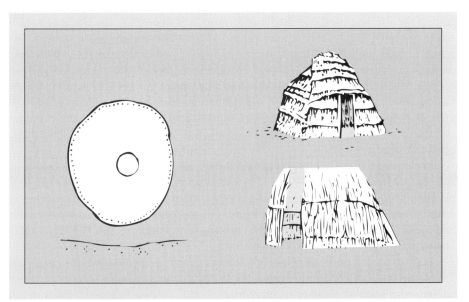

FIGURE **9.13**

These historic wickiups are probably similar to those constructed by peoples of the Middle and Late Desert Archaic tradition.

SOURCE: Jesse D. Jennings (ed.), *Ancient Native Americans* (New York: W.H. Freeman & Company, 1978), Figure 4.10b.

FIGURE **9.14**

This plan and section view of pit houses illustrate the types of dwellings used by both Basketmaker and Fremont peoples.

SOURCE: Jesse D. Jennings (ed.), *Ancient Native Americans* (New York: W.H. Freeman & Company, 1978), Figure 4.10a.

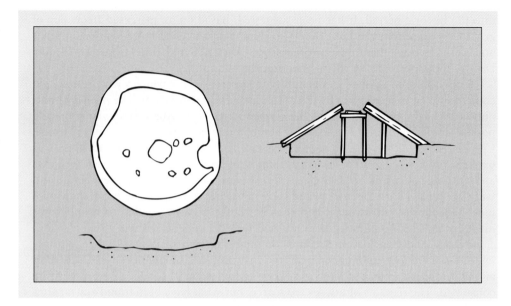

**Ball courts:** long rectangular or I-shaped areas, often with sloping sides, used to play the Mesoamerican ball game—a game something like a combination of soccer and basketball.

**Caldwell Village** (Utah, Fremont)

**Early Hohokam** (2000–900 B.P.)

**Early Anasazi** (1300–700 B.P.)

**Early Mogollon** (2000–1000 B.P.)

**Snaketown** (Arizona, Early Hohokam)

wild resources such as piñon nuts, juniper berries, and the like. While Basketmaker peoples raised maize, wild foods apparently remained the staple of the diet.

Peoples of the Fremont tradition became settled village agriculturalists, who relied on domesticated maize, beans, and squash, supplemented by hunted and gathered foods. Typical Fremont communities range from hamlets of 2 to 5 pit houses up to villages of a dozen or more pit houses. These appear to be permanent settlements located adjacent to fertile agricultural soils and near water and fuel sources. Pit houses are similar to those constructed by Basketmaker peoples, but become rectangular and somewhat larger over time (Figure 9.14). They appear to have housed a single family, suggesting that hamlets may have consisted of a single extended family or several related families, while villages probably held several families. There is no evidence of social or political organization beyond the family, even in villages.

A typical Fremont site is **Caldwell Village** in northeast Utah. It is located near Deep Creek, a reliable freshwater source that is at the base of the Uinta mountains, where wood for fuel and building, juniper, piñon, desirable plant foods, and a wide variety of game animals were all readily available. Twenty-two pit houses were uncovered at the site, and several show superpositioning with other pit houses, suggesting the site was used repeatedly over time. It is likely that the site was used by a single extended family over a long period of time and was regularly rebuilt. In the house remains and the village garbage midden a wide range of tools were found, including a variety of chipped and ground stone tools. Simple coiled grey-ware ceramics were also found in abundance. The image we get of Fremont life from Caldwell Village is that of a small agricultural hamlet whose residents made all the utensils they needed. They farmed maize, collected and hunted in the mountains, and fished in the nearby river. Social organization was egalitarian and based on the bonds of family.

Peoples of the **Early Hohokam** (2000–900 B.P.), **Early Anasazi** (1300–700 B.P.), and **Early Mogollon** (2000–1000 B.P.) traditions made a transition from life in simple agricultural hamlets to more centrally organized village life. Peoples of these traditions lived in pit houses arranged around plazas or courtyards, and many villages had public architecture in the form of ball courts and mounds (Early Hohokam) and kivas (Early Anasazi and Early Mogollon).

Perhaps the best-known Early Hohokam site is **Snaketown**, located about 25 kilometers from Phoenix, Arizona (Figure 9.15). Snaketown is a large agricultural village, consisting of more than forty houses, at least two "capped" trash mounds, and two **ball courts**. Houses were arranged in clusters of three to six, each cluster

FIGURE **9.15**
The Snaketown site during excavations.

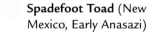

having an open courtyard onto which houses opened. These probably represent an extended family or small group of related families. Houses were rectangular and semisubterranean, with a hearth and storage pits in the floor, and measured roughly 4 to 5 meters on a side. There were a number of very large pit houses as well, and the combination of these large houses and public architecture suggest that there was a formal leadership hierarchy in place at Snaketown, probably organized around descent groups. The people at Snaketown subsisted on a diet of maize, beans, and squash, supplemented by hunted and collected foods. Two irrigation canals fed people's fields from the Gila River. There appear to be special ceramic workshops on the edge of Snaketown, where distinctive and well-made red-on-buff ceramics were produced using locally available schist as temper.

The Early Anasazi tradition is marked by a transition from pit houses to above-ground adobe **pueblos,** a transition that took place around 900 B.P. Before that time, villages were much like those of the Fremont tradition—a half dozen or so pit houses organized around a central courtyard. After about 900 B.P. villages changed to clusters of above-ground rooms divided into separate living quarters for individual families. Room blocks were built from adobe bricks with beam and thatch roofs. Each family had one or more living rooms within the room block, several storerooms, and a work area in front of the room block. Most room blocks remained small, with perhaps three to five families inhabiting each. A good example is the **Spadefoot Toad** site in the Martha's Rincon area of Chaco Canyon, New Mexico (Figure 9.16). The Spadefoot Toad site is a small pueblo with nine rooms built in an arc around a pit house or **kiva,** a round, semisubterranean structure used primarily for public gatherings and rituals. A **ramada,** or covered courtyard, was located in front of most of the rooms, and the debris from these areas suggests that most daily activities took place in these ramadas. The rooms themselves were fairly small—roughly 2 meters by 4 meters—and were built from adobe bricks set on stone foundations. The rooms shared common walls (usually the short wall) with neighbors, forming a single block of rooms. It appears that a group of families, probably related through descent, lived together at this small site, farming nearby fields and hunting and collecting in the Chaco Canyon region.

**Pueblos:** blocks of mud-brick or adobe rooms built together to form a single, large structure.

**Kiva:** a round, semisubterranean structure used primarily for public gatherings and rituals.

**Ramada:** a roofed courtyard.

**Spadefoot Toad** (New Mexico, Early Anasazi)

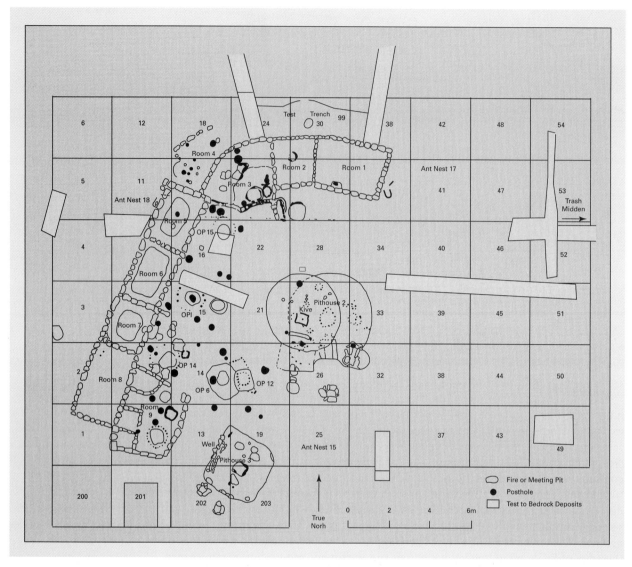

FIGURE **9.16**

Plan map of the Spadefoot Toad site in Chaco Canyon, New Mexico.

SOURCE: Thomas C. Windes, *The Spadefoot Toad Site Investigations at 29SJ 629 Chaco Canyon, New Mexico, Artifactual and Biological Analyses*, Volume II (Santa Fe, N.M.: Southwest Cultural Resources Center, Branch of Cultural Research, Division of Anthropology, National Park Service, 1993), Figure 1.3.

**Bluff Ruin** (Arizona, Early Mogollon)

Early Mogollon tradition villages remained clusters of pit houses, but they grew markedly in size over time. Early in the tradition villages contained five to ten pit houses, while late in the tradition villages tended to have twenty or thirty, and some more than 200, pit houses. Large communal structures or kivas also began to be constructed late in the tradition. Early Mogollon pit houses themselves were round to square and roughly 4 to 5 meters on a side, often with a long, sloping entrance. They were arranged in clusters around courtyards, and several such clusters might be present in larger villages. A single family probably resided in each pit house, and clusters probably represented an extended family or descent group. At **Bluff Ruin** in the Forestdale Valley of east-central Arizona, for example, there were forty-five pit houses uncovered as well as a larger public structure. Both ground and chipped stone were found in abundance at the site, but relatively few ceramics. The site seems to have been a community of maize agriculturalists who hunted and gathered broadly in the Forestdale Valley.

Over time, the peoples of these traditions became more politically centralized and established trade networks reaching as far as Mesoamerica and the Pacific coast. At Snaketown, for example, a shell workshop contained material from the California coast, and items made at Snaketown appear to have been exchanged widely among Early Hohokam villages.

The **Late Hohokam** (900–500 B.P.) tradition saw a remarkable increase in volume and scale of public architecture and the development of substantial adobe houses. Houses were rectangular and on the order of 4 by 5 meters in size. Houses were clustered around courtyards similar to the way they were in the Early Hohokam tradition. Communities consisted of a group of such house clusters and, in larger communities, substantial public architecture. There appears to have developed a hierarchy of settlements, with a group of smaller villages, consisting of perhaps only two or three house clusters, each associated with a larger village that also contained public facilities. Some of the largest communities had thirty or more house clusters and more than 1,000 residents. Irrigation agriculture was the foundation of life in all these communities, regardless of their size.

Public facilities in these large communities included platform mounds, ball courts, and large buildings. For example, at the **Marana** site located near the Santa Cruz river in the northern Tuscon basin, two earlier ball-court communities apparently coalesced into a single, large center. A platform mound was constructed between the earlier communities, and a canal was built to support the 500 to 700 people that occupied the site. A structure on top of the platform mound has been interpreted as the home of the community leader, but it is not significantly different from the houses of ordinary residents. Even so, the clear distinction of this residence has led scholars to suggest that Marana was headed by a formal chief. The Marana community, then, appears to represent the concentration of population into centers and the emergence of formal leaders who resided on top of platform mounds. Similar changes took place throughout Late Hohokam populations.

Similar changes in community organization also occurred in the **Late Anasazi** (700–400 B.P.) and **Late Mogollon** (1000–600 B.P.) traditions, with the development of large, multistoried pueblos. Political centralization continued with the emergence of what appear to be powerful regional chiefdoms. One of the best known was likely centered at the site of **Pueblo Bonito** in Chaco Canyon (Figure 9.17), which is

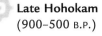
**Late Hohokam**
(900–500 B.P.)

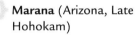
**Marana** (Arizona, Late Hohokam)

**Late Anasazi**
(700–400 B.P.)

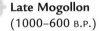
**Late Mogollon**
(1000–600 B.P.)

**Pueblo Bonito**
(New Mexico, Late Anasazi)

FIGURE **9.17**
Aerial view of Pueblo Bonito.

## Pueblo Bonito

Pueblo Bonito is the primary town in Chaco Canyon, one of the most important areas of Early Anasazi settlement. Located in northwestern New Mexico, Chaco Canyon is in the middle of the San Juan River basin, an area of rolling brushland cut by shallow canyons and surrounded by mountains on all sides. The area is marginal for agriculture today, but during the Early Anasazi tradition wetter conditions may have made rainfall agriculture supplemented by irrigation highly productive. Chaco Canyon contains the remains of a variety of Early Anasazi communities, from small pueblos of five to fifty rooms to "great houses"—large, multistoried pueblos like Pueblo Bonito. In all there are eleven "great houses" in Chaco Canyon, and Pueblo Bonito is the largest.

Construction of Pueblo Bonito began about A.D. 860, with a small block of about sixteen rooms. I use dates in years *anno domini* (A.D.) here because of the nature of the dating used in understanding the construction history of Pueblo Bonito. Some 4,294 wood samples were taken from the structure, and were dated using dendrochronology, which you will recall provides dates accurate to the year the tree from which the sample was taken died. These dates were used to develop a remarkably detailed chronology of Pueblo Bonito's construction—a chronology accurate to single years. In A.D. 891 an addition was built, creating a small arc of rooms that resembles many of the smaller pueblos in Chaco Canyon. At this point in its history, Pueblo Bonito was constructed using long sandstone slabs, uncoursed, with wide mud-mortar joints. Later builders would include long, thin pieces of stone in parallel rows within these large mortar joints. Large timbers were used to support roofs constructed from small beams, matting, and clay-sand plaster. It is from these support timbers and roof beams that wood samples for dendrochronology were obtained.

**Arroyo Hondo**
(New Mexico, Late Anasazi)

**Grasshopper Pueblo**
(Arizona, Late Mogollon)

described in the box feature, but there were other important sites as well. At **Arroyo Hondo** near Santa Fe, for example, Late Anasazi peoples built a multistoried pueblo that contained twenty-four terraced room blocks and more than 1,000 rooms. The room blocks were arranged to form thirteen enclosed plazas, within which circular, subterranean kivas were built. The kivas may have been places where public meetings and rituals were held for groups inhabiting the rooms in the blocks surrounding the plaza. This suggests that the kivas may have been powerful integrating tools in these communities, and that a single large kiva built outside the main room blocks at Arroyo Hondo may have been a focus for communitywide meetings and ritual.

Around 700 B.P. the Late Mogollon peoples living in small room blocks in the basin and range area of central Arizona began to coalesce into large pueblo communities. One of these was **Grasshopper Pueblo,** located atop Grasshopper Butte in the White Mountains. There a small room block of perhaps ten to fifteen rooms (obliterated by later construction) grew rapidly into a large, multilevel pueblo of over 500 rooms. The rooms were built in three large blocks, each surrounding an open plaza. Two room blocks were on the west side of the Salt River Draw, a spring-fed

Small additions were added to Pueblo Bonito throughout the A.D. 900s, and second-story rooms were perhaps added. In the A.D. 1040s an outer ring of small rooms were added to the arc of existing rooms. It is thought that these may have been storage rooms, perhaps built to house material moving along the extensive network of roadways that ran out from Chaco Canyon, but this interpretation is controversial. Expansion of Pueblo Bonito continued in the A.D. 1050s, with the construction of multistory room blocks on either end of the existing structure. A wall connecting these ends was also built, completing the great house's characteristic D-shape. Wall construction changed during this construction period as well, with a course of large brick-shaped blocks alternating with three or more courses of smaller, thinner stones. Over time, builders stopped including the large brick courses and used smaller, thinner tabular stones alone.

The final phases of major construction at Pueblo Bonito began about A.D. 1077 and ended about A.D. 1082. In that period large, three-story room blocks were added on both the east and west sides of the town arc, forming the existing outer walls of the town. Minor additions were made, particularly within the central area of the town's D-shaped plaza, until A.D. 1127—the last firm construction date. By around A.D. 1150 Pueblo Bonito was abandoned and never fully reoccupied. At Pueblo Bonito we have a remarkable record of an Early Anasazi great house community. Over the course of three centuries the town grew to include some 350 ground-level rooms and three stories of additional rooms, making it one of the architectural marvels of pre-Columbian North America.

SOURCES: Lekson, Stephen, *Great Pueblo Architecture of Chaco Canyon, New Mexico* (Albuquerque: University of New Mexico Press, 1986); Windes, Thomas, and Dabney Ford, 1996, "The Chaco Wood Project: The Chronometric Reappraisal of Pueblo Bonito," *American Antiquity* 61: 295–310.

stream running through the community, and the other on the east side. The influx of population to Grasshopper pueblo appears to have depopulated many sites in the surrounding area, and both the attraction of the large community and violence appears to have played a role, as a number of small sites were burned and destroyed at this time. Indeed, with little water and arable land, Grasshopper Butte is an unlikely spot for a large community unless defense is an important consideration. Complex social organization was needed to maintain the large Grasshopper community in a marginal environment, and many scholars think that political authority centered around ceremonial societies and their leaders, much like in modern-day Pueblo societies.

## PLATEAU

The Plateau comprises what is today the northwestern United States and includes the Cascade and northern Sierra Nevada mountain ranges (Figure 9.1). This is a region of mountainous uplands and deep canyons, with the Columbia and Frasier

FIGURE **9.18**

Native Americans harvesting salmon from a fish trap. Annual salmon runs provided abundant food to peoples of the Plateau.

**Early Sierra Nevada**
(10,000–3800 B.P.)

**Cascade**
(8000–5000 B.P.)

**Tucannon**
(5000–2500 B.P.)

river basins being dominant features of the landscape. The entire area is dissected by deep river valleys and canyons cut into the basalt bedrock of the Columbia plateau. Obsidian, fine-grained basalt, and cherts are found throughout the region, both in source deposits and secondary deposits in river gravels. The region contains steppelike canyon and upland forest environments, both of which supported a wide variety of animal and plant species. Salmon were abundant in the rivers and streams of the region, while the canyons and uplands were rich with game species such as deer and elk.

In the same way that bison was a key aspect of life on the Great Plains, so salmon played a key role in the lives of prehistoric Plateau peoples. Each year, tens of thousands of adult Pacific salmon congregate in major rivers of the Plateau, swimming upstream to spawn far inland. This rich concentration of food attracted people seasonally to particular locations where salmon could be readily caught and processed (Figure 9.18). As early as the **Early Sierra Nevada** (10,000–3800 B.P.) and **Cascade** (8000–5000 B.P.) traditions, and continuing through the **Tucannon** (5000–2500 B.P.) tradition, peoples of the Plateau came together at annual salmon runs to catch and process fish, and to socialize. During salmon runs enough fish could be netted or speared, then filleted and dried, to support the group for many months. During this time peoples worked together to harvest and process fish, and then relaxed, socialized, and performed ceremonies while the supplies of fish lasted. As winter neared, groups would again split up to hunt and gather independently.

Peoples of the Early Sierra Nevada, Cascade, and Tucannon traditions lived during most of the year as nomadic hunter-gatherers in the rich forests of the Plateau uplands and mountains. Game such as elk, deer, and antelope were hunted, and plant foods such as acorns were collected. As with other North American hunter-gatherers, technology was simple and portable. Chipped stone tools were basic and included projectile points, knives, and scrapers. Bone and antler were used extensively for such things as needles, awls, and chisels. Ground stone mortars and pestles were used to process plant foods. Ceramics were not made, but a variety of both twined and coiled baskets were used. Settlements were small and short-term, and houses appear to have been simple brush structures. During the time of the Tucannon tradition, however, some more substantial pit houses were constructed, which may point to an increasingly sedentary way of life.

Sedentary villages came to occupy prime fishing locations by the time of the **Late Sierra Nevada** (3800–150 B.P.) and **Harder** (2500–500 B.P.) traditions. Houses were circular, with a conical, timber framed roof covered with brush and earth. Each of these dwellings was 5 to 8 meters in diameter and housed a single family. Villages ranged in size from only one or two such houses to over a dozen, these larger villages having up to 100 residents. Large villages seem to have functioned as centers for regional religious and economic activities. Burials were located near large villages, and long-distance trade probably centered on these locations. Traded items included such things as shell, obsidian, and animal pelts. Large villages also likely had headmen or other informal leaders, but there is no evidence of social differentiation or specialization.

While salmon were central to the economy of Late Sierra Nevada and Harder peoples, other fish (such as trout) and mussels were taken when salmon were not present. Hunting and gathering in the deep canyons and mountain uplands of the region was also important, and a wide variety of game animals and plants were used. Technology included chipped stone projectile points, knives, drills, scrapers, and the like. Small, triangular projectile points were used, suggesting the bow and arrow was present. Stone mortars and pestles, grinding slabs, and mullers, were used to process seeds and nuts. A wide variety of bone and antler tools were used as well, including needles and awls employed in manufacturing twined and woven baskets. Ceramics were also made. These were thick and relatively crude plain wares, typically in simple open pot or bowl forms.

Along the coast, peoples of the **Archaic Oregon Coast** (10,000–2000 B.P.) tradition exploited the rich marine resources of the Pacific Ocean as well as those of the mountain uplands. They lived in small, mobile groups, but over time developed more sedentary lifeways. The few houses that have been excavated are small, circular pit houses. Otherwise, sites are simple scatters of shell or lithic debris. These sites are typically located along rivers or the coast and tend to be small. For example, the **Blacklock Point** site is located on a terrace about 40 meters above the Pacific Ocean in southern Oregon. The site consists of a scatter of lithic debris covering an area of roughly 160 meters by 125 meters along the terrace edge. The most common artifacts at the site are projectile points, bifaces, cores, hammer stones, and flakes, suggesting that this site was used as a place to manufacture or rework chipped stone tools. Several hearths were also found, and radiocarbon dates span almost 5,000 years—from 7560 B.P. to 2750 B.P., suggesting the site was used repeatedly over a very long period of time. The **Tahkenitch Landing** site, on the other hand, is a large marine shell midden covering an area of nearly 7,000 square meters on the shore of Tahkenitch Lake in south-central Oregon. In addition to a variety of stone and bone tools, personal ornaments such as bone and shell beads, stone pipes, and even a bird bone whistle were found. A wide variety of marine fish bones were part of the midden, as were the remains of sea mammals such as seal, dophin, and whale. Although no houses were found, Tahkenitch Landing appears to be a long-term village where people subsisted on the rich resources of the sea.

By the time of the **Formative Oregon Coast** (2000–150 B.P.) tradition, most people were living in coastal villages. These villages consisted of a number of rectangular semisubterranean plank houses, the distinctive feature of the Formative Oregon Coast tradition (Figure 9.19). The houses were large, often on the order of 10 meters wide and 30 meters long. They were constructed from beams supporting wood plank walls and roof. Floors were often dirt, but were sometimes planked as well. Sleeping and storage platforms were built along the walls, and internal

**Late Sierra Nevada** (3800–150 B.P.)

**Harder** (2500–500 B.P.)

**Archaic Oregon Coast** (10,000–2000 B.P.)

**Blacklock Point** (Oregon, Archaic Oregon Coast)

**Tahkenitch Landing** (Oregon, Archaic Oregon Coast)

**Formative Oregon Coast** (2000–150 B.P.)

FIGURE **9.19**
These historic Native American houses are probably very similar to houses constructed by Formative Oregon Coast peoples.

divisions to separate spaces for each of the several families living in the house were sometimes constructed. Typically five or so related families might inhabit such a house, perhaps thirty to fifty people in all. Villages typically contained from one to more than a dozen plank houses, and thus would have populations on the order of fifty to perhaps nearly 1,000 people. Houses were typically arranged in rows following the contours of the landscape.

Meier (Oregon, Formative Oregon Coast)

The **Meier** site is a good example of a small Formative Oregon Coast village. It is located on a gravel terrace above the lower Columbia River. The site consisted of the remains of a single large plank house, 14 meters by 35 meters in size, and estimated to have been over 6 meters high at its ridgepole. Four hearths were found regularly spaced along the center line of the house, suggesting four families shared the structure. The faunal remains from the site were dominated by freshwater shellfish, salmon, sturgeon, deer, and elk. A large number of tools were also recovered, and these included representatives of most of the range of the Formative Oregon Coast tool kit. Chipped stone included small narrow-necked projectile points, knives, scrapers, and other worked bifaces, stone grinders, a variety of bone tools such as needles and harpoons, and locally made plainware ceramics. The Meier site, therefore, appears to be a permanent settlement for a group of perhaps thirty people who hunted, fished, and collected in the rich lower Columbia river valley.

## CALIFORNIA

California represents a unique region of North American prehistory. Separated from the rest of the continent by the Sierra Nevada mountains and Mojave Desert (Figure 9.1), the prehistoric peoples of California developed distinct ways of life. These were focused on two primary sets of resources—fish, shellfish, and sea mammals for people living on the coast, and nuts for people living inland. Unlike most other areas in North America, domesticates played only a minimal role among the prehistoric peoples of California. The relative paucity of domesticates may be due to California's rich natural resources. The coastal areas have numerous rocky coves and off-shore islands that provide shelter and breeding grounds for sea mammals and birds. Parts of the central valley were marshlands that provided fish, reptiles, waterfowl, and seed-bearing plants, while other areas were oak savannahs that offered both large game animals such as deer and elk as well as a plentiful supply of nuts. Uplands and mountains also offered nuts and large game animals. The entire area has a mild climate, with wet, cool winters and dry, warm summers.

The earliest inhabitants of California were peoples of the **Windmiller** (8000–3000 B.P.) tradition. Windmiller peoples were hunters and gatherers who lived in small communities primarily in the central valley of the Sacramento and San Joaquin rivers. These communities consisted of perhaps fifteen to thirty people who moved seasonally between the swampy river bottoms in the summer and the foothills of the Sierra Nevadas in the winter. In summer, the Windmiller peoples took fish and waterfowl and collected plants, while in winter they hunted larger game such as deer and elk and collected acorns and other nuts, which, judging from the large number of grinding stones found on some Windmiller sites, may have been an essential part of the diet. Hunting was done with spears armed with large bifacially flaked projectile points, often stemmed. Chipped stone was also used for knives and scrapers. Ground stone tools included mortars and pestles and net sinkers. Bone was used for items such as awls and needles. Evidence of twined baskets in the form of impressions in baked soil have been found, though no baskets have survived.

The Windmiller peoples apparently carried on a lively trade with populations both on the coast and in the Sierra Nevada mountains. Shell from the coast was imported and used in personal ornaments; minerals and obsidian from the Sierra Nevadas was imported and used for a variety of purposes. Whether the Windmiller peoples ventured to these locations or material was traded down-the-line is not clear, nor is it clear precisely what the other populations received in return for their goods.

The general way of life established in the Windmiller tradition continued through the **Cosumnes** (3000–1500 B.P.) tradition, the primary difference between the two being distinctive diagonally flaked projectile points made by the Cosumnes peoples and their extensive bone tool industry. But by the time of the **Hotchkiss** (1500–150 B.P.) tradition, people in the central valley had begun to live in larger and more sedentary villages. For example, the **Patrick** site near Chico, contained the remains of numerous large, semisubterranean houses. Houses were larger by about half from earlier periods, increasing from about 4 meters on a side to about 6 meters, and the construction of the houses was more substantial. The increase in size and stability suggests that the houses were meant to be permanent residences.

Food for these large villages was obtained through a combination of hunting, fishing, and gathering, along with the intensive harvest of acorns, which became a primary subsistence food since they could be harvested in the fall but stored to be used throughout the year. A wide variety of other nuts and fruits were also collected. Animals hunted included deer, elk, and pronghorn, along with a diversity of smaller game animals and waterfowl. Fish were also taken by the Hotchkiss peoples, particularly sturgeon and salmon. Hunting was done with spears armed with serrated projectile points, and the bow and arrow was also used by groups in some parts of the Central Valley. Chipped stone was used for knives and scrapers. Ground stone tools included mortars and pestles and net sinkers. Bone was used for items such as needles and also used in making coiled baskets. Ceramics were made in limited quantities, while coiled baskets formed the basic storage utensils (Figure 9.20).

**Windmiller**
(8000–3000 B.P.)

**Cosumnes**
(3000–1500 B.P.)

**Hotchkiss**
(1500–150 B.P.)

**Patrick** (California, Hotchkiss)

FIGURE **9.20**

Net bags like these were used for carrying and storing goods by prehistoric peoples in California's central valley.

SOURCE: After Gifford and Schenck 1926, courtesy of the R.H. Lowie Museum of Anthropology, University of California, Berkeley.

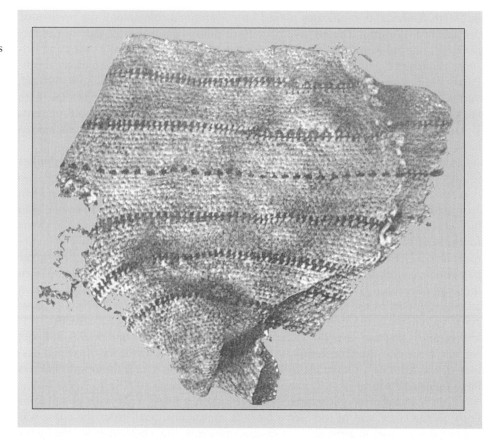

**Early Southern California**
(8000–3000 B.P.)

**Rincon Point**
(California, Early Southern California)

The Hotchkiss peoples traded extensively with surrounding populations. Shell from the coast was imported and used in personal ornaments, minerals and obsidian from the Sierra Nevadas was imported and used for a variety of purposes. Ethnographic sources suggest that chiefs may have controlled trade in some items.

Sedentary life developed much earlier along the Pacific coast of southern California, where marine resources supplemented by plants allowed peoples of the **Early Southern California** (8000–3000 B.P.) tradition to develop small sedentary coastal communities. These communities consisted of several to perhaps several dozen round dwellings, 4 to 8 meters in diameter and constructed from a domed wood framework covered with thatch. Each dwelling housed a single family, so communities ranged in size from twenty to perhaps more than 100 people. Particularly good locations, like **Rincon Point** at the mouth of Rincon creek south of Santa Barbara, were occupied continuously for thousands of years, providing evidence of long-term stability in both subsistence and social organization.

For coastal groups, like those at the Rincon Point site, subsistence included both coastal plant foods and marine resources such as fish, shellfish, and marine mammals, while away from the coast terrestrial animals such as deer, rabbit, and squirrel were important. Seed-bearing plants appear to have been particularly important, and walnuts were collected in large numbers. Hunting was done with spears aided by a spear thrower and armed with large, round-based projectile points. Butchering was done with chipped stone knives and hides worked with chipped stone and bone scrapers as well as bone awls and needles. Fishing was done with bone fishhooks and barbed spears. Seeds and nuts were collected in twined baskets and processed with stone mortar and pestle or mano and metate.

In addition to tools, a wide variety of personal ornaments were also manufactured by Early Southern California peoples. These included shell disk beads and small drilled shells, which were either strung to make necklaces or bracelets or sewn onto clothing or other items. Bone was carved into hairpins. Over time these items became a measure of wealth, and some individuals were able to acquire, and be buried with, large numbers of such personal ornaments. These individuals may have been political leaders in the larger Early Southern California communities.

Peoples of the **Late Southern California** (3000–150 B.P.) tradition developed larger communities and a hereditary chiefdom form of political organization. Communities were regularly spaced and controlled distinct territories where their residents hunted, fished, and collected plants and shellfish. Each community was apparently independent but intermarried with neighbors. Communities themselves consisted of a group of houses set around an open plaza, with an associated cemetery and ceremonial enclosure, which was a circular area surrounded by a windbreak of poles and woven mats (Figure 9.21). Houses were circular domed structures made of a pole framework covered with thatch or woven mats. A single family resided in each house, and communities typically contained fifteen to thirty such houses, or around 100 to 250 people. Each Late Southern California community was headed by a hereditary chief, who adjudicated conflicts and coordinated communal ritual and labor.

**Late Southern California**
(3000–150 B.P.)

FIGURE **9.21**

Reconstruction of what a Late Southern California tradition village may have looked like.

SOURCE: Michael J. Moratto, *California Archaeology* (*New World Archaeological Record Series*) (San Diego, CA: Academic Press, 1984), Figure 4.12. Reprinted by permission of the author.

## ◉ SUMMARY

Painted in broad strokes, the prehistory of North America creates a picture of human cultural adaptation over a 10,000-year period. Nomadic hunter-gatherers moved into the continent at the end of the Pleistocene following herds of big-game animals. As the glacial climate ameliorated these hunter-gatherers began to settle into discrete territories and to focus subsistence on seasonally abundant resources. In some areas (particularly within the Plateau, the Great Plains, and California), these general ways of life continued until the historic period. Elsewhere, particularly in riverine settings, people became more sedentary as time went on, focused on more broad-based exploitation of the local environment, and began experimenting with domesticated plants. Peoples in the Southwest, Eastern Woodlands, and major river valleys of the Great Plains developed large sedentary villages, apparently aided by the introduction of the corn-bean-squash agricultural regime from Mesoamerica. In a few areas large centralized polities emerged.

## ◉ DISCUSSION QUESTIONS

1. What is similar about the places where chiefdoms developed in North America? What is different about them?

2. How did domesticated plants initially affect the traditions that developed them? How did they affect later traditions?

3. Similar patterns of cultural evolution took place in very different environments in North America, such as the Southwest and the Eastern Woodlands. What processes or factors may have led cultures in very different environments to develop along fairly similar lines?

## ◉ ESSAY QUESTIONS

1. Trying to summarize all of North American prehistory in a single chapter is an exercise in futility. Much is missing; much is simplified or glossed over. It is important to realize, however, that the same could be said for any area of the world. Humanity has a rich prehistory, and the extent of our knowledge and understanding of it in North America should point out how little we know about other areas of the world—areas that certainly had an equally rich prehistory but have not had the richness of archaeological research lavished upon them. Write an essay in which you consider how the relatively large amount of time and money that have been focused on the prehistory of North America affects our knowledge of North American prehistory. Does effort and funding create knowledge? If so, what does that suggest about how our knowledge of the past is constructed? Are there political ramifications to the connection between effort, funding, and knowledge? Are there social implications?

2. North American prehistory here is presented in a cultural evolutionary framework. One tradition is seen not only to precede another but to lay a groundwork for developments in the later tradition. Write an essay in which you critically reflect on this underlying evolutionary framework. How does a cultural

evolutionary framework affect the way in which information is presented and interpreted?

3. This chapter is organized around what anthropologists call "culture areas." Culture areas are regions where a particular environment gives rise to similar cultural adaptations; thus, culture areas share similar environments and cultures. Explore the culture area concept by considering the following question: Are culture areas self-fulfilling prophecies or real products of cultural adaptation?

## ✒ RESEARCH PROJECT

Use library and Internet resources to examine three ethnographically described chiefdoms. Consider one aspect of these chiefdoms, such as food production, housing, the activities of chiefs, or the like. Write an essay explaining how ethnographic information might be used to help identify and understand prehistoric chiefdoms. How can ethnographic information about chiefdoms help archaeologists interpret the archaeological record?

## ✦ KEY SOURCES

### Eastern Woodlands

Anderson, 1994; Anderson and Sassaman, 1996; Blitz, 1993; Brose and Greber, 1979; Brown, 1991; Brown and O'Brien, 1990; Caldwell and Hall, 1964; Carstens and Watson, 1996; Chapman, 1985; Christiansen, 2001; Cowan, 1987; Dancy and Pacheco, 1997; Daniel, 2001; Dent, 1995; Dragoo, 1963; Dye and Cox, 1990; Ellis and Ferris, 1990; Emerson, 1997; Emerson and Lewis, 1991; Farnsworth and Emerson, 1986; Fitting, 1972; Gibbon, 2001; Green, 1995; Hasenstab, 2001; Hays, 2001; Henderson, 1992; Henderson and Pollack, 2001; Hunter, 2001; Johnson, J.K., 2001; Mason, 1981; McNett, 1985; Milanich, 1994; Muller, 1997; Pauketat, 1994; Pauketat and Emerson, 1997; Phillips and Brown, 1983; Richie, 1980; Rogers and Smith, 1995; Sassaman, 2001a, 2001b; Sassaman and Anderson, 1996; Scarry, M., 1993; Scarry, J., 1996; Smith, B.D., 1976, 1990; Smith, D., 2001; Snow, 1980, 2001; Stoltman, 1991; Tankersley, 2001; Williams and Elliott, 1998; Williams and Shapiro, 1990; Wright, J.V., 1972b; Wright and Anderson, 1963; Yerkes, 1988.

### Great Plains

Bell, 1984; Chapman, 1975; Frison, 1991; Gregg, Bozell, and Vehik, 2001; Hoffmann, 1996; Holder, 1970; Larson, 2001; Lehmer, 1971; Logan and Ritterbush, 2001; Schlesier, 1994; Wedel, 1986; Wood, 1998; Zimmerman, 1985, 2001.

### Southwest

Adler, 1996, 2001; Cordell, 1994, 1997; Cordell and Gumerman, 1989; Crown and Judge, 1991; Dean, 2001; Doyel, 2001; Grayson, 1993; Gumerman, 1991, 1994; Haas, 2001; Haury, 1985; Huckell, 1996; Jennings, 1978; Lekson, 2001; Masden, 1989; Matson, 1991; Plog, 1997; Reid, 2001; Reid and Whittlesey,

1997, 1999; Rogers, 1966; Roth, 2001; Sebastian, 1992; Smiley, 2001; Vierra, 1994; Vivian, 1990; White and Lekson, 2001; Wills, 2001; Wills and Leonard, 1994; Windes, 1993.

## Plateau

Aikens, 1993; Ames, Dumond, Galm, and Minor, 1998; Ames and Maschner, 1999; Campbell, 1985; Chatters, 1986; Davis, 2001; Greengo, 1986; Lyman, 1991; Mack, 2001; Matson and Coupland, 1995; Minor, 2001a, 2001b; Minor and Toepel, 1986; Ross, 1990.

## California

Arnold, 2001; Chartkoff and Chartkoff, 1984; Johnson and Berry, 2001; King, 1990, 2001; Moratto, 1984; Ragir, 1972.

# HOMOLOVI SOCIAL ORGANIZATION

The great American Southwest is comprised of four arid regions centered on the Four-Corners area (the intersection of the boundaries of Colorado, Arizona, New Mexico, and Utah). This dry region has been home to many people who have created some of the most fantastic architecture in prehistoric North America. Names such as Pueblo Bonito, Chaco Canyon, Mesa Verdi, Snaketown, Casa Grande, and many others adorn maps of the prehistoric Southwest. The Late Anasazi, Late Hohokam, and Late Mogollon were the preeminent archaeological traditions in the Southwest. Much of their architecture was what is called pueblo (from the Spanish word for "home"). This architecture has survived through time along with remains of their pottery. Southwestern pottery, mostly made using a coiled technique and fired with dung and wood in open hearths, comes in many styles and is easy to trace. These great peoples were farmers. They irrigated their crops of corn and beans. Their social organization was highly advanced due to the need for cooperation. Yet by 600 B.P., they were all gone, leaving much behind, including questions as to why they disappeared.

The Media Lab can be found in Chapter 9 on the *Companion Website*™ http://www.prenhall.com/peregrine

## WEB ACTIVITY

The contemporary Hopi (meaning "well-behaved") are an austere group. They occupy a series of mesas in eastern Arizona called First Mesa, Second Mesa, Third Mesa, and Black Mesa. These contemporary pueblo peoples live in much the same way as the ancient puebloans lived. The disappearance of the ancient Anasazi, Hohokam, and Mogollon is no mystery to the Hopi. They trace their ancestry to them. Hopi social structure may mirror the social structure of their ancestors and because of this it is important for archaeologists to study them. In this activity, you will view footage of an interview about Hopi social structure.

## Activity

1. View the video. Who owns the homes and lands of the Hopi? What is the role of men in relation to the land?

2. What is Hopi religion like? How does it differ from modern ecclesiastical religions?

3. How can Hopi pottery styles show marriage patterns in and between villages? How might archaeologists use this information to study ancient Southwest archaeological sites?

# Middle America

Middle America includes modern Mexico, the long isthmus that makes up Central America, the northwestern portion of South America, and the Caribbean (Figure 10.1). While the area is diverse, there is a level of cultural unity that gives the region coherence when looking at its prehistory. Four distinct subregions are often identified as areas of archaeological specialization. From north to south these areas are: Northern Mesoamerica, which includes Mexico north of the Tropic of Cancer; Highland Mesoamerica, which includes Mexico from Oaxaca to the Tropic of Cancer; Lowland Mesoamerica, which includes the Mexican

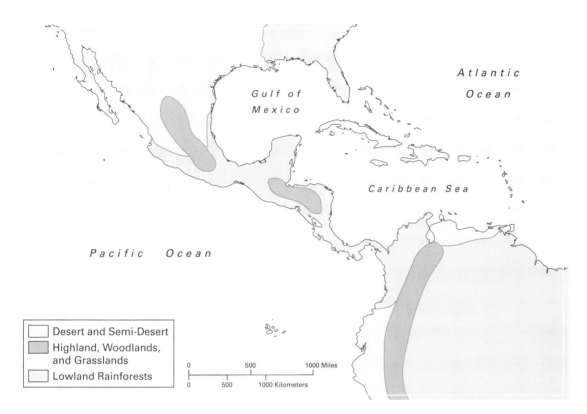

Desert and Semi-Desert
Highland, Woodlands, and Grasslands
Lowland Rainforests

Gulf of Mexico

Atlantic Ocean

Pacific Ocean

Caribbean Sea

0     500     1000 Miles
0     500     1000 Kilometers

FIGURE 10.1

Environments of Middle America.

states of Chiapas, Tabasco, and the Yucatan, Guatemala, Belize, Honduras, and El Salvador; and the Intermediate Area, which includes Nicaragua, Costa Rica, Panama, western Colombia, and Ecuador, as well as the Caribbean (Figure 10.2). Although this organization has its problems (the areas do not have clear boundaries), it does provide a useful framework for looking at the prehistory of Middle America.

Middle America contains, in a relatively small land area, virtually all of the environments known on earth (Figure 10.1). Northern Mesoamerica is a region dominated by deserts and mountains. It is hot and arid year-round. Highland Mesoamerica is more diverse. Highland valleys are dominated by grasslands that merge into thorn, oak, and piñon forest as altitude increases. These highland valleys are generally cool and semiarid. Coastal valleys are hot and humid and have tropical and subtropical forests and savannahs. Lowland Mesoamerica is dominated by tropical forests and marshlands and, like coastal regions of Highland Mesoamerica, is hot and humid year-round. The Intermediate Area is also dominated by tropical forest and is generally hot and humid. It is no surprise that such diverse environments would give rise to diverse cultures and cultural histories.

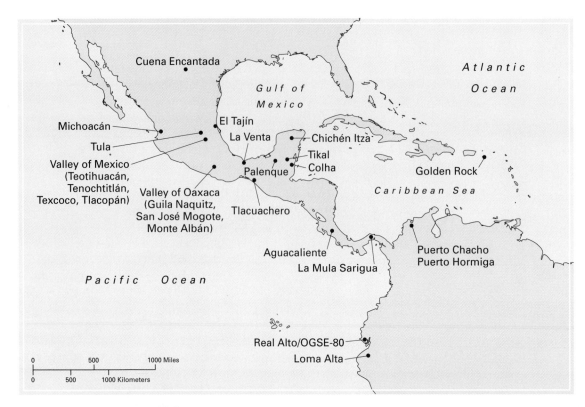

FIGURE **10.2**
Sites discussed in Chapter 10.

## The End of the Upper Paleolithic

**Early Mesoamerican Archaic**
(9600–7000 B.P.)

At the end of the Upper Paleolithic, peoples of the **Early Mesoamerican Archaic** (9600–7000 B.P.) tradition inhabited most of the region today called Middle America. These people were mobile hunters and gatherers, who moved regularly to take advantage of seasonally abundant resources. In the summer dry season, for example, they might move to river valleys or other areas with water, while in fall they might move to upland areas to harvest nuts and fruit. Local populations were small, perhaps only thirty or so people inhabiting a territory of several hundred square kilometers. These people lived in autonomous bands of five to ten individuals, but came together seasonally to collectively hunt and harvest, and to perform rituals.

**Guila Naquitz Cave**
(Mexico, Early Mesoamerican Archaic)

**Guila Naquitz Cave** in Oaxaca, Mexico, is one of the best examples of an Early Mesoamerican Archaic campsite. The cave is located in a canyon in thorn forest above a rich valley floor. Above the cave the thorn forest gives way to oak forest. Thus the cave is located among three major environmental zones, offering access to resources in all three. The cave was occupied repeatedly by a small group of people over more than 6,000 years, and during the Early Mesoamerican Archaic, the cave had at least eight occupations. The inhabitants of the cave collected agave, cactus fruits, nuts, squash, legumes, roots, and many other plants from the surrounding area. They hunted deer, peccary, rabbit, and other small animals. They used a wide variety of chipped stone and bone tools, and used knotted nets and baskets for storage. This basic broad-spectrum hunting and gathering way of life would continue in some parts of Middle America until the historic period.

## NORTHERN MESOAMERICA

Northern Mesoamerica refers to the arid regions of northern Mexico and the Gulf of California (Figure 10.1). Like much of Middle America, the region is diverse and includes arid, temperate, and tropical climates with mean annual temperature ranging from 12.5 degrees C to 28 degrees C and rainfall varying from less than 500 mm in Sonora to over 1,500 mm in Jalisco. Rainfall tends to be seasonal, with 90 percent falling between May and September in some of the coastal areas. Upland areas are dominated by oak forests, changing to pine and fir forests at higher elevations. Coastal areas are dominated by semitropical and tropical forests. The area is rugged in most places, as the region lies within the central volcanic axis running east-west across Mexico, and contains numerous volcanic cones and faults. Volcanic action has produced large obsidian deposits as well as deposits of basalt and granite. The Sierra Madre Occidental mountains contain rich deposits of metals and minerals, including gold, silver, and copper.

Northeastern Mexico is one of the places where the hunting and gathering lifestyle that emerged during the Early Mesoamerican Archaic tradition persisted until the historic period. Here peoples of the **Coahuilan** (8000–500 B.P.) tradition subsisted on succulents and grassland game, such as antelope, deer, and rabbit. They moved seasonally to locations that were used year after year, with caves and rockshelters being preferred. **Cueva Encantada** was one such location. It is a long, shallow rockshelter on the eastern rim of the Valle Colombia in northern Coahuila, Mexico. Cueva Encantada was inhabited repeatedly for nearly 3,000 years and contained at least 1.5 meters of occupational debris when excavated. Probably a single family of five to seven people inhabited the cave at any one time, but the combined debris from perhaps thousands of seasonal occupations left a striking array of materials, including sandals, woven baskets, netting, and a variety of wooden utensils. In addition, a number of plant-lined basins have been interpreted as sleeping pads or beds.

In northwestern Mexico, the story is much different. Here, peoples of the **Trincheras** (3000–450 B.P.) tradition adopted agriculture and developed a lifestyle that appears to have blended elements from the North American Southwest, particularly the Hohokam. Peoples of the Trincheras tradition lived in large, sedentary villages that contained distinctive dry-laid stone terraces, called *trincheras*, from which the tradition derives its name. These terraces were used as house platforms, and a variety of houses are found on Trincheras sites. They range from circular pit structures to dry stone masonry structures to wattle and daub structures. Regardless of their construction, houses were only large enough for a single family, although on some sites there appear to be compounds that may have been locations where extended families resided together. Most villages were quite large, ranging from a few dozen to over 900 terraces. Sites where structures are visible on the surface range from 77 to 232 individual houses.

Trincheras people subsisted primarily on maize, which was grown in river bottoms using both floodwater and canal irrigation. Wild plants were also collected and animals hunted, but maize seems to have dominated the diet. Trincheras peoples also played a role in local exchange systems. Large shell workshops have been found on a number of Trincheras sites, and shell from these sites has been found in both Hohokam and northern Mesoamerican contexts. Trincheras peoples also made purple-on-red ceramics that are similar to Hohokam styles, and a number of Trincheras settlements are within areas that are otherwise dominated by Hohokam settlements, suggesting that Trincheras peoples were well integrated into the Hohokam regional system. Trincheras communities likely had formal leaders or chiefs, and a few sites have obvious public architecture in the form of walled enclosures and mounds supporting structures with apparent ritual functions.

**Coahuilan**
(8000–500 B.P.)

**Cueva Encantada**
(Mexico, Coahuilan)

**Trincheras**
(3000–450 B.P.)

## Huatabampo
(1800–500 B.P.)

The **Huatabampo** (1800–500 B.P.) tradition follows and partially overlaps the Trincheras tradition. These village agriculturalists lived along the coastal plains and river valleys of the Gulf of California, but they appear to have expanded settlement into the Sierra over time. Villages were relatively small, ranging from hamlets of only a few houses to larger communities with several dozen. Houses themselves were constructed of wooden frames covered with woven matting. Huatabampo villages appear to have been economically independent, with simple political leadership. Subsistence was based on maize agriculture, supplemented by fish and shellfish on the coast, and hunted and gathered wild foods in the Sierra. Huatabampo peoples made distinctive thin, polished, red-slipped ceramics. These sometimes had unique shapes, including "chimney" spouts and large "scoop" handles. Otherwise the tool kit was much like others in northern Mesoamerica, consisting of chipped stone projectile points, knives, scrapers, drills, and the like, and ground stone manos and metates. In short, the peoples of the Huatabampo tradition appear to have been relatively independent small farmers.

## West Mexico Classic
(1800–1100 B.P.)

The **West Mexico Classic** (1800–1100 B.P.) tradition also follows the Trincheras tradition. This tradition appears to represent a distinctive regional civilization, one which archaeologists have only recently come to recognize. Large villages with monumental architecture, irrigation agriculture, political hierarchy, and economic specialization all seem to be present. Excavated tombs show clear evidence of social ranking. Fine obsidian mirrors and jewelry, spectacular ceramic figurines and finewares, and some standardization of plainware ceramics suggests that craft specialization was widespread. West Mexico Classic society was supported by intensive agriculture employing irrigated terraced fields. In all these ways, the West Mexico Classic tradition appears to represent a virtually unknown prehistoric Mesoamerican state.

## States

**States** are formally defined as having leaders with the power to govern by force. In chiefdoms, leaders may have some ability to use force, but most of their power comes from status, respect, and perceived supernatural authority. Leaders of states may have status, respect, and supernatural authority, but they don't need any of those to govern—they can force people to follow their authority even if they are disliked and disrespected. Power in states is often implemented through a standing army or police force. States often have a formal set of laws that are enforced by the military or police. There is also a bureaucracy in most states that administers the law and maintains the military or police forces. Finally, since leaders, bureaucrats, and members of the military or police do not contribute to food or craft production, there are typically specialists in these tasks and markets where such materials are bought and sold. The government in states usually supports itself through taxation or tribute taken from the specialist producers.

There is a problem, however, in identifying states in the archaeological record, as many of the things that define states may not leave unambiguous archaeological remains. West Mexico Classic is a case in point, since some scholars think the evidence is clear that a state was present, while others find the evidence lacking. The primary evidence put forward for West Mexico Classic states are the presence of monumental architecture, agricultural intensification supported by public water and land management, and large-scale craft specialization. Monumental architecture in the West Mexico Classic tradition takes two forms. At the beginning of the tradition the West Mexico Classic peoples built large, multichambered, subterranean tombs at depths of 8 meters or more below the ground surface. Digging these tombs would have required massive coordinated labor, and since many of the individuals buried in the tombs are elites bedecked with exotic ornaments and surrounded by fineware ceramics and figurines, it

**States:** polities in which leaders govern by force.

PLATE **2**
The main plaza of Monte Albán.

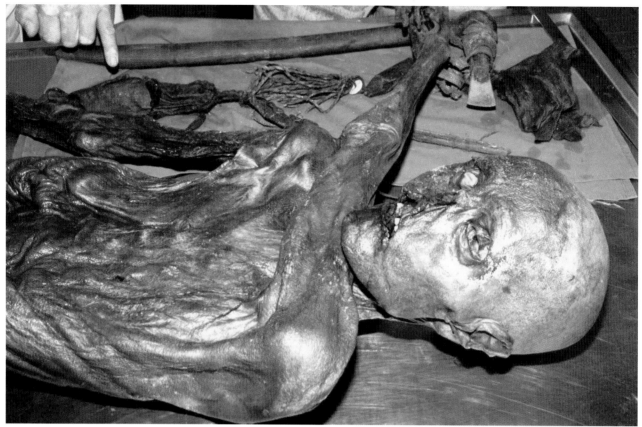

PLATE **3**
The "Ice Man" and some of the personal effects found with him. Note the copper axe in the background that helped to establish the "Ice Man's" antiquity.

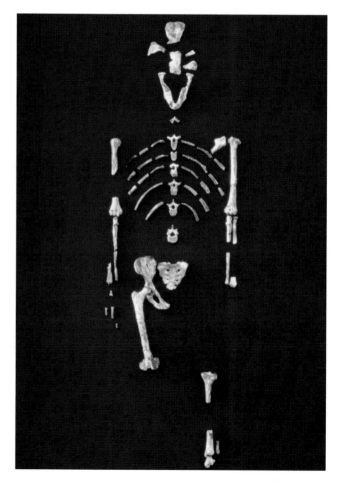

PLATE **4**
The *Australopithecus afarensis* skeleton nicknamed "Lucy."

PLATE **5**
Two *Australopithecus afarensis*
individuals walk through
newly laid ash at Laetoli in this
reconstruction of the event that
formed the famous footprints
some 3.6 million years ago.

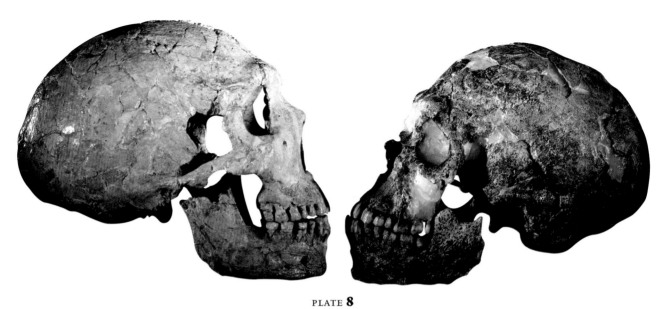

PLATE **8**

Comparison of a Neandertal skull from Amud (*left*) and a modern human skull from Qafzeh (*right*). The two species lived near one another in the eastern Mediterranean for perhaps as long as 60,000 years.

PLATE **9**

Artist's reconstruction of a Neandertal burial.

PLATE **10**

A group of Upper Paleolithic bone tools from Europe.

PLATE **II**
Paintings on the wall of Ardeche cave in France, found in 1994.

**PLATE 12**

A Kwakiutl mask with an eagle face.

PLATE **13**
Typical Hopewell ornaments—
copper ear spools and a pearl
and copper necklace.

PLATE **14**
A West Mexico terracotta
figurine of a ball player.

PLATE **15**

A group of Olmec figurines found buried together in a pit at La Venta.

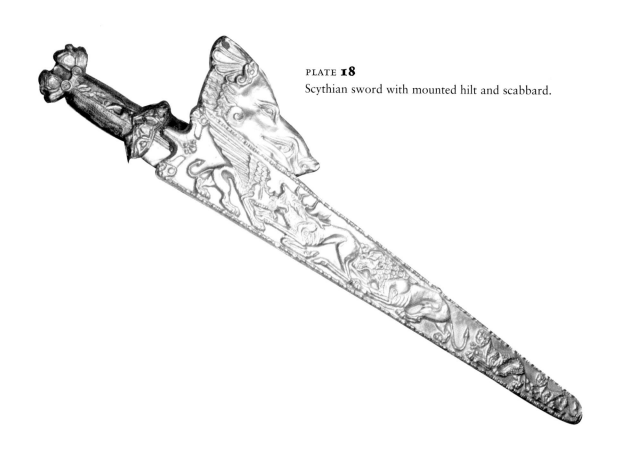

PLATE **18**

Scythian sword with mounted hilt and scabbard.

PLATE **19**

A row of Easter Island *moai*.

PLATE **20**

The "Standard of Ur."

PLATE **21**

One of two "Ram in a Thicket"
statues from Ur.

PLATE **22**
This photograph illustrates the tremendous genetic variation in domesticated maize.
Such variation has made it difficult to identify the direct ancestor of maize, but it is one of
the characteristics of maize that has led it to be one of the world's most important domesticated plants.

PLATE **23**
These terraced Incan fields and ruins illustrate the labor that is often put into
building substantial settlements once food production is adopted.

PLATE **24**
Aztec nobles as depicted in a contact period codex.
Note the distinctive regalia they each wear.

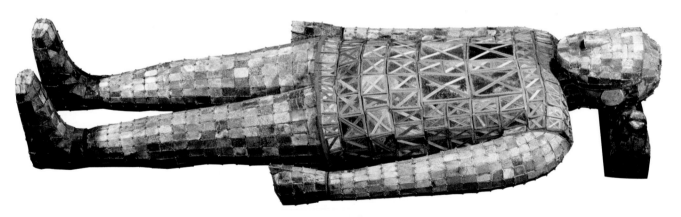

PLATE **25**
The jade burial suit of Han Princess Tou Wan.
The presence of such elaborate grave ornaments is a clear indication of elite class.

FIGURE **10.3**

Reconstruction of what a West Mexico Classic pyramid and surrounding community may
have looked like.

SOURCE: Richard Townshend (ed.), *Ancient West Mexico* (London: Thames and Hudson, 1998), Figure 22.

seems clear that these were built to house elites who were capable of amassing
and controlling a large labor pool.

Later in the West Mexico Classic tradition, above-ground monumental architecture was built. This architecture may have developed out of the platform mounds
that were often built over tomb shafts and, in essence, moved the location of labor
from the unseen below-ground tombs to highly visible circular stepped pyramids
(Figure 10.3). These pyramids were the center point for residential compounds,
which were build around them on low platforms, and ball courts, built adjacent to

major pyramid compounds. Again, considerable labor would have been required to build these pyramids, platforms, and ball courts that surrounded them—so much labor, in fact, that some archaeologists suggest force, and hence a state form of government, would have been needed to amass and coordinate this labor.

Considerable labor would have been needed for the construction and maintenance of West Mexico Classic agricultural fields as well. During the tradition, population apparently rose to the point where standard agricultural practices were not sufficient, and large complexes of terraces and raised-field agricultural systems were built. The terraces were cut into steep hillsides, allowing them to be brought into production. The raised fields were built in lowlands, and these included complex irrigation facilities that diverted streams into the field canals. Both systems appear to have been carefully planned, and this, in turn, suggests that a bureaucracy capable of designing and building such agricultural facilities was present in West Mexico Classic polities.

Finally, craft specialization seems to have been present. The architecture of the circular pyramids was sophisticated, and archaeologists have suggested that their construction would have required specialist stone masons. Massive obsidian workshops have been found on a number of West Mexico Classic sites, particularly near local sources of fine obsidian. Shell workshops, particularly specializing in *Spondylus*, which was available in large quantities along the West Mexico coast, were present, and apparently exported finished shell beads and other items to locations as far away as the North American Southwest and perhaps even Ecuador. Special salt production facilities were also present at a number of West Mexico Classic sites. These are particularly interesting, since the volume of salt produced at these sites far exceeded what would have been needed in West Mexico, so that salt was clearly being produced for export. Ceramics, too, were made by specialist craftsmen in large workshops, and exchanged widely (see Color Plate 14).

Was a state present in the West Mexico Classic tradition? The answer depends on how one views and weighs the archaeological evidence. West Mexico Classic polities had the ability to coordinate large labor pools for the construction of pyramids, ball courts, and residential terraces. Labor was also coordinated to build and maintain agricultural facilities. Specialist craftsmen produced a variety of items that were exchanged both within West Mexico and to locations across Middle America. Was a state therefore present? Perhaps, or perhaps not.

**West Mexico Postclassic (1100–480 B.P.)**

There is less doubt about the presence of a state in the **West Mexico Postclassic** (1100–480 B.P.) tradition, for at the end of the period both Aztec and Spanish chroniclers describe what is known as the Tarascan state. The Tarascans fell to the Spanish during the conquest period, but they had withstood attempted invasions by the Aztecs for more than a century. The Tarascan's tenacity was accomplished through a well-coordinated army and a series of garrisons that defended their frontier. Outlying polities were tightly attached to the core of the Tarascan state through bonds of tribute and labor that were reciprocated by the Tarascan system of defense. Indeed, many archaeologists suggest that the Tarascan state should be considered an empire.

## Empires

**Empires** differ from states in that they incorporate a number of otherwise independent polities within an overarching political structure. Usually this takes place in the context of military conquest. The polities conquered are allowed to function independently on a day-to-day basis, especially in terms of food supply and local bureaucratic or judicial issues, but are subject to the empire in terms of extra-local matters such as defense. Conquered polities are also expected to provide taxes or tribute to the empire as a means of paying for the empire's military.

In the West Mexico Postclassic tradition, the peoples of Michoacán appear to have developed an empire. How can one tell? What features of the archaeological

**Empires:** incorporate a number of independent polities within an overarching political structure, usually through military conquest.

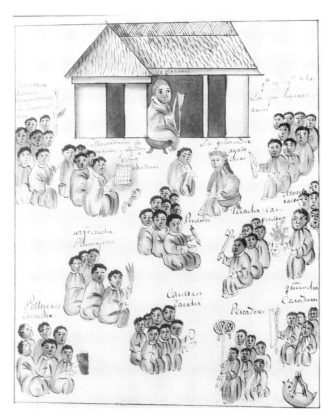

FIGURE **10.4**
This image from the *Relación de Michoacán* illustrates the economic organization of a Tarascan village. Each group of people represents a different group of specialists, such as fishermen and artists, while the village chief sits at the top in his house, apparently overseeing them.

record suggest that an empire was present in Michoacán? One piece of evidence is the widespread distribution of common traditions of metallurgy, ceramic forms (especially pipes), and polychrome ceramics which spread rapidly into polities that did not employ them before. Another piece of evidence is the dramatic increase in the size of the Tarascan capital, the site of Tzintzuntzan. A third piece of evidence is the creation of defensive sites on the imperial frontier. But by far the best evidence for the West Mexico Postclassic Tarascan empire is the *Relación de Michoacán*, an account of the history and culture of Michoacán by a Franciscan monk, first published in 1541. The *Relación de Michoacán* details the nature and extent of the Tarascan empire and how it allegedly developed (see Figure 10.4).

The Tarascan empire was said to have been founded by a warrior-leader named Taríacuri, who may have been from the Chichimec region of northern Mexico, early in the fourteenth century. The empire was expanded by his son and nephews to the very edge of the Aztec empire. For more than a century the Aztecs attempted to conquer the Tarascans, but with little success. The standoff meant that there was little interaction, either political or economic, between the two empires, likely to the detriment of the Tarascans, who were largely encircled by areas of Aztec control. The border areas of the Tarascan empire were patrolled by local peoples put into service of the empire as a part of local tribute. Military personnel from the imperial government apparently led these patrols, but the rank-and-file military personnel were local conscripts. In addition to labor, the imperial rulers demanded gold, silver, copper, and other minerals and ores, as well as salt, shell, and other trade goods as tribute. The empire, in turn, provided security, land and water resources, and a system of merchants and markets to distribute goods around the empire.

The West Mexico Classic Tarascan empire seems remarkably similar to other empires I will discuss in this chapter and a later chapter. In Chapter 17 I will provide a comparative discussion of both states and empires, how they develop and collapse, and their effect on the peoples who live within them.

## HIGHLAND MESOAMERICA

Life in Highland Mesoamerica was focused on the large intermontaine valleys that dominate the region. While the climate of Highland Mesoamerica fluctuated during prehistory, it was generally similar to the contemporary climate. Summers were warm and wet, while winters were cooler and dry. Typical temperatures ranged between 15 and 30 degrees C, with cooler temperatures at higher elevations and warmer temperatures along the coast. Precipitation also varied by altitude from less than 500 mm a year in some highland areas to more than 3,000 mm along the coasts of Veracruz. In the highlands, broad valleys are separated by steep volcanic mountains rising to more than 2,000 meters, and most highland valleys are above 800 meters. Soils in the valleys are fertile loams. Valleys tend to have scrubby, grassland vegetation, while foothills and mountains have oak and pine forests. A wide range of other plants as well as animal resources lived in these contrasting environments.

**Highland Mesoamerican Archaic (7000–4000 B.P.)**

The earliest peoples to live in these highland valleys, peoples of the **Highland Mesoamerican Archaic** (7000–4000 B.P.) tradition, were hunters and gatherers who lived in family bands moving seasonally between valley floor and upland locations. Like their predecessors, the peoples of the Early Mesoamerican Archaic tradition, Highland Mesoamerican Archaic peoples used a wide variety of resources and effectively timed movements to take full advantage of seasonal availability of acorns, piñon nuts, and cactus fruits. They also hunted deer, peccary, and small animals. Through their use of a broad spectrum of resources and effective scheduling of movements, the Highland Mesoamerican Archaic peoples were able to live within discrete territories and spread throughout the Highland valleys with apparent ease.

In addition to effective scheduling, the peoples of the Highland Mesoamerican Archaic tradition also began to actively domesticate local plants. The earliest domesticate appears to have been bottle gourds, which were used to carry water (see Figure 10.5). The bottle gourd may have been domesticated through a process in which groups actively planted desirable varieties of bottle gourds in locations where they did not naturally grow, in order to ensure their availability throughout a group's territory. Two other early domesticates, squash and runner beans, probably grew wild in the disturbed soil near inhabited caves and rockshelters. Highland Mesoamerican Archaic peoples may have actively selected preferred varieties and planted them, knowing they would grow well in those locations. The most important domesticate of the Highland Mesoamerican Archaic peoples was maize, which I will discuss in detail in Chapter 16 on the origins of agriculture.

**Early Highland Mesoamerican Preclassic (4000–2600 B.P.)**

The use of domesticates became more widespread and intensive, and peoples of the **Early Highland Mesoamerican Preclassic** (4000–2600 B.P.) tradition began to settle into permanent agricultural communities. While most of these communities were small hamlets with only a few resident families, others were very large, with more than 1,000 residents. Indeed, some scholars have suggested a hierarchy of settlements had developed by the time of the Early Highland Mesoamerican Preclassic tradition, with hamlets at the bottom of the hierarchy, larger villages that served as an economic center for surrounding hamlets, and a preeminent village that served as the political and religious center for a number of village groups. Hamlets and villages appear to have been largely egalitarian, but social stratification appears to have been present in preeminent villages, where political leaders may have become a hereditary elite class.

Early Highland Mesoamerican communities of all sizes were located within easy access to good agricultural soils, in which maize, beans, squash, avocados, and chilis were grown. Rainfall was sufficient for these crops in most areas, but irrigation and raised fields were used in more arid locations. Planting and cultivation were done with simple digging sticks, and harvesting was accomplished with chert or obsidian blades. Crops were dried and stored in net bags and baskets, or in ceramics, which were manufactured in a wide variety of forms and with widely

FIGURE **10.5**
A bottle gourd, perhaps the
first domesticated plant in the
New World.

varying decoration. Wild plants were also collected, and deer, peccary, rabbit, water-fowl, fish, and reptiles were all hunted. Trade was also important to some Early Highland Mesoamerican communities as a wide range of goods began to be traded across Mesoamerica at this time. Basic trade items included obsidian, which was used by all members of society. Emergent elites appear also to have traded exotic goods such as incised jade and shell, magnetite mirrors, and beads.

One of the best-known Early Highland Mesoamerican Preclassic communities is **San José Mogote** in Oaxaca, Mexico. It is located on prime agricultural soils over-looking the Atoyac river. During the Early Highland Mesoamerican Preclassic, the site grew from a small village covering about 8 hectares to a large one covering more than 70 hectares, the largest community in the Valley of Oaxaca. While residential architecture—wattle-and-daub houses built on stone platforms—remained the same during this time, public architecture underwent significant changes. Lime-plastered buildings built on low earthen platforms have been interpreted as public buildings, perhaps religious structures. Quantities of obsidian, magnetite, and other materials of nonlocal origin increased over time, suggesting that the site was becoming a cen-ter for regional exchange that was perhaps controlled by elites. The presence of carved images of captives also suggests that war was part of life in San José Mogote (Figure 10.6).

In the **Late Highland Mesoamerican Preclassic** (2600–1600 B.P.) tradition some communities developed into cities with plazas, pyramidal mounds, and other public architecture. Perhaps the best example is **Monte Albán**, which became the primary urban center for the Valley of Oaxaca, Mexico. Unlike San José Mogote, which was built adjacent to both agricultural fields and a source of fresh water, Monte Albán was built on a high prominence, distant from the fields that produced food for its residents and requiring every drop of water to be hauled up a steep 400-meter slope.

**San José Mogote**
(Mexico, Early Highland
Mesoamerican
Preclassic)

**Late Highland
Mesoamerican
Preclassic**
(2600–1600 B.P.)

**Monte Albán**
(Mexico, Late Highland
Mesoamerican
Preclassic)

FIGURE **10.6**

This *danzante* from San José Mogote probably represents a sacrificed war captive, and illustrates the importance of conflict in Early Highland Mesoamerican Preclassic polities.

Why build a city of perhaps 17,000 residents in such an unlikely place? The answer seems to be both for defense and because the site was not previously inhabited. Monte Albán was built in a "neutral" location, near the center of the valley, as a new ruling capitol. Among the first constructions were pyramidal mounds and walled compounds that make up the spectacular main plaza of Monte Albán, and which were the center of government (Figure 10.7). Some of these early constructions

FIGURE **10.7**

The main plaza at Monte Albán, the center of the polity that came to control the Valley of Oaxaca.

included depictions of executed captives and glyphs recording the polities conquered by the leaders of the Monte Albán state (like Figure 10.6). It appears that the leaders of Monte Albán conquered the other polities in the Valley of Oaxaca and established a central state government in a new, defensible location.

Of course not all Late Highland Mesoamerican Preclassic peoples lived in urban centers like Monte Albán. Indeed, much of the population remained in small agricultural villages and hamlets. A typical house in one of these smaller villages was a rectangular wattle-and-daub or adobe brick structure roughly 3 meters by 5 meters in size. A courtyard work area and external kitchen would have been located adjacent to the house. Daily life would have been centered around agricultural chores—preparing fields and planting, weeding and watering, and harvesting. Plant processing—drying and grinding with a stone mano and metate—took a great deal of labor as well. Maize, beans, and squash were the primary domesticates, which together provided a well-balanced diet. Amaranth, tomatoes, chilis, cotton, tobacco, and other plants were also grown, and turkeys were kept. Wild cactus fruits, agave hearts, acorns, and other wild foods were collected, and hunting of deer, peccary, and small game was common. For a typical farmer of the Late Highland Mesoamerican Preclassic, this rural way of life was largely unaffected by the developments going on at places like Monte Albán.

Political centralization continued during the Central Mexico Classic and Southern Mexican Highlands Classic traditions. **Teotihuacan,** perhaps the most important city in the prehistoric New World (Figure 10.8), came into power during

**Teotihuacan**
(Mexico, Central Mexico Classic)

FIGURE **10.8**
The facade of the Feathered Serpent Pyramid at Teotihuacan illustrates both the scale and craftsmanship of this ancient city.

# Teotihuacan

Teotihuacan sits in the northeastern part of the Valley of Mexico, near present-day Mexico City. It is a propitious location, for just as Mexico City is one of the world's largest cities and the center of an important state, so Teotihuacan at its height, some 1,800 years ago, was one of the great cities of the world and center to a powerful empire. Over a century of research has provided a detailed picture of this ancient city and its environs, and archaeological survey in the surrounding Basin of Mexico has provided an unprecedented understanding of the world of Teotihuacan.

Eighteen hundred years ago Teotihuacan had a residental area covering about 25 square kilometers and a population of perhaps 150,000. The city was laid out on a grid with a major north–south axis called the "Street of the Dead" at its core. At the northern end of the "Street of the Dead" was the Pyramid of the Moon and its plaza, surrounded by a series of platform mounds, temples, and elite residences. To the south, on the east side of the "Street of the Dead," was the massive Pyramid of the Sun—the largest pre-Columbian structure in the New World and one of the largest structures of the ancient world. The area encompassing these two pyramids has been interpreted as the religious center of the Teotihuacan polity.

Farther south along the "Street of the Dead," at the geographic center of the city, were two large compounds, the Ciudadela enclosure, which includes the Feathered Serpent pyramid (Figure 10.8), and the "Great Compound," a large open space surrounded by a low wall and numerous buildings. These have been interpreted as the political and economic center of the Teotihuacan polity. The Ciudadela is a unique structure, with the Feathered Serpent pyramid at its center, surrounded by a large plaza, which is enclosed by what are essentially a series of low pyramids connected by a single massive wall. It is thought to have been a political and military compound, a place where political and military leaders would meet with outsiders and citizens. Across the "Street of the Dead" is the "Great Compound." This large open plaza is thought to have been a central marketplace for Teotihuacan, a place where the numerous craftspeople who worked in the city could exchange their wares for food and other necessities, and where people from outside the polity could come to trade foreign goods.

Craft production was widespread within Teotihuacan, and there is good evidence that foreigners made regular trade and perhaps diplomatic visits to the city.

**Central Mexico Classic (2150–1350 B.P.)**

the Central Mexico Classic (2150–1350 B.P.) tradition, and is described in some detail in the box feature. Teotihuacan integrated the whole of the Valley of Mexico into a single political entity, and its influence was felt throughout Highland and Lowland Mesoamerica. A combination of militarism and trade were the foundation of Teotihuacan's influence, and it is worth taking a look at both.

But as much as scholars focus on the international aspects of this ancient city, with its "barrios" of foreigners and evidence of regular interaction with peoples of the Gulf Coast and the Maya region, its purpose was to serve its residents. A typical resident of Teotihuacan lived in an apartment compound. An apartment consisted of a suite of rooms—probably one or more storage rooms and one or more rooms for sleeping and daily activities. Several adjoining apartments made up a compound. Apartments were arranged around a central courtyard, and the compound itself surrounded by a wall that provided only one or two access points. There was typically a small platform temple within the courtyard, where censers were burned and offerings made, perhaps to ancestors. Some scholars have suggested that these apartment compounds were owned by patrilineal descent groups, but the evidence is unclear.

The scale of these apartment compounds and their construction and ornamentation varies considerably. Some compounds are very large, and these have been interpreted as elite residences or palaces, particularly those located at the northern end of the "Street of the Dead." Others seem much less substantial. There is marked variation even within some compounds, with some individual apartments having large rooms and lavish wall paintings, and others having neither. Some archaeologists have interpreted these differences as illustrating marked social stratification, but the evidence is not clear since the fact that apartments of varying types occupy single complexes might also suggest that social equality was emphasized in Teotihuacan society.

One of the more interesting aspects of Teotihuacan is the lack of obvious political leaders. There are no stelae depicting rulers or describing their exploits as are found elsewhere in Mesoamerica, and even the presence of elite residences and palaces is equivocal. Teotihuacan seems a state without a head. Some scholars have suggested that equality may have been emphasized even in the political structure of Teotihuacan, with leaders being "first among equals" and serving not as powerful individuals but as individuals taking on positions of power for the good of society. Despite over a half century of sustained research at Teotihuacan, the city leaves many unanswered questions.

SOURCES: Cowgill, George, 1997, "State and Society at Teotihuacan, Mexico," *Annual Review of Anthropology*, 26: 129–161; Kurtz, D.V., 1987, "The Economics of Urbanization and State Formation at Teotihuacan," *Current Anthropology* 28: 329–353; Manzanilla, Linda, 1996, "Corporate Groups and Domestic Activities at Teotihuacan," *Latin American Antiquity* 7: 228–246; Millon, René, *Urbanization at Teotihuacan, Mexico, Volume 1: The Teotihuacan Map* (Austin: University of Texas Press, 1973); Spence, Michael, 1981, "Obsidian Production and the State in Teotihuacan," *American Antiquity* 46: 769–788; Storey, Rebecca, 1991, "Residential Compound Organization and the Evolution of the Teotihuacan State," *Ancient Mesoamerica* 2: 107–118.

While the origins of Teotihuacan are not entirely clear, it is certainly clear that militarism played an important role. For example, some 200 people, dressed as warriors and accompanied by weapons, were sacrificed as part of the construction of the Feathered Serpent Pyramid (Figure 10.8). The pyramid itself is ornamented with images associated with war, and the Feathered Serpent deity itself is thought to have been a god of war. In addition, small figurines of warriors are found in abundance at Teotihuacan, and war is a common theme on some ceramic forms, such as incense burners. This emphasis on war makes considerable sense when one considers the area that Teotihuacan ruled—some 25,000 square kilometers. It is unlikely that any polity could have incorporated and ruled such a large area without being strongly militaristic. Teotihuacan's armies were apparently well organized, with warrior ornaments depicting at least four military orders (rattlesnake, jaguar, coyote, and raptorial bird), and effective weapons including atl-atl propelled spears. Teotihuacan's influence across Mesoamerica may also have been aided by its militarism, as military symbolism is the most prominent feature of Teotihucan influence in places like Lowland Mesoamerica.

In addition to warfare, however, Teotihuacan trade was a powerful influence, and, indeed, the two probably went hand in hand. Teotihuacan imported large amounts of raw materials and produced craft goods on a huge scale. Indeed, one estimate suggests 400 obsidian workshops were present at Teotihuacan. In addition to obsidian, there were large numbers of lapidary and ceramic workshops in the city. Materials manufactured in these workshops, particularly green obsidian and ceramics, are found throughout Highland and Lowland Mesoamerica. More importantly, however, individuals from Teotihuacan established trade enclaves within foreign polities, and foreign polities apparently did the same in Teotihuacan. For example, there are two well-established "barrios" of foreign peoples at Teotihuacan—one from the Valley of Oaxaca and the other from the Maya region. These people may have been special craftsmen who came to Teotihucan to practice their trade, or, more likely, merchants trading foreign goods. Again, this is not surprising, as Maya inscriptions record formal political ties between Teotihuacan and Lowland Mesoamerican cities like Tikal, and people in the Valley of Mexico had been interacting with peoples in the Valley of Oaxaca for centuries before the rise of Teotihuacan.

Teotihuacan was not the only state to be flourishing in the Mesoamerican highlands at this time, for peoples of the **Southern Mexican Highlands Classic** (1700–1300 B.P.) tradition lived within a powerful state centered at Monte Albán (see Figure 10.7). Like Teotihuacan, Monte Albán integrated an entire highland valley, the Valley of Oaxaca, into a single polity. And like Teotihuacan, militarism and trade seem to have been key aspects of the state's influence. One of the first public structures built at Monte Albán was the so-called Danzantes Gallery, a platform built at the southern end of a large plaza and faced with rows of carved stone slabs. The stone slabs depict naked people in odd poses that were originally thought to be dancers, hence the name *danzante*—dancer in Spanish. However, closer examination has demonstrated that these are images of dead captives, often disemboweled or sexually mutilated (see Figure 10.6). Most have several glyphs which name the location from which the individual came. The Danzantes Gallery, then, appears to depict the murdered rulers or military figures from locations around the Valley of Oaxaca—a clear statement of Monte Albán's power, and a clear indication of the role militarism must have played in its ascendancy.

Trade was also central to the Monte Albán state, if only for provisioning its residents. The area around Monte Albán could not possibly have supported the population with food, so food must have been imported to the city in large quantities. Much of this may have been in the form of tribute, but trade may also have taken place. A number of archaeologists think that markets emerged during the Southern Mexican Highlands Classic tradition as a way for food to be exchanged for other goods. A possible market area found near Monte Albán has evidence that ceramics, chipped stone, raw stone, and processed food were all exchanged at the site. Ceramics underwent a dramatic transformation in the Southern Mexican Highlands Classic tradition, becoming standardized in form—simple flat-bottomed

⊛ **Southern Mexican Highlands Classic** (1700–1300 B.P.)

bowls that are easily stackable—and wholly lacking in decoration. These ceramics were mass-produced at sites around the valley, and their production may have been controlled by the state since production of local ceramic forms entirely ceased. Thus it appears that the Monte Albán state had profound influence over the valley's economy.

While states like those centered at Teotihuacan and Monte Albán were able to integrate large areas of highland Mexico into single polities, during the **Central Mexico Postclassic** (1300–429 B.P.) and **Postclassic Southern Mexican Highlands** (1300–430 B.P.) traditions these large polities dissolved into smaller, more regionally diverse ones. Teotihuacan was "selectively" destroyed—temples and elite areas were burned and idols were smashed—and large parts of the city were abandoned. What happened is an intriguing question. Some archaeologists argue that the city was conquered by an external army—perhaps Nahua or Chichimec peoples from the north, but the fact that large parts of the city show little or no damage makes conquest improbable. Others argue that an internal conflict erupted within the city, and the population rose up against the elites and priests. The selective destruction of the site seems to make this more plausible, but the underlying cause is still unknown.

Monte Albán was also largely abandoned, but its dissolution seems to have been less violent. People simply left the city, and apparently moved to one of several regional centers that appeared at the same time as Monte Albán declined. Over time even these regional centers broke down, and the population of the Valley of Oaxaca lived primarily in small, agricultural communities that were part of a small regional polities. Historic documents suggest that twenty-seven distinct polities were present in the Valley of Oaxaca in the early sixteenth century, each having a ruling nobility. What happened? Why did the Monte Albán state dissipate so rapidly? One answer is that production and trade moved out of government control and into the hands of local craftsmen and merchants. Without the government funneling goods to the population at Monte Albán, the residents could not support themselves and the city, and its power as a focus of regional integration rapidly declined. But this isn't a wholly satisfactory answer since one still has to ask why government control might have ceased. That question has no clear answer at this point. We will return to examine the rise and decline of the states centered at Monte Albán and Teotihuacan in a comparative framework in Chapter 17.

By 1000 B.P. a new power arose in Highland Mesoamerica—the Toltecs—with their political center at the site of **Tula,** in Hidalgo, just north of the Valley of Mexico. In most ways the ascendancy of the Toltecs is reminicent of Teotihuacan, and many archaeologists see Tula largely as a replacement for Teotihuacan. The Toltecs were said to have been warlike invaders from the north, who conquered the Tula region and established their capital there. Thus the Toltecs were clearly militaristic like the peoples of Teotihuacan. The Toltecs were also engaged in trade in a way reminiscent of Teotihuacan and established a formal trade relationship between Tula, the Lowland Mesoamerican site of Chichén Itza (discussed on pages 248–249), and the Gulf Coast site of **El Tajín,** in order to move goods from Highland Mesoamerica to Lowland Mesoamerica and back across the Gulf of Mexico. However, Tula never achieved the size or regional power that Teotihuacan did, and its reign lasted only until about 800 B.P. when another power entered Highland Mesoamerica—the Aztecs.

The Aztecs, who called themselves the Mexica, entered Highland Mesoamerica like the Toltecs—as migrants from the north. They found themselves unwelcome and were driven from place to place until they found **Tenochtitlan**—an island in Lake Texcoco located in the very center of the Valley of Mexico. Their patron diety, Huitzilopochtli, is said to have told them that Tenochtitlan was to be their land, and with a stable location to call home, the Mexica began what must be one of the greatest political ascendancies in world prehistory. They began by forming alliances

**Central Mexico Postclassic**
(1300–429 B.P.)

**Postclassic Southern Mexican Highlands**
(1300–430 B.P.)

**Tula** (Mexico, Central Mexico Postclassic)

**El Tajín** (Mexico, Gulf Coast Classic)

**Tenochtitlan** (Mexico, Central Mexico Postclassic)

**Texcoco** (Mexico, Central Mexico Postclassic)

**Tlacopan** (Mexico, Central Mexico Postclassic)

with neighboring peoples at **Texcoco** and **Tlacopan.** Over the next century, this "Triple Alliance" would become centered at Tenochtitlan, with the Mexica ruler being preeminent over rulers at the other two cities. Begining about 570 B.P. the "Triple Alliance" began to form the historic Aztec empire. They launched military campaigns against polities across highland Mesoamerica, bringing most of the central and southern highlands under their control. Once incorporated into the growing empire, these local polities had to supply tribute in the form of food, clothing, and craft products to Tenochtitlan, along with labor for public construction projects and, most important, military service. Goods and services were then distributed out from Tenochtitlan to the populace of the other Aztec cities and military garrisons.

Tenochtitlan itself was one of the great cities of the prehistoric world. It was connected to the shores of Lake Texcoco by three massive causeways which met in the central ceremonial district. There, a massive walled compound housed the royal palace, the houses of lower-ranking rulers, administrative buildings, and pyramidal temples to the Mexica deities (see Figure 10.9), especially Huitzilopochtli, to whom the Mexica regularly sacrificed war captives. It is estimated that 500 to 1,000 people resided within this central religious and administrative compound. Outside of the central compound the city was divided into four quarters, each of which was further divided into smaller administrative districts, with some eighty districts in all. Each district had a ceremonial and administrative center and a school. Houses were built around these district centers and consisted of several rooms surrounding a patio. All together, the city of Tenochtitlan covered an area of 12 square kilometers and had a total population of perhaps 200,000 people at the time of the Spanish conquest— an amazing size given that London had only 50,000 residents and Seville only 70,000 residents at the same time.

FIGURE **10.9**

The Stone of the Sun, some 3.5 meters in diameter, was found in the central administrative district of Tenochtitlan. At the center of the stone is the god Tonatiuh, who governed the universe. Surrounding him are band of symbols representing each of the 20 days of the 18 month Aztec year. Coiled around the outside are two fire serpents. Most scholars believe the Stone of the Sun represents basic facets of Aztec cosmology.

## LOWLAND MESOAMERICA

Lowland Mesoamerica refers primarily to the Yucatan peninsula and the coastal regions of Guatemala, Honduras, and Belize. The region varies from mountainous highlands to level coastal plains and swampy estuarine lowlands. The highlands are dominated by a group of active volcanoes with peaks rising above 4,000 meters, while the lowlands are dominated by rolling hills and shallow basins. Climate is temperate in the highlands, with a mean annual temperature ranging between 15 degrees and 25 degrees C, and tropical in the lowlands, with a mean annual temperature ranging between 25 degrees and 35 degrees C. Water is available from rivers and lakes, except in the northern lowlands where subsurface drainage often limits access to sinkholes (*cenotes*). There are distinct wet (May–December) and dry (January–April) seasons, with mean annual rainfall in the range of 2,000 to 3,000 mm. Deep volcanic or alluvial soils are typical of the highlands and the Pacific coastal plain, while many lowland areas have shallow tropical forest soils. The mountains provided rich sources of stone, including obsidian and jade, while lowland limestone was used for masonry, burned and mixed with water for plaster, and mined for chert.

The flora and fauna of the region are highly diverse Highland forests included evergreen and deciduous trees, while lowland rain forests contained a vast variety of hardwoods, palms, and other species. Animals included deer, tapir, and rabbit, as well as carnivores such as pumas and jaguars. Reptiles and amphibians were present in large numbers in all environments, as were birds. Rivers and lakes provided fish, while the Pacific and Gulf coasts yielded shellfish and reptiles in addition to fish.

Peoples of the **Lowland Mesoamerican Archaic** (7000–3800 B.P.) tradition were hunters and gatherers. Unfortunately, few sites have been excavated, so little is known about the Lowland Mesoamerican Archaic way of life. Most sites have been found in coastal areas, where populations may have lived in semisedentary communities, subsisting on fish, shellfish, and reptiles. Many inland sites may have been special-function sites for things like stone tool production or gathering forest resources, but there are also larger sites that may have been residential base camps. The few excavated Lowland Mesoamerican Archaic houses are small, oval structures built from a domed wood frame covered with thatch. Most communities probably consisted of only a few of these structures, and perhaps fifteen to twenty people.

> **Lowland Mesoamerican Archaic**
> (7000–3800 B.P.)

The technology used by Lowland Mesoamerican Archaic peoples was simple and included chipped stone tools made from locally available cherts, especially massive stemmed projectile points, large blades and blade tools, and a variety of smaller scrapers, drills, and the like made from both flakes and blades. Large cobbles and choppers were apparently used to crack open shellfish. Ceramics were not made, and cooking and food storage may have been done with baskets or hide bags, but these have not survived.

A good example of a coastal Lowland Mesoamerican Archaic site is **Tlacuachero** on the coastal plain of Chiapas, Mexico. The site consists of a large, artificial island within a shallow estuary, constructed largely from crushed clam shells. The island covers about 18,000 square meters and rises some 7 meters above the estuary. The remains of fish, reptiles, shrimp, and, of course, clams were found within the Archaic levels of the mound. The tool kit includes hammer and milling stones, obsidian flakes, and a few other stone artifacts, all apparently related to processing shellfish and clams. The remains of two oval structures were also found, which are interpreted as having wattle-and-daub walls and a thatched roof. The excavators of the site suggest it may have been used seasonally by inland agriculturalists as a location to harvest and process coastal resources.

> **Tlacuachero**
> (Mexico, Lowland Mesoamerican Archaic)

A good example of an inland Lowland Mesoamerican Archaic site is **Colha** in northern Belize (Figure 10.10). Colha is a relatively late site, dating to the time when agriculture was beginning to dominate subsistence practices. The site is essentially

> **Colha** (Belize, Lowland Mesoamerican Archaic)

FIGURE **10.10**

Excavations in a Lowland Mesoamerican Archaic lithic deposit at the Colha site.

an agricultural village, built adjacent to a swamp where seasonally flooded, raised agricultural fields were built. Near the edge of the swamp, and adjacent to an outcrop of high-quality chert, is an area of dense lithic debris with diagnostic artifacts dating to the Lowland Mesoamerican Archaic tradition. This has been interpreted as a small village, although no house remains have been found. Excavations in the agricultural terraces have uncovered remains of manioc and maize dating to the Archaic period, giving some weight to the idea that a small village was located at Colha, with residents taking advantage of both the excellent lithic resources and the resources of the swamp.

By around 5000 B.P., maize was incorporated into the Lowland Mesoamerican Archaic diet, and soon Lowland Mesoamerican peoples began to focus more subsistence activity on domesticates and to become more sedentary. Peoples of the **Preclassic Maya** (3800–1850 B.P.) tradition developed a fully agricultural economy and settled into permanent communities. Communities tended to be located in relatively broad river basins or highland plains where agriculture could readily be practiced. Often these flat areas served as natural communication routes, and there are indications that many of these sites were engaged in trade with other settlements and even with other regions of Middle America. A range of settlement sizes have been identified from small hamlets of a dozen or so people to large communities of approximately 1,000 individuals. The larger Preclassic Maya sites have a core area which is devoted to nonresidential, civic-ceremonial earthen platform mounds not found at smaller sites. These platform mounds occur both singly and clustered in courtyard arrangements. It appears that these sites served as civic and political centers.

Other Preclassic Maya sites appear to have been trade centers. Jade and obsidian from highland quarries have been found in contemporary sites in many parts of Mesoamerica, indicating that highland sites were participating in these early interregional exchange networks. In addition to these nonperishable items it is likely that perishable goods such as cacao beans, cloth, and feathers moved through these exchange networks as well. In lowland areas, clear connections with the Olmecs of Veracruz are found, demonstrating that these lowland areas also participated in interregional exchange systems.

**Preclassic Maya** (3800–1850 B.P.)

The Preclassic Maya peoples appear to have lived in a largely egalitarian society; however, toward the end of the Preclassic there are indications at some sites that a division of society into elites and commoners had begun. For example, at the site of **Las Mangales** an important individual was buried with not only elaborate grave goods but with the remains of twelve sacrificial victims. This suggests that Preclassic Maya elites had some formal control over commoners. The exact role of elites in society is not well documented but it is likely that they organized public construction projects, public ceremonies, and long-distance trade, activities which were of interest to the community as a whole. The evidence suggests that this was a time of increasing political centralization and political stratification, which carried over into the Classic Maya tradition when sites such as Kaminaljuyu and Tikal became major regional political centers.

**Las Mangales**
(Mexico, Preclassic Maya)

Peoples of the **Classic Maya** (1850–1100 B.P.) tradition developed large states with regional ceremonial centers and powerful rulers. A four-tiered settlement hierarchy is evident across the Classic Maya region. At the base of the hierarchy were small agricultural hamlets. Next were villages that integrated surrounding hamlets. Third were subregional centers integrating a group of villages and finally there were the regional political and ceremonial centers where Mayan kingdoms were headquartered. Some forty to fifty separate polities were located throughout Lowland Mesoamerica, each with its own regional center and a number of smaller centers, sometimes connected by formal roads or causeways. At times these polities might be unified into larger groups, but the number and size of polities continually fluctuated during the Classic Maya tradition.

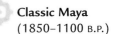

**Classic Maya**
(1850–1100 B.P.)

Communities at all levels of the hierarchy were organized in similar ways. Structures built of stone, adobe, or wattle and thatch were grouped around a courtyard that was shared by an extended family. A typical nuclear family had a main residence and several outbuildings surrounding a smaller internal courtyard. Clusters of these courtyard groups surrounded a central public area. At larger sites courtyard groups of related families clustered near one another, forming kin-based barrios. The public area of communities ranged from a simple open plaza to a complex arrangement of pyramidal mounds, ballcourts, elite residences, and plazas.

Perhaps the most important Classic Maya polity was centered at **Tikal** in Peten, Guatemala, which is described in the box feature (see Figure 10.11), but many

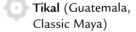

**Tikal** (Guatemala, Classic Maya)

FIGURE **10.11**
The Classic Maya site of Tikal in Guatemala.

# Tikal

Tikal is located in lowland Guatemala within a dense tropical rainforest environment. The site itself consists of five major temple pyramids surrounding a plaza bounded by an acropolis of smaller pyramids to the north, an acropolis of linear pyramidal structures to the south, and additional complexes to the east. This central district lies at the intersection of causeway systems extending to the north and to the east, connecting the central temple compound with smaller temple compounds. Surrounding these temple complexes were dense residential areas, reservoirs, and raised agricultural fields. At its height, the site of Tikal covered perhaps 60 square kilometers and had perhaps 50,000 residents.

Tikal was the focus of one of the most extensive research programs in Lowland Mesoamerica, and deservedly so, for the site played a vital role in Classic Maya society. From 1956 to 1971 the University of Pennsylvania worked at the site under the direction of William Coe and Edwin Shook. This research produced a detailed understanding of the development of Tikal and its role in the Classic Mayan world. A generation of archaeologists were trained at the site, and the reports, which are still being published by the University of Pennsylvania Museum, are exemplars of fine archaeological research and interpretation.

Tikal was founded in the Preclassic Maya tradition, around 2400 B.P. It grew into an important site in the Classic Maya tradition and was the residence of a series of important Mayan rulers, whose lives are well documented on the site's stelae. The "Temple of the Inscriptions" provides a record of dynastic succession reaching back into the mythical past, but historic figures are also recorded. These include Jaguar Paw, the first identified ruler of Tikal, whose reign began about A.D. 320. Chitam, one of Tikal's last rulers, whose reign began about A.D. 768, is

**Palenque**
(Mexico, Classic Maya)

other polities are also well known. One such polity was centered at **Palenque,** located in Chiapas, Mexico. At the center of the site are some of the most remarkable buildings in the Maya world, especially the palace with a four-story tower, numerous courtyards and galleries, and three adjacent temples. North of the palace the site's plaza is surrounded by additional temples and a ball court. Surrounding this central public area are clusters of courtyard groups, but the extent of the site is not yet known, although it is clear that at least several thousand people lived in and around Palenque.

One of the most important features of Palenque are the large number of inscriptions that have been found at the site (Figure 10.12). The Classic Maya peoples developed a sophisticated writing system that was used primarily to record historical events. The records from Palenque are among the most extensive in the Classic Maya world. They begin in A.D. 431 with Palenque's founder, Bahlum Kuk, and end nearly 300 years later with Palenque's defeat by another Mayan polity. During the three centuries of Palenque's existence two women were rulers, a nonroyal family took the throne and altered the historical record to justify their actions, and several great rulers built and expanded the Palenque polity. Pacal, for example, reigned for said to be the twenty-ninth ruler of Tikal. There are others recorded too—Curl Nose, Stormy Sky, Ah Cacaw—but clearly many whose records are lost or were destroyed in antiquity, perhaps by political successors.

It is interesting to note the differences between Tikal and Teotihuacan. The two were contemporaries for centuries, and there is good evidence for regular interaction between the two polities (indeed, the Tikal stelae tell of a ruler named Stormy Sky who integrated the two polities in the middle of the fourth century A.D.). But while Tikal provides striking images of individual rulers on massive stone stelae located both within the special "Temple of Inscriptions" and on the site's central plaza, no such rulers are depicted at Teotihuacan. Teotihuacan seems "faceless" in comparison to the distinct personalities preserved at Tikal. Clearly the cities had very different ideas about government and power. Power at Tikal resided in distinct individuals descended through a carefully recorded series of dynastic succession. Power at Teotihuacan apparently resided in positions of authority that individuals held, but the positions, not the individuals, were the central features.

Despite these differences in governance, both polities seem to have functioned in much the same way. Craft production was widespread at Tikal, and in the compound to the east of the great plaza was a marketplace and a ball court—areas where the residents of Tikal would have come to trade and, perhaps, to watch the semiceremonial game of ball being played. Tikal interacted with polities across the Maya region, from the Guatemalan highlands to the Gulf Coast, and even with polities in highland Mesoamerica. The site provides us with a stark skeleton of what must once have been a vibrant city.

SOURCES: Coe, Michael, *Breaking the Maya Code* (New York, Thames and Hudson, 1992); *The Maya* (New York: Thames and Hudson, 1993); Coe, William, *Tikal, A Handbook of the Ancient Maya Ruins* (Philadelphia: University of Pennsylvania Museum, 1967); Ferguson, William, and John Royce, *Maya Ruins in Central America in Color* (Albuquerque: University of New Mexico Press, 1984).

67 years, from A.D. 615 to A.D. 683. During Pacal's reign Palenque formed an alliance with Tikal, creating a stable political climate in which Palenque's population flourished. Interestingly, Pacal is one of the rulers whose legitimacy seems questionable and who altered historical records to justify their rule. The picture we get from these texts is of a polity like many others in the world at the same time—full of intrigue, political maneuvering, great figures, failures, and conquest.

Classic Maya states dissolved into smaller polities during the **Postclassic Maya** (1100–400 B.P.) tradition. Explanations for the Classic Maya collapse are varied, but most scholars believe environmental degradation from thousands of years of agriculture finally took its toll. In Peten, for example, all the hardwood forests had been cut down or seriously degraded by the end of the Classic Maya tradition. Population seems to have declined markedly too, and some scholars have argued that disease may have played a role in the Classic Maya collapse. Still another explanation is that the endemic warfare that took place between Classic Maya polities finally caused enough disruption to bring the entire political system down. Whatever the reason, Postclassic Maya polities, while still having powerful rulers and complex networks of trade and warfare, were fewer and smaller than their Classic Maya predecessors.

**Postclassic Maya**
(1100–400 B.P.)

FIGURE **10.12**

One of the many panels with inscriptions found at Palenque.

**Chichen Itza**
(Mexico, Postclassic Maya)

A good example of a Postclassic Maya polity is the one centered at the site of **Chichen Itza** in northwest Yucatan (Figure 10.13). Chichen Itza is one of the most striking Mayan sites, both because of its architecture and because of its location. It is situated on a flat limestone plain between two large natural wells, called *cenotes*. The southern well was apparently used for drinking water, but the northern well was a special place of sacrifice. Food, exotic goods, and humans were thrown into the *cenote* as gifts to the gods. A long causeway linked the northern Cenote of Sacrifice to the main plaza of Chichen Itza, which was surrounded by pyramids

FIGURE **10.13**

Arial view of the Temple of the Warriors at Chichen Itza.

and ball courts. These pyramids and ball courts were built using a mosaic of limestone masonry over a core of rubble (called the *puuc* style) and were decorated with elaborate carvings, many showing military themes (warriors and skull racks, for example). Chichen Itza was apparently both a military and trade center. As I discussed earlier, the Toltecs made the Gulf of Mexico a major route for trade between Highland Mexico and the Intermediate Area, and Chichen Itza was at one end of that trade. Its rulers controlled both ports and inland trade routes through the Yucatan. In order to maintain control of trade, the rulers of Chichen Itza also commanded a military force, and indeed one of the most imposing structures at the site is the Temple of the Warriors, where rituals surrounding war and the sacrifice of prisoners apparently took place. Even though the period is called the Postclassic, powerful rulers were still present building enduring cities.

## Gulf Coast

Before moving on to the Intermediate Area, it is important to note that the civilizations that emerged in both highland and lowland Mesoamerica are thought by many scholars to have roots in the **Olmec** (3400–2100 B.P.) tradition of the Gulf coast. The Olmec peoples built regional centers with large populations earlier than in other regions of Mesoamerica, and they developed a unique artistic style and belief system that has parallels in both highland and lowland Mesoamerica (Color Plate 15). These include human-animal hybrids, especially humans with feline features, images of caves or humans emerging from caves, monumental sculptures, pyramidal mounds, and the orientation of public architecture to the four cardinal directions. All these are thought to represent a set of religious ideas that spread across Mesoamerica.

**Olmec**
(3400–2100 B.P.)

Large Olmec communities at La Venta, San Lorenzo, and Tres Zapotes appear to have been regional centers for a hierarchical settlement system that included small agricultural hamlets, larger villages, and smaller, perhaps seasonal, shellfishing and collecting sites. Most research has been focused on the large communities, and it is those we know most about. **La Venta,** for example, was excavated beginning in the late 1950s, and work has been done sporadically on the site ever since. La Venta occupies an island within a swampy lowland area between the Mexican states of Tabasco and Veracruz. The island is 4.5 kilometers long and 1.5 kilometers wide, and the site covers the entire island. The main focus of research has been a central complex of low pyramidal mounds built of clay, stone blocks, and colored clay bricks, arranged around a ceremonial court, with a larger, conical mound built on platform at the southern end. This complex resembles many of the later temple complexes built in both Highland and Lowland Mesoamerica, and may have been a model for them.

**La Venta**
(Mexico, Olmec)

Many of the mounds were built upon tombs, and the tombs themselves are impressive. They contain basalt columns that form a central crypt. Several burials were housed within large stone sarcophagi with elaborate carvings. The most famous carvings from La Venta, however, are the four colossal stone heads, each more than 2 meters in diameter and representing a helmeted individual (Figure 10.14). Numerous stela and altars were also found at La Venta. Perhaps the most intriguing finds, however, have been large caches of exotic objects and works of art, almost all of which have been found along a central north–south axis running through the site. These caches usually occur in pairs, and include items such as celts, figurines, and mosaic floors. All these items, even the mosaic floors, were apparently placed in the ground and buried at one time; that is, they were never used, but were created specifically as sacrifices. The meaning of these sacrificial caches remains unknown.

Despite the size and complexity of Olmec sites, scholars are not certain about the organization of Olmec polities. Some suggest they represent emergent states, while others suggest there is little or no evidence of coercive power. By the time of the **Gulf Coast Classic** (2100–800 B.P.) tradition, however, states had clearly developed. A hierarchical settlement pattern similar to the Classic Mayan emerged, with

**Gulf Coast Classic**
(2100–800 B.P.)

FIGURE **10.14**
One of the colossal stone
heads from La Venta.

most people living in small, agricultural hamlets integrated by local centers which
where further integrated by large regional political and ceremonial centers. Typical
centers contained one or more stone-faced pyramidal mounds facing onto an open
plaza. Some of these mounds were topped by tall ritual structures, while others
had long residences for elites. Nonelite houses surrounded the mound and plaza
area and are themselves surrounded by open work and garden areas. Houses were
rectangular wattle-and-daub structures, often built on low platforms.

The Gulf Coast Classic economy was based in maize-bean-squash agriculture,
but there is also clear evidence for craft specialization, and for regular trade with
contemporary polities in other areas of Mesoamerica. While individual households
probably produced their own ceramics, clothing, and basic tools (manos and metates
and obsidian blades), specialization in the production of fineware ceramics and
ceramic figurines, obsidian, and stone carving seem apparent because of both the difficulty in manufacturing these items and the skill with which they were produced.
Trade may also have been a specialist activity since fineware ceramics were traded
widely, obsidian was obtained from Highland Mesoamerica, and jade, serpentine,
magnetite, and other stone was obtained from as far away as Guatemala. It appears
that Gulf Coast Classic elites may have controlled at least some of this trade because
items obtained from long distances are found almost exclusively in elite areas. Workshops for the production of obsidian, carved stone, and ceramic figurines have been
found associated with elite houses, suggesting that craft production in these items
may have been controlled by elites as well.

Some Gulf Coast Classic elites were apparently hereditary rulers with considerable political and religious authority. Statuary and other iconography depicts rulers
leading public ceremonies of bloodletting, human sacrifice, and feasting. Ritual

FIGURE **10.15**
A Gulf Coast Classic relief sculpture showing a priest making an offering.

seems to have centered around a cult of death, where the ruler's blood and the life of other humans were offered to the gods, some of whom appear to be the same as those later recorded by Aztec scribes. Gulf Coast Classic iconography depicts priests or shamans who aided the ruler in ceremonies and apparently performed some ceremonies themselves (Figure 10.15). Monuments also record the military exploits of rulers and the capture and sacrifice of foreign warriors. Warriors are also depicted, and may have formed a separate class of society. In addition, the ball game seems to have played an important ceremonial role among Gulf Coast Classic polities, with players depicted as being sacrificed following matches.

## INTERMEDIATE AREA

The Intermediate Area is the region between Mesoamerica and South America. It includes Central America (El Salvador, Honduras, Nicaragua, Costa Rica, and Panama), northeastern South America (the eastern lowlands of Colombia, northern Venezuela, and Ecuador), and the Caribbean. This large area is dominated by tropical forests and lowland tropical savannah, both of which support a wide array of plant life. The region is generally hot and humid year-round, with most areas having mean annual temperatures in the range of 20 degrees to 25 degrees C and receiving several thousand millimeters of rain each year. The wettest time of the year is between September and November, while the dry season falls between January and March.

The topography of the Intermediate Area varies enormously. There is a chain of volcanic mountains running along the isthmus that forms Central America, with a broad lowland zone to the east and a narrow coastal zone to the west. The highland zone has scattered individual volcanos, rugged mountains, and broad highland valleys. The Pacific coast has rolling foothills, changing to more rugged hills, inlets, and bays as one moves south. The Caribbean coastal plain is generally flat.

The earliest distinct tradition in the region is the **Early Northwest South American Littoral** (9000–5000 B.P.) tradition. These were hunter-gatherers living

**Early Northwest South American Littoral**
(9000–5000 B.P.)

in small bands moving regularly between coastal and inland sites. Fish and shellfish provided abundant resources on the coast, while deer, rabbits, and other small animals could be easily obtained. Fruits, roots, and grasses were collected, and there is good evidence of sites located to take advantage of seasonal plant resources. Tools were simple chipped and ground stone items made from locally available materials. Settlements were small and short-term, and the scant evidence of housing suggests simple domed huts. However, the **OGSE-80** site represents a unique divergence from this general pattern. Located on the Santa Elena peninsula of southwestern Ecuador, OGSE-80 was a very large site, perhaps over 13,000 square meters, with deep deposits suggesting long-term use. Nearly 200 burials were found on the site, intermixed with habitation areas. Both primary and secondary internments were found, as well as four ossuaries containing numerous intermixed burials. It appears that OGSE-80 was a location where Early Northwest South American Littoral peoples returned regularly to bury their dead, perhaps as part of rituals of group cohesion and maintenance.

People of the **Late Northwest South American Littoral** (5500–3000 B.P.) tradition became sedentary, adopted agriculture, and developed some large villages. However, settlements varied considerably, as did subsistence. Coastal sites tended to have large accumulations of discarded shell, and populations were heavily dependent on ocean resources. At inland sites, populations were more dependent on agriculture, although hunting and collecting remained important. Houses were typically simple domed huts or rectangular wattle-and-daub structures, often organized around an oval or U-shaped plaza. A typical Late Northwest South American Littoral community might have six to twelve such houses and perhaps thirty to fifty people. At **Loma Alta** in southwestern Ecuador, for example, a large U-shaped plaza was cleared on a hill 12 meters above the Valdivia river about 5000 B.P., and houses were built around it. The community remained in the location for many centuries, with the site's inhabitants gathering and hunting in the surrounding hills. The basis of subsistence, however, was a combination of maize, squash, beans, and probably manioc, which were cultivated in the river bottom. The combination of hunting, collecting, and agriculture allowed the Loma Alta peoples to remain sedentary for many generations.

Many coastal Late Northwest South American Littoral populations retained a heavy emphasis on marine resources. **Puerto Chacho** and **Puerto Hormiga,** both on the lower Magdalena river in Colombia, represent villages located in estuarine environments whose inhabitants lived on the rich local resources. Both sites consist of large shell middens that include habitation debris, but no evidence of domesticated plants. Fish, mollusks, and reptiles make up much of the faunal remains, while palm nuts and roots constitute much of the floral materials. These foods were processed with chipped stone bifaces and grinding stones made from locally available materials. Foods were stored and cooked in ceramics, which were made as early as 5100 B.P. The earliest of these ceramics were fiber tempered and hand formed, while later ones were sand tempered and coiled. Bowls were the predominant form and were decorated by incising and punctating. Both sites may have had as many as 100 residents, demonstrating the richness of the estuarine environment.

Some Late Northwest South American Littoral communities became very large, and may have developed into incipient chiefdoms. The most famous of these is **Real Alto** in the Chanduy river valley of southwestern Ecuador. Real Alto is a remarkable site for many reasons; perhaps the most important is because it may represent one of the earliest ceremonial centers in the New World. Real Alto began as a small, agricultural community, but perhaps as early as 5000 B.P. the site began to grow in size and its residents began to construct large public works. Over time, the site came to cover more than 12 hectares and had a population of perhaps 1,500. A large U-shaped ridge was constructed around a sunken plaza. Large structures were built along the ridges, and these have been interpreted as elite residences. Two mounds were constructed at opposite ends of the plaza, and each had temples on their summits. The plaza and mounds appear to have been the focus of feasting and

## Sidebar

**OGSE-80** (Ecuador, Early Northwest South American Littoral)

**Late Northwest South American Littoral** (5500–3000 B.P.)

**Loma Alta** (Ecuador, Late Northwest South American Littoral)

**Puerto Chacho** (Colombia, Late Northwest South American Littoral)

**Puerto Hormiga** (Colombia, Late Northwest South American Littoral)

**Real Alto** (Ecuador, Late Northwest South American Littoral)

mortuary rituals. Exotic goods from as far away as Peru were distributed at these feasts, and some scholars have suggested that Real Alto was the center of an early chiefdom, whose leaders based authority on sponsoring religious rituals and controlling long-distance trade.

Agriculture became the dominant subsistence mode in the Intermediate Area during the **Early Chibcha** (3500–1200 B.P.) tradition. Before about 2000 B.P. Early Chibcha peoples lived in villages of perhaps 100 people who raised a wide variety of domesticated plants. Tree and root crops such as palm, arrowroot, manioc, and sweet potato were emphasized, although maize, beans, and squash were also raised. Wild plants were collected and deer, peccary, and small game were hunted. Fish and shellfish were important for Early Chibcha peoples and were heavily relied upon in coastal communities. Indeed, dried and salted fish were traded from coastal communities inland in return for forest products.

Technology was simple among the Early Chibcha peoples, with ground stone axes, manos and metates, and mortars and pestles being basic utensils in every household. Chipped stone was not widely used, perhaps because bamboo and thorns were widely available for making cutting tools. Early Chibcha peoples also made ceramics, which developed into distinctive regional styles. Most are sand tempered and heavily decorated. Decoration was not limited to ceramics, however, for the Early Chibcha peoples were among the first goldworkers in the Americas. Gold was obtained by panning from rivers and was hammered into thin sheets, which were then worked into a wide variety of personal ornaments and ritual objects (Figure 10.16). Jade and other stone such as agate, serpentine, and quartz were also carved into personal ornaments. Ornaments included beads, pendants, necklaces, earspools, and arm bands.

After about 2000 B.P. some Early Chibcha villages began to grow into very large communities. For example, the village at **La Mula-Sarigua** in central Panama grew from roughly 9 hectares to almost 60 hectares in about a 200-year period. The population of the site rose from under 100 to perhaps nearly 1,000 residents. The site itself was located in an estuarine environment with mangrove forests, ocean resources, and alluvial deposits suitable for agriculture all nearby. It may be that the rich environment

 **Early Chibcha**
**(3500–1200** B.P.**)**

**La Mula-Sarigua**
**(Panama, Early**
**Chibcha)**

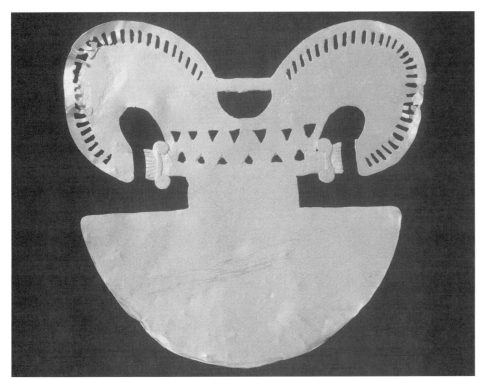

FIGURE **10.16**
A gold Chibcha ornament depicting a stylized shaman-bird in flight.

of the site attracted people to the location. The site also contained an important deposit of chalcedony cobbles that were traded widely, and it has been suggested that one group at La Mula-Sarigua may have taken control of this resource to build a political power base. In either case, political centralization was beginning throughout the Intermediate Area, and La Mula-Sarigua was an emergent political center.

Political centralization continued during the **Late Chibcha** (1200–500 B.P.) tradition, when a series of regional centers, perhaps the primary villages for regional chiefdoms, and special-purpose communities were built. For example, the site of **Aguacaliente**, near Cartago, Costa Rica, became the center for a regional hierarchy of sites. Aguacaliente itself had a population of 1,000 or more residents in a residental area with a plaza and housemounds, and a cemetery. Surrounding it were smaller, special-purpose sites and agricultural hamlets. Special-purpose communities included coastal villages that produced dried and salted fish, and communities near important raw material sources. However, most of the population resided in agricultural communities of 200 to 500 residents. These were simple clusters of houses surrounding an open plaza and located near fertile agricultural soils. Houses were round and ranged widely in size, some housing a single family and some multiple families. Most houses were built on low platforms faced with stone. Some of these agricultural communities were connected to larger centers by formal paths or even stone-lined causeways.

Similar political centralization was happening elsewhere on the isthmus that forms Central America, and several distinct groups of archaeological traditions emerged. Peoples of the **Chiriqui** (1200–500 B.P.) tradition, located in western Panama and southern Costa Rica, and the **Gran Cocle** (2000–400 B.P.) tradition, located in central Panama, lived in distinct regional chiefdoms. Both were agricultural, but neither appear to have made extensive use of marine resources like most of their neighbors. They are further distinguished from their neighbors, and from one another, by their distinct ceramic styles—Chiriqui, in particular, by a thin, well-fired ceramic called "biscuit ware," and Gran Cocle by unique geometric and zoomorphic design imagery. But in many ways peoples in these traditions appear to have had similar ways of life.

Chiefdoms also emerged on the coast of Ecuador, and during the **Central Coast Regional Chiefdoms** (2500–1500 B.P.) tradition, regional civic-ceremonial centers developed. These were the centers of regional polities, apparently controlled by powerful chiefs. Regional chiefdoms continued during the **Manteño** (1150–410 B.P.) tradition, and, in the highlands, during the **Ecuadoran Highlands** (1500–500 B.P.) tradition. Like those of Panama, these Ecuadoran chiefdoms are distinguished from their neighbors by ceramic styles and unique design imagery. All are known for their artistry in gold.

Historical documents from early Spanish explorers suggest that these Pacific coast chiefdoms were organized along fairly similar lines. There were two social ranks—commoner and elite, and both were ascribed to a person at birth through their descent group (Figure 10.17). Birth order was the key to this organization. Higher ranking descent groups were perceived as being descended from elder founding members of the society. Within descent groups, rank was also determined by birth order, so that elder members were of higher status than younger members. Preeminent chiefs, then, were the eldest son of the previous preeminent chief, subchiefs were the brothers of the preeminent chief, other elites were members of the chiefly descent group. Apparently, daughters of a chief were also of high status, and the elder daughters had higher status than younger sons; thus birth order was clearly of primary importance. However, one could apparently also be elevated to the elite rank by success or bravery in war.

War was endemic among the Pacific coast chiefdoms, and organizing the populace for war and defense was a key responsibility of the chiefs. Chiefs also adjudicated disputes and meted out punishment. In addition to dealing with internal and external conflicts, a key role of chiefs among the Pacific coast chiefdoms was

**Late Chibcha**
(1200–500 B.P.)

**Aguacaliente**
(Costa Rica, Late Chibcha)

**Chiriqui**
(1200–500 B.P.)

**Gran Cocle**
(2000–400 B.P.)

**Central Coast Regional Chiefdoms**
(2500–1500 B.P.)

**Manteño**
(1150–410 B.P.)

**Ecuadoran Highlands**
(1500–500 B.P.)

The Indians marching upon a Visit, or to Feast. P. 140.

Lacenta. his Lady. Attendants.

FIGURE **10.17**

A Panama chief with his wife
and attendants. Chiefly rank
was ascribed at birth among
the Pacific coast chiefdoms
and was based on descent.

supporting craft production and interregional trade. Chiefs used the exotic goods
produced in distant locations as a way to symbolize their status and authority, and
they gave exotic goods away to followers in return for their support. In order to
acquire foreign goods, chiefs supported local artisans, who produced the magnificent gold items for which the area is famous, as well as merchants who exchanged
items with other polities, sometimes over very long distances. There is good evidence, for example, that Manteño traders obtained *Spondylus* shell from as far
north as West Mexico and traded it as far south as central Peru—a region of trade
covering more than 4,000 kilometers.

While they interacted with other polities over very long distances, Pacific coast
chiefdoms were themselves fairly small. Each chiefdom had a center, often called a
*bohío* in Spanish documents, where the chiefs, other elites, craftspeople, traders, and
commoners supporting these people resided—perhaps 500 to 1,000 people in all.
These chiefly *bohíos* were often defended with stone walls or palisades and a moat.
In addition to residences, one or more public buildings were typically found in
chiefly *bohíos*, ranging from simple longhouses of poles and thatch in Panama to
buildings constructed atop pyramidal mounds in Ecuador. The majority of the population lived in small agricultural and fishing villages along waterways or the coast.
Each chiefdom appears to have controlled an area roughly 40 kilometers wide
extending from the coast inland to where mountains or rivers formed a clear boundary. Often these areas corresponded with river drainages, or had boundaries marked
by rivers or mountains.

In contrast to developments elsewhere in the Intermediate Area, peoples of
the **Nicoya** (3600–500 B.P.) and **Paya** (1500–500 B.P.) traditions of Nicaragua,
Honduras, and northern Costa Rica appear to have remained village-dwelling
hunter-fisher-gatherers who used marine aquatic resources extensively. Both groups
made use of domesticated plants as well, but neither appear to have relied upon
them to the same extent that peoples both north and south of them did.

Typical Nicoya and Paya settlements are composed of a cluster of houses
surrounding an open work space. Some communities had larger, perhaps ceremonial, platform mounds, and some Nicoya communities appear to have had separate
residential and ritual areas. Many Paya settlements were either located in defensible

**Nicoya**
(3600–500 B.P.)

**Paya**
(1500–500 B.P.)

positions or had defensive works surrounding them. Houses of both traditions were wattle and daub, sometimes constructed above a cobblestone foundation.

Paya ceramics were well-made polychrome types, with bowls and globular vessels being common forms. Incising and punctating were common decorative practices in addition to polychrome painting, which was often done in red and black on orange. Nicoya ceramics include distinctive shell-stamped and white or orange slipped types. Lithics in both traditions are diverse and include obsidian blades and large grinding stones. Paya peoples made distinctive chipped T-shaped axes. A variety of imports from Mesoamerica suggests trade was an important part of both the Nicoya and Paya economies. Obsidian, copper, textiles, and food were likely the major trade items in both traditions.

There is little archaeological evidence for either Paya or Nicoya sociopolitical organization. Ethnohistoric documents suggest small chiefdoms were scattered across the region, and this does seem to fit the general settlement pattern seen in the archaeological record. Communities may have each contained several lineages, each with its leaders, one of whom served as the community chief. The defensive nature of many Paya settlements suggests conflict between communities may have played a major role in political life.

## The Caribbean

**Early Caribbean** (3000–1000 B.P.)

**Golden Rock** (Caribbean, Early Caribbean)

**Late Caribbean** (1000–500 B.P.)

Finally, the islands of the Caribbean represent an interesting case. They were settled, probably from northern Colombia and Venezuela, around 3000 B.P., initiating the **Early Caribbean** (3000–1000 B.P.) tradition. These early colonizers were horticulturalists, but also used a wide variety of land and marine resources. They lived in small, egalitarian villages, often near prime agricultural land. The **Golden Rock** site on St. Eustatius island is a good example of an Early Caribbean tradition village. It is located near the center of the small island, roughly 1.5 kilometers from either coast, and in the middle of a broad plain with rich volcanic soils. The remains of six large, round houses, ranging from 7 to 19 meters in diameter, were uncovered. Each of these dwellings probably housed an extended family, although the larger ones could have easily housed several families. The houses were arranged around an open plaza, beneath which eleven burials were found. Faunal remains from the site suggest a heavy reliance on fish, while the site's location on prime agricultural land suggests cassava and sweet potato were important. Utensils found at the site included simple ceramics, and shell scrapers, knives, hoes, and fishhooks.

Peoples of the following **Late Caribbean** (1000–500 B.P.) tradition developed some larger villages and became politically centralized under hereditary chiefs. When first contacted by Columbus, the peoples of the Greater Antilles were reportedly living in large permanent villages, each composed of family houses arranged around a plaza (Figure 10.18). Each village was divided into nobles and commoners, and each had its own set of religious specialists. Nobles' houses were larger than those of commoners, but all houses were round, with conical thatch roofs. Commoners apparently slept in hammocks and stored food in bags hanging from house rafters, while nobles used wooden benches and received visitors while seated on a wooden stool. The central plaza of these villages was used as a ceremonial and dance ground, and many villages also had a stone-lined ball court upon which was played the Mesoamerican ball game.

Late Caribbean communities supported themselves through intensive agriculture and fishing. Cassava and sweet potato were the main crops, although maize, beans, squash, peanuts, cotton, tobacco, peppers, and other domesticates were also grown. Fish were speared or caught using nets or hooks and line. Fish poisoning also took place and weirs were set in rivers. Technology was relatively simple and included ceramics, woven nets, bags, cloth, a wide variety of shell tools, and both chipped and ground stone utensils. Most of these were made by individuals or families for their own use.

FIGURE **10.18**
A rather fanciful drawing of
Columbus meeting peoples of
the Late Caribbean tradition.

## SUMMARY

Similar patterns of cultural evolution seem to be apparent in the different regions of
Middle America. Egalitarian hunters and gatherers first moved into the region and
begin exploiting seasonally abundant resources. They became more sedentary over
time and adopted agriculture as a supplement to wild plant and animal foods. Villages grew larger and political complexity emerged. Over time powerful chiefdoms
and states developed, often collapsed, and were redeveloped in another location or
with a somewhat different sociopolitical form. By the time of Spanish conquest,
virtually the entire region was controlled by these fluid regional chiefdoms and
states.

## DISCUSSION QUESTIONS

1. In what ways did cultural evolution differ between highland and lowland areas
   of Middle America? In what ways did cultural evolution proceed along similar
   lines?

2. What effect did domestication of plants have on the peoples who domesticated
   them? Why was there such a long period between the development of domesticated plants and peoples' reliance on them for subsistence?

3. What role did trade play among prehistoric Middle American peoples? Why did
   trade appear to be relatively important in some areas, and not as important in
   others?

## ESSAY QUESTIONS

1. Reflect upon the use of archaeological traditions as organizational units in this
   chapter. What is the effect of cutting prehistory up into discrete chunks? What
   is gained by doing this? What is lost? How do the traditions affect our view of
   the past?

2. Find plan maps for an ancient Maya city and a Highland Mesoamerican city (many excavation reports have such maps). Examine the organization and layout of the two cities. In what ways are they similar? In what ways are they different? What might these differences mean in terms of how these cities were organized and how they functioned?

3. Construct a "horizontal" view of Middle America at a particular point in time. Consider all of the traditions that existed at the same point in time, comparing and contrasting them. How does this "horizontal" picture differ from the more "vertical" one presented in the chapter?

## ✦ RESEARCH PROJECT

Use library and Internet resources to examine ethnographically described nonindustrial states. Choose four or five states to examine in detail. What characteristics do they have in common? How might we use those common features to more readily identify states in the archaeological record? In what ways do these states vary? How might we see this variation in the archaeological record?

## ✿ KEY SOURCES

### Northern Mesoamerica

Alvarez Palma, 1990; Berry and Doyon, 2001; Downum, Fish, and Fish, 1994; Fish, 2001; Foster and Gorenstein, 2000; Foster and Weigand, 1985; Hosler, 1994; Johnson, 1963; Kan, Meighan, and Nicholson, 1989; Ohnersorgon and Varien, 1996; Pollard, 1993, 1997, 2001; Taylor, 1988; Townshend, 1998; Turpin, 2001; Weigand, 2001.

### Highland Mesoamerica

Berdan, 1982; Blanton, 2001; Blanton, Feinman, Kowalewski, and Nicholas, 1999; Blanton, Kowalewski, Feinman, and Finsten, 1993; Cowgill, 1997, 2001; Diehl, 1983; Diehl and Berlo, 1989; Feinman, 2001; Finsten, 2001; Flannery, 1976, 1986; Healan, 1989; Kowalewski, 1990; MacNeish, 2001; MacNeish and Nelken-Terner, 1983; Marcus and Flannery, 1996; Millon, 1981; Nichols and Charlton, 2001; Pasztory, 1997; Sanders, Parsons, and Santley, 1979; Smith, M.E., 1996; Spores, 1984; Storey, 1992; van Rossum, 2001; Weaver, 1993.

### Lowland Mesoamerica

Adams, 1977; Andrews, 1993; Arnold, 1994; Benson, 1981; Benson and Guthrie, 1996; Chase and Rice, 1985; Coe and Diehl, 1980; Culbert, 1991; Fowler, 1991; Fox, 1987; Fry, 2001; Grove, 1997; Herrera, 2001; Iceland and Hester, 2001; Pool, 2001; Sabloff, 1990; Sabloff and Andrews, 1986; Schele and Freidel, 1990; Sharer, 1994, 2001; Sharer and Grove, 1989; Stark and Arnold, 1997; Zeitlin, 1984.

### Intermediate Area

Bruhns, 1994; Cooke, 2001; Corrales Ulloa, 2001; Deagan, 1988; Engwall, 2001a, 2001b; Helms, 1979; Hoopes, 2001a, 2001b; Keegan, 1992, 1994, 2001; Labbe, 1986; Lange, 1988, 1992, 1996, 2001; Lange and Stone, 1984; Lange et al., 1992; Lathrap, Marcos, and Zeidler, 1977; Linares, 1968; Linares and Ranere, 1980; Meggers, 1966; Myers, 2001; Piperno and Pearsall, 1998; Rouse, 1992; Salomon, 1986; Scott, 1998; Stothert, 1985, 2001; Weeks, 2001; Wilson, 1997; Zeidler, 2001.

# RUINS OF THE MAYA

Middle America includes Mexico, Central America, the northwestern portion of South America, and the Caribbean. This region has some level of cultural unity that gives it coherence when looking at its prehistory. One of the sub-regions that comprises what we call Middle America is Lowland Mesoamerica, primarily the Yucatan Peninsula and the coastal regions of Guatemala, Honduras, and Belize. Mountainous highlands and coastal plains dominate its terrain. People of the Classic Maya (1850–1100 B.P.) tradition developed large states with regional ceremonial centers and powerful rulers here. A four-tiered settlement hierarchy existed during Classic Maya time. At its base was the agricultural hamlet; at its apex were the regional political and ceremonial centers where Mayan kingdoms were headquartered. These large regional political and ceremonial centers were dominated by monumental architecture.

## WEB ACTIVITY

This chapter develops the history of the Maya. Forty to fifty polities existed at the zenith of the Maya tradition. Each polity was represented by a regional center complete with powerful rulers, religious leaders, a population that could number in the thousands, and written histories. Clearly monumental architecture held meaning for these people; palaces, ball courts, temples, large plazas, courtyards, galleries, and towers defined each of these cities. Huge resources were obviously required to build these elaborate ceremonial and trade centers. Finally, Classic Maya society collapsed into Postclassic Maya society (1100–400 B.P.). Ceremonial centers became less important or were completely abandoned and it appears that population declined rapidly during this period. In this activity, you will view footage of a Mayan ceremonial center exemplifying its monumental architecture.

The Media Lab can be found in Chapter 10 on the *Companion Website*™ http://www.prenhall.com/peregrine

## Activity

1. View the video. What level of organization would be required to build such large structures as those depicted? How could a society support such large public ceremonial, religious, and political centers?

2. What value are the temples to the general public of the time? Why invest so much into their construction?

3. How can archaeologists study such large cities? What techniques might be useful in describing an entire city? What conclusions can we draw about a society that invests so much of itself into such large ceremonial centers?

# South America

South America is a continent of amazing diversity (Figure 11.1). On the west coast the Andes rise abruptly from the Pacific Ocean and climb rapidly to more than 6,000 meters, then descend into the broad Amazon and Pampas basins. The Amazon is an equatorial rainforest, while the Pampas is a rich grassland. On the east coast the land rises again to a broad upland known as the Brazilian Highlands. These uplands are situated above 2,000 meters and stretch from the north coast of Brazil south to Uruguay. Thus South America can be divided into four major regions: the Andes, the Amazon, the Pampas, and the Eastern Highlands.

FIGURE **11.1**

Environments of South America.

Archaeological work has proceeded largely separately in these regions, with the Andes receiving the vast majority of research efforts (Figure 11.2). In some ways this makes sense because the unique features of each region produced a unique set of cultures, and the Andes produced a great prehistoric civilization that deserved close study. On the other hand, all areas of South America have a rich prehistory, and it is unfortunate that not all have received the same attention as the Andes. In this chapter I will offer a basic overview of the prehistory of each of these four areas of

FIGURE **11.2**
Sites discussed in Chapter 11.

South America in order to give a sense of the rich diversity of cultures that existed during the continent's prehistory.

## ANDES

The Andes region consists of three major environmental zones: the coast, the mountains, and the upland valleys or *puna*. The Pacific coastline of the Andes is a cool desert environment that has changed little since humans first inhabited the area. Rivers descend from the Andes and deposit rich alluvial fans where they meet the coastline. This alluvium is fertile and relatively lush with grasses, scrub bushes, and small trees, while surrounding areas are hyperarid and almost completely lacking in vegetation. While deer, birds, and small mammals were present, fish, shellfish, and marine mammals were vital to the peoples who lived along the Andean coasts.

The Andes proper are massive mountains rising steeply to a height of 3,800 to 4,500 meters before opening into the *puna*. The Andes are cut by rivers flowing

*Puna:* a high-altitude plateau in the Andes that lies between roughly 2,500 and 4,500 meters above sea level.

down the steep mountain slopes to the sea, and these rivers, combined with uplifts and flows from ancient volcanoes, make the terrain extremely rugged. The volcanic peaks of the Andes occur as two chains, or *cordillera,* between which lies the *puna.* The steep slopes of the Andes form a series of distinct environments that change as one goes up the mountains. These environments are also affected by generally decreasing rainfall from north to south. The high mountains receive little rainfall (500 mm per annum in the north to 1 mm per annum in the south) that generally supports scrub and thorn forests on the western flanks of the Andes. The few west-flowing streams and rivers that drain into the Pacific Ocean present crucial resource zones and are, for all practical purposes, the only places human habitation is possible.

The *puna* (sometimes called the **altiplano**) is a high-altitude plateau that lies between roughly 2,500 and 4,500 meters above sea level. The *puna* is a treeless plain dotted with large marshes, lakes, and streams. Some areas, particularly in the vicinity of Lake Titicaca, are characterized by large expanses of grasslands, bounded on the east and west by two parallel mountain ranges. Further north, in Peru, the two ranges are closer, resulting in fractured expanses, with grasslands along meandering ridges separated by deep valleys. Altogether, the region constitutes roughly 25 percent of the area of Peru and Bolivia, and, apart from the coast, was the major area of human habitation. The *puna's* high altitude means that freezing temperatures are common and oxygen levels are low. Both present special problems for plant and animal life. Only a few hardy varieties of domestic plants such as potatoes and quinona can be grown. Consequently, human habitation in the *puna* has always depended upon animal life, particularly Andean camelids such as guanaco, alpaca, and llama.

As I discussed in the chapter on the Upper Paleolithic, the earliest archaeological tradition in the Andes is the Old South American Hunting-Collecting tradition, and it may be the oldest established archaeological tradition in the New World, currently predating all other recognized traditions. Peoples of the Old South American Hunting-Collecting tradition were, as the name implies, nomadic hunters and gatherers of Pleistocene megafauna and plant species. They were followed by peoples of the **Late Andean Hunting-Collecting** (ca. 8000–6000 B.P.) tradition, who were also nomadic hunters and gatherers. By the time period of this tradition, the Pleistocene fauna had disappeared, and peoples were hunting and gathering a wider variety of plant and animal species. This "broad spectrum" foraging was also true for peoples of the **Early Highland Andean Archaic** (7000–4500 B.P.) tradition, but these peoples also started experimenting with plant cultivation, particularly starchy seed plants and perhaps some root crops including potato, and there is some evidence that alpacas were beginning to be kept.

Plant and animal domestication was in place by the time of the Late Highland Andean Archaic and Coastal Andean Archaic traditions. **Coastal Andean Archaic** (ca. 7000–4100 B.P.) settlements, as the name suggests, were located along the coastline with access to fresh water from springs. Most settlements were relatively compact agglomerations of dwellings built up without any obvious community plan or layout. The typical dwelling appears to have been circular and semisubterranean with a roof composed of saplings covered with woven mats. However, a wide diversity of dwellings were used by the Coastal Andean Archaic peoples, ranging from circular to rectangular and built from materials as diverse as stone, reed mats, and packed clay. Regardless of their form, most dwellings were relatively small and only large enough to house a single family. Late in the tradition what appear to be larger dwellings and compounds were present, as were the first large public structures such as pyramids and temples, which came to prominence among the Early Coastal Andean Formative peoples.

The large communities inhabited by the Coastal Andean Archaic peoples suggest some degree of political centralization was likely present, if only to maintain peaceful relationships in these communities. Large public works such as pyramids

**Late Andean Hunting-Collecting** (ca. 8000–6000 B.P.)

**Early Highland Andean Archaic** (7000–4500 B.P.)

**Coastal Andean Archaic** (ca. 7000–4100 B.P.)

**Altiplano:** another name used for the *puna,* a high-altitude plateau in the Andes that lies between roughly 2,500 and 4,500 meters above sea level.

and temples would have required some degree of labor organization. However, evidence for social stratification is not present until late in the tradition, and is modest even then. It seems likely that leaders were present but were not strongly differentiated from other members of society. Leaders' roles would have been as coordinators and facilitators rather than as strong figures of authority.

The Coastal Andean Archaic peoples subsisted on a combination of domesticated and wild foods. Domesticated plants raised by the Coastal Andean Archaic peoples included squash, gourds, beans, maize, potatoes, and cotton, among others. Some scholars have suggested that domesticated llamas, guinea pigs, and ducks were also kept, but their context is uncertain. Wild foods came almost exclusively from the sea and included fish, shellfish, and sea mammals. Some inland mammals, such as deer, were also hunted, as were birds, reptiles, and land mollusks. Technology was relatively simple and was available to everyone. Basic tools included chipped stone knives, scrapers, and projectile points; stone grinding slabs, mortars, and pestles; bone tools of various kinds; shell hoes and scrapers; wooden digging sticks; and a range of twined textiles such as bags, fishing lines, and nets. Ceramics were not manufactured by the Coastal Andean Archaic peoples. Their ornaments included textiles and beads made from shell, bone, and stone. Trade between neighboring communities took place, but most items were manufactured from locally available materials.

**Late Highland Andean Archaic** (4500–3500 B.P.) peoples were seasonally sedentary and maintained a fairly high reliance on wild foods, particularly early in the tradition. Settlements varied tremendously, from large villages to small campsites. Larger settlements were likely seasonal macroband villages occupied during wet seasons, while the smaller settlements reflected individual bands hunting and collecting during dry seasons. The peoples of these villages hunted and gathered, but there is also evidence that potatoes, beans, chile peppers, and camelids were domesticated during this tradition. The **Tulan 52** site in northern Chile appears to reflect a typical Late Highland Andean Archaic village. About 30 semisubterranean, stone-walled houses were present on the site at roughly 4300 B.P. Each housed a single family who supported itself by hunting vicuna and guanaco, and by collecting wild plant foods. Large grinding stones suggest that grains were being used, and the excavators have suggested that domesticated quinona was grown. Similarly, at the **Asana** site in southern Peru evidence for domesticates is found by 4400 B.P., when large numbers of grinding stones appear along with remains of domesticated quinoa. Domesticates became more important over time, and at about 3600 B.P. a rapid transition to camelid pastoralism occurred at Asana, with bones of llama coming to dominate the faunal assemblage.

Asana also has some evidence of increasing size and permanence. Houses increased in size over time, and several works of public architecture, including a large stone platform, were constructed. Asana is not the only Late Highland Andean Archaic site where public architecture has been found. Indeed, several larger villages with ceremonial architecture date to the Late Highland Andean Archaic tradition, and these raise the possibility that regional ceremonial centers emerged as peoples became increasingly sedentary. **Huaricoto**, for example, in north-central Peru, has thirteen ceremonial structures that date as early as 4300 B.P. These structures are rectangular or U-shaped rubble platforms and walls and with large hearths, apparently for burnt offerings. Despite the presence of these apparent ritual centers, there is little evidence for political centralization or social differentiation.

Ceramics were first made by peoples of the **Highland Andean Formative** (3500–2200 B.P.) tradition. These ceramics were fiber tempered and developed quickly into a number of distinctive forms, including tripod bowls, pedestal vases, and both bichrome and polychrome forms (Figure 11.3). Weaving also emerged from simple twining techniques and began to develop into the sophisticated design and production systems that are known in the historic period. New skills in metalwork also developed during the Highland Andean Formative tradition, including

**Late Highland Andean Archaic** (4500–3500 B.P.)

**Tulan 52** (Chile, Late Highland Andean Archaic)

**Asana** (Peru, Late Highland Andean Archaic)

**Huaricoto** (Peru, Late Highland Andean Archaic)

**Highland Andean Formative** (3500–2200 B.P.)

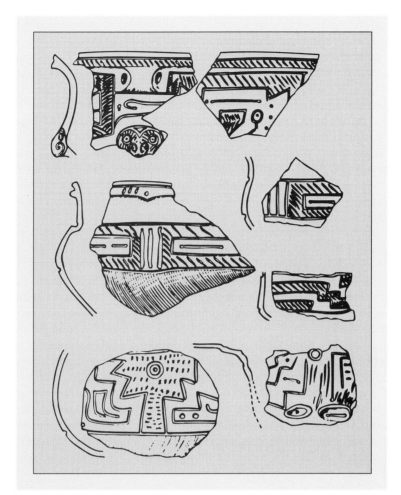

FIGURE **11.3**

Examples of the distinctive decorations found on some Highland Andean Formative ceramics.

SOURCE: Luis G. Lumbreras, *Peoples and Cultures of Ancient Peru.* Translated by Betty J. Meggers (Washington, D.C.: Smithsonian Institution Press, 1974), p. 132. Reprinted by permission of Betty J. Meggers.

copper smelting. By the end of the tradition, the basic tool kit known in the historic period was in place. This included ceramics, woven bags and cloth, stone-blade cutting tools, wooden digging sticks, and simple copper fishhooks and needles.

Trade also began between the highlands and both the coast and the interior of South America during the Highland Andean Formative tradition; indeed, the first evidence of roads dates from this tradition. Highland products such as dried llama meat, wool, stone, and woven textiles were traded for lowland products such as dried fish and jungle produce.

Highland Andean Formative peoples lived in small agricultural villages and moved seasonally. In the dry season, people moved to the highlands to pasture their flocks of llama and alpaca. At the beginning of the wet season they would return to the valleys to plant potatoes and other root and grain crops, including maize. The wet season villages typically had populations between 100 and 300. Houses were built from adobe and fieldstone, and housed a single family. It is thought that villages may have represented individual descent groups, or *ayllus,* that became important social and political entities in later centralized polities. However, there is no clear evidence of political centralization taking place until the very end of the Highland Andean Formative tradition.

Political development occurred somewhat more rapidly on the Andean coast. During the **Early Coastal Andean Formative** (4100–3000 B.P.) tradition, a settlement hierarchy emerged with large, regional centers containing groups of carefully arranged platform mounds. There were also smaller centers with only one platform mound, and both agricultural and fishing villages, within which most of the population resided. Centers were clearly planned, with a central axis along which main

*Ayllus:* individual descent groups that resided in a single village and formed an important organizing element in Andean polities.

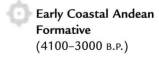

**Early Coastal Andean Formative** (4100–3000 B.P.)

mounds and plazas were arranged. Smaller mounds surrounded the plazas, and elite residences surrounded the mound areas. Elite houses were built from quarried stone and were on the order of 4 meters by 6 meters in size. Nonelite housing at both centers and villages were smaller, on the order of 2 meters by 4 meters in size, and with wattle-and-daub walls built on a stone foundation. Villages often had less than 100 residents, while large centers had perhaps as many as 2,000 or more.

Agricultural villagers of the Early Coastal Andean Formative tradition developed sophisticated irrigation systems, where rivers carrying rain and meltwater from the Andes to the sea were diverted through a complex network of canals and fields. With irrigation, Early Coastal Andean Formative farmers were able to grow crops in otherwise marginal locations, and to raise as many as three crops a year in places. Peanuts, beans, squash, potatoes, guava, and other domesticates were grown. Villagers living on the coast intensively harvested fish and shellfish, which they traded inland for agricultural products. Elites appear to have exercised some control over both trade and access to water.

The basic pattern of life established during the Early Coastal Andean Formative tradition continued through the **Late Coastal Andean Formative** (3000–2200 B.P.) tradition, with regional centers growing into true urban communities and fortified military sites appearing on defensible hilltops. The regional centers developed a unique layout, with numerous single mound plazas surrounded by rooms. Each of these room complexes may have represented a single extended family or a group of related families. The presence of hilltop forts suggests conflict was regular between communities. More of the population was living in large communities, perhaps for defensive purposes, and even small agricultural and fishing villages seem to have been closely tied to centers as foci of trade, ritual, and perhaps defense. Craft specialists in ceramics, textiles, and metalwork (particularly gold) probably operated out of the regional centers, and may have been attached to elites.

The **San Diego** site on the south side of the lower Casma Valley in Peru illustrates a Late Coastal Andean Formative center. The site is located in the foothills of the Andes and was supported by irrigation agriculture and by fish and shellfish traded from the ocean some 5 kilometers away. The site itself consists of a series of interconnected compounds covering an area of almost 50 hectares. Each compound had a low, narrow platform mound connected to a plaza that was entered through a "baffled" entrance. On top of the mound was a small open structure that was probably used for ritual. Surrounding the mound and plaza were houses built of stone and wood. Each compound may have represented a single group of related people.

In the highlands, ritual and political centralization came together in a more significant way as peoples of the **Chavín** (2800–2200 B.P.) tradition developed what may have been a centralized polity focused at the large temple center of **Chavín de Huantar,** described in the box feature. The Chavín tradition appears to represent the spread of an iconographic and, presumably, religious ideology across the Peruvian highlands and into coastal valleys. The iconography is distinctive, representing deities from the two temples at the Chavín de Huantar site. These include a fanged male deity, who appears to be the supreme supernatural being, and numerous secondary deities including eagles, caymans, snakes, and jaguars. These beings were rendered using modular design elements that were combined and rotated to make optical illusions. For example, Figure 11.4 can be rotated 180 degrees to produce a completely different image. Chavín iconography was found on ceramics, gold, silver, and bone jewelry and in public places on statuary and friezes. It appears that these design elements and the ideas behind them were not only grafted onto existing ideas and designs in areas away from Chavín de Huantar itself, but may have been used by elites to differentiate themselves from the rest of society. At some sites, "branch" temples or oracles were even built to provide a location for the exclusive worship of Chavín deities.

**Late Coastal Andean Formative**
(3000–2200 B.P.)

**San Diego**
(Peru, Late Coastal Andean Formative)

**Chavín**
(2800–2200 B.P.)

**Chavín de Huantar**
(Peru, Chavín)

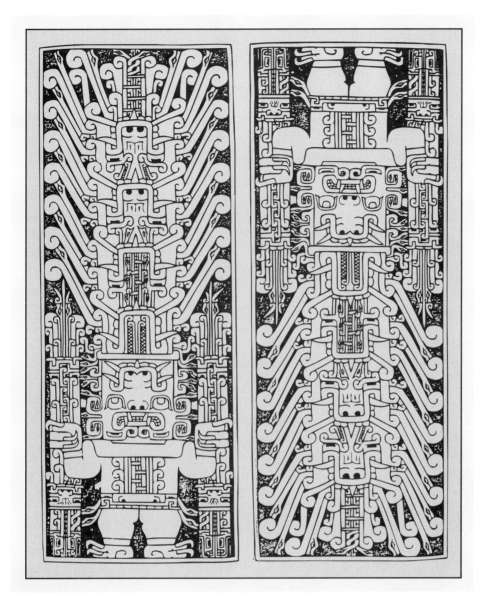

FIGURE **11.4**
This drawing of the Raimondi Stone from Chavín de Huántar shows one of the more interesting aspects of Chavín art—when rotated 180 degrees an alternative image is formed. Granite, 195 cm × 74 cm.
SOURCE: Courtesy Dr. John Rowe.

During the **Andean Regional Development** (2200–1300 B.P.) tradition, temple centers spread throughout the highlands as the foci of numerous regional polities. The extent to which the spread of Chavín iconography and ideology affected political centralization is a highly debated one, but seems a reasonable inference. In the Andean Regional Development tradition, regionally distinct polities appear to have formed in geographically circumscribed areas of the highlands. Each polity had a center that contained platform mounds and temples, and which served as the religious and political hub of the polity. For example, **Nawimpukio,** in the Ayacucho valley of Peru, grew rapidly from a village to a political center. Located on a defensible hilltop, the site was probably attractive both because of this position and also because of easy access to water and agricultural land. The core of the site had relatively large elite residences built on terraces. Houses were built along streets that also had granaries, public architecture, and clay-lined canals. Surrounding the hilltop core of the site were numerous commoner households and their associated agricultural fields.

Individual Andean Regional Development villages were located near agricultural or pasture lands and water sources, and often on defensible hilltops. The

**Andean Regional Development**
(2200–1300 B.P.)

**Nawimpukio**
(Peru, Andean Regional Development)

# Chavín de Huantar

Chavín de Huantar is an enigmatic site in many ways. Its architecture is at once functional and mysterious. It has platforms rising to the sky and tunnels sinking deep into the ground. Its iconography is full of images that seem, at one level, representative of the natural world and, at another, full of fantastic beasts. From Chavín de Huantar an iconographic system and, probably, an associated ideology spread across the Andes and formed the foundation for all the later ideological systems of the region. Yet the polity of Chavín de Huantar seems not to have been powerful, and the site itself declined quickly.

Chavín de Huantar was among the first sites in Peru to be systematically studied. The legendary Peruvian archaeologists Julio Tello and Luis Lumbreras both conducted extensive work at the site—Tello between 1919 and 1941, and Lumbreras between 1966 and 1972. Their work established the importance of the site and identified its major features. The most recent work was done by Richard Burger in the mid-1970s. Together, the work of these scholars suggests that the site can be best understood as the center for a regional cult that spread across the north and central highlands of Peru in the period between 2400 and 2200 B.P. The site's location, midway between the western coast and the eastern jungle, might also have made it an important trade and communications center, but it appears never to have been an important political center.

Occupation of Chavín de Huantar began around 2900 B.P., and the period of its greatest influence was not until the very end of its main occupation. It may be that once the Chavín cult spread and regional cult centers emerged, Chavín de Huantar itself was no longer needed. Habitation at Chavín de Huantar covers an area of some 40 hectares, but the most important part of the site is a group of monumental stone platform mounds that cover an area of about 3 hectares. These stone mounds are not as large as others in prehistoric Peru, but they are among the most impressive in terms of their construction and complex features. They were built using finely polished stones carefully fitted together to form tall

defensive location of many Andean Regional Development villages suggests that interregional conflict may have fostered the development of centralized regional polities. Villages themselves consisted of several dozen small adobe and fieldstone houses, with a total population of 200 to 300 people. Each village is thought to have been the residence of a single descent group or *ayllu*, which, in the historic period, controlled access to pasture and water, and the distribution of land. These *ayllus* became the basic organizational units of the later Huari and Inca empires, in part because they were readily made integrated into a hierarchical system. Members of an *ayllu* trace descent from a common ancestor. Individual *ayllus* also recognize kinship with other *ayllus* who trace descent to siblings or other related kin. In this way, *ayllus* can be brought together by tracing ancestry back to more and more distant kin. *Ayllus* (or groups of *ayllus*) tracing descent from particularly important (some over 10 meters) facades for the mounds. Near the top of the walls monstrous carved heads were inserted to look out menacingly at those approaching the mounds.

There are two main mounds at Chavín de Huantar; one, called the "Old Temple," is a U-shaped mound with a circular courtyard located within the U and decorated with stone friezes depicting a procession of mythical figures and jaguars. The second mound, called the "New Temple," is rectangular in form and was built against the south arm of the "Old Temple." The "New Temple" has a sunken, rectangular courtyard. Many parts of the "New Temple" are also decorated with friezes depicting supernatural beings. Both mounds are unique in having internal, mazelike galleries that were supplied with fresh air through ventilation shafts and with conduits to allow water to run out. The purpose of these internal galleries is unknown. Some were clearly meant for religious rituals. Others may have been places for solitude or meditation. Others appear to have been storerooms. Lumbreras argued that some were designed as acoustic resonating chambers that provided unusual sounds for religious rituals.

Also unique to the Chavín de Huantar is an abundance of sculpture depicting a range of natural and supernatural beings, all thought to be important figures in the Chavín cult. The most significant are probably those that represent what has come to be known as the "supreme being" of the Chavín cult—a human figure with large fangs, usually depicted wearing a short skirt, anklets, ear spools, and a large headdress. These sculptures were executed in a unique style that reduces figures to a series of lines, curves, and scrolls. In addition, there are images that are regularly repeated within Chavín art, such as snakes used to depict whiskers or hair, and lines of caiman teeth to depict wing bones. This stylized form of depicting natural and supernatural beings spread widely across the northern and central Andes, and it is the primary feature identifying the spread of the Chavín cult.

SOURCES: Burger, Richard, *The Prehistoric Occupation of Chavín de Huantar, Peru* (Berkeley: University of California Press, 1984); *Chavín and the Origins of Andean Civilization* (London: Thames and Hudson, 1992).

ancestors have higher status and power than other *ayllus* (or groups of *ayllus*), thus providing an inherent hierarchy.

Leaders in Andean Regional Development polities, then, controlled the population through the *ayllu* system. Preeminent leaders controlled those lower down in the hierarchy of their elite *ayllu*. Leaders lower down, in turn, controlled those lower than them. At the level of individual villages, the *ayllu* leader, often an elder, controlled land, pasture, water, and labor. Andean Regional Development polities were apparently supported through tribute in the form of food, textiles, and labor provided by local *ayllus*. Textiles became particularly important and were major items of both tribute and trade (Figure 11.5). Weaving became highly sophisticated during the Andean Regional Development tradition, with fabrics of thread counts of 300 to 500 per inch being common. Metallurgy also became more sophisticated,

FIGURE **11.5**
An Andean Regional
Development textile.

**Moche**
(1950–1200 B.P.)

**Nasca** (2200–1300 B.P.)

**Cahauachi**
(Peru, Nasca)

with techniques of embossing, repousse, plating, soldering, acid pickling, smelting, and casting (both simple and lost wax methods) developing. Fine ceramics, too, were produced in new ways, and mass production of some forms developed. These innovations were developed by craft specialists, many of whom were probably attached to elites.

Similar developments also took place along the Andean coast. On the northern Peruvian coast, peoples of the **Moche** (1950–1200 B.P.) tradition developed large urban centers with several thousand residents, supported by a complex system of irrigation agriculture. Large centers were also locations where political leaders resided and contained platform mounds and ritual enclosures where religious ceremonies were performed. On the southern coast, peoples of the **Nasca** (2200–1300 B.P.) tradition also built large ceremonial centers, but these do not appear to have had large resident populations. Indeed, the site of **Cahauachi**, perhaps the primary ceremonial center in the area, appears to have had no resident population. The site contains more than fourty platform mounds and numerous ceremonial enclosures covering an area of some 25 hectares. Since the site has no residential architecture, it appears to have been a location solely for pilgrimage and ritual.

Despite the presence of urban centers, most people in both the Moche and Nasca traditions lived in agricultural villages in river valleys. Irrigation agriculture allowed large populations to inhabit these valleys, and villages grew to have 300 to 500 residents. Housing was in rectangular adobe or wattle-and-daub structures, roughly 4 meters by 6 meters in size. Fishing villages along the coast were similar in size and housing, but residents there subsisted by harvesting the vast resources of the sea using balsa and reed boats. As is the case in the highlands, most scholars think that these villages each represented a single descent group and that both Moche and Nasca polities were built upon these local descent groups.

Both the Moche and Nasca stand out in the artistic achievements they made in ceramics and metalwork. Moche artisans produced fineware ceramics using simple molding and modeling techniques that stand among the finest ceramics ever produced. Standard forms included restricted neck bottles, stirrup-handled bottles, and high-collared jars. The globular part of the bottle or jar was often shaped into a life-like effigy and painted using realistic colors (see Color Plate 16). Images depicted on Moche ceramics range from individual people to groups to animals to fantastic beings to everyday objects. The entire range of human and animal behavior is found as well, including a wide variety of sexual behavior. Nasca ceramicists were also highly skilled, particularly in the production of complex polychrome decoration.

FIGURE **11.6**
A hummingbird geoglyph on
the Pampa de San Jose.

Nasca metalwork was restricted to elite ornaments and ritual paraphenalia, though Nazca artisans produced masterpieces in these realms, particularly gold masks that were apparently used in rituals. Moche metalworkers produced a wider range of both utilitarian and ornamental goods, and perfected techniques of gilding and lost wax casting.

One aspect of the Nasca tradition that cannot be ignored is the creation of intaglio **geoglyphs,** or designs incised in rock, that cover the **Pampa de San Jose** (Figure 11.6). The surface of the Pampa is covered by dark desert varnish caused by oxidation of the surface layers of stone and sand. When this desert varnish is scraped aside, the light, unoxidized sand and stone are revealed, creating a stark contrasting line. Nasca peoples realized this, and created a vast array of lines and at least eighteen images on the Pampa. Since the area is extremely arid and there appears to have been little wind erosion in at least 2000 years, the lines and images have remained intact on the desert floor. The lines have been interpreted as road-ways, as ritual paths for pilgrimages or ceremonies, as indicators of water courses under the Pampa, and as calendrical markers. Most scholars believe the images represent Nasca dieties.

In the southern highlands of Peru and Bolivia, peoples of the **Tiwanaku** (1600–900 B.P.) tradition developed a powerful, centralized state in the area around Lake Titicaca. The state was supported by large-scale herding of llama and alpaca and coordinated raised-field agriculture. The state was centered at the site of **Tiwanaku.** Covering an area of more than 420 hectares and with a population estimated to be more than 40,000 people, Tiwanaku was one of the great cities of the prehistoric world (Figure 11.7). It was laid out according to the cardinal directions, with the ceremonial and administrative precinct at the center, surrounded by a wall and moat, apparently to keep commoners out. The surrounding nonelite residential areas were divided into rectangular, walled barrios, with each of these subdivided into groups of houses surrounding a courtyard. It is thought each courtyard group represented a single extended family while the larger barrios represented the

**Pampa de San Jose**
(Peru, Nasca)

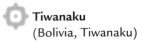

**Tiwanaku**
(1600–900 B.P.)

**Tiwanaku**
(Bolivia, Tiwanaku)

**Geoglyphs:** designs incised
in rock.

FIGURE **11.7**
Aerial view of the central
administrative precinct at
Tiwanaku.

separate *ayllus* that made up the city's population. At least seven secondary administrative centers were located within the Lake Titicaca basin and had similar layouts to Tiwanaku, although smaller populations—on the order of 10,000 residents.

Most people within the Lake Titicaca basin were engaged in large-scale llama and alpaca herding and raised-field agriculture. Over 120,000 hectares of raised-field systems were cultivated, and crops included potatoes, *oca, olluco,* and quinona. With such extensive agricultural systems, much of the population must have lived in smaller villages. These are ubiquitous, ranging from a few to a few dozen households. Houses themselves were simple wattle-and-daub structures, roughly 4 meters by 6 meters in size, and typically sharing a courtyard with several other houses, probably part of an extended family.

The nature of political authority in the Tiwanaku state appears to have rested on both the *ayllu* structure and religious ideology. Strong local traditions in ceramics and other tools continued throughout the Tiwanaku tradition, suggesting that local autonomy remained strong. Tiwanaku, therefore, may have been more of a confederation of autonomous communities and *ayllus* than a single overarching political structure. The Tiwanaku polity sponsored rituals and festivals, and the city may have been a place of pilgrimage or worship for people dwelling in the Lake Titicaca basin. In return, Tiwanaku received tribute from local communities, but it is not clear whether there was any strong coercive force or administrative authority issuing from Tiwanaku.

**Huari** (1200–950 B.P.)

**Huari** (Peru, Huari)

In the northern highlands of Peru, peoples of the **Huari** (1200–950 B.P.) tradition developed a similar, centralized polity. Communities appear to have been planned, and common forms of dress and iconography suggest that Huari leaders were integrated into a complex, multiregional political system (see Figure 11.8). The **Huari** site itself is situated atop an oval mesa roughly 3 kilometers by 4 kilometers in size. Water was fed to the mesa by a canal running along a ridge connecting the mesa to the eastern slope of the Huamanga basin. Some 50,000 people inhabited Huari at its height. In addition to distinctive D-shaped buildings forming ceremonial complexes, and subterranean corridors and rooms, also thought to be ceremonial structures, the architecture of Huari was based on courtyard groups. Several stone-walled houses

FIGURE **11.8**
Massive stone walls at the Huari site of Piquillacta demonstrate the ability of Huari leaders to coordinate labor and construct large, planned communities.

were arranged around courtyards and surrounded by narrow galleries. Each courtyard group was probably inhabited by a single extended family.

The widespread integration of peoples sharing similar iconography and, presumably, ideology appears to have dissolved into regionally distinct polities in the **Andean Regional States** (900–530 B.P.) and **Aymara Kingdoms** (900–530 B.P.) traditions. The Andean Regional States tradition was located in the northern and central Andes while the Aymara Kingdoms tradition was located in the Lake Titicaca region. Despite the differences in location, they share many similarities. In both traditions fortified sites are common, suggesting a high level of conflict. Settlements were often placed on hilltops or ridges, and houses placed on terraces cut into the slope. Housing in both traditions consists of small rectangular or circular nuclear family dwellings built of stone and adobe or wattle and daub. There is also a general absence of the very large regional centers that existed in previous traditions; rather, centers tend to be small, with perhaps 1,000 residents. Overall, then, there appears to have been a general decentralization of population in the Andean Regional States and the Aymara Kingdoms traditions.

On the north coast of Peru the **Chimu** (1050–480 B.P.) tradition followed a different pattern, and centralization continued or even increased. The political center of **Chan Chan**, described in the box feature, had as many as 50,000 residents and was the center of a hierarchical state (Figure 11.9). Regional centers like Manchan, smaller communities like Cerro de la Virgen, and agricultural hamlets filled out the hierarchy. These communities were integrated into a single polity through a king and a group of provincial and local elites.

The Chimu state was supported by irrigation agriculture and the intensive harvesting of ocean resources. If sufficient rain and snow fell in the Andes, enough water would flow through the complex irrigation systems that surrounded Chimu communities so that they could produce two crops a year. Maize, beans, and squash were staples, while schools of anchovy, sardine, and tuna provided abundant protein. Technology was simple, and included digging sticks and foot plows, fishing nets and copper fishhooks, cloth, and ceramics. Metalwork included both utilitarian items like fishhooks and needles as well as personal ornaments. Obsidian blades and flakes were used as cutting tools.

**Andean Regional States**
(900–530 B.P.)

**Aymara Kingdoms**
(900–530 B.P.)

**Chimu** (1050–480 B.P.)

**Chan Chan**
(Peru, Chimu)

FIGURE **11.9**
Aerial photograph of one
of the nine administrative
compounds at Chan Chan.

**Cerro de la Virgen**
**(Peru, Chimu)**

A typical Chimu agricultural village is **Cerro de la Virgen,** located 5 kilometers north of Chan Chan and 2.5 kilometers from the coast, in what is today a desert. Agriculture was possible here because of irrigation, brought to the area through a large canal. The village itself consists of some 400 rooms that vary from single structures to multiroom clusters. The walls of these structures were built from wattle and daub supported on a stone foundation. Larger rooms probably represent single-family dwellings, and those few that have been excavated contained hearths, storage vessels, and storage pits. Smaller rooms were apparently storerooms. Weaving was an important activity at Cerro de la Virgen, and households also contain remains of looms, spindle whorls, and needles. It is thought that cotton was a major agricultural crop, and perhaps the site's residents specialized in cloth production for the state.

**Manchan (Peru, Chimu)**

**Manchan** represents a provincial center of the Chimu state. It is located at the northern end of the state, in the Casma valley of Peru, some 9 kilometers from the sea. The site covers over 60 hectares and contains several distinct residential and administrative or religious areas. There are numerous blocks of adobe rooms, consisting of both small and large rooms with common walls and doorways opening onto large walled plazas. Some of the smaller room blocks are interpreted as compounds for elite residents of the site. Most inhabitants of Manchan, however, lived in simple wattle-and-daub rooms surrounding a central courtyard that likely comprised the residence of a single nuclear or extended family. These courtyard groups were linked by sinuous alleyways that wandered through Manchan. Excavation of these courtyard groups indicated that a wide range of activities took place, including spinning and weaving, woodworking, and metalwork. It appears that individual families at Manchan were largely self-sufficient and supported the elite with both agricultural products and craft goods.

**Inca (c. 800–468 B.P.)**

Sometime around 800 B.P. the **Inca** (c. 800–468 B.P.) tradition, which saw the integration of much of highland and coastal Peru and Bolivia into a single empire, began to develop and expand. Because of Spanish chronicles and colonial records, we have a rich set of historical documents to aid in our understanding of the Inca empire. The Inca empire was centered at **Cuzco,** located in the south-central highlands of Peru. In 500 B.P. the city of Cuzco had some 20,000 residents and perhaps as many as 100,000 people living within its vicinity. The Inca empire as a whole integrated most of highland and coastal Peru and may have had as many as 10 million citizens. How did this massive empire operate?

**Cuzco (Peru, Inca)**

Subsistence was based on agriculture, and production was controlled by the Inca. The Inca owned all land, but gave a portion to each local *ayllu* for their support. The remaining portion was worked by local *ayllus,* with the food produced going to the empire. The Inca government also constructed and maintained agricultural terraces, irrigation canals, and dams. The labor for these projects came from a system called *m'ita,* in which each *ayllu* was expected to supply a set number of people each year to work on imperial projects. In addition to agriculture, *ayllus* also kept herds of llama and alpaca, whose wool was spun and woven into cloth. Cloth was given to the Inca as tribute, and was an important part of the imperial economy.

The Inca government supported itself through agricultural products, cloth, and *m'ita* labor received from *ayllus,* and in return offered *ayllus* a stable government, a standing army (largely composed of *m'ita* conscripts), and the benefit of government-funded public works such as irrigation canals and roads. The empire was divided into four quarters, and each quarter was divided into provinces, which generally corresponded with political divisions before Inca conquest and unification. Each quarter had a lord, and each province had a governor. Below the governor were a hierarchical set of bureaucrats, each with a smaller group of families to administer—from 1,000 down to the local *curacas* who each administered 100 families. This complex bureaucracy was able to keep close control of people and to maintain clear lines of command and information flow throughout the empire.

In addition to public works, the Inca government supported religion and the arts. The Inca controlled the production of polychrome ceramics, fine cloth, and precious metals, all of which were symbols of status and authority. The Inca also built, supported, and controlled religious facilities and rites. The Inca himself was considered to be a direct descendent of the sun. There was a pantheon of deities subordinant to the sun (and his heir, the Inca), as well as the earth, mountain, and water, which all possessed supernatural qualities. The Inca built shrines to the deities and maintained a range of ritual attendants at each shrine; their job was to maintain the shrine and perform day-to-day rituals for the deity (Figure 11.10). They also

*M'ita:* a system of labor mobilization in the Inca empire in which each *ayllu* was expected to supply a set number of people each year to work on imperial projects.

FIGURE **11.10**
Atahualpa, the last ruler of the Incas.

# Chan Chan

Chan Chan, the ancient capital of the Chimú state, rests in a most inauspicious environment—a barren coastal desert in the Moche Valley of Peru, virtually devoid of life and completely lacking in any obvious signs that, at one time, the area housed one of the great civilizations of the world. While the site's location has been known since its fall to the Incas about A.D. 1465 (indeed, the Spanish apparently looted the site for gold and silver artifacts in the A.D. 1540s), it was not the focus of archaeological research until Michael Moseley and Carol Mackay began systematically mapping and excavating the site in 1969.

Moseley and Mackay found that the site covers a vast area, some 20 square kilometers in total. Much of the site is in ruins, the adobe walls of the numerous residences broken apart by earthquakes, eroded by wind and water, and covered by windblown soil. The core of the city, with densely packed residences and monumental architectural compounds, covers an area of over 6 square kilometers. This was the center of the Chimú state. The main architectural remains in this area of the site are ten large, rectangular enclosures, called "ciudadelas," each enclosing an area of about 10 hectares. Each ciudadela is surrounded by a large adobe wall up to 9 meters high, with a single entrance on the north side. Within the ciudadela are three main sections, a north section, a central section, and a side section or wing. Each section was similar in form. They had a large entry hall that opened onto a series of smaller courtyards with U-shaped structures within them

met with individuals who sought the deity's help, performed curing ceremonies, and offered sacrifices for individuals.

The Inca empire gives us a unique picture of how many prehistoric states may have been organized. The Inca used force when necessary, particularly to conquer autonomous polities, but much of their power came from their ability to harness and coordinate agricultural production and labor for public works. In addition, the Inca provided a relatively peaceful and stable political situation, and they supported religious institutions used by all citizens. They accomplished this by adopting the ancient *ayllus* and molding them into useful state entities. This is a recipe for state organization that was probably very common in the prehistoric world, and I will discuss it further in Chapter 17 on the rise of states.

**South Andean Ceramic (ca. 2500–500 B.P.)**

Finally, along the southern Andean coasts, peoples of the **South Andean Ceramic** (ca. 2500–500 B.P.) tradition appear to have been influenced by political developments to the north and began coalescing into large communities and regional polities that persisted until the Spanish conquest. South Andean settlements tended to be along major river valleys. Settlements varied in size from small villages to large fortified towns. Dwellings were small and rectangular, typically built on terraces with walls made from stone, adobe, or woven cane. Larger dwellings were also present, as were large, multistructure compounds at some sites. These compounds may have been for elites, and would have contained special-purpose rooms for storage and administrative duties. Most communities were not internally organized but were more of an "agglutination" of dwellings and compounds. The South

and, beyond these, numerous storage rooms. On the south end of the ciudadela is a fourth area, separated from the others, that seems to have housed residents who took care of the ciudadela. Associated with the ciudadelas are elite residential compounds, often built as annexes. Since there are ten ciudadelas and there were ten recorded Chimú kings, some have suggested that a ciudadela was built for each king as a combination governmental building and palace.

While Chimú kings lived in these palaces, most of Chan Chan's estimated 30,000 residents lived in what Moseley calls "small, irregularly agglutinated rooms," or SIAR. Most SIAR were located on the southern and western sides of the site (with ceremonial areas on the northern and eastern sides), and these tended to merge into one vast urban sprawl. SIAR tend to be associated with elite compounds, wells, and cemeteries, forming distinct barrios. Wells were often located within elite compounds, and this suggests that individual elites may have maintained some control over the resources used by barrio residents. Construction of the SIAR apparently began with the creation of exterior walls that enclosed a large area, which was then divided into individual rooms. Rooms varied considerably, but usually included a kitchen with a large hearth and often with an adjacent area that appears to have housed llamas, guinea pigs, and ducks, sleeping or living rooms, storage rooms, and craft workshops. Craft workshops were present both within domestic areas and in separate structures that must have functioned as special industrial areas.

SOURCE: Moseley, Michael, and Kent Day, *Chan Chan: Andean Desert City* (Albuquerque: University of New Mexico Press, 1982).

Andean economy was primarily agricultural, but it was supplemented with fishing, hunting, and collecting. Irrigation was used in many places, and crops were diverse. Domestic plants included corn, potatoes, manioc, legumes, squash, and chili pepper. Domesticated animals included the llama, guinea pig, and muscovy duck.

Tools used by the South Andean peoples included chipped stone hoes, knives, and arrows. Bone was used for tools as well. Textiles included bolas, fishing lines, and nets. A wide variety of ceramics were also employed by the South Andean peoples. All were handmade, and early forms lacked decoration. Forms included bowls, globular storage jars, cups and beakers, and urns, among others. Later ceramics were more often decorated than earlier ones, often adopting styles from the northern Andes.

Large residential compounds in some communities suggest the presence of elites, and the overall scale of society with large communities, irrigation, and the like suggests the presence of formal political leaders. Neighboring regions to the north were, of course, developing large states and empires at the same time as the South Andean Ceramic tradition, and it is reasonable to think that parallel processes were under way.

## AMAZON

The Amazon basin is a vast region covering nearly 7 million square kilometers in northeast South America—roughly 40 percent of the continent. Through it runs the second largest river in the world—the Amazon, nearly 6,500 kilometers long and discharging the greatest volume of water of any river in the world. This water comes from the rainforests that dominate the Amazon basin and receive several thousand millimeters of rainfall a year. Temperature averages about 20 degrees C, with little annual variation. While it has long been assumed that Amazonian soils were unsuitable for intensive agriculture, deep organic soils are found throughout the basin, particularly at both its far eastern and western ends. These soils were used widely for agriculture. In addition to agriculture, the Amazon basin was a rich environment for fishing and gathering. The backwaters, side channels, and lakes of the rivers were full of fish, easiest to catch in the dry season, but available year-round. Terrestrial game was less abundant, but still plentiful. Wild plant food was abundant, especially in river forests and swamps.

As I discussed in the chapter on the Upper Paleolithic, peoples of the Old Amazonian Collecting-Hunting tradition began to populate the Amazon as early as 11,000 years ago. By the time of the **Early Amazonian** (7000–2000 B.P.) tradition, peoples living in the Amazon basin appear to have begun settling in small villages, making ceramics, and experimenting with plant cultivation. They also hunted, fished, and collected widely. At **Taperinha**, located on the lower Amazon in Para, Brazil, remains of mussels, fish, and turtles dominated the faunal assemblage, suggesting a heavy reliance on the Amazon itself for food. The site consists of a large mound some 6 meters high and perhaps 5 hectares in area, composed largely of discarded mussel shell. No housing has been found at Taperinha, but at other Early Amazonian sites evidence for large communal houses built of poles and thatch have been found. Sand-tempered ceramics, mostly plain but some with red paint or incised decoration, were found in abundance at Taperinha, along with a variety of bone and shell tools, and some stone flakes and bifaces. Taperinha appears to represent the remains of a small, egalitarian village of fisher-gatherers who lived on the resources of the Amazon.

Peoples of the **Late Amazonian** (2000–50 B.P.) tradition were village-dwelling horticulturalists who both planted domestic crops and cultivated wild trees and other plants. There is evidence that some villages were led by elites, and there is even evidence of regional site hierarchies in some areas. In both the eastern Amazon basin of Brazil and the western Amazon of Bolivia and Ecuador, sites consist of large mounds that served to raise houses above swampy river floodplains. On **Marajo Island** in eastern Brazil, the mounds vary from 1 hectare to almost 20 hectares in area and are typically several meters high. Platforms occur singly or in groups, sometimes with several dozen together. Each platform would have formed the foundation for a single house to perhaps as many as twenty large communal houses, with several families related by descent residing in each. The people of Marajo island subsisted on fish and on forest and swamp plants, supplemented by domestic plants. Raised agricultural terraces were used in wet areas, but uplands could be farmed using basic slash-and-burn methods. In these areas, houses were apparently built directly on the forest floor, rather than on raised mounds. Manioc and sweet potato were the most important crops raised, but maize was found as well.

Late Amazonian peoples made ceramics in several regionally distinct styles. Polychrome types are found in both the western and eastern Amazon basin (Figure 11.11). They are generally well made and are typically painted in red and brown or black on white. In the central Amazon incised and punctuated ceramics are more common. Shapes are diverse and include plates, bowls, jars, funnels, rattles, figurines, and many more. Tools were simple and made from locally available stone, bone, and wood. Woven hammocks, nets, bags, and cloth bands were also made. One interesting feature of the Late Amazonian tradition is burial. Many individuals were buried in large ceramic urns after having been defleshed and wrapped in cloth.

Historic period texts suggest that Late Amazonian peoples lived in simple chiefdoms, and the archaeological record seems to provide some support for that idea. The large communities in places like Marajo Island would have probably required some individuals to maintain order. There seems clear evidence for descent groups

---

**Early Amazonian**
(7000–2000 B.P.)

**Taperinha**
(Brazil, Early Amazonian)

**Late Amazonian**
(2000–50 B.P.)

**Marajo Island**
(Brazil, Late Amazonian)

FIGURE **11.11**

Examples of Late Amazonian polychrome ceramics.

SOURCE: Jesse D. Jennings (ed.), *Ancient Native Americans* (New York: W.H. Freeman & Company, 1978), p. 570.

in the large communal houses at the site, and these may also have had formal leaders. Certain individuals were buried with extensive personal ornaments, and historic records describe some personal ornaments as symbols of rank. Success in hunting and war may have led to achieved status, but it may be that ascribed positions of status were also present among Late Amazonian societies.

## PAMPAS

Three major environments are included within the Pampas region. These include the northern Parana river lowlands and alluvial plains, the flat grasslands of the Pampas proper, and the southern arid flatlands of northern and eastern Patagonia. Thus flat grassland topography dominates the region. Large rivers flow west-to-east across these flatlands at rather wide intervals. Game animals such as the guanaco and rhea were plentiful on these grasslands, as were fish in the rivers.

These vast grasslands and arid flatlands were home to humans for more than 10,000 years. Unfortunately, the remains of their lives have proven difficult to find and recover, and archaeological knowledge of the region is in a comparatively unsophisticated state. The earliest distinct tradition is the **Early Parana-Pampean** (7000–1500 B.P.) tradition. Early Parana-Pampean settlements are small and

**Early Parana-Pampean**
(7000–1500 B.P.)

ephemeral, often consisting of little more than a scattering of kitchen and stone-tool production refuse. In some areas caves were inhabited, and these have provided a better picture of the material culture of the Early Parana-Pampean peoples, but not much more information about their settlements or dwellings. The Early Parana-Pampean peoples were hunter-gatherers. Guanaco, rhea, and deer were hunted on the grasslands, fish were taken in the rivers, and a diversity of plant foods were collected from both areas. Hunting was done with distinctive triangular stemmed projectile points, often with concave bases. These are often small, and may indicate the use of the bow and arrow. **Bolas** were also used for hunting on open grasslands. Scrapers, knives, and flat grinding stones were used to work hide by the Early Parana-Pampean peoples.

They were followed by peoples of the **Late Parana-Pampean** (1500–500 B.P.) tradition. These peoples were also hunters and gatherers, but some groups, particularly in the larger river valleys, also practiced agriculture and lived in sedentary villages, sometimes quite large. A wide variety of Late Parana-Pampean settlements have been found, from cave sites to large villages. All seem to have access to water and tend to be located near major river valleys. Dwellings, where found, appear to be of two major styles, round or rectangular, but were only large enough to house a single family. They were made from either stone or adobe, with adobe dwellings sometimes having a stone foundation. Communities varied in size from small hamlets of perhaps only a few related families to villages of perhaps 300 or more people.

The Late Parana-Pampean people were primarily hunter-gatherers, but some groups, particularly in the river valleys in the northern range of the tradition, may have supplemented their diet with domesticated plant foods. Animals such as the guanaco and deer were hunted with the bolas and bow and arrow. Arrows armed with small, triangular arrow-points were manufactured from chipped stone. Ground-stone implements included bolas stones and a variety of hammer and grinding stones. Bone was used for a variety of tools, including awls, fishhooks, and arrow points. Ceramics were manufactured by the Late Parana-Pampean peoples. These ceramics were red-brown wares in a variety of forms, with bowls predominating. Some were decorated with geometric designs, often using a stab-and-drag technique. In the northwestern range of the tradition, influences from the Andes led to a greater diversity of ceramic styles and forms, which included the use of polychrome decoration.

To the far south, peoples of the **Magellan-Fuegian** (6300–50 B.P.) tradition lived on the rugged Patagonian coasts in small, nomadic groups. They hunted, gathered, and fished, with a particular emphasis on sea mammals and shellfish. Magellan-Fuegan peoples used technology as simple as clubs to dispatch seals on shore, but also employed ocean-going canoes, harpoons with detachable ivory heads, and bows and arrows armed with chipped stone points. Ceramics were not made, but rather rush baskets and skin bags were used for collecting and storage. Settlements were small and short-term; groups moved regularly to maintain adequate access to resources. Housing was of two kinds: one was a dome of branches covered with brush or skins; the other was a conical tent made of straight poles tied at the top and covered with skin. In either case they housed a single family. Most groups consisted of two or three related families.

## EASTERN HIGHLANDS

The highlands of eastern Brazil are so vast, north and south, and have so much variation in altitude from the coastal mountain range to the bottom of the river valleys that no single environment characterizes the region. The interior on the west side is a tropical savanna. The northwest is tropical and subtropical steppe. The northern

---

**Late Parana-Pampean** (1500–500 B.P.)

**Magellan-Fuegian** (6300–50 B.P.)

**Bolas:** a hunting tool consisting of three stones connected by three strings tied together. When thrown around the legs of an animal, the strings wrap around the legs and prevent the animal from running away.

half of the highlands are always hot, and the southern half has hot summers and mild winters. The climate along the Brazilian coast is subtropical and humid, with rainfall throughout most of the year. The coast itself is rocky, and there are often a series of dunes paralleling the water. Mangrove swamps, lagoon forests, and dune forests grow along the coast, while tropical rain forests grow farther inland.

The first archaeological tradition in the Eastern Highlands is the **Early East Brazilian Uplands** (11,000–5000 B.P.) tradition. Peoples of this tradition were hunters and gatherers who lived in rockshelters or small open-air sites. Most sites were probably occupied by individual families, but larger rockshelters may have had several families residing in them if area resources were plentiful. Open sites tended to be located along streams. No remains of housing have been uncovered. A typical site is the **Abrigo do Pilao,** a rockshelter located at the base of a limestone ridge near the town of Central in Bahia, Brazil. The rockshelter itself is about 17 meters long and would have provided space for several families. The site contains abundant flakes, cores, and flake tools made from locally available quartz and quartzite, along with shell scrapers and bone projectile points. While the first Early East Brazilian Uplands peoples hunted the last of the Pleistocene megafauna, later members of the tradition, like those who lived at Abrigo do Pilao, hunted peccaries, deer, and small mammals such as agouti, armadillos, marmosets, lizards, and snakes. The forest surrounding the rockshelter would have provided cacti and trees producing edible fruits, and a variety of nuts, roots, and other edible plants.

The peoples of the ensuing **Late East Brazilian Uplands** (5000–50 B.P.) tradition, who continued to hunt and gather, supplemented those wild foods with domesticated horticultural products. They also constructed villages of up to a dozen round, semisubterranean houses and produced ceramics. At **Lagoa Sao Paulo,** located by the city of Presidente Epitacio in the state of Sao Paulo, a group of circular houses with diameters from 5 to 10 meters were uncovered. Ceramics included both decorated and undecorated types in a variety of forms. Stone tools included local quartz and silicified sandstone flakes, worked flakes, cores, and scapers. A similar assemblage of artifacts was found at **PR-FO-17** near the bank of the Parana River in the state of Parana. Here houses were arranged in an oval around an open plaza. Both villages probably had seven to ten houses, each housing an extended family, and a population of 50 to 100 people. Subsistence was based on hunting peccaries and small game, gathering a wide variety of plant foods, fishing and shellfishing, and raising manioc and other domestic crops.

Peoples of the **Sambaqui** (7000–500 B.P.) tradition lived during the same time as both the Early and the Late East Brazilian Uplands peoples, but they occupied the coastal areas and focused subsistence on marine resources. They built distinctive mounds of shells, called *sambaqui,* some of which were apparently used to support houses (Figure 11.12). The Sambaqui da Caieira, for example, located adjacent to the coastal town of **Laguna,** Santa Catarina, was clearly built as a platform mound. The mound was constructed of shells, sand, and occupational debris that were deposited in parallel layers, some separated by layers of windblown sand. Thus it appears that the mound was purposely constructed as a flat platform and was periodically abandoned and re-occupied. Within the mound were found post-holes and living floors from circular houses. In contrast, the **Sambaqui de Camboinhas,** located on the edge of a lagoon near Niteroi in the state of Rio de Janeiro, was simply a trash mound. Deposits of shells, occupational debris, and pockets of dark sand and ash are all jumbled from simple accretion. There are no features or evidences of housing in the mound. The mound was apparently built as a simple refuse mound adjacent to where a group of Sambaqui people lived.

Despite the differences in the *sambaquis* they created, the peoples of the Sambaqui tradition lived very similarly across the entire range of the tradition. Shellfish was obviously central to their diet. Fish, turtles, sea mammals, and land mammals were all taken as well. Plant foods such as beach grasses and fruits and

**Early East Brazilian Uplands** (11,000–5000 B.P.)

**Abrigo do Pilao** (Brazil, Early East Brazilian Uplands)

**Late East Brazilian Uplands** (5000–50 B.P.)

**Lagoa Sao Paulo** (Brazil, Late East Brazilian Uplands)

**PR-FO-17** (Brazil, Late East Brazilian Uplands)

**Sambaqui** (7000–500 B.P.)

**Laguna** (Brazil, Sambaqui)

**Sambaqui de Camboinhas** (Brazil, Sambaqui)

FIGURE **11.12**
The Sambaqui do Tambor
near Rio de Janeiro, Brazil.

nuts from coastal forests were collected. Tools used by Sambaqui peoples to collect these foods were simple, and included projectiles armed with bone points, bone fishhooks, weighted fishing nets, pitted hammer stones, ground stone axes, and a variety of flaked stone tools made from locally available quartz. Sambaqui communities were relatively large, with as many as thirty or forty small, circular houses arranged around an open plaza or, in some cases, on top of a platform *sambaqui* raised well above sea level (typically several meters, although some *sambaquis* are over 20 meters high). Several hundred people would have lived in these villages, but despite their size and the obvious coordinated labor it took to create large platform *sambaquis*, there is no evidence of social differentiation or formal political leaders.

**Tupi (1500–150 B.P.)**

**Almeida (Brazil, Tupi)**

Finally, peoples of the **Tupi** (1500–150 B.P.) tradition lived in villages along the Brazilian coast and the interior regions of the Parana, Paraguay, and Uruguay rivers. Most villages were small—simple hamlets of one or two houses to villages of fifteen or twenty houses. Houses themselves varied greatly, ranging from circular single-family dwellings to large communal dwellings that, in the historic period, reportedly housed up to 600 people. Most archaeologically known houses are of the smaller variety, and most Tupi villages probably had populations on the order of 50 to 100 people. For example, at the **Almeida** site near Tejupa in the state of Sao Paulo, Brazil, nine circular areas of darkened soil, between 12 and 20 meters in diameter, were interpreted as houses. They were oriented in a line near a low sandstone hill with outcrops of silicified sandstone that was used by the site's inhabitants for tools. The houses probably held extended families, and the entire village had a population of perhaps sixty people.

The people living at Almeida fished, hunted, and raised a variety of domestic plants, including manioc, sweet potato, taro, peanut, and maize, among many others. Technology was simple, and was made by individual households. Hunting was done with bow and arrow, the arrows armed with bone or chipped stone points. Fishing was done with nets, harpoon, hook and line, and traps. Food was cooked and served in a variety of ceramic pots, jars, and bowls. Tupi peoples also wove hammocks and textile bands for loincloths. Socially, the large houses on some Tupi sites have been interpreted as habitations for groups of families related by descent, and such descent groups are reported in the historic literature. Politically, the villages like Almeida appear to have been largely autonomous. Some larger villages may have had headmen, but most communities were probably egalitarian. In the historic period village chiefs were present and village warfare was endemic, but it is unclear whether either was common in the prehistoric period.

## ⚙ SUMMARY

The prehistory of South America seems one of disparate regional evolution, with Andean populations rapidly evolving village life and political centralization, and other populations maintaining a fairly stable way of life for thousands of years. The lifeways of peoples in the interior of the continent and the eastern coasts seem to have remained largely unchanged after the adoption of agriculture, and all seem to have followed similar hunting and gathering ways of life before agricultural crops were introduced. Perhaps this picture is biased because of the relative paucity of information for areas outside of the Andes, but it does appear that the Andes were a particularly vibrant region for sociopolitical evolution.

## ⚙ DISCUSSION QUESTIONS

1. What accounts for the dynamic nature of Andean cultural evolution when compared to the rest of the continent and, indeed, to much of the rest of the New World?

2. While the Andes are a particularly dramatic region of cultural evolution, parts of Patagonia and the Pampas seem comparative backwaters, where little changed for thousands of years. What accounts for cultural stability in some regions of South America?

3. How did the adoption of agriculture affect people in the many fertile areas of eastern South America?

## ⚙ ESSAY QUESTIONS

1. The archaeological record of the Andes region has been one of the most heavily explored in the world. In contrast, comparatively little research has been done in the Amazon basin and the Parana-Pampas regions—an area comprising more than half the South American continent. Write an essay in which you explore this difference and its ramifications. Why has so much archaeological research been done in the Andes? Why has so little archaeological research been done on the eastern half of South America? How does this difference in the amount of research affect our understanding of South American prehistory?

2. The historian Marc Bloch once wrote that "Explorers of the past are never quite free. The past is their tyrant. It forbids them to know anything which it has not itself, consciously or unconsciously, yielded to them." In what ways are Bloch's ideas manifested in the archaeological record of the Andes region. In what ways is the past an unyielding tyrant to archaeologists working on Tiwanaku, for example, or Chan Chan? What knowledge, or realms of knowledge, remain hidden? What knowledge, or realms of knowledge, does the archaeological record most readily yield?

3. Use this text and any other resources you can locate to compare and contrast the central Andes with the northern and southern Andes. How do the three

regions differ in terms of cultural evolution? Why did the southern Andes seem to lag behind the other two areas? Why were the central Andes the location where the most complex and politically centralized societies evolved?

## ✒ RESEARCH PROJECT

Use library and Internet resources to research the geoglyphs drawn by Nasca peoples on the Pampa de San Jose. Find as many explanations for the purpose and meaning of the geoglyphs as you can (including the more bizarre ones such as those suggesting they were messages to or from aliens). Evaluate these explanations using the information in this chapter and the knowledge of archaeological research you gained through the first three chapters of this text. What makes one explanation better than another? Do all the explanations fit the facts equally well? Do all the explanations explain the purpose and meaning of the geoglyphs equally well? Do all the explanations mesh with the general archaeological record of the Andes equally well? Which explanation do you think is the best one? Why?

## ⬢ KEY SOURCES

### Andes

Aldenderfer, 1989, 1993, 1998, 2002; Arsenault, 2002; Aveni, 1990; Bauer, 1992; Bawden, 1996; Bermann, 1994; Browman, 2002a, 2002b; Bray, 2002; Burger, 1984, 1992; Church, 2002; D'Altroy, 1992; Dillehay, 2000, 2002; Dillehay et al., 1992; Donnan, 1985; Earle, 2002; Goldstein, 2002; Haas, Pozorski, and Pozorski, 1987; Hastorf, 1993; Hyslop, 1990; Isbell, 1997; Isbell and McEwan, 1991; Keatinge, 1988; Knobloch, 2002; Kolata, 1993, 1996; Kuznar, 2002; Lumbreras, 1974; Lynch, 1980; MacNeish, Patterson, and Browman, 1975; MacNeish et al., 1981, 1983; Masuda, Shimada, and Morris, 1985; Moore, 1996, 2002; Moseley, 1992; Moseley and Cordy-Collins, 1990; Moseley and Day, 1982; Murra, 1980; Nuñez, 1983; Pozorsky and Pozorsky, 1987, 2002a, 2002b; Proulx, 2002; Rick, 1980, 2002; Rivera, 1991; Silverman, 1993; Stanish, 1992, 2002; Wilson, 1988.

### Amazon

Magalhaes, 1994; Meggers, 1971, 1988; Piperno and Pearsall, 1998; Roosevelt, 1980, 1991, 1995, 1998a, 1998b, 1999a, 1999b, 2002a, 2002b, 2002c.

### Pampas

Bird, 1988; Borrero and Franco, 1997; Nami, 1995; Orquera, 1987; Piana, 2002.

### Eastern Highlands

Brochado, 2002; Bruhns, 1994; Bryan and Gruhn, 1993; Hurt, 1974, 1998, 2002a, 2002b, 2002c; Noelli, 1998.

# LORDS OF SIPAN

South America had numerous kingdoms, one of which was the Moche. The Moche lived in splendor while being situated on the northern coastal plain of Peru's desert interface, with the Pacific Ocean to the west and the towering Andes' volcanic peaks to the east. This wedge of land is part of one of the driest desert environments in the world. Rain and snowfall in the Andes feed the few westward-flowing rivers, which allowed for agricultural surplus in societies like the Moche, Chimu, and Inca. Fishing also occupied these people's economic lives, as agriculture was not always ample due to little snow and rainfall in some seasons. The tomb of the Lord of Sipan is located in Huaca Rajada, on the coastal plains of Lambayeque, along the Northern Coast of Peru, in a pyramid complex erected around 290 A.D.

The Media Lab can be found in Chapter 11 on the *Companion Website*™ http://www.prenhall.com/peregrine

## WEB ACTIVITY

This chapter develops the history and prehistory of South America. South America is treated as four major environmental regions: the Andes, the Amazon, the Pampas, and the Eastern Highlands. The great societies of the Inca, Chimu, Moche, Chavin, and many others, grew up in the great desert environment that flanked the western face of the Andes. Perhaps these civilizations elicit some interest in almost all people because of their elaborate cultures. Whether discussing Inca, Chimu, or Moche, the burial practices of all these people were intricate and sophisticated. The burial known as the Lord of Sipan is comprised of a warrior priest who is interred in the center of a tomb and sealed in a chamber with copper straps. Sacrificial victims surround him, as if to act as guards. The entire brick-lined chamber was completely intact when discovered in the late 1980s. In this activity, you will view a video of coastal Peru and a description of this famous burial.

## Activity

1. View the video. What does this type of burial tell us about the beliefs of the Moche?
2. Why would archaeologists call this warrior priest a lord? What type of political organization would be required to produce such a burial?
3. Why do archaeologists show such interest in burials, whether they are Inca, Ancient Egyptian, or Moche? What can burials of common people tell us about a society, especially in comparison to those of the nobility?

# Africa

The end of the Upper Paleolithic saw dramatic changes in the environment of Africa, particularly in the north. During the Pleistocene most of Africa was relatively cool and arid. Egypt was a desert of windblown sand, and the Nile River ran at less than 20 percent of its current flow. Central Africa was covered with deciduous woodlands rather than rain forest, and southern Africa was dominated by mixed woodlands and grasslands. Around 15,000 years ago the climate became milder. Trees and shrubs began to grow in what were once barren deserts, and

rainfall increased throughout the continent. Much of what is today the Sahara desert was vegetated, and large portions of the eastern Sahara were covered in marshlands. These mild conditions continued until the onset of the **Younger Dryas,** a cold and arid period that persisted from roughly 11,000 to 10,000 B.P. After 10,000 B.P. the climate shifted toward a modern pattern and became similar to the modern climate after about 8000 B.P.

The continent of Africa today is as environmentally diverse as any region of the world, and its prehistory is no less varied. For the purposes of this chapter I have divided Africa into five major regions: (1) North Africa; (2) the Nile Valley; (3) Southern and Eastern Africa; (4) Central Africa; and (5) West Africa (Figure 12.1). Though each of these regions blends into its neighbors, each also shares a somewhat distinct environmental and cultural history.

## NORTH AFRICA

Two environmental regions dominate northern Africa: the Mediterranean and the Sahara (Figure 12.2). The topography of the Mediterranean zone varies from coastal plains to rugged mountains. The region is relatively warm and arid and is covered with scrub forests and grasslands. A variety of plant foods are available, including nuts from pistachio, oak, and pine trees. Game animals flourish in the region and include both small animals and larger game such as Barbary sheep, gazelle, boar, hartebeest, and auroch. On the coast an abundance of fish and shellfish is available. The other major environmental region of northern Africa is the Sahara—an unforgiving desert stretching across north Africa from the west coast to the Rift Valley, essentially isolating the Mediterranean region from the south. Major rivers running across the Sahara provide local water sources, and in both the northern and southern parts of the region vast grasslands support large animals such as gazelle, giraffe, and elephant.

As I noted in the chapter on the Upper Paleolithic, both regions supported Upper Paleolithic hunters and gatherers, and the Mediterranean zone would continue to do so for thousands of years. However, the increasing aridity of the Younger Dryas depleted game and plant foods across both the Mediterranean and Sahara regions. The Sahara zone was particularly affected. At 10,000 B.P. there were numerous rivers, large lakes, and vast marshlands across the Sahara. By 8000 B.P. the region was dominated by arid grasslands, and by 5000 B.P. the region was dominated by desert. After 8000 B.P. hunting and gathering had become difficult in North Africa away from the Mediterranean coast, and people turned to pastoralism as a basic means of subsistence.

### Pastoralism

**Pastoralism** refers to subsistence based on domestic animals. But pastoralism refers as much to a way of life as it does to a means of subsistence. The demands of domesticated animals, especially in marginal zones, take precedence over all other aspects of life. Settlement, social and political organization, and even patterns of sleep are

**Younger Dryas:** a cold and arid period at the end of the last ice age, about 11,000 B.P. to 10,000 B.P.

**Pastoralism:** subsistence based on domesticated animals.

FIGURE **12.1**
Sites discussed in Chapter 12.

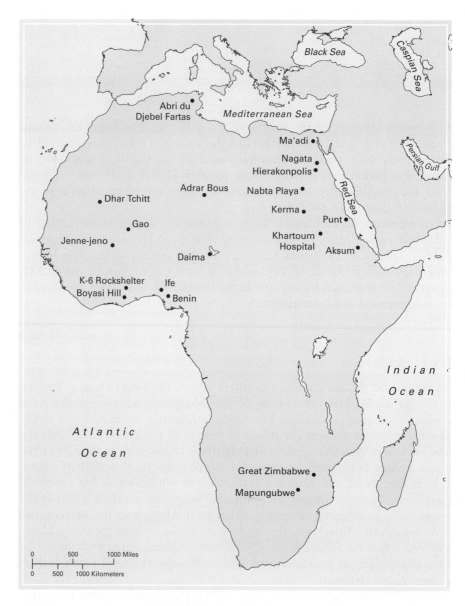

**Age sets:** groups of people who were born during the same period of time. Individuals in the same age set share social roles and go through important life events together.

shaped by the daily routine set by the animals. Animals are not commonly eaten by pastoralists, but rather kept for their products—milk, blood, dung, and hair. Life is structured in a seasonal round, sometimes moving daily to fresh pastures and often moving seasonally between uplands and lowlands or steppe lands and river valleys. In arid lands, movement is always dependent on being near sources of fresh water.

Animals are the source of wealth and status among pastoralists, and thus animals are highly valued and guarded (Figure 12.3). Most pastoralists maintain large numbers of animals, both to support themselves and as a way of "banking" their wealth and safeguarding their future. A group of domestic animals is, however, always in danger from contagious and insect-borne diseases, from predators, and from poachers. Pastoralists must always be on guard against these dangers, and yet the very basis of pastoral life—constant movement—makes such protection difficult. Not only is it difficult to avoid dangers in new and unknown lands, but pastoral groups tend to be very small, and thus there are often very few people available to guard the animals. For these reasons pastoralists also tend to have formal associations such as **age sets** (Figure 12.4) or descent groups that create close bonds between individual pastoral groups. These close ties provide a way for groups to

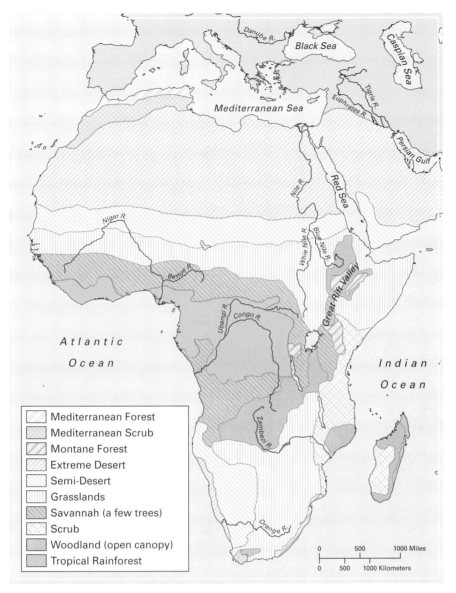

FIGURE **12.2**
Environments of Africa.

Mediterranean Forest
Mediterranean Scrub
Montane Forest
Extreme Desert
Semi-Desert
Grasslands
Savannah (a few trees)
Scrub
Woodland (open canopy)
Tropical Rainforest

FIGURE **12.3**
Two Maasai boys herd cattle. The daily life of pastoral peoples like the Maasai revolves around the needs of their animals.

Infants

Children

Young Adults

Mature Adults

FIGURE **12.4**

Each group of figures in this illustration represents an age set. The individuals within each age set all have the same role in society (such as herder, warrior, parent, etc.). When the group "graduates" to the next age set (a transition usually marked by a formal ceremony), all the members take on new roles. In this way age sets provide a means for societies to organize people into distinct roles that change as the people grow older.

come together quickly in times of danger (as when predators are numerous or poachers are raiding a particular area) and also provide a measure of protection if animals are lost, since one group can join another until they again become self-sufficient.

Many pastoral groups also have hierarchical social and political organizations, which create yet another way to tie individual groups together. Often both social and political status rests on achievement as an animal husbandman (that is, on the number of animals a person is able to maintain), or on success as a warrior. War is often a constant threat among pastoralists since wealth and status reside in animals, and often animals can be acquired simply by ambushing a small group far away from allies. Success as a warrior, both defending one's own animals and coming to the aid of other groups, is often a key element in gaining social and political status in pastoral societies. In addition, deadly animals like lions and hyenas are often seen to be at war with pastoralists in the same way that poachers are—they seek to steal wealth away. Thus success in killing dangerous animals may also lead to social and political status among pastoral groups.

With regular movement such a normal part of life, pastoralists tend to have few material possessions, and their settlements tend to be ephemeral. Neither provides much that might survive in the archaeological record, making the archaeological study of pastoral peoples difficult. Yet even pastoralists leave traces of their activities behind, and archaeologists, particularly in Africa, have found ways to recover those traces and learn about the past through them.

## Pastoralists of North Africa

In northern Africa the first domesticated animals were cattle, appearing as early as 9500 B.P. and becoming well established by 6500 B.P. About the same time (6500 B.P.) sheep and goats were added to the domesticated flocks. The origins of these domestic animals has been contested, with some arguing that they were domesticated locally and others that they were imported from Southwest Asia. The early dates for domesticated cattle, however, suggest that they were domesticated in North Africa from local aurochs, and genetic evidence supports that idea. The archaeological traditions in which domesticated animals first made their appearance in North Africa include the Saharo-Sudanese Neolithic, the Neolithic of Capsian, and the Southern Mediterranean Neolithic traditions.

Peoples of the **Saharo-Sudanese Neolithic** (8000–3000 B.P.) tradition were apparently the first to incorporate domestic cattle, sheep, and goats into their subsistence regime and adopt a fully pastoral way of life. Because these people were nomadic, the remains of settlements are extremely rare. One locale where a number of very early settlements have been found is the **Nabta Playa** in the western Egyptian desert, just north of the Egypt-Sudan border (Figure 12.5). Here, on the edge of what was a large seasonal lake, the remains of some twenty encampments have been excavated. All are situated on what would have been the lake margins and were likely a location where pastoralists came seasonally to take advantage of the abundant water and grass. Houses used in the Nabta Playa were round and semisubterranean. Associated with them were storage pits, hearths, and wells (which would have allowed the people living there to avoid wading into the mucky lake to get water). The remains of both cattle and sheep have been found in the Nabta Playa, including some cattle that appear to have been purposely buried under mounds and are associated with megalithic stone blocks. There are other interesting "ceremonial" features in the region as well. At one site a line of large stones arranged on a north–south axis have been interpreted as a crude solar calendar.

The Nabta Playa may have been a location where separate groups of Saharo-Sudanese peoples congregated during the wet season (roughly September to December) to interact and perform rituals, such as initiation ceremonies for age sets.

**Saharo-Sudanese Neolithic** (8000–3000 B.P.)

**Nabta Playa** (Egypt, Saharo-Sudanese Neolithic)

FIGURE **12.5**
A view of the Nabta Playa region.

**Adrar Bous** (Niger, Saharo-Sudanese Neolithic)

During the lengthy dry season peoples probably separated into small groups, perhaps individual families, and dispersed across the landscape in search of water and fodder for their animals. During this time period shelter was probably little more than a skin windbreak or tent, and small stone rings found at the site of **Adrar Bous** in Niger may be the remains of such tents. In mountainous regions caves and rockshelters were commonly used to house both people and animals. Some of the walls of these rockshelters have been extensively painted and provide clear depictions of the cattle that were central to Saharo-Sudanese life.

The tools used by the Saharo-Sudanese people were simple, and they were likely made from skin and bones which have long since decayed. The remains of ceramics that were manufactured by coiling and fired in open pits have, however, been found. They tend to be globular in form and have small, impressed decorations around their rims. The Saharo-Sudanese peoples also used a variety of stone tools which have survived. These tend to be flake rather than blade tools and include scrapers, knives, and drills, as well as projectile points with distinctive "hollow" (inverted) bases. The Saharo-Sudanese peoples also made a variety of personal ornaments, especially beads, from stone, ostrich eggshell, and ivory. Workshops for the manufacture of both stone tools and beads have been found, and since the raw materials for both are found in widely separated locations, it seems clear that Saharo-Sudanese peoples were trading raw materials. The basis of this trade is unclear, but may have taken place when groups came together at common locations in the wet season.

Although sheep and cattle were central to Saharo-Sudanese subsistence, hunting and gathering also played an important role, and may have been the primary source of meat. Animals hunted included antelope, Barbary sheep, giraffes, hippos, and small game. Along the Atlantic coast marine mollusks and fish were collected and may have been very important in the diet. In some areas the presence of large grinding stones suggests wild nuts and cereals were collected and processed. Indeed, by roughly 4000 B.P. there is good evidence that some domesticated plants had entered the diet, and these are associated with a period of increasing sedentism. For example, along the **Dhar Tchitt** escarpment of Mauritania, peoples appear to have begun to settle into small agricultural villages along the edges of small lakes. These settlements were close enough to the coast to allow regular foraging of marine resources, and, with regular access to water and grass, little need for the entire group to move. Over time domesticated grains, particularly millets and sorghum, were added to the diet.

**Dhar Tchitt** (Mauritania, Saharo-Sudanese Neolithic)

There is little evidence of social or political organization for the Saharo-Sudanese peoples. During most of the period it seems clear that people lived in small, egalitarian groups. This is probably even true for the larger seasonal communities. However, some have argued that later in the period, when villages appeared, more centralized political authority must have been present. Clear evidence for this authority is, however, lacking.

In the Mediterranean zone, the peoples of the **Neolithic of Capsian** (7500–3500 B.P.) tradition developed a seasonal round of settlements among which they moved to ensure good pasturage for their sheep, goats, and cattle. Settlements tended to be in uplands during the summer, providing easy access to water, pasturage, and wild food resources. In the winter, settlements were in lowlands, often on well-watered slopes. Caves and rockshelters were used frequently for shelter. Open upland sites are also found, but no obvious structures have been identified. It is likely that people relied upon skin tents when at these open sites. Neolithic of Capsian groups were small, probably consisting of a single family and their flocks. No large, seasonal villages have been identified for the Neolithic of Capsian, and it appears that these small, nomadic groups interacted only infrequently with one another.

While products from domesticated animals were essential to the diet of the Neolithic of Capsian peoples, wild foods were also eaten. Particularly interesting for the Neolithic of Capsian peoples was the intense collection of large land snails by some groups. These are found on sites such as **Abri du Djebel Fartas** in Tunisia, where a midden of land snail shells more than a meter thick was discovered. A wide variety of plant foods have been found on Neolithic of Capsian sites as well, including fruits such as grapes, cherries, and plums, nuts such as acorns and pine nuts, legumes, mushrooms, and herbs. Small game including foxes, rabbits, tortoises, and birds were taken, as were larger game animals such as gazelles, ostriches, and zebras. Altogether, the Neolithic of Capsian peoples appear to have used a great variety of foods in addition to the products of their domestic animals.

Neolithic of Capsian peoples made coiled ceramics tempered with snail shell and fired in open pits. These ceramics were decorated by stamping with shell or were left undecorated. Most were jars with conical bases and handles, although handled bottles with restricted necks are also common. Ostrich eggshells were used as containers, as were tortoise shells and animal-skin bags. Flaked knives, scrapers, and projectile points are common, but also common are ground-stone tools, which were used to process nuts and fruits and to work wood (Figure 12.6). Personal ornaments are common, too, and include beads and pendants made from shell, bone, and stone, in some cases processed to create distinctive colors and surfaces. Many of the stones used for both ornaments and tools were nonlocal, suggesting that when Neolithic of Capsian groups met trade was a frequent activity.

Also living along the Mediterranean, the peoples of the **Southern Mediterranean Neolithic** (7500–4000 B.P.) tradition retained a nomadic, hunting and gathering lifestyle reminiscent of their Upper Paleolithic predecessors. They also kept domesticated sheep and pigs, but these seem to have been a supplement to a diet based primarily on wild foods. Mollusks were important to groups on the coast, while gazelle and hartebeest were hunted in large numbers inland. The Southern Mediterranean Neolithic peoples were nomadic, and it is likely that a single group of perhaps ten to twenty people moved seasonally between coastal and inland campsites. They made ceramics similar to those of peoples on the north coast of the Mediterranean, and this may reflect cultural ties across the Straits of Gibraltar.

## Later North Africans

Following the Neolithic of Capsian and Southern Mediterranean Neolithic traditions, the peoples of the **North African Protohistoric** (4000–3000 B.P.) tradition continued pastoralism as their basic way of life, although hunting remained important for some groups, and for others agriculture was added to the subsistence regime. In general, the North African Protohistoric peoples were more sedentary than their

**Neolithic of Capsian**
(7500–3500 B.P.)

**Abri du Djebel Fartas**
(Tunisia, Neolithic
of Capsian)

**Southern
Mediterranean
Neolithic**
(7500–4000 B.P.)

**North African
Protohistoric**
(4000–3000 B.P.)

FIGURE **12.6**

Neolithic of Capsian tradition artifacts, including bone projectile points (1, 12), flake (4, 9), and blade (2, 3, 6–8, 10, 11) tools, and a fragment of decorated ostrich eggshell (5).

SOURCE: David W. Phillipson, *African Archaeology* (New York, NY: Cambridge University Press, 1985), p. 93. Reprinted with the permission of Cambridge University Press.

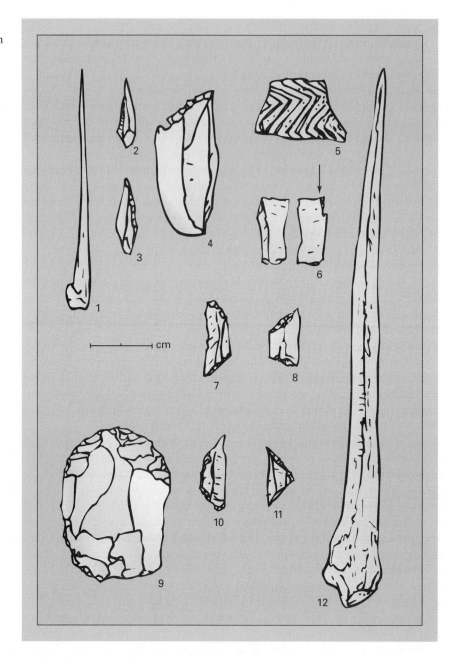

predecessors, and some large villages and even protourban settlements developed. For example, along the Dhar Tichitt escarpment in Maruitania, where peoples of the Saharo-Sudanese Neolithic tradition had initially settled in permanent villages, the North African Protohistoric peoples built cites with stone buildings and thousands of residents. At the far eastern end of the tradition, in what today is the eastern Sudan, the peoples of **Punt** built stone "beehive" structures in large villages of several hundred people.

Along with sedentism, a more formal political organization evolved among many North African Protohistoric groups, which apparently included powerful rulers. Texts from Egypt suggest the peoples of Punt lived in a hierarchical chiefdom, perhaps with a preeminent chief (called Parahu in the Egyptian texts) who was equivalent to a king. Later, the region of what is today Ethiopia and Eritrea would see the emergence of the powerful **Aksum** state (Figure 12.7), which is described in the box feature. Egyptian texts also describe raids made by pastoralists from Libya,

**Punt** (Sudan, North African Protohistoric)

**Aksum** (Ethiopia, North African Protohistoric)

FIGURE **12.7**
Monumental stelae marking royal tombs at Aksum.

suggesting that they, too, had leadership that could coordinate large groups of people for a military expedition. In the western Sahara a great diversity of groups is apparent, but some had a clearly hierarchical organization. Some scholars have suggested the diversity in the western Sahara resulted from the mixture of North African, Sub-Saharan African, and European populations.

The material culture of the North African Protohistoric peoples are as varied as their settlements and political organization. Pastoral groups tended to have a simple tool kit, consisting of ceramic and hide containers, stone and metal tools (with metal—bronze and iron—both manufactured locally and traded), small, portable ornaments, and an extensive tradition of rock art, particularly among those groups living in the Maghreb and central Sahara. Agricultural and coastal groups tended to have a somewhat more sophisticated tool kit, which included a variety of ceramics, some locally manufactured and some traded from other North African Protohistoric groups, from West Africa, from Egypt, and even from Europe (including bell beakers, which are discussed in Chapter 13). Metal tools were common and were both manufactured locally and traded.

## NILE VALLEY

The Nile River valley is a remarkable environment, both in its contrasts and in its regularities. The contrasts are stark. The Nile itself is the sole major river in North Africa and drains roughly one tenth of the continent. The Nile basin is fairly narrow—only 15 to 25 kilometers wide, cutting gently through the limestone bedrock of North Africa. Outside of this basin the landscape is barren, but within the floodplain the land is lush. The climate is hot and dry, with no rainfall during the winter months and often less than 250 mm in the summer. Temperatures regularly exceed 100 degrees in the summer, and only fall to the 50s during the coolest evenings in winter. Until the damning of the Nile, annual floods spread a layer of rich alluvium across the floodplain, providing the basis for plant and animal life in the Nile Valley. The Nile River is the source of life itself in Egypt—without its waters humans would have a difficult time living in the region and certainly could not settle down or practice agriculture there. The Nile also provided life to a wide variety of

# Aksum

The ancient city of Aksum sits atop a fertile plateau in northern Ethiopia at an elevation of more than 2,200 meters above sea level. After its founding sometime after 2000 B.P., Aksum quickly became one of the most important cities in ancient Africa. Its location provided for abundant crops, and it was situated to take advantage of trade between Southwest Asia and the rest of Africa. Ivory, gold, and other precious materials flowed through Aksum to the Red Sea and on into the Roman Empire and beyond.

The first major excavations at Aksum began in 1906, but most of the information we have about the site comes from excavations in the mid-1970s and from 1993 onward by the British Institute in eastern Africa. The primary focus has been on burials and monumental architecture, but the information recovered from them has been rich. The site of Aksum is dominated by the palaces of the ancient Aksumite kings. These are massive, multistoried stone constructions that must be among the wonders of ancient architecture. The palace Ta'akha Mariam, for example, was an eight-story structure with each floor measuring 24 meters square. Each floor had four or five large rooms with enormous staircases connecting them to the other stories. The palace was surrounded by an ensemble of buildings measuring 120 meters by 80 meters in all, and containing, in addition to the palace, three courtyards built on different levels and hundreds of rooms for servants, retainers, guards, and other nobles.

In addition to archaeological work, we also know much about Aksum from documents written by Roman, Byzantine, Himyarite, and various other sources,

plants and animals. Fish were abundant in the river, as were shellfish, mollusks, and reptiles. Antelope, gazelle, hartebeest, and hippo were common in the Nile basin, along with a wide variety of smaller mammals and birds. Water-loving plants such as papyrus and Egyptian willow thrived near the river, while on the desert margins grasslands and small groves of savannah trees and shrubs were present.

## The Heartland of Egyptian Civilization

The Upper Paleolithic peoples of the Nile Valley exploited fish, large mammals, and a variety of plants using a microlithic technology. In this way they were not much different from the other Upper Paleolithic peoples of North Africa. But by 7000 B.P. peoples of the **Upper Egypt Predynastic** (7000–5000 B.P.) tradition had incorporated domestic crops into their hunting-fishing-gathering lifestyle and had created sedentary agricultural villages in the Nile floodplain. Some of these villages, such as Hierakonpolis and **Nagata,** were quite large and appear to reflect a two-tiered village hierarchy. Smaller agricultural villages consisted of a few to a few dozen mud brick houses with associated hearths and storage pits. Larger villages had hundreds of houses arranged along streets. These larger villages also contained public buildings, perhaps temple or administrative complexes, manufacturing areas, defensive

**Upper Egypt Predynastic** (7000–5000 B.P.)

**Nagata** (Egypt, Upper Egypt Predynastic)

as well as from Aksumite inscriptions in both the local Ge'ez language and in Greek. Together these works paint an interesting picture of a powerful kingdom on the very edge of the Roman world, and one taking great advantage of that position. For the most part, the government of Aksum was the king and his household. The king was supported internally by his personal estate consisting of slaves, animals, and farmland, as well as by tribute and sacrificial offerings given to him by the populace. These resources were used to both support the kingly household and to raise armies with which the king raided neighboring peoples to extract wealth and slaves. The king appears to have also controlled export and import trade, which provided additional wealth to the kingly household.

With wealth and power resting largely in the person of the king, the vast majority of the citizens of Aksum (perhaps some 400,000 in all) were farmers and craftspeople. Farmers grew wheat, barley, millet, legumes, and other crops, and raised cows, sheep, and goats. Craftspeople produced cloth, ceramics, metal goods, and carved stone. Markets provided the basis for economic transactions, but money was not used until late in Aksum's history. Thus, we essentially see a feudal-like kingdom in northern Ethiopia some 2,000 years ago, one that could amass large amounts of labor for construction projects, could launch military campaigns against neighboring polities, and which actively controlled trade between Africa and the classical empires of Europe and Asia.

SOURCES: Connah, Graham, *African Civilizations* (Cambridge: Cambridge University Press, 1987); Kobishchanov, Yuri, *Axum* (University Park: Pennsylvania State University Press, 1979).

walls, and formal extramural cemeteries. They may have been locations where river travel and trade were controlled, and they appear to have functioned as regional political and ceremonial centers.

The Upper Egypt Predynastic economy was rooted in wheat and barley agriculture produced in rich alluvial fields lining the Nile and irrigated with Nile water. Domesticated sheep, goats, pigs, and cattle all contributed to subsistence, not only for meat, milk, and wool, but also for fuel in the form of dung and as traction animals. Fish were also essential to the diet, and antelope, hippo, crocodile, and other large animals were hunted and eaten. Wild plant foods such as dates and figs were also collected.

Ceramics were made both by individual families and by craft specialists, and these varied widely in quality and style. Lithics were manufactured from local Nile river cobbles and were generally simple, expedient flake tools, although more sophisticated stone tools are also found and may have been produced by specialist artisans. A unique group of Predynastic utensils are stone bowls, often made from very hard or exotic materials such as diorite, porphyry, and serpentine. These almost certainly were made by skilled craftsmen. Metalwork was also present, with cold-forged copper being used for a variety of tools and gold used for personal ornaments. Exotic goods of other kinds, such as lapis, ivory, turquoise, faience, and carnelian, just to name a few, were used to make beads, amulets, pendants, and other ornamental items. Again, it seems clear that both craft specialists and long-distance trade were involved in the production of these goods.

With a clear two-level hierarchy in settlement and the presence of both craft specialists and long-distance trade, it is not surprising that most scholars believe that a hierarchical political structure was in place by this time. Indeed, it has been argued that trade and craft specialization were the basis of this hierarchy. Political leaders were apparently able to control both trade and the products of craft specialists working within their communities. Over time it is thought that these local political leaders merged into larger and more hierarchical polities, resulting in two or three large chiefdoms by the end of the Upper Egypt Predynastic tradition. One such chiefdom, probably located at Hierakonpolis, is thought to have controlled a region stretching from roughly the first cataract to the area around what is today the site of Luxor.

The **Hierakonpolis** site itself is located on the west bank of the Nile river and north of the modern town of Edfu. The site covers an area of more than 300,000 square meters, although the size of the ancient city changed dramatically over time, expanding and ultimately nucleating into an area of roughly 40,000 square meters. It is estimated that about 1,000 people lived at Hierakonpolis at any given time. The site contained numerous domestic compounds, with mud-brick dwellings and storehouses or outbuildings, and walled "barnyards." Special workshops for bead, stone bowl, and ceramic production were also present. There were also large, public buildings that have been interpreted as temples and a massive stone platform thought to have supported an administrative structure. Outside of the city, formal cemeteries contained bodies of both common and elite people. Individuals were typically buried with utilitarian grave goods, including food, but elites had additional wealth items included and sometimes were buried in brick- or stone-lined tombs.

In the north Nile Valley and the Nile delta region, the peoples of the **Lower Egypt Predynastic** (7000–5000 B.P.) tradition had developed a similar way of life. Their villages varied in size from small agricultural hamlets to large villages, and both round wattle-and-daub and more substantial rectangular mud-brick houses were made. They practiced agriculture in the rich Nile alluvium, raised domestic animals, fished and hunted, and gathered wild fruits. Craft specialization also appears to be present in the manufacture of stone bowls, finely crafted flaked stone tools, and metalwork. However, ceramics appear to have remained an item produced by households rather than by specialists. Trade was also important in the Lower Egypt Predynastic economy. Trade took place both between peoples of the Upper Egypt Predynastic tradition and with other peoples in northern Africa and the Levant. The presence of craft specialization, long-distance trade, and some burials with rich grave goods suggests that some degree of social differentiation and political centralization was present in the Lower Egypt Predynastic tradition, but the evidence is not as clear as that for the Upper Egypt Predynastic tradition.

One of the best-known Lower Egypt Predynastic sites is **Ma'adi**, located on the eastern side of the Nile south of Cairo. The site covers an area of roughly 18 hectares, and it has been estimated that perhaps as many as 1,000 people resided there. Houses were round or oval wattle-and-daub structures, loosely organized in separate areas of the site. Workshops for metal and stone craftsmen were present, and it appears that craft production played an important role in the community. Trade may have played an important role as well since many foreign raw materials and finished goods were found on the site. Nearby cemeteries that likely served Ma'adi's residents contained graves that varied from simple pit inhumations with minimal grave goods to mud-brick tombs containing richly adorned burials. Again, this seems to point to some form of social differentiation and perhaps political centralization among the Lower Egypt Predynastic peoples.

The two regions became unified as part of a single large state in the **Early Dynastic Egypt** (5000–4700 B.P.) tradition, the direct ancestor of classical Egyptian civilization. Many scholars believe that the peoples of Lower Egypt were conquered

**Hierakonpolis** (Egypt, Upper Egypt Predynastic)

**Lower Egypt Predynastic** (7000–5000 B.P.)

**Ma'adi** (Egypt, Lower Egypt Predynastic)

**Early Dynastic Egypt** (5000–4700 B.P.)

by a polity centered at Nagada; perhaps under the leadership of an individual identified as Narmer, but the evidence is equivocal. We will come back to the Early Dynastic Egypt tradition and the rise of classical Egyptian civilization in Chapter 17 on the rise of states.

## The Southern Nile

At the far southern end of the Nile valley two traditions have been defined, the Early Khartoum and Khartoum Neolithic. Peoples of the **Early Khartoum** (10,000–5700 B.P.) tradition were semisedentary hunter-fisher-gatherers who exploited the rich resources of the Sahara and Sahel during a period before the region became desertified. People lived in large villages during most of the year, venturing out from these villages regularly to hunt and gather seasonal plants. Houses were made from wattle and daub and may have been semisubterranean in some areas. Villages themselves were simple clusters of these houses, consisting of perhaps several dozen houses providing shelter for 200 or so people in each village. Fish from the Nile and surrounding wetlands were essential to subsistence, as were other aquatic plants and animals such as hippos, reptiles, mollusks, and wild sorghum, which was later domesticated. Antelope and wild cattle were also frequently hunted, and fruits and nuts were gathered from wild groves when in season. The Early Khartoum peoples made thin, well-fired ceramics from Nile clays, and they used river cobbles and several sources of chert to manufacture flaked stone tools. Bone and ivory were used for harpoon and barbed projectile points.

**Early Khartoum (10,000–5700 B.P.)**

The **Khartoum Hospital** site is illustrative of Early Khartoum life. Here the excavation of a large mound on the east bank of the Nile exposed a lengthy occupation and a vast array of lithics, ceramics, bone tools, and animal remains. No houses were found, but there were plentiful remains of daub, suggesting houses were constructed from wattle and daub. Even though the site was used for perhaps 500 years, its size (about 7,500 square meters) suggests a population of only a few dozen people. The presence of grinding stones attest to the importance of seeds and nuts in the diet, and net sinkers attest to the importance of fish. Bone was used extensively for tools, which included bone harpoon and barbed spearheads used for fishing (Figure 12.8). Animal remains included a large amount of fish, mollusks, reptiles, and antelope. The picture we have from the Khartoum Hospital site, then, is of a sedentary people living in modest, egalitarian villages and subsisting largely on aquatic resources from the Nile. Although evidence is scant, it is likely they interacted with the Nile-dwelling peoples to the north and with the pastoralists who lived in the grasslands and marshlands surrounding them.

**Khartoum Hospital (Sudan, Early Khartoum)**

The peoples of the **Khartoum Neolithic** (5700–3550 B.P.) tradition continued this general way of life, but supplemented collected foods with domesticated plants and animals. Villages became larger, some as large as 40,000 square meters, and may have had more than 100 residents. These villages appear to have been simple clusters of wattle-and-daub houses with thatched roofs, without any clear organization. Like those of the Early Khartoum tradition, most of these villages were probably egalitarian in organization. Sorghum and millet were planted in the vicinity of these villages, and goats, sheep, and cattle were kept. This mixed economy appears to have been very successful, and the number of sites increased dramatically over the Early Khartoum tradition. Larger sites tend to be somewhat farther away from the Nile than smaller sites and were situated on natural rises that kept them dry during annual floods. Smaller sites are typically located within 5 kilometers of the Nile, and these sites may have been used only during the dry season for fishing and pasturing animals.

**Khartoum Neolithic (5700–3550 B.P.)**

The material culture of the Khartoum Neolithic peoples was relatively simple. They made thin, grit-tempered ceramics that they burnished and decorated with

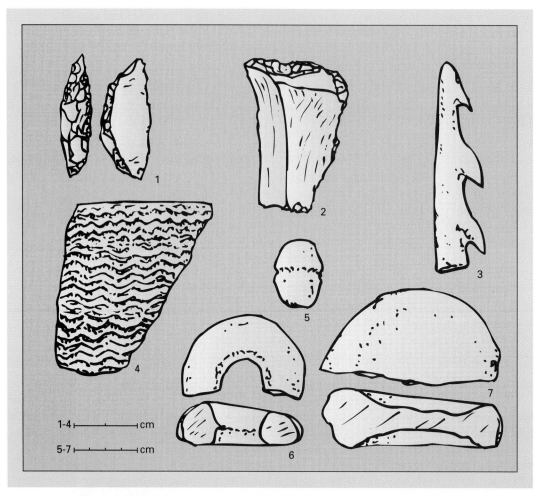

FIGURE **12.8**

Tools of the Early Khartom tradition, including (1) a backed microlith, (2) a scraper, (3) a bone harpoon, (4) a ceramic fragment, (5) a stone net weight, (6) a digging stick weight, and (7) a grinding stone.

SOURCE: David W. Phillipson, *African Archaeology* (New York, NY: Cambridge University Press, 1985), p. 102. Reprinted with the permission of Cambridge University Press.

incised or impressed designs. Local stone was used to make blades and microliths. Bone was used extensively, particularly for harpoon and barbed spear points. Grinding stones were used to process cereals and nuts, and ground stone celts and gouges were used to work wood. The Khartoum Neolithic peoples imported some materials including rhyolite, which they made into mace heads, amazonite and carnelian, used for beads, and zeolite, used for lip plugs. Some of these items made from imported raw materials have been found together in single burials along with highly decorated ceramics, and scholars have suggested this indicates that social differentiation was present in some Khartoum Neolithic communities, and perhaps there was also some degree of formal political leadership.

Between the Egyptian border and Khartoum a number of different groups lived. Nomadic pastoralists of the North African Protohistoric tradition crossed the Nile valley regularly to seek water and pasturage, and some lived in relatively settled communities in the Nile valley itself. Indeed, the Nubian site known as **Kerma** appears to be a pastoral-based city. Kerma consisted of mud-brick dwellings, domestic spaces, and workshops surrounding a walled temple complex. The city was laid out according to a grid pattern, with several distinct neighborhoods. Priests and

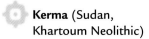

**Kerma** (Sudan, Khartoum Neolithic)

nobility apparently lived in the temple complex, while craftsmen, merchants, and farmers lived in the residential neighborhoods. Cattle breeding and grain agriculture supported the city, which functioned as both a trade and manufacturing center for a vast region of pastoralists and small farmers.

## SOUTHERN AND EASTERN AFRICA

Southern and eastern Africa is a region situated between the north-south-running rift valley and the Indian Ocean. There is great diversity across this vast area, but there are two major environmental types that are common in the area—savannahs and forested highlands. Savannahs are dominated by grasses and mixed woodlands and typically contain a wide variety of grassland species. Forested uplands are more diverse in their composition and in the fauna that inhabit them. Some are dominated by succulents and thorny plants, while others are dominated by deciduous or evergreen forests. Rainforest environments are even present in the central rift valley. Rifting and volcanism have created an abundance of obsidian sources and have exposed a wide range of stone and minerals. The climate throughout the area is relatively warm, with temperatures typically ranging between 20 and 30 degrees C. Rainfall is markedly seasonal through most of the region, with total annual rainfall typically ranging between 250 mm to well over 1,000 mm.

As discussed previously, the Upper Paleolithic hunters and gatherers of eastern and southern Africa developed a lifestyle that, one could argue, has the greatest longevity of any in the world since it has persisted from perhaps 40,000 years ago until today. Though by no means equal in longevity, the peoples of the **East African Neolithic** (5000–1200 B.P.) tradition developed a pastoral way of life that could be argued survives today. Cattle were the center of life for East African Neolithic peoples, and both their subsistence and their culture revolved around the needs of their animals. Habitation sites were small and were usually located on well-drained slopes, and most consist of a circular concentration of debris and decomposed or burnt dung. Houses were round with interior partitions and were built from wattle and daub. A typical settlement might consist of a dozen such houses and perhaps thirty to fifty people. Rockshelters were also used for habitation in the Rift Valley.

**East African Neolithic** (5000–1200 B.P.)

Ceramics and lithics are the primary materials found on East African Neolithic sites. Ceramics are both diverse and highly distinctive of particular groups (Figure 12.9). For example, Eburran ceramics from the Naivasha and Nakuru basins of Kenya are typically cord marked, while Elementian ceramics from adjacent regions to the south and west are typically burnished and undecorated. Similarly, lithics tend to have highly distinctive differences. Eburran blades are made solely from obsidian and have very thick and wide striking platforms, while Elementian blades are relatively long and have very small striking platforms, suggesting that they were manufactured using a punch, where Eburran blades were manufactured using a hammer. The regularity of these differences in material culture suggest that several culturally (and perhaps linguistically) distinct pastoral groups were present in East Africa from the very beginning of the Neolithic. Indeed, it may be that these distinct groups represent migrants from the Sahara and Sahel who moved south down the rift valley into the rich pasture lands of the East African savannah.

In southern Africa, peoples of the **Southern African Iron Age** (2000–500 B.P.) developed a sedentary, agricultural lifestyle which included large villages with formal leaders and the use of metal tools. The source of these changes is highly contested, but most scholars agree they were brought to the region by speakers of Bantu languages migrating from West Africa beginning about 3000 B.P. There appear to be three major types of Southern African Iron Age settlements. The smallest are in caves or rockshelters and may represent encampments of hunting or

**Southern African Iron Age** (2000–500 B.P.)

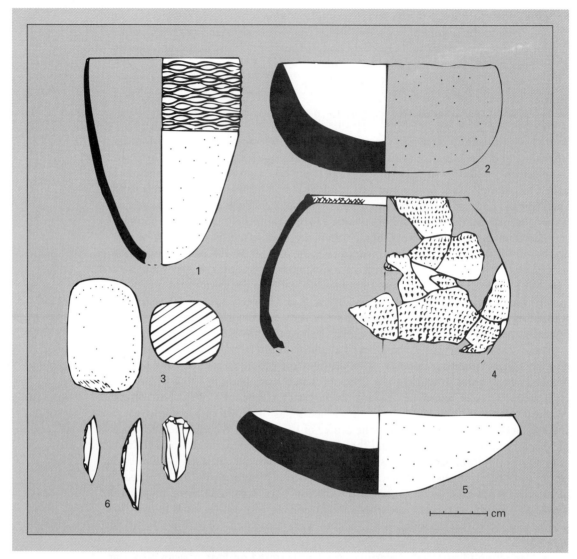

FIGURE **12.9**

Tools of the East African Neolithic tradition, including (1, 4) ceramics, (2, 5) stone bowls, (3) a pestle, and (6) microliths.

SOURCE: David W. Phillipson, *African Archaeology* (New York, NY: Cambridge University Press, 1985), p. 145. Reprinted with the permission of Cambridge University Press.

foraging parties. Moderate in size are agricultural hamlets, housing perhaps several families living in round wattle-and-daub structures. Finally, there are large, permanent villages with better-made houses, including houses constructed from stone, and with more than 100 residents. Several of these large villages have been extensively excavated, including the site of **Great Zimbabwe**, described in the box feature (Figure 12.10).

**Great Zimbabwe** (Zimbabwe, Southern African Iron Age)

People living in both small and larger villages subsisted primarily on domesticated foods, especially sorghum. The remains of domesticated cattle are found rarely. More common are the remains of hunted animals. Metal was an important part of the Southern African Iron Age tool kit, and iron was used for a wide variety of tools including spear points, knives, hoes, and razors. Some iron tools may have been obtained through trade, but most appear to have been made locally. Ceramics were also important. These were typically small and globular in shape and only

FIGURE **12.10**
The "Great Enclosure" at Great Zimbabwe. Note the tower in the center of the enclosure.

lightly decorated. In addition to tools, the South African Iron Age peoples created a variety of personal ornaments. These included copper bangles and rings; stone, shell, glass, and metal beads; and carved ivory pieces, among other items. Many of these items, and the raw materials from which they were created, were traded across the continent and even found their way into South Asia through trade across the Indian Ocean.

Political organization appears to have varied between different South African Iron Age groups. Some, particularly those in small villages, appear egalitarian, while others, such as those residing at sites such as Great Zimbabwe and Mapungubwe, must have been complex chiefdoms or kingdoms. **Mapungubwe**, for example, is a site dating to about 800 B.P. that is situated on a hill overlooking the Limpopo River in the nation of South Africa. Large residences were constructed on top of this hill, with smaller, densely packed houses surrounding it. Rich burials were also found on the hill, which included many articles obtained through trade. Trade seems to have been a primary activity at the site, and there is good evidence of cowrie shells, glass beads, and perhaps iron and copper being traded from the coast in return for ivory and animal skins. It appears that political elites at Mapungubwe controlled this trade and built their political and social power upon that control. It also appears that the elites at Mapungubwe controlled a large surrounding area since there seems to be a hierarchy of sites, from large villages to small hamlets, in a roughly 100-kilometer radius around Mapungubwe that are contemporary and appear to share similar site planning and material culture.

**Mapungubwe**
(South Africa, South African Iron Age)

## CENTRAL AFRICA

The environment of Central Africa is dominated by the Congo River, which runs from the East African rift valley across the continent and into the Atlantic Ocean between the modern nations of Zaire and Congo. The river drains nearly one quarter of sub-Saharan Africa. The Congo basin is a region of dense equatorial rainforests, teeming with wild plants and animals. The climate in the Congo basin is consistently hot and humid, with average temperatures near 30 degrees C, 85 percent humidity, and over 2,000 mm of rain annually. Surrounding the Congo basin are the mountains of Cameroon to the north, the rift valley to the east, and the undulating highlands of Angola to the south. The environment varies in these

# Great Zimbabwe

The site of Great Zimbabwe is one of a number of large, circular stone complexes built by peoples of the South African Iron Age tradition, but it is by far the biggest and most impressive of all of them. Construction of Great Zimbabwe began sometime around 900 B.P., and the site was occupied until about 500 B.P. During that time, Great Zimbabwe was the seat of a regional Karanga kingdom and an important trade center where goods moved between coastal cities to the interior of Africa and vice versa. The rulers at Great Zimbabwe controlled a large area of perhaps 100,000 square kilometers between the Zambezi and Limpopo Rivers, and the site itself had a resident population of some 15,000 to 20,000 people.

The Great Zimbabwe site is dominated by what is called the "Great Enclosure"—a massive stone wall built from dry-laid stone and standing some 10 meters high and 5 meters thick at the base. The "Great Enclosure" encompasses an area of more than 7,000 square meters, within which are the remains of other stone buildings which likely made up a palace complex for the king. The most distinctive of the stone structures within the "Great Enclosure" is a conical tower rising 9 meters above the other buildings. It has been interpreted by many scholars as a kingly symbol of power and fertility.

On a hill to the north of the "Great Enclosure" is a second large complex of dry-laid stone structures known, appropriately, as the "Hill Complex." The "Hill Complex" was apparently the earliest group of structures built at the site, and indeed was started before the techniques of dry-laid stone masonry were being used. Over time stone structures and what appear to be defensive walls and

regions from equatorial rain forest to upland deciduous forests to dry savannah. The upland areas vary in their underlying geology and provide a variety of resources from volcanic obsidian and basalt to quartz and sandstone. The Atlantic coast of Central Africa is relatively wide and contains numerous lagoons and mangrove swamps. Like the Congo basin, average temperatures on the coast are typically near 30 degrees C, and there is abundant rainfall.

As in eastern and southern Africa, ways of life very much like those of the Upper Paleolithic peoples living in the region continued until relatively recently. Over time, however, some of these hunters and gatherers began to incorporate domesticated plants and animals into their subsistence regime, and slowly they developed a more sedentary, agricultural lifestyle. This was a slow process that took place at different times within the large region that is Central Africa, but by about 3000 B.P. it seems reasonable to distinguish a **Central African Neolithic** (4000–2000 B.P.) tradition, with a sedentary way of life based on domesticated foods.

Central African Neolithic villages consisted of ten to twenty round wattle-and-daub houses and tended to be located on hilltops close to a good water source and near stands of wild oil palms. Agricultural fields for crops of yams and plantains surrounded the villages. In addition to these agricultural products, many wild plant

**Central African Neolithic** (4000–2000 B.P.)

towers encircling the site were constructed. Finally, between the "Hill Complex" and the "Great Enclosure" are a series of smaller walled compounds called, collectively, the "Valley Ruins." These appear similar to the "Great Enclosure" but are on a much smaller scale. Both the "Hill Complex" and the "Valley Ruins" are thought to be secondary settlements where important individuals within the Great Zimbabwe polity resided. Surrounding these stone enclosures were numerous residences of farmers, cattle herders, and craftspeople. They lived in round wattle-and-daub structures with conical thatched roofs.

Why was Great Zimbabwe built? The answers to that question have been numerous. Perhaps the simplest is defense—these constructions provided a place of refuge for elites and the surrounding populations in time of war. A second answer is that they were built not to keep invaders out, but to keep ritual secrets in. That is, the stone walls were ritual enclosures surrounding elite compounds where important ceremonies and other activities not to be witnessed by commoners took place. Yet neither of these answers seems adequate, for the walls and towers, particularly in the "Great Enclosure," seem far too massive to have been built strictly as defenses or ritual enclosures. The stone constructions appear to demonstrate the vast labor and skill that the rulers of the Great Zimbabwe polity could put to work. This is a third answer to the question of why Great Zimbabwe was built—as a display of power. Each answer seems to have some evidence to support it, and perhaps the real answer to the question is a combination of all three.

SOURCES: Connah, Graham, *African Civilizations* (Cambridge: Cambridge University Press, 1987); Garlake, P.S. *Great Zimbabwe* (New York: Stein and Day, 1973).

foods were collected. Most important were palm oil and palm wine, wild nuts and fruits, and even cereals such as wild millet. Sheep and goats were kept by Central African Neolithic peoples, but fish were also taken as well as game such as bush pig, primates, and small forest antelopes.

The material culture of the Central African Neolithic peoples was fairly simple and included utilitarian ceramics, often highly decorated, polished stone axes and adzes, grinding stones, and a wide variety of bone and ivory tools (Figure 12.11). Shell beads were also made by Central African Neolithic peoples; these were apparently basic personal ornaments worn by most people. Socially, the Central African Neolithic peoples appear to have been egalitarian, with informal political leadership. Some scholars have argued that the Central African Neolithic peoples were members of the Bantu language family, who moved into Central Africa from West Africa at the beginning of their expansion toward the south and thus formed a population intrusive to the existing hunting and gathering peoples of the region. At this point there is no clear archaeological evidence to support this idea, but linguistic data does seem to provide reason for further investigation.

The peoples of the **Central African Iron Age** (2000–500 B.P.) tradition are the last prehistoric peoples in Central Africa. They continued the agricultural lifestyle

**Central African Iron Age** (2000–500 B.P.)

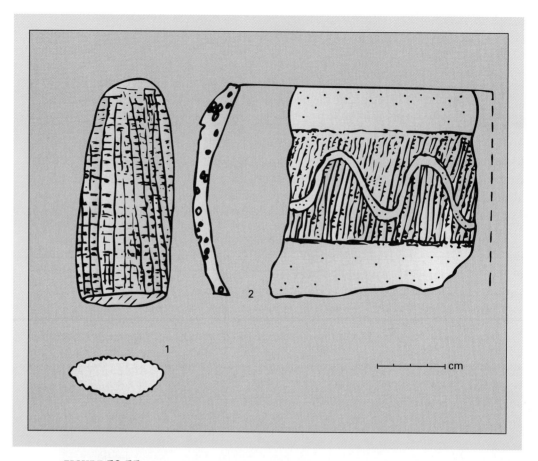

**FIGURE 12.11**

Central African Neolithic stone rasp (1) and decorated ceramic fragment (2).

SOURCE: David W. Phillipson, *African Archaeology* (New York, NY: Cambridge University Press, 1985), p. 137. Reprinted with the permission of Cambridge University Press.

of their predecessors, but added to it iron tools. Like their predecessors, it has been suggested that some Central African Iron Age groups represent Bantu populations continuing to spread across central and southern Africa. Iron was manufactured throughout Central Africa from locally available ores, and with several local innovations in smelting technology. Iron was used to make a wide range of tools, including knives, axes, and hoes, as well as weaponry such as spear and arrow points. As iron working became more sophisticated, personal ornaments such as bracelets, bangles, and rings were also manufactured. The other major category of utensils used by Central African Iron Age people was ceramics, which were well made and often highly decorated.

Central African Iron Age settlements are largely indistinguishable from Central African Neolithic settlements apart from the presence of iron tools and iron working debris. Subsistence was similar as well, with yam and plantain being primary crops, and sheep and goats being a source of milk and meat. There is some evidence that communities of specialized fishers were present on major rivers, and trade with them and with hunter-gatherers who lived in the dense rain forests certainly contributed to the diet. There is also evidence that some Central African Iron Age communities specialized in the production of ceramics and copper, and traded them widely. It is likely that these items, as well as many of the ceramic and iron items made locally in Central African Iron Age communities, were manufactured by part-time specialists. The reason for this supposition is the general uniformity and craftsmanship on some Central African Iron Age ceramics and the overall technological knowledge needed to manufacture many iron objects used by the Central African Iron Age peoples.

## WEST AFRICA

West Africa varies in its environment and climate, but most of the region is warm and relatively wet. There is a marked north–south difference in precipitation, with northern areas getting as little as 250 mm of rain a year, and southern areas more than 1,500 mm. Correspondingly, savannah areas and gallery forests are typical of the north, while tropical and equatorial rain forests are typical of the southern and coastal regions. The coast itself is relatively narrow, and the land rises quickly to a relatively flat plain at about 200 meters above sea level. Major north–south-running rivers drain this large plain, while the Niger river runs roughly northeast from the Guinean highlands into Mali, then turns southeast until it reaches the Gulf of Guinea in Nigeria. Deposits of iron, gold, copper, and workable stone are found in bedrock and volcanic outcroppings throughout the region. Plant and animal species are found in abundance in both the southern forested areas and the savannah areas to the north.

As in the rest of sub-Saharan Africa, people following a hunting and gathering way of life survived in West Africa well into the Holocene. But around 5000 B.P. domestic animals and, later, domestic plants began to be adopted by people of the **West African Neolithic** (4000–2500 B.P.) tradition. Cattle, sheep, and goats were introduced to the area from the north, perhaps by Saharan pastoralists seeking refuge from **tsetse** infestations. Later, millet and yams were domesticated along with oil palms, which, while remaining typologically wild, were carefully managed and nurtured. Hunting of both small and large game remained important to West African Neolithic peoples, and fishing and shellfishing were vital to some groups. Wild plant foods were also collected even after millet and yams were domesticated. The tools used by West African Neolithic peoples were simple and included well-made ceramics with extensive decoration, a diverse array of stone tools including both simple flake tools and microliths, and polished stone tools including axes, adzes, and hoes, and grinding stones for processing seeds and nuts.

**West African Neolithic** (4000–2500 B.P.)

As agriculture became more important, some West African Neolithic peoples began to develop sedentary villages. Villages of groups who remained heavily reliant on wild foods were small and seasonal. Villages of groups who adopted animal husbandry were more substantial and larger while villages of agriculturalists were sometimes quite large and contained structures of both wattle and daub and stone. Some of these villages were large enough so that scholars have suggested they may represent the political centers of emerging chiefdoms. Certainly there were interesting political and economic changes taking place. In central Ghana, for example, peoples of what are known as the Kintampo Complex developed what appears to be a relatively integrated sphere of economic interaction. Permanent agricultural villages such as **Boyasi Hill** contained substantial dwellings with stone foundations, while smaller sites such as the **K-6 Rockshelter** appear to be seasonal encampments of people still reliant on hunting and gathering. Interestingly, both sites demonstrate extensive economic interaction. Boyasi Hill contains shell and stone bead workshops, while the K-6 Rockshelter contains marine shell beads that were perhaps manufactured at Boyasi Hill, and which were certainly obtained through long-distance trade. K-6 Rockshelter also contained more than 100 greenstone axes, suggesting they were being accumulated and perhaps manufactured for trade.

**Boyasi Hill** (Ghana, West African Neolithic)

**K-6 Rockshelter** (Ghana, West African Neolithic)

**West African Iron Age**
(2500–1200 B.P.)

Political and economic change continued during the subsequent **West African Iron Age** (2500–1200 B.P.) tradition. The peoples of the West African Iron Age tradition continued the generalized agricultural subsistence regime of their predecessors and added iron utensils to their tool kit. Both iron and copper were smelted, using a number of different and locally varying techniques. Iron was used initially to make tools and weapons such as hoes and spear points, but soon came to be used in personal ornaments such as bracelets, bangles, and pendants. Stone and bone tools continued to be used even after the emergence of copper and iron tools. Ceramics were also manufactured and continued to be generally well made and highly decorated. Distinctive regional ceramic traditions were present, and both fine-ware ceramics and painted ceramics were produced. Also appearing for the first time were terra cotta figurines depicting both humans and animals (see Color Plate 17). The purpose of these figurines is unknown, but they are most commonly found in houses, which suggests they may have been decorative rather than ritual objects.

West African Iron Age peoples also continued to develop agriculture, adding several additional varieties of domesticated yams to their diet, along with sorghum and African rice. It is important to note that not all peoples in West Africa adopted iron or domesticates—many still lived by hunting and gathering. However, both iron and agriculture began to spread rapidly during the West African Iron Age. Iron tools allowed agricultural settlements to move into heavier soils and made clearing forests for cultivation easier. With these developments it is not surprising that larger and more substantial villages began to appear at locations such as Jenne-jeno (Mali) and Daima (Nigeria) that would ultimately develop into cities during the subsequent West African Regional Development tradition. Both sites also provide evidence of the kind of long-distance trade that would become essential to West African cities in the form of nonlocal stone, iron, and exotic materials such as Mediterranean glass beads and gold. Finally, the region around Jenne-jeno contains what appears to be a hierarchy of sites, from the large central site of **Jenne-jeno** proper, to smaller villages, to agricultural hamlets. It has been suggested that this represents the emergence of a hierarchical chiefdom that would later develop into a powerful state during the historic period.

**Jenne-jeno** (Mali, West African Iron Age)

**West African Regional Development**
(1200–630 B.P.)

The **West African Regional Development** (1200–630 B.P.) tradition marks the emergence of the historically known West African states. While many scholars have argued that it was the impact of Islamic traders that fostered the development of states in West Africa, the clear evidence of increasing political complexity in the West African Iron Age, and archaeological evidence from the West African Regional Development tradition itself suggests the process was a complex one. For example, the historic cities of Ife and Benin, both in Nigeria, grew slowly over a period of perhaps several centuries, beginning as early as 1000 B.P. Both were walled, and one can see from the expansion of the walled area how both grew slowly in population and organization, requiring larger and larger areas to be enclosed, and a clearer organization of residences within the city. The layout of many West African Regional Development villages, with distinct areas for local agriculturalists and craftsmen and Muslim traders, suggests Islamic visitors were intrusive into an already well-organized social system and not integral to it.

Both communities and residences varied dramatically in the West African Regional Development tradition. Small villages and hamlets of agro-pastoralists and hunter-fisher-gatherers still existed, as did larger agricultural and merchant villages. But in the West African Regional Development tradition true cities also appeared, as did styles of architecture that demonstrate both a stability of residence and wealth that go well beyond the typical wattle-and-daub structures of the preceding periods. Residences made from mud brick, both round and square in floor plan, and apparently with both peaked and flat roofs, became common at larger villages and

FIGURE **12.12**
This cast bronze head from Nigeria illustrates the skill in metalwork that developed during the West African Regional Development tradition.

cities. Many houses in cities had paved floors, made by pounding pottery sherds and small rocks into the ground surface. Some of these floors were artistically arranged, with sherds placed on edge in a herringbone pattern. Housing was quite dense within the walled cities, and residential compounds of what were likely individual nuclear or extended families can be identified. As mentioned previously, some of the larger villages and cities had clearly identifiable neighborhoods housing craftsmen, merchants, Islamic traders, and the like.

Material culture became more diversified in the West African Regional Development tradition, and production began to be taken over by craft specialists, particularly in metal and ceramic work. Ceramics became more diverse in both form and decoration, and a variety of unique local styles emerged. Metal shows even more dramatic development (Figure 12.12). Several new smelting technologies were developed, and an indigenous West African lost-wax casting process was perfected. Some of the brass and bronze cast items made by West African Regional Development artisans rank among the world's greatest works of art. Personal ornaments and jewelry also emerged as outstanding works of art. Beads and combination bead and metalwork bracelets, belts, necklaces, and pendants represent both a highly developed artistic tradition and extensive trade with areas outside of West Africa. Camel caravans crossed the Sahara bringing glass, brass, shell, and stone from North Africa, Southwest Asia, and even Europe to West Africa through cities such as Jenne-jeno and Gao, both in Mali, where they were traded for West African gold and ivory.

These extensive trade contacts and the presence of cities and craft specialists all suggest a complex political system had developed by the time of the West African Regional Development tradition. Historic texts from Arabs and Europeans who traveled into the region after about 500 B.P. describe hierarchical systems of local chiefs, priests, and bureaucrats integrated through a preeminent chief or king. The king typically held power both through supernatural legitimation and through physical control of trade and materials obtained through trade. In some of these kingdoms a standing army also helped the king to wield power, and in others craft specialists and their products were controlled by local chiefs, who provided some goods to preeminent chiefs in the form of tribute and obtained exotic raw materials and what were essentially guild rights to use them to produce goods. While there is little direct archaeological evidence of the political system of the West African Regional Development tradition, there are a number of mound or tumuli burials of individuals interred with vast amounts of wealth.

## ✪ SUMMARY

African prehistory is fascinating in its diversity. Complex states arose in at least two areas (Nile Valley and West Africa). Ceramics, metals, writing, and monumental architecture were all developed. Trade links cut across the continent and into Southwest Asia. Yet at the same time Neolithic and even Paleolithic lifestyles were retained, in some cases to the present day. That diversity speaks to processes of cultural adaptation, interaction, and innovation that we can only begin to examine today. Of all the regions of the world covered in this text, Africa is perhaps the richest in the prehistoric record it has to offer and the poorest in terms of the amount of work that has been done. We know little about much of the continent, and while there are areas where intensive research has been carried out, no scholar would argue that the work has been adequate to answer the many questions with which the prehistory of Africa presents us.

Painted in broad strokes, the prehistory of Africa looks something like the following. Africa was dominated by hunters and gatherers until roughly 8,000 years ago. At that time some North African populations began utilizing domesticated animals. Whether these people domesticated animals themselves or imported already domesticated animals from Asia is a lingering question. There is no question, however, that indigenous plants were domesticated, and by 5,000 years ago there were agriculturalists across most of Africa. As agriculture spread, so did settled life and formal political leaders. Egypt is the earliest and best-known of the African states, but by 2,000 years ago all of Africa had sedentary populations, and powerful political leaders had appeared in a number of locations.

## ✪ DISCUSSION QUESTIONS

1. The Nile Valley provided the basis for one of the world's great civilizations, but other civilizations also arose in Africa. What similarities do you see among the prehistoric states of Egypt, Aksum, Great Zimbabwe, and West Africa? What differences are there?

2. Why did pastoralism take hold in northern and eastern Africa and not elsewhere on the continent?

3. What differences in cultural evolution were there between the forests of West Africa and the savannahs of East Africa? What similarities were there?

## ✪ ESSAY QUESTIONS

1. This chapter (and the book as a whole) largely avoids discussion of ritual and belief. Why do you think I avoid such discussions? How does the avoidance of

ritual and belief effect the way I present and explain the prehistory of Africa? How might more discussion of ritual and belief change the way I present and interpret African prehistory?

2. Use library or Internet resources to find excavation reports for one of the sites discussed in this chapter. Compare and contrast those reports with the discussion of the site here. How do the two differ? How are they similar? What is missing in the descriptions I provide here? Is there any benefit to the brief overviews I present versus the thorough excavation reports?

3. Several of the traditions discussed in this chapter existed for very long periods of time. For example, the Southern and Eastern African Later Stone Age persisted from the end of the Upper Paleolithic until the modern era with apparently very few changes. What accounts for the longevity of some archaeological traditions? What cultural practices or processes might allow for such stability? How might change come about in these long stable traditions?

## ⚶ RESEARCH PROJECT

Pastoralists are perhaps the most difficult peoples to study through the archaeological record. Pastoralists move regularly and leave behind relatively little debris. Use ethnographic descriptions of pastoralists and reports from archaeological work on pastoral traditions in Africa to identify a group of artifacts, ecofacts, or features that are associated with pastoralists. With these in hand, develop a strategy for studying pastoralism in prehistory. How can archaeologists learn about prehistoric pastoral ways of life?

## ⬢ KEY SOURCES

### North Africa

Close, 1987; Fattovich et al., 1984; Gilman, 1974, 1975; Kitchen, 1993; Lubell, Sheppard, and Jackes, 1986; Phillipson, 1993; Roubet, 2001; Smith, 1986a, 1992a, 1992b, 2001; Wendorf and Schild, 1980; Wyroll, 2001.

### Nile Valley

Adams, 1988; Bard, 1994; Caneva, 1988; Clark and Brandt, 1984; Connah, 1987; Debono and Mortensen, 1988; Haaland, 1987; Hassan, 1988; Hoffman, 1979; Kemp, 1989; Köhler, 2001; Marks and Mohammed-Ali, 1991; Mohammed-Ali, 1982; Phillipson, 1993; Proussakov, 2001; Rice, 1990; Rizkana and Seeher, 1987–1990; Savage, 2001; Spencer, 1995; Trigger et al., 1983; van den Brink, 1988, 1992; Wendorf and Schild, 1976, 1980; Wendorf, Schild, and Close, 1984; Wenke, 1989, 1991; Wetterstrom, 1993; Wilkinson, 1999; Williams and Faure, 1982; Winchell, 2001a, 2001b.

### Southern and Eastern Africa

Ambrose, 1997, 2001; Barut, 1994; Clark and Brandt, 1984; Deacon, H., 1976; Deacon, J., 1984; Huffman, 1989; Klein, 1994; Marean, 1992; Mitchell, 1997; Phillipson, 1977, 1993; Robbins, 1984, 1998; Robertson, 2001; Robertshaw, 1989, 1993; Sampson, 1974; Wadley, 1987, 1993, 2001.

## Central Africa

Clark, 1959; Clist, 1989; Connah, 1987; de Maret, 1985; Denbow, 1990; Eggert, 1992, 1997; Miller, 2001a, 2001b; Phillipson, 1977, 1993; Sampson, 1974; Sutton, 1996; Van Noten, 1982; Vansina, 1990; Wotzka, 2001a, 2001b.

## West Africa

Connah, 1981, 1987; DeCorse and Spiers, 2001a, 2001b; MacDonald and Allsworth-Jones, 1997; McIntosh, 1999, 2001a, 2001b; McIntosh and McIntosh, 1983, 1988; Phillipson, 1993; Schmidt, 1996; Shaw, 1977, 1978.

# TASSILI N'AJJER

Fifteen thousand years ago, the climate of Africa became milder. The onset of the Younger Dryas about 11,000 B.P., a cold and arid period that persisted 1,000 years, ended this mild climate. Climate in Africa shifted to what it is today over a couple of thousand years. This chapter divides Africa into five major regions: North Africa, the Nile Valley, Southern and Eastern Africa, Central Africa, and West Africa. Each of these regions shares a somewhat distinct environmental and cultural history. One of these regions, North Africa, contained a pastoral tradition known as the North African Protohistoric (4000–3000 B.P.). These people also relied on hunting or agriculture, depending on the resources available to them. The material culture of this tradition included bronze and iron tools, ceramic and hide containers, and even stone tools. One thing they are noted for is their rock art.

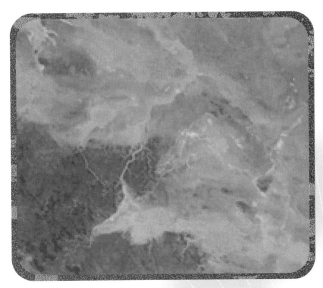

The Media Lab can be found in Chapter 12 on the *Companion Website*™ http://www.prenhall.com/peregrine

## WEB ACTIVITY

Tassili N'Ajjer is located in a strange landscape of great geological interest in the southwest portion of what is now Algeria. This site contains one of the most important groupings of prehistoric cave art in the world. More than 15,000 drawings and engravings record the climatic changes, the animal migrations, and the evolution of human life on the edge of the Sahara from 8000 B.P. to sometime after 2000 B.P. The geological formations are of outstanding scenic interest, with eroded sandstones forming broad areas of reds and blacks. In this activity, you will view a video detailing the environment of the Sahara and the rock art at this famous site. Today this archaeological site is a World Heritage Site, so designated by UNESCO.

## Activity

1. View the video. What does the emphasis on animals in these paintings tell us?

2. Since these artworks span a great period of time, including the pastoral cultures of the North African Protohistoric tradition, what can archaeologists infer about the development of this cultural region?

3. Why do archaeologists pay so much attention to rock paintings such as these? What can we learn about the environment from paintings of animals?

# chapter thirteen

# Europe

**overview**

**Mesolithic**

**Neolithic**

**Bronze Age**

**Iron Age**

**The Eurasian Steppe**

**BOXES**

**Stonehenge**

**Knossos**

The prehistory of Europe has been the subject of scholarship for longer than any other part of the world, and although environmentally and culturally diverse, its prehistoric diversity has been more intensively chronicled and thoughtfully organized than any other region on earth (Figure 13.1). By the 1920s the **age/area concept** had become established as a way of organizing European prehistory. I follow the age/area concept in this chapter, and, indeed, the concept shapes the way I have organized many of the archaeological traditions presented in this book.

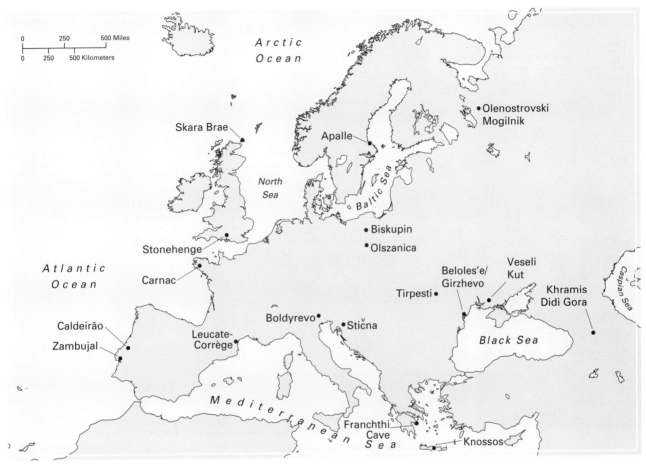

FIGURE **13.1**
Sites discussed in Chapter 13.

A basic principle of the age/area concept is that prehistory can be usefully organized on the basis of technology, and most scholars recognize at least five major ages: the Paleolithic (literally, the Old Stone Age), the Mesolithic (or Middle Stone Age), the Neolithic (or New Stone Age), the Bronze Age, and the Iron Age. Although this organization has its problems (technology and culture change in ways that are not as clear-cut as this organization implies), it does provide a useful framework for looking at the prehistory of Europe.

Members of the genus *Homo* first entered the European continent more than a million and a half years ago. We have examined the traditions of these Paleolithic Europeans in previous chapters on the origins of culture, the evolution of modern humans, and the Upper Paleolithic world. In this chapter we will examine what happened in Europe after the end of the Paleolithic era. Before doing so, however, I need to give you a sense of the European environment.

**Age/area concept:** a way to organize prehistory into temporal units, called ages, usually defined by technology, and located in a particular area. European Bronze Age or Southeastern European Chalcolithic are examples of age/area designations.

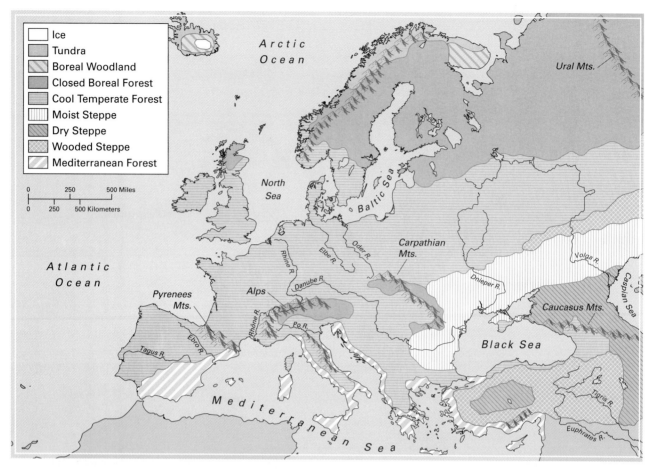

FIGURE **13.2**

Environments of Europe.

Oceans and mountains dominate the landscape of western Europe (Figure 13.2). Europe is surrounded by oceans on three sides—the Atlantic to the north and west, the Mediterranean to the south. Virtually any location in western Europe is within 300 kilometers of a coast, and the oceans have a profound effect on the environments of Europe. Because of the oceans' warming effects, Europe is much more temperate than other areas of the earth at the same north latitude. The surrounding oceans also provide Europe with more precipitation than other areas. Mountains also have an important effect on Europe's environment, since they constitute much of the southern part of the continent and form the continent's watersheds. Major rivers such as the Rhine and Danube are formed from waters running off these mountains. The mountains and oceans also effect the flora and fauna of Europe. The tempering effect of the oceans allows broadleaf forests to dominate most of western Europe, while mountain areas have alpine meadows and pine forests in higher altitudes.

Eastern Europe, lacking both oceans and mountains, is dominated by plains that were formed during the glacial periods that affected Europe during the Paleolithic era. Forests and grasslands dominate this area, and much of the region is low and marshy. Mixed broadleaf and conifer forests give way to boreal forest and tundra as one moves north in eastern Europe, while forested grasslands give way to open steppe as one moves south and east. The tempering effect of the Atlantic and Mediterranean also disappears as one moves east, and the region becomes colder and drier. For example, mean annual temperature in Paris today is 12 degrees C and annual precipitation is 650 mm, while in Kiev, at roughly the same latitude as Paris but 2,000 kilometers to the east, the mean annual temperature is only 7 degrees C and annual precipitation is 600 mm.

## MESOLITHIC

The Mesolithic is a period of transition from subsistence based primarily on hunting large game animals to one focused on a wider range of animal and plant species. Humans across Europe began this transition at the end of the last ice age, roughly 11,000 years ago. This corresponds to a period of increasingly warm conditions and the northward spread of conifer and broadleaf forests as the European glaciers melted. Pleistocene megafauna and the large herds of reindeer and horse that roamed the glacial plains of Europe were replaced by deer, elk, boar, and other smaller forest-dwelling game. A wide range of edible plant foods also emerged, including nut- and fruit-bearing trees, legumes, and seed-bearing grasses.

The **Western European Mesolithic** (11,000–6000 B.P.) tradition is characterized by the development of a microlithic blade technology and the emergence of ground stone tools, particularly axes and adzes, which probably relate to an increased use of wood and plant products. The bow and arrow also may have been developed by Western European Mesolithic peoples, and would have made hunting forest-dwelling animals much easier than with spear and spear thrower. Subsistence was based on hunting and gathering locally abundant resources, including fish and waterfowl, over the course of a seasonal round of movements by small bands of people. Settlements were small and short-term, and tended to be near sources of fresh water. Housing varied from small, skin tents to larger semisubterranean dwellings, which may have been winter houses. Typical settlements consisted of several families, probably no more than fifteen to twenty people in all.

Peoples of the **Eastern European Mesolithic** (11,000–6500 B.P.) tradition also developed microlithic and ground stone tool industries, but appear to have developed more locally specific adaptations than their Western European neighbors. For example, shellfish were found in abundance at the **Beloles'e** site on the Sarata River in Ukraine, and may have been a primary resource collected when people lived at the site. In contrast, at the **Girzhevo** site, also in Ukraine, horse dominated the faunal assemblage. Housing at these sites was apparently much like the Western European Mesolithic—skin tents or semisubterranean structures, although rock-shelters and caves were also used. Several human burials were found at the Girzhevo site, and burials are remarkably common at Eastern European Mesolithic sites. Burials tend to be placed in shallow pits in an extended position and covered with red ochre. Grave goods such as stone tools and personal ornaments also were commonly included in burials.

While Eastern European Mesolithic peoples seem to have lived in small groups of perhaps fifteen to twenty individuals, some of the cemeteries are very large. **Olenostrovski Mogilnik,** in Karelia, for example, contained 177 burials in 141 graves. The site is located on an island in Lake Onega, and appears to have been a special cemetery site. Most of the graves are oriented to the east, and individuals were buried in a similar extended position. Some of the burials have extensive grave goods such as flint knives and daggers, composite harpoon points, bone incised with elk, snake, and human figures, elk, beaver, and bear-teeth pendants, and the like. The number of graves, their similarities, and the amount of effort put into their construction suggests that the Olenostrovski Mogilnik cemetery was carefully organized. The nature of authority that organized the cemetery and the labor to undertake interments must have superceded the individual bands that used the site, but it is not clear what form such authority took.

The **Northern Mediterranean Mesolithic** (11,000–8000 B.P.) tradition was the most distinctive of the Mesolithic traditions of Europe, in part because the region

**Western European Mesolithic** (11,000–6000 B.P.)

**Eastern European Mesolithic** (11,000–6500 B.P.)

**Beloles'e** (Ukraine, Eastern European Mesolithic)

**Girzhevo** (Ukraine, Eastern European Mesolithic)

**Olenostrovski Mogilnik** (Karelia, Eastern European Mesolithic)

**Northern Mediterranean Mesolithic** (11,000–8000 B.P.)

was less strongly effected by environmental change at the end of the last ice age. Northern Mediterranean Mesolithic peoples practiced broad-spectrum hunting and gathering, with an increasing emphasis on marine resources over time. In fact, some coastal sites appear to have become sedentary through their reliance on the sea. One such site is **Franchthi Cave,** located on the east shore of the Gulf of Argolis in southern Greece. The cave itself was about 2 kilometers from the coast in Mesolithic times and was in a region covered with open oak forests. Both forest and coastal resources were used by the people inhabiting Franchthi Cave. Deer and boar, which would have lived in large numbers in the oak forests, dominate the faunal assemblage, but there are also large numbers of fish. By combining forest and coastal resources, the peoples of Franchthi Cave were able to reside year-round in the same location, shifting their reliance on available resources rather than moving from resource to resource as most other Mesolithic peoples did.

**Franchthi Cave
(Greece, Northern
Mediterranean
Mesolithic)**

The remains of some fifteen to thirty-four individuals have been found at Franchthi Cave, and provide some insight into social organization at the time. Both sexes and all age groups are represented, but burial treatment varies. Some individuals were interred in shallow pits, while others were cremated. It is not clear why this variation exists, and some archaeologists suggest it points to variations in social roles or social status. Some of the burials contain personal ornaments such as pebble pendants and shell beads, but again this varies and may indicate emergent social differences.

Franchthi Cave also offers evidence of long-distance trade. Obsidian from the island of Melos in the Agean has been found in large quantities in the cave, and Melos obsidian found elsewhere in Peloponnisos may have been obtained through the Franchthi area, as it is the closest coastal region to Melos. The fact that this material comes from Melos is remarkable, as it means that Northern Mediterranean Mesolithic peoples had seafaring knowledge and boats that could cross 150 kilometers of open ocean.

Other Northern Mediterranean Mesolithic sites are less impressive and seem more like Mesolithic sites elsewhere in Europe. The **Romagnano** site in northern Italy is a good example. Romagnano is located in a rich upland valley which was surrounded by pine and oak forests. The peoples of Romagnano apparently used the location as a base camp to which they would return regularly between foraging trips to the surrounding uplands. Deer, boar, and ibex were the primary animals hunted, and fish and freshwater mollusks were taken in a lake at the bottom of the valley. Lakeshore plants were probably also collected, as were nuts and roots from the surrounding forests. Life at the Romagnano site probably consisted of a seasonal round of trips to upland locations to harvest specific resources (such as nuts or berries) when in season, hunting trips, and trips to obtain quality stone, separated by long periods of time in residence at the site, living off of the collected resources and hunting, fishing, and gathering in the valley itself. This way of life was probably very common throughout Mesolithic Europe.

**Romagnano
(Italy, Northern
Mediterranean
Mesolithic)**

## NEOLITHIC

The Neolithic period is defined by three primary developments: sedentary communities, ceramics, and domesticated foods. The three appeared together as something of a "package." Domesticated plants and animals, which were acquired from Southwest Asia, allowed a more sedentary existence than had been possible in most locations during the Mesolithic era. Ceramic technology, also acquired from Southwest Asia, was used by Neolithic Europeans to both store and cook domesticated foods. The relative fragility and weight of ceramics made them impractical for seminomadic peoples like the Mesolithic Europeans, but once sedentism became more common, ceramics became more common as well.

Since both domesticated foods and ceramic technology were borrowed from Southwest Asia, it is not surprising that the first Neolithic traditions in Europe are the Southeastern European Neolithic and Caucasian Neolithic traditions. While I define a transition at 8000 B.P. between the Mesolithic and Neolithic, clearly the transition to sedentary agricultural lifestyles was a slow one, occurring on the level of individual families and communities over hundreds, if not thousands, of years. Hunting and gathering remained important in many Neolithic traditions, and people remained mobile in many locations well after farming had taken hold elsewhere.

**Caucasian Neolithic** (8000–6500 B.P.) peoples lived in the region of the Caucasus Mountains, between the Black and Caspian seas. Their communities varied tremendously. Caves and rockshelters were used in the north and west Caucasus, while communities of round mud-brick houses were present in the south and east. These mud-brick communities had ties to peoples in Southwest Asia, and their lifestyles were more strongly influenced by developments in the Fertile Crescent and Mesopotamia (discussed in the next chapter). They raised wheat, barley, rye, lentils, oats, and numerous other crops in the fertile alluvial valleys of the region. Domesticated animals, particularly goat and sheep, but also cow and pig, were more important to Caucasian Neolithic peoples in the north and west. These people were relatively mobile, moving their herds regularly to new pastures, and they maintained a significant reliance on hunting and gathering.

A good example of a sedentary Caucasian Neolithic settlement is **Khramis Didi Gora**, located in southeastern Georgia. The site is situated in the fertile alluvial valley of the Khrami river, surrounded by grasslands and upland forests. Houses at the site were circular, constructed of crude mud bricks, and organized around courtyards. Hearths and other work areas were found in these courtyards, suggesting they were the location where most chores were performed. The site as a whole was very large, covering an area of more than 4 hectares, and having perhaps more than 1,000 residents. These people supported themselves by a combination of farming (primarily wheat and barley) and raising domestic animals (especially goat and sheep). Tools used by the people of Khramis Didi Gora were simple, consisting of stone blades and flakes, ground stone axes and adzes, bone and antler tools of various kinds, and simple ceramics. Given the size of the site, archaeologists would typically assume that formal political organization of some kind must have been present, but there is no evidence for formal political authority or for differences in social roles or statuses.

Peoples of the **Southeastern European Neolithic** (8000–6500 B.P.) tradition lived in what is today southern Italy, Greece, the Balkans, and western Turkey. Their way of life was similar to that of the Caucasian Neolithic peoples. Settlements were located in fertile alluvial valleys where crops of wheat, barley, and a variety of legumes could be grown. Sheep, goats, and cattle were pastured in surrounding grasslands. Hunting, fishing, and gathering remained important, particularly fruits and nuts, gathered in forest areas, and fish, which were taken in large numbers. Houses were simple wattle-and-daub structures or, in some cases, of mud brick built on a stone foundation. Typical communities had thirty to fifty houses and perhaps 300 residents. Technology was simple and included stone blade and flake tools, ground stone tools, bone and antler, and simple ceramics. These communities appear to have been completely autonomous, and there is no evidence for formal political authority or social differentiation.

While both the Caucasian Neolithic and the Southeastern European Neolithic communities appear to have been autonomous and egalitarian, trade did take place between them, and long-distance interaction with peoples in other regions appears to have become more important over time. Again, this should not be surprising since agriculture was clearly introduced from Southwest Asia, but the extent of long-distance interaction seems significant for these otherwise simple communities. Obsidian, flint, and chert were obtained from several sources in the Mediterranean

**Caucasian Neolithic**
(8000–6500 B.P.)

**Khramis Didi Gora**
(Georgia, Caucasian Neolithic)

**Southeastern European Neolithic**
(8000–6500 B.P.)

FIGURE **13.3**
A Cardial Ware vase showing
cardial shell impressions.

and were traded widely in southeastern Europe. The Caucasus had local obsidian sources, but even these were traded between communities as well as traded to other regions—some Caucasian obsidian has been found 900 kilometers to the east in Iran. Caucasus peoples obtained lapis and turquoise from Southwest Asia, and they may have been influenced in terms of religious ideas since numerous small figurines in northern Mesopotamian styles have been found at Caucasian Neolithic sites.

Regional interaction seems to have continued to be important during the Impressed Ware and Linear Pottery traditions, which mark the beginnings of the Neolithic period in Western Europe. Both traditions get their names from the unique designs on ceramics made by the peoples of each tradition. Impressed Ware peoples decorated ceramics with impressions of cardial shells (and sometimes these ceramics are called cardial ware instead of impressed ware—see Figure 13.3). Linear Pottery peoples decorated ceramics with incised or impressed lines or bands. The widespread distribution of these distinctive ceramic forms suggests that interaction between communities had become very important and that both ideas and individuals were likely moving between communities on a regular basis. This interaction may not have always been friendly; some Linear Pottery communities are fortified.

**Impressed Ware** (6800–6000 B.P.) peoples lived along the northern Mediterranean coast from southern Italy to Portugal. Most sites are located either in upland caves or along the coast. Cave sites may have been locations where families pastured herds during the summer months since they tend to be small and have relatively scanty archaeological deposits. For example, the cave site of **Caldeirão**, in southern Portugal, had only a small living area near the front of the cave and a burial area in the back. A total of seven ceramic vessels were found, and five burials. Thus it appears the site was used by a very small group of people—perhaps a single family, over the course of several generations. Coastal sites are larger and have more significant archaeological deposits. **Leucate-Corrège**, in France, was apparently a year-round village. It was located directly on the coast (indeed, it is now submerged

**Impressed Ware**
(6800–6000 B.P.)

**Caldeirão** (Portugal,
Impressed Ware)

**Leucate-Corrège**
(France, Impressed
Ware)

under 6 meters of water owing to the rising level of the Mediterranean over the last 6,000 years), and it would have been in a prime location for taking advantage of marine resources. The site produced large amounts of ceramics and stone tools, and evidence for small, circular huts, which would have housed no more than a single family. Although the site is relatively large, there is no evidence for political authority or social differentiation.

**Linear Pottery** (6500–6000 B.P.) peoples lived throughout northwestern and central Europe. Linear Pottery settlements ranged from individual farmsteads and small hamlets to large villages. Villages typically consisted of from one to perhaps a dozen longhouses (Figure 13.4). These were constructed with wooden posts supporting wattle-and-daub walls and a gabled roof. Longhouses varied from 4 to 7 meters in width and from 7 to 45 meters in length. Several families resided within each longhouse, from two or three in the smaller longhouses to more than a dozen in the largest. Most archaeologists think a single descent group, probably matrilineal, shared each longhouse, implying that each village consisted of several separate descent groups living together. Villages were sometimes palisaded, and were often located in groups of three or more within a small area, which suggests that warfare may have been taking place between village groups or regions. Given the size and organization of these villages, some archaeologists think that there may have been village leaders coordinating defense. Others argue that Linear Pottery societies were wholly egalitarian.

**Linear Pottery**
(6500–6000 B.P.)

Hunting and gathering remained important for both Impressed Ware and Linear Pottery peoples, but domestic plants and animals were also raised. At the **Olszanica** Linear Pottery site in southeastern Poland, for example, remains of a wide variety of domesticated crops, including emmer, einkorn, and spelt wheat, barley, millet, and oats were all found. Animal bones were not preserved at the site, but in neighboring areas remains of pigs and sheep are common. Remains of wild horse, red and roe deer, and wild boar are also found at these sites. Olszanica was a large village, covering an area of 50 hectares. At any given time in the site's long history (about 400 years of continuous occupation), only about a quarter of that area was used, but there were perhaps a dozen or more longhouses occupied, and perhaps 200 to 300 residents. These people made their living through the grain and animals they grew, but clearly hunting and gathering continued to be practiced.

**Olszanica** (Poland, Linear Pottery)

Trade also was important to the people of Olszanica since some 80 percent of the stone tools found on the site were made from nonlocal raw materials. Both obsidian and ceramics from Slovakia and Hungary were found on the site, so clearly

# Stonehenge

Stonehenge, located on the Salisbury plain in southern England, is a place of wonder for all who visit it, and a place of great mystery for many who do not know anything about the European Megalithic tradition. It has been identified as a node in the "planetary grid" of supernatural power, as structure built by residents of the mythical city of Atlantis, and as the center of an ancient Druidic world. In some ways, however, Stonehenge is actually a rather unimportant site. It is a well-preserved example of a Megalithic structure, but it is only one of many that dot Western Europe, and there are others that are considerably larger and probably played a much more important role in European Megalithic society. Why has Stonehenge been made into a mystery, while related constructions have not?

In part, the answer lies in Stonehenge's construction. Nowhere else were massive lintels used, and they provide an important part of the site's aura, for a visitor to the site has to ask "How did they get those massive stones up there?" The lintels give a sense of completeness to the site that other henges, composed of large, standing stones alone, seem to lack. The fact that the stones at Stonehenge were shaped into rectangular forms also adds to the site's feeling of completeness, while other henges, built from rough stones, seem comparatively unfinished. But probably most important is the site's exquisite preservation. Although a large number of the stones were robbed for other uses in antiquity, those that remain are mostly in the original locations where they were set some 4,500 years ago. The site has not been buried by wind or water-borne soils, and erosion has not significantly damaged the stones. Stonehenge looks as good as a 4,500-year-old site can.

Stonehenge itself consists of about 162 large stone blocks arranged in five concentric circles. The outermost circle has thirty rectangular stone uprights supporting horizontal stone lintels. The uprights are made of sandstone, about 4 meters

---

the people of Olszanica were importing goods. More significantly, the excavators were able to determine that the Olszanica peoples were also exporting stone blades. The site is located near a flint source, and the site's residents apparently mined and worked the flint. By measuring the ratio of flint cores to blades found on the site, the excavators determined that roughly 25 percent of the blades manufactured at Olszanica were exported from the site. Thus, by the time of the Linear Pottery and Impressed Ware traditions, sedentary agricultural communities were regularly interacting with one another, and perhaps not always peacefully.

**European Megalithic (6000–4500 B.P.)**

The **European Megalithic** (6000–4500 B.P.) tradition follows the Impressed Ware and Linear Pottery traditions in Western and Central Europe. Sedentarism, ceramics, and domesticates are highly variable in this tradition. Sites vary from small camps to walled communities, and European Megalithic populations in some areas appear to have been highly mobile. Hunted and gathered foods remained important for some European Megalithic peoples, but domesticated animals (cattle, sheep, and goats) and plants (wheat and barley) were also raised by most groups.

high, and are separated from one another by about a meter. The lintels, also of sandstone, add another meter to the height of the outer circle, which is, in total, about 30 meters in diameter. The lintels are held in place by bulbs projecting out of the uprights fitted into round sockets in the lintels. Immediately within the outer circle is a second circle of upright stones without lintels, about 2 meters in height, and made from distinctive bluish granite. The third circle is not complete, but forms a U composed of five sets of two sandstone uprights supporting a single lintel. The U opens to the northeast, and the height of the sets of uprights and lintel gets higher towards the back of the U. The uprights and lintel forming the base of the U are the tallest, standing about 8 meters high. Within this U is another set of bluish granite stones, increasing in height toward the base of the U from about 2 meters to nearly 3 meters. Finally, in the center of the U is a single large slab of green sandstone.

Clearly this structure was built for some specific purpose, but what was it? Arguments have ranged from human sacrifice to celestial observations. The best answer today is that the site was a solar calendar used to mark the dates for important events. Seen in the context of the surrounding area, which includes several contemporary henges, dense residential occupation, and numerous burial mounds, many archaeologists see Stonehenge as a multipurpose ritual center serving area communities, perhaps something like a parish church or town hall. Solar observances were likely made at the site, but many other activities probably took place there as well. These may have included burial rituals, religious ceremonies, and public meetings, but in truth, we really don't know. Perhaps it is the very nature of this structure, clearly built with specific purposes in mind, but with those purposes lost in the distant past, that gives Stonehenge its enduring power.

SOURCES: Chippendale, Christopher, *Stonehenge Complete* (London: Thames and Hudson, 1994); Wainwright, Geoffrey, *The Henge Monuments* (London: Thames and Hudson, 1989).

The most distinctive aspect of the European Megalithic tradition are the massive stone and earth constructions that give the tradition its name. These were often built to house collective burials, in some cases several hundred individuals or more.

The most famous European Megalithic site is **Stonehenge,** which is described in the box feature (Figure 13.5). But there are other Megalithic sites that are equally, if not more, impressive. For example, **Carnac,** located in northwestern France, consists of a series of stone alignments and enclosures stretching nearly 4 kilometers and consisting of more than 3,000 stones. The stones themselves are in some cases massive—on the order of 100 tons—although most are much smaller. It is not clear what these stone alignments and enclosures mean, but they were certainly important to the people who built them since massive labor would have been required to move and position these thousands of stones. In some cases the alignments appear to form a calendar marking celestial events. In some cases enclosures appear to outline places of ritual. But other alignments and enclosures have no clear function, and it may be that a single explanation does not cover the numerous features at Carnac.

**Stonehenge** (England, European Megalithic)

**Carnac** (France, European Megalithic)

FIGURE **13.5**
Aerial view of Stonehenge.

**Skara Brae**
(Scotland, European
Megalithic)

One of the few excavated European Megalithic villages is the site of **Skara Brae** on the west coast of Scotland. The location seems a harsh one for an agricultural village—the land is treeless, windy, and there is frequent rain. For early agriculture and animal husbandry, however, this location may have been highly desirable. Rainfall is plentiful and the inhabitants of Skara Brae could have used seaweed as contemporary people do as an excellent fertilizer for their crops. Pasture for the sheep and cattle kept by the Skara Brae people was plentiful as well. In addition, fish and shellfish could have been harvested easily and were used in abundance. Houses at Skara Brae were small (4 to 7 meters on a side), square structures built of rougly cut and dry-laid sandstone, which was plastered with clay on the outside to keep out the wind and rain. The houses probably had thatched roofs. Each house was connected to its neighbors by narrow roofed passages. Within each house was a central hearth, storage pits, stone shelves, and sleeping platforms. The compactness of Skara Brae and the fact that houses were connected to one another suggests that an extended family or small descent group inhabited the site. The picture we get from Skara Brae of a small, closely knit community of simple farmers, fishers, and herdsmen is probably characteristic of many European Megalithic villages.

**Scandinavian Neolithic**
(6000–3800 B.P.)

In far Northern Europe peoples of the **Scandinavian Neolithic** (6000–3800 B.P.) tradition also began cultivating wheat and barley and raising cattle, pigs, and sheep. Like other areas of Europe, hunting and gathering remained important, and some groups remained mobile. The primary features that differentiate the Scandinavian Neolithic from other European Neolithic traditions are tool forms. In northern Denmark, southern Sweden, and Norway, for example, a unique form of ceramics called Pitted Ware is found. In southern Denmark and northern Germany so-called "battle axes"—large, butterfly shaped stone axes—are characteristic of Neolithic peoples. In these areas settlements tend to be small coastal communities located to take advantage of both good agricultural soils and marine resources. In northern Norway, Sweden, and Finland hunting and gathering remained more important. Projectile points and knives made from slate are characteristic, and sites tend to be small and ephemeral.

The other characteristic aspect of the Scandinavian Neolithic tradition is extensive trade in exotic goods. Several unique artifact types are found across a wide area

FIGURE **13.6**
Corded Ware tradition ceramics from Denmark. In the foreground are examples of ground stone "battle axes" that are also characteristic of the Corded Ware tradition.

of Scandinavia, particularly amber beads and finely crafted flint axes and daggers. Amber and flint were apparently traded from northern and central Europe in exchange for furs from Scandinavia. Some of the objects came into southern Scandinavia in raw form and were made into finished products there, and often again traded once complete. In addition, some items are so well made and required such technical skill that they were likely manufacued by craft specialists. These include flint axes and daggers and finely crafted ceramics called funnel beakers. The presence of this trade and craft specialization has led some scholars to suggest that a group of elites must have been present among Scandinavian Neolithic peoples, but the evidence is ambiguous.

Finally, in northern and western Russia, peoples of the **Corded Ware** (6000–3800 B.P.) tradition followed a similar way of life. The artifacts for which the tradition is named are ceramics decorated with impressed cord markings, usually in the form of parallel lines around the vessel's neck (Figure 13.6). These ceramics are relatively crude, often flat-bottomed, and with beaker forms common. Peoples of the Corded Ware tradition lived in small and ephemeral settlements. The ephemeral nature of Corded Ware settlements has led some scholars to suggest that Corded Ware peoples were seminomadic in parts of their range. A more likely explanation for the lack of archaeological materials is that peoples of the Corded Ware tradition moved regularly as soils, game, and local plant foods became depleted. The small, ephemeral settlements suggest political organization was informal.

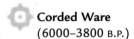

**Corded Ware**
(6000–3800 B.P.)

There has been a long debate about the importance of domestic foods in the economy of the Corded Ware peoples, in part because there seems to be a great diversity in the intensity of their use. In some areas domesticated plants and animals played an important role in the economy. In others, particularly in northern regions, they played little if any role. Domesticated pigs, sheep, and cattle were present in most regions of the Corded Ware tradition, and there is evidence of wheeled carts being used in some areas. Evidence for domesticated wheat and barley is less extensive but is present on many sites. In addition to domestic foods, Corded Ware peoples hunted large game in the forests and grasslands and collected a variety of plant foods, perhaps the most important being acorns and chestnuts. Fishing was important too, and the remains of pike and carp are found in large numbers on some sites.

Tools used for hunting and gathering included the bow and arrow, the arrows typically armed with small, triangular stone points. Fish were taken with spears and nets. Flint blades were used for knives and scrapers. The Corded Ware people manufactured a variety of ceramics as well, but they are most clearly identified with globular beakers having cord-impressed designs. Technology, then, through the Mesolithic and Neolithic, remained largely unchanged. However, a major innovation was on the horizon that would emerge as a vital part of later European societies—bronze.

## BRONZE AGE

The use of bronze defines the Bronze Age, but like domesticated plants and animals, bronze use had a slow development in most parts of Europe and was preceded by periods where people used copper, often termed Chalcolithic (literally, copper stone age). Bronze itself is a combination of copper and tin, sometimes with arsenic or other minerals added as well. Bronze is stronger and more brittle than raw copper, and it can hold a sharp edge and wear longer than raw copper. To make bronze, copper is melted and tin (and sometimes other minerals) added in precise quantities. The molten bronze is then either made into ingots to be reheated and cast later, or immediately poured and cast into a bronze object. Thus bronze working is technologically much more sophisticated and labor intensive than copper working, and in many ways more technically challenging that stone knapping. Bronze work also requires smelting and casting facilities that are not easily moved, and the process usually requires long-distance trade to obtain at least some raw materials.

**Bell Beaker**
(4500–3600 B.P.)

In Western Europe the peoples of the **Bell Beaker** (4500–3600 B.P.) tradition began using copper for distinctive tanged daggers and personal ornaments (Figure 13.7). The name of the tradition comes from a unique ceramic form which became widespread across Central and Western Europe. Both the spread of these bell-shaped ceramics and the presence of exotic materials such as amber, ivory, and gold suggests that trade was an important activity for Bell Beaker peoples. Typical Bell Beaker communities were small hamlets or villages of ten to twenty houses, usually on fertile soils near a good source of fresh water. Houses were oval or rectangular and varied widely in size from as small as 2 meters by 3 meters to as large as 7 meters by 20 meters. They were constructed from wattle and daub. Some villages were surrounded by a wooden palisade and others with large stone fortification walls, suggesting that conflict was present in some areas.

FIGURE **13.7**
Bell Beaker burial. Note the beaker held in the individual's hands and the copper dagger next to it.

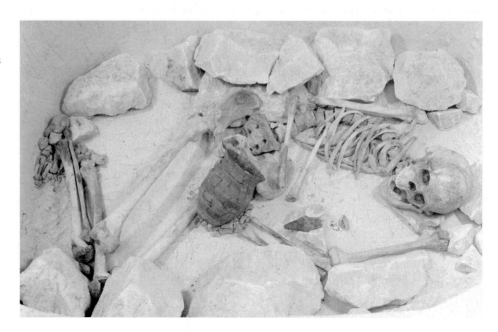

Bell Beaker people lived by growing wheat, barley, rye, oats, and legumes, and by raising sheep, goats, pigs, and cattle. There were some important innovations during the Bell Beaker period that intensified agricultural production. Perhaps most important were the development of the plow and cart and the use of cattle (oxen) as traction animals. This allowed areas of land that could not have been cultivated by hand to be brought into production. Carts provided the ability to transport goods, allowing farmers to live more distant from their fields. Carts would have also been a boon for trade, and this may be one reason why interregional trade in goods such as bell-shaped ceramics becomes so apparent. These innovations, however, had other effects as well. The importance of wild foods appears to have declined during the Bell Beaker tradition as large areas of Western Europe became deforested and large game animals scarce. Still, some 10 to 20 percent of the meat consumed by Bell Beaker peoples came from wild animals.

With the majority of the population living in small farming villages, the presence of long-distance trade, fortified settlements, and new exotic items such as gold and ivory in the Bell Beaker tradition suggests that there may have been a group of elites who coordinated labor for trade and defense, and who acquired and controlled access to unique exotic goods. At the fortified site of **Zambujal** in Portugal, for example, there is evidence of special copper production areas in two houses at the center of the settlement. These house also had imported Bell Beaker ceramics. It has been suggested that these were the houses of the settlement's leaders, who controlled both copper production and trade, and who coordinated labor to maintain the settlement's stone fortifications and to defend the settlement if besieged. Certainly some labor coordination was needed to construct Zambujal's fortifications; they consisted of a double bastion wall and several stone defensive towers, all of which were regularly added to and updated.

**Zambujal** (Portugal, Bell Beaker)

In southeastern Europe and the Caucasus, peoples of the **Southeastern European Chalcolithic** (6500–4500 B.P.) and **Caucasian Chalcolithic** (6500–5500 B.P.) traditions also began to use copper, initially for small tools such as awls and knives as well as for personal ornaments, but also for larger and more complex axes and adzes. Peoples of both traditions lived primarily in large (100 to 300 people) farming villages and participated extensively in trade with other communities. A good example is the Caucasian Chalcolithic site of **Leilatepe** in Azerbaijan. Leilatepe is located on a hill overlooking the Karabakh steppe, which contains both excellent pasture and good agricultural soils. The site covers an area roughly 60 meters in diameter and contains extensive debris from daily life, including obsidian blades used to make sickles and knives, grinding stones, mortars, and pestles, used to process grain crops, and a variety of both utilitarian and fineware ceramics. Six rectangular mud-brick houses were uncovered at Leilatepe, as well as a ceramic production area with two kilns and a copper smelting area where the residents of Leilatepe were apparently experimenting with adding arsenic and nickel to molten copper before casting it. Three copper awls, a knife, and pieces of copper wire have also been found. If Leilatepe is representative of other Caucasian Chalcolithic sites, it suggests that people in many small farming and herding communities were involved in craft production and perhaps trade.

**Southeastern European Chalcolithic** (6500–4500 B.P.)

**Caucasian Chalcolithic** (6500–5500 B.P.)

**Leilatepe** (Azerbaijan, Caucasian Chalcolithic)

A good example of a Southeastern European Chalcolithic village is **Tirpesti**, located in northeastern Romania. The site is built on a hill overlooking the Topolita river and was surrounded by oak forests. Farming was apparently done in the river valley, and hunting, collecting, and herding animals was done in the upland forests. The village consisted of ten wattle-and-daub houses, and was surrounded by a defensive ditch some 2 meters deep and 3 meters wide. The houses themselves varied in size, and three appear larger and more substantial than the others. These were constructed with wooden floors and contained a much richer assortment of stone tools and ceramics than the other houses. They were also constructed with accompanying ritual since anthropomorphic figurines were placed in the foundations of

**Tirpesti** (Romania, Southeastern European Chalcolithic)

## Knossos

The Southeastern European Bronze Age city of Knossos on the north side of the island of Crete is one of the most famous sites in the ancient world. It is the fabled home of the Minotaur, a monstrous bull who lived within a giant labyrinth that was part of the Palace of King Minos, as well as the childhood home of the Greek god Zeus. It was the center of Minoan culture and was, during its height, the most important city in Europe.

Research at Knossos was first undertaken by the legendary archaeologist Sir Arthur Evans, who began work at the site in 1900 and completed excavation and conservation work in 1929. Research since Evans has been largely focused on solving specific problems of chronology or assisting in the reconstruction and conservation of the city.

The primary structure at Knossos is the palace, which was constructed beginning perhaps as early as 4200 B.P., but which reached is completed form around 3900 B.P. The palace had numerous rooms and corridors, the internal complexity of which probably gave rise to the myth of the great labyrinth (which otherwise has not been found). The first palace was destroyed by an earthquake around 3700 B.P., and that structure was leveled and a new palace built on top of it. The second palace stood until around 3375 B.P., when it was destroyed, allegedly by Minoans revolting against Mycenaean overlords who apparently took control of Crete around 3400 B.P.

The complexity of the palace of Knossos can be reduced to a fairly simple plan. The structure was organized around a large, rectangular courtyard, some 1,800 square meters in size, and oriented with the long sides running north–south. At the north end of the courtyard was a pillared entrance hall through which important

these houses before construction. The excavators suggest these houses were the residences of elites who had, perhaps, important religious or political functions.

There seems clear evidence that social stratification had emerged among Southeastern European Chalcolithic peoples. Communities became larger and better organized, and special craft areas and elite residences appeared. Trade became important, and metal goods, fineware ceramics, and symbols of power such as gold and copper ornaments moved throughout Southeastern Europe and beyond to the European steppe. Some communities emerged as centers of trade and economic activity, such as **Veseli Kut** in Ukraine. Veseli Kut was a large site, with concentric rings of structures positioned around a central open space and covering an area of roughly 150 hectares. Many of the structures were simple one-room houses, roughly 5 meters by 10 meters in size. Others, however, were more complex, and there appear to have been a large number of houses with attached workshops for flint, bone, and leather work. There were also large houses, some over 100 square meters in size, that appear to have been residences of elites or political leaders. Several large ceramic production facilities were located on the periphery of the site. The picture

**Veseli Kut** (Ukraine, Southeastern European Chalcolithic)

visitors to the palace would enter. On the west and south sides of the courtyard were official rooms, including the king's throne room and numerous religious shrines, as well as a huge staircase going up to the other two floors of the palace's west wing. Beyond these official rooms was a large west courtyard, and between the two were long narrow rooms, called "magazines," used for storage. The west courtyard was probably where goods stored in the "magazines" were delivered. On the east side of the central courtyard were the private apartments of the royal family. These were built down a slope, and they actually went several stories below the level of the central courtyard.

What was life like at Knossos? The major functions of the palace seem to have been a combination of economic activity and religious ritual. Large areas of the palace were dedicated to storage. Some areas contained enormous quantities of foodstuffs such as olive oil, wine, and grain, while others contained valuable raw materials such as gold, ivory, and stone. These raw materials were turned into precious finished goods at workshops on the east side of the central courtyard and elsewhere surrounding the palace, and the combination of foods and raw materials suggests that craftspeople were fully supported by the palace. Clay sealings and tablets attest to the fact that an important activity of the palace was the creation and trade of precious wealth items.

A vast number of religious artifacts found in the palace attest to the importance of religious activities. Stone, ceramic, and metal figures, libation vessels, and other ritual items are found in numerous shrines within the palace. Frescos on the palace walls illustrate a fertility goddess whose worship was apparently channeled through the palace and, indeed, directly through the king

SOURCES: Cotterell, Arthur, *The Minoan World* (New York: Scribners, 1980); Mellersh, H.E.L., *Minoan Crete* (New York: Putnam, 1967).

we get from Veseli Kut is of a mixed community of farmers, craftsmen, and their leaders—a bustling center of trade and activity like many villages in Southeastern Europe today.

In the **Southeastern European Bronze Age** (5100–3100 B.P.) tradition, social stratification crystallized into hierarchical polities with powerful political rulers. This is the tradition associated with the first Greek civilizations (Minoan and Mycenaean) and the first writing systems in Europe (Linear A and B). Large towns with a central palace complex, communal storage facilities, and large defensive works were built, perhaps the best-known example being **Knossos,** which is described in the box feature (Figure 13.8). While powerful kings, priests, and craftsmen lived in these urban centers, most peoples of the Southeastern European Bronze Age lived in smaller communities and agricultural hamlets. There they raised crops of wheat and barley, and cared for herds of sheep and goats. Whether in cities or agricultural villages, people lived in well-made mud-brick houses, often with stone foundations or basements and typically two stories tall. Craftsmen usually had workshops attached to their houses, while farmers had attached storage facilities and animal pens.

**Southeastern European Bronze Age** (5100–3100 B.P.)

**Knossos** (Crete, Southeastern European Bronze Age)

FIGURE **13.8**
Aerial view of the Palace
of Knossos.

Trade was extensive in the Southeastern European Bronze Age tradition, and reached across the Mediterranean to the Near East and North Africa. Linear B texts and shipwrecks have provided a detailed perspective on this trade (see Figure 13.9). Olive oil, used both as lamp oil and in food, was produced in large quantities in Europe and exported across the Mediterranean to the Levant and Egypt. Wool was spun into thread and woven into cloth that were both also exported in large quantities. In return, European traders received obsidian, ivory, precious metals and stones, carved seals, scarabs, and metal objects. Many of these goods were objects used by elites to display prestige, and it appears that this trade was controlled through these elites. Production of some of the trade items, particularly bronze, may also have been controlled by elites. Bronze work became highly developed in the Southeastern European Bronze Age, and weapons were the most frequently produced items. Daggers, swords, spear and arrow points, armor, shields, and helmets were all manufactured. Woodworking tools such as chisels, axes, knives, and saws were also manufactured of bronze, but these were often less ornate and less well made than bronze weaponry. The fact that most identified bronze workshops are found in association with palace complexes, as well as the military nature of the goods produced, suggests a close connection between bronze work and the elites.

Linear B texts also provide a record of political and religious life in the Southeastern European Bronze Age that nicely augments the archaeological record. The presence of palaces and rich burials suggests that elites were the center of both political and religious life in the Southeastern European Bronze Age, and the texts bear out that conclusion. Linear B documents describe centrally controlled territories that are each divided into smaller administrative (and taxation) districts. Each district was administered by a local official who reported directly to the king. Large areas of land were owned by elites, who had peasants and slaves working it to support the palaces and temples. Religious life focused around temples at which sacrifices were made to specific resident gods. There were also annual festivals for particular gods, at which ceremonies such as pouring libations would be performed by priests. These festivals were accompanied by feasting and gift-giving.

Elsewhere in Europe social complexity did not arise in the Bronze Age, although society did become more integrated. Most peoples of the **European Early Bronze Age** (4700–3500 B.P.) lived in small agricultural hamlets or villages which were

**European Early Bronze
Age** (4700–3500 B.P.)

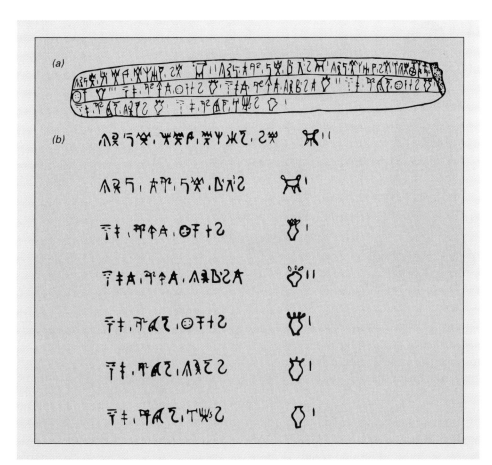

FIGURE **13.9**

A Linear B text from the palace of Pylos known as the "Tripod tablet" (a) with each phrase copied below (b) to make the organization of the text easier to understand. The text gives an accounting of a shipment of bronze cauldrons, and roughly translates "Two Cretan *ai-ke-u* tripod-cauldrons; one single-handled tripod cauldron; one unusable Cretan tripod-cauldron, with legs burned away; three wine jars; one large *dipas* with four handles; two large *dipas* with three handles; one small *dipas* with four handles; one small *dipas* with three handles; one small *dipas* without handle."

SOURCE: Timothy Champion, Clive Gamble, Stephen Shennan, and Alastair Whittle, *Prehistoric Europe* (London: Academic Press, 1984), p. 234.

linked to larger towns that probably served as regional economic, religious, and perhaps political centers. Agricultural hamlets housed a group of a half-dozen or so related families, who worked the land surrounding the hamlet, raised sheep, goats, cattle, and pigs, and produced craft goods such as yarn, textiles, and ceramics. Plow agriculture using oxen as traction animals became standard in the European Early Bronze Age, and large areas of land that were impractical to farm by hand were brought into production. For this reason settlements were no longer restricted to alluvial valleys, but were found in all areas of Europe. Houses were rectangular wattle-and-daub structures, typically something like 5 meters by 7 meters in size, but size varied widely. In some areas small pit houses were also used, perhaps as winter dwellings.

Larger European Early Bronze Age villages typically occupied a hilltop and were fortified with walls, ditches, or palisades. These sites seem to have functioned as both political and trade centers for the hamlets in the surrounding areas. Craft activities were common in these large villages, and they are the only locations where a diversity of bronze items are found. These include swords, daggers, battle axes, and spears, as well as personal ornaments. Large villages sometimes also contain richly adorned burials that have been interpreted as the remains of political leaders. Because of their defensive works and common presence of bronze weaponry, these large villages are often seen to be fortifications where area populations could retreat in times of war. They appear also to have functioned as places were craft goods were produced and exchanged, a market town for the regional economy.

Peoples of the **Western European Earlier Bronze Age** (3800–3300 B.P.) tradition continued this general pattern of small hamlet life tied to larger regional centers. Hamlets consisted of several small, square structures, probably housing one or more

 **Western European Earlier Bronze Age** (3800–3300 B.P.)

FIGURE **13.10**
Bronze items from Western Europe including an axe, bracelet or torc, and dagger.

extended family groups. Centers were usually built on an easily defended prominence and surrounded by a series of walls and ditches. Houses in both hamlets and fortified towns were built using a wooden frame of posts supporting a thatched roof and walled with wattle and daub. Within the houses were usually a hearth and one or more storage pits. In some parts of Iberia circular or oval houses were also constructed, but their size suggests that, like the houses in other parts of Europe, only a single family inhabited them. In parts of central Europe larger houses with several internal divisions have been found, but these, again, seem to be nuclear family residences with the additional rooms in place for storage or to house livestock in harsh weather.

The peoples of the Earlier Bronze Age subsisted primarily on domesticated plants and animals. They grew wheat, barley, rye, and other grains using a shifting method of cultivation, though in some areas they also tended more permanent stands of olive trees, grape vines, and the like. They also raised pigs, sheep, and cattle. While agricultural products provided the bulk of the diet, a variety of game animals were also hunted, the most important being deer and boar, and locally available wild plant foods were collected when in season.

Bronze was obviously used by the Earlier Bronze Age peoples, but its uses were surprisingly limited. Bronze was widely used for weapons, particularly swords, for axes, and for clothing pins, but otherwise bronze use was largely restricted to personal ornaments such as **torcs**, anklets, and the like (Figure 13.10). In many ways the Earlier Bronze Age saw no marked departure from earlier technology, despite the beginnings of bronze production. Stone, wood, and bone were still used quite extensively for basic tools. Ceramics were also used extensively, and were made in a variety of forms and decorative styles.

The presence of bronze, however, does suggest some important changes in the economy of the Earlier Bronze Age peoples in comparison with their predecessors. First, it seems likely that bronze was manufactured by specialists, perhaps only part-time specialists, but specialists nonetheless. Second, since sources of copper, arsenic, and tin are limited, the widespread use of bronze required trade networks to be established and maintained in order to link sources with production sites and consumers. While trade in raw materials such as stone and shell had been in place for thousands of years before the Bronze Age, the bronze trade networks seem more substantial. Quarry sites were linked with sites producing raw bronze ingots (which often resemble torcs). Bronze ingots were traded to local artisans who worked them into objects, which were then traded to consumers. Thus several distinct steps stood

**Torcs:** thick metal neck-rings, often of gold or bronze and highly decorated, which were thought to provide good fortune to the wearer.

between the quarrying of the raw material and the finished product—a more complex system than that which had been (and apparently was still) in place for stone or shell.

The production of bronze objects has suggested to many scholars that just as trade became more complex, sociopolitical organization may have become more complex as well. This idea seems to be reinforced by the presence of fortified towns, suggesting some degree of political integration, at least at a local level. Unfortunately, there is little formal data on sociopolitical organization for the Earlier Bronze Age. Scholars analyzing the contents of burials have suggested a two-tiered division was present in Earlier Bronze Age society, with one tier being elites buried with considerable wealth and the other being commoners buried with very few goods. Most scholars believe that such differences were probably achieved during the life of the individual, particularly since many of the "elite" burials contain goods associated with warriors. However, both women and men, and even some children, were buried in the elite style, suggesting that ascribed status differences may have been present.

During the **Western European Late Bronze Age** (3300–2800 B.P.) tradition some interesting social changes took place. Most obvious were death rituals, which became highly uniform across most of Western Europe. Individuals were cremated and the deceased's remains, sometimes along with a few personal items, were placed into a large ceramic urn. The urn was then buried in a simple, unmarked pit within a large cemetery containing, by the end of the Late Bronze Age, many hundreds or thousands of such burial urns. These "urnfields," as they are called, were enclosed by a ditch or were located in caves, but most were unmarked. There are few elite graves dating to the Late Bronze Age, and these are always located outside of urnfields. The image we have is of a shift to a strongly communal society, where individual differences in wealth or status were downplayed and where individuals saw themselves as a member of a society more than as a member of a family. During the Late Bronze Age peoples also left hordes of bronze, gold, silver, and other goods at locations such as caves, springs, fords, and wells, and these have been interpreted as gifts to spirits residing at those locations.

While urnfields suggest a generally egalitarian society, the hordes of exotic goods indicate that there were still individuals or groups able to obtain and amass wealth. The persistence of fortified central towns and the continuing production of large numbers of bronze weapons suggests that conflict was common and that regional leaders, perhaps chiefs, were present. However, diversity seems to characterize the Bronze Age in Western Europe, with some regions having what appear to be "warrior" chiefs residing in central fortified towns, and others apparently lacking both.

Outside of Western Europe there was also diversity in Bronze Age societies. In Northern Europe peoples of the **Scandinavian Bronze Age** (3800–2500 B.P.) and **Northeastern European Bronze Age** (3800–2800 B.P.) traditions lived in small agricultural hamlets that appear to have been largely autonomous, though some larger communities are found in the southern range of both traditions. Scandinavian Bronze Age peoples resided in longhouses shared by several families, while Northeastern European Bronze Age peoples lived in single-family houses. Both types were of wattle-and-daub construction. Scandinavian Bronze Age settlements consisted of only one or two longhouses, and Northeastern European Bronze Age settlements were no larger, consisting of a few to perhaps ten individual family dwellings. Social differentiation within and between villages seems to have been modest or nonexistent. Most craft goods were made within hamlets, although bronze ores, gold, and salt must have been imported. Since both bronze items and gold have been found in large numbers, the trade in these items must have been extensive.

A good example of a Scandinavian Bronze Age settlement is **Apalle**, located north of Stockholm, Sweden. Forty-five longhouses were uncovered at the site, all in excellent preservation. They were typically 15 to 20 meters long, roughly 5 meters

**Western European Late Bronze Age** (3300–2800 B.P.)

**Scandinavian Bronze Age** (3800–2500 B.P.)

**Northeastern European Bronze Age** (3800–2800 B.P.)

**Apalle** (Sweden, Scandinavian Bronze Age)

wide, and were internally divided into two or three rooms. One room in each long-house had a hearth, while another typically had a clay rather than wood floor and may have housed animals during the winter. Oxen and pigs are the dominant animal bones. Oxen were probably used as draft animals, while pigs were consumed. Locally made ceramics and bone and stone tools were found in abundance, along with moulds used in bronze casting and the remains of crucibles, suggesting bronze work took place at the site as well. Probably ten to twenty families occupied the site at any given time—perhaps fifty to one hundred people. They appear to have been largely self-sufficient, although they must have obtained bronze ingots from elsewhere, and so were tied into a larger sphere of trade.

**Caucasian Bronze Age (5600–3000 B.P.)**

In the Caucasus, peoples of the **Caucasian Bronze Age** (5600–3000 B.P.) lived in a variety of settlements, ranging from small agricultural hamlets to large towns. Mud-brick houses were common in steppe regions, while stone houses were built in highland areas. Along the Caspian plain, peoples built large and deep pit houses. Regardless of their location, Caucasian Bronze Age peoples were farmers and herders who relied on crops of wheat, barley, and millet, and on flocks of sheep, goats, cattle, and pigs for subsistence. Horses were also used, and may have been ridden or used as traction animals by Caucasian Bronze Age peoples. Plows, carts, and chariots were all used, and were drawn by either oxen or horses. Technology was simple and included both stone and bronze tools. Metalwork, however, became highly sophisticated, and Caucasian Bronze Age artisans created sophisticated bronze, gold, and silver ornaments, horse tack, and goblets, among other items. Ceramic artisans also produced fine wares of exceptional quality. While there is little evidence of social stratification in most of the Caucasus, there are extraordinarily rich burials in some areas (particularly in the south), suggesting the presence of powerful elites in some parts of the Caucasus.

## IRON AGE

The Iron Age is formally identified by the use of iron tools, often weapons initially and later agricultural and woodworking implements. The making of iron is a logical step beyond bronze for societies that have already made the transition from stone to metal. Iron is stonger, more durable, and more flexible than bronze. It is harder to transform from raw ore to cast object, particularly because iron does not usually come in ingots in the way that copper does. However, once obtained from ore, raw iron can be smelted, cast, and worked in much the same way as bronze, making the two technologies in many ways complementary. Iron lacks the visual appeal of bronze, which, when first cast, shines much like gold. Iron is dull by comparison, and it is perhaps for this reason that iron was rarely used to make ornaments or prestige objects. Rather, iron was used for tools, and its strength and durability made it uniquely suited for a particular class of tools—weapons.

**Northeastern European Iron Age (2800–1843 B.P.)**

Iron weaponry may have emerged as part of the endemic warfare characteristic of many Iron Age societies, including the **Northeastern European Iron Age** (2800–1843 B.P.) tradition, located in what is today Poland, the Czech Republic, Slovakia, Austria, Hungary, and the northern Balkans, and who were among the first people in Europe to adopt iron technology. Peoples of the Northeastern European Iron Age were agriculturalists who lived in fortified villages linked to regional centers, which apparently functioned as both central market places and as places of refuge in time of war. Typical agricultural villages were small, containing perhaps a dozen houses and perhaps 100 people. Larger centers were fortified with earthen ramparts, stone walls, or timber palisades (Figure 13.11). Craft specialists and merchants apparently resided at these centers and produced iron, bronze, ceramic, leather, and other goods in special workshops. Merchants traded these goods and agricultural products widely, including into the steppe regions and to the Mediterranean. Elites residing at these centers apparently controlled much of this trade and gained political power

FIGURE **13.11**

This artist's reconstruction of the hill fort at Klucov in eastern Germany illustrates the extensive fortifications that were built to defend Northern European Iron Age communities.

SOURCE: Barry Cunliffe (ed.), *The Oxford Illustrated Prehistory of Europe* (New York, NY: Oxford University Press, 1994), p. 478.

through the wealth they amassed. Elite status may have been tied to descent, but the emphasis on war also suggests that warriors were part of the elite class, and success or ability in war may have been a key element in creating and maintaining status and political power in Northeastern European Iron Age society.

Peoples of the **Scandinavian Iron Age** (2500–1500 B.P.) apparently also succumbed to warfare. Hill forts become common throughout the region, and a group of warrior-elites seem to have been the political leaders and may also have controlled the extensive trade to the south. The typical farmstead of the Scandinavian Iron Age consisted of one or more structures surrounded by a low stone wall. The primary, and sometimes only, structure was a longhouse built with a stone foundation, thick walls, and timber-frame roof. These were usually some 7 meters wide and 20 or more meters long. They had an internal division which is thought to have separated the family's living space, usually at the western end of the house, from the space where animals were kept in cold weather. Farmsteads were often solitary, but were also built in small hamlets of some three to five farmsteads. Both farmsteads and hamlets were located with access to good agricultural soils and forest lands. Hill forts appeared late in the Scandinavian Iron Age. These were walled and fortified strongholds located at the tops of easily defendable hills (thus the name "hill fort"). Within the defensive fortifications were a dozen or more houses, arranged along planned causeways that allowed easy movement within the fort.

The peoples of the Scandinavian Iron Age had mixed agricultural economy. They raised barley, rye, wheat, and other grains. They also kept sheep, pigs, goats, horses, and cattle. Cooler temperatures during the Iron Age apparently led to cattle and other livestock being kept indoors during at least part of the year, and this, in turn, forced people to raise and collect feed for their animals. Hunting and fishing remained

**Scandinavian Iron Age**
(2500–1500 B.P.)

important parts of the Iron Age economy, and it may have been that some individuals became specialists in these activities. A lively trade in animal furs, particularly reindeer, was ongoing with peoples to the south and, ultimately, with the Roman Empire. Who hunted these animals and prepared their furs and how those furs were collected and marketed is not well understood; however, it seems likely that some specialists were involved, and scholars have identified several apparent trade centers.

Despite the wealth of archaeological data, we have only an imperfect understanding of Scandinavian Iron Age sociopolitical organization. It seems clear from burials that there were both powerful warriors and chieftains and that the two, indeed, went hand-in-hand; thus we can envision a warrior-led political system. How this political system integrated the majority of the population, living in small and relatively autonomous farmsteads, is unclear; however, the presence of hill forts suggests that war, or the threat of war, was present, and that the warrior-leaders may have exercised authority only when war threatened. It has also been suggested that trade with polities to the south was controlled by these warrior-leaders, and that this control formed an additional basis for their authority.

Hoards of weapons and wealth items were deposited in bogs, streams, lakes, or in the ground. The reasons are not entirely clear, and may be as simple as hiding wealth in times of war. However, historical accounts suggest that at least some hoards were offerings to the gods following success in war. Similar sacrifices of wealth, animals, and humans were made to the gods both to encourage their action and to offer thanks for actions performed.

The wealth items given to the gods often were the products of artisans who, by late in the Scandinavian Iron Age tradition, produced some of the finest gold objects ever known (Figure 13.12). Among the more common gold items were large ornamental "collars" made from long gold tubes set parallel to one another and covered with filagree and human and animal figures, medallions with stamped designs and

FIGURE **13.12**
Examples of the magnificent gold items created by Scandinavian Iron Age artisans.

FIGURE **13.13**
Reconstruction of the city walls of Biskupin.

usually with a human profile in the center, and sword pommels decorated in a variety of styles and often incorporating semiprecious stones.

There was tremendous variation in burial rites during the Scandinavian Iron Age. Both cremation and inhumation were practiced, and variation in both forms existed. Within this variation two recurrent types are clear. One is the burial of a "warrior" with sword, spear, shield, and often other items (sometimes quite luxurious, and frequently imported from the Roman world). The other is the burial of a "chieftain," often in a monumental grave with a large volume of grave goods. Chieftains' grave goods were often luxurious imports from the south, such as Roman glass, bronze caldrons and vessels from Italy and Gaul, and even Roman coins and medallions.

Peoples of the **West-Central European Early Iron Age** (2800–2400 B.P.) tradition (who are often referred to as peoples of the Hallstatt culture) used iron plows to open up new areas to agriculture. Most people lived in small agricultural villages or hamlets that were widely dispersed across the landscape and were apparently linked to larger, fortified towns that served as regional political and economic centers. The site of **Biskupin** in northeastern Poland provides a remarkable picture of life in an Early Iron Age town (Figure 13.13). The site was located on the shores of a lake, but today it is buried in a peat bog that built up over the course of centuries. The peat preserved the site, and today whole buildings, wooden walkways, and birch-bark boats all exist intact. Biskupin was a relatively small town, covering about 1.5 hectares within a timber rampart and breakwater that encircled the town. Some fifty or more houses were within the fortifications. All the houses were remarkably similar—8 meters by 9 meters in size with an internal division separating a room housing animals from living quarters. The houses were built from logs and were roofed with thatch above an attic used for storage. Houses were laid out on a grid pattern, and caches of sling stones and arrows placed against the fortification walls suggest centralized planning in both the construction and defense of Biskupin.

**West-Central European Early Iron Age** (2800–2400 B.P.)

**Biskupin** (Poland, West-Central European Early Iron Age)

Warfare was apparently endemic among West-Central European Early Iron Age populations, and the defenses like those at Biskupin, with weapons cached and at the ready, are common. Also common are sites that suffered violent destruction (indeed Biskupin burned once, though whether that was due to war is unknown), are abandoned, and have burials of individuals with traumatic injuries. All these point to high levels of war. It would make sense in this situation to have leaders skilled in warfare, and that is precisely what burial evidence suggests. Elite burials during the West-Central European Iron Age are often stocked with weapons, armor, and other utensils of war. At the **Stična** site in Slovenia, for example, more than 140 burial mounds contain rich evidence of the importance of warfare to elite status. There elite burials include bronze armor and iron axes and spears, along with iron and bronze tack for war horses. These burials also include Etruscan ceramic and bronze items, providing clear evidence that an extensive trade system was also present which linked West-Central European elites to the rest of the European world.

During the West-Central European Late Iron Age and East-Central European Iron Age traditions, trade and interaction expanded, and became the center of life. The **East-Central European Iron Age** (2700–2050 B.P.) was centered around the Black Sea and the Balkans, an area which was colonized by Greeks and became a major area in trade from the Eurasian steppes to the Mediterranean world. According to the historian Heroditus, the Tracians, as the peoples of the East-Central European Iron Age were called, exported slaves in large numbers in return for Greek wine, olive oil, and craft goods. They lived in strictly hierarchical societies, with warrior elites at the top, craftspeople and merchants in the middle, and farmers at the bottom. Although Heroditus claims that the Tracians sold their children into slavery, it seems more likely, given the strong evidence of endemic warfare, that war captives were sold, and that acquiring slaves may have been a powerful factor behind war.

Endemic warfare meant that many agricultural settlements were destroyed and all were lightly constructed. Farmers raised crops of wheat and barley and kept sheep, goats, pigs, cattle, and horses. Over time more people seem to have become mobile herders, perhaps because the threat of war, and colonization by Greeks, meant that permanent settlement was impractical. The only permanent settlements of the East-Central European Iron Age appear to be fortified sites occupied by elites. In addition to being fortifications, these sites also served as centers of craft production and trade, and rather than being located in highly defensible positions or in places where the local populace could easily retreat in time of war, as was the case earlier, fortified sites appeared to be located along riverine trade routes.

The **West-Central European Late Iron Age** (2400–2033 B.P.) tradition is marked by the expansion across Western Europe of La Tène peoples, known to the Romans as the Celts. The Celts are thought to be the direct descendents of the Halstatt peoples, who expanded across Western Europe militaristically, both through their own conquest of neighboring societies and through mercenary work for Thracians and others in southern and eastern Europe fighting against Greek, Scythian, and Persian expansion (Figure 13.14). Most West-Central European Late Iron Age people lived in small agricultural villages of five to ten rectangular wattle-and-daub houses located within easy access to both fresh water and good agricultural land. They subsisted on plow agriculture and animal husbandry. Many people were engaged in cottage industries as well, and there was an extensive system of marketing these craft products. Items produced within farming villages included ceramics, bronze and iron tools and weapons, bronze and gold ornaments, and textiles. These were traded widely, and material from throughout Europe are found in West-Central European Late Iron Age contexts.

The peoples of both the West-Central European Late Iron Age and the East-Central European Iron Age were conquered by the Romans, who had been preceded in southeastern Europe by the Greeks. The Romans and Greeks left detailed

**Stična** (Slovenia, West-Central European Early Iron Age)

**East-Central European Iron Age** (2700–2050 B.P.)

**West-Central European Late Iron Age** (2400–2033 B.P.)

FIGURE **13.14**
Panel from a silver cauldron showing Celtic warriors.

records of the world they found in Europe at the time of conquest. According to the Greek ethnographer Posidonius (ca. 2135–2050 B.P.), Celtic society was divided into three classes: nobles, druids, and commoners. Nobles were political and military leaders who mobilized armies, conducted trade, and apparently maintained power within local areas by providing rich feasts and gifts to their followers. It is not clear whether nobility was ascribed at birth, as nobles apparently had to continually demonstrate their bravery, strength, and generosity.

The druids were essentially priests in Celtic society, but also served as judges, historians, and learned advisors (Figure 13.15). An important part of their role in society was to remember and interpret customary law and to maintain the record of Celtic history. In this way the druids had tremendous power, and they were closely

FIGURE **13.15**
Panel from a silver cauldron showing a druid.

allied to nobles whom they supported through legal decisions and recounting of historical occurrences in which nobles or their ancestors played important roles. For this reason nobles supported the druids, and they were free from taxation and military services and were allowed to move freely throughout Celtic lands. The movement and authority of the druids probably played a major role in the cultural uniformity that developed across the Celtic world.

Commoners were closely bound to individual nobles. Nobles provided commoners with protection from violence and the guarantee that they could stay on their lands to produce food. In return, the commoners offered nobles their support, tribute in the form of food and goods to maintain the noble household, and military service in time of conflict. There was great competition between nobles to acquire more commoner supporters. The more followers a noble had, the greater his prestige, and, perhaps more important, the greater the supply of goods and labor he could mobilize. Often such competition took the form of generous gifts or offers of protection, but competition between nobles could also turn violent, drawing commoners into a vicious cycle of internecine warfare. By around 2100 B.P. some nobles did succeed in completely subverting rivals, and these men emerged as the historic Celtic kings who struggled with the Romans over the control of Western Europe.

## THE EURASIAN STEPPE

I have separated off the cultures of the Eurasian steppe because in many ways they participated in a distinct evolutionary trajectory. The Eurasian steppe is a unique environment. Stretching from central Russia to western China, the steppe is a broad, open land of rolling hills and deep river valleys. Grasses dominate the flora, although forests grow in the river valleys. The steppe supported a wide variety of game, but was an inhospitable region for both gatherers and farmers. There was not enough diversity in plant foods to gather, and the deep roots of the grasses and general aridity of the region made farming difficult. Nomadic pastoralists and farmers whose livelihood depended in large part on cattle were the peoples who could take best advantage of the Eurasian steppelands, and it is they who evolved there.

**Kelteminar**
**(8000–4000 B.P.)**

The **Kelteminar** (8000–4000 B.P.) tradition represents the earliest Eurasian steppe peoples. The Kelteminar peoples lived in the area around the Aral sea and to the west as far as the Caspian sea. Kelteminar settlements were most frequently located on forested river terraces with access to both fish and steppe game animals. Settlements usually consisted of only a few houses, and had perhaps a total of 150 to 200 people in them. Houses were of two forms. The most common was a very large (80 to 150 or more square meters in area), rectangular structure made of a wood framework covered by matting. Multiple hearths were usually associated with these structures, and they are interpreted as having been multiple-family dwellings, probably associated with descent groups. In addition, smaller, semisubterranean dwellings were also present, often on the same sites as larger dwellings. These may have been winter or special-purpose residences, but no clear interpretation has been offered. The size of these settlements, and the possibility of both summer and winter dwellings, suggests they were permanent or semipermanent.

Kelteminar subsistence was based on hunting, fishing, and gathering. Remains of game animals from both the forest (deer and pig, for example) and steppe (auroch and gazelle, for example) are common. Waterfowl remains are also found in large quantities on some sites. Fish remains are found in great quantities on some sites, with the most common type being pike. Remains of a wide variety of gathered foods are also found on Kelteminar sites, including fruits, nuts, shellfish, and eggs.

Stone projectile points made from microblades were used for hunting. Scrapers based on microblades were used for working hides, and the blades themselves, probably hafted into a bone or wood handle, served as basic cutting tools. Bone was

FIGURE **13.16**
A modern yurt, probably very similar to those used by the Andronovo peoples.

also used for knives and scrapers. Fishing was done with nets and spears. The Kelteminar peoples used ceramics for storage and cooking. Globular forms with rounded bases were the most common ceramics. These were formed by coiling and finished by smoothing. Designs were incised or stamped into the paste, often employing parallel wavy or zigzag lines as basic design elements.

The Kelteminar peoples were followed by peoples of the **Andronovo** (4000–2800 B.P) tradition, who adopted cattle breeding as a primary base to subsistence, but retained a settled village lifestyle. Andronovo villages were located in fertile river valleys where crops such as wheat, millet, and rye could be raised, and near good pasturage for sheep, cattle, and horses. Many Andronovo villages were large, and may have been winter settlements for people who spent much of the summer pasturing herds on the steppe. For example, at **Atasuin** in central Kazakstan the remains of twenty-seven structures were recovered. The earliest were large, rectangular, semisubterranean dwellings, roughly 10 meters by 20 meters in size. Later structures were round, and probably represent large tents or **yurts** used by a single nuclear family (Figure 13.16). Structures were built around an open workspace that had both ceramic and bronze production areas. Bronze work appears to have been important at the site, and it appears that metalwork was a central activity. Bronze-working areas are a common feature at Andronovo sites, and must have played an important role in the economy.

One measure of the importance of bronze is the volume that is found in Andronovo burials. The Andronovo peoples built substantial mounds, called **kurgans,** under which important people were buried (Figure 13.17). Kurgans were often surrounded by stone slabs, and secondary burials were frequently added to the mound. For example, at the **Alakul** site in south-central Russia, some sixty-six mounds were constructed. Each had a central log-lined tomb which usually contained the remains of a man and woman, probably a married couple, and sacrificed horses and sheep. The grave goods included in these tombs varied widely, but it is clear that the death of particular individuals prompted Andronovo society to perform elaborate rituals and bury the individuals with great wealth. Some of the individuals buried in these central tombs appear to have been warrior-elites. As I noted in the last chapter, many pastoral socities have formal leaders because raiding by predators and other groups requires pastoralists to be able to mount a defense quickly. The central tombs in many Andronovo kurgans may reflect the emergence of such leaders.

To both the east and west of the Andronovo peoples, nomadic pastoralism developed. To the east was the Early Nomad tradition of Central Asia (discussed in

**Andronovo** (4000–2800 B.P.)

**Atasuin** (Kazakstan, Andronovo)

**Alakul** (Russia, Andronovo)

**Yurt:** a large domed tent constructed by covering a wooden framework with thick felt mats.

**Kurgans:** large conical burial mounds built by the peoples of the Eurasian steppe.

FIGURE **13.17**

The Pyat Bratya kurgan in the southern Ural steppes.

**Eurasian Steppe Nomad**
(6500–4000 B.P.)

**Boldyrevo** (Russia, Eurasian Steppe Nomad)

**Scythian**
(4000–1700 B.P.)

the next chapter), and to the west was the **Eurasian Steppe Nomad** (6500–4000 B.P.) tradition. The Eurasian Steppe Nomad peoples practiced nomadic pastoralism of sheep, goats, and cattle and used horses as a basic means of transportation. Hunting remained important for most Eurasian Steppe Nomads, and some groups also planted wheat and millet. They also appear to have been more mobile than Andronovo peoples, and the only form of housing that has been identified is the yurt. Like the Andronovo peoples, the Eurasian Steppe Nomads are best known by their burial mounds or kurgans. At **Boldyrevo** in central Russia, for example, a large number of kurgans are present. Those that have been excavated contain a central pit with a ledge, upon which a timber roof was lain. Burials were placed into these pits, covered with red ochre, and provided with widely varying amounts of grave goods. The differences in grave accompaniments has been suggested to be a reflection of social role or status.

The **Scythian** (4000–1700 B.P.) tradition represents the culmination of the nomadic pastoral life on the Eurasian steppes. The Scythians were not only well known for their complex political organization and ability to field large, mobile armies, but also for their exquisite skills in metalwork. The Scythians were nomads throughout most of their range, and their settlements were, in most cases, short-term and impermanent. There is evidence of more long-term settlement, perhaps winter encampments, in river valley locations, and there are some unique fortified sites that may have been gathering places, political centers, or pure fortifications during times of war. These more sedentary and fortified sites appear to be restricted to the northern and western forested regions of the Scythian tradition. Settlements in these regions tended to be located on hilltops near rivers and good agricultural land.

The Scythians primarily lived in hide tents or felt yurts, similar to those still in use by Eurasian nomads. These were carried in ox-drawn wagons, apparently fully assembled in some cases, then removed to the ground when the group and its herds came to a halt. Some wagons apparently had wooden structures built upon them, and these may have served as houses themselves. In the northern and western forested areas of the Scythian tradition there is evidence of more permanent housing in the form of rectangular, wood-framed, semisubterranean dwellings.

The Scythian economy was based on the breeding of cattle, sheep, goats, and horses. The Scythians relied on all these animals for milk, hides, and meat. Milk was

FIGURE **13.18**
A magnificent silver vase made by a Scythian artisan. Note the quiver of arrows and compound bow at the figure's side.

drunk fresh and made into butter and cheese. Hides were tanned both with and without fir, and wool was both spun and felted. Meat from all these animals was eaten, but based on remains found in kurgans (which may only reflect ceremonial occasions), horse was preferred above all the rest. Some Scythian groups, particularly in the northern reaches of the Scythian tradition, also raised crops of grain such as wheat, barley, millet, and oats; legumes such as lentils, peas, and beans; and roots such as radish and onion. These were planted in gardens that were likely not tended carefully, but rather were left to grow following spring planting and then harvested in the late summer or fall when the group returned from summer pastures, perhaps to set up winter encampments in the river valleys.

The Scythians were both great artisans and expert craftsmen. They employed wood, bone, ceramic, and metal with equal ability. While many items used daily by the Scythians were likely made by the individuals or family members of those who used them, the great craftsmanship demonstrated in some items strongly suggests the presence of formal artisans or craft specialists, particularly in metalwork (Figure 13.18).

Scythians used a variety of utensils in daily life. Among these were handmade and pit-fired ceramics decorated by cord marking and incising. A variety of ceramic forms were used, including globular vessels, often flat-bottomed, amphorae, and jars. Bronze cauldrons were used for cooking, and bronze was used extensively for other utensils as well, including knives, axes, and weapons. Key utensils for the Scythians were the tack used for horses—bridles, saddles, harnesses—as well as for carts and wagons. The remains of wagons found in kurgans, along with toy wagons fashioned from clay, suggest the Scythians used a variety of designs, from ones with large, covered frameworks that would have been like moving houses, to ones that apparently could be completely dismantled and carried on horseback over difficult terrain.

The Scythians also had a sophisticated tool kit for hunting and war. Their primary weapon for both was the bow and arrow. Bows were composite and powerful (see Figure 13.18). Arrows were armed with bronze points, often barbed, and were apparently sometimes poisoned. Long lances, armed with large bronze blades, were also used when on horseback. When on foot, bronze swords and daggers were used. The Scythians developed a variety of metal and leather armor for both themselves and, to a lesser extent, their horses for use in war, and they used wood and bronze or iron shields as well.

In addition to their tools, tack, and weapons, the Scythians produced some of the most exquisite personal ornaments in all of human history (Color Plate 18). These range from simple gold rings to entire suits of what is essentially gold mail. Decoration often depicted scenes from daily life and the world of the steppe—animals, hunting, horse training, war, and the like. Designs were often not simply engraved or embossed on an item, but rather the item would itself be formed as a three-dimensional figure. For example, the handle of a bronze dagger might take the form of a ram's body with the back legs forming the hilt and the head forming the pommel.

Some of the materials produced by Scythian artisans were traded, but an important trade in pastoral products existed as well. Trade routes crisscrossed the Scythian world, and the Scythians were apparently eager participants in it. By the middle of the tradition they were actively trading with Greek colonies in the Black Sea region as well as with peoples to the east, making ties as far as East Asia. Precious metals and textiles were an important part of this trade, but grain, milk products, meat, wool, hides, and other bulk goods, along with animals themselves, were also extensively traded.

The Scythians were apparently a clan-based society, likely patrilineal. Both primogeniture and age seems to have played a role in social status, and Scythian society was apparently divided into three hereditary classes as well: nobility, middle class, and commoner. The burials in large kurgans attest to the fact that the nobility had access to extreme wealth and could assemble labor not only for the building of these large tombs but also for feasts and sacrifices that surrounded their interment. Historical documents report that the Scythians had powerful hereditary political leaders who are typically referred to as kings, but who, in practice, seem to have acted more like powerful chiefs.

War became a central feature of Scythian life early on, and it continued to be a focal point of life throughout the tradition. Scythian warfare is well described by the literate adversaries they fought, particularly the Greeks. Scythians attacked on horseback, using much-feared barbed and poisoned arrows first, lances as they came closer to their enemies, and finally a combination of long and short swords for hand-to-hand combat. Scythian warriors took heads or scalps as trophies, and these apparently brought great social prestige to their bearers.

## ◉ SUMMARY

The prehistory of Europe was the basis for nineteenth-century evolutionary schemes, which theorized that technological change drove changes in social and political organization. It is easy to see why. Sedentarism arrives with the arrival of ceramics and domesticated plants and animals. Social stratification appears when bronze does. The appearance of iron sees the appearance of centralized polities. Those who achieved these technological milestones first, like the peoples of Southeastern Europe, were seen as leaders in a progressive march toward civilization. Unfortunately, the scheme does not actually work, for during all these periods of change there is diversity in European society, and indeed, the lifestyle of most individuals probably did not change drastically from the Neolithic period through the Iron Age.

There are, however, broad patterns of change that followed a similar pattern across the entire continent. Painted in broad strokes, the prehistory of Europe looks something like the following. During the last Ice Age humans lived a mobile life following migrating herds of big-game animals across the European continent. As the ice age ended and more plant and forest resources became available, people turned to more broad-spectrum hunting and gathering, often within fairly restricted territories. Resources available to some groups even allowed them to become semisedentary. Domesticates were introduced to Europe from the Near East, and with them settled, agricultural life began. Ceramics were manufactured to carry water and to store and perhaps cook harvested plant and animal products. Microlithic stone tool industries were adopted to make more efficient use of stone, which became less accessible once sedentary lifestyles predominated. Copper, bronze, and later iron industries were developed, and along with them, elites and centralized polities. Whether control of metalworking techniques, raw material sources, or trade were key to the rise of elites and political centralization is unclear, but there do seem to be connections. Warfare and conquest also seem to have developed along with metalworking and political centralization, culminating in the rise of the Roman Empire and the conquest of much of the European continent.

## ✪ DISCUSSION QUESTIONS

1. How are Eastern and Western Europe different in their cultural histories? How are they similar? What might account for these similarities and differences?

2. In what ways did environment affect cultural evolution in different areas of prehistoric Europe?

3. In what ways did technology affect cultural evolution in different areas of prehistoric Europe?

## ✪ ESSAY QUESTIONS

1. Reflect on the organization of this chapter into technological periods rather than geographic areas. How does the focus on technology influence or change your understanding of the prehistory of Europe?

2. Here and elsewhere in the book I have relied on written documents to augment the archaeological record. For most of the prehistory of Europe, however, there are no written documents. What types of information might we be missing by only being able to examine the material remains of prehistoric European life? What information might be gained if we had written documents? How does the lack of this information affect our understanding of European prehistory?

3. Compare and contrast the origins, spread, and use of metal in Europe and Africa. How were metals used? How did they spread from one society to another? How did the invention of metalwork affect cultural evolution on the two continents?

## ✦ RESEARCH PROJECT

War seems to have played an important role in European societies, particularly in the Bronze and Iron Ages. We have seen in previous chapters that war has played an important role in many other world areas, particularly in chiefdoms and states. Choose two world areas and undertake research on ancient war in those areas. Examine both theoretical discussions and regional or site reports documenting prehistoric warfare. What effects, both positive and negative, has war had on prehistoric cultures in these areas?

## ⊙ KEY SOURCES

### Mesolithic

Cullen, 1995; Dickson, 2001; Haeussler, 1996, 2001; Milliken, 2001; Peterkin, Bricker, and Mellars, 1993; Runnels, 1995; van Andel and Sutton, 1987; Zvelevbil, 1986.

### Neolithic

Barker, 1985; Barnett, 2001; Bogucki, 1988; Champion et al., 1984; Gregg, 1988; Hodder, 1990; Howell, 1983; Kiguradze, 2001b; Lillios, 2001; Mallory, 1989; Milisauskas, 2001; Milisauskas and Kruk, 1989; Mohen, 1990; Prescott, 2001; Price, 2000; Renfrew, 1983; Scarre, 1983; Sherratt, 1994, 1997; Sulimirski, 1968, 1970; Whittle, 1985, 1996; Zvelebil, 1986.

### Bronze Age

Alexander, 1972; Bailey and Panayotov, 1995; Barker, 1985; Briard, 1979; Chadwick, 1970; Champion et al., 1984; Chernykh, 1992; Coles and Harding, 1979; Davies, 1992; Dickinson, 1994; Fernandez Castro, 1995; Galaty, 2001; Gheorghiu, 2001a, 2001b; Greenfield, 2001; Harding, 1983, 1994; Kiguradze, 2001a; Kohl, 2001; Kovács, 1977; Kristiansen, 1987; Kushnareva, 1997; Mantu, Dumitroaia, and Tsaravopoulos, 1997; Marinescu-Bilcu, 1981; Milisauskas, 1978; Murray, 2001; Peltenburg, 1989; Renfrew, 1997; Rutter, 1993; Shelmerdine, 1997; Shennan, 1993; Sorensen and Thomas, 1989; Sulimirski, 1970; Thrane, 2001; Wells, 1984.

### Iron Age

Arnold, B., 2001; Arnold and Gibson, 1995; Boardman, 1999; Collins, 1997; Cunliffe, 1994, 1997; Frere, 1987; Green, M., 1995; Hedeager, 1992; Hoddinott, 1981; Kristiansen, 1984, 1998; Taylor, 1994, 2001a, 2001b; Todd, 1992; Wells, 1980, 1981, 1984.

### Eurasian Steppe

Basilov, 1989; Dolukhanov, 1986; Frumkin, 1970; Kuzmina, 2001; Matyushin, 1986; Melyukova, 1990; Okladnikov, 1990; Rice, 1961; Rolle, 1980; Shishlina, 2001.

## STAR CARR

The Mesolithic is a period of transition from subsistence based primarily on hunting large game animals to one focused on a wider range of animal and plant species. Across Europe people began this transition at the end of the last ice age, about 11,000 years ago. Average temperatures rose across Europe and with that conifer and deciduous forests spread. Deer, elk, boar, and other smaller forest-dwelling animals replaced Pleistocene megafauna and the large herds of reindeer and horses that roamed the glacial plains of Europe. Star Carr is a very famous site situated in northeastern England. Star Carr was discovered in 1947 by an amateur archaeologist and then excavated by Graham Clark from 1949 through 1951. A team led by Paul Mellars re-excavated it starting in 1999. The new team also did extensive field surveys and excavated test pits. A parallel program of high-resolution pollen and sedimentological studies was undertaken by Dr. S.P. Dark. Calibration of radiocarbon dates shows that Star Carr occupation spans about 350 years, c. 10,700–10,350 B.P.

### WEB ACTIVITY

These new investigations at Star Carr are aimed at placing this site in the wider context of later Upper Paleolithic and early Mesolithic occupation of the former Lake Pickering. Studies of lithics, pollen, and other ecological factors are leading modern archaeologists to various conclusions about this site. Aside from its long-term occupation, it is apparent that the occupants used fire for brush control to easily gain access to the lake. Recent findings also show a 6-meter-long worked-wood platform. This platform was placed to provide easy access from dry land to the lake. Found in association with this platform are lithic artifacts and worked red deer antlers. In this activity, you will view a map of Star Carr and artifacts recently found at this famous site.

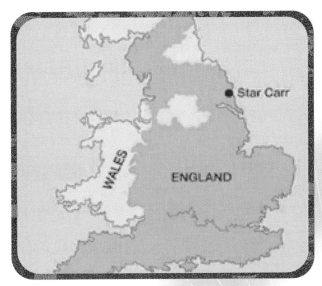

The Media Lab can be found in Chapter 13 on the *Companion Website*™ http://www.prenhall.com/peregrine

### Activity

1. View the video. What types of artifacts are shown? What do they tell us about the people of the Western European Mesolithic?

2. What was the environment like at Star Carr ca. 10,000 B.P.? How do archaeologists make these determinations? How are ecological and environmental knowledge of past environments useful to us today?

3. How does Star Carr fit into the Western European Mesolithic as discussed in Chapter 13?

# chapter fourteen

# East Asia and Oceania

### Holocene Food Collectors

---

### Food Production and Complex Societies in East Asia

---

### Colonization of the Pacific

---

**BOXES**

**Anyang**

**Easter Island**

East Asia refers to the Asian landmass to the south of Siberia and east of the Tibetan Plateau and Taklamakan Desert. The area is environmentally diverse, ranging from the vast loess plateau of northern China to the great river valleys of central China to the mountainous tropical forests of Southeast Asia (Figure 14.1). Oceania refers to Australia, New Guinea, and the islands of the Pacific, and, again, the area is environmentally diverse (Figure 14.2). While Australia and New Guinea are huge land masses, the islands of the Pacific are often tiny, and while flora and fauna that were established in the Paleocene are found in Australia and New Guinea, the Pacific islands were inhabited only by recent chance colonizers until humans arrived.

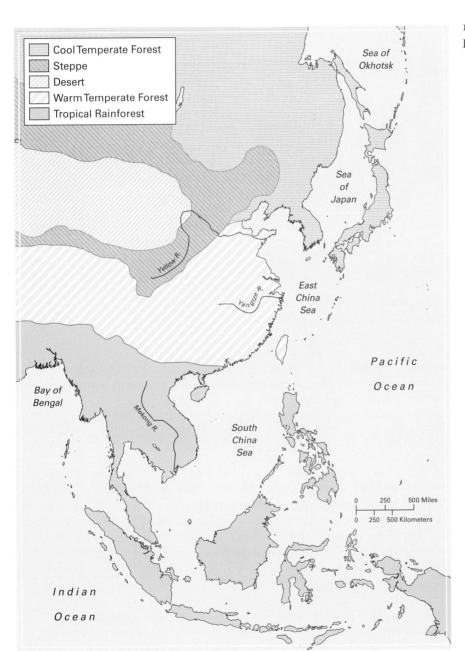

FIGURE **14.1**

Environments of East Asia.

It should be clear that East Asia and Oceania are as environmentally and culturally diverse as any region of the world, and the region's prehistory is no less varied (Figure 14.3). To give coherence to the diversity presented in this chapter, I find it useful to divide the prehistory of East Asia and Oceania into three broad categories: (1) Holocene food collectors; (2) food producers and complex societies

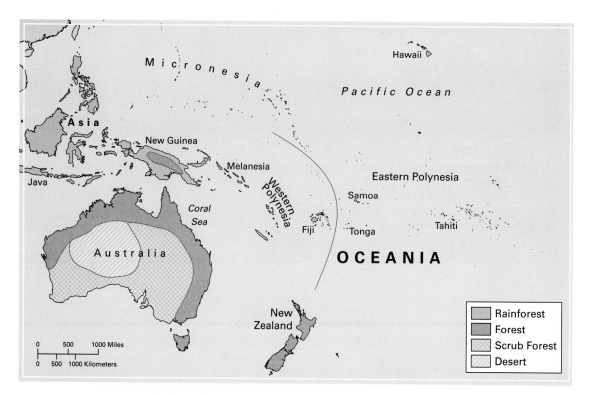

FIGURE **14.2**
Environments of Oceania.

of East Asia; and (3) the peoples of Oceania. Each of these categories blends into the others, but each also contains a set of common elements and, to some extent, a history of cultural development.

## HOLOCENE FOOD COLLECTORS

Lifestyles based on food collection did not end in East Asia and Oceania with the end of the Upper Paleolithic era. Like other places on earth, the end of the Upper Paleolithic saw significant environmental changes. In East Asia one of the most significant changes was the rise in ocean levels, which flooded large areas of land and forced many populations to relocate and to change their patterns of seasonal movement. Climate also changed as the region slowly warmed to present conditions, and rainfall appears to have increased. Broadleaf forests moved northward, and tropical forests expanded. The range of edible plants, especially those bearing nuts and fruits, expanded tremendously. However, the large game animals of the Upper Paleolithic were replaced with smaller game animals, and hunting took on lesser importance.

**Jomon**
**(12,000–2500 B.P.)**

In Japan, the **Jomon** (12,000–2500 B.P.) tradition followed the Upper Paleolithic era. Peoples of the Jomon tradition were broad-spectrum hunters and gatherers who lived in seasonal camps and small pit house villages. Pit houses in these villages were arranged in a horseshoe pattern around a central plaza that often served as a burial ground. Pit houses themselves were a meter or more deep, circular in form, and roofed with a wood superstructure covered with thatch or matting. Most villages appear to have been used over long periods of time, with hundreds of overlapping pit houses. At **Sannai-Maruyama** on Honshu Island, for example, more than 500 pit houses were uncovered. Most scholars think that only a handful of these would have been occupied at any given time, perhaps five or six at most, but the large

**Sannai-Maruyama**
**(Japan, Jomon)**

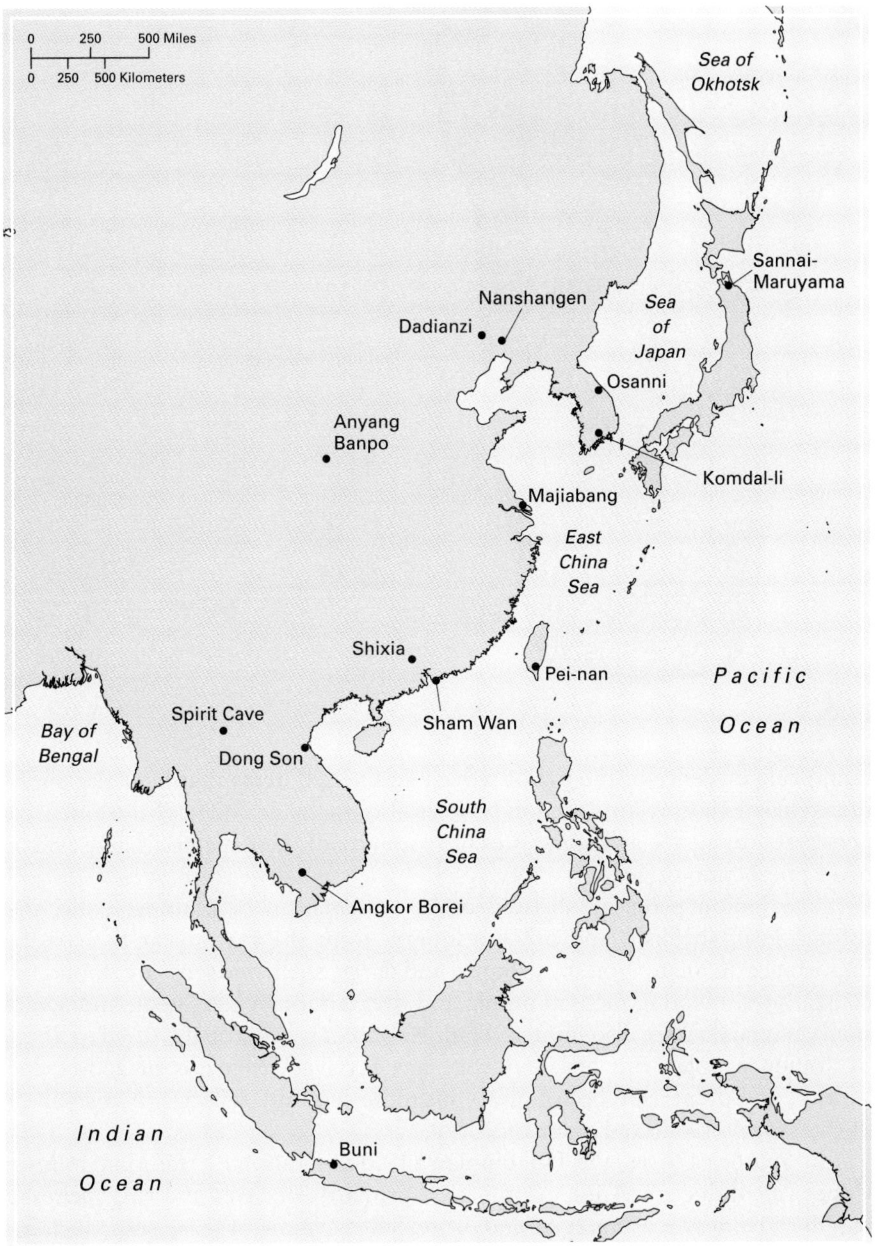

FIGURE **14.3**
Sites mentioned in Chapter 14.

number of these dwellings attests to long-term use of the site. Long-term use of the Sannai-Maruyama site is also evidenced by burials. More than 100 adult and 700 infant burials have been recovered. Jomon burials here, as elsewhere, were placed in formal cemetery areas adjacent to the settlement. Individuals were buried in pits, usually without grave goods, while infants were buried in ceramic urns.

Ceramics were developed early in the Jomon tradition, and the name of the tradition itself means "cord mark," which is the predominant form of decoration on these ceramics (Figure 14.4). Jomon ceramics are found in a wide variety of forms, but all share some type of cord-marked decoration. Other tools used by Jomon peoples included a wide variety of core and flake stone tools, ground and chipped stone azes, and ground stone querns, among many others. Early Jomon projectile points were relatively large and were probably used to arm spears. By the middle of the tradition small projectile points appeared, suggesting the adoption of the bow and arrow. At Sannai-Maruyama the remains of a woven bag and matting offer

FIGURE **14.4**
A Jomon vase. Note the intricate designs, including cord marking.

Hoabinhian
(10,000–4000 B.P.)

Spirit Cave (Thailand, Hoabinhian)

tantalizing evidence of the use of woven and netted items that have not survived in the archaeological record. Jomon peoples also used jade and nephrite extensively for personal ornaments, and some sites near sources of these materials give evidence for mass production of beads.

The Jomon peoples subsisted on a combination of hunting, collecting, and fishing. Fish, shellfish, and other resources from the sea appear to have been of importance to many Jomon groups, and large shell middens are found at most coastal sites. Hunting focused on pig and deer, although bear, goat, and a variety of small mammals were also hunted. Plant resources were probably used in abundance by Jomon peoples, but little evidence has survived. Remains of acorn, chestnut, walnut, and plum have been found, but these certainly reflect only a small portion of the range of collected plant foods.

In Southeast Asia, the **Hoabinhian** (10,000–4000 B.P.) tradition followed the Upper Paleolithic era. These people lived primarily in caves and rockshelters, probably located near seasonally abundant resources. Some of these sites, such as **Spirit Cave** in northwest Thailand, were regularly occupied over thousands of years. Spirit Cave overlooks the Khong valley and was surrounded by tropical forests, probably much like those in the region today. Other cave sites are in similar locations, providing a good view of the surroundings, easy access to water, and access to a range of hunting and gathering areas. Spirit Cave and similar sites were probably occupied seasonally. The size of the main habitation area at Spirit Cave, some 10 meters by 7 meters, suggests these sites were occupied by small bands of only five to ten people, probably a single nuclear or extended family.

The Hoabinhian peoples hunted both large and small mammals and gathered a wide variety of plant foods. At Spirit Cave the remains of wild cattle and buffalo, deer, and a variety of small mammals, reptiles, and birds were found. Plant remains included a variety of nuts, legumes, cucurbits, and gourds. Along the coasts, Hoabinhian peoples made extensive use of ocean resources. The tools used by Hoabinhian peoples seems relatively crude. Stone tools include large, flaked cobbles and worked flakes. It is likely that these tools were used only for cutting or crushing very hard materials, and that bamboo, bone, and shell were used for most cutting and scraping tools.

# FOOD PRODUCTION AND COMPLEX SOCIETIES IN EAST ASIA

The first food producers in East Asia were located in southeast China. The region has a tropical climate with high levels of precipitation and humidity. Its topography is rugged, with rivers dissecting deep valleys as they run from the inland plains through coastal mountains to the sea. The region's dense woodlands and tropical rain forests hold a great variety of animals, from primates to carnivores to large game animals.

Peoples of the **Southeast China Early Neolithic** (9000–5500 B.P.) may be among the earliest agriculturalists in the world. While few plant remains have been reported, the presence of hoes and what appear to be digging stick weights makes gardening likely for most Early Neolithic communities, especially in the coastal region. The bones of domesticated pigs have been found in some Early Neolithic deposits. Much more plentiful, however, are the remains of wild game such as deer and boar, in addition to fish, shellfish, and turtles. The Southeast China Early Neolithic peoples were also the first in the region to make ceramics. These were thick, grit-tempered wares, fired at low temperature. Most were cord marked, and they often had incised geometric designs around the rim. Cords were likely used for fishing lines and nets as well. Hunting was done with spears armed with bone, chipped stone, or slate points. Chipped stone was also used for cutting and scraping tools. Ground stone adzes and axes were used for working wood, and polished scythes, hoes, and grinding slabs were used for producing, collecting, and processing plant foods.

Caves were a primary settlement location for these peoples, but open coastal and riverine sites are also found, and these may have been used seasonally for fishing and collecting shellfish. Caves were often selected because of their access to both fresh water and woodlands. While some of the caves are large, it is likely that no more than several families shared them; thus communities were likely on the order of thirty to fifty people. No evidence of freestanding structures or dwellings have been reported. With such small communities and a semisedentary lifestyle, it is likely that the Southeast China Early Neolithic peoples were both egalitarian and acephalous. Numerous burials have been found, and these do not indicate social stratification. It is likely the primary social and political unit was the family.

Peoples of the **Southeast China Late Neolithic** (5500–2500 B.P.) tradition were the first in East Asia to develop sedentary agricultural communities. During this tradition rice agriculture became more important and, combined with fishing and some hunting, developed into a subsistence regime that has persisted in some areas to the modern era (Figure 14.5). At the **Shixia** site in Guangdong province, remains of rice were found in storage and cooking pits dating to slightly before 5000 B.P. The peoples of Shixia apparently used rice fairly intensively, although hunted and gathered foods were still very important. Elsewhere, domesticates were not as important. For example, the peoples of the **Sham Wan** site in Hong Kong apparently subsisted on marine resources, and may not have used domesticates at all.

Both the Shixia and Sham Wan sites are relatively extensive in area, but this likely comes from repeated use over time. Most Southeast China Late Neolithic communities were probably small, on the order of fifty to one hundred people. People appear to have lived in small, circular wattle-and-daub houses, but evidence is not well preserved and no clear housing or community patterns are known. The Southeast China Late Neolithic peoples had a relatively simple tool kit, which included distinctive complex stamped ceramics. Some of these ceramics, particularly from late in the tradition, show enough regularity and sophistication in their manufacture that some archaeologists have suggested they were made by craft specialists. There is clear evidence of craft specialization in stone and jade work, from which finely carved ornaments were made. Items of daily use, such as chipped and polished stone tools, shell and bone implements, and woven items and cordage, were made by individual households for their own use.

**Southeast China Early Neolithic**
(9000–5500 B.P.)

**Southeast China Late Neolithic**
(5500–2500 B.P.)

**Shixia**
(China, Southeast China Late Neolithic)

**Sham Wan**
(China, Southeast China Late Neolithic)

FIGURE **14.5**
Modern rice fields in southern China reflect a subsistence regime going back to the Southeast China Late Neolithic tradition.

There is some evidence of social stratification among the Southeast China Late Neolithic peoples. At the cemetery at Shixia, for example, there seem to have been two distinct types of burials. The most complex were secondary inhumations placed in large graves with abundant grave goods, including some finely made items of stone and jade. After interment the burial pits were apparently burned, and then covered with soil. These are interpreted as burials of elites. The far more common, type of burial was a simple pit inhumation, often lacking grave goods. Because many of the more complex graves contained ritual objects, archaeologists have speculated that these individuals may have been important ritual practitioners.

## Southeast Asia

**Southeast Asia Neolithic and Early Bronze**
(6500–2500 B.P.)

**Pei-nan**
(Taiwan, Southeast Asia Neolithic and Early Bronze)

In areas adjacent to Southeast China a similar subsistence regime combining rice agriculture with fishing and hunting was also developed. Peoples of the **Southeast Asia Neolithic and Early Bronze** (6500–2500 B.P.) tradition adopted rice agriculture from China and began living in settled agricultural communities. Unfortunately, very little from this tradition has been preserved in the archaeological record apart from burials. The only known village is **Pei-nan** in southeastern Taiwan. Pei-nan was a village that covered an area of about 8 hectares. It consisted of two terrace-like alignments of houses, each constructed of dry-laid stone and roughly 6 meters by 12 meters in size. Behind each house was a series of smaller storehouses. Each house held a single family, and the storehouses probably held the rice and millet produced in the family's fields. Burials were placed in stone-lined crypts beneath the house floors, and many individuals were buried with extensive grave goods. The picture we get from Pei-nan, of a large agricultural village composed of numerous independent family farmers, is probably representative of most Southeast Asia Neolithic and Early Bronze communities.

**Island Southeast Asia Late Prehistoric**
(2500–1500 B.P.)

By the Late Prehistoric period a clear separation had emerged in Southeast Asia between those living in the islands of Malaysia and Indonesia and the Philippines and those living on the mainland. The **Island Southeast Asia Late Prehistoric** (2500–1500 B.P.) peoples focused on fish and rice and developed a complex trade network that moved both foodstuffs and other goods throughout the region and to

China and India. They lived in a wide variety of communities and under a similar variety of political systems. A typical site from the Island Southeast Asia Late Prehistoric tradition is **Buni,** on the northwest coast of Java. Buni was a village of rice agriculturalists who lived in houses built on wooden piles thrust into estuarine mud. They made extensive use of fish, but rice was the staple of the diet. Trade was also important for the people of Buni, and materials from mainland Southeast Asia, China, and India, as well as ceramics, stone tools, bronze and iron tools, and other items from elsewhere in Island Southeast Asia were all found at the site. Indeed it is this reliance on rice, fish, and trade that best characterizes the lifestyle of the Island Southeast Asia Late Prehistoric peoples.

**Buni** (Java, Island Southeast Asia Late Prehistoric)

The **Mainland Southeast Asia Late Prehistoric** (2500–1500 B.P.) peoples continued to rely on hunting and gathering as a supplement to rice agriculture. They lived in what appear to be small and diffuse communities that were linked into increasingly complex political systems—political systems which ultimately evolved into the classical civilizations of Southeast Asia. A typical village of this tradition might be **Dong Son,** located along the Ma river in northern Vietnam. The site's location made it a natural trade entrepôt, as people moving goods from the mountains to the sea and back could easily sail up the Ma river. The site is also located on rich alluvial soils which would have been excellent for wet rice agriculture. Both trade and agriculture were vital to the residents of Dong Son. Among the many trade items found were both Chinese and local bronzes (drums, vases, figurines, tools, and weapons) and various Han Chinese materials, including coins. Food production is evidenced by the presence of various locally made agricultural tools and ceramics, as well as abundant bones of water buffalo and pig. The peoples of Dong Son lived in woven mat-and-thatch houses built on wooden stilts above flood level. Dong Son appears to have been a thriving agricultural and trade community, much like many larger rural communities in Southeast Asia today.

**Mainland Southeast Asia Late Prehistoric** (2500–1500 B.P.)

**Dong Son** (Vietnam, Mainland Southeast Asia Late Prehistoric)

Some people of the Mainland Southeast Asia Late Prehistoric tradition, however, lived in very large communities that have been called cities. These urban places are associated with temples and elite residences, and must have been both political and religious centers. One such center is the site of **Angkor Borei,** located in the Mekong delta of Cambodia. Angkor Borei was a very large community, covering an area of roughly 300 hectares and completely enclosed by a wall and ditch fortification. At the center of the enclosed area was a large complex of temples and elite residences, which were the center for a polity that was called the "Kingdom of Funan" in Chinese records. Beyond its role as a religious and political center, Angkor Borei was also a manufacturing and trade center. Ceramics were mass-produced at the site and used throughout the polity. Canals led from Angkor Borei to numerous nearby communities as well as to a large ocean trading center 90 kilometers away (Figure 14.6). These canals allowed easy travel and trade between Angkor Borei and other areas of the polity. The image we get is of a small, well-integrated state of a kind that probably dotted Southeast Asia before Chinese, Indian, and European conquest of the region.

**Angkor Borei** (Cambodia, Mainland Southeast Asia Late Prehistoric)

## Northern China

Northern China is dominated by a vast loess plateau. The area consists of rolling hills and broad tablelands cut by rivers flowing through rich loess soils. The climate is variable, with cold and dry winters and hot and wet summers. The annual precipitation is about 500 mm, with most of the rain falling in the summer. Much of the area is covered in grasslands, but alluvial valleys and other areas contain hardwood forests.

In northern China the move from hunting and gathering to food production was also made. Peoples of the **Peiligang** (8500–6200 B.P.) tradition were the first agriculturalists in the region. They raised millet, pigs, and chickens in the rich

**Peiligang** (8500–6200 B.P.)

FIGURE **14.6**

An extensive canal system connected the Mainland Southeast Asia Late Prehistoric site of Ankor Borei with other important sites in the Lower Mekong valley.

SOURCE: Charles Higham, *The Archaeology of Mainland Southeast Asia from 10,000 B.C. to the Fall of Angkor* (Cambridge: Cambridge University Press, 1989), p. 246. Reprinted with the permission of Cambridge University Press.

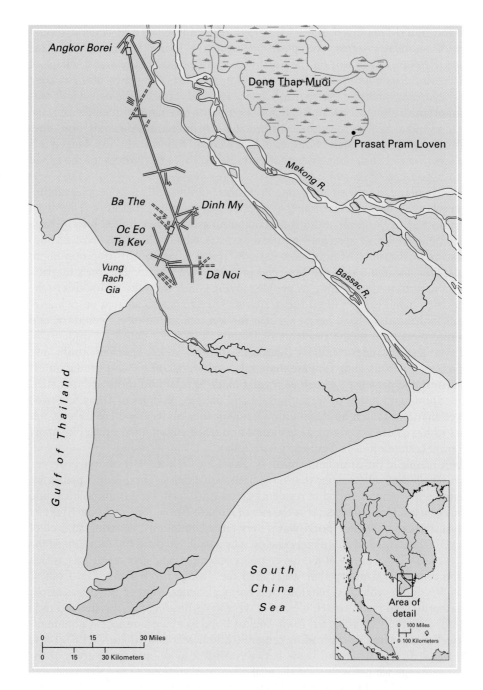

alluvial plains of the Yellow River valley and expanded agriculture out into the North China plains. Communities appear to have been extensive (10,000 to 20,000 square meters in surface area), but archaeological deposits from these communities are relatively shallow. Houses were typically small, round, and semisubterranean, with plastered floors containing a hearth and associated storage pits. They were too small to house anything larger than a single family.

Peiligang technology was simple. Ground stone tools were the most common and included axes, hoes, serrated scythes, and distinctive rectangular mortars with four legs. A microlithic industry was also present, and microliths apparently were used as cutting and scraping tools, and perhaps to arm arrow shafts. More common were arrows and harpoons armed with bone points, and bone was used for a variety of other tools as well. Ceramics were handmade and fired in low-temperature kilns.

Red and brown slipped wares were common, and their decoration showed tremendous variation. Common ceramic forms included two-handled, narrow-necked jars and deep, tripod-footed bowls.

Peoples of the subsequent **Hongshan** (7000–4500 B.P.) tradition raised wheat, millet, pigs, sheep, and cattle. They were the first in the region to use plows, and were able to cultivate the soils and thus settle in a wider range of locations across North China than their predecessors. The Hongshan peoples lived in agricultural villages scattered across the landscape. These villages consisted of 50 to 100 small, semisubterranean dwellings, which were densely concentrated in one area and surrounded by a ditch, perhaps to alleviate flooding. Each dwelling was only large enough for a nuclear family, so the population of these villages must have been on the order of 200 to 300 people.

The Hongshan peoples also constructed ceremonial mound centers and burial grounds. These centers included large stone-mounded tombs, stone-faced platforms, and stone circles. While interpreting the meaning of these constructions is pure speculation, some archaeologists have suggested that the combination of square and round constructions reflects the later division between earth (square) and heaven (round), pointing to rituals where humans attempted to create or strengthen bonds between heaven and earth. Some of the stone-mounded tombs constructed by Hongshan peoples were elaborate, suggesting an elite class of individuals was present. Since these individuals were buried at ceremonial centers, and communities show little in the way of social differentiation, archaeologists have suggested these elites may have had important roles in religious practices.

Social differentiation continued in the **Early Xiajiadian** (4500–3600 B.P.) tradition, in which a three-tiered settlement hierarchy was established. At the top of this hierarchy were large, fortified sites like **Dadianzi**, located on a flat hilltop in Inner Mongolia. Dadianzi has a fortification wall roughly 3 meters high and made of **tamped earth** faced with stone (Figure 14.7). Outside the wall is a ditch 8 meters wide and 3 meters deep. Within the walls is a roughly rectangular space within which are the remains of circular, semisubterranean houses built of mud brick and stone. Dadianzi apparently served as the center for a regional polity that included numerous smaller fortified villages and agricultural hamlets or farmsteads.

**Hongshan**
(7000–4500 B.P.)

**Early Xiajiadian**
(4500–3600 B.P.)

**Dadianzi** (China, Early Xiajiadian)

**Tamped earth:** a method of making walls in China, where earth is pounded into a mould made by two parallel boards that are raised as the walls grow higher.

FIGURE **14.7**
Constructing a raised tamped-earth floor. The logs serve as a form to hold the earth in place while it is compacted using a heavy tamper.

The Early Xiajiadian peoples were agriculturalists who raised millet and other crops in the rich loess plateau of northern China. They also kept pigs, sheep, goats, and cattle. The tool kit of the Early Xiajiadian peoples was fairly simple and included ground stone hoes, axes, and grinding stones, flint blades and microliths, and ceramics. Early Xiajiadian ceramics were sophisticated and were made by craft specialists. These ceramics were brown, sand-tempered wares made on a fast wheel and decorated with net or cord impressions. Most were flat-bottomed or had legs. Craft specialists also produced the numerous jade, shell, and semiprecious stone beads, pendants, rings, bracelets, and other personal ornaments that are often found in Early Xiajiadian graves. Some graves have more goods than others, and this, combined with the presence of political centers, suggests social differentiation must have been present in Early Xiajiadian society.

Political centers with complex fortification systems in the Early Xiajiadian point to conflict, and conflict may have brought political centralization in the region to an end, for **Late Xiajiadian** (3600–2500 B.P.) peoples lived in small villages lacking defensive works and with no evidence of settlement hierarchy, although social differentiation does appear to have continued. A typical Late Xiajiadian site is **Nanshangen,** located on a hill overlooking the Laohahe river in Inner Mongolia. The site consists of numerous storage pits and eleven graves. The fact that no remains of houses was found suggests they were lightly built, perhaps only semipermanent. The graves give evidence of marked social differentiation, with some having wooden coffins and others not, and those with wooden coffins having bronze and even gold objects, many imported from the south.

Late Xiajiadian peoples appear to have begun to emphasize animal husbandry, although agricultural villages do exist along major rivers. Agricultural villages have more substantial housing than the Nanshangen site, with both surface and semi-subterranean dwellings made of mud brick or tamped earth. Millet appears to remain the staple among Late Xiajiadian peoples, but large numbers of animal bones found at many sites suggest that animal husbandry was very important as well. Also common are horse remains and tack, suggesting that horses may have become important elements in the herding economy. Bronze also became common, and local bronze workers produced both tools such as axes, chisels, and horse fittings, as well as weapons like daggers and arrowheads. Taken all together, the picture we get of the Late Xiajiandian tradition is one of a mixed agricultural and pastoral economy, with society held together by wealthy elites.

## Eastern Central Asia

On the peripheries of East Asia similar developments also took place. In the eastern portions of Central Asia, those areas that are today the eastern Tibetan Plateau and Taklamakan Desert, the Gobi Desert, and Mongolia, peoples of the **Eastern Central Asia Neolithic and Bronze Age** (6000–1500 B.P.) tradition developed a nomadic pastoral economy based upon the herding of cattle, sheep, goats, and horses on the fertile grasslands of the region, a way of life shared by peoples of the later **Early Nomad** (3000–2300 B.P.) tradition.

The Eastern Central Asia Neolithic and Bronze Age peoples lived in both sedentary communities located along rivers and at oases and nomadic communities wandering across Central Asia. Sedentary communities were relatively large, often covering areas of 10,000 square meters or more. Houses in these communities were square or rectangular and built of stone or mud brick. In contrast, Early Nomad peoples were completely nomadic, and because of this, their remains are scarce. It is very likely that the Early Nomad peoples lived in large round tents similar to yurts still in use in the Eurasian steppes. Most information about the Early Nomad peoples has been recovered from their burials. These generally took the form of coffins or above-ground sarcophagi made of stone slabs. In some cases these coffins

**Late Xiajiadian**
(3600–2500 B.P.)

**Nanshangen**
(China, Late Xiajiadian)

**Eastern Central Asia Neolithic and Bronze Age** (6000–1500 B.P.)

**Early Nomad**
(3000–2300 B.P.)

were themselves enclosed in round structures made of rubble, which may have been symbolic of the round tents the Early Nomads are thought to have lived in.

Wheat and millet agriculture supplemented by fishing and hunting formed the economic basis of the sedentary Eastern Central Asia Neolithic and Bronze Age communities, while herding cattle, horses, sheep, and goats was the economic basis of the nomadic communities of both traditions. Peoples of both traditions used a variety of stone tools including pebble tools, scrapers, knives, and projectile points. These were manufactured from locally available stone (often of poor quality) and using a variety of techniques. Coiled ceramics were used by peoples of both traditions as well. Axes, adzes, sickles, and other tools of ground stone were also manufactured and used; however, many of these were replaced with bronze forms as bronze manufacture developed and spread across Central Asia.

Bronze working appeared early in the Eastern Central Asia Neolithic and Bronze Age tradition (by 5000 B.P.), but seems to have developed slowly. Woodworking tools appear to have been the first manufactured of bronze. Later, personal ornaments, projectile points, knives, and other items were produced from bronze. Bronze itself was smelted from locally available copper and tin, and a variety of molding and forging techniques, some quite sophisticated, were used to produce bronze items. Bronze items used in both traditions include daggers, axes, and horse fittings.

Little is known about the sociopolitical organization of either the Eastern Central Asia Neolithic and Bronze Age peoples or the Early Nomad peoples. Some scholars suggest that burial patterns demonstrate a lineage organization, but the evidence is in no way clear. The presence of large communities, probably with several hundred residents among the Eastern Central Asia Neolithic and Bronze Age peoples, does suggest some positions of political authority were present. Similarly, there seems clear evidence of regular interaction between sedentary agricultural and nomadic pastoral peoples, and these interactions may have been facilitated by formal leaders on both sides.

## Korea and Japan

On the Korean peninsula, peoples of the **Chulum** (8000–4000 B.P.) tradition relied on fish and shellfish along with other hunted and gathered foods, but supplemented them with millet and domestic pigs. They lived in small, egalitarian villages near the coast or in major river valleys. These villages consisted of a group of ten to twenty houses loosely arranged together. Houses were semisubterranean, roughly 3 meters by 8 meters, and constructed from posts that leaned in toward one another to form a peaked roof that was covered with thatch. These structures housed a single family, and the population of a typical village was probably around 100 people.

**Osanni**, located on the northeast coast of South Korea, is a good example of a Chulum village. The village was situated on the seacoast and a short distance from a freshwater stream. Houses were informally arranged and contained a full range of the items of daily use, including ceramic pots and jars, some with stamped or incised patterns, a range of fishhooks and net sinkers, obsidian flake tools, and stone hoes, axes, and grinding stones. This tool kit illustrates the diverse nature of Chulum subsistence. Fishhooks and net sinkers were used in fishing, and fish and shellfish provided much of the Osanni people's needs. However, stone hoes and grinding stones point to millet cultivation, which probably supplemented their diet. Axes and grinding stones were probably also used to collect and process wild plant foods. The image we get from Osanni is of a settled community of mixed fisher-farmer-collectors, and this probably is representative of many Chulum communities.

They were followed by peoples of the **Mumun** (4000–2300 B.P.) tradition, who adopted rice agriculture from China and developed a complex political system. Villages grew significantly in size during the Mumun tradition, and larger villages

**Chulum**
(8000–4000 B.P.)

**Osanni**
(South Korea, Chulum)

**Mumun**
(4000–2300 B.P.)

**Komdal-li**
(South Korea, Mumun)

became fortified. For example, the **Komdal-li** site, located in southeastern South Korea, grew from a small farming hamlet to a village of thirty-seven houses grouped into several clusters that have been interpreted as representing descent groups. The site was also fortified with a large moat. One of the houses was much larger than the others, and has been interpreted as the house of a village chief. Tombs associated with Komdal-li support the idea that elites of some kind resided at the site. These tombs were large mounds covering a single interment, and the interred individual was usually accompanied by significant wealth.

There appears to be at least two tiers in Mumun settlement, which further supports the idea that chiefdoms developed during the tradition. At the higher level were larger, often fortified villages like Komdal-li. Many of these villages have what appear to be elite or chiefly residences and associated tombs. At the lower level were smaller villages of a dozen or so houses and agricultural hamlets or farmsteads that housed only one or two families. The emergence of extensive trade networks with China also supports the idea that the Mumun people had developed chiefdoms. Trade was almost exclusively in the form of prestige objects, especially jade beads and bronze weapons. There was some local production of these prestige goods as well, and this production appears to have been done by craftsmen associated with chiefly households.

A significant change in subsistence also occurred in the Mumun tradition as rice was introduced from China. Rice agriculture often requires significant investments in agricultural fields and water control, and these investments may have fostered the development of chiefs and defensive facilities. Agricultural fields would have needed to be defended and water control mechanisms built and maintained. Chiefs may have emerged as individuals who controlled the labor necessary for these activities.

**Yayoi (2500–1500 B.P.)**

Beginning around 2500 B.P. rice agriculturalists moved into Japan, probably from the Korean peninsula, and initiated the **Yayoi** (2500–1500 B.P.) tradition, which was ancestral to classical Japanese civilization. The typical Yayoi settlement was a small village of a dozen or so houses. The community shared wells and water control ditches used to flood surrounding rice paddies. Houses were round or square post-frame structures, roughly 6 meters in diameter, with floors cut a half meter or more below the surrounding ground surface. Walls were constructed from a wooden framework covered with thatch or perhaps adze-cut boards, and topped with a pitched thatch roof. Benches were built against the house walls, and a single hearth is typically found in the center of Yayoi houses. The basis of social and political life in these villages was the nuclear family. Chinese chronicles, particularly the *Wei Zhi,* suggest class distinctions and a political hierarchy among the later Yayoi peoples. These differences seem to be evident in variation in burial treatments, with some individuals buried in a manner suggesting they were social or political elites.

The Yayoi economy was based on wet rice agriculture and animal husbandry. In addition to rice, wheat, millet, gourd, melon, and some tree crops were grown. Evidence of domestic animals is scarce, but includes pigs, cows, and chickens. Hunting and fishing supplemented this diet, and collecting plant foods, particularly fruits and nuts, was an important activity. The tool kit used by Yayoi peoples included distinctive flat-bottomed ceramics, as well as stone, bronze, and wooden tools. Common Yayoi artifacts are copper and bronze bells (*dotaku*) that have a truncated cone shape (Figure 14.8). However, their decorations are individualized and unique, including both geometric designs and depictions of humans and animals. It has been suggested that they may have been rung when an offering was made or a ritual performed (as in modern Shinto worship). They have often been found in isolation from other artifacts and may have been deliberately hidden or cached.

The Yayoi peoples buried their dead in organized cemeteries and, in some cases, with grave goods. Grave goods included both personal ornaments and ceramics, although by the later Yayoi period some individuals were buried with large numbers

FIGURE **14.8**
Yayoi bronze bell or *dotaku*.

of grave goods including bronze mirrors and weapons of Chinese origin. Some individuals were also interred in stone-lined pits or chambers, while most lacked such enclosures. Single burials were typical although multiple internments have been found. By the late Yayoi period most individuals were buried in large ceramic jars. Cemeteries themselves were apparently laid out so that kin groups buried their dead in specific sections.

## Central China

Central China is dominated by the two great East Asian rivers, the Yellow and the Yangtzee. The area also includes the mountainous regions of western Szechwan and eastern Hsikang, which are dissected by deep valleys and fast-flowing rivers, and, to the east, a vast coastal basin surrounded by mountains and dissected by the Yangztee, Min, T'o, and Chia-ling rivers. The basin itself consists of rolling hills and fertile but clayey soils. The climate of central China is generally mild and wet, with hot, humid summers and cool winters.

Complex political systems developed in the great river valleys of central China as agricultural communities stabilized and spread. The **Yangshao** (7000–4500 B.P.) tradition of the middle Yellow River valley witnessed the emergence of relatively large agricultural communities organized around a public courtyard, many with a defensive moat, which may have been built for flood control rather than to defend against invaders. Most Yangshao communities were located on the banks of small rivers on rich alluvial farmland where crops of millet could be readily grown. Yangshao houses were either circular and semisubterranean or rectangular and above ground. In either case, houses were well built, often with plastered floors and plastered

**Yangshao**
(7000–4500 B.P.)

FIGURE **14.9**

Reconstructions of houses built by Yangshou peoples.

SOURCE: From *Archaeology of Ancient China,* 4E by K-C. Chang, p. 323. Reprinted by permission of Yale University Press.

wattle-and-daub walls (Figure 14.9). Community sizes varied from several dozen to several hundred residents.

The internal organization of Yangshao villages suggests that there were three important social groups in Yangshao society. The first was the family, which resided in a single house. The second was a descent group, consisting of perhaps five to ten houses. The third was the village as a whole, typically made up of three to five descent groups. Villages were autonomous and appear to have been egalitarian. However, descent group leaders probably served as village leaders as well and coordinated labor for public construction projects such as the moats that surround some Yangshao villages. At the site of **Banpo** near Xian there is more direct evidence for some form of village authority. The village at Banpo consisted of some fifteen or twenty semisubterranean houses built around a single large rectangular structure. The large structure has been interpreted as a public building, providing a clear image of village cohesion and the presence of some village authority. Interestingly, burials uncovered at Banpo and other sites show little variation in burial treatment,

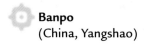

**Banpo**
(China, Yangshao)

suggesting that, despite the presence of village-level political authority, social organization remained egalitarian among Yangshao peoples.

Peoples of the **Dawenkou** (6200–4500 B.P.) tradition of the lower Yellow River valley also appear to have developed stable agricultural communities with substantial houses. Most sites were located with easy access to prime agricultural soils and water. Typical villages were composed of a dozen or more wattle-and-daub houses ranging in size from 10 to 40 square meters, but all likely housing a single nuclear family. Subsistence in the Dawenkou tradition was based on millet and perhaps rice agriculture and domesticated pigs and chickens, supplemented by hunted and gathered foods. The Dawenkou tool kit was simple, and each community was largely self-suffcent. However, there was trade in prestige goods such as ornaments of jade and ivory. These prestige goods are sometimes found in large quantities in particular burials, and these indicate that social stratification was present. Since these high-status burials are all male, archaeologists have suggested that a system of status based on patrilineal descent may have been present.

In the lower Yangzi River valley peoples of the **Majiabang** (7000–5000 B.P.) tradition combined rice agriculture with pig and water buffalo husbandry, establishing a subsistence regime that would last until the present day. The **Majiabang** site, from which the tradition gets its name, is a representative community. It is located south of Shanghai in a low, salt-marsh area. The site's first inhabitants lived in round pit houses but soon began to construct rectangular above-ground structures built on tamped earth platforms. While rice was the primary agricultural product, the peoples at Majiabang continued to hunt and later added domesticated pig and water buffalo to the subsistence regime. The Majiabang peoples made a variety of ceramics, and these were found in abundance at the site. Bone tools were also found in abundance. There were also some thirty burials found at the site, and only six had grave goods. The combined information from the Majiabang site suggests a largely autonomous and egalitarian agricultural village with perhaps some individuals having greater access to goods than others.

Peoples of the **Daxi** (7000–4500 B.P.) tradition created sedentary agricultural communities in the middle and upper Yangztee River valley. Daxi settlements tended to be located on low terraces in the river valley built against the base of the valley walls. No villages and only a few houses have been excavated. Most sites consist of a scatter of building debris and ceramics. Houses were apparently made of square or rectangular bamboo or wooden frames covered with clay, which was then burnt or baked to a hard finish. Roofs were presumably covered with a wooden lattice and matting. Hearths were located in the floor of the houses. Storage pits were located outside of the houses.

The economy of the Daxi peoples was based on rice agriculture supplemented with fish and meat from domestic pigs and chickens. The technology used for subsistence was apparently quite basic, as no tools beyond simple hoes, axes, sickles, and the like have been found. Stone tools were made by grinding and polishing, and few flaked tools are found. Bone and shell were also used extensively for tools. Ceramics were abundant, and largely manufactured by coiling and smoothing. Red wares predominated, and these were largely undecorated. The most common ceramic forms had flat to rounded bases or ring feet. Cups, bowls, plates, and bottles were all present. One form unusually common among the Daxi people was a cylindrical bottle.

Social ranking based on descent appears to have been present in all four of these early central China traditions, and during the **Longshan** (4500–3900 B.P.) tradition descent-based political leadership seems to have developed into a complex and centralized form. The Longshan tradition came to dominate much of central China. Shared forms of ceramics were found over a wide area during the Longshan tradition, and these suggest that interregional interaction had increased markedly.

**Dawenkou**
(6200–4500 B.P.)

**Majiabang**
(7000–5000 B.P.)

**Majiabang**
(China, Majiabang)

**Daxi** (7000–4500 B.P.)

**Longshan**
(4500–3900 B.P.)

## Anyang

Anyang is the site of the ancient capital of the Shang dynasty, the earliest clearly identified royal dynasty in ancient China. It is located in the modern-day city of Anyang, on the rich loess plains of central China. Excavations began at the site in 1928 after hundreds of oracle bones were uncovered by local farmers. Fifteen years of work uncovered a city of immense size and numerous magnificent tombs. Excavations continue to this day, although they are minor compared to those conducted in the 1930s.

The most impressive finds at Anyang were the remains of palaces and royal tombs. The main palace complex was found at Xiaotun, interpreted as the ritual and political center of the city. There, fifty-three large tamped-earth building platforms were uncovered, the largest of which was approximately 70 meters long and 40 meters wide. Associated with this massive platform were twenty additional large rectangular or square platforms, some associated with burials. This area of Xiaotun is interpreted as having been a palace complex, with grand houses, official structures, and royal temples. To the north were fifteen smaller rectangular house platforms, arranged in parallel, and these are interpreted as being the dwelling area for the royal retinue. To the south was a cluster of seventeen tamped-earth platforms of various sizes arranged in a precise U-shaped form, interpreted as forming a ceremonial area. Around the house platforms are the remains of numerous smaller residences and workshops, which must have housed the many people who supported the royal palace and its retinue.

Some of these ceramics were remarkably sophisticated, indeed one form, often found in burials, is less than one millimeter thick and is rightly given the name "eggshell ware"(Figure 14.10). The skill to make these and other sophisticated forms of ceramics must have required craft specialists. There are also indications of the beginnings of copper or bronze work that again point to emergent craft specialization.

Settlement appears to have been organized hierarchically, ranging from small agricultural villages to large, fortified political centers. Some have suggested the largest of these political centers represent the first states in East Asia. At most sites, houses were circular, built at ground level, and had walls of wattle and daub. At larger sites, there were often large, square houses built on platforms of tamped earth with adobe brick walls, and these are interpreted to be elite houses. Longshan settlements of all kinds supported themselves through a combination of agriculture and animal husbandry. Domesticated animals were the pig, chicken, cattle, and water buffalo. Millet was the most important domesticated plant in the Yellow River valley, although rice has been reported for sites in Henan, Shandong, and Shaanxi.

There are marked differences among Longshan burials (quality and quantity of grave goods, size and construction material of graves), and some scholars have suggested that these reflect the presence of ranked patrilineal descent groups. The presence of craft specialists, settlement hierarchies, and large, walled communities

Eleven royal tombs were excavated at the Xibeigang cemetery, which also contained the graves of over 1,000 ordinary citizens of Anyang. The eleven tombs are thought to be those of the eleven kings who ruled from Anyang. Each tomb consists of a massive square or rectangular grave pit, oriented north–south, with a ramp leading into the pit on each of its four sides. Tomb 1,001, for example, has a grave pit that is 19 meters long (north to south), 14 meters wide, and 10 meters deep. The north and south ramps leading into the grave pit are each about 30 meters long. A wooden chamber was built in the middle of the grave pits and the coffin of the king placed within it. Numerous human sacrifices were placed within the wooden chamber, surrounding it, and on the entrance ramps to the grave pit. Some of the sacrificial burials were supplied with coffins, but most were not, and some were even buried lacking their heads. Both the wooden burial chamber and the grave pit were provided with extensive grave goods including numerous utensils, a variety of foodstuffs, and abundant works of art. The royal tombs were plundered in antiquity, but the relatively minor, unplundered tomb of Fu Hao, a consort of the second king residing at Anyang, contained no less that 440 bronze vessels and 590 jade items. The royal tombs must have been supplied with phenomenal amounts of goods, illustrating the power of these early Shang rulers.

SOURCES: Chang, K-C., *Shang Civilization* (New Haven: Yale University Press, 1980); Chi, Li, *Anyang* (Seattle: University of Washington Press, 1977).

all indicate that centralized polities, perhaps chiefdoms, were present. Some scholars have proposed that city-states developed in some regions, and that Longshan sites in western Henan and southern Shanxi are precursors of the Xia Dynasty, the earliest state-level society in China, described in later Zhou and Han texts.

Whether or not states were present in the Longshan tradition is a question that will require much more research to answer, but it is clear that the **Shang** (3900–3100 B.P.) tradition witnessed the emergence of powerful states in the central Yellow River valley. The capital, at least for the last nine rulers of the Shang state, was at the site of **Anyang,** described in the box feature. With the Shang tradition we enter the realm of the historic period. One of the most important finds from the site of Anyang are thousands of inscribed **oracle bones**—mostly turtle shells and cattle scapula—that describe divinations (Figure 14.11). In addition, ritual bronzes are inscribed with information about who made them, for whom, and for what event or purpose. There are also later Zhou and Han texts that describe the Shang world, although these are less reliable than the Shang period texts themselves. For one thing, some were written in part to legitimate Zhou rule over all of central China, and in doing so the authors elevated the Shang state, which Zhou conquered, to an empire that allegedly controlled much of central China. The archaeological evidence and even much of the information from Shang texts themselves makes this idea highly circumspect. Secondly, these texts were written centuries after Shang had

**Shang** (3900–3100 B.P.)

**Anyang** (China, Shang)

**Oracle bones:** turtle shell or cattle scapula that were cracked by heat and then "read" by a diviner to predict the future.

been conquered and are in some ways intended to be stories or myths rather than purely factual accounts of the past.

The presence of sophisticated written script on Shang oracle bones and bronzes suggests that writing had developed long before the tradition of writing on oracle bones or bronzes had begun. It is likely that earlier forms of writing were on perishable materials such as bamboo, silk, or paper, and that these have decayed over the millennia. The records we do have, albeit highly focused texts, do provide a wealth of information about the Shang world. What these texts tell us the most about is the practice of divination. Tortoise shells and cattle scapula would be consecrated and then heated to form cracks. The cracks would then be read by an interpreter, and the meaning of the cracks would be written on the bone. The inscribed bones would be kept for a time and then deposited in pits or accompanying burials. It is from these pits and burials that the oracle bones were recovered.

Divination was a primary occupation of Shang kings, and the practice seems to have become increasingly important during the course of the Shang dynasty, for which twenty-nine kings are recorded, the last nine of whom resided at Anyang and left direct records of their deeds. Some 120 diviners are also named on the oracle bones. These individuals prepared the bones, heated them, and interpreted the cracks. The king listened to the diviner's interpretations, examined the bones, and offered a final pronouncement based on the cracks. Consecration and preparation of the bones took place in temples dedicated to particular patrilineal ancestors of the king. The king's position as the ultimate authority on the meaning of the cracks resulted from his being the closest living relative of these ancestral kings. In a sense, the Shang king served as the mediator between the ancestral kings and the living world. As part of his role, the Shang king was also expected to maintain ancestral temples and to perform a cycle of rituals at each of them.

When Shang kings died, they became supernatural powers with whom the new king communicated through oracle bones and rituals. Therefore, a Shang king's death was an important event since it marked the ascension of a new deity, and Shang royal tombs are among the most impressive in the ancient world. Shang leaders took with them vast amounts of wealth and, perhaps more important,

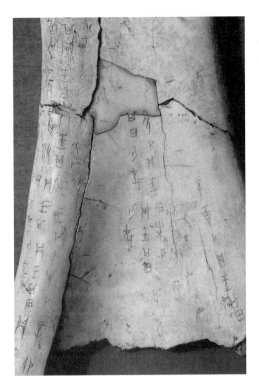

FIGURE **14.11**
A Shang oracle bone from Anyang.

numerous retainers who were sacrificed to accompany the king into his tomb. Tombs themselves were massive works. Ramps were dug into the earth to a depth of 10 to 20 meters, and a large, square hole, perhaps 10 meters on a side, was dug several more meters into the ground as the central tomb. Into this tomb would go the wooden coffin of the king, numerous bronzes and jade pieces, and sacrificed palace guards and other elites in coffins. Above the tomb were numerous sacrificial victims, many of whom were beheaded and placed along the ramps leading down to the central tomb. Horses with chariots were also sacrificed and placed on the ramps. Much of the physical information we have about Shang technology and material culture comes from the vast amount of goods placed in these royal tombs.

Beyond the royal community and the system of ancestor worship, Shang inscriptions also tell us much about Shang life and culture. Patrilineal descent groups were the basis of social organization and social status. The royal lineage was at the head of the social, political, and religious order, but beneath them were lesser noble lineages of the king's sons and minor lineages of more distant relations. Commoners were members of local patrilineal descent groups that were themselves ranked, with higher-ranking local lineages providing the local social, political, and religious elite; they are identified in inscriptions as local officers or local chiefs. Peoples far away from Anyang are only identified as "allies" or "enemies," and much of the divination efforts had to do with predicting success or failure in war against, or defense against, these outsiders. War was a constant concern for Shang kings, and this alone demonstrates that Shang was not an empire that controlled much of the Yellow River valley since they apparently had numerous rivals.

The oracle inscriptions also deal with agriculture and the hopes for good crops. Shang society was based on millet agriculture and raising pigs, cattle, and chickens. Shang villages, including Anyang, were self-sufficient in most items, but bronzes were cast at Anyang or other facilities controlled by the kings, while the kings received cattle scapula in vast numbers from villages. We know this because the place of origin and date of consecration are often noted on these scapula. The king did have large farms, worked by laborers who were apparently provided to the king by lesser nobles and villages as part of tribute. The military seems to have been organized in a similar fashion, with conscripts being offered as a regular part of village tribute to the king. In return for tribute, the Shang kings offered mediation with the supernatural world, and this, in turn, ensured the safety and stability of Shang society.

## COLONIZATION OF THE PACIFIC

As discussed in previous chapters, there is good evidence that *Homo erectus* was in Southeast Asia more than a million and a half years ago, even though many of what are today islands were part of large landmasses such as Sunda and Sahul. New Guinea, Australia, New Zealand, and the many smaller islands of Melanesia, Micronesia, and the Pacific were separated from the mainland and inaccessible to these early humans. Sometime around 40,000 years ago (and perhaps earlier) humans made the voyage to New Guinea and Australia, presumably by boat, and initiated the colonization of the Pacific.

These Upper Paleolithic people were followed by peoples of the Late Australian and New Guinea Neolithic traditions. Peoples of both these traditions developed unique adaptations to their environments—adaptations so satisfactory that they were able to maintain relatively stable lifestyles for thousands of years. Peoples of the **Late Australian** (7000–200 B.P.) tradition were hunters and gatherers who, like their predecessors, tended to focus on regionally abundant resources. Plant foods were of primary importance, and some of the more common plant remains found on Late Australian sites include yams and tubers, grass seeds, and nuts. In coastal areas fish, shellfish, and marine mammals were taken, while elsewhere a wide variety of animals were hunted. However, there is clear evidence that the Late Australian peoples went beyond simple food collecting and actively began to manage wild food resources, for example, through controlled burning of secondary plant growth.

The Late Australian peoples lived in small communities which moved regularly. Some locations, however, were used repeatedly over long periods of time. One such location is **Malangangerr,** located in northern Arnhem Land. The site is a large rockshelter covering an area of some 10 meters by 30 meters, and was used by humans from as early as 23,000 B.P. until the modern era. The site overlooks the Alligator River and is surrounded by woodlands. Faunal and floral remains from the site show that the location offered its Late Australian inhabitants access to a wide range of resources, from riverine fish and shellfish to animals living in the open woodlands, and a wide range of plant resources. Malangangerr was occupied repeatedly by small bands of ten to fifteen people, probably representing several families. The tool kit of these people was simple and included crude flake and core tools, as well as chipped and ground stone axes, flaked projectile points, and knives. Wooden tools preserved rarely in archaeological contexts included digging sticks, boomerangs, and a range of woven and netted items.

The **New Guinea Neolithic** (10,000–100 B.P.) peoples, on the other hand, adopted agriculture as their subsistence base and lived in small sedentary villages of perhaps fifty to one hundred people near their agricultural fields. These villages showed little internal organization, but rather consisted of groups of household clusters. Houses themselves were insubstantial, post-wall constructions, often with several internal subdivisions, but apparently they housed only a single family. While there is little formal archaeological evidence, it seems clear that kinship was the basis of sociopolitical organization for the New Guinea Neolithic peoples. The trade networks that appear by 2000 B.P. suggest that the "big man" system so prominent among historic New Guinea groups may have developed by that time. Prior to 2000 B.P. it is likely that political authority was based solely on age and kinship.

**Late Australian**
(7000–200 B.P.)

**Malangangerr**
(Australia, Late Australian)

**New Guinea Neolithic**
(10,000–100 B.P.)

FIGURE **14.12**
These modern yam gardens reflect a type of agriculture that has been practiced for thousands of years in Highland New Guinea.

Three main agricultural crops were central to the New Guinea Neolithic economy: taro, yam, and banana. All three were grown in small, raised fields and terraces cross-cut with drainage ditches (Figure 14.12). By 6000 B.P. pigs had been domesticated as well, and these became equally central to the diet of the New Guinea Neolithic peoples. The New Guinea Neolithic peoples used simple tools to produce food—ground stone axes and mortars; chipped stone bifaces; wooden digging sticks; and woven bags and nets. Ceramics did not appear until roughly 2000 B.P. The New Guinea Neolithic peoples began to participate in extensive trade networks of shell, stone, and other items at about the same time ceramics were introduced.

## Melanesia

Melanesia exists in a purely tropical environment. Temperatures are warm year-round, and there is abundant rainfall, although there is marked seasonality to rainfall in areas away from the equator. There are distinct microclimatic differences both within and between the individual islands of Melanesia, and these differences create a complex landscape where even small islands may have a great diversity of plant and animal life. Regular volcanism creates a dynamic landscape, and major eruptions have been both devastating and transforming in the history of the region.

In coastal New Guinea and the islands of Melanesia, the predecessors of the **Melanesian** (2500–200 B.P.) tradition began to manufacture ceramics sometime around 3500 B.P. These ceramics are diagnostic of the **Lapita** (3500–2000 B.P.) tradition, and their presence marks the beginning of the colonization of the remote Pacific. Lifeways of the Lapita and Melanesian peoples were focused on the sea, and they located their villages within easy access of the water. Unfortunately, there are few excavated settlements dating from this time period. Historic settlements in Melanesia tended to be small clusters or neighborhood groupings of houses containing, in total, perhaps 100 to 200 people. Houses themselves were rectangular and built of large posts supporting walls of woven leaf matting. Typically, several families inhabited a single house, and several houses of related individuals formed a local cluster.

**Melanesian**
(2500–200 B.P.)

**Lapita** (3500–2000 B.P.)

FIGURE **14.13**
A fragment of a Lapita
ceramic. Note the intricate
designs incised on its surface,
which are characteristic of
Lapita ceramics.

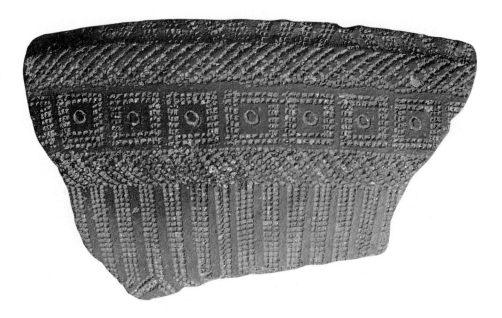

The economy of both the Melanesian and Lapita peoples was based on fish and shellfish. While there are some examples of fishhooks and sinkers in the archaeological record, it is likely that nets were used extensively for fishing, and these have not survived. Both the bow and arrow and spears were used to hunt fish, land animals, and birds. These were tipped with wood or bone points, often barbed. Gathered nuts and fruits were also an important part of the diet, and there is tantalizing evidence in the form of digging sticks and shell hoes that taro and yam may have been grown. There is good evidence for long-distance trading in shell, obsidian, ceramics, and other items, perhaps as far away as mainland Southeast Asia.

Between 3200 and 2900 B.P. peoples of the Lapita tradition expanded out into the remote Pacific, colonizing all of Melanesia and much of western Polynesia, including Fiji, Tonga, and Samoa. Lapita is technically defined by the presence of ceramics. Lapita ceramics are distinctive wares fired at low temperatures and decorated with complicated stamped designs (Figure 14.13). After firing, these designs were filled in with white lime to make them stand out. Lapita peoples also began using domesticates, both plants and animals, probably obtained from New Guinea and Southeast Asia. These included root crops, such as yams and taro, and tree crops, such as coconut and pandanus. Domesticated animals were pigs, chickens, and dogs. These domesticates, especially animals, certainly aided the Lapita peoples in their colonization of Pacific islands because domesticates allowed them to shape whatever resources they found into ones that would produce both familiar and useful foods.

What may have most significantly aided the Lapita peoples in colonizing the Pacific was the development of the outrigger sailing canoe (Figure 14.14). While no physical remains of sailing canoes have been found since they are made entirely of perishable plant materials, there is good linguistic evidence that many of the words referring to the sailing canoe, its construction, and its operation have ancient roots that go back to the Lapita era. The best evidence for the development of the sailing canoe by the Lapita peoples is simply the distances they covered on a regular basis. Not only did Lapita peoples reach the remote islands of the Pacific, but they maintained regular connections among those islands in the form of long-distance trade for items such as obsidian, chert, stone adzes, shell, and cooking stones. Animals and seedlings, and perishable items such as woven mats and pandanus cloth, were

probably traded as well, but these have not survied in the archaeological record. While most of this trade probably took place between communities within a range of 50 kilometers or so, some goods, such as obsidian, moved as far as several thousand kilometers from its source, and some of the distances covered over the open ocean must have been hundreds of kilometers at a time.

## Micronesia

Micronesia consists of more than 1,000 small islands covering almost 8 million square kilometers of the Pacific Ocean east of the Philippines and north of Melanesia. The islands are of two types: volcanic and coral. Both tend to be only a few square kilometers in surface area, but the volcanic islands are mountainous and rugged, while the coral islands tend to be low and relatively flat. Volcanic islands often have rainfall-fed steams, rich alluvial soils, and stone and mineral resources lacking on the coral islands. Coral islands, on the other hand, have thin soils and less diverse vegetation than the volcanic islands but provide more open spaces for dwellings and easier access to the sea. The climate is warm year-round with little fluctuation in temperature, which averages around 27 degrees C. Rainfall is plentiful throughout the region, but seasonal storms are a hazard to central Micronesia. Plant life is diverse on volcanic islands, less so on coral islands, though palms and tropical grasses dominate the landscape on both. Land animals and birds are relatively scarce.

Peoples of the **Micronesian** (3000–200 B.P.) tradition were horticulturalists who raised banana, coconut, breadfruit, and other crops and supplemented these domestic foods with wild foods from the sea. Micronesian settlements tended to be located near the Pacific Ocean and were spread linearly along high beach terraces. Houses were substantial post structures with open walls covered with mat screens and steeply pitched roofs covered with thatch. Foundations were stone or stone pilings while floors were either stone or, more commonly, planks. Houses themselves were very large, frequently more than 15 meters long and 6 meters wide. They were also very tall, with roof posts reaching 12 or more meters in height. Although large,

**Micronesian**
(3000–200 B.P.)

these structures apparently housed single nuclear or extended families. Some of the very large structures (e.g., those more than 30 meters long or with multiple stories) were likely for public use and not residences at all. In addition, the Micronesians living on some of the larger islands (e.g., Kosrae and Pohnpei) built large stone enclosures around house groups and public or sacred structures. Some of these enclosures are massive, with walls of stacked basalt blocks over 6 meters high and nearly as thick at the base. Coral or stone raised walkways often connected these enclosures.

The large stone enclosures on some of the islands suggest individuals there had the ability to pool and coordinate labor. Such coordinated labor, however, would also have been necessary for such mundane tasks as building, launching, and operating the large outrigger canoes used for fishing and trading. With this in mind, it seems reasonable to suggest that the hierarchical sociopolitical organization found historically throughout Micronesia had ancient roots. A system of ranked clans gave authority to chiefs who could call upon the resources and labor of their own or of subordinate clans. Chiefs inherited their positions and also inherited unique knowledge of the ancestors and gods, which they also used to legitimate and consolidate their authority. The location of what appear to be chiefly house compounds associated with what appear to be "sacred" precincts at, for example, **Leluh** on Kosrae, may be evidence of this historic sociopolitical organization existing in antiquity.

**Leluh** (Micronesia, Micronesian)

## Western Polynesia

Polynesia consists of island groups spread across the Pacific Ocean from Fiji to Easter Island. Western Polynesia typically includes the Fiji, Tongan, and Samoan Islands, while Eastern Polynesia includes all the islands to the east of Samoa. These islands are volcanic in origin and typically contain one or more large primary islands and dozens of smaller islands and coral atolls. The primary islands are mountainous, volcanic, and often quite rugged. The climate is extremely mild and varies only slightly with the seasons. Most of the islands have areas of broad littoral plains that open onto the ocean or, more commonly, a reef-sheltered beach or lagoon. Some large deep valleys run far inland. The islands' flora varies by location (inland versus coastal) and altitude but is tropical and relatively diverse. Fauna, on the other hand, is sparse, with only a few species of birds and reptiles, and few mammals until they were introduced by humans.

On the islands of western Polynesia, the direct descendants of the Lapita colonizers developed unique archaeological traditions—**Fijian** (2400–200 B.P.), **Samoan** (2500–200 B.P.), and **Tongan** (2500–200 B.P.)—but continued a focus on ocean resources supplemented by domestic animals and horticulture. In all three traditions, Lapita ceramics were replaced by Polynesian plainware ceramics. Peoples in all three traditions also began to build large architectural features that included fortifications, elite residences and burials, large stone platforms, and causeways that linked fortified communities. Houses tended to be built on low mounds. These house mounds were themselves either of earth or stone, and if of earth, they were typically faced with pebbles or stone slabs. Smaller, often round, mounds were apparently substructures for small, round houses, while larger, rectangular mounds often served as substructures for chiefs' houses and community houses. Houses themselves were built of a wooden frame covered with thatch or woven mats. House floors were often "paved" with river gravel. Houses tended to be clustered in small groups surrounded by a low stone wall and one or more raised pathways. Earth ovens were apparently shared by house clusters, suggesting houses cooked together, and probably represent extended family compounds.

**Fijian** (2400–200 B.P.)

**Samoan** (2500–200 B.P.)

**Tongan** (2500–200 B.P.)

Powerful chiefs were present on all three island groups in the historic period, and while there is little direct archaeological evidence about social or political organization for these traditions, there is a wealth of oral tradition and ethnohistory on the subject, particularly for Tonga. Oral traditions suggest that a powerful chiefdom developed on the island of Tongatapu by roughly 1000 B.P. and extended out to incorporate the other islands in the group. The mound burials and fortified community at **Mu'a** are thought to be archaeological manifestations of these developments. By roughly 500 B.P. the chiefdom reorganized and a formal division between political and religious chiefs was created. Additional divisions and segmentation of society into formal status groups and specialists continued into the historic period. Although patrilineages formed the basic structure underlying Tongan society, sisters were perceived to outrank their brothers. The marriage of Tongan women to Fijian men and Tongan men to Samoan women avoided potential problems between a Tongan high chief and his sister's son. Primogeniture was key to status and authority in both the secular and religious worlds.

⊕ **Mu'a** (Tonga, Tongan)

By the beginning of the historic period, there was a sharp division between commoner and chiefly classes. Ethnohistoric documents suggest that chiefs were seen as incarnations of deities, and deities themselves were seen as connected or ancestral to particular lineages. Thus chiefs, ancestors, and deities were all considered sacred. Archaeological manifestations of these beliefs are thought to be evidenced in the distinctions between commoner and chiefly burials. Commoners were typically buried in low, circular mounds, while high-status people and chiefs were buried in more elaborate rectangular mounds faced with stone or coral. These flat mounds resemble "council" mounds and ceremonial structures found on other Polynesian islands. Rarely, ethnohistoric documents have enabled the sites of former religious structures to be identified.

## Eastern Polynesia

The descendants of the Lapita peoples also continued to expand into the eastern Polynesia, establishing the Marquesan, Tahitian, Easter Island, Hawaiian, and Maori traditions. It is interesting that all of these traditions developed complex sociopolitical structures and dense population centers, neither of which were known in the ancestral Lapita tradition itself. In the Society Islands, for example, peoples of the **Tahitian** (1400–200 B.P.) tradition built large religious and political structures that are found throughout the Society Islands. *Marae* (religious structures) consist of a plaza, often defined by a low wall, with a long stone platform at one end. Upright stone slabs provided (according to ethnohistoric sources) resting places for deities. *Marae* vary greatly in size and complexity of construction, depending on their exact function and the size of the social group which built them. Secular structures indicative of social complexity include large, isolated platforms interpreted as council meeting places, specialized platforms believed to be for the chiefly sport of archery, and curbstone outlines of large, round-ended buildings. Ethnohistoric records suggest that relatively strong clan chiefs were present and that some may have integrated several clans into regional chiefdoms by the early historic period.

⊕ **Tahitian**
(1400–200 B.P.)

Fishing was central in the economies of these eastern Polynesian traditions. For example, at the **Marquesan** (1700–175 B.P.) tradition site of **Hanamiai**, located on Tahuata island, there is evidence that fish were taken with hooks, spears or arrows, and nets. Faunal remains show that the inhabitants of the site were skilled marine hunters, taking fish such as tuna, turtles, and dolphins as well as lagoon fish. Pigs, dogs, and chickens also contributed meat to the diet. Cultivated plants, including taro, banana, plantain, and breadfruit were also grown. These introduced plant and animal species, as well as human hunting and fishing, had a tremendous impact on the environment. At Hanamiai there is evidence that seven species of native birds were hunted to extinction and that indigenous land snails were completely replaced by introduced species. These kinds of dramatic transformations occurred

⊕ **Marquesan**
(1700–175 B.P.)

⊕ **Hanamiai** (Marquesan)

*Marae:* a religious structure found throughout Polynesia.

FIGURE **14.15**
Drawing of a moa about to be speared by a Maori hunter.

Maori (900–200 B.P.)

Wairau Bar
(New Zealand, Maori)

Hawaiian
(800–200 B.P.)

**Moas:** flightless birds indigenous to New Zealand that went extinct soon after human colonization.

throughout the Marquesas, and indeed throughout the islands of eastern Polynesia as humans arrived and began to hunt, fish, and produce domestic foods.

The human effect on indigenous species is perhaps nowhere more evident than in New Zealand, where peoples of the **Maori** (900–200 B.P.) tradition lived. The earliest inhabitants focused subsistence on sea mammals and large flightless birds called **moas** (Figure 14.15). At the **Wairau Bar** site, located near the tip of the South island of New Zealand, the first inhabitants made extensive use of moas and their eggs. Moa joints were placed in burials along with perforated eggs, which may have been used as water containers. Moa bone was also used for personal ornaments. Over time, moa remains become less and less common, so that by the end of the site's occupation their are no longer any moa remains. The archaeological deposits at Wairau Bar reflect the gradual extinction of the moa, most likely caused by humans overhunting them. Fur seal remains show a similar pattern at sites on the North island of New Zealand, where they completely disappear by roughly 500 B.P. The Maori peoples also introduced new animals and plants to New Zealand, particularly the pig and dog, and the sweet potato, yam, taro, and gourd. These were able to survive and flourish with human assistance, driving other, indigenous species either to remote areas or to extinction. Human colonization of the Pacific, then, came at a huge cost to the indigenous flora and fauna.

Perhaps the best known of the eastern Polynesian archaeological traditions is the **Hawaiian** (800–200 B.P.) tradition. It is well known both because of the extensive archaeological work that has been done on the Hawaiian islands, but also because of extensive historical records that describe the cultures of the Hawaiian peoples at the time of European contact. Both the archaeological and historical records show that peoples of the Hawaiian tradition lived in two distinct types of settlements: agricultural villages and regional centers. Villages were formal organizations that controlled a strip of land running from a mountain top to the coast, typically bounded by streams or ridges. In this way, each village had access to a wide range of resources, from upland hunting areas to lowland agricultural areas to coastal fishing and shellfishing areas. Each village consisted of a number of compounds, each of which contained a single family. Separate eating structures were used by the men and women of each family, and there were other structures for activities such as food storage, cooking, sleeping, and worship. A typical village might have several dozen such compounds, and perhaps a hundred or more residents.

Regional centers had, in addition to house compounds, elite residential areas and large religious complexes. Elites were organized hierarchically, and elite status was determined by patrilineal descent. At the time of European contact there were four levels of elite hierarchy: (1) community leaders, who were the elders of local villages; (2) regional chiefs, who oversaw several communities and who lived in regional centers; (3) island chiefs, who lived in the largest center on a given island; and (4) the paramount chief, who resided on the large island of Hawaii. The paramount chief was the supreme political and religious leader, and he owned all land and resources. He gave land to villages for their use, but expected in return tribute, which he used to support his household. The paramount chief also supported an extensive array of priests and temples, at which ceremonies of sacrifice were offered to the gods. Huge feasts and extensive gift exchanges accompanied many of these ceremonies, and required the paramount chief to acquire, and then distribute, great amounts of wealth.

Perhaps the most enigmatic of all the traditions of Oceania is the **Easter Island** (1500–400 B.P.) tradition. The Easter Island tradition is enigmatic, both for the remoteness of Easter Island itself, located some 1,800 kilometers away from the nearest island (Pitcairn), and because of the massive stone sculptures of stylized humans, called *moai,* that are found by the hundreds along the coast of Easter Island (Color Plate 19). One of the great fables in popular archaeological literature is that we know nothing about these *moai,* who made them, or how they were made and transported (see the box feature). In truth, we know much about the prehistory of Easter Island. The peoples of the Easter Island tradition lived in a complex chiefdom like others in eastern Polynesia. The chief was both a secular and religious ruler, part of whose job was to convey the power of ancestral gods to humans. This was accomplished, in part, through rituals performed at ceremonial centers. The *moai* were built as part of these centers. For example, at Akivi-Vai Teka, a ceremonial platform, or *ahu,* was built around 500 B.P. that served as a place for cremation and burial. About 100 years later, the *ahu* was rebuilt and seven moai were erected. A second cremation area was also created, and the site continued to be used for cremation and burial. In this context the *moai* clearly represent a connection to the ancestors—probably those whose remains were cremated and buried at the site.

At the time of European contact, these *ahu* were no longer in use, and Easter Island as a whole had only a small population living on it. Part of the tradition's mystery has to do with what must have been a massive collapse of the prehistoric chiefdom. Traditional histories suggest that two competing chiefs, one controlling the eastern part of the island and one the west, went to war sometime around 400 B.P. This war may have caused political collapse. However, environmental deterioration probably played an important role as well. When colonized by humans, Easter Island was forested with palms, at least in low areas. By the time of European contact the island was treeless and grass-covered. While there is debate over the mechanisms, it seems clear that humans dramatically altered the Eastern Island environment. It also seems clear that population rose to high levels—perhaps to as high as seventy-five people per square kilometer. Fresh water, fuel, and food would all have been in short supply for a population of this density, and it may be that the environment of Easter Island simply could not support them.

**Easter Island**
(1500–400 B.P.)

*Moai:* massive stone figures in human form found on Easter Island.

*Ahu:* a low platform, usually faced with stone, used for religious rituals throughout Polynesia.

## Easter Island

The history of archaeological research on Easter Island must be among the strangest for any location on earth, the primary reason being that much of the best-known research was conducted by nonarchaeologists, and much of that done in order to demonstrate that the inhabitants of Easter Island must have had outside help to live on the island and create a unique, local civilization. Two figures in this history stand out: Thor Heyerdahl and Erich von Daniken. Thor Heyerdahl believed that Easter Island (and the rest of the Pacific) had not been colonized from Asia but from the Americas. In 1947 he undertook a voyage from Peru on a large balsa raft (named Kon Tiki) and crossed 8,000 kilometers of ocean on it successfully. In 1955 he began excavations on Easter Island to demonstrate Peruvian connections, which proved tentative at best. Von Daniken, on the other hand, has never done formal research on Easter Island, but his theory, published in his 1969 book *Chariots of the Gods?*, that Easter Island had been visited by aliens from outer space who erected the giant stone figures (*moai*) that are so prominent, has been widely disseminated and was even made the subject of a popular film.

Why has Easter Island been the subject of such unusual ideas? There are several likely reasons. Part of the answer is probably the island's location, isolated in the middle of the Pacific, nearly 4,000 kilometers from the Chilean coast. One has to ask, how did people get there? A second part of the answer is probably the island's current environment, which is barren, treeless, and rocky. How did people live there? A third part of the answer is certainly the enigmatic stone *moai*. How were they erected? Why were they erected? Finally, where are the inhabitants now? When first contacted Easter Island had only a few hundred residents. Today there are even fewer. But Easter Island must have been home to thousands of people at one time. Where did they go? In short, Easter Island begs questions that have no easy answers, and that makes it a place of mystery.

##  SUMMARY

*Homo erectus* moved into East Asia more than a million and a half years ago. Modern humans appeared in the region by 40,000 years ago and colonized New Guinea and Australia. For 30,000 years life changed very little. People across East Asia lived in small, mobile, hunting and gathering groups. About 9,000 years ago agriculture was developed and spread rapidly across the region. By 6,000 years ago most people were living in sedentary agricultural villages. Social and political complexity increased within these agricultural communities, and centralized polities emerged some 4,000 years ago. Those living near the coast and on the islands of Melanesia had always relied on ocean resources to supplement agriculture, but

Happily, recent research has provided clear answers to some of the enduring questions raised by Easter Island. First, Easter Island was peopled by Polynesians who arrived around 1600 B.P. There were probably only a dozen or so colonists, perhaps blown off course or perhaps following a discovery of the island by earlier fishermen or traders. The fact that they brought with them pigs, chickens, and dogs (the pigs and dogs soon died out), along with bananas, sweet potatoes, and breadfruit (the breadfruit also died out), suggests that their voyage to the island may have been purposeful. The environment they found was very different from the one today as the island at the time of colonization was covered in tropical rainforest. The population of these colonists grew over the succeeding centuries, and by about 1000 B.P. the first of the large *moai* statues were erected. These are thought to represent ancestors, perhaps the original voyagers who first came to the island.

Around 500 B.P. construction of the large *moai* and associated ritual platforms ceased, and weapons became common. It appears that warfare erupted among the island's populace, warfare that ended in the overthrow of the existing social order, the toppling of many of the *moai*, and the creation of political system based on chiefs who were selected annually (this system still existed during the early historic period). What happened to the people of Easter Island, then? The answer seems to be that they were the victims of their own success. From about 800 B.P. onward the island was deforested, and by the early historic period there were virtually no large trees left. Without large trees canoes could not be built, and without canoes, deep ocean fishing was impossible. Chickens and domestic crops became the only foods, but domestic crops suffered, too, as the loss of forest cover led to massive soil erosion. Starvation and population collapse was the end result, so that when Europeans first "discovered" the island on Easter Sunday, 1722, the Dutch sailors found it desolate and virtually uninhabited.

SOURCES: Bahn, Paul, and John Flenley, *Easter Island, Earth Island* (London: Thames and Hudson, 1992); Tilburg, Van, and Jo Anne, *Easter Island* (Washington, DC: Smithsonian Institution Press, 1994).

by 3,000 years ago they began to venture farther out to sea and, over the next 2,000 years, colonized the Pacific.

This summary may suggest that there is a uniform evolutionary trend to the prehistory of East Asia and Oceania, but that would not be an accurate interpretation. While some areas did follow a parallel trajectory toward food production, settled life, and sociopolitical complexity, others did not. In Japan and Australia, for example, hunting and gathering persisted long after agriculture had spread across most of East Asia. The areas which tended to remain more stable over time should not be viewed as "backward" or somehow less evolutionarily developed than other areas—on the contrary, people there developed such a successful way of life early on that change was not needed.

## ❂ DISCUSSION QUESTIONS

1. Explain the importance of rice in the prehistory of East Asia. How did the domestication of rice affect cultural evolution?

2. Many areas of Southeast Asia are poorly known, both because of poor preservation in the archaeological record and because of a lack of research. How might the paucity of data from Southeast Asia affect our understanding of the prehistory of the region?

3. How did Lapita peoples colonize the Pacific? What tools and knowledge must they have brought with them? How did they survive on previously uninhabited islands?

## ◉ ESSAY QUESTIONS

1. Reflect on the inherent ecological bias in this chapter. Why is the focus on settlement and subsistence? How does this focus effect the way the prehistory of East Asia is presented and interpreted? What might be missing in this presentation? What might be gained through the focus on subsistence and settlement?

2. The major center of cultural evolution in East Asia was the Yellow River valley. Use library and Internet resources to examine the Yellow River valley. Why did complex, centralized polities first arise in the Yellow River valley and not elsewhere in East Asia?

3. Although colonized sequentially over perhaps a 500-year period, all the major island groups of Polynesia had developed centralized polities by the time of European contact. Provide at least two explanations, backed up by archaeological data, to explain why such similar patterns of cultural evolution are found throughout Polynesia. What makes the pattern of cultural evolution in different parts of Polynesia so similar?

## ✐ RESEARCH PROJECT

China has a history of archaeological research that is largely separate from the rest of the world. Most of the world's archaeologists have been trained in either an American or European institution, but not most Chinese archaeologists. Until recently, few non-Chinese were allowed to work in China. This has given Chinese archaeology a unique perspective that is strongly attached to Marxist historical materialism yet seems focused on elite goods and corroborating historical texts. Find books, journal articles, and Web pages authored by Chinese archaeologists, and compare and contrast them with research on similar topics or places by non-Chinese archaeologists. How does Chinese archaeological scholarship differ from work done on similar topics or areas by non-Chinese scholars? How might these differences illustrate differences in political ideology; that is, how might the cultural world of Chinese scholars affect the way in which the past is presented and interpreted? How might the cultural world of Western scholars affect the way the past is presented and interpreted?

## ◉ KEY SOURCES

### Holocene Food Collectors

Aikens and Higuchi, 1982; Akazawa and Aikens, 1986; Barnes, 1990, 1999; Bellwood, 1997; Charoenwongsa and Bronson, 1988; Glover, 1977; Gorman,

1971; Higham, 1989; Higham and Thosarat, 1998; Hiscock, 2001b; Keiji, 1996; Kenrick, 1995; Lourandos, 1996; Matsui, 2001; Mulvaney, 1975; Murray, 1998; Pearson, 1992; Pearson, Barnes, and Hutterer, 1986; Shoocongdej, 2001.

## Food Production and Complex Societies in East Asia

Chang, 1986, 1999; Chung-Tong and Wai-ling, 1995; Higham, 1996a, 1996b; Higham and Lu, 1998; Meacham, 1978, 1983; Underhill, 1997.

## Southeast Asia

Bellwood, 1987, 1992, 1997, 2001; Bentley, 1986; Bulbeck, 2001; Charoenwongsa and Bronson, 1988; Glover and Syme, 1993; Hall, 1985; Higham, 1989, 1996a, 1996b; Higham and Thosarat, 1998; Stark, 1998, 2001; Van Heekeren, 1958.

## Northern China

Chang, 1986, 1999; Nelson, 1995, 1996, 2001b; Rawson, 1996; Shelach, 1998, 1999, 2001a, 2001b.

## Eastern Central Asia

Askarov, Volkov, and Ser-Odjav, 1992; Binghua, 1996; Chen and Hiebert, 1995; Frumkin, 1970; Okladnikov, 1990; Zhimin, 1992a, 1992b.

## Korea and Japan

Aikens and Higuchi, 1982; Barnes, 1990, 1999; Kim, C., 1978; Kim, W., 1986; Nelson, 1993, 2001; Pearson, 1992; Pearson, Barnes, and Hutterer, 1986; Rhee, 2001; Rhee and Choi, 1992; Yun, 1987.

## Central China

Bagley, 1999; Barnes, 1993; Chang, 1980, 1986, 1999; Cheng, 1957, 1966; Gao and Lee, 1993; Keightly, 1999; Lee, 2001; Liu, 1996; Ming, 2001; Murowchick, 1994; Treistman, 1974; Underhill, 1994, 1997, 2001a, 2001b; Zhimin, 1988.

## Colonization of the Pacific

Bulmer, 1975; Feil, 1987; Golson, 1977, 1989; Golson and Gardiner, 1990; Gosden, 1989; Jennings, 1979; Kirch, 1997; Sullivan, Hughes, and Golson, 1987; White, 1972; White and O'Connell, 1982.

## Melanesia

Allen and Gosden, 1991; Garanger, 1982; Smith, Spriggs, and Fankhauser, 1993; Spriggs, 1997.

## Micronesia

Alkire, 1977; Cordy, 1993; Craib, 1983; Graves, 1986; Morgan, 1988.

## Western Polynesia

Burley, 1998; Gifford, 1951; Green and Davidson, 1969; Jennings, 1979; Jennings and Holmer, 1980; Jennings, Holmer, Janetski, and Smith, 1976; Kirch, 1988; Kirch and Hunt, 1993; McKern, 1929; Parry, 1984; Poulsen, 1968, 1977; Thompson, 1940.

## Eastern Polynesia

Cordy, 1981; Davidson, 1984, 2001; Earle, 1978; Emory, 1933; Englert, 1970; Garanger, 1967; Graves and Green, 1993; Green, 1996; Green et al., 1967; Heyerdahl and Ferdon, 1961; Jennings, 1979; Kirch, 1985, 1990; Kolb, 1994, 2001; Linton, 1925; Oliver, 1974; Rolett, 1993, 1998, 2001; Thomas, 1990; Van Tilburg, 1994, 2001; Wilson, 1987.

# PRINCESS OF KHOK PHANOM DI

East Asia comprises a substantial portion of Asia. It extends south of Siberia and east of the Tibetan Plateau and Taklamakan Desert. Vast loess plains cover northern China, great river valleys occupy central China, and mountainous tropical forests cover Southeast Asia. In Southeast Asia, the Southeast Asia Neolithic and Bronze Age tradition extended from 6500 to 2500 B.P. The Southeast Asia Neolithic and Bronze Age people were agriculturalists, who raised rice and lived in large villages composed of numerous independent family farmers. Only a few sites of the Southeast Asia Neolithic and Bronze Age tradition have been excavated. One of these is Khok Phanom Di.

The Media Lab can be found in Chapter 14 on the *Companion Website*™ http://www.prenhall.com/peregrine

## WEB ACTIVITY

The site of Khok Phanom Di in Thailand was situated on the Bang Pakong River. Excavation was begun by Charles Higham and Rachanie Thosarat in 1984. A large burial chamber was discovered which contained a very elaborate burial of a woman of obvious high status—a princess. She was buried wearing beaded clothing consisting of over 120,000 shell beads. She also had a shell bracelet on her left wrist and two horned disks made of shell on her shoulders. The beads were made from shellfish only found in clear coral waters. As the site is not near clean seas (Khok Phanom Di is on a muddy estuary), the shells would have been obtained through trade. The princess was a potter and it is thought that she gained her prestige from her work. Altogether approximately 139 burials were discovered here, spanning 17–20 generations. Khok Phanom Di was occupied from 4000 B.P. to 3500 B.P.

## Activity

1. View the video. What types of artifacts are shown? What do they tell us about the people of the Southeast Asia Neolithic and Bronze Age tradition?

2. What does the elaborateness of the funeral artifacts mean to you? Does this compare to other agricultural societies you have studied?

3. What do the artifacts found in this burial tell us about the level of trade in Southeast Asian Neolithic and Bronze Age societies? What did the people of Khok Phanom Di trade for the vast quantities of shells that they imported?

# chapter fifteen

# South and Southwest Asia

**o v e r v i e w**

**Indian Subcontinent**

**Indus Valley**

**Iranian Plateau**

**Arabian Peninsula**

**Levant**

**Mesopotamia**

**BOXES**

**Harappa**

**Uruk**

South and Southwest Asia includes the entire area east of the Bay of Bengal, north of the Indian Ocean, east of the Mediterranean, and south of the Caucasus and the Tibetan Plateau (Figure 15.1). It is a region of generally warm to hot climates, low rainfall (except in southern India, where summer monsoons bring abundant rainfall), and rugged terrain. It is also where plants and animals were first domesticated and where the first states developed. Indeed, the region

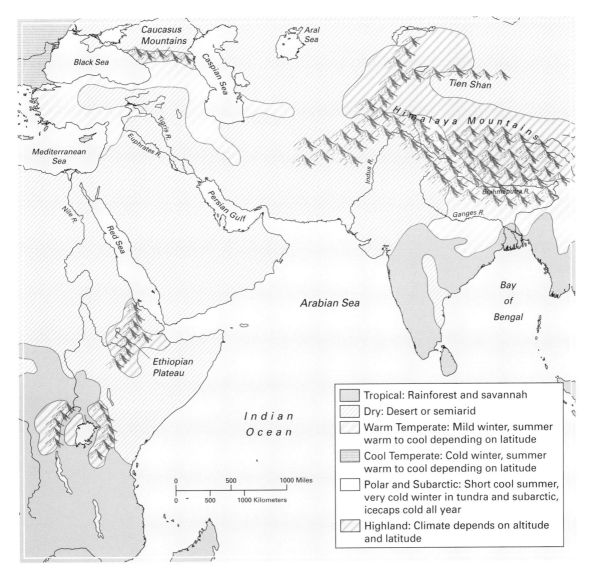

FIGURE **15.1**

The environments of South and Southwest Asia.

is home to two great civilizations, the Harappan in the Indus Valley and the Sumerian in southern Mesopotamia. But the region is also home to a great number of other civilizations, from the states of the Ganges plain to the Bronze Age of the Levant (Figure 15.2). In this chapter I hope to provide a brief overview of this region and the remarkable patterns of cultural evolution within it.

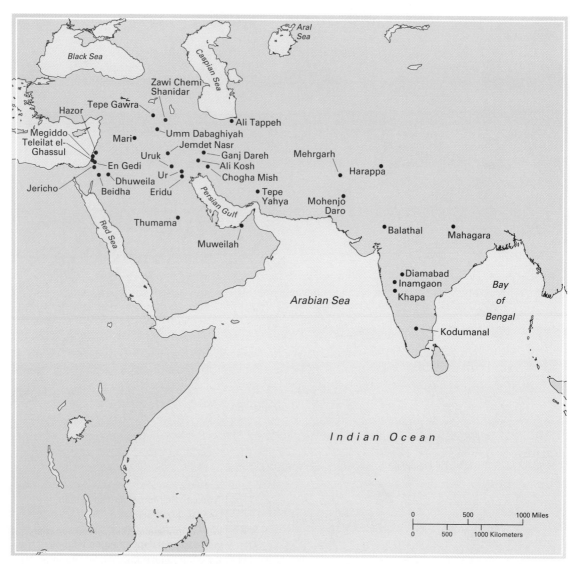

FIGURE **15.2**
Sites discussed in Chapter 15.

## INDIAN SUBCONTINENT

In this section I only discuss the Indian subcontinent east of the Indus valley. The region includes the vast Gangetic plain of northeastern India and the rolling Deccan plateau that forms the foundation of peninsular India. The entire area is subject to a markedly seasonal climate. From June to September the weather is hot and wet, with regular periods of monsoonal rain. The climate becomes cooler between October and February, then heats up again for a hot and dry period between March and mid-June, when the monsoons start again. Elevation alters these conditions, as does distance from the coasts and rain shadows on the lee side of the Ghat mountains. The plants and animals generally follow the pattern of rainfall. In areas where the monsoon rains are most active, particularly in the southern parts of the subcontinent, there are dense tropical and deciduous woodlands. Deciduous forests and grasslands dominate central India. Dryer areas in northern India have thorn forests. A wide range of animals inhabit the Indian subcontinent, from monkeys to tigers to elephants. Of most importance to human groups living in the subcontinent are large ruminants like the water buffalo and ungulates like deer.

The peoples of the **South Asian Microlithic** (7000–3500 B.P.) tradition followed the Upper Paleolithic. They were the first peoples in the region to domesticate animals and, perhaps, plants, although evidence for the latter is equivocal. Remains of domesticated sheep and goats are found in abundance on South Asian Microlithic sites. Whether these animals were locally domesticated or imported from Southwest Asia is unclear. South Asian Microlithic peoples also hunted and fished extensively, and a wide variety of plant foods were collected. In a sense, the South Asian Microlithic economy was much like the hunting and gathering economy of their Upper Paleolithic predecessors, but with domestic sheep and goats replacing a large quantity of hunted game.

South Asian Microlithic peoples were highly mobile, and their settlements were small and short-term. Caves and rockshelters were used where present, and open-air sites are found throughout the subcontinent. Some sites appear to have been seasonal base camps, while others were hunting or special-purpose camps. The largest sites may have had a dozen or more families in residence, while only a few families probably resided at the more common small sites. Houses were small, circular structures, likely built from brush. Some had stone foundations, which perhaps served to secure their coverings from wind, while others had floors paved with pebbles.

As their name suggests, peoples of the South Asian Microlithic tradition developed a stone tool industry based on microlithic blades. These were combined and placed in handles to make composite tools such as knives and projectile points. Blades and flakes were also used for knives, scrapers, burins, and projectile points, among other tools. Polished stone was used to make anvils and hammer stones, perhaps for processing nuts and wild grains, and stone rings that may have been weights for digging sticks.

Over time, peoples of the South Asian Microlithic tradition began to incorporate domesticated plants into their economy, to become more sedentary, and to make ceramics and metals. These changes ushered in the various neolithic and chalcolithic traditions of the Indian subcontinent.

In the Ganges Valley of northeastern India, people of the **Ganges Neolithic** (4500–2500 B.P.) tradition were among the first to develop a settled agricultural lifestyle. Domesticated goats and sheep remained important, and the pig and **zebu** were added to the group of animals that were kept (Figure 15.3). Agriculture was based on rice, apparently an import from Southeast Asia. Some sites also have evidence of wheat, barley, and lentils, imports from Southwest Asia. Thus northern India even at this early date is a crossroads of Asia—a pattern that will continue throughout prehistory and, indeed, to the modern day.

Most Ganges Neolithic sites are situated near the tributaries of the Ganges on good agricultural soils. These were long-term habitations and included special facilities for craft production (especially bone and antler tools) and cattle raising. At **Mahagara**, located near Allahabad in Uttar Pradesh, for example, houses were arranged around a large enclosure containing hoof marks of both adult and juvenile cattle—a cattle pen of some kind. Such an arrangement suggests that cattle may have been the property of the Mahagara community as a whole, rather than of individual families. Houses at Mahagara were circular wattle-and-daub structures, likely with a conical thatch roof. It appears that two or three adjacent huts formed a single compound that shared a courtyard where much of daily activity took place. At Mahagara eight such compounds were identified, each housing perhaps five to ten people.

The material remains from the floors of house clusters at Mahagara provide a good picture of the tool kit of Ganges Neolithic peoples. Stone blades, ground stone food-processing equipment, and a variety of ceramics were present. Ceramics were

**South Asian Microlithic** (7000–3500 B.P.)

**Ganges Neolithic** (4500–2500 B.P.)

**Mahagara** (India, Ganges Neolithic)

**Zebu:** a type of cattle domesticated in South Asia with a distinctive hump and dewlap.

FIGURE **15.3**
A zebu, the first domesticated cattle in South Asia.

simple and handmade at Mahagara, but elsewhere (especially late in the tradition) ceramics were made on a slow wheel and sometimes took on complex forms. Common ceramic types are bowls, platters, vases, and jars. Mahagara has a relative paucity of bone and antler tools, which are found in great abundance at sites that do not have access to workable stone. Mahagara gives us a picture of a simple, egalitarian community of farmers and cattle herders, and the site probably represents a common way of life in the Ganges Neolithic.

The relatively egalitarian agricultural lifestyle of the Ganges Neolithic peoples persisted for nearly two millenniums, but by 2500 B.P. developments elsewhere on the Indian subcontinent brought about dramatic change. Peoples of the **Gangetic India** (2500–2000 B.P.) tradition were incorporated into the world of caste-based state societies that were already present in much of the rest of India. **Castes** are social groups that are defined by occupation and are ascribed to a person at birth. Within caste-based states, people are born into an occupation which they cannot choose and cannot leave. Castes in India typically have three major groups—brahmans, who are elites and take on leadership roles; commoners, who do craft, farm, and merchant work; and untouchables, who are engaged in ritually or physically "unclean" occupations like public sanitation.

Peoples of the Gangetic India tradition lived in either agricultural villages or regional centers. The primary occupants of villages were farmers, but there were also craftsmen, local bureaucrats, and merchants in all but the smallest villages. Houses were made from wattle and daub, mud brick, or, occasionally, fired brick. Houses were placed along streets, normally oriented along cardinal directions. In addition to houses for farmers and craftsmen, villages also had one or more temples, a community hall where public meetings were held, and a place where cremations were performed. In larger villages and regional centers individual streets would be associated with different craft items, and larger areas would be set aside for temple and public spaces. Some larger villages and centers also had public wells and sanitation systems.

**Gangetic India**
(2500–2000 B.P.)

**Castes:** social groups that are defined by occupation and are ascribed to a person at birth.

Gangetic India farmers typically produced two crops a year—a summer rice crop and a winter crop of wheat and barley. Cattle, oxen, sheep, and goats were all kept, providing milk and meat. Meat was also obtained by fishing and, to a lesser extent, hunting. Farmers produced enough to support a wide variety of craftsmen, bureaucrats, and priests. Of particular importance were metal and ceramic craftsmen. Copper and bronze had been used for several thousand years in India, but by the time of the Gangetic India tradition iron was becoming common and was being used for a wide variety of household and agricultural items. Ceramics were made on a fast wheel by skilled artisans. The ceramics from the Gangetic India tradition are typically slipped in black or red and fired in a high-temperature kiln to give them a lustrous surface. Typical forms of these ceramics are dishes and bowls with straight or inverted sides and *handi*, which is a rounded cooking vessel quite typical on the Indian subcontinent. According to historic documents of the time, craftsmen were organized into guilds, and each guild inhabited particular sections of villages where they lived and worked together. Guilds were so close-knit that they often formed distinctive subcastes within the overall caste-based social hierarchy.

Social hierarchy played a central role in Gangetic India society. Historic documents describe rigidly organized states headed by kings. The king presided over the executive and judicial departments and acted as the supreme commander of the army in battles. Subordinate to the king were a large group of ministers and lesser officials, military officers, diplomats, and lower bureaucrats. Under the **Mauryan Empire,** which encompassed the entire Ganges region by 2300 B.P., the Ganges region was divided into into provinces called *prant*. Each province had a governor who was part of the imperial family. Provinces were further divided into districts headed by local rulers under the control of the provincial governor. Finally, each district was further divided into units of ten villages headed by another local ruler who answered to the district ruler.

The Mauryan Empire expanded to control virtually the entire Indian subcontinent, even though states had developed elsewhere in India before Maghada, core state of the Mauryan Empire, had developed. In central India, the region between the Thar desert in the north and the Ghat mountains in the south, the process of state development began in the **Central Indian Chalcolithic** (5000–3100 B.P.) tradition. Here small communities of farmers began settling in river valleys where large tracts of rich alluvial soil, plentiful fresh water, and abundant pasturage were all available. In these locations the peoples of the Central Indian Chalcolithic raised crops of wheat, barley, rice, lentils, and other domesticated plants. They pastured sheep, goats, and zebu in the surrounding grasslands.

**Central Indian Chalcolithic** (5000–3100 B.P.)

The site of **Balathal** in Rajasthan is one of the earliest Central Indian Chalcolithic farming communities. The site's first residents constructed simple wattle and daub structures, but by about 4500 B.P. the people were building more substantial mud-brick structures with dung or lime plastered floors. Many of these mud-brick structures were multiroomed, with separate areas for storage, cooking, sleeping, and craft activities. In the middle of the settlement was a large stone structure that has been interpreted as a granary. Special copper and ceramic workshops have been found at Balathal. The copper workshops have U-shaped furnaces for heating and smelting copper, which was made into axes, chisels, daggers, fishhooks, and beads and bangles. Ceramics were made at Balathal on a slow wheel and included dishes, pots, and bowls in both fine and coarse forms.

**Balathal** (India, Central Indian Chalcolithic)

Because villages like Balathal have public facilities and evidence of craft specialization, many scholars believe that there must have been some form of centralized political leadership in the Central Indian Chalcolithic tradition. Some sites that appear larger than agricultural villages like Balathal have been interpreted as regional centers, and this further suggests that a chiefdom form of political organization might have been present. However, archaeological evidence is equivocal, and

**Mauryan Empire:** an empire located in the Ganges River valley, dating to roughly 2300 B.P.

at this point the specific form of political organization that was present among Central Indian Chalcolithic societies is unknown.

Peoples of the **Central Indian Iron Age** (3100–2100 B.P.) added iron utensils and weapons to the tool kit. Unfortunately, few Central Indian Iron Age sites have been excavated. Those that have vary in size, and these suggest that both agricultural villages and regional centers were present. Remains of both wattle and daub and mud-brick structures have been found, with both round and rectangular floor plans. Central Indian Iron Age peoples supported themselves by growing millet, rice, barley, and various legumes. Cotton was also grown. Domestic cattle were the most important animal resource, remains of domestic horse, water buffalo, sheep, and goat have also been identified. Horses were probably not consumed, but were important both for riding and as status goods.

Iron was used by Central Indian Iron Age peoples for a variety of tools and weapons, including arrow and spear points, knives, and axes, among many others. Ceramics were wheel-made and came in a diversity of forms. Ground stone was used for processing grains, and the common occurrence of ceramic spindle whorls suggests spinning and weaving of both cotton and wool. Many of these items, particularly metals and ceramics, were likely made by craft specialists. Trade was also common in the Central Indian Iron Age, and exotic goods include carnelian and gold.

Evidence from mortuary contexts and the limited settlement evidence suggest that Central Indian Iron Age societies were organized into multiple competing political units, at least some of which contained social hierarchies. These societies are probably best classified as simple chiefdoms. The kind of evidence that mortuary remains provide is illustrated at **Khapa**, located on a bend in the Krishna River, in the semiarid Deccan plateau of Maharashtra. The site contains twenty-six stone circles, ranging from 12 to 27 meters in diameter. The circles were constructed of large unmodified boulders, and in their centers were burials placed in small pits covered with clay and stone rubble. Remains of both primary and secondary burials were identified. Horse remains were also found in some of the stone circles. Artifacts recovered in graves included ceramics, iron implements and weapons, and copper vessels and ornaments, as well as carnelian, crystal, agate, chalcedony, jasper, and glass beads. The form of these burial monuments and the large amount of exotic and prestige items included within them suggest these were elite graves, and they give clear evidence for social stratification during the Central Indian Iron Age.

In Southern India, the region south of the Ghat mountains, peoples of the **South Indian Chalcolithic** (5000–3100 B.P.) tradition were the first sedentary agriculturalists. Agricultural villages are usually found near fertile tracts of land and good sources of water, and these are often extensive settlements with thick habitation deposits, suggesting long-term occupation by large populations. South Indian Chalcolithic sites have produced evidence of rectangular or circular mud houses with low mud walls and wattle and daub screens. Floors were made of layers of silt and black clay and periodically plastered with cow dung. Larger houses with special-purpose rooms and in central locations within these villages have been interpreted as homes of elites.

Settlements that were strategically located at crossroads on trade routes may have served as regional centers. One such site is **Daimabad**. Daimabad is a large, fortified site located on the Pravara river in Maharashtra. The site consists of several occupation layers of houses, workshops, and a remarkable religious complex. Houses at the site are of mud brick and are rectangular in floor plan. In one area eight houses formed a complex that may have been a merchant's house, since it had a unique assortment of artifacts—a terracotta lamp, a terracotta figurine, a terracotta cylindrical seal, thirteen pottery spindle whorls, one conical pendant, and two beads. Elsewhere a lapidary workshop was found, and the house of a coppersmith, complete with two copper-smelting furnaces. Two pottery kilns were also

**Central Indian Iron Age (3100–2100 B.P.)**

**Khapa** (India, Central Indian Iron Age)

**South Indian Chalcolithic (5000–3100 B.P.)**

**Daimabad** (India, South Indian Chalcolithic)

found at the site. These kilns each had a domed outer mud wall, a central ash packing, and an inner burnt wall. They had two stoke-holes at the base and would have been capable of firing ceramics at very high temperatures. The religious complex at Daimabad is comprised of a large mud platform with several altars for burnt offerings. Three postholes near the altars were probably for wooden posts to which animals to be sacrificed were tied.

The South Indian Chalcolithic people subsisted on agriculture, animal husbandry, fishing, and hunting. They raised sheep, goat, zebu, and pig, and the large numbers of animal bones on most sites suggest that the people relied heavily on meat from both domestic and wild animals. Fish were also important in the South Indian Chalcolithic diet. The South Indian Chalcolithic peoples grew barley, rice, millet, lentils, and other legumes. Craft production was also an important part of the economy, even for farming villages. Foodstuff and animal products were traded for goods such as pottery, beads, lime, and metals produced by craft specialists. Copper work was relatively simple, with most objects made by cold hammering. Pottery manufacture was the largest specialized craft industry, with most ceramics being wheel-made, and finewares were of outstanding quality.

This wide variety of developed crafts, agriculture, herd animals, and industrial activity at sites such as Daimabad shows specialization, division of labor, and the existence of a stratified community organization. One elite household that was larger and had more goods than others was found at Daimabad, but the best evidence of social stratification comes from burials at the site. Some individuals were richly accompanied with beads of shell, terracotta, and semiprecious stones, and a wide variety of tools. At **Inamgaon**, located on the River Ghod near Pune, Maharashtra, a five-roomed structure in the middle of the settlement has been interpreted as an elite residence. Within the structure was a unique burial of a 35-year-old man in a four-legged clay jar, a man who has been identified as a chief of the community (Figure 15.4). The site also has fortification walls, an irrigation channel, and a granary. Although the social organization of South Indian Chalcolithic communities is not entirely clear, the existing evidence supports the idea that simple chiefdoms were present.

**Inamgaon**
(Indian, Central Indian Chalcolithic)

The evidence from mortuary contexts and historical documents suggests that **South Indian Iron Age** (3100–2100 B.P.) societies were organized into multiple competing political units, probably best classified as chiefdoms, though there was likely great diversity in South Indian Iron Age political organization, ranging from more egalitarian communities to, near the end of the period, incipient states.

**South Indian Iron Age**
(3100–2100 B.P.)

Mortuary sites are by far the most common sites of the South Indian Iron Age, with nearly 2,000 such sites known. These sites range in size from one grave to regional centers with more than 1,500 graves, suggesting a hierarchical structure. In contrast to cemeteries, less than 200 settlement sites have been documented. This appears to be in large part a function of sampling biases, though it may be that large settlements were rare in some areas. Where settlement sites have been well documented there is evidence for a settlement hierarchy, with the large and best-known settlements ranging from 20 to 50 hectares in area. Smaller settlements and occupied rock shelters have also been found.

Large settlements are found most frequently in defensible locations on the slopes of hills and outcrops, and sometimes along major transport routes. Evidence for terracing of habitation areas, defensive walls, and reservoirs or water catchment basins is known from several settlements. One such settlement is at **Kodumanal**, located on the Noyyal River in Tamil Nadu. The site consists of a settlement area and a cemetery. The settlement is a low mound with roughly 2 meters of stratified deposits that extends over an area of about 20 hectares. Structures were rectangular, of mud-brick construction, and with lime-plastered floors. Ceramics were found in abundance and were in a wide variety of forms and styles. There was extensive evidence for craft production at the site, including remains of iron furnaces, furnaces

**Kodumanal**
(India, South Indian Iron Age)

FIGURE **15.4**
This unique jar burial from the South Indian Chalcolithic site of Inamgaon may contain the remains of a community chief.

associated with the production of crucible steel, and abundant evidence for manu-facture of beryl, sapphire, and crystal beads. Numerous spindle whorls were also recovered, as were a small number of Roman imports and coins.

The cemetery at Kodumanal consists of some 150 megalithic graves covering an area of 40 hectares. Burials were placed in stone crypts beneath heaped mounds of stones, which were themselves enclosed within single or double stone circles (Figure 15.5). Grave goods included ceramics, iron implements, weapons, and horse tack, as well as ornaments including copper, silver, and gold objects and beads. One grave contained more than 2,000 imported carnelian beads and thus illustrates clearly that these graves were reserved for elites. The evidence from graves at sites like Kodumanal illustrates that trade in prestige goods was widespread throughout and beyond South India during this period. Elite fineware ceramics may also have moved widely, and by the end of the Iron Age, Roman goods began to appear in South India.

Subsistence in the South Indian Iron Age was, as in preceding periods, based on agriculture and animal husbandry. A wide array of hunted animals were also impor-tant to subsistence, as were fish and shellfish. Basic tools of everyday life included ground and chipped stone tools, as well as bone and copper artifacts. Ceramics of various kinds, both handmade and wheel-made, are found. Iron implements were widespread at both habitational sites and in mortuary deposits. Both ceramics and iron were made by craft specialists. Given the paucity of settlement excavations it is unknown to what extent households were economically self-sufficient in food and tool production.

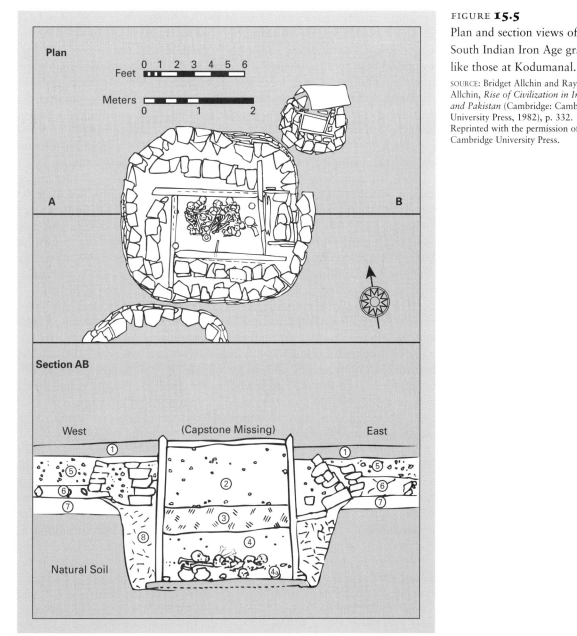

FIGURE **15.5**

Plan and section views of a
South Indian Iron Age grave
like those at Kodumanal.

SOURCE: Bridget Allchin and Raymond
Allchin, *Rise of Civilization in India
and Pakistan* (Cambridge: Cambridge
University Press, 1982), p. 332.
Reprinted with the permission of
Cambridge University Press.

## INDUS VALLEY

The Indus valley encompasses two major rivers, the Indus and the Ghaggar-Hakra.
Surrounding these two rivers is a vast alluvial plain that has provided humans a rich
environment for hunting and gathering, fishing, agriculture, and animal husbandry.
Indus valley sites are not strictly confined to the alluvial plain, however, but are also
found in the uplands and mountain foothills to the north and west. These mountains held important sources of flint, chert, quartz, granite, and minerals. The valleys also provided access to peoples and materials in Central Asia. The climate of
the area is generally mild to hot and is dominated by two distinct seasons. The winter is mild and relatively dry, while the summer is hot and wet, with regular
monsoons bringing abundant rainfall.

Following the Paleolithic era in the Indus Valley, peoples of the **Indus Neolithic**
(9000–6800 B.P.) tradition began to settle into permanent or semipermanent villages.

**Indus Neolithic**
**(9000–6800 B.P.)**

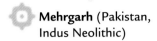

**Mehrgarh** (Pakistan, Indus Neolithic)

At the site of **Mehrgarh** at the base of the Bolan Pass in central Pakistan, the earliest structures are square and built of mud brick. Roofs were of thatch or woven mats. Early in the tradition, hunting was the basis of the economy at Mehrgarh, and it appears that hunting focused on "crop robbers" such as wild goat, gazelle, deer, antelope, wild cattle, and pig. Soon domesticated forms of sheep, goat, and cattle appeared. These may have been locally domesticated or imports from Southwest Asia. Plant exploitation early in the tradition included collecting of wild grains such as barley and fruits such as dates. Later, domesticated forms of wheat and barley appeared, probably imported from Southwest Asia. Fields must have been irrigated by controlled flooding or situated along oxbows or marshy areas.

No pottery making is found in the earliest levels at Mehrgarh, but there are some unfired clay containers and crudely formed clay figurines. Ceramics, at first crude but becoming steadily more sophisticated, appeared by 7500 B.P. Other tools found at Mehrgarh include bone awls and antler tools, ground stone bowls, celts, mortars and pestles, chipped stone scrapers, blades, and microliths. Craft production at Mehrgarh included the manufacture of beads and pendants from soft local limestone. Disc beads made using *Spondylus* shell, turquoise, steatite, and lapis lazuli have also been found, but there is no evidence they were manufactured at the site.

The presence of *Spondylus* shell beads at Mehrgarh indicates trade with the coast over 500 kilometers to the south. Similarly, beads of turquoise, steatite, and lapis lazuli must have been obtained through trade extending to Afghanistan or Iran. How this trade was organized is unknown. Some scholars have suggested that trade may have occurred through contacts made in the western highlands during summer movements to pasture animals in those regions. It is also possible that some individuals undertook trade expeditions down the Indus to obtain whole shell or shell beads from the coast. On the other hand, traders from the coast may have traveled inland to market their goods, either directly up the Indus Valley or via the highland routes.

**Early Indus**
(7500–4600 B.P.)

By the time of the **Early Indus** (7500–4600 B.P.) tradition, trade links up and down the Indus valley were well established. Trade during the Early Indus period was basically an extension of networks that had been established during the Neolithic period combined with exploration and exploitation of new resource areas. This is represented by an increase in the importation of raw materials from distant resource areas, rather than finished goods. In the Early Indus tradition Mehrgarh became a central place for trade, and raw materials (copper, shell, chert, and others) were processed there for local and regional consumption. Mehrgarh also began producing specialized ceramics for exchange. Trade was apparently controlled by elites who used ceramic **seals** to monitor the movement and ownership of trade goods (Figure 15.6). The discovery of standardized cubical limestone weights suggests that there may have been some form of taxation or regulation of value. In return for these exotic raw materials, elites at Mehrgarh would have provided locally produced items such as wool, cotton, grain, oil, and perhaps meat.

Early Indus settlements are found throughout most of modern Pakistan and parts of northwestern India, and there appears to have been at least a three-tiered settlement system. Mounded sites such as **Harappa** (described in the box feature) represent the largest urban centers (Figure 15.7). They are surrounded by smaller towns located at variable distances. Interspersed between and around these are small agricultural hamlets or farmsteads. Many of the Early Indus sites are made up of single mounds of habitation debris, while larger sites are sometimes divided into two distinct mounded areas. These large villages had formal streets, some with open drains, walls built to prevent flooding, and distinct areas of habitation and craft production, such as pottery and metalwork. At both large and small sites houses are made of mud brick with roofs constructed of wooden beams and thatching. Several houses built next to each other define open areas or passageways that were used for craft activities and burials. Cylindrical pits were used for garbage disposal and bell-shaped pits lined with clay were used for storage.

**Harappa**
(Pakistan, Early Indus)

**Seals:** pieces of carved ceramic or stone used to make impressions in wet clay used to seal the contents of materials being shipped. Typically seals identify the owner of a shipment.

FIGURE **15.6**
Early Indus seals from
Harappa.

Agriculture and animal husbandry supported these Early Indus communities. Two crops a year were raised. In the winter, wheat, barley, and legumes were grown, while in the summer monsoon season cotton, dates, melon, and other water-loving crops were produced. Animal husbandry appears to have focused on cattle, water buffalo, sheep, and goat. Fishing and hunting supplemented the diet. Trade and craft production were also important features of the economy, particularly at larger sites, where specialized craft production facilities suggest increasing localization and control of production.

FIGURE **15.7**
Excavations to uncover a
brick culvert near the main
gate of Harappa.

# Harappa

Harappa sits on the southern bank of the Ravi river, a major tributary of the Indus river, in Punjab Province, Pakistan. It is one of three known cities of the Mature Indus tradition (the others are Mohenjo Daro and Ganweriwala) and was the first to be extensively researched. The site was identified in 1826, and systematic excavations were first conducted in 1920. Work continued throughout the 1920s and 1930s by the Archaeological Survey of India. Sir Mortimer Wheeler worked at the site for one season in 1946. In 1986 an ongoing research project was launched under the direction of George Dales and Richard Meadow.

Harappa itself consists of three large mounds and several smaller mounds that cover an area of approximately 150 hectares. The main part of the site is located on Mound AB, which is a north–south oriented parallelogram approximately 7 hectares in area and rising some 6 to 8 meters above the surrounding plain. The mound was called a "citadel" by Wheeler because it is surrounded by a massive mud-brick fortification wall. To the north is a lower area covering approximately 10 hectares and labeled Mound F. It houses the remains of what are interpreted as a large granary and threshing area that may have held food for the city. Southeast of Mound AB are two long east–west mounds: Mound E, 13 hectares in area and rising some 7 meters above the plain, and Mound ET, which is approximately 5.5 hectares. Between Mounds AB and E is a large pottery workshop area with kilns, and south of Mound AB is a large cemetery area.

Harappa began as a small village on the Ravi river about 5200 B.P. Over time the community grew, and by 4600 B.P. had emerged as a center of Indus civilization.

By around 4800 B.P. there is clear evidence for the use of writing, which may have been an outgrowth of marks made by potters to identify the ceramics they made. Potters marks and clay seals, along with the emergence of Indus script, suggest that individuals were carefully controlling the products they produced and exchanged. While there is no clear evidence of social classes in the Early Indus tradition, the presence of writing and the importance of trade both suggest that wealthy elites were present. No centralized structures for political, economic, or ideological control have been found at Early Indus sites, yet the emergence of relatively large urban centers indicates that people living at some sites developed more complex forms of social organization.

**Mature Indus**
(4600–3900 B.P.)

**Mohenjo Daro**
(Pakistan, Mature Indus)

Powerful leaders were clearly present by the time of the **Mature Indus** (4600–3900 B.P.) tradition, and sites like Harappa and Mohenjo Daro became capitals of regional states. **Mohenjo Daro** is located in the Indus River valley in Sindh Province, Pakistan (Figure 15.8). The site covers some 80 hectares, all of which contain dense residential debris. On the western side of the site is a larger mound, called the "citadel," that is roughly 7 hectares in area and is enclosed by a massive mud-brick wall. Mohenjo Daro is divided into sectors by four major north–south streets and four equally wide east–west streets that run across the site. Numerous smaller streets and alleyways further subdivide the city. The site is best known for its well-preserved architecture, which provides a unique picture of life in a Mature Indus

At its height, around 4500 B.P., Harappa covered an area of about 200 hectares and may have had a population of more than 20,000 people. Although most of the architecture of the city has been badly disturbed by brick robbing, it is still possible to determine the overall layout of the different neighborhoods and identify the presence of drains and streets. Most residents lived in multiroomed houses built of mud-brick. These were densely packed into residential neighborhoods, both within the walled area of Mound AB, and on the other mounds. Although houses differed in size, nearly all had private wells, and many had staircases leading to an upper floor or roof.

Most residents of Harappa were farmers and craftspeople. Workshops of various types are found throughout the city. Evidence for ceramics, copper and bronze work, stone work, brick making, bead making, and many other crafts have been found. A variety of weights have also been found, along with numerous stamp seals and seal impressions. The presence of these latter items implies that scribes, administrators, and perhaps merchants were also an important part of the Harappan community. The presence of the large defensive wall around Mound AB, and of a well-designed drainage system through which water ran in covered drains from houses into the street and out of the community, suggests a powerful central government was in place as well. Unfortunately, excavations have uncovered little about the political leaders at Harappa, and at this point we have only a derivative sense of their presence and role.

SOURCES: Allchin, Bridget, and Raymond Allchin, *The Rise of Civilization in India and Pakistan* (Cambridge: Cambridge University Press, 1982); Meadow, Richard, *Harappa Excavations 1986–1990* (Madison: Prehistory Press, 1991).

city. Most of the excavated architecture reflects blocks of mud-brick houses with associated bathing platforms, wells, and small internal courtyards. The density of settlement was very high in Mohenjo Daro, and the cramped courtyards and narrow alleyways must have teemed with activity.

In addition to large cities like Mohenjo Daro, there were also smaller cities, each of which appears to have been associated with a large city. These smaller cities were located along rivers and overland trade routes, and were likely outposts that linked the major cities into a network of information and exchange. There were also smaller towns surrounding both the larger and smaller cities, as well as numerous agricultural villages, hamlets, and farmsteads. The general layout of most of these nonurban settlements was fairly irregular, unlike the rigid grid pattern of urban centers. Larger towns and cities usually had several mounds, one often serving as a central religious–political area like the "citadel" at Mohenjo Daro. Most settlements were built up within or on top of massive mud-brick walls or platforms, which may have been defensive but would also have served to prevent flooding. In addition to perimeter walls numerous smaller mud-brick platforms were constructed inside the settlement as house foundations.

Three basic types of structures have been uncovered at Mohenjo Daro. The most common are mud-brick houses built around a central courtyard and isolated from the street by a discrete street entrance. Groups of houses are often associated

FIGURE **15.8**
Ruins of Mohenjo Daro, showing residences in the foreground and the citadel rising in the background.

with a well, and the presence of wells, bathing platforms, sewers, and public garbage bins is one of the hallmarks of Mature Indus settlements. Apparently, peoples of the Mature Indus tradition were greatly concerned with sanitation and spent considerable energy maintaining the cleanliness of their cities. A second common type of structure is a large house surrounded by smaller structures. The smaller structures may have been houses and workshops for individuals attached to the larger house. Finally, there are large public structures. These include water tanks, granaries, and city walls and platforms.

The peoples of Mohenjo Daro supported themselves through agriculture, animal husbandry, craft production, and trade. Farmers planted grains such as wheat and barley in the fall to be harvested in the spring, then planted water-loving crops such as cotton and melon to grow during the monsoon season and be harvested in late summer. Goats, sheep, zebu, cattle, water buffalo, and pigs were all kept. Fish and hunted meat supplemented the diet. Specialized crafts of many types were produced at Mohenjo Daro, including ceramics, metals, beads (from shell, stone, and many exotic materials), wood, and flaked stone. Some crafts appear to have been produced by local guilds or family groups, based on the fact that there are specific areas of the city dedicated to specific crafts. Other crafts were clearly supported by elite households, as evidenced by the workshops attached to elite houses. These craft goods were used locally at Mohenjo Daro, but were also exchanged throughout the Indus valley region.

Trade was apparently closely controlled by the state. Evidence for this control includes the presence of standardized stone weights found at all major Mature Indus sites, seals used to mark bundles of goods, and ceramics inscribed to indicate owners, the commodities being shipped, and the intended destination (Figure 15.9). External trade during the Indus period can be documented with the Arabian Gulf, Afghanistan, and Mesopotamia. Most trade ran though large urban centers like Mohenjo Daro, which were directly connected to each other and to external regions. Smaller cities and towns obtained goods from the urban centers, from which hamlets and farmsteads, in turn, obtained goods.

This highly developed trade, the control of craft production, and the presence of urban centers leads most scholars to think that Mature Indus cities were

FIGURE **15.9**
Mature Indus seals with pictographs which may indicate the owner, contents, or destination of materials being shipped.

organized as state-level societies with a considerable degree of decentralization. This decentralization may have meant that various peoples or groups held power, perhaps within distinct areas of the society. Instead of one social group with absolute control, the rulers or dominant members in the various cities would have included merchants, ritual specialists, and individuals who controlled resources such as land, livestock, and raw materials. These independent city-states were integrated with one another primarily through shared economic and ideological systems. Each city served as a central place within a specific region, and they all appear to have used a shared script and a standardization of economic exchange that may reflect a form of taxation. They had a common material culture, and there is clear evidence for a common ideology as represented by symbolic objects such as seals, figurines, ornaments, ceramics, and other artifacts.

## IRANIAN PLATEAU

The Iranian Plateau is a rugged highland ringed by mountains that reach elevations of 4,000 meters above sea level in some places. These mountains create microenvironments that change with elevation. Limestone makes up much of the underlying geology of the Iranian Plateau, and in many areas it has been metamorphosed and uplifted. Deposits of various minerals, flint, and chert are common throughout the region. Solution caves and natural springs are also common and provide good sources of shelter and fresh water. Much of the area is relatively treeless and is dominated by steppe vegetation. Wooded areas around the Caspian sea and in some mountain areas contain both broadleaf deciduous trees and conifers. The modern climatic of the Iranian Plateau is marked by hot, dry summers and cool, moist winters, a pattern that appears to extend back to the Mesolithic era.

Peoples of the **Iranian Mesolithic** (12,000–8000 B.P.) tradition followed a way of life in many ways similar to those of their Paleolithic predecessors. They lived primarily in caves and rockshelters that would have been occupied by small bands made up of one or two extended families. These peoples hunted and gathered broadly in the surrounding environments. Tools used by Iranian Mesolithic peoples included various types of stone microblades and retouched microblades. Bone tools included awls and scrapers. Ground stone tools included querns, mullers, mortars and pestles, stone vessels, celts, maceheads, and abraders.

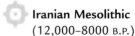 **Iranian Mesolithic**
(12,000–8000 B.P.)

**Ali Tappeh**
(Iran, Iranian
Mesolithic)

**Zawi Chemi Shanidar**
(Iraq, Iranian
Mesolithic)

**Iranian Neolithic**
(11,500–7500 B.P.)

**Ganj Dareh**
(Iran, Iranian Neolithic)

A good example of an Iranian Mesolithic site is **Ali Tappeh,** a cave site located in what is today northern Iran. The cave is situated near the coast of the Caspian Sea, in an area that was probably covered with oak forests at the time of the site's habitation. Ali Tappeh was inhabited by small bands of hunting and gathering peoples who may have used the cave as a seasonal base camp. A broad range of animal resources was utilized by the inhabitants of Ali Tappeh including boar, cattle, deer, horse, goat, sheep, waterfowl, fish, and shellfish; however, primary emphasis was on gazelle and Caspian seal. Plant remains were not recovered from the site, but it is likely that the inhabitants of Ali Tappeh used the oak forests extensively for nuts, fruits, and legumes. Microliths and bone tools were found in abundance at the cave, and these illustrate a tool industry that was simple and available to everyone.

Another Iranian Mesolithic, **Zawi Chemi Shanidar,** located near Shanidar Cave, discussed earlier as a Mousterian tradition site, illustrates the slow process of settling down that took place on the Iranian Plateau during the Mesolithic era. Zawi Chemi Shanidar is an open site situated in the alluvial plain of a 13-kilometer-long valley of the Shanidar river in what is today northern Iraq. The environment during the Iranian Mesolithic would have varied from open steppe-forests to fairly dense oak woodlands. People living at Zawi Chemi Shanidar would have had a wide range of resources to exploit in these diverse environments, and the Shanidar river and a nearby spring would have provided plenty of water. The site's inhabitants built small, roughly 2-meter diameter, circular hut foundations of stone. These are the first substantial structures on the Iranian Plateau and may suggest long-term habitation at the site. Certainly, Zawi, Chemi Shanidar was located in a prime environment that would have provided abundant resources, and the site's residents apparently took advantage of them.

The people living at Zawi Chemi Shanidar hunted a wide variety of game, but deer and sheep appear to have been the most commonly taken. The sheep remains indicate a relatively high proportion of individuals under the age of twelve months, and some scholars have suggested that this manipulation of wild sheep herds is evidence for the beginnings of domestication. On the other hand, the large number of young animals may simply reflect seasonality in the site's habitation. If the site was primarily inhabited in the summer and fall (with the residents retreating to Shanidar cave or to some other well-sheltered place during the winter) then the wild sheep population would have had many young individuals who were born in the spring. Whether the peoples of Zawi Chemi Shanidar were beginning to domesticate sheep is unclear, but it is clear that they resided at the site for long periods of time, beginning a process of settling down that would continue through the Iranian Neolithic tradition.

Peoples of the **Iranian Neolithic** (11,500–7500 B.P.) tradition began living in villages of fifty to one hundred people. Initially, they built semisubterranean huts of wood, wattle and daub, clay slabs, or packed mud. Later they constructed aboveground rectilinear houses of clay or packed mud, often built adjacent to each other with little or no space between them. Over time villages became larger and some may have housed as many as 400 individuals. These later villages consisted of multiroom houses, often with adjacent courtyards. Houses of these later villages were separated from each other by narrow alleyways.

A good example of one of these larger Iranian Neolithic villages is the site of **Ganj Dareh,** located in the central Zagros mountains of western Iran. The site was at a relatively high elevation surrounded by oak and pistachio forests, and the region was probably home to numerous wild goats. The site itself consists of an oval mound roughly 40 meters in diameter. The lowest level of the mound has evidence of small semisubterranean huts. In the main Neolithic levels of the site, however, rectangular structures of mud slabs or mud brick are present. These houses were built against one another in an agglutinated pattern that shows little evidence of

FIGURE **15.10**
A painted Ceramic Neolithic
jar from Syria.

formal organization. The peoples at Ganj Dareh lived by hunting and gathering, but
there is good evidence that domesticated goats were present, and the presence of
abundant wheat, barley, and legume remains well above the elevation where these
normally grow suggests they may have been domesticated as well.

One of the earliest sites with evidence of domestication is **Ali Kosh**, located on
the Deh Luran plain of western Iran. Here in the earliest phases of the site's habitation (around 9800 B.P.) people lived primarily on emmer wheat and barley that were
harvested from nearby wild stands. Sheep and goat were also eaten in abundance,
and since these had not yet undergone the physical changes associated with domestication they may have been wild as well. Over time, both developed domesticated
traits, which I will discuss in more detail in the next chapter. What is interesting to
note is that, unlike Middle America where domesticated plants proceeded settled life
by thousands of years, Ali Kosh illustrates a pattern of domestication developing
hand-in-hand with settled life. I will discuss this in more detail in the next chapter
on the origins of agriculture.

Also developing hand-in-hand with settled life were ceramics, which first
appeared at about 8500 B.P., well after domesticated plants and animals had already
become an important part of the subsistence economy. These early ceramics were
chaff-tempered and either wet-smoothed or burnished (Figure 15.10). They were
often decorated with geometric designs in red paint or with red slip. Bowls were the
most common form, but beakers, large storage jars, and trays or plates were also
produced. Other utensils used by the Iranian Neolithic peoples were microlithic
blades and composite blade tools such as sickles and knives. Ground stone querns
and mullers were used both to process food items and to grind mineral-based pigments. The ground stone assemblages from Iranian Neolithic sites frequently contain
pierced stones, which may have functioned as maceheads. Items made of worked
bone include needles, awls, and spatulas that may have been used to work hides.

While the social and political organization of Iranian Neolithic villages is not
known, there is no evidence to suggest that there were formal leaders or any social
inequality beyond individual differences in ability. This egalitarian lifestyle would
largely continue, but with some interesting changes, during the Iranian Chalcolithic
tradition.

**Ali Kosh**
(Iran, Iranian Neolithic)

## Iranian Chalcolithic (7500–5500 B.P.)

**Chogha Mish** (Iran, Iranian Chalcolithic)

**Tepe Yahya** (Iran, Iranian Chalcolithic)

The **Iranian Chalcolithic** (7500–5500 B.P.) tradition saw the emergence of regional centers with large populations. One of these was located at the site of **Chogha Mish,** located on the Susiana plain of southwestern Iran. The area was a rich steppe parkland that would have provided abundant pasturage for domestic animals and, with irrigation in years when rains did not provide adequate moisture, was a fertile location for grain agriculture. During the Chalcolithic period Chogha Mish became the largest site in the region, covering an area of about 15 hectares. Most of the site consisted of large multiroom houses containing both living spaces and smaller storage rooms. Houses were set close together and separated by narrow alleyways. Most houses had courtyards with associated pottery kilns. There was also a large public structure built on a massive brick platform. The building was roughly 12 meters by 15 meters in size and had 2-meter-thick buttressed walls. Within the building was an "L"-shaped hall and a number of small rooms. One room had been stacked full of painted ceramics. Another room contained a large number of flint nodules and blades, suggesting it was a lithic workshop. The remains of a large brick platform or terrace extended more than 15 meters from the east side of the building. The purpose of the large public building is unclear, but it suggests some centralized control over ceramic distribution and lithic production.

The size of the site and the nature of its architecture and material remains indicate that Chogha Mish was an important regional administrative center. However, the precise nature of the administrative activities carried out here remains unclear. Lithic production was apparently controlled by some centralized authority, and the amount of debris suggests that production far exceeded what was needed by the site's residents. The presence of courtyard kilns associated with domestic structures suggests that pottery production existed as a household industry. Textile production is indicated by the large number of spindle whorls and possible loom weights recovered from the site, and this too appears to have been a household industry. However, the storeroom filled with ceramics at the large public structure indicates that while these items may have been produced at the household level, their distribution may have been controlled at a higher administrative level.

**Tepe Yahya,** located in southeastern Iran, represents a more typical Iranian Chalcolithic village. The site is located in a semiarid steppe environment, with average precipitation only about 250 mm. However, monsoons often bring torrential rains, and rainfall amounts can vary tremendously from year to year and from location to location. The water table in the region is quite high, and wells for both drinking and irrigation could easily be used when rainfall was inadequate.

The village at Tepe Yahya was inhabited for over 5,000 years and changed form dramatically even during the Chalcolithic era. The earliest Chalcolithic village consisted of mud-brick houses organized around what was probably a large communal storage area, which consisted of a cluster of small cell-like compartments each about 2 square meters in size. The houses each had four or five small rooms, none of which had interior features. Most of the interior walls and floors were faced with green plaster, and exterior walls were coated with thick mud plaster. Entrances to the houses looked out toward the communal storage area. Over time the houses became larger and the rooms appear to have taken on distinct functions such as cooking, storage, and sleeping. Some rooms contained hearths and some of the smaller rooms had been paved with sherds. By the end of the Iranian Chalcolithic tradition, the houses at Tepe Yahya became more segregated. By this time each house had its own walled courtyard which contained several storage buildings, and the large communal storage complex was no longer used.

The changes in architecture and village organization at Tepe Yahya probably reflect changes in social and economic organization. During the earlier phases of occupation, either the community itself or a large collection of kin-related households seem to have been the basic economic unit, as indicated by the presence of the large communal storage complex. This may imply relatively equal access to the stored resources and probably reflects egalitarian social and economic relations among individuals and households. The shift to individual household storage areas and courtyards may reflect a change in the ownership and control of production modes, with each household being the primary economic unit. The shift in size of the basic economic unit may have paralleled a shift to greater social and economic differentiation.

The subsistence economy at Tepe Yahya was almost completely dependent on domesticated plants and animals. The high water table and winter precipitation together with terracing used to catch surface runoff provided sufficient water for agriculture. Wheat and barley were the staple crops, and sheep, goats, and cattle provided most of the meat protein. At some sites the close proximity of upland and lowland terrain and the major seasonal differences between these regions made it possible to develop a specialized subsistence strategy based on herding sheep and goats. This strategy involved the movement of herds between winter and summer pastures. Originally this movement probably involved relatively short distances and was a part of a mixed village economy, but herding sheep and goats appears to have become more specialized though the course of the Iranian Chalcolithic tradition. The distances involved became greater, and new modes of interaction between settled agriculturalists and relatively mobile pastoralists must have developed.

Trade between agriculturalists and pastoralists, and between people at regional centers and smaller sites, was probably undertaken as simple barter exchanges. However, the emergence of stamp seals, the presence of regional centers like Chogha Mish, and the growth of elite houses at many sites suggests some sort of centralization in the storage and distribution of various commodities was becoming increasingly organized and perhaps under the control of specific individuals. Items that may have been exchanged by more formal mechanisms than individual barter included fineware ceramics, obsidian, copper, and marine shells.

Even with the emergence of elite houses, large regional centers, and more formal exchange networks, the Iranian Chalcolithic appears largely egalitarian in terms of overall wealth and political authority. Most villages appear to have been autonomous with extended families making up the basic social and economic units. Villages may have been overseen by a council of village elders. If individuals did have differential access to wealth or power it may have involved less archaeologically visible items such as staples, access to water, and control over labor.

Peoples of the **Iranian Bronze Age** (5000–3500 B.P.) tradition were sedentary agriculturalists who raised wheat, barley, rye, and millet, and herded goats, sheep, and cattle. There were also a large number of pastoral peoples who interacted regularly with sedentary agriculturalists, trading animal products for agricultural products and craft goods. Agricultural peoples lived in villages and cities, some of which were quite large. Settlements were located in areas providing an abundance of water and vegetation for their herds and an ample supply of water for domestic and agricultural purposes. Houses were of mud brick and often had numerous rooms built adjacent to an enclosed courtyard. Each dwelling had at least one large domed bread oven, an external stairway protected by a low wall leading to the upper floor or terrace, smaller internal staircases, square-bench hearths, and narrow doors.

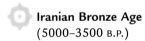

**Iranian Bronze Age**
(5000–3500 B.P.)

The presence of workshops for ceramic, lithic, and metal production suggests the presence of craft specialists. Clay spindle whorls found at some of the sites also indicate that fibers, perhaps wool from the sheep, were being spun for use in woven textiles. Ceramics were diverse in form and well made. Forms included bottles, pots, spouted vessels, and beakers. These were decorated with painted geometric designs, although uniform gray and gray-black ware became common late in the tradition. Other ceramic items included spindle whorls, molds (for metal casting), and human and animal figurines. Chlorite, a soft, green stone, was carved into bowls, which formed a major item of trade with the cities of Mesopotamia.

FIGURE **15.11**
A proto-Elamite tablet
from the Iranian Bronze Age
tradition.

Trade with Mesopotamia, particularly goods such as steatite and lapis lazuli, and with other areas for tin used in making bronze, led to the rapid diffusion of ideas and technological improvements. Indeed, Proto-Elamite **tablets** found at Tepe Yahya provide clear evidence of trade with Mesopotamia and the Indus Valley, and also the important role of this writing, an idea borrowed from Mesopotamia, in the organization of long-distance trade (Figure 15.11). The archaeological record does not provide clear information about how this trade was organized, but the presence of craft specialists and literate people suggests that Iranian Bronze Age society was divided into clear social groups. There was probably an elite group, who based their status on wealth and the control of exotic goods and items derived from long-distance trade. Craftsmen, scribes, and other skilled individuals may have formed a separate status group. Farmers and pastoralists probably formed a group of commoners. A possible confirmation of this may be noted in the quantity and quality of grave goods found in Iranian Bronze Age burials. Some individuals were buried with great wealth while others were interred with little.

In the **Iranian Iron Age** (3500–2550 B.P.) tradition one can see these social differences expand into clear social classes and a state form of political organization. Akkadian, Bablyonian, Assyrian, and Elamite texts suggest that Iranian Iron Age political organization was based on a complex hierarchy of authorities. At the top was a "king" or "overlord" who ruled over local "governors," probably representing individual cities. Individual cities apparently had their own hierarchy of priests, priestesses, judges, and bureaucrats. Interpreting the cuneiform titles in modern terms is probably misleading, but it is reasonable to view these descriptions as representative of a complex political system with hierarchical authority and a formal bureaucracy. The political bureaucracy was apparently supported through government-owned lands worked by government-employed laborers.

During this tradition the large walled cities of Susa, Choga Zanbil, and Malyan appear. These cities had palaces, temples, and workshops along with residences for several thousand inhabitants. Houses were made of mud brick and consisted of a complex of rooms surrounding a courtyard. Several related families apparently lived in each house complex. Historical texts suggest that Iranian Iron Age social organization was rooted in "brotherhoods," probably representing patrilineal descent groups. These descent groups resided in a single compound, shared land and other resources, and worked together as a single economic unit. Upon the death of the father or patriarch of the compound, resources were distributed to the male heirs.

**Iranian Iron Age**
(3500–2550 B.P.)

**Tablets:** rectangular pieces of clay that were written upon using a stylus. Tablets were dried or baked to form a permanent written record of a transaction or event.

At this point the "brotherhood" might split, or a new patriarch would be chosen. Slaves were also kept and formed part of the property of the "brotherhood." Historical texts also describe some two dozen deities that were worshipped by Iranian Iron Age peoples, and each city had temples where sacrifices of food and libations were presented to the deities and where rituals were performed. While poorly known at present, it is likely that smaller agricultural villages were also present during the Iranian Iron Age, and pastoralists in Luristan and Kurdistan probably lived in seminomadic groups for at least a part of the year.

The Iranian Iron Age economy was based on agriculture and animal husbandry. In river valleys and irrigable lands agriculture was the primary subsistence base. Wheat and barley were the primary crops, supplemented by legumes, fruits, spices, and other domesticated plants. Sheep, goats, and cattle were kept, and fish were important as well. In upland areas sheep, goats, and cattle formed the basis of subsistence, and peoples moved in a seasonal round between winter and summer pastures. Both bronze and iron were used for utensils and were produced in workshops by metalwork specialists. Stone blades persisted early in the tradition, but were replaced by metals later on. Ceramics of various styles including both plainwares and painted finewares were produced in specialist workshops. These utensils were created and distributed within a market economy where both barter and sale were present and where there was a marked division of labor between craftsmen, farmers, and politico-religious bureaucrats.

## ARABIAN PENINSULA

The Arabian Peninsula can be divided into two main regions, the western deserts and the eastern coast. The western deserts, the Rub al Khali and Nafud, are true sand deserts and in places are almost devoid of life. The region is hot and arid year-round. Rivers do run through these deserts and create locally fertile environments. The coast has the benefit of the southeast monsoons that provide abundant summer rain along with streams that run from the interior of the peninsula to the sea. Here too the climate is warm year-round. A wide variety of plants grow, including a number of distinctive succulents like frankincense and myrrh. A range of grassland and desert fauna were found on the Arabian Peninsula, including lions, camels, rabbits, cattle, and a variety of other ungulates. Along the coasts marine mammals, fish, and shellfish were plentiful.

As I discussed in the chapter on the Upper Paleolithic, the earliest populations in the region are recognized primarily from a small number of lithic scatters unassociated with architecture and most likely represent ephemeral seasonal camps. By contrast, sites of the **Early Arabian Pastoral** (11,000–5750 B.P.) tradition are small settlements defined by rings of large stones that are thought to be the foundations for simple skin tents or brush huts. Typical communities have a group of houses with a common work area, associated animal pens, and some specialized areas for activities such as stone working. Early Arabian Pastoral peoples may have practiced seasonal transhumance, with people living in larger winter base camps located where water and fodder were abundant, and smaller summer camps dispersed over the landscape.

**Early Arabian Pastoral**
(11,000–5750 B.P.)

An example of a winter base camp is **Thumama**, located northwest of Riyadh, Saudi Arabia, in a location where there are fertile soils, seasonal streams, and springs. The site consists of a number of circular, semisubterranean houses with low stone walls that likely supported a wood and skin or brush roof. Several of the excavated houses contained clear evidence of partitions and internal hearths. They were likely winter dwellings for those periods when the weather in the region turns cool. There were also burials at the site, the individuals placed in shallow pits topped with piles of stone. Stone projectile points, projectile point blanks, bifacial knives, scrapers,

**Thumama**
(Saudi Arabia, Early Arabian Pastoral)

blades, and drills were found. Thumama also yielded limestone mortars, pounders, and pestles, suggesting some collection and processing of wild plant foods.

**Dhuweila** (Jordan, Early Arabian Pastoral)

A summer camp is likely represented by **Dhuweila**, located in eastern Jordan on a rocky outcrop overlooking a large valley. Two periods of occupation include an earlier camp constructed of irregular stone circles and a later camp with larger stone circles within which are stone-paved floors. The inhabitants of Dhuweila hunted a variety of wild animals using projectile points made from blades. Blades were also used to make knives and scrapers. In addition to wild gazelles and horses, the faunal remains from Dhuweila include domestic sheep and goats.

While Early Arabian Pastoral peoples were, as the name suggests, primarily pastoralists herding sheep, goats, cattle, and horses, they also interacted regularly with sedentary agriculturalists in the Levant, Mesopotamia, and Egypt. This interaction involved trade for agricultural products and raw materials, but the Early Arabian Pastoral peoples, being mobile, were also able to act as middlemen in trade between sedentary communities, and they became a vital link in the flow of information and goods throughout Southwest Asia. Some of the goods that have been recovered from Early Arabian Pastoral sites include obsidian, greenstone, amazonite, and jadeite, which were likely being traded between their sources and sedentary communities elsewhere.

**Middle Arabian Pastoral** (5750–4200 B.P.)

By the time of the **Middle Arabian Pastoral** (5750–4200 B.P.) tradition, trade had brought bronze into the Arabian Peninsula. Indeed, the presence of bronze is the primary feature distinguishing the Middle Arabian Pastoral tradition from the Early Arabian Pastoral tradition. In most other ways, life remained largely the same. Middle Arabian Pastoral people still built small, round structures with stone foundations and skin or brush superstructures. They herded sheep, goats, and cattle, and they traded regularly with peoples in the Levant, Mesopotamia, and Egypt. However, during this time populations in these other areas were consolidating into large cities, and this must have effected both the nature and scale of trade across the Arabian Peninsula and may have led to social and political changes among Middle Arabian Littoral populations as well.

While the beginning of the Middle Arabian Pastoral tradition may be vague, the end is clear. By 4200–4000 B.P. major ecological, political, and social changes occurred across Southwest Asia, and the Arabian Peninsula was not spared. Peoples of the **Late Arabian Pastoral** (4200–3595 B.P.) tradition lived a more mobile life than their predecessors. Pit houses and houses with paved floors are no longer found. In the Late Arabian Pastoral tradition all that is found are small stone rings that likely held down the edges of skin or felt tents, or perhaps brush huts. The Late Arabian Pastoral peoples herded sheep, goats, and cattle, and they used horses to trade between Egypt and the Horn of Africa, the Levant, and Mesopotamia.

**Late Arabian Pastoral** (4200–3595 B.P.)

There appear to have been distinct changes in social and political organization during the Late Arabian Pastoral tradition. Texts from Mesopotamia and Egypt describe individuals that might be translated as paramount sheikh, sheikh, great man, and mayor. Patrilineal descent groups are also described, and membership in high-ranking patrilineal groups was apparently a major basis for social status and authority. These texts also describe raiding between Late Arabian Pastoral groups, which suggest that conflict was a major part of life.

**Early Arabian Littoral** (11,000–7000 B.P.)

Along the coast, developments appear to have taken a very different course. The first coastal peoples of the Arabian Peninsula, peoples of the **Early Arabian Littoral** (11,000–7000 B.P.) tradition lived in settlements located on elevated coastal terraces providing access to both coastal and inland resources. These settlements usually consist of a cluster of small (roughly 2 meters in diameter) rings of stone, which likely formed the foundation for light frame huts or tents. Some five to seven of these stone rings are usually found together, likely representing a single band of perhaps twenty related people.

The Early Arabian Littoral peoples were broad-spectrum hunter-fisher-gatherers. They hunted gazelles, horses, and other large game on the grasslands adjacent to stable dunes, and they collected mollusks and shellfish on the coast. Fish were taken in large quantities, though many are small species such as sardines and herrings. The bow and arrow armed with thin blade arrows was used for hunting, while both nets and hook and line were used for fishing.

During the **Middle Arabian Littoral** (7000–3300 B.P.) tradition significant changes took place. Middle Arabian Littoral settlements are located primarily on coastal terraces with access to both agricultural soils and coastal resources. Houses were made of stone and mud brick and were quite substantial in some areas, while in others houses were apparently frame huts and quite insubstantial. Few settlements have been excavated, and no clear community plans are known. Communities appear to have varied in size from small agricultural hamlets of perhaps only a few families to cities, where trade with civilizations in Mesopotamia, Iran, and South Asia encouraged large population concentrations.

Agriculture, animal husbandry, and exploitation of coastal and ocean resources formed the foundation of Middle Arabian Littoral subsistence. Sorghum and date palm were two of the more important domesticated crops, and sheep, goats, and cattle were kept. Middle Arabian Littoral peoples collected mollusks and shellfish on the coast and fished extensively in the Persian Gulf and Arabian Sea using both nets and hook and line. Sea turtles were particularly important in some areas. Hunting for gazelle, oryx, and other animals also took place. Trade became central for some Middle Arabian Littoral communities. Bahrain (ancient Dilmun) became an important port for oceanic trade through the Persian Gulf, with particularly strong ties to Southern Mesopotamia. Oman became a center for copper extraction and a further link for oceanic trade with Mesopotamia, South Asia, and Africa.

The sociopolitical organization of Middle Arabian Littoral society is largely unknown, but it appears to have been quite varied. Documents from Southern Mesopotamia suggest at least some politically centralized and socially stratified societies existed in the region, and archaeological evidence of differences in burial practices and the presence of public architecture (such as temples and towers) seems to support that idea. However, some areas lack such evidence and appear to have only small, perhaps egalitarian, communities.

The Middle Arabian Littoral peoples buried their dead in tombs or cairns, often in large areas containing thousands of such burials (Figure 15.12). Tombs and cairns varied over time and location, but typically contained a central stone chamber containing from one to several hundred individuals. Utilitarian grave goods such as ceramic and stone vessels, tools, and weapons, as well as personal ornaments, were included in burials, and some burials of apparently elite individuals contained considerable quantities of such goods.

Peoples of the **Late Arabian Littoral** (3300–2300 B.P.) tradition continued this pattern of life. They lived in large stone and mud-brick houses consisting of two or three living rooms and several storage rooms surrounding a courtyard, some built atop mud-brick platforms. They raised cereal crops and date palms, using **falaj irrigation** (Figure 15.13). Falaj irrigation involves tapping mountain aquifers and then transporting the water in subterranean channels to lower-lying agricultural areas. This technique allowed the fertile soils in many dry wadis to be brought into production. Sheep, goats, and cattle were also kept, and the resources of the sea, especially fish and shellfish, were an important part of the subsistence economy. Domesticated camels also made their first appearance during the Late Arabian Littoral tradition.

The site of **Muweilah** is a good example of a Late Arabian Littoral settlement. Muweilah is located in the sand-dune belt near the coast of the United Arab Emirates. The present-day environment consists of scattered scrub vegetation and sand dunes. Muweilah consists of several hectares of artifactual debris scattered on

**Middle Arabian Littoral**
(7000–3300 B.P.)

**Late Arabian Littoral**
(3300–2300 B.P.)

**Muweilah** (United Arab Emirates, Late Arabian Littoral)

**Falaj irrigation:** a type of irrigation in which water from mountain aquifers is transported through subterranean channels to lower-lying agricultural fields.

FIGURE **15.12**
Aerial view of one of the many Middle Arabian Littoral tomb fields. Both unexcavated mounds and excavated tombs can be seen.

and between several sand dunes and a hard, dune platform. The site contains several large stone-built ovens, and numerous buildings constructed of stone and mud. One of these had a number of internal rooms, and some of the buildings appear to have been placed around an open courtyard. Within the buildings were fireplaces, clay-lined bins, grinding stones, and clay storage jars, and they have been interpreted as single-family residences.

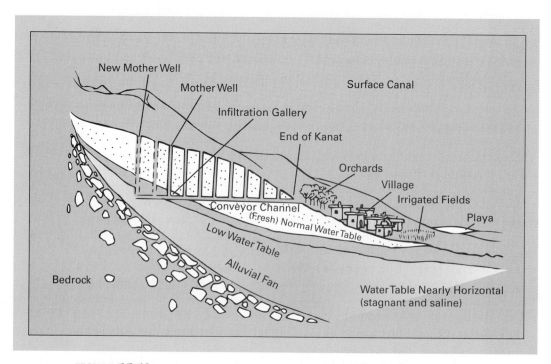

FIGURE **15.13**

Diagram of how one type of falaj irrigation system works.

SOURCE: From George B. Cressey, "Qanats, Karez, and Foggeras," *The Geographical Review* Vol. 48, No. 1, p. 28. Adapted with permission from the American Geographical Society.

Another stone and mud building at Muweilah has a large central room with twenty stone column bases. The column bases are arranged in a 4 × 5 pattern and supported wooden beams. The interior of the room was plastered, and it appears that the floor area within the columned space was plastered as well. The central room was flanked by several ancillary rooms. Most of these could only be accessed directly from the central room and not from outside the building. Unlike the central room, some of the floors in these rooms were made from a hardened mud surface and were at a much higher level than the central room. Concentrations of bronze nodules were found in several of these rooms, along with a cache of recently cast objects. Clearly this was a bronze production and perhaps marketing facility, which seems to have been directly associated with an elite household.

This bronze production facility illustrates that in addition to the subsistence economy, there was also a rich economy of craft production and trade in the Late Arabian Littoral tradition. Bronze was clearly being produced in workshops and may have been controlled by elites. Workshops for the production of steatite objects, especially bowls, and ceramics have also been found. Materials produced at these workshops were traded widely, and goods from Iran, Mesopotamia, the Levant, and Egypt have been found in Late Arabian Littoral contexts. The mechanics and organizational aspects of trade are not clear, but it appears that goods such as iron and imported ceramics were a controlled resource that were probably used by elites to support their status positions.

## LEVANT

The Levant is an environmentally diverse region. It includes the coastal plain of the eastern Mediterranean, hilly and mountainous terrain extending from the Sinai north through Lebanon and western Syria, the foothills of the Taurus and Zagros mountains, and the steppe and desert regions of eastern Jordan, Syria, and western Iraq. Like the environment, the flora and fauna are also diverse. The hilly and mountainous regions were dominated by oak-pistachio woodlands that harbored deer, aurochs, wild boar, and other animals. In open areas on these slopes broad stands of the wild progenitors of domesticated cereals such as wheat and barley grew. Many lowland areas were steppes in which the dominant vegetation was small shrubs and the fauna included gazelles, hares, hyaenas, onagers, and ostriches. The Jordan and Orontes Valleys and Azraq oasis were major stops for migratory birds, such as ducks and storks.

The **Aceramic Neolithic** (10,500–7500 B.P.) tradition marks the beginnings of village life in the Levant. Aceramic Neolithic settlements were primarily small agricultural villages with substantial mud-brick architecture, although there were also cave sites and, in steppe and desert regions, open-air sites that may have been seasonal camps. Villages were typically located close to permanent springs and near good agricultural soils. Most of the settlements showed no clear organization, although some had clusters of houses. Houses often had several rooms, and were constructed of mud brick, sometimes on stone foundations, and sometimes with plastered walls and floors. Houses appear to have been individual family dwellings, but the clusters of houses that occur on some sites may represent extended-family households.

**'Ain Ghazal** is a good example of an Aceramic Neolithic agricultural village. It is located near Amman, Jordan, close to a reliable spring and with oak-pistachio forest to its west and steppe not far to the east. Thus, the residents of 'Ain Ghazal had easy access to a variety of environments as well as good agricultural soils in the area around the site. The community at 'Ain Ghazal consisted of rectangular mud-brick houses arranged along the terraced lower slopes of the Zarqa valley. The houses were about 5 by 7 meters in size, often single-roomed, and with a well-laid plaster floor.

**Aceramic Neolithic** (10,500–7500 B.P.)

**'Ain Ghazal** (Jordan, Aceramic Neolithic)

Aceramic Neolithic subsistence was based on agriculture and animal husbandry supplemented by hunting and gathering. Wild plant foods included barley, wheat, pistachios, and acorns. Hunting focused on large game such as gazelles, onagers, deer, aurochs, and boars. Domesticated plants included wheat, barley, peas, and lentils. Late in the tradition domesticated goats and cattle made their first appearance in the region. The basic tool kit included blades, blade projectile points, microblades used to create sickles, ground stone querns, mullers, mortars and pestles, and bone awls and spatulas. Aceramic Neolithic peoples also created beautiful stone bowls from marble and other decorative stone.

Although most of the resources that Aceramic Neolithic communities used were locally abundant, there were also extensive exchange networks. Obsidian from Turkey is found in southern Jordan. There may have been trade in bitumen (asphalt) from the Dead Sea. Shells from the Mediterranean and Red Seas, polished stone bracelets and beads of stone, shell or wood occur in many sites of this tradition. **Beidha**, located in southern Jordan, is a small settlement, but provides strong evidence for craft specialization and interregional trade. There a number of distinctive structures had numerous small chambers that may have served as basement storage pits or workrooms. Some contained large numbers of shells, worked stone, or bead blanks, suggesting they were places were craft production was taking place or craft goods were stored. The site's location, on a route connecting Mesopotamia, Egypt, and the Levant, may have made the location one where goods from one area could be exchanged for goods from others, and where craft goods could be produced and traded throughout the region.

How these communities and the trade between them was organized is still an open question. Most villages appear to have been egalitarian, with the nuclear or extended family being the most important social, economic, and political unit. However, the clustering of houses and treatment of the dead suggest that descent groups may have been present. At **Jericho**, located in southern Israel, for example, the skulls of some individuals were removed, coated with plaster and modeled into a lifelike face, complete with cowrie shell eyes (Figure 15.14). These were kept in residences, sometimes in below-floor caches. Such plastered and curated skulls have been found on other sites as well, and they suggest ancestor worship, perhaps of founding members of a descent group.

Jericho is a very large site and has massive public works that include a large stone wall and tower (Figure 15.15). Other sites also have large walls, and some show evidence of formal organization. The presence of these public facilities and planned settlements suggests that villagewide authority was present in some communities.

Life remained similar in the **Ceramic Neolithic** (8000–6100 B.P.) tradition, but ceramics were added to the tool kit. Most settlements were still small agricultural villages. Settlements were often densely packed with mud-brick houses, and storerooms, and in some cases settlements, were enclosed by mud-brick walls. Large houses and some clusters of houses may represent extended-family households. In some communities there were also large storage facilities that may have been used by descent groups.

Ceramic Neolithic subsistence was based on growing domesticated plants and raising sheep, goats, and cattle. Wild plants and animals played only a minor role in the subsistence economy. Tools included blades and blade tools, microblades that were combined to make composite tools such as sickles, flakes and flake tools, ground stone axes and adzes, grinding stones, mortars and pestles, bone awls and spatulas, among many others. Most of these tools were relatively simple and were probably manufactured by the individuals using them. However, some blades and blade tools, and perhaps some polished stone tools and bowls, were probably manufactured by specialists. Ceramics were, of course, used by the Ceramic Neolithic peoples. There was great diversity in pottery forms, including jars and deep bowls

**Beidha** (Jordan, Aceramic Neolithic)

**Jericho** (Israel, Aceramic Neolithic)

**Ceramic Neolithic** (8000–6100 B.P.)

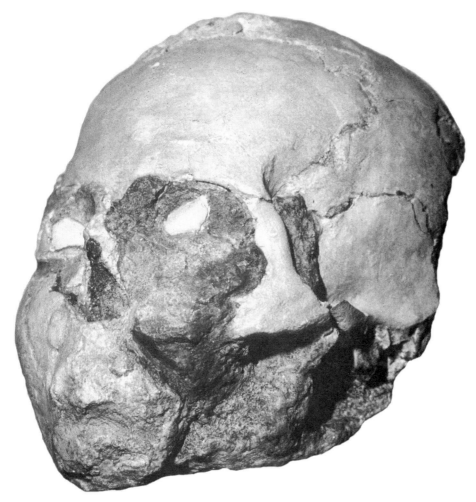

FIGURE **15.14**
Skulls like this one, with plaster and cowrie shells used to reconstruct facial features, were kept within houses at Jericho and may represent ancestor worship in the Aceramic Neolithic tradition.

(many of which are probably cooking pots), and many bowls and cups probably used in serving food, and they are often burnished or decorated.

Most of the resources that Ceramic Neolithic communities used were locally abundant, but there was some exchange of obsidian, shells, bitumen, and semi-precious stones. However, **Umm Dabaghiyah,** located in an arid region of northern Iraq, provides unique evidence of trade in subsistence items. Umm Dabaghiyah contains a number of large, multichambered buildings that have been interpreted as storehouses (Figure 15.16). The chambers in these large buildings are only about 1 meter square and are located on either side of long hallways lacking evidence of doors, so that they must have been entered from above. These buildings were arranged around a large rectangular plaza. There were also houses at the site, so these were clearly special-purpose buildings. Faunal remains are dominated by onager and gazelle, and a cache of clay balls in one of the storehouses may be sling projectiles used to hunt them. Indeed, the abundance of onager remains suggests that the site may have functioned as a special-purpose site for hunting and processing onager. The multichambered buildings may have been locations where onager meat or hides were stored before being transported to other locations.

While individual Ceramic Neolithic villages appear to be autonomous and largely egalitarian, trade in exotic goods and perhaps some subsistence goods suggests that social and political organization may have been more sophisticated than the archaeological record might suggest. Broad similarities in material culture and the growing importance of good agricultural lands suggest the possibility that

**Umm Dabaghiyah
(Iraq, Ceramic
Neolithic)**

FIGURE **15.15**
This massive wall and tower at Jericho suggests that some form of village-wide political authority was present.

descent groups or formal political leaders might have integrated large regions by the end of the period.

During the **Chalcolithic** (6500–5500 B.P.) tradition formal political leaders and centralized polities appeared in the Levant. One of the most striking features of the Chalcolithic tradition is the emergence of numerous distinct regional cultures

 **Chalcolithic**
(6500–5500 B.P.)

FIGURE **15.16**
Plan map of the large, multi-chambered buildings found at Umm Dabaghiyah.

SOURCE: Charles L. Redman, *The Rise of Civilization* (New York, NY: W.H. Freeman, 1978), p. 299.

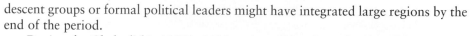
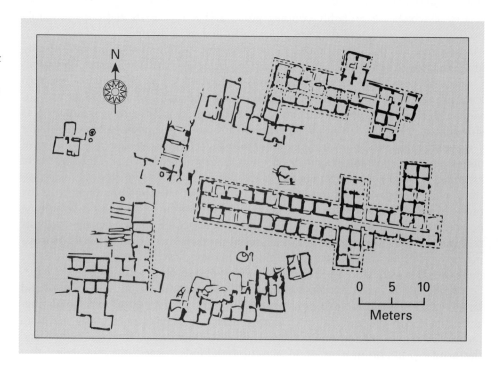

sharing common artifact forms and decorations. Some archaeologists have suggested that each of these regional cultures represents a separate social or political group, and there is some supporting evidence in the form of settlement hierarchies. Some Chalcolithic villages are much larger than earlier ones, and these have been interpreted as regional centers. For example, **Teleilat el-Ghassul** in Israel covered an area of approximately 20 hectares. The site had several distinct occupation areas. One area was densely packed with large rectangular buildings that were situated in conjunction with courtyards, small storage rooms, ovens, and alleyways. There is a clear distinction between small domestic houses and these larger buildings that suggests the larger buildings may have served some kind of public function, perhaps corporate buildings for elite lineages resident at the site. The layout of Teleilat el-Ghassul, with closely built compounds separated by alleyways, suggests the presence of a central authority that organized the public labor needed to build these planned settlements.

**Teleilat el-Ghassul**
(Israel, Chalcolithic)

These large villages supported themselves through irrigation agriculture, and a wide range of water control systems appear to have been developed. These include cisterns, dams, and canals, all used to divert and trap floodwater for agricultural purposes. The organization of labor needed to carry out floodwater farming may be another indication of the existence of centralized social and political authority in the Chalcolithic tradition. The investment made in these agricultural facilities, and the emergence of new perennial crops like dates and olives, may have made the distinction between agriculturalists and pastoralists more marked, as focused pastoral economies appear during the Chalcolithic tradition. Although most agricultural villagers kept sheep, goats, and cattle, there also appear to have been communities that specialized in production of meat, milk, and wool. Keeping sheep and goat herds away from the critical floodplain areas during growing and harvesting periods was probably an important factor in promoting the need for specialized pastoralists.

There also appears to have been increasing specialization in craft production during the Chalcolithic tradition, particularly in ceramics and copper working. Copper working required a number of specialized activities, including procurement of raw materials, processing of the raw copper, and the production of copper items. It is interesting to note that most items produced from copper were ritual objects or personal ornaments—items that would have been used solely by elites. This suggests that copper working and the emergence of elites were strongly tied together. Axes, adzes, chisels, maceheads, and other tools were also made from copper, so it was not solely an elite material. Ceramics began to be wheel-made during the Chalcolithic tradition, and there was a dramatic increase in both the quality and quantity of ceramics. There is also evidence for specialization in the production of some stone tools, particularly blades and blade tools.

Peoples of the Chalcolithic tradition, then, appear to have developed the first centralized polities in the Levant. These were probably chiefdoms, with chiefs basing their authority on descent, on their control over craft production and trade, and perhaps on the control or support of agricultural facilities. The creation, support, and perhaps control of religious facilities may have played a role in the development of centralized Chalcolithic polities as well. At the site of **En-Gedi**, for example, a temple complex was built overlooking the Dead Sea (Figure 15.17). The En-Gedi complex consists of four structures connected by a stone fence that encloses a roughly rectangular courtyard. These structures include a main gatehouse, a secondary gatehouse, a lateral chamber, and a sanctuary. A circular installation was built in the center of the courtyard. The site is isolated from other settlements and may have been a temple built to serve a wide region. Similar temple sites are found elsewhere in the Levant, and these suggest a widespread religious system that must have been supported by local populations, perhaps with the coordination and support of local chiefs.

**En-Gedi**
(Israel, Chalcolithic)

FIGURE **15.17**
Ruins of the Ein Gedi temple complex overlooking the Dead Sea.

**Early Bronze Age**
(5500–4000 B.P.)

**Megiddo** (Israel, Early Bronze Age)

States appeared in the Levant during the **Early Bronze Age** (5500–4000 B.P.) tradition, and society became increasingly urban. These emergent cities are often located on alluvial soils near perennial water sources. Apart from these urban centers, each containing 100 to 150 households and perhaps 500 to 1,000 residents, peoples of the Early Bronze Age tradition also lived in villages of ten to twenty households and small farmsteads having only one or two households. The cities appear to have functioned as central places that dominated a much broader area, economically and, perhaps, politically. For example, **Megiddo,** located in Israel near a perennial water source and on a main route between the coast and inland sites, is a good example of an Early Bronze Age regional center. Megiddo served as the primary economic, religious, and political center for the Jezreel Valley and was one of the wealthiest cities in the southern Levant. It became a prominent city because it controlled trade routes connecting the coast with the entire southern Levant. The remains of donkeys found at the site suggest pack animals were used for transport. Megiddo was also a center for craft production. High-quality flint used to manufacture blades was imported to the site from a nearby quarry and made into finished goods. Kilns near the site were used to produce large quantities of ceramics, and bronze working is evidenced through the presence of molds used to cast adzes.

A hallmark of urban centers like Megiddo are their massive fortification systems. Megiddo was surrounded by 3- to 4-meter-wide fortification walls with square bastions, which were regularly maintained and improved (Figure 15.18). If these defensive systems were constructed in reaction to an increase in conflict, it is possible that they served as havens for the population living in the surrounding region. There is evidence from Egyptian texts that Early Dynastic rulers led regular military expeditions into the southern Levant. There is also evidence that large areas of the northern Levant were depopulated during the Early Bronze Age, perhaps because of environmental degradation. The influx of these people may have led to conflict as well.

Cities like Megiddo might also have attracted population because of their roles as religious centers. At Megiddo, there is a distinct religious complex comprising a double temple with annex rooms, and a third cultic structure. Each temple was built with exterior walls nearly 2 meter thick and was based on the "broad room" plan with a wide entrance leading to a broad hall (ca. 130 square meter) and annex

FIGURE **15.18**
Aerial view of Megiddo,
showing its massive
fortification walls.

room. Inside the temples some of the column bases were dressed with elaborate designs, and two of the temples had raised platforms that may have been used for the display of cultic figures and/or as a place for rituals. The cultic structure was associated with a large courtyard paved with flat stones incised with images of animals and humans holding musical instruments and weapons, suggesting this area may have been the scene of performances and/or rituals. Late in the Bronze Age the entire precinct was surrounded by an enclosure wall. Whether temples were used for public rituals or served as restricted areas is unknown.

There is also evidence at Megiddo for secular public architecture. A large (800 square meter) public building constructed on the eastern side of the site may have been a palace. It was replaced late in the Bronze Age by a new structure, possibly a ceremonial gate, with a monumental staircase leading toward the sacred area. Direct evidence for social control mechanisms and political authority is limited. The presence of a granary at some sites clearly indicates economic integration, and it is likely that some political figure or group held control over redistribution of a staple surplus. There are also clearly elites in the Early Bronze Age, who had greater access to, and likely control over, goods being traded long distances, particularly from Egypt. The presence of these elites and their ability to control the economy must have played an important role in the development and function of cities like Megiddo, but the precise nature of those functions are unclear.

The emergence of cities has led to much speculation about population movement and growth. The process occurred so rapidly that its causes were initially thought to stem from population influx from the north. However, the material culture remained the same, and in recent years archaeologists have highlighted internal factors such as population increases and reorganization of the economic system. At present, Early Bronze Age cities appear to stem largely from population concentrating rather than population growth, and this suggests that there was a significant reorganization of society. The question is, what kind of reorganization occurred? This is a question taken up in detail in the chapter on the rise of states, but I will outline some of the apparent changes here.

Peoples of the Early Bronze Age moved away from independent village-based agriculture and toward more specialized agriculture, with an emphasis on production for trade. It is difficult to determine how this was organized, but there is evidence for the storage and perhaps redistribution of surplus subsistence goods in the

**Beth-Yerah** (Israel, Early Bronze Age)

form of large granaries at sites like **Beth-Yerah,** on the southern shore of the Sea of Galilee. As part of this move toward specialized agriculture, certain settlements seem to have emerged as special-purpose communities, usually associated with the exploitation of some strategic location or ecological niche. Settlements adjacent to the broad inland valleys, like Megiddo, benefited from their proximity to trade routes. Sites located on the coast probably functioned as ports. Settlements in the rain-fed hilly areas may have focused on the production of horticultural goods such as wine and olive oil, while small villages and pastoral groups in the semiarid zones focused on pastoral production.

Craft production and distribution became more centralized as well, and an urban-based market system probably developed. Ceramics were mass-produced on wheels and fired in large kilns. Metalworking technology improved and became a large-scale industry. Change in the organization of metal production is also suggested by a growing distinction between miners and smiths as tasks were broken down in stages performed at different sites. Lithic production also became more standardized and large lithic workshops appeared. Trade with Egypt probably played an increasingly important role in urban-based marketing. Timber was particularly valuable in Egypt, and there appears to have been a brisk trade. Agricultural products such as wine, olive oil, and wools were probably also traded.

Trade activity between Egypt and the Levant probably involved elites, and in the course of the Early Bronze Age these relations became formalized. Maintaining trade and market systems, both with Egypt and within the increasingly specialized economic sectors within the Levant, may have become a primary role of Early Bronze Age leaders.

The urban states of the Early Bronze Age collapsed rapidly at the end of the tradition. Some were conquered by Mesopotamians (particularly Sargon of Akkad, who took control of the entire Tigris Valley by about 4150 B.P.), others appear to have simply declined. At the beginning of the **Middle Bronze Age** (4000–3550 B.P.) tradition, urban life was no longer a part of life in the Levant. The Middle Bronze Age, then, marks a resurgence of urban life. While less than one-third of Early Bronze settlements were reinhabited in the Middle Bronze Age, a large number of new settlements were created, especially on the Mediterranean coast. A system of urban centers linking agricultural villages and hamlets also reemerged, and perhaps became more complex, with more special-purpose sites than in the Early Bronze Age. Urban centers such as Meggido, which was reoccupied, and **Hazor,** located on the Sea of Galilee, functioned as economic, political, and religious hubs. Lower-order centers functioned as gateways between villages and urban centers, and as places where staple goods produced in the countryside were converted into specialized, labor-intensive goods such as metal. These centers also served as the nexus for long-distance trade with the cities of Egypt and Mesopotamia.

Middle Bronze Age cities were fortified with massive sloping earthen ramparts that were roughly square in outline. A number of cities had impressive gate structures built into the ramparts, and in some cases the gate areas incorporated open plazas with large roads leading up to them, perhaps to accommodate chariot and cart traffic. Cities were well planned, with large thoroughfares directing traffic to central points and allowing movement through the city, and with smaller alleyways giving access to workshop and residential areas. Middle Bronze Age houses were built of mud brick on stone foundations. They generally had several small rooms enclosing a central courtyard. Many cities had distinct residential and craft production quarters, in some cases with separate quarters for individual crafts. Cities also had large palace complexes and temple precincts (Figure 15.19).

The founders of the Middle Bronze Age tradition are thought to have been seminomadic people subsisting largely on pastoral resources. Over time, however, the population grew and sedentary agricultural communities were established, though the process by which this occurred is not well understood. Wheat and barley

**Middle Bronze Age** (4000–3550 B.P.)

**Hazor** (Israel, Middle Bronze Age)

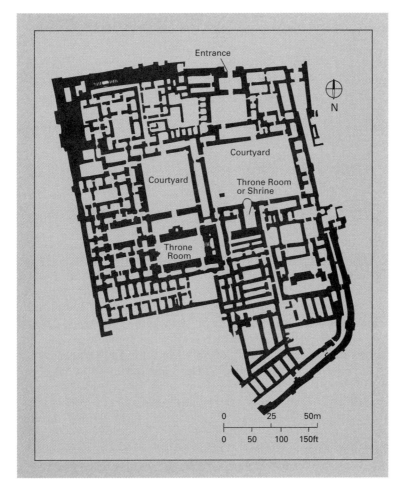

FIGURE **15.19**

Plan map of the Zimri-Lim palace at Mari, illustrating the massive scale of many Middle Bronze Age palace complexes.

SOURCE: From *Cultural Atlas of Mesopotamia and the Ancient Near East,* by Michael Roaf, 1990, p. 119. Reprinted by permission of Andromeda Oxford Limited.

continued to be the primary staple during the Middle Bronze Age, with legumes such as lentils and chickpeas forming a significant part of the diet. Sheep and goats dominate the faunal assemblage.

The material culture of the Middle Bronze Age, particularly luxury items such as intricate bronze weapons, gives the overall impression that this was a period of significant technological development. One technological breakthrough was the use of true tin-bronze, which allowed for an expansion in casting techniques. Despite the practical advantages of this new metal, much of it saw only limited or no use as many of the Middle Bronze Age bronzes were created specifically for burial. Finished goods, such as hoards of gold jewelry, including earrings, finely worked pins, and rings attest to a high level of craftsmanship. Mesopotamian texts indicate that there may have been private enterprise and merchant guilds.

Trade with Anatolia and Egypt is well documented in the archaeological record and in historical texts, and there are indications of trade with Cyprus and the Aegean. Historical texts gives some indication of how this trade was organized. Texts from **Mari** on the Euphrates river in Syria refer directly to Hazor and Laish (Tel Dan) as the recipients of tin. Tin had become a vital trade commodity because of its use in the production of bronze. Specific references to Hazor, the most important exchange center in the southern Levant, also point to a relation between the royal court and trade activities. For instance, in a letter from the Assyrian king, Shamshi Adad, to his son Iasmah Adad, ruler of Mari, it is implied that envoys from Hazor were afforded high status, in one case receiving a special escort from Qatna. Mari texts also describe people on the Syrian and Lebanese coasts engaged in maritime trade with Egypt and to a lesser extent with Cyprus and the Aegean world.

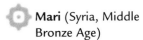 **Mari** (Syria, Middle Bronze Age)

FIGURE **15.20**
A cylinder seal and the impression it makes when rolled across clay. This is the seal of Sharkali-Sharri, an Akkadian king.

During the later Middle Bronze Age, a system of social organization involving distinctions between a wealthy and powerful social group associated with political and religious institutions and commoners emerged. The elite group probably functioned in a variety of specialized roles such as priests, administrators, traders, merchants, and warriors. The archaeological record also suggests that some craftspeople worked as "attached specialists." For example, the discovery of molds used to cast images of a horned goddess in the vicinity of a temple suggests that the religious establishment had some link with production. In addition, textual evidence from Mesopotamia and Syria points to a relationship between producers and the elite institutions. Another link between producers and elite consumers can be seen in the glyptic art of **cylinder seals** (Figure 15.20). Cylinder seals produced at Hazor, for example, may represent the work of specialists since their production involved both intricate carving and knowledge of the artistic canons. The style and trappings of the elite and royal families depicted on the cylinder seals also suggest an association between the producers and the nobles and merchants who used them for commercial activities.

Archaeological evidence suggests that at least some cities had local rulers or kings. Massive buildings with elaborate design found at sites such as Megiddo and Hazor have been interpreted as palaces or the homes of governors and kings. These palaces commonly included large courtyards, storage rooms, and broad halls. In certain cases, such as Megiddo, there appears to have been an association between the royal court and temple, at least in terms of physical proximity. Historic texts also support the idea that Middle Bronze Age cities had royal institutions, though little is said about individual rulers. The historical texts depict a political landscape where numerous city-states of various sizes functioned as distinct entities ruled by kings.

Perhaps the best evidence that political institutions or individuals were able to command and mobilize resources are the massive fortifications found at many Middle Bronze Age cities. While it is not always clear whether these earthen ramparts functioned as fortification systems, in all cases they would have required the efforts of a substantial labor force. Fortifications might well have been a necessity in the Middle Bronze Age Levant, and the region seems to have been rife with conflict. The array of bronze weapons themselves suggest that there was conflict. Historical texts also describe growing animosity among Egyptians toward the peoples of the southern Levant, and some of the conquests described in these texts appear to correlate with archaeological evidence for mass burning and destruction. By the end of the Middle Bronze Age, there was a major breakdown in the Levant, as virtually every urban center experienced destruction, abandonment, or significant depopulation. Many scholars now agree that this process of deurbanization may have taken over a century and that while Egyptian interference may have hastened their demise, internal problems already threatened the stability of Levantine cities.

**Cylinder seals:** cylinders with carved designs in them that are rolled across wet clay in order to mark and seal shipments.

# MESOPOTAMIA

Mesopotamia is essentially a large basin lying between the Zagros mountains and the desert uplands of the Arabian Peninsula. The Tigris and Euphrates rivers run through this basin, creating a vast plain of marsh and riverine environments. To the east of the Tigris and Euphrates rivers is an open steppeland, while to the west is the Syrian desert. Thus a diversity of plants and animals are present. Stands of willow, poplar, tamarask, palm, and other trees and bushes are found near the rivers, and these support populations of deer, boar, and smaller animals and birds. On the steppes a wide variety of wild grasses are present, supporting gazelle, deer, and onager, as well as the carnivores that feed on them. Marshlands provide a rich environment for reptiles and fish, as well as migratory waterfowl. Temperatures in Mesopotamia vary from highs well below 20 degrees C in winter to over 40 degrees C in summer. Rainfall also varies tremendously and is not sufficient for agriculture in most parts of the region, so agriculture is dependent on irrigation.

There is a great question in Mesopotamian archaeology about the area's earliest inhabitants. No sites contemporary with post-Upper Paleolithic settlements in other areas of Southwest Asia are known. This may be due to buildup of alluvium deeply burying these early sites, or they may be under the waters of the Persian Gulf. In any case, the first clearly identified peoples of Mesopotamia are of the **Halafian** (7500–7000 B.P.) tradition. Most Halafian settlements are small agricultural villages, but even at this very early time there are at least six very large sites which may have functioned as regional centers of some kind. Housing is quite distinct, consisting of a **tholoi**, or circular, domed room, with a rectangular anteroom (Figure 15.21). Tholoi appear to have had a range of functions, including residence, storage, and communal activities. Houses are not large and are constructed of mud brick, often on stone foundations. Communities consisted of loose agglomerations of these houses. There is some evidence for special craft and production activities, especially pottery production, within communities.

Dry-farming was the basis of Halafian subsistence. The primary plants were wheat, barley, lentils, flax, and peas. Domesticated sheep, goats, cattle, and pigs were kept. Wild plants such as raspberry, almond, fig, and pistachio were collected in season, and large game animals such as gazelle, deer, and onager were hunted. The basic technology used by Halafian peoples was simple and available to everyone. However, there does appear to have been some specialized production of

**Halafian**
(7500–7000 B.P.)

**Tholoi:** a circular, domed structure.

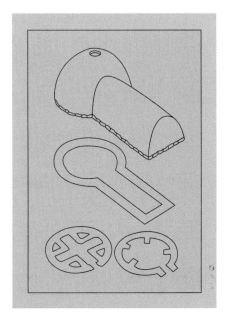

FIGURE **15.21**
A typical Halafian house, called a tholoi. The top image illustrates how such houses looked from the outside, while the middle and lower images illustrate the ground plan and various ways in which the interior of the house might be divided.

SOURCE: Michael Roaf, *Cultural Atlas of Mesopotamia and the Ancient Near East*, 1990, p. 49. Reprinted by permission of Andromeda Oxford Limited.

fineware ceramics. These were created in complex forms and richly decorated. Analysis of ceramics from a variety of Halafian sites suggests that these finewares were only manufactured in a handful of places but were distributed widely.

The little evidence that we have so far indicates that Halafian communities were egalitarian, structured principally on family lines. There is no unequivocal evidence of social stratification or formal political authorities. However, the presence of a few very large Halafian sites may indicate a genuine political, as well as settlement and economic, hierarchy of the type that would appear during the Ubaid tradition.

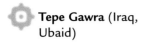

**Ubaid** (8000–6000 B.P.)

The peoples of the **Ubaid** (8000–6000 B.P.) tradition were settled agriculturalists who primarily lived in villages averaging 1 to 2 hectares, organized around larger centers of up to 10 hectares. In contrast to the smaller settlements, the centers contained religious architecture. These centers probably served both ritual and economic functions for chiefdoms based on the mobilization of staple goods. These centers also appear to have been the focus of important cemeteries used by elites from the surrounding region.

Villages contained a number of extended family dwellings made from mud brick. The typical house consisted of a tripartite structure in which a large, roofed central T-shaped hall was flanked by a series of rooms on either side. Most structures have evidence of a stairway or ramp, most likely leading up to the roof. Other structures that were probably used by the community as a whole were used to house livestock, store fodder, and possibly store equipment. These contained small compartmentalized cells, often sealed with bitumen, flanked by long narrow courtyards. Kilns used for localized ceramic production were also present at some sites. Excavations at **Tepe Gawra** in northern Iraq revealed a densely packed community consisting largely of houses with a long central hall flanked on either side by a series of smaller rooms. They frequently abutted each other, though sometimes they were separated by narrow alleyways and roads.

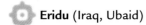

**Tepe Gawra** (Iraq, Ubaid)

In larger villages, the community was organized around a large public structure, which may have had an administrative function as well as serving as a residence. Villages which served as regional centers also contained at least one temple precinct. Early Ubaid temples, such as the one excavated at the site of **Eridu** in southern Iraq, were small, but contained elements characteristic of later temple architecture such as a cult-niche, a central offering-table, and an orientation along the cardinal axis of the earth. Temple architecture became increasingly sophisticated, the Eridu temple ending up as a structure with a long central sanctuary flanked on either side by a series of smaller rooms (Figure 15.22). This temple also had thick walls and was formally decorated with alternating recesses and buttresses.

**Eridu** (Iraq, Ubaid)

Ubaid subsistence was based on irrigation agriculture aided by draft animals and animal husbandry. Primary staples were wheat and barley. Domesticated sheep, goat, cattle, and pig were all important animal resources. Production was organized and controlled at the local level. In some cases, such as with pottery manufacture, production may have been organized and controlled at the level of the community, but most production seems to have been organized at the level of the extended family household and organized along sex and age lines. Agricultural implements included rough flaked stone and ground stone hoes. Other tools included flint sickle blades and, where flint was more rare, clay sickles. Ground stone axes or adzes may have been used for both agriculturally related activities and for wood working. Woven textiles, baskets, and mats were important household items during the Ubaid tradition. The production of woven goods is evidenced by the presence of spindle whorls, bone awls, and spatulate tools. Evidence for basketry and matting is present in the form of impressions left by these items on living surfaces at several Ubaid sites. Although metal was used in small amounts, stone, wood, clay, and other perishable materials formed the primary raw materials for Ubaid material culture.

One of the most distinctive features of Ubaid material culture was its ceramics (Figure 15.23). Well-fired painted, incised, and impressed wares as well as cruder

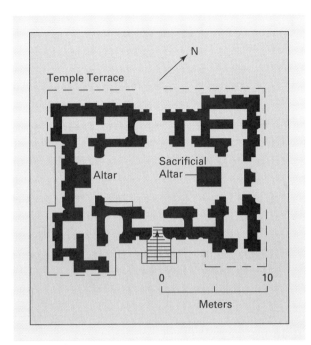

FIGURE **15.22**
Plan map of the level 8 temple at Eridu, illustrating the standard form of a Mesopotamian temple. There is a large central altar room with smaller rooms at either end. One altar would hold the statue of the god, while the other would be used for making sacrifices. The complex plan, including numerous buttresses and niches, is also typical of Mesopotamian temples.

SOURCE: Charles Redman, *The Rise of Civilization* (San Francisco: W.H. Freeman, 1978), Fig. 8.6, p. 251.

plain wares were all utilized. Most vessels were made by hand although some appear to have been finished on a slow wheel. The slow wheel was also used to apply painted decorations to vessels. A wide range of vessel shapes were produced including various types of bowls, jars, jugs, beakers, and cups. Painted pottery consists of a light-colored paste decorated with geometric motifs executed in a dark-colored monochrome paint. Incised decorations were commonly executed using a comb to produce parallel horizontal or wavy bands, parallel arcs, and dotted lines. Other incised decorations include diagonal slashes, herringbone patterns, crosshatched bands, and crosshatched triangles. Occasionally painted and incised decorations were used together. Other decorations were executed by impressing the wet clay with various objects. Common designs include reed, string, or fingernail impressed and fingertip dimpled patterns.

FIGURE **15.23**
A painted Ubaid ceramic vessel.

# Uruk

The ancient city of Uruk was the principle city of the Sumerian empire and arguably the most important city in the world during the era of the Uruk tradition. The city itself sat near the Euphrates (although the river has now shifted course to the east) about 250 kilometers south of present-day Baghdad, Iraq. Uruk was surrounded by a 10-kilometer-long rampart wall which enclosed an area of about 100 hectares.

Research at Uruk began in the mid-1800s, but it was not until 1912 when the Deutsche Orient-Gesellschaft began sustained research at the site. They have worked there, except during times of war, continually, making Uruk one of the best-studied cities of the ancient world.

Uruk was established during the Ubaid tradition and developed into a true city in the Uruk tradition. During the Uruk tradition, the city of Uruk was divided into two main precincts: Eanna, with a large temple complex dedicated to the city goddess Inanna; and Kullaba, with a temple complex dedicated to the god An. The Kullaba temple complex, part of which was plastered with gypsum and has come to be known as the "White Temple," is unusual in that it was not leveled before each rebuilding, so that by the time of the Uruk tradition it stood more that 13 meters high and resembled the ziggurats that would be constructed later in the Early Dynastic Mesopotamian tradition. About 5000 B.P. the Kullaba complex was leveled and buried under a massive platform, leaving the Eanna temple precinct as the center of religious and secular power during the Early Dynastic Mesopotamian tradition.

The Eanna temple complex is among the best-researched areas in Mesopotamia. Part of the reason for the intensive study of this area is that each temple complex was razed before subsequent rebuildings, so that all that remains of early temples are their foundations. The earliest building, dating to around 6000 B.P., is known as the "Limestone Temple," and this was some 76 meters long and 30 meters wide. It was constructed with numerous niches and buttresses and had the typical "tripartite" plan of Mesopotamian temples: an offering table at one end, a central room surrounded by numerous smaller rooms, and an altar at

Given the complexity of Ubaid society, trade was important. However, emphasis appears to have been on localized rather than long-distance exchange networks. Most trade was confined to utensils and agricultural staples. Small amounts of obsidian from southeastern Anatolia, Azerbaijan, and Armenia, carnelian from Iran, and copper from southeastern Anatolia indicate that there was some contact with groups over a wide area. However, these trade items were never in large quantities, suggesting that the trade for exotic goods was not of great importance. Mesopotamian-made Ubaid ceramics found at sites along the shores of the Persian Gulf in Saudi Arabia and Bahrain indicate contact by sea. This maritime network probably involved either the trade for or direct exploitation of marine resources and the end of the room opposite the offering table. The next temple complex (built around 5500 B.P.) had two buildings reached by a huge, colonnaded staircase and decorated with an intricate mosaic of small red, white, and black clay cones (the bases of these cones were painted, and the pointed end inserted into wet clay to make the mosaic). Beyond this "Mosaic Court" were several temples as well as residences for temple officials or priests. Adjacent to the temple complex was a large, square structure with a central courtyard, which has been interpreted as a public building or perhaps even a palace.

In the final major construction, dating to around 5200 B.P., a complete reorganization of the Eanna precinct was undertaken. A large temple was built over the pillared staircase and entrance of the earlier temple complex. Adjacent to this large temple a smaller temple was built, connected to a magnificent pillared hall with complex mosaic decorations made from red, white, and black clay cones. Also connected to the pillared hall (and adjacent to the public building or palace) was a large, 50-meter-square, sunken court with benches running along its walls. This is thought to have been a public meeting place. The entire complex was apparently surrounded by a wall at this point.

What do the changes in the Eanna temple complex tell us about the emerging Uruk state? They seem to suggest a growing connection between secular and religious matters, with public buildings being placed within the temple complex and even connected to other temple buildings. The changes in the Eanna complex also seem to suggest an increasing separation between the public and the elites or priests using the temple buildings. In the second reconstruction of the complex, access was through a large pillared staircase, while in the third reconstruction a pillared hallway appears to have served as an entrance. Both would have served to restrict access to the temple complex. Also in the third reconstruction, the temple complex appears to have been walled off from the rest of the city. These changes suggest increasing division between the political and religious authorities and the populace of Uruk during the period when the Sumerian empire was beginning to take shape.

SOURCES: Redman, Charles, *The Rise of Civilization* (San Francisco: W.H. Freeman, 1978); Roaf, Michael, *Cultural Atlas of Mesopotamia and the Near East* (New York: Facts on File, 1990).

perhaps animal hides by Ubaidian "merchants." There is no evidence that it involved the procurement of significant amounts of exotic prestige items.

By the time of the **Uruk** (6000–5100 B.P.) tradition, states had emerged in Mesopotamia. These states were highly urbanized, and one of the best known of these city-states, **Uruk,** from which the tradition derives its name, is described in the box feature (Figure 15.24). What also distinguishes this tradition is the mass production of goods and a general increase in craft specialization. Cottage industries are evident in utilitarian wares including pottery making, cloth making, flint knapping, and bead and seal carving. As early as 5800 B.P., specialized buildings for textile manufacture and woodworking were present. The increase in craft specialization

**Uruk** (6000–5100 B.P.)

**Uruk** (Iraq, Uruk)

FIGURE **15.24**
The ruins of Uruk.

was supported through irrigation agriculture, which became phenomenally productive in southern Mesopotamia. Estimates of yields for southern Iraqi fields based on third-millennium texts indicate more grain per acre than in many modern industrial farms.

At the same time, production of surplus foods probably served as a basis for the emergence of centralized political power. Indeed the creation of city-states in southern Mesopotamia may have been a response to periodic agricultural shortfalls. Central storage facilities could be placed in cities to provide for the populace in times of want. Because Mesopotamia lacked a wide range of resources, such as timber for large constructions, metals, quality chipping stone, basalt for utilitarian tools, bitumen for waterproofing boats and baskets, and many precious and semiprecious goods, exchange of goods across a wide area was typical. Centrally controlled cities would have been useful in the organization of this trade as well, and trade appears to have been a central aspect of political control in the Uruk tradition.

During the Uruk tradition an administrative system based on clay seals developed. Covers were placed over vessels, tied with string, and clean clay was placed over knots; then a stamp or cylinder seal was applied to the wet clay. Only authorized individuals could break the seal and access goods stored inside. Based on the distribution of clay seals, archaeologists have demonstrated that over time extended family control gave way to elite control and finally to state bureaucrats. By the end of the Uruk tradition, the sealing system was replaced by writing on clay tablets. These tablets also recorded a series of official positions and professions, which provide some idea of the complexity of the administrative system at the end of the tradition.

At the end of the Uruk tradition there appears to have been a general collapse of the trade system that held the Uruk tradition together. Although city-states continued to exist, they became more locally focused. This period of more local urban cultures defines the **Jemdet Nasr** (5100–4900 B.P.). A good example of a city-state from this tradition is the **Jemdet Nasr** site itself. A number of sun dried and baked brick buildings have been excavated at Jemdet Nasr and are similar to those found on both earlier and later Mesopotamian sites. One large building, 98 by 48 meters in size, contained a large open room surrounded on three sides by long, narrow rooms. The size and organization of the structure suggest it was an administrative

**Jemdet Nasr**
(5100–4900 B.P.)

**Jemdet Nasr**
(Iraq, Jemdet Nasr)

center of some kind. Jemdet Nasr as a whole covers an area of more than 10 hectares and was certainly a city. Other settlements were probably similar to Jemdet Nasr, and indeed thirteen other cites, including Kish, Larsa, Nippur, Ur, and Uruk are named in seal impressions on tablets found at Jemdet Nasr. Smaller agricultural villages and hamlets, like those from the preceding Uruk tradition, were certainly also present, though few are known archaeologically

The Jemdet Nasr economy was based, like that of the preceding Uruk tradition, on irrigation agriculture and sheep/goat pastoralism. Grain crops were the major agricultural focus, and were tremendously productive. The main domestic crops were wheat, barley, pulses (lentils, beans, and peas), and fruit (apples, dates, and figs). The main domestic animals were sheep and goats, which were raised primarily for wool, milk, and dung. Cattle were also kept, as were ducks, geese, pigs, and dogs.

The sociopolitical organization of the Jemdet Nasr tradition appears to be a continuation of that which developed during the preceding Uruk tradition. A hierarchical administrative system centralized in cities controlled decision making and some production activities. Bureaucratic and craft specialization were supported through surplus production controlled by state leaders either on their own estates and/or through tribute or taxation. Administration was aided by the use of stamps, cylinder seals, and protocuneiform writing that was used to mark economic transactions and keep track of both administrative and economic activities.

A distinct regional culture developed during the Jemdet Nasr tradition that likely had some economic and political unity. Society was essentially urban, with administration centralized within temple complexes that shared a common symbolic language and ideology in which certain designs or goods designated elite status and in which a group of common styles in utilitarian products like pottery was shared. Such cultural similarity had long been present in Mesopotamia by the Jemdet Nasr tradition, but it seems to have become more pronounced and focused during this period, which some scholars view as the aftermath of the collapse of the much more broadly distributed Uruk tradition.

Settlement in the **Early Dynastic Mesopotamia** (4900–4334 B.P.) tradition was dominated by city-states. There were some 20 to 30 city-states, each with a principle center that linked smaller towns and villages dispersed across its countryside. The centers themselves were also dispersed fairly evenly across the Tigris-Euphrates floodplain, separated from one another by 30 or so kilometers. Most of the population, some 80 percent by one estimate, lived in cites larger than 40 hectares, while less than 10 percent lived in villages smaller than 4 hectares.

**Early Dynastic Mesopotamia** (4900–4334 B.P.)

Cities were dominated by two features: temples and fortifications. The temples formed the center of the cities, while the fortifications formed their peripheries. An irregular plan of streets with houses and workshops filled the space between the temples and the walls, and cities such as Uruk and Lagash had dense settlements extending well outside the city walls. Temples were surrounded by auxiliary buildings that formed a complex of religious and political activity. Palace complexes were also present in some cities, and these may have replaced temples as the centers of political activity. These complexes were both the physical and political heart of the city, the location where most resources were controlled and most decisions were made.

Each city had a principle deity who was believed to inhabit the city's main temple, although there were temples for other deities as well. A statue of the deity resided in the temple, which was regarded as its home, and was cared for by temple priests. Temple priests also made offerings and supplications and carried out rituals to the deities. Some individuals apparently had access to the temples as well and left small votive statues to represent their continuing presence before the deities (Figure 15.25). Sacrifices were apparently made to deities on altars in the temples. Prayer and supplication to the deities is evidenced by the votive statues left in temples. Cylinder seals depict feasts and libation ceremonies presented to the deities.

Texts and images describe ceremonies where the statues of the deities were taken from the temples and paraded through the streets. There are also descriptions of the consecration of temples and the "animation" of the deity statues.

Powerful leaders, often referred to as kings, headed a complex hierarchical political system centered in the city palace complex. Their primary task, it appears, was to ensure that all the proper forms of worship toward the city deity were observed and that the deity received sufficient gifts and praise to support the polity. Thus politics and religion were closely linked in Early Dynastic societies, and the earliest rulers may have been priests. By the end of the Early Dynastic tradition, however, texts describe secular, hereditary leadership. Texts also describe assemblies of citizens that may have approved decisions made by the rulers. Courts were present in Early Dynastic society, but their operation is not well known. Written contracts and documents demonstrate the importance writing was to take on in terms of social control. Writing allowed authorities to keep records of important events (judicial and otherwise) and economic transactions, to write messages for emissaries to covey to friends and adversaries, and to create texts for the formal instruction of bureaucrats and other political or judicial agents.

Outside of the temple and palace complexes was a dense network of streets that fed into gates in the city walls. The gates controlled entrance to the city. Often there were also areas of the city set aside for ceramic production, flintworking, and other industrial activities. Some streets were paved with mud brick or pottery sherds and had drains to carry water away. Other streets were simply packed earth. House walls bordered directly on the streets, making streets appear an intricate maze of habitations and shops. Houses were made of mud brick with mud-plastered walls and floors, and a mud and wood roof. Most houses consisted of several rooms organized around a central courtyard. Houses ranged in size from 40 to 100 square meters, and they likely held a single nuclear or extended family.

The total population of Southern Mesopotamia increased during the Early Dynastic tradition from perhaps 100,000 persons to over 200,000. The corresponding density increased from about 100 persons per hectare to over 200 persons per hectare. These large populations were able to maintain themselves through irrigation agriculture and animal husbandry. The main domestic crops were wheat, barley, pulses (lentils, beans, and peas), and fruit (apples, dates, and figs). The main domestic animals were sheep and goats, which were raised primarily for wool, milk, and dung. Cattle were also kept, as were ducks, geese, pigs, and dogs. Fishing was important in the marshlands to the south, as was harvesting wild reeds. Small game (such as rabbits) and larger game (such as gazelle) were also hunted to supplement the diet.

The Early Dynastic peoples used a wide variety of utensils. For agriculture, animal-drawn plows were employed, and images on cylinder seals suggest some had seed funnels for planting. Shovels and hoes with either copper or stone blades were used for weeding and planting. Flint sickles were used for harvesting. Ceramics were used in abundance by Early Dynastic peoples. These were manufactured by specialists using a fast wheel, and often working in large "factories" which mass-produced the most common forms. Most ceramics were plain and simple in form—they were utilitarian and designed to be easily manufactured and used. On the other hand, metal containers were elaborate, with complex forms and intricate decoration in some cases. Metals were used for a variety of objects, from ornaments and statues to weapons and agricultural tools. Specialists worked in a variety of methods, including cold hammering, molding, and lost wax. Both copper and bronze were used, and different alloys were employed for different objects, suggesting metalsmiths had a detailed knowledge of their properties. Woven goods were important in Early Dynastic life. Clothing, rugs, pillows, and other items were all woven from wool. Texts describe a variety of cloths distinguished by weave and weight. Statues show figures with embroidery, elaborate fringes and tassels, and beadwork on their clothing.

There was a bustling exchange system in the Early Dynastic tradition. Copper was apparently a standard of value, but there was no formal money. Local trade involved utilitarian goods and foodstuffs. Foreign trade involved raw materials, often precious metals and semiprecious stones. Lapis and other semiprecious stones were imported from Afghanistan and the east, metals and obsidian from Anatolia, and copper, shell, and pearls from the Persian Gulf and Indus valley.

An extensive division of labor was present in the Early Dynastic tradition. While most individuals were probably farmers, some farming their own lands and most others working for a public official or temple, there were also a wide variety of specialized occupations, including potters, flintworkers, metalworkers, and builders. Manufacturing was apparently controlled largely through temples and palaces. Many craft specialists worked in "factories" run by the temples and produced goods such as ceramics, leather, textiles, furniture, and luxuries that were consumed by priests and elites, or were exchanged for exotic raw materials. The government supported a variety of its own specialists, including scribes, soldiers, minor officials and bureaucrats, palace and temple attendants, and priests.

There appears to have been a clear division between elites and commoners in Early Dynastic society, evidenced in both architecture and burials. Status also appears to have been hereditary, as both young and old elites have been identified through elaborate burial treatment. This is perhaps best evidenced in the royal cemetery at **Ur.** There many individuals were buried in simple graves with no grave goods, while others, particularly those in the 16 "royal" graves, were buried with elaborate ceremony (including human sacrifice) and extraordinary wealth (Color Plates 20 and 21). Elites apparently served as priests or political figures. There is little evidence of secular wealth or power in Early Dynastic society. Temples and palaces controlled most of the land and labor, and most citizens were likely employed by them. These institutions apparently also rented land to public officials,

 **Ur (Iraq, Early Dynastic)**

who used it to support themselves and their families. The temples and palaces also controlled enormous flocks of sheep and goats—hundreds of thousands of individual animals by some accounts. Like land, these were apparently distributed to officials and others who used their milk and wool in return for shepherding the animals.

# ❂ SUMMARY

South and Southwest Asia provide some of the most fascinating and complex images of prehistory that we have. At the end of the Upper Paleolithic era people throughout the region, particularly those in the Levant, Iran, and northern India, began settling down into small communities and subsisting upon rich local plant and animal resources that had emerged at the end of the last ice age. In the Levant and Iran, the intensive use of seed-bearing grasses led to their domestication. Similarly, though perhaps in a more widespread area, intensive use of sheep and goats led to their domestication. Once these first domesticates were established, the peoples of South and Southwest Asia developed a wide range of domesticated plants and animals and soon became fully reliant upon them for subsistence.

The development of domesticates and settled village life went hand in hand in South and Southwest Asia, and it appears that technological innovation accompanied them as well. Copper and ceramics began to be used early on by these settled food producers, and soon bronze was developed. Settled life also appears to have fostered intercommunity interaction, particularly trade. Raw materials for stone and metal tools, as well as a wide variety of exotic goods such as gold and lapis lazuli, were exchanged across a wide area of South and Southwest Asia, and into neighboring regions as well. Domesticates, too, spread widely, creating a vast area across which similar subsistence regimes flourished.

Settled life seems also to have fostered political centralization. Over time centralized polities emerged in all areas of South and Southwest Asia. Most of these polities appear to have been expansionistic, and conflict, conquest, and collapse seems to have been the normal course for most South and Southwest Asian polities. Those that survived emerged as powerful empires that themselves regularly expanded and collapsed. By the time we reach the historic era, we read of a complex world of social classes, political conflicts, economic interactions, and religious beliefs that are only hinted at by the archaeological record.

# ❂ DISCUSSION QUESTIONS

1. The earliest domesticates in Southwest Asia include wheat, barley, sheep, and goats. Why were these plants and animals the first to be domesticated? What characteristics do they have that might have made them easy or desirable domesticates?

2. In what ways is the Indus Valley civilization similar to Southern Mesopotamian civilization? How do they differ?

3. Long-distance trade appears to have been an important feature of many societies in South and Southwest Asia. What characteristics of the environment might have promoted the development of long-distance trade?

# ❂ ESSAY QUESTIONS

1. Unlike many other parts of the world, every area of South and Southwest Asia witnessed the emergence of state societies. What might have made this region so prone to state development? Are there unique elements of the environment, both physical and social, that might promote the rise of states?

2. States emerged in all areas of South and Southwest Asia, but their forms seem very different. Compare and contrast the apparent forms of state leadership, control, and militarism in at least three areas of South and Southwest Asia. How do these states vary? In what ways are they similar?

3. Philosopher of science Karl Popper complained in *The Open Society and Its Enemies* (1945) that "There is no history of mankind, there are only many histories of all kinds of aspects of human life. And one of these is the history of political power. This is elevated into the history of the world." To what extent is Popper's complaint applicable to the prehistory of South and Southwest Asia? That is, to what extent has the prehistory of South and Southwest Asia been written with a focus on the origins and expansion of political power rather on other aspects of human life?

## ✦ RESEARCH PROJECT

States are found in all areas of South and Southwest Asia, and there is great diversity in the types of societies that are defined as states. Might this be, in part, an effect of research tradition or focus? If North American chiefdoms were put in South Asia, would they be seen as states? Do research on a particular North American chiefdom, such as Cahokia or Chaco Canyon, and on an early South Asian state, such as Uruk or Harappa. What features of the archaeological record tell us that the North American cases are chiefdoms and the South Asian cases are states? What ambiguities are there in the archaeological record that might make the distinction between chiefdoms and states difficult? What role does theory and ideology play in the way the archaeological record might be interpreted in these cases?

## ✪ KEY SOURCES

### Indian Subcontinent

Agrawal, 1982; Allchin, 1990; Allchin and Allchin, 1982; Banerjee, 1965; Chattopadhyaya, I., 2002; Chattopadhyaya, U., 2002a, 2002b; Deo, 1982; Dhavalikar, 1988; Erdosy, 1987; Ghosh, 1973, 1990; Gururaja Rao, 1972; Narain, 1979; Narayan, 1996; Ray, 1987; Roy, 1983; Sankialia, 1974; Sant, 1991; Sharma, 1980; Sharma et al., 1980; Shinde, 1989, 1990, 1991, 1994, 2002a, 2002b; Sinha, 1994; Sinopoli, 2001a, 2001b; Verma, 1988.

### Indus Valley

Allchin and Allchin, 1997; Jarrige, 1991, 1993; Jarrige et al., 1995; Kenoyer, 1998, 2000, 2002a, 2002b, 2002c; Meadow, 1991; Possehl, 1993, 1999; Wheeler, 1968.

### Iranian Plateau

Carter and Stolper, 1984; Delougaz and Kantor, 1996; Diakonoff, 1985a, 1985b; Hole, 1987; Hole and Flannery, 1967; Hole, Flannery, and Neely, 1969; Kohl, 1978; Lamberg-Karlovsky, 1971; Lamberg-Karlovsky and Beale, 1986; Peasnall, 2002a, 2002b, 2002c; Potts, 1980, 1999; Smith, P., 1986; Solecki, 1981; Voigt, 1983.

### Arabian Peninsula

Biagi et al., 1984; Bibby, 1969; Crawford, 1998; Edens and Wilkinson, 1998; Keall, 1998; Magee, 1996a, 1996b, 2002; Magee and Carter, 1999; Newton and Zarins, 2000; Potts, 1990; Rice, 1994; Tosi, 1986; Uerpmann, 1992; Zarins, 1989, 2002a, 2002b, 2002c.

## Levant

Akkermans, 1993; Anati, 1963; Banning, 1998, 2002a, 2002b; Bar-Yosef, 1980, 1995; Ben-Tor, 1992; Braidwood and Braidwood, 1986; Byrd and Monahan, 1995; Dever, 1987; Epstein, 1977, 1998; Esse, 1991; Gilead, 1988; Golden, 2002a, 2002b; Gopher and Gophna, 1993; Henry, 1986, 1989; Hershkovitz, Bar-Yosef, and Arensburg, 1994; Joffe, 1993; Kirkbride, 1968; Kislev, 1984; Kislev and Bar-Yosef, 1988; Knapp, 1992; Kohler-Rollefson, 1992; Kramer, 1982; Levy, 1983, 1998, 2002; Maisels, 1993; Mazar, 1990; McCorriston and Hole, 1991; Mellaart, 1975; Moore, 1985; Peasnall, 2002d; Pigott, 1999; Stein and Rothman, 1994; Watkins, 1992; Wright, 1985.

## Mesopotamia

Adams, 1981; Adams and Nissen, 1972; Algaze, 1989, 1993; Banning, 2002b; Braidwood and Howe, 1960; Crawford, 1991; Delougaz and Kantor, 1996; Finkbeiner and Röllig, 1986; Hijjara, 1997; Johnson, 1973; Kubba, 1987; Matthews, 1992a, 1992b, 1999, 2002; Nissen, 1988, 1993; Pittman, 1993; Pollock, 1999; Postgate, 1992; Roaf, 1990; Rothman, 1998, 2000, 2002; Schwartz, 1994; Stein, 1989; Wilkinson, 1990; Wright and Johnson, 1975; Yoffee, 1995; Yoffee and Clark, 1993; Zettler and Horne, 1998.

# THE TEMPLE OF ERIDU

Mesopotamia is essentially a large basin lying between the Zagros Mountains and the desert uplands of the Arabian Peninsula. The Tigris and Euphrates rivers run through this basin, creating a vast plain of marsh and riverine environments. Grasslands are found to the east of the rivers and the Syrian Desert is to the west. Willow, poplar, tamarask, palm, and other trees and bushes are found near the rivers, and these support populations of deer, boar, and smaller animals and birds. Temperatures in this large river valley range from 20 degrees C in the winter to over 40 degrees in the summer. Rainfall is not sufficient for agriculture, so agriculture is based on irrigation. There is no evidence of Upper Paleolithic people in this region. It is thought that their settlements are either buried under tons of sediment or under the waters of the Persian Gulf. The first known culture in this region is the Halafian (7500–7000 B.P.) tradition, followed by the Ubaid (8000–6000 B.P.) tradition. The Ubaid peoples were settled agriculturalists who primarily lived in small villages averaging 1 to 2 hectares (an area of land 100 meters on a side or 2.47 acres) organized around larger centers of up to 10 hectares. The larger centers contained religious architecture. The large centers probably served both ritual and economic functions for chiefdoms based on the mobilization of staple goods. They were also the focus of large cemeteries used by elites from the surrounding region.

## WEB ACTIVITY

The site of Eridu sits on the delta of the Tigris–Euphrates Rivers near the Persian Gulf. Eridu is important to our understanding of the Ubaid tradition because it contains an early temple. It is small, but contains elements characteristic of later temple architecture, such as a cult-niche, a central offering-table, and an orientation along the cardinal

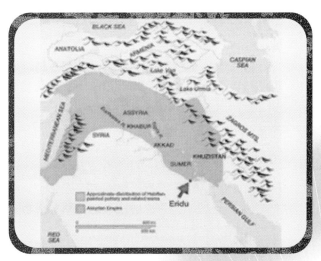

The Media Lab can be found in Chapter 15 on the *Companion Website*™ http://www.prenhall.com/peregrine

axis of the earth. Temple architecture became increasingly sophisticated, with the Eridu temple ending up as a structure with a long central sanctuary flanked on either side by a series of smaller rooms. In this activity, you will view a map of Mesopotamia and its surrounding region, along with imagery of Eridu.

## Activity

1. View the video. What types of artifacts are shown? What do they tell us about the people of the Ubaid tradition?

2. The people of the Ubaid tradition utilized draft animals in agricultural production. What does this tell us about their ability to produce agricultural surplus? How do we link this to large structures found in essentially small cities?

3. What was the environment of Mesopotamia at the time of the Ubaid tradition? Why would it be conducive to agriculture? What about this form of agriculture provided such large surpluses for such a long period of time? What is this very environment like today?

# The Evolution of Food Production

In the previous eight chapters we have seen that humans in every part of the world learned to domesticate plants and animals. In most cases humans came to rely upon these domesticates for subsistence; that is, most humans made a change from food collection to food production. Twelve thousand years ago all humans were food collectors. Today, only a few thousand people remain food collectors. Why did this transformation occur? This chapter will try to answer that question.

Before considering why humans all over the world made the shift from food collection to food production, we need to consider a few other basic questions—where and when did this transformation occur? The preceding chapters provide some basic answers to those questions. Before proceeding to the larger question of why people adopted food production, let's review what domestication means, as well as where and when the major domesticated plants and animals appeared.

## Domestication

Recall that domestication refers to the process through which humans modify plants and animals to enhance characteristics that humans desire. For example, during the process of domestication wild wheat and barley developed a tough **rachis**—the seed-bearing part of the stem. Wild forms of wheat and barley have a brittle rachis, which shatters easily, releasing the seeds. Domesticated grains have a tough rachis, which does not release seeds until they are torn from the stem by human hands. In addition, grains of wild barley and wheat have a tough shell, which protects the seed from premature exposure, while domesticated grains have a brittle shell that can be easily separated, which facilitates preparing the seed for grinding into flour (see Figure 16.1).

How did domesticated plants get to be different from their wild ancestors? The simple answer is that humans, either purposefully or accidentally, facilitated the growth of plants having characteristics humans desired. Consider how the rachis of wheat and barley may have changed. When wild grain ripens in the field, the rachis shatters easily, scattering the seed. When humans began harvesting wild wheat with sickles, many of the seeds probably fell to the ground rather than being collected

**Rachis:** the seed-bearing part of a plant stem.

FIGURE **16.1**

Weed heads of wild and domestic wheat. Note the larger and more numerous seeds on domesticated wheat.

SOURCE: From *Past in Perspective* by K. Feder, p. 338. Copyright © 2000 by Mayfield Publishing Company. Reprinted by permission of the publisher.

Wild      Domesticated

with the cut stalk. Those that were collected had a tougher rachis and did not fall off when the stalk was cut. If humans sowed these seeds, the next years' crop would likely have many tough-rachis plants. If in each successive harvest seeds from tough-rachis plants were the least likely to be lost, tough-rachis plants would come to predominate, and the plant would become domesticated. It would have the tough-rachis characteristic desired by humans and, perhaps more significantly, would have difficulty reproducing without human intervention because seeds would rarely fall off tough-rachis plants on their own.

In some species the process of domestication is even more dramatic. Maize, for example, has become entirely dependent upon humans for reproduction. Although the origins of maize (corn) are controversial, most scholars believe that maize was domesticated from **teosinte**, a tall, wild grass that still grows widely in Mexico. Teosinte is quite different from maize in several important ways. Teosinte stalks do look a lot like maize, but teosinte has a "spike" to which seven to twelve individual seeds are attached in a single row, unlike the maize cob, which has many seeds in many rows. Each teosinte seed has its own brittle shell, while the entire maize cob is covered with a tough husk (see Figure 16.2). This is a profound change because maize requires a human to open the husk without damaging the seeds in order for the seeds to be exposed and disperse.

Domesticated species of animals also differ from the wild varieties. For example, the horns of wild goats in the Near East are shaped differently from those of

**Teosinte:** a tall, wild grass that grows widely in Mexico and is thought to be ancestral to maize.

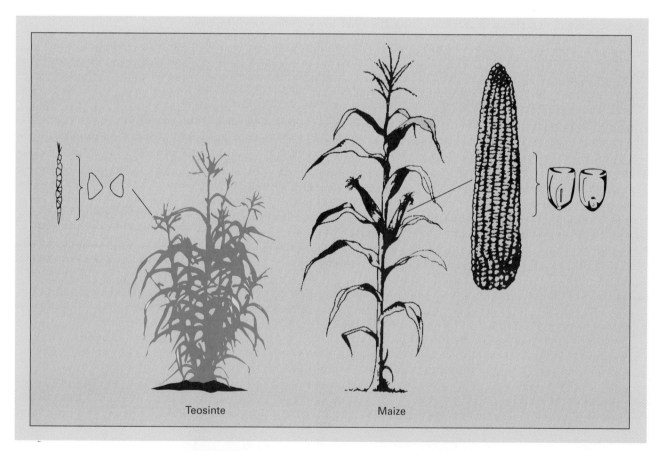

Teosinte                    Maize

FIGURE **16.2**

Teosinte plant, spike, and seeds and maize plant, cob, and kernels. Note how much larger the domesticated maize spike and seeds are.

SOURCE: From *Past in Perspective* by K. Feder, p. 340. Copyright © 2000 by Mayfield Publishing Company. Reprinted by permission of the publisher.

domesticated goats. Differences in physical characteristics are not the only indicators of domestication. Archaeologists also use statistics to examine sex and age ratios of animal remains to determine if there are imbalances that suggest domestication had occurred. For example, at Zawi Chemi Shanidar in Iraq, introduced in the previous chapter, the proportion of young to mature sheep remains was much higher than the ratio of young to mature sheep in wild herds. One possible inference to be drawn is that the animals were domesticated, the adult sheep being saved for breeding purposes while the young were eaten.

## WHERE AND WHEN DID FOOD PRODUCTION EVOLVE?

The previous eight chapters have explained where and when food production evolved. It is interesting that no area of the world lacks food production—even in the tundra of the Siberian arctic, humans of the Siberian Protohistoric tradition domesticated reindeer. But there are only a small number of significant domesticated species of plants and animals—about ten of each—upon which most humans on earth rely (Figure 16.3). Where and when were these plants and animals domesticated?

In the Old World, the earliest domesticates are wheat and barley, which appear in the Levant during the Aceramic Neolithic tradition, about 10,500 B.P. Sheep and goats were domesticated somewhat later, perhaps by 9000 B.P. The earliest clear evidence of cereal cultivation outside of the Levant is from southwest China were peoples of the Southeast China Early Neolithic tradition cultivated millet as early as 9000 B.P. Southeast China Early Neolithic peoples also had domesticated pigs about 9000 B.P. Rice was domesticated somewhat later, probably about 6000 B.P. In Africa sorghum appears to have been an early domesticate, appearing by 8000 B.P. among peoples of the Early Khartoum tradition. While the cattle, sheep, and goats relied upon by many African pastoral groups were first domesticated in the Levant, recent studies of cattle genetics has demonstrated that several African groups independently domesticated cattle, perhaps as early as 9500 B.P.

Maize was domesticated in the highland valleys of Mesoamerica during the Highland Mesoamerican Archaic tradition, some 9,000 years ago. Bottle gourds, runner beans, and squash were also domesticated about the same time. Outside of Mesoamerica, evidence of independent domestication of plants comes from at least two areas in the New World: South America and eastern North America. The

## Major Domesticated Plants and Animals

| NAME | WHERE DOMESTICATED | WHEN DOMESTICATED |
| --- | --- | --- |
| Wheat | Southwest Asia | 10,500 B.P. |
| Maize | Mexico | 9000 B.P. |
| Rice | China | 9000 B.P. |
| Barley | Southwest Asia | 10,500 B.P. |
| Sheep/Goat | Southwest Asia | 9000 B.P. |
| Cow/Ox | Southwest Asia/North Africa | 9000 B.P. |
| Pig | Southwest Asia | 8000 B.P. |
| Horse | Central Asia | 6000 B.P. |

FIGURE **16.3**
The ten most important domesticated plants and animals. While thousands of species have been domesticated, these ten account for most of the food consumed in the world.

first clear South American domesticate was the chili pepper, which appears in the Andes about 9000 B.P., making domestication in the Andes nearly as old as in Mesoamerica. Potatoes, lima beans, peanuts, amaranth, and quinoa were domesticated by peoples of the Late Andean Hunting-Collecting tradition sometime before 7000 B.P. Many of the plants grown in eastern North America such as corn, beans, and squash were apparently introduced from Mesoamerica. However, at least three seed plants were domesticated independently in eastern North America at an earlier time—sunflowers, sumpweed, and goosefoot. These plants were cultivated by peoples of the Middle Eastern Archaic tradition, perhaps as early as 7000 B.P.

Domestic animals were not as important to subsistence in the New World as they were in the Old World. In North and Middle America, dogs and turkeys were the only domestic animals before the arrival of the Spanish. In the Andes, however, domesticated alpaca and llama were a significant part of the economy and were used for meat, transportation, and wool. They were domesticated by people of the Late Andean Hunting-Collecting tradition sometime before 7000 B.P. Guinea pigs, raised for their meat, were domesticated in the Andes at about the same time. The reason for the relatively few domesticated animals in the New World probably has to do with the available species. The Old World plains and forests were the homes for the wild ancestors of the cattle, sheep, goats, pigs, and horses we know today. In the New World, the Pleistocene herds of horses, mastodons, mammoths, and other large animals were long extinct, allowing few opportunities for domestication of large animals.

Figure 16.4 summarizes where and when food production began. One can readily see that food production began all around the world within a relatively short period of time. Between 10,000 and 7,000 years ago people everywhere were actively domesticating plants and animals. In the two million years since our genus

FIGURE **16.4**

Timeline of the evolution of domestication.

SOURCE: Dates for animal domestication are from Juliet Clutton-Brock, "Domestication of Animals," in Stephen Jones, Robert Martin, and David Pilbeam, eds., *The Cambridge Encyclopedia of Human Evolution* (New York: Cambridge University Press, 1992), p. 384. Reprinted with the permission of Cambridge University Press.

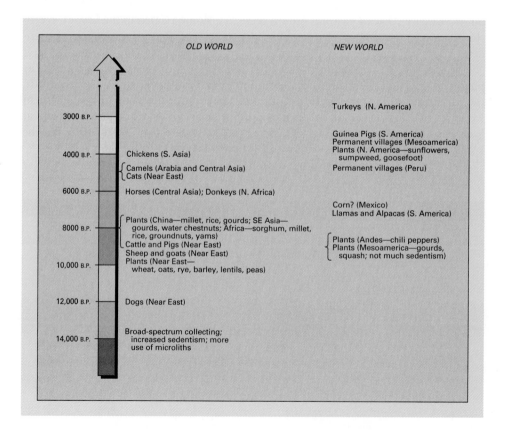

first made its appearance, this is a remarkably brief period of time, and forces us to ask an interesting question: Should we think about the shift to food production on the scale of traditions or on a larger, perhaps global, scale? Was the transition to food production a human phenomenon, or a local one that just happened to occur at about the same time all over the world? How could the transition to food production be a global phenomenon?

One of the first answers was provided by archaeologists Robert Braidwood and Gordon Willey. They argued that the reason food production began at about the same time all over the world was because people did not undertake domestication until they had learned a great deal about their environment and until their culture had evolved enough for them to handle such an undertaking. In their view, no human culture was capable of making the shift to food production until after the last ice age. Before that time the environment was too cold in most of the places humans lived for food production to be successful (northern climates even today generally lack food production). Perhaps more important, human culture did not display the sophisticated toolmaking and artistic expression suggesting complex abstract thought before the last ice age. In short, humans may not have had the intellectual abilities to become food producers until after the last ice age.

Alternatively, physical anthropologist Mark Cohen argued it was population pressure on a global scale that explains why food production was adopted by so many of the world's peoples within the span of a few thousand years. He suggested that hunter-gatherers all over the world gradually increased in population so that by about 10,000 years ago the world was more or less filled with food collectors. Thus people could no longer relieve population pressure by moving to uninhabited areas. To support their increasing populations, they would have had to exploit a broader range of less desirable wild foods; that is, they would have had to switch to broad-spectrum collecting, or they would have had to increase the yields of the most desirable wild plants by weeding, protecting them from animal pests, and perhaps deliberately planting the most productive among them. Cohen thinks that people might have tried a variety of these strategies but would generally have ended up depending on cultivation because that would have been the most efficient way to allow more people to live in one place.

Is there evidence to support either of these theories? As I noted earlier, Upper Paleolithic art, sophisticated stone and bone tools (and potentially modern language ability) emerged just prior to the last ice age, and as soon as the ice age was over and conditions ameliorated, domestication began. These may be simple coincidences, but it is interesting that there is some tantalizing evidence suggesting that horses may have been kept (though probably not domesticated) by Upper Paleolithic peoples. The evidence includes unique wear on horse teeth caused by gnawing on wood that today is only found among horses kept in corrals or stalls, and a carving of a horse that appears to have a nose bridal (see Figure 16.5). There is also evidence for selective killing of young male reindeer at some European Upper Paleolithic sites, and in Neolithic contexts such selective killing is often associated with domesticated herds. So the process of domestication may have emerged at the same time as art and sophisticated tools, but it had to wait until the climate ameliorated before it could be used to develop dependable domestic plants and animals.

It is also clear that that population and food production are strongly associated with one another. Figure 16.6 presents a table based on information from all of the archaeological traditions discussed in the previous eight chapters, demonstrating the association between population and agriculture. I created the data for this table and the others in this and the next two chapters, using the codebook presented in Appendix I. A **codebook** provides definitions used to assign values to cases on specific variables. Here the cases are archaeological traditions, and in Figure 16.6 the variables are Agriculture and Density of Population. Each variable has three values.

**Codebook:** provides definitions used to assign values to cases on specific variables.

FIGURE **16.5**
This carved horse from the Upper Paleolithic site of Grotte des Espelunges in France appears to have a bridle. It is one of several tantalizing pieces of evidence that suggest Upper Paleolithic peoples may have domesticated horses.

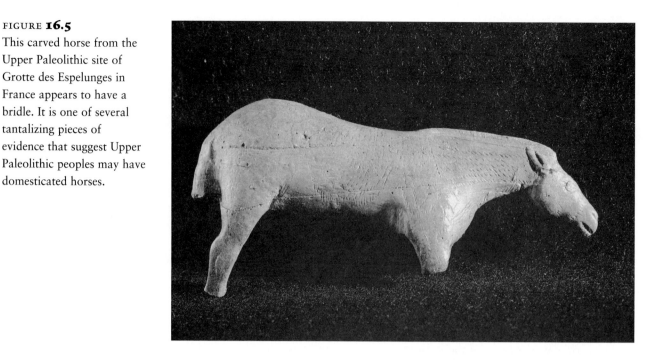

For Agriculture these values are 1, no food production; 2, 10 percent or more of food is produced, but it is still secondary to food collection; and 3, food production is the primary source. The values for Density of Population are 1, less than 1 person per square mile; 2, 1 to 25 persons per square mile; and 3, more than 26 persons per square mile.

Figure 16.6 is called a **cross-tabulation** table. It shows the number of cases that have a particular value on two variables. For example, the cell at the top left shows the number of cases with a value of 1 on both the Agriculture and the Density of Population variables (here there are 113 such cases), while the bottom right shows the number of cases with a value of 3 on both variables (here there are 28 cases). The other number in each cell of the table is the number of cases expected to have a given value on the two variables if there is no association between the two; that is, the expected number of cases with those values by random chance. Here one could expect 58 cases with a value of 1 on both variables by chance, and 15 cases with a value of 3 on both variables by chance. By comparing the actual number of cases in each cell with the expected number, we can see if, and how, two variables are associated. If the actual and expected numbers are about the same, the two variables are not associated because their values follow a random pattern. If the actual

**Cross-tabulation:** shows the number of cases that have a particular value on two variables.

FIGURE **16.6**
Crosstabulation of Agriculture and Density of Population.

| | | | DENSITY | | |
|---|---|---|---|---|---|
| | | | 1 | 2 | 3 |
| Agriculture | 1 | Count | 113 | 6 | 0 |
| | | Expected Count | 58 | 49 | 12 |
| | 2 | Count | 17 | 5 | 2 |
| | | Expected Count | 12 | 10 | 2 |
| | 3 | Count | 10 | 108 | 28 |
| | | Expected Count | 71 | 60 | 15 |

FIGURE **16.7**

Line graph of Agriculture and
Density of Population.

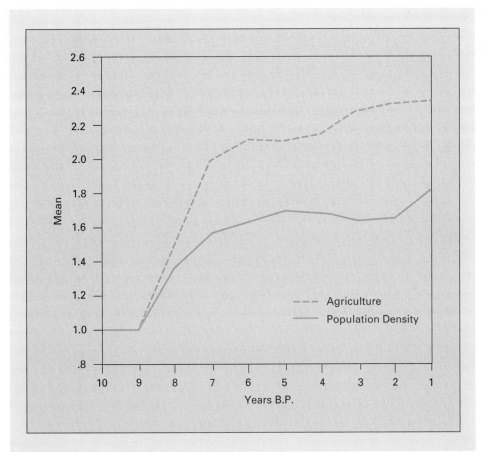

and expected values differ, those differences tell us how the two variables are associated.

Looking at Figure 16.6 we can see that there are almost twice as many cases with a value of 1 for each variable as is expected by chance, and almost the same with cases having a value of 3 for each variable. There are also far more cases with a value of 2 for Density of Population and 3 for Agriculture than expected by chance (there are 108 such cases and only 60 expected). On the other hand, there are far fewer cases with a value of 1 for Density of Population and 3 for Agriculture than expected by chance. What Figure 16.6 tells us is that Density of Population and Agriculture are strongly associated. As Density of Population goes up, so does Agriculture, and vice versa. This would seem to support Cohen's argument.

However, there is a "chicken and egg" problem here. While population and food production are strongly associated, as Cohen argues, there is no way here to tell which came first or whether one caused the other. In fact, the two seem to go hand in hand so that neither seems causal for the other, as we can see from Figure 16.7. Figure 16.7 is a graph of Agriculture and Density of Population over time for the last 10,000 years. To make this graph, the average value of Agriculture and Density of Population were calculated for all cases at 1,000-year intervals and then charted. The horizontal axis shows the time in years B.P. and the vertical axis the average value for all cases on each variable. What you can see is that Agriculture and Density of Population parallel one another throughout prehistory, and one does not seem to precede the other.

In addition to this "chicken and egg" problem there also seems to be a logical problem with Cohen's argument, as Density of Population was not high everywhere that saw food production emerge. Indeed, even today there are areas of the earth where population density is very low, so to argue that global population rose to the point that food production was necessary seems a problematic argument. In addition, some scholars would argue that the time period within which domestication occurred around the world was at least 3,000 years, and 3,000 years is a long, long time no matter how you look at it. These scholars also argue that the processes through which domestication occurred were very different in different parts of the world. Before going on to consider other theories for why people made the shift from food collection to food production, then, let's first gain a more complete understanding of how this transition occurred by comparing the process of domestication as evidenced in the archaeological record from the Iranian Neolithic site of Ali Kosh and the Highland Mesoamerican Archaic site of Guila Naquitz.

## FOOD PRODUCTION IN SOUTHWEST ASIA

For some time most archaeologists have thought that the Fertile Crescent (see Figure 16.8), the arc of land stretching up from Israel and the Jordan Valley through southern Turkey and then downward to the western slopes of the Zagros

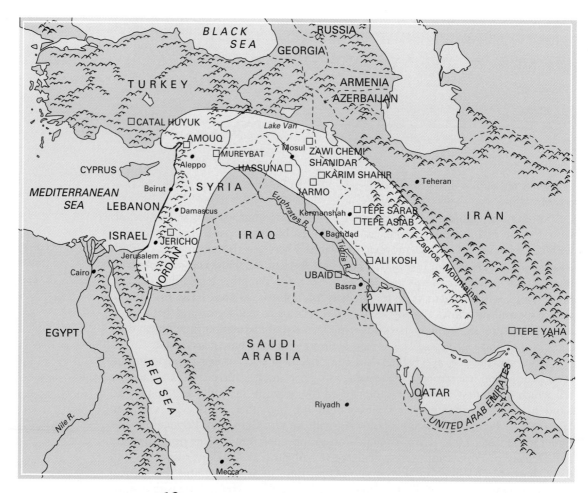

FIGURE **16.8**

The "Fertile Crescent" and important sites of early domestication.

SOURCE: Peter N. Peregrine, Carol R. Ember, and Melvin Ember, *Archaeology: Original Readings in Method and Practice* (Upper Saddle River, NJ: Prentice Hall, 2002), p. 177. Reprinted by permission of Pearson Education, Inc., Upper Saddle River, NJ.

Mountains in Iran, was the earliest center of plant and animal domestication. We know that several varieties of domesticated wheat were being grown there after about 10,000 B.P., as were oats, rye, barley, lentils, peas, and various fruits and nuts (apricots, pears, pomegranates, dates, figs, olives, almonds, and pistachios). It appears that the first animals were domesticated in the Near East. One of the most important sites with evidence of early domestication is Ali Kosh.

## Ali Kosh

At the stratified site of **Ali Kosh** in what is now southwestern Iran (see Figure 16.8) are preserved the remains of an Iranian Neolithic community that started out about 9500 B.P., living mostly on wild plants and animals. Over the next 2,000 years, until about 7500 B.P., agriculture and herding became increasingly important. After 7500 B.P. we see the appearance of two innovations—irrigation and the use of domesticated cattle—that seem to have stimulated a minor population explosion during the following millennium.

**Ali Kosh**
(Iran, Iranian Neolithic)

From 9500 to 8750 B.P., the people at Ali Kosh built small, multiroom structures from unbaked clay bricks. The excavated rooms are small, seldom more than 2 meters by 3 meters, and there is no evidence that the structures were definitely houses where people actually spent time or slept. Instead they may have been storage rooms. On the other hand, house rooms of even smaller size are known in other areas of the world, so it is possible that the people at Ali Kosh in its earliest phase were actually living in these tiny houses. There is some evidence that the people at Ali Kosh may have moved for the summer (with their goats) to the grassier mountain valleys nearby, which were just a few days' walk away.

We know a lot about what the people at Ali Kosh ate. They got some of their food from cultivated emmer wheat and a kind of barley and a considerable amount from domesticated goats. We know the goats were domesticated because wild goats do not seem to have lived in the area. Also, the fact that virtually no bones from elderly goats were found in the site suggests that the goats were domesticated and herded rather than hunted. Moreover, it would seem from the horn cores found in the site that mostly young male goats were eaten, so the females probably were kept for breeding and milking. But with all these signs of deliberate food production, there is an enormous amount of evidence—literally tens of thousands of seeds and bone fragments—that the people at the beginning of Ali Kosh depended mostly on wild plants (legumes and grasses) and wild animals (including gazelles, wild oxen, and wild pigs). They also collected fish, such as carp and catfish, and shellfish, such as mussels, as well as waterfowl that visited the area during part of the year.

The stone tools used during this earliest phase at Ali Kosh were varied and abundant, and they included numerous microliths. About 1 percent of the chipped stone was obsidian, which came from what is now eastern Turkey, several hundred kilometers away. Thus, the people at Ali Kosh during its earliest phase definitely had some kind of contact with people elsewhere. This contact is also suggested by the fact that the emmer wheat they cultivated did not have a wild relative in the area.

From 8750 to 8000 B.P., the people increased their consumption of cultivated food plants; 40 percent of the seed remains in the hearths and refuse areas were now from emmer wheat and barley. The proportion of the diet coming from wild plants was much reduced, probably because the cultivated plants have the same growing season and grow in the same kind of soil as the wild plants. Grazing by the goats and sheep that were kept may also have contributed to the reduction of wild plant foods in the area and in the diet. The village may or may not have gotten larger, but the multiroom houses definitely had. The rooms were now larger than 3 meters square; the walls were much thicker; and the clay bricks were now held together by a mud mortar. Also, the walls now often had a coat of smooth mud plaster on both sides. The stamped-mud house floors were apparently covered with rush or reed mats. There were courtyards with domed brick ovens and brick-lined roasting pits. Understandably, considering the summer heat in the area, none of the ovens found were inside a house.

Even though the village probably contained no more than 100 individuals, it participated in an extensive trading network. Seashells were probably obtained from the Persian Gulf, which is some distance to the south; copper may have come from what is now central Iran; obsidian was still coming from eastern Turkey; and turquoise somehow made its way from what is now the border between Iran and Afghanistan. Some of these materials were used as ornaments worn by both sexes—or so it seems from the remains of bodies found buried under the floors of houses.

After about 7500 B.P., the area around Ali Kosh begins to show signs of a much larger population, apparently made possible by a more complex agriculture employing irrigation and plows drawn by domesticated cattle. In the next thousand years, by 6500 B.P., the population of the area probably tripled. This population growth was apparently part of the cultural developments that culminated in the rise of urban civilizations (see Chapter 17).

Population growth may have occurred in and around Ali Kosh but did not continue in all areas of Southwest Asia after domestication. For example, the Aceramic Neolithic site of 'Ain Ghazal on the outskirts of what is now Amman, Jordan, suffered a decline in population and standard of living over time, perhaps because the environment around 'Ain Ghazal could not permanently support a large village.

## FOOD PRODUCTION IN MESOAMERICA

A very different pattern of domestication is seen in Mesoamerica. Here the seminomadic Highland Mesoamerican Archaic hunting and gathering lifestyle persisted long after people first domesticated plants. How can this be? Don't people have to settle near their crops to take care of them? Once they have domesticated plants, don't they stop collecting wild plants? The answer is no. In Mesoamerica people sowed a variety of plants, but after doing so they went on with their seasonal rounds of hunting and gathering, coming back later to harvest what they had sown. Many of the early domesticates in Mesoamerica were not basic to subsistence, even if they were highly desirable. Domestication may have been a way for Highland Mesoamerican Archaic peoples to make desirable plants more common in their environment. For example, one of the first domesticates was the bottle gourd. These were not eaten, but rather were used to carry water. Joyce Marcus and Kent Flannery hypothesize that the bottle gourd was domesticated by deliberately planting them in areas where they did not grow naturally, so that as groups moved through those areas they always had access to gourds for carrying water.

Bottle gourds are only one of many early domesticates from highland Mesoamerica. Others include tomatoes, cotton, a variety of beans and squashes, and, perhaps most important, maize. As noted earlier, these were probably domesticated by simple manipulation of wild varieties. Runner beans, for example, grow naturally in the soils on the slopes outside of rockshelters and caves. It is not a stretch of the imagination to envision Highland Mesoamerican Archaic peoples harvesting these beans (for their roots to begin with—nondomestic runner bean seeds are tiny and probably were not eaten) and selectively planting those with desired qualities like large seeds. Similarly, only the seeds of wild squashes were likely eaten by Highland Mesoamerican Archaic peoples since the flesh of wild squashes often has an unattractive smell and taste. But they may have selectively planted seeds from individual squashes with better tasting flesh and larger seeds than others, eventually producing the domestic varieties over time.

People who lived in Mesoamerica are often credited with the invention of planting maize, beans, and squash together in the same field. This planting strategy provides some important advantages. Maize takes nitrogen from the soil; beans, like all legumes, put nitrogen back into the soil. The maize stalk provides a natural pole for the bean plant to twine around, and the low-growing squash can grow around the base of the tall maize plant. Beans supply people with the amino acid lysine, which is missing in maize. Thus, maize and beans together provide all the essential amino acids that humans need to obtain from their food. Whether teosinte was or was not the ancestor of maize, it may have provided the model for this unique combination since wild runner beans and wild squash occur naturally where teosinte grows.

## Guila Naquitz

The **Guila Naquitz** cave, excavated in the 1960s by Kent Flannery, provides a good picture of early domestication in highland Mesoamerica. Here small groups of people—probably only a single family at a time—lived intermittently (and probably seasonally) over a period of 2,000 years (ca 10,900 B.P. to 8700 B.P.), the period during which plants were domesticated. The cave itself is located in the thorn forest of the upper piedmont above the floor of the Valley of Oaxaca (Figure 16.9). The residents of Guila Naquitz hunted deer and peccary (a wild piglike animal) with spears and spear throwers, and trapped small animals such as rabbits. They also collected plant foods from the surrounding area, particularly prickly pear fruits, cherries, acorns, and pinion nuts from the forests above the cave, along with agave hearts, onions, and various other nuts and fruits from a variety of thorn forest plants.

Also found in Guila Naquitz cave are the remains of domesticated plants, including bottle gourd and several varieties of squashes. How did these come to be

**Guila Naquitz**
(Mexico, Highland
Mesoamerican Archaic)

FIGURE **16.9**
The thorn forest in the Valley of Oaxaca.

in the cave? Were the inhabitants planting fields of squashes? Probably not in the way one thinks of planting a field today. Squashes are common wild plants in Highland Mesoamerica, and they thrive in disturbed soils such as those outside of caves. It may be that the inhabitants of the Guila Naquitz cave knew squashes would grow easily near their cave and so actively planted some with better tasting flesh or larger seeds than those that might naturally grow there. Domestication and the use of domesticated plants would be rather informal—a supplement to a diet already rich in animal and plant species. This picture seems much different from that presented by Near Eastern sites such as Ali Kosh and Catal Huyuk. Domestication in Guila Naquitz appears to have been accomplished by hunters and gatherers who supplemented their basic diet with some desired plants (squashes with tasty flesh, for example); there was no "revolution" that enabled the people to rely on domesticated plants.

## WHY DID FOOD PRODUCTION EVOLVE?

The comparison of the emergence of food production at Ali Kosh and Guila Naquitz demonstrates how diverse the patterns of domestication were across the world. With this kind of diversity, one might wonder how archaeologists can hope to develop a general answer to the question of why food production developed. Archaeologists Lewis Binford and Kent Flannery suggested that a general answer must begin with the idea that a change in external circumstances must have induced or favored food production over food collection. As Flannery pointed out, there is no evidence of a great economic incentive for hunter-gatherers to become food producers. In fact, some contemporary hunter-gatherers obtain adequate nutrition with far less work than many agriculturalists. So what might push food collectors to become food producers?

Binford and Flannery thought that the incentive to become food producers may have been a desire to reproduce what was wildly abundant in the most bountiful or optimum hunting and gathering areas. Because of population growth in the optimum areas, people might have moved to surrounding areas containing fewer wild resources. It would have been in those marginal areas that people might have first turned to food production in order to reproduce what they used to have. The Binford-Flannery model seems to fit the archaeological record in the Levant, the southwestern part of the Fertile Crescent, where population increase did precede the first signs of domestication. But as Flannery admitted, in some regions, such as southwestern Iran where Ali Kosh is located, the optimum hunting-gathering areas do not show population increase before the emergence of domestication.

Some archaeologists have recently returned to an older idea that climatic change might have been the change in external circumstances that encouraged the development of food production. It seems clear from the evidence now available that the climate of Southwest Asia about 13,000 to 12,000 years ago became more seasonal: The summers got hotter and drier than before and the winters became colder. These climatic changes may have favored the emergence of annual species of wild grain, which archaeologically one can see proliferating in many areas of Southwest Asia. People such as the Natufians intensively exploited these seasonal grains, developing an elaborate technology for storing and processing the grains and giving up their previous nomadic existence to do so. The transition to agriculture may have occurred when sedentary foraging no longer provided sufficient resources for the population. This could have happened because sedentarization led to population increase and therefore resource scarcity, or because local wild resources became depleted after people settled down in permanent villages. In the area of Israel and Jordan where the Natufians lived, some of the people apparently turned to food production, probably to increase the supply of grain, whereas other people returned to nomadic food collection because of the decreasing availability of wild grain.

Change to a more seasonal climate might also have led to a shortage of certain nutrients for food collectors. In the dry seasons certain nutrients would have been less available. For example, grazing animals get lean when grasses are not plentiful, so meat from hunting would have been in short supply in the dry seasons. Although it may seem surprising, some recent hunter-gatherers have starved when they had to rely on lean meat. If they could have somehow increased their carbohydrate or fat intake, they might have been more likely to get through the periods of lean game. So it is possible that some wild-food collectors in the past thought of planting crops to get them through the dry seasons when hunting, fishing, and gathering did not provide enough carbohydrates and fat for them to avoid starvation.

Mesoamerica presents a very different picture, because the early domesticates were not important to subsistence. Theories about population pressure and nutrient shortage don't seem to fit Mesoamerica well. However, there were apparently shortages of desired plants, such as bottle gourds, and domestication may well have occurred as humans actively sowed these desired plants. The difference between this model and those just discussed is that humans in Mesoamerica were apparently not forced into domestication by climate change or population pressure, but actively turned to domestication to obtain more of the most desired or useful plant species. The most interesting case is maize, which only became a staple food some 2,500 or more years after it was first domesticated. Why did it become a staple? Probably both because is was a suitable staple crop (especially when intercropped with beans and squash, as discussed earlier) and because people liked it, so they grew it in large quantities. Over time, and perhaps because of conflict, population pressure, and other forces similar to those that apparently led to domestication in Southwest Asia, people in Mesoamerica and later North and South America came to rely upon maize as the dietary mainstay.

Unlike Binford and Flannery, who argued a change in external circumstances must have led to food production, archaeologist Barbara Bender argued that internal changes, particularly the emergence of status differences and formal leaders, may have fostered food production. In her model the desire to have a surplus of storable foods to support feasting, craft production, and public works would have encouraged food production. She points out that among the Natufians there is not only evidence for intensive harvesting and storage of wild grains, but also some of the earliest evidence for status differences.

Is there evidence to support Bender's model? Figure 16.10 shows a crosstabulation of Agriculture and Social Stratification. What we see is that cases lacking Agriculture also lack Social Stratification (stratification value 1), while cases dependent upon Agriculture tend to have moderate or high levels of Social Stratification

| | | | STRATIFICATION | | |
|---|---|---|---|---|---|
| | | | 1 | 2 | 3 |
| Agriculture | 1 | Count | 110 | 6 | 3 |
| | | Expected Count | 56.0 | 34 | 29 |
| | 2 | Count | 16 | 7 | 1 |
| | | Expected Count | 11 | 7 | 6 |
| | 3 | Count | 10 | 70 | 66 |
| | | Expected Count | 69 | 42 | 35 |

FIGURE **16.10**
Crosstabulation of Agriculture and Social Stratification.

FIGURE **16.11**

Line graph of Agriculture and Social Stratification.

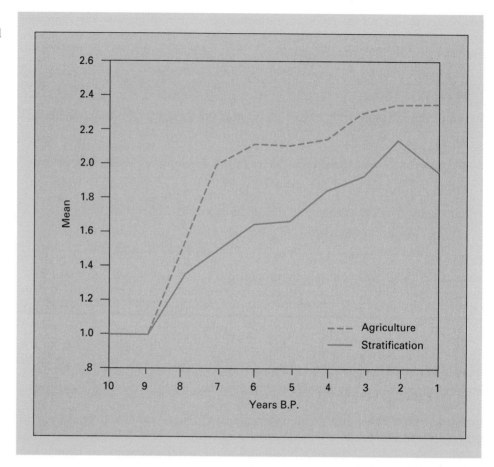

(values 2 and 3). The association between Agriculture and Social Stratification appears to support Bender's model, but we face the same "chicken and egg" problem that we did with Cohen's model—which came first, and did one cause the other? Looking at a graph of Agriculture and Social Stratification over the last 10,000 years in Figure 16.11, we can see that like Density of Population the two seem to increase together, with neither clearly preceding the other.

What, then, is the answer to our question? Why did food production develop? At present archaeologists are not sure. There are a number of reasonable theories with good supporting evidence. The best answer is probably that no single answer will suffice. In some places population growth may have been key, in others the emergence of social stratification, and in still others the desire to have a regular supply of particular plants. No single theory will likely ever apply to the development of food production in every part of the world, but as archaeologist Richard MacNeish (whose work is described in more detail in the box feature) explained, our knowledge of the archaeological record for the emergence of food production is only at a very basic level. As our knowledge improves, our answers to the question of why food production evolved will surely improve as well.

## CONSEQUENCES OF FOOD PRODUCTION

We have already seen, in Figure 16.7 and 16.11, that as food production became more important both Density of Population and Social Stratification increased. There were other consequences of food production too. Paradoxically, perhaps, health seems to have declined. Material possessions, though, became more elaborate.

## Accelerated Population Growth

As we have seen, Density of Population and food production are strongly associated. Looking over a longer period of time, and at existing cultures, it seems clear that population growth definitely accelerated after the emergence of food production, possibly because the spacing between births was reduced further and therefore fertility (the number of births per mother) increased. Increased fertility may have been advantageous because of the greater value of children in farming and herding economies; there is evidence from recent population studies that fertility rates are higher where children contribute more to the economy. Not only may parents desire more children to help with chores, the increased workload of mothers may also (but inadvertently) decrease birth spacing. The busier a mother is, the less frequently she may nurse and the more likely her baby will be given supplementary food by other caretakers such as older siblings. Less frequent nursing and greater reliance on food other than mother's milk may result in an earlier resumption of ovulation after the birth of a baby. (Farmers and herders are likely to have animal milk to feed to babies, and also cereals that have been transformed by cooking into soft, mushy porridges.) Therefore the spacing between births may have decreased (and the number of births per mother, in turn, increased) when mothers got busier after the rise of food production.

## Declining Health

Although the rise of food production may have led to increased fertility, this does not mean that health generally improved. In fact, it appears that health declined sometimes with the transition to food production. The two trends may seem paradoxical, but rapid population growth can occur if each mother gives birth to a large number of babies, even if many of them die early because of disease or poor nutrition.

The evidence that health may have declined sometimes after the rise of food production comes from studies of the bones and teeth of some prehistoric populations, before and after the emergence of food production. Nutritional and disease problems are indicated by such features as incomplete formation of tooth enamel (see Figure 16.13), nonaccidental bone lesions (incompletely filled-in bone), reduction in stature, and decreased life expectancy. Many of the studied prehistoric populations that relied heavily on food production seem to show less adequate nutrition and higher infection rates than populations living in the same areas before the emergence of food production. Some of the food producing populations are shorter and had lower life expectancies.

The reasons for a decline in health in those populations are not yet clear. Greater malnutrition can result from an overdependence on a few dietary staples that lack some necessary nutrients. Overdependence on a few sources of food may also increase the risk of famine because the fewer the staple crops, the greater the danger to the food supply posed by a weather-caused crop failure. But some or most nutritional problems may be the result of social and political factors, particularly the rise of different status groups of people and unequal access, between and within communities, to food and other resources.

As we saw in Figure 16.10 and Figure 16.11, social stratification seems likely to develop with the rise of food production. The effects of stratification and political dominance from afar on the general level of health may be reflected in the skeletal remains of prehistoric Native Americans who died in what is now Illinois between 1050 B.P. and 700 B.P., the period spanning the changeover in that region from hunting and gathering to food production. The food producing people living in the area of Dickson's Mounds—burial sites named after the doctor who first excavated them—were apparently in much worse health than their hunter-gatherer ancestors.

# Richard MacNeish

Richard MacNeish is a legendary archaeologist. He is perhaps the greatest field archaeologist ever to live (in 1993 he claimed to have spent 7,200 days in the field since 1936), and he pioneered research in two important areas—the origins of domestication and the peopling of the New World. Richard MacNeish was born in New York City in 1918 and grew up in Eastchester, New York. He attended Colgate University as an undergraduate, and in 1936 took part in his first archaeological excavation, an Iroquois village in central New York State. The experience apparently transformed him, and he transferred to the University of Chicago, which at the time had the top archaeology program in the country. He earned bachelors, masters, and doctoral degrees from the University of Chicago.

In 1949, MacNeish began working in his first professional position, as an archaeologist at the National Museum of Canada. He conducted field work all over Canada and became interested in the earliest human occupations, particularly in the Yukon, where he continued to work until his death in 2001. In the 1950s he began working in dry caves in northern Mexico, seeking both evidence for early human occupations and evidence for early domestication—a topic about which he had become interested following the discoveries of early farming communities in

FIGURE **16.12**
Richard MacNeish.

Southwest Asia. In 1962 the work paid off with the discovery of ancient corn cobs, dated to 5,600 years ago, in the Tehuacan Valley. These were the first evidence that corn was an ancient domesticate. Through continuing work in dry caves in the Tehuacan Valley as well as the Ayacucho Valley of Peru, MacNeish also found evidence of early domestication of squash, bean, chili pepper, and avocado.

Work in these dry caves also offered evidence for early human occupations, and in 1992 MacNeish produced the most controversial evidence to date, preserved human palm and fingerprints in clay dated to 28,000 years ago—almost twice as old as any other evidence of human occupation in the New World. The site where these prints were found, Pendejo Cave in New Mexico, also produced evidence of hearths dating to 38,000 years ago, and fragments of human hair. The site remains controversial, but if the context and dates of these prints and associated materials stand after further evaluation, they may mark one of the most important archaeological discoveries of our time.

MacNeish's interest in plant domestication led him to China to investigate the origins of rice, about which comparatively little was known. In the 1990s his work at sites along the Yangtzee River demonstrated the presence of domesticated rice some 9,000 years ago, much earlier than had been thought, and much farther north. Most scholars though rice was a Southeast Asian domesticate, but MacNeish's findings have caused that idea to be reconsidered. At the time of his death, MacNeish was planning fieldwork in Turkey to examine the origins of domesticated wheat. We can only wonder what he may have discovered.

MacNeish also had a profound impact on archaeological training in North America. In 1964 he founded the Department of Archaeology at the University of Calgary, and began offering the first archaeology degree in an autonomous department of archaeology in North America. From 1968 to 1980 he directed the Peabody Museum of Archaeology at Phillips Academy—a boys' boarding school—and although the museum never had the impact on secondary education that MacNeish and the museum's founders had hoped, the unique position as director of a world-class archaeological museum and research facility connected to a secondary school seemed to fit MacNeish well. In 1982 he made his final move, to Boston University, where he helped to establish the first autonomous department of archaeology in the United States.

His work as an educator, a field worker, and a researcher on the origins of domestication have made Richard MacNeish one of the world's most renowned archaeologists.

SOURCES: "Richard MacNeish, Agricultural Archaeologist, Dies at 82," *New York Times*, January 30, 2001, C.16; "Richard MacNeish," *Times* (London) January 26, 2001, F.27.

FIGURE **16.13**
The horizontal lines visible on the front teeth of this individual are called "enamel hypoplasias" and are caused when tooth growth stops during times of starvation.

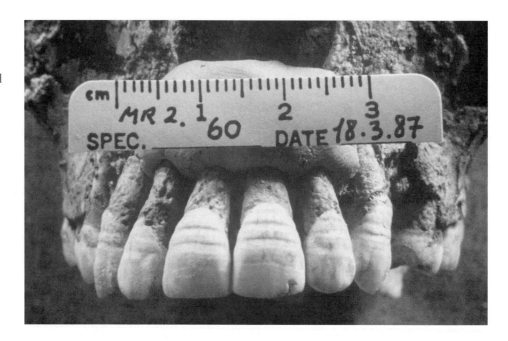

But curiously, archaeological evidence suggests that they were still also hunting and fishing. A balanced diet was apparently available, but who was getting it? Possibly it was the elite at the Mississippian center Cahokia, about 150 kilometers away, who were getting most of the meat and fish. The individuals near Dickson's Mounds who collected the meat and fish may have gotten luxury items such as shell necklaces from the Cahokia elite, but many of the people buried at Dickson's Mounds were clearly not benefiting nutritionally from the relationship with Cahokia.

## The Elaboration of Material Possessions

In the more permanent villages that were established after the rise of food production, houses became more elaborate and comfortable, and construction methods improved. The materials used in construction depended on whether timber or stone was locally available or whether a strong sun could dry mud bricks. The interiors of houses became more complex, and where furnishings have survived, such as in European Neolithic lake dwellings, they suggest increasing number and sophistication of household possessions. For example, many Linear Pottery tradition longhouses had doors, beds, tables, and other furniture that closely resembled those in modern-day societies (see Figure 16.14). We know the people had furniture because miniature clay models have been found at their sites. Several of the chairs and couches seem to be models of padded and upholstered furniture with wooden frames, indicating that Linear Pottery tradition artisans were creating fairly sophisticated furnishings. Such furnishings are the result of an advanced tool technology put to use by a people who, because they were staying in one area, could take time to make and use furniture.

Woven textiles also appeared after the rise of food production. This development was not simply the result of the domestication of flax (for linen), cotton, and wool-growing sheep. These sources of fiber alone could not produce cloth. It was the development of the spindle and loom for spinning and weaving that made textiles possible. Textiles can be woven by hand without a loom, but to do so is a slow, laborious process, impractical for producing garments.

While ceramics preceded food production in some parts of the world, the ceramics of the early food producers became more diverse and complex. In

FIGURE **16.14**
A preserved door from
the neolithic village of
Robenhausen, Switzerland,
dating to around 6000 B.P.
The shift from food collection
to food production often led
to more substantial housing
and house furnishings.

Southwest Asia, for example, these included large urns for grain storage, mugs, cooking pots, and dishes. To improve the retention of liquid, potters in Southwest Asia may have been the first to glaze the earthenware's porous surface. Later ceramics became more artistic. For example Ubaid potters shaped the clay into graceful forms and painted colorful patterns on the vessels.

It is probable that virtually none of these architectural and technological innovations could have occurred until humans became fully sedentary. Nomadic hunting and gathering peoples would have found it difficult to carry many material goods, especially fragile items such as pottery. It was only when humans became fully sedentary that these goods would have provided advantages, enabling villagers to cook and store food more effectively and to house themselves more comfortably.

There is also evidence of increased long-distance trade following the emergence of food production. As I noted in the discussion of Ali Kosh, obsidian from southern Turkey was being exported to sites in the Zagros Mountains of Iran and to what are now Israel, Jordan, and Syria in the Levant. Great amounts of obsidian were exported to sites over 200 kilometers from the source of supply; more than 80 percent of the tools used by residents of those areas were made of this material. Marble was being sent from western to eastern Turkey, and seashells from the coast were traded to distant inland regions. Such trade suggests a considerable amount of contact among various food-producing communities.

About 5500 B.P., cities first appeared in Southwest Asia. These cities had political assemblies, kings, scribes, and specialized workshops. The specialized production of goods and services was supported by surrounding farming villages, which sent their produce to the urban centers. A dazzling transformation had taken place in a relatively short time. People had not only settled down, but they had also become "civilized," or urbanized. (The word *civilized* literally means to make "citified.") Urban societies seem to have developed first in Southwest Asia and somewhat later around the eastern Mediterranean, in the Indus Valley of northwestern India, in northern China, and in Mexico and Peru. In the next chapter we turn to the rise of these earliest civilizations.

## ❖ SUMMARY

The shift from food collection to food production took place relatively rapidly all over the world between 10,000 B.P. and 7000 B.P. To date, the earliest evidence of domestication comes from Southwest Asia about 10,500 B.P. Dating for the earliest domestication in other areas of the Old World is not so clear, but the presence of different domesticated crops in different regions suggests that there were independent centers of domestication in China, Southeast Asia, and Africa sometime around 9000 B.P. In the New World, there appear to have been several early areas of cultivation and domestication: the highlands of Mesoamerica (about 9000 B.P.), the central Andes around Peru (about the same time), and the Eastern Woodlands of North America (about 7000 B.P.).

Theories about why food production originated remain controversial, but most archaeologists think that certain conditions must have pushed people to switch from collecting to producing food. Some possible causal factors include (1) climate change at the end of the last ice age; (2) population growth, especially in regions of bountiful wild resources (which may have pushed people to move to marginal areas where they tried to reproduce their former abundance); and (3) the desire to create surpluses of storable or particularly sought-after foods. No single theory seems to apply to all cases of food production, especially since the evolution of food production appears to have taken widely different paths in the Old World and the New World. In the Old World sedentarism appears to predate food production, while in the New World the reverse is true. In the Old World staples such as wheat and barley were the first domesticated plants, while in the New World gourds, peppers, and other nonstaples were the first domesticates. Domesticated animals were not significant in most New World economies, while they quickly became central to many Old World economies.

Regardless of why food production originated, it seems to have had important consequences for human life. Populations generally increased substantially *after* plant and animal domestication. Even though not all early cultivators were sedentary, sedentarism did increase with greater reliance on agriculture. Somewhat surprisingly, some prehistoric populations that relied heavily on agriculture seem to have been less healthy than prior populations that relied on food collection. In the more permanent villages that were established after the rise of food production, houses and furnishings became more elaborate, and people began to make textiles and to paint pottery. These villages have also yielded evidence of increased long-distance trade.

## ❖ DISCUSSION QUESTIONS

1. Plants of various types are present in the arctic and subarctic, yet none were domesticated. Why weren't plants domesticated in the arctic or subarctic?
2. How might people have domesticated sheep, goats, and cattle?

3. Which of the various theories for the evolution of food production best explains why domestication occurred in the New World? In the Old World?

## ✱ ESSAY QUESTIONS

1. It is a strange irony that food producers today work five or six hours a day in subsistence activities while food collectors work only three or four hours a day. Why would people be willing to work harder to produce food? Use the information in this text and any library or Internet resources you can find to explore at least two factors that may have provided the impetus for people to work harder to get food.

2. Current theories for the evolution of food production focus on either external or internal factors as causing the shift to food production, but not both. Describe these theories and then propose a way in which both external and internal factors might have combined to foster food production. Use library or Internet resources, along with the information in this textbook, to demonstrate that the combination you propose is feasible.

3. In this chapter I have argued that the evolution of food production marked an important turning point in human prehistory—one important enough to warrant a special chapter. Why single out food production in this way? What was so significant about food production? What other developments in human prehistory might be singled out for similar, detailed treatment?

## ✎ RESEARCH PROJECT

Visit a nearby grocery or convenience store and select ten to fifteen packaged items. Write down all of the plant and animal products contained in these items. Make a chart listing the domesticated plant and animal products found in these foods. Which domesticated plants and animals are the most common among the items you chose? Where and when were these plants and animals domesticated? Which are the least common among the items you chose? Where and when were these less common plants and animals domesticated? Did any of the food items contain domesticated plants or animals that originated on different continents? On continents different from the one you are living on now? Using the information you have and your answers to the previous questions, reflect on the ways in which domestication has altered the range and types of foods we eat.

## ✱ KEY SOURCES

### Where and When Did Food Production Begin?

Binford, 1971; Braidwood and Willey, 1962; Cohen, 1977; Cowan and Watson, 1992; Flannery, 1969, 1973; MacNeish, 1991; Phillipson, 1993; Reed, 1977; Smith, B., 1992, 1995.

### Food Production in Southwest Asia

Braidwood, 1960; Braidwood and Braidwood, 1969; Cowan and Watson, 1992; Flannery, 1965; Henry, 1989; Hole, Flannery, and Neely, 1969; MacNeish, 1991; Reed, 1977; Wright, 1971; Zohary, 1969.

## Food Production in Mesoamerica

Cowan and Watson, 1992; Flannery, 1986; MacNeish, 1991; Marcus and Flannery, 1996; Reed, 1977.

## Why Did Food Production Develop?

Bender, 1978, 1985; Blumler and Byrne, 1991; Byrne, 1987; Cowan and Watson, 1992; MacNeish, 1991; McCorriston and Hole, 1991; Price and Gebauer, 1995; Pringle, 1998.

## Consequences of Food Production

Cohen, 1989, 2002; Cohen and Armelagos, 1984; Goodman and Armelagos, 1985; Hassan, 1981; Hodder, 1990; Konner and Worthman, 1980.

# MEN'S AND WOMEN'S WORK AT ABU HUREYRA

Abu Hureyra is a tell (mound) site on the Euphrates River in Syria. The site was excavated in 1972–73 as a cultural resource management project because of the flooding of Lake Assad. Two major phases of occupation have been discovered. The first dates to the Epipaleolithic and Natufian traditions. This site was later reoccupied after a long period of abandonment by peoples of the Aceramic Neolithic tradition. It was finally abandoned about 7800 B.P. The earlier settlement is particularly important because of the early development of farming in the Levant. The Aceramic Neolithic settlement is also of great importance, in this case because of its enormous size. Abu Hureyra was 15 hectares, larger than any other recorded site of this period. Rectangular houses of pise (rammed earth) were built up into a mound approximately 5 meters high; both floors and walls were sometimes plastered and some wall plaster bears traces of painting. Most of the Neolithic levels were aceramic. After about 8000 B.P., a dark burnished pottery appears.

## WEB ACTIVITY

This transition from the hunting, fishing, and gathering of the Natufian culture to that of cereal grain agriculture is quite telling in the physical remains of the Neolithic farmers of the Aceramic Neolithic tradition. Fragmentary remains of 162 people were recovered in the excavations of Abu Hureyra. Many skeletons displayed collapsed lower vertebrae, grossly arthritic big toes, and very muscular arms and legs. The cause of these deformities and others was grain milling or grinding. In the case of these early Neolithic farmers, grain was ground by kneeling and curling the toes under the feet. This posture would put tremendous strain on the knees, lower back, and toes of the people doing the grinding. In

The Media Lab can be found in Chapter 16 on the *Companion Website*™ http://www.prenhall.com/peregrine

this activity, you will see a video about the physical implications of farming and milling, with Abu Hureyra used as the example.

## Activity

1. View the video. What might have driven these people of the Euphrates River to agriculture, even though it is apparently much harder work, with physical pain as one of its byproducts?

2. What health implications existed with the advent of cereal grain farming? (You might want to consider the new diet of farmers compared with their ancestors, who were hunter–gatherers.)

3. What ultimately made food production successful? Why did the entire world eventually move in this direction?

# The Rise of Civilization

In the previous chapter we saw that the transition from food collection to food production was a human event that occurred on every continent of the globe and affected all the peoples of the earth. The development of states is another human event. Like food production, states arose independently across the world and spread rapidly once they were established. Six thousand years ago not a single human was living in a state. Today all humans live under state authority of some kind. Where, when, how, and why did states evolve? Those are the questions I hope to answer in this chapter.

First let's review what we've learned about states in previous chapters. Recall that states are polities in which leaders are capable of governing by force. These leaders are typically distinguished from others in the society as a separate noble class. Force is usually exercised through police or the military, and the implementation of force is often regulated through formal laws. States, then, have a variety of formal positions through which power is exercised, including through the nobility, members of the police or military, judges and legal bureaucrats, and often many others.

To support the nobility and others who work for the state government, states typically collect tribute or taxes from food producers and craftspeople. Tribute and taxes often require a formal monetary and market system so that members of the government can obtain all the goods they need. To keep track of such things as the exchange of goods and of laws and legal precedents, states often develop formal writing systems. State governments are also typically centered in locations where markets, offices, courts, and the like are within close proximity, meaning that most states are urban. States, then, are centralized, urban polities with a complex bureaucracy and social classes.

How do archaeologists infer that a particular people in the past had a state? One way is through the analysis of burials. Archaeologists generally assume that inequality in death reflects inequality in life, at least in status and perhaps also in wealth and power. Thus, we can be fairly sure that a society had differences in status if only some people were buried with special objects, such as symbols of power or exotic goods. And we can be fairly sure that high status was assigned at birth rather than achieved in later life if we find noticeable differences in children's tombs. For example, some (but not all) child burials from as early as 7500 B.P. at the Ceramic Neolithic site **Tell es-Sawwan** in Iraq are filled with statues and ornaments, suggesting that some children had high status from birth.

**Tell es-Sawwan** (Iraq, Ceramic Neolithic)

Another way archaeologists can determine if a society had social classes is by analyzing housing and house furnishings. High status individuals typically have larger and more complex houses than others. Often these houses also have more furnishings than others, and sometimes they contain unique goods such as ceremonial ceramic wares. They are typically built with better materials and techniques than other houses and often have exterior decorations that demonstrate the high status of the occupants (Figure 17.1). If a community only has one or a few houses that are very large, contain unique goods, and are more substantially constructed than others, most archaeologists would infer that social classes were present.

The presence of social classes, however, is not enough to define a state. Archaeologists do not always agree on how a state should be defined, but most think that hierarchical and centralized decision making affecting a substantial population is the key criterion. Archaeologists Henry Wright and Gregory Johnson developed a widely accepted method focusing on the presence of settlement hierarchies. They argued a state should have at least three levels of political hierarchy, and that these should be evident in settlements. There should be hamlets and villages (first level) integrated through regional centers (second level) which are, in turn, integrated through a political capital (third level). But how might archaeologists infer that such a hierarchy existed in some area? Wright and Johnson suggested that the way

FIGURE **17.1**
This Louisiana mansion serves
as a clear symbol of its
owner's wealth and power.

settlement sites differ in size is one indication of how many levels of administration there were in an area.

During the early Uruk period (just before 5500 B.P.) in what is now southwestern Iran, there were some fifty settlements that seem to fall into three groups in terms of size. There were about forty-five small villages, three or four larger towns, and one large center, **Susa.** These three types of settlements seem to have been part of a three-level administration hierarchy, since many small villages could not trade with Susa without passing through a settlement intermediate in size. Because a three-level hierarchy is Wright and Johnson's criterion of a state, they think a state had emerged in the area by early Uruk times.

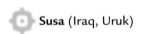
**Susa** (Iraq, Uruk)

In addition to a clear settlement hierarchy, most archaeologists also look for evidence of control over the movement of goods and people. In the case of Uruk, clay seals provide this evidence. Seals were used to keep shipments of goods closed until they reached their destination, and they were also used to keep track of goods sent and received. The clay seals found in Susa include many seals and **bullae,** clay containers that served as bills of lading for goods received. The villages, in contrast, had few message seals and bullae. Again, this finding suggests that Susa administered the regional movement of goods and that Susa was the "capital" of the state.

Finally, most archaeologists also look for evidence of state control over labor. Evidence for labor control is most often sought in public works and the amount of time and effort those works required. States should be able to amass enough labor to build large public works such as defenses, roads, and water-control systems. States should also be able to maintain a standing army and police force that might be identified through the presence of military regalia or garrisons. Gregory Johnson found evidence for labor control in the case of Uruk by analyzing ceramics. During the Uruk tradition crude bowls with a beveled rim became ubiquitous (Figure 17.2). Johnson found that, despite their simple forms and crude manufacture, they were highly standardized in terms of their volumes. Indeed, Johnson found that these beveled-rim bowls were universally made in three sizes and were being mass-produced at what appeared to be state-run facilities. Johnson argued that these beveled-rim bowls were ration containers, given to workers on the basis of the amount or type of labor they performed for the state.

**Bullae:** clay containers made during the Uruk tradition that served as bills of lading for goods.

FIGURE **17.2**
Bevel-rim bowls.

## WHERE AND WHEN DID STATES ARISE?

The locations where early states arose are seen in Figure 17.3, and a timetable is presented in Figure 17.4. The first states appeared in Mesopotamia during the Uruk tradition, about 6000 B.P. These were city-states; that is, they were based in a particular city and their direct sphere of control was apparently quite limited. However, the Uruk states interacted regularly and developed a complex regional economy, often referred to as the Sumerian empire, that influenced populations throughout the Tigris and Euphrates river valleys. To the west, in the Levant, states appeared by at least 5000 B.P. among peoples of the Early Bronze Age tradition, and these states were strongly influenced by the Sumerian states. To the east, peoples of the Iranian Bronze Age had also developed states by 5000 B.P., and also at least in part through Sumerian influence.

Almost at the same time as the peoples of the Uruk tradition were developing states, the great dynastic age was beginning in the Nile Valley in Egypt. Leaders in

FIGURE **17.3**

The locations of the six "pristine" states.

SOURCE: Adapted from *The Origins of the State and Civilization: The Process of Cultural Evolution* by Elman R. Service. Copyright © 1975 by W. W. Norton & Company, Inc. Used by permission of W. W. Norton & Company, Inc.

FIGURE **17.4**

Timeline of the rise of states.

SOURCE: Peter N. Peregrine, Carol R. Ember, and Melvin Ember, *Archaeology: Original Readings in Method and Practice* (Upper Saddle River, NJ: Prentice Hall, 2002), p. 193. Reprinted by permission of Pearson Education, Inc., Upper Saddle River, NJ.

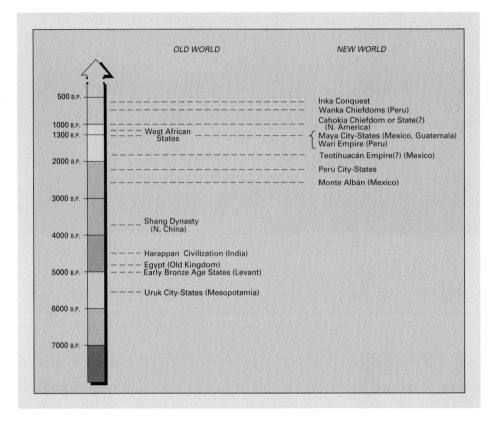

the Lower Egypt Predynastic and Upper Egypt Predynastic traditions began to centralize power into what appear to be states by around 5500 B.P., and by the time of the Early Dynastic Egypt tradition, which begins at 5000 B.P., a powerful state had already come to control the Nile valley. Because many of the changes that led to state development in Egypt appear to have happened at about the same time as the Sumerian states were first emerging in Mesopotamia, many scholars think that these developments were independent and that Egypt represents a second location (after Mesopotamia) where states arose without conquest or formal influence from other states.

Elsewhere in Africa states also arose. In what is present-day Ethiopia the Axum (or Aksum) state evolved among peoples of the East African Neolithic tradition sometime after 2000 B.P., ultimately becoming a center of trade and commerce between Africa and the Arabian peninsula. The savannah and forest zones of western Africa had a succession of city-states beginning in the West African Iron Age, again around 2000 B.P. Farther south, states apparently arose in several areas beginning around 1000 B.P. among peoples of the South African Iron Age tradition. All these states appear to have emerged through interactions with existing states in Egypt and Southwest Asia.

At about the same time as states were emerging in the areas around Mesopotamia, states also arose in the Indus Valley. There the Harappan state developed in the Early Indus tradition, sometime after 5000 B.P. While interaction was regular between Mesopotamia and the Harappans later, it is not clear whether early interactions could have fostered state development in the Indus valley in the same way they did in the upper Tigris and Euphrates valleys. For this reason, the Harappan state is also thought to be one of the rare examples of a state emerging outside the influence of another state.

The Longshan tradition represents a fourth example of a state that arose without influence from other states. At about 6000 B.P., peoples of the Longshan tradition were apparently developing regional states that spread across north and central China. By the time of the Shang tradition (5900 B.P.) historical texts suggest the presence of states throughout much of China.

In the New World states appeared in Mesoamerica and the Andes at around the same time. In Mesoamerica, peoples of the Highland Mesoamerican Late Preclassic tradition developed states around 2100 B.P. States arose at about the same time along the Gulf Coast, but may have been present earlier in the Olmec tradition (perhaps as early as 3000 B.P.), although the evidence is equivocal. The emergence of states in Highland Mesoamerica and the Gulf Coast strongly influenced surrounding areas, so that by about 1800 B.P. states were present throughout Highland and Lowland Mesoamerica.

In South America, a group of distinct state societies emerged during the Highland Andean Formative and Coastal Andean Late Formative traditions. By 2200 B.P. states were clearly present in the puna and in many of the major river valleys leading from the Andes to the sea. State development may have been influenced by the widespread system of religious symbols and beliefs that emerged during the Chavín tradition, around 2800 B.P. Indeed, some scholars believe that Chavín represents the first states in South America.

Interestingly, states may not have emerged in North America. A few scholars have argued that some Mississippian polities, particularly Cahokia, represent states, but the evidence is ambiguous and not widely accepted.

States emerged in the New World quite a bit later than they did in the Old World. The later appearance of New World states is an interesting problem. Some scholars have linked the delay to the later emergence of agriculture in the New World and to the near-absence of large domesticated animals. Interestingly, New World states appear to have developed much more rapidly than Old World states, and this suggests that different processes may have been at work in the two areas of the world, much like the different processes we saw in the emergence of food production. What might some of these processes have been? Let's consider some of the theories for state origins that have been put forward.

## HOW AND WHY DID STATES ARISE?

As with food production, the question of how states arose and why they arose seem to be closely linked. Most archaeologists believe that states arose because some change in external or internal conditions forced the development of centralized control over the use of force. A number of theories have been proposed for how and why states arose, and here I consider those that have been discussed the most frequently by archaeologists.

### Diffusion

Once states arise they tend to expand and to conquer other polities, particularly nonstate polities. Often the conquering state will impose a state form of government on areas they have conquered, and thus states tend to spread, or diffuse. The process of diffusion was one of the earliest theories put forward to explain the rise of states. Antiquarians, for example, put forward the idea that the ancient Greeks developed the state, and state forms of government spread from Greece across the rest of the world. It was the Greek genius that caused the state to arise, and its diffusion was due to its clear superiority over other forms of political organization. This was a Eurocentric view of prehistory, and as new and better data emerged it became clear that Europe was a relative latecomer to the world of states.

However, the idea that states arose under rare conditions and then diffused rapidly is still widely held in archaeology. Today, four centers of "pristine" state development are commonly accepted—Mesopotamia, China, Highland Mesoamerica, and Peru. Many scholars also see Egypt and the Indus Valley as "pristine" centers of state emergence. The problem with the idea that there are "pristine" states and "secondary" states arising by diffusion is that interaction between and among societies seems to be a central feature of even the "pristine" states, so to argue that they arose in some kind of political or economic vacuum seems as biased as the earlier view that Europe must have been the birthplace of states.

It does seem clear that the emergence of a state fosters the emergence of states among neighboring polities. This process has been identified by archaeologists Colin Renfrew and John Cherry as "peer-polity interaction." Renfrew and Cherry argue that neighboring polities regularly interact and that these interactions are important because they provide a means through which information, goods from other areas, and mutual assistance can move. As changes take place in one polity involved in such interactions, they tend to spread rapidly to other polities. The others, it seems, change in order to maintain the ongoing interactions. While Renfrew and Cherry provide an excellent model for how states might diffuse among a group of peer-polities, they do not offer a model for the rise of the initial state among those polities.

## Resource Control

Anthropologist Elman Service (whose work is introduced in more detail in the box feature) developed a theory for the rise of states that focused on what a state government might offer to the people living within it. He argued that a state would not arise unless it functioned in some important way to maintain the society. Service examined the rise of states all over the world (much as we have done) and came to the conclusion that in all cases states serve to control access to resources in situations where resources are highly diverse and localized. In Highland Mesoamerica, for example, good agricultural soils are limited to river valleys while important resources like obsidian are located in mountain areas. Service argued that in such cases a state might function to collect and redistribute important goods. The state would collect both agricultural products and obsidian, for example, redistributing obsidian to the agriculturalists living in river valleys and agricultural products to peoples living near obsidian sources in the mountains. In this way, the state would serve an important function in ensuring that all members of the polity had access to all the resources they needed.

Economic historian Karl Wittfogel suggested control of a single resource—water—was essential to the rise of states. He noted that irrigation was vital in many of the areas in which early state societies developed. Irrigation made the land habitable or productive in parts of Mesoamerica, southern Iraq, the Nile Valley, China, and South America. Wittfogel argued that the labor and management needed for the upkeep of an irrigation system led to the formation of a political elite, the overseers of the system, who eventually became the governors of the society.

However, recent work has shown that neither redistribution nor water control were important in all early states, and where they were important they seem to have developed well after a state had first emerged. For example, in southern Iraq, the irrigation systems serving the early cities were generally small and probably did not require extensive labor and management. Large-scale irrigation works were not constructed until after cities had been fully established (see Figure 17.5). Thus, irrigation

FIGURE **17.5**
Large-scale irrigation projects like this one in Washington require constant supervision and maintenance. Some scholars have suggested the need for overseeing irrigation works may have promoted the rise of states.

could not have been the main stimulus for the development of cities and states in Mesopotamia. Even in China, for which the irrigation theory was first formulated, there is no evidence of large-scale irrigation as early as Shang times.

## Population Growth

Cultural anthropologist Robert Carneiro has suggested that states may emerge because of population growth in an area that is physically or socially limited, what he calls "circumscription." Competition and warfare in situations of circumscription may lead to the subordination of defeated groups, who are obliged to pay tribute and to submit to the control of a more powerful group. Members of the more powerful group, then, become the leaders of the emergent state. Carneiro illustrated his theory by describing how states may have emerged on the northern coast of Peru.

After the people of that area first settled into an agricultural village life, population grew at a slow, steady rate. Initially, new villages were formed as population grew. But in the narrow coastal valleys—blocked by high mountains, fronted by the sea, and surrounded by desert—this splintering-off process could not continue indefinitely. The result, according to Carneiro, was increasing land shortage and warfare between villages as they competed for land. Since the high mountains, the sea, and the desert blocked any escape for losers, the defeated villagers had no choice but to submit to political domination. In this way, chiefdoms may have become kingdoms as the most powerful villages grew to control entire valleys. As chiefs' power expanded over several valleys, states and empires may have been born.

Carneiro noted that physical or environmental circumscription may not be the only kind of barrier that gives rise to a state. Social circumscription may be just as important. People living at the center of a high-density area may find that their migration is blocked by surrounding settlements just as effectively as it could be by mountains, sea, and desert.

# Elman Service

Elman Service was born in Michigan in 1915 and began his career as "the most influential cultural evolutionist of the past half century" (Harding, p. 163) in an inauspicious way. With the Great Depression in full swing, Service was happy to find a job after graduating from high school and worked for several years in a California aircraft factory before saving enough money to pursue higher education. Even then, his future as a preeminent anthropologist seemed unlikely since he majored in English at the University of Michigan and left in his first year to fight in the Spanish Civil War with the Abraham Lincoln Brigade. He returned to Michigan in 1938 and completed a bachelors degree in English before enlisting in the U.S. Army for the duration of World War II. The experiences of war, of other cultures, of political oppression, and conversations with friends and teachers led Service to anthropology, and through the G.I. Bill he was able to enroll in graduate school at Columbia University, where he completed his doctorate in anthropology in 1950.

At Columbia, Service worked with a group of fellow students who shared an interest in cultural evolution and the empirical analysis of culture. Foremost

FIGURE **17.6**
Elman Service.

among his colleagues was Morton Fried, and together Service and Fried developed many of the concepts that anthropologists use today to talk about cultural evolution. Among their most important contributions were Fried's *Evolution of Political Society* (New York: Random House, 1967), in which the concepts of egalitarian, ranked, and class-based societies were developed, and Service's *Primitive Social Organization* (New York: Random House, 1962), in which Service developed the concepts of bands, tribes, chiefdoms, and states. Indeed, Service's idea that chiefdoms were a special form of social organization, one that typically precedes and may be foundational to the rise of states, launched an astounding range of ethnographic and archaeological research that continues to this day. For that alone, Service would be well remembered.

But Service was not content to simply develop concepts and outline research agendas. *Primitive Social Organization* argues a strong position—that the development of political oppression could not have taken place if such developments were not beneficial to society. Service strongly believed that people would not willingly submit to political oppression by developing chiefdoms or states unless they gained much more than they lost. His belief was undoubtedly rooted in his experiences in the Spanish Civil War and World War II, where people fought to overthrow oppressive regimes, but he also had sound ethnographic and archaeological data to support his ideas. These data were brought together in *Origins of the State and Civilization* (New York: Norton, 1975).

*Origins of the State and Civilization* is a classic in comparative anthropology and the study of cultural evolution. In it Service put forward the idea that government functions to maintain society and that the evolution of new political forms is rooted in their ability to solve problems. He described the origins and operation of five ethnographically known states and the six "pristine" states we have discussed in this chapter. By comparing and contrasting these cases he found that neither conflict, population growth, irrigation and agricultural intensification, nor any of the other ideas scholars at the time had put forward to explain the rise of states worked very well. On the other hand, he argued that in the cases he looked at the state provided important services to the population, especially in redistributing localized resources throughout the polity. While additional research has demonstrated that Service's conclusions do not hold true in many of the cases he thought they did, his ideas have had a profound impact on anthropology and have offered a refreshing alternative to the notion that the rise of states must have been forced, rather than voluntary.

SOURCES: Harding, Thomas, 1999, "Elman Rogers Service (1915–1996)," *American Anthropologist* 101: 161–164; Fried, Morton, *Evolution of Political Society* (New York: Random House, 1967); Service, Elman, *Primitive Social Organization* (New York: Random House, 1962), *Origins of the State and Civilization* (New York: Norton, 1975).

FIGURE 17.7

Crosstabulation of Political
Integration and Density of
Population.

|  |  |  | DENSITY | | |
|---|---|---|---|---|---|
|  |  |  | 1 | 2 | 3 |
| Integration | 1 | Count | 114 | 2 | 0 |
|  |  | Expected Count | 56 | 48 | 12 |
|  | 2 | Count | 26 | 80 | 10 |
|  |  | Expected Count | 56 | 48 | 12 |
|  | 3 | Count | 0 | 37 | 20 |
|  |  | Expected Count | 28 | 23 | 6 |

Cultural anthropologist Marvin Harris suggested a somewhat different form of circumscription. He argued that the first states with their coercive authority could emerge only in areas that supported intensive grain agriculture (and the possibility of high food production) and were surrounded by areas that could not support intensive grain agriculture. Only people in such areas could put up with the coercive authority of a state because they would suffer a sharp drop in living standards if they moved away.

Archaeologist William Sanders and his colleagues took yet another tack on the relationship between population growth and the rise of states. They used the ideas of agricultural economist Esther Boserup, who argued that under conditions of population pressure societies will develop innovations in order to increase subsistence production to support the growing population. Sanders and his colleagues argued that one such innovation might be the rise of centralized political control to coordinate subsistence production and distribution. Their research in the Valley of Mexico showed that there was population growth before the emergence of the Teotihuacan state.

There is a clear association between population density and states in the data from the archaeological traditions described in Chapters 8 to 15. Figure 17.7 shows this association in a cross-tabulation similar to those we looked at in the previous chapter. Here we see that as Political Integration increases (1 = local community; 2 = 1 or 2 levels above local community; 3 = 3 or more levels above local community, which means a state is present) so does population density. Indeed, there are no cases of low population density where a state is present (Political Integration = 3). Can we say that Density of Population causes a state to form? Not from these data, and even the line graph shown in Figure 17.8 makes us question this idea. Figure 17.8 shows the average for Density of Population and Political Integration over the last 10,000 years at 1,000-year intervals. Until about 8,000 years ago the two increased in basically the same way, but after about 8,000 years ago Political Integration increased more rapidly than Density of Population and Density of Population seems to have leveled off, suggesting that population growth may not have been primary in state formation.

But neither population growth nor population density necessarily means that there was population pressure. For example, the populations in the Valley of Mexico apparently did increase prior to state development, but there is no evidence that they had even begun to approach the limits of their resources. More people could have lived there without starving. Nor is population growth definitely associated with state formation in all areas where early states arose. For example, according to Henry Wright and Gregory Johnson, there was population growth long before states emerged in southwestern Iran, but the population apparently declined just before the states emerged. Richard Blanton and his colleagues have argued a similar population decline before the rise of the state at Monte Albán in the Valley of Oaxaca.

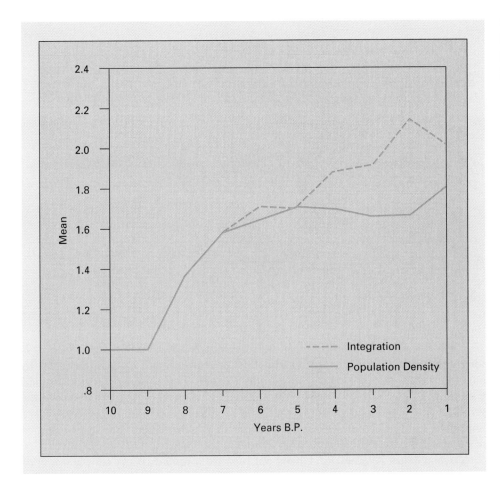

FIGURE **17.8**
Line graph of Political
Integration and Density of
Population.

## Interregional Interaction

In recent years some archaeologists have argued that interactions between societies may have played an important role in the rise of states. Local polities interact with one another and, as Renfrew and Cherry noted, such interaction seems to be important to the ongoing maintenance of societies since the interactions provide information and material exchanges over large areas. However, interactions between polities also encourage boundary maintenance, with each polity working to define and maintain its boundaries relative to the others. Richard Blanton and his colleagues have argued that in the Valley of Oaxaca such boundary maintenance may have played a vital role in the rise of the state. Maintaining boundaries in the face of important long-distance interactions with the Maya lowlands, the Valley of Mexico, and the Gulf Coast may have led to the creation of what Blanton calls a core-periphery system in the Valley of Oaxaca. The core of this system was **Monte Albán,** while peripheral towns maintained formal links to the core, even as they interacted with the peripheral towns of neighboring polities.

**Monte Albán**
(Mexico, Southern
Mexican Highlands
Classic)

Trade would have been an important part of interregional interaction, and many archaeologists have suggested that trade was a factor in the emergence of the earliest states. Henry Wright and Gregory Johnson, for example, theorized that the organizational requirements of producing items for export, redistributing the items imported, and defending trading parties would foster state formation. Does the archaeological evidence support such a theory?

In southern Iraq and the Mayan lowlands, long-distance trade routes may indeed have stimulated bureaucratic growth. In the lowlands of southern Iraq, people needed wood and stone for building, and they traded with highland people

FIGURE **17.9**

The Chinese "interaction sphere."

SOURCE: From *Archaeology of Ancient China, 4E* by K-C. Chang. Reprinted by permission of Yale University Press.

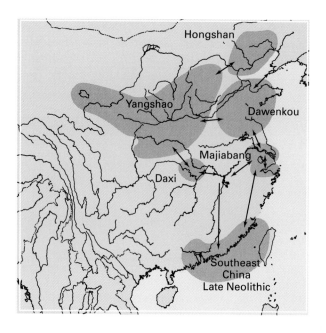

for those items. In the Mayan lowlands, the development of civilization seems to have been preceded by long-distance trade. Farmers in the lowland regions traded with faraway places in order to obtain salt, obsidian for blades, and hard stone for grinding tools. In southwestern Iran, long-distance trade did not become very important until after Susa became the center of a state society, but short-distance trade may have played the same kind of role in the formation of states.

Archaeologist Kwang-chih Chang put forward a similar theory for the origin of states in China. He suggested that Neolithic societies in the Yellow River valley developed a long-distance trade network, which he called an "interaction sphere," by about 6000 B.P. (see Figure 17.9). Trade spread cultural elements among the societies in the interaction sphere, so that they came to share some common elements. Over time, these societies came to depend on each other both as trade partners and as cultural partners, and around 4000 B.P. they unified into a single political unit under the Shang Dynasty. Thus Chang sees political unification in China as an outgrowth of a preexisting system of trade and cultural interaction.

## The Various Theories: An Evaluation

How and why do states form? As of now, no one theory seems to fit all the known situations. The reason may be that different conditions in different places may have favored the emergence of states. After all, the state, by definition, implies an ability to organize large populations for a collective purpose. In some areas, this purpose may have been the need to organize trade with local or far-off regions. In other cases, the state may have emerged as a way to control defeated populations in circumscribed areas. In still other instances, a combination of factors may have fostered the development of the state type of political system.

## THE CONSEQUENCES OF STATE FORMATION

I have discussed several places where states arose and several theories to explain the origin of states, but what were the consequences for the people living in those societies? The consequences seem to have been dramatic.

One of the ways states change the lifestyles of people is by allowing for larger and denser populations. As we have already seen, agriculture itself gives populations the potential to grow, and the development of a state only furthers that potential. Why? Because a state is able to build infrastructure, such as irrigation systems, roadways, and markets, that allow both the production and distribution of agricultural products to become more efficient. States are able to coordinate information as well, and can use that information to manage agricultural production cycles and to anticipate or manage droughts, blights, or other natural disasters. States are also able to control access to land (through laws and a military), to maintain farmers on the land, and to prevent others (from either within or outside of the state) from removing them or interfering with their abilities to produce food.

With increased efficiency of agricultural production and distribution, states also allow many (if not most) people in the society to be removed from food production. These people are freed to become craftspeople, merchants, and artists, as well as bureaucrats, soldiers, and political leaders. People may also live apart from agricultural fields, and thus cities with dense populations can arise. Cities can also arise in locations that are not suited to agriculture but that perhaps are suited to trade (such as the cities on rivers in southern Mesopotamia) or defense (such as on top of a mountain—as in the case of Monte Albán). Art, music, and literature often flourish in such contexts, and these too are often consequences of the rise of states. Organized religion, too, often develops after states appear. Thus all the hallmarks we associate with civilization can be seen as resulting from the evolution of states.

The development of states can have many negative impacts as well. When states develop people become governed by force and are no longer able to say "no" to their leaders. Police and military forces can become instruments of oppression and terror (see Figure 17.10). On a less obvious level, the class stratification of states

FIGURE **17.10**
One of the consequences of the rise of states is that police or military can be turned against the population as a force of political repression.

creates differences in access to resources and an underclass of poor, uneducated, and frequently unhealthy people. Health issues are exacerbated by the concentration of people in cities, an environment in which epidemic diseases can flourish. Without direct access to food supplies, people in cities also face the threat of malnutrition or outright starvation if food production and distribution systems fail.

All states appear to be expansionistic, and the emergence of state warfare and conquest seem one of the most striking negative impacts the evolution of states has had. In fact, more human suffering can probably be linked to state expansion than to any other single factor. Why do states expand? One basic reason may be that they are able to. States have standing armies ready to fight or be sent to conquer enemies. Another reason for state expansion might be related to the threat of famine and disease, which is more likely with intensive agriculture. A third answer might be that belligerence is simply part of the nature of states. States often arise through military means, and it may be vital to the continuation of some states that military power be continually demonstrated. Regardless of the causes, war and conquest are the consequences of state formation. Often too, defeat in war is the fate of states.

## THE DECLINE AND COLLAPSE OF STATES

When one looks over the list of ancient states discussed in this chapter (Monte Albán, Sumer, Pharaonic Egypt, etc.) one will notice a common element to all of them: All collapsed eventually. None of them maintained their power and influence into historic times. Why? It is an important question because, if collapse is the ultimate fate of many if not all states, then we can anticipate that our own state is likely to collapse eventually. Perhaps knowing something about how and why other states have collapsed can prevent (or at least hold off) the collapse of ours.

One suggested explanation for the decline and collapse of states is environmental degradation. If states originally arose where the environment was conducive to intensive agriculture and harvests big enough to support social stratification, political officials, and a state type of political system, then perhaps environmental degradation—declining soil productivity, persistent drought, and the like—contributed to the collapse of ancient states. Archaeologist Harvey Weiss has suggested that persistent drought helped to bring about the fall of the Akkadian empire. By 4300 B.P., the Akkadians had established an empire stretching 1,300 kilometers from the Persian Gulf in what is now Iraq to the headwaters of the Euphrates River in what is now Turkey. But a century later the empire collapsed. Weiss thinks that a long-term drought brought the empire down, as well as other civilizations at that time. Many archaeologists doubted there was such a widespread drought, but new evidence indicates that the worst dry spell of the past 10,000 years began just as the Akkadians' northern stronghold was being abandoned. The evidence of the drought, windblown dust in sediment retrieved from the bottom of the Persian Gulf, indicates that the dry spell lasted 300 years. Other geophysical evidence suggests that the drought was worldwide.

Environmental degradation may occur for other reasons than natural events. The behavior of humans may sometimes be responsible. Consider the collapse of **Cahokia**, the Mississippian tradition city we discussed in Chapter 9. By around 1000 B.P., Cahokia had large public plazas, a city wall constructed from some 20,000 logs, and massive mounds. But within 300 years only the mounds were left. Silt from flooding covered former croplands and settled areas. Geographer Bill Woods thinks that overuse of woodlands for fuel, construction, and defense led to deforestation, flooding, and persistent crop failure (see Figure 17.11). The result was the abandonment of Cahokia. Timber depletion is also indicated by studies of

**Cahokia** (United States, Mississippian)

FIGURE **17.11**
Midwestern farms today are highly productive, but have altered the landscape tremendously. What were once forests and prairies are now vast agricultural fields. Such radical alterations of the landscape may be one of the factors behind the collapse of states.

charcoal from excavations in the area. Apparently the quality of wood used in construction declined over time, suggesting that choice trees got scarcer. Cahokia is just one example of degradation that may have been caused by human behavior. Another example is the increasing saltiness of soils caused by evaporation of water from fields that have been irrigated over long periods of time, as in what is now southern Iraq.

Civilizations may sometimes decline because human behavior has increased the incidence of disease. For example, many lowland Mayan cities were abandoned between 1200 and 1000 B.P. Explanations of this collapse have ranged from over-population to resource depletion. But another factor may have been the increasing incidence of yellow fever. The clearing of forests and the consequent increase of breeding sites for mosquitoes may have favored the spread of the disease from areas farther south in Central America. Or the planting of particular trees by the Mayans in their urban areas may have increased the populations of co-resident monkeys who carried the disease (which mosquitoes transmitted to people).

Another reason that some states have collapsed appears to be overextension. This is often one of the reasons given for the decline of the Roman Empire. By the time of its fall, beginning about 1,800 years ago, the Empire had expanded through-out the Mediterranean region and into northwestern Europe. That huge area may simply have been too large to administer. "Barbarian" incursions on the peripheries of the Empire went unchecked because it was too difficult, and too costly, to reinforce these far-flung frontiers. Sometimes these incursions became wholesale invasions, which were exacerbated by famines, plagues, and poor leadership. By the time the last Roman Emperor of the West was deposed in A.D. 476, the Empire had withered to virtually nothing.

Finally, internal conflict because of leaders' mismanagment or exploitation have been put forward to explain the collapse of states. For example, historian Peter Charnais has argued that the Byzantine Empire (the eastern half of the Roman Empire) collapsed because large, powerful landholders had been allowed to absorb the land of too many smallholders, creating a group of overtaxed, exploited peasants with no interest in maintaining the empire. When the landholders began vying with the emperors for power, civil wars erupted, leading to disunity that left the empire vulnerable to conquest.

Many other ideas have been put forward to explain collapse—ranging from catastrophes to almost mystical factors such as "social decadence," but, as with theories for the origin of states, no single explanation seems to fit all or even most of the situations where states have collapsed. While it is still not clear what specific conditions led to the emergence, or collapse, of the state in each of the early centers of civilization, the question of why states form and decline is a lively focus of research today, so more satisfactory answers may come out of ongoing and future investigations.

## ⚙ SUMMARY

Archaeologists do not always agree on how a state should be defined, but most seem to agree that hierarchical and centralized decision making affecting a substantial population is the key criterion. States maintain power with a monopoly on the use of force. Force or the threat of force is used by the state to tax its population and to draft people for work or war. States arose all over the world. The first arose about 5000 B.P. in Mesopotamia. In the New World the first state did not arise until about 2500 B.P.

There are a wide variety of theories for how and why states arose. Theories of diffusion argue that states arose in one location because of the genius of the people or unique circumstances, and then spread across the rest of the world. Theories of resource control argue that states arose because they functioned to efficiently control and distribute important resources. Theories of population growth argue that states arose in order to deal with the problems associated with overpopulation. Finally, theories of interregional interaction argue that states arose in order to maintain social and political boundaries while simultaneously maintaining important interactions with neighboring societies. While each of these theories has some merit, no single theory seems to adequately explain the rise of states.

Regardless of how and why they arose, states have a dramatic impact on the people living within them. Populations grow and become concentrated in cities. Agriculture becomes more efficient, allowing many people to be removed from food production. States provide a context in which what we commonly call civilization— art, music, literature, and organized religion—can develop and flourish. But states also provide a context in which warfare and political terror can flourish. The social differentiation found in states produces an underclass of poor and often unhealthy people. States are prone to epidemic disease and periodic famine.

All ancient states collapsed eventually. While we have no good answers to the question of why states collapse, research into this question may have implications for prolonging the lives of our modern state systems.

## ⚙ DISCUSSION QUESTIONS

1. States did not appear until after the emergence of food production. Why might food production be necessary, but not sufficient, for states to develop?
2. The earliest states developed within a few thousand years of each other in the Old World. What might be the reasons?

3. What similarities are there in the locations where the first states evolved? What differences are there?

## ⚙ ESSAY QUESTIONS

1. It is a sobering thought that all of the ancient states we have discussed in this book collapsed. Consider at least two states and use this text and any library or Internet resources you can find to investigate their collapse. Why did these states collapse? Are there similarities between their collapses?

2. While population pressure does not alone seem to explain the rise of states, it is clear that a large and dense population is needed for a state to emerge. Examine at least two states discussed in this text and, using any library or Internet resources you can find, consider the role of population density, growth, or decline in the emergence of these states. What is the relationship between population and the rise of states?

3. The earliest states in the New World emerged several thousand years after those in the Old World. Use information from this text and any library or Internet resources you can find to examine the rise of states in both areas. What differences between the Old World and the New World might account for the New World's lag relative to the Old World in terms of the timing of the rise of states?

## ↗ RESEARCH PROJECT

The Sumerian, Egyptian, Shang, and Mayan states are unique in that all developed writing that can be read and understood today. Libraries and the Internet contain a wide variety of translated texts of these early writings. Find a body of literature from at least two of these early states and read carefully through it, noting the subject matters covered, the purposes of the writing, and the Intended audience of the written material. Then compare and contrast these bodies of literature. What differences are there in the literature? What similarities? What appears to be the primary purposes of written documents in these early states?

## ⚙ KEY SOURCES

### Where and When Did States Arise?

Cohen and Service, 1978; Feinman and Marcus, 1998; Flannery, 1972; Lamberg-Karlovsky and Sabloff, 1979; Redman, 1978; Service, 1975.

### How and Why Did States Arise?

Blanton et al., 1999; Brumfiel, 1983; Carniero, 1970, 1988; Chang, 1986; Cohen and Service, 1978; Feinman and Marcus, 1998; Flannery, 1972; Haas, 1982; Harris, 1979; Hole, 1994; Johnson, 1987; Johnson and Earle, 1987; Redman, 1978; Sanders, 1968; Sanders, Parsons, and Santley, 1979; Sanders and Price, 1968; Service, 1975; Upham, 1990; Wittfogel, 1957; Wright, 1986; Wright and Johnson, 1975.

## The Consequences of State Formation

Claessen and van de Velde, 1991; Cohen and Toland, 1988; Demarest and Conrad, 1992; Feinman and Marcus, 1998; Johnson and Earle, 1987; Tainter, 1988; Yoffee and Cowgill, 1988.

## The Decline and Collapse of States

Charnais, 1953; Kerr, 1998; Tainter, 1988; Weiss et al., 1993; Wilkinson, 1995; Yoffee and Cowgill, 1988.

# PHAISTOS DISK

Long before the invention of the Gutenberg press, there was the Phaistos Disk. This 16 cm (6 in.) diameter disk was discovered in Crete in 1903. In a century that has seen the cracking of many other complex linguistic systems, the Phaistos Disk has eluded decipherment. The disk is thought to date from around 3700 B.P. It is a round disk of clay, with symbols stamped into it. The stampings spiral inward from the outer ring. The text consists of 45 different symbols occurring 241 times. The symbols are repeated many times, suggesting that the text is a song or a prayer. The symbols portray recognizable objects, such as human figures and body parts, animals, weapons, and plants. Since the text of the disk is so short, decipherment by statistical cryptographic techniques employed in cracking Linear B is impossible. No other artifact like this exists anywhere in the world.

## WEB ACTIVITY

The island of Crete was the home of the Minoan Civilization, which was ruled by wealthy sea-kings. The Phaistos Disk comes from the New Palace period of Minoan culture. Besides having a written language, the Minoans also had ceramic plumbing and even full-size bathtubs. These Mediterranean people were quite well-versed in advanced technology at a very early time. Questions arise about the disk: What is it? What does it mean? Why is it stamped, almost as if by a large typewriter? Is the stamping technology an adjunct to any other? Does the technology of this disk carry through to later times? Theories abound but no one can answer these questions completely. In this activity, you will view the disk, its symbols, and its mystery.

The Media Lab can be found in Chapter 17 on the *Companion Website*™ http://www.prenhall.com/peregrine

## Activity

1. View the video. Just how far ahead of technology is the Phaistos Disk? Why do you think the technology shown in this disk was not adopted?

2. In reference to the Phaistos Disk, how do you react to the old adage that "necessity is the mother of invention?"

3. Since the Minoans were creating ceramic plumbing and bathtubs (and those certainly caught on), why do you think that there is only one example of stamped printing in the early historic world?

# chapter eighteen

# Trends in World Prehistory

**o v e r v i e w**

**Progress**

—◦—

**Interdependence**

—◦—

**The Big Picture**

—◦—

BOX

**Vere Gordon Childe**

By this point you should understand that archaeologists know prehistory only by finding, recovering, and interpreting objects that ancient peoples discarded or lost. Prehistory, in this sense, exists only in the present, in the interpretations made of the ancient items archaeologists find. But these items were left by real people, and prehistory must therefore also be a direct representation of the past—if only we can find the right tools to interpret the items that were left. Prehistory, then, is something of a puzzle that we assemble from ancient material. The purpose of this chapter is to try to piece together enough of the puzzle to find out if we can recognize the picture it shows.

If the last paragraph sounds vaguely familiar, it should: It is taken from the opening paragraph of this book. In that opening chapter I suggested that by the end of the book the picture archaeologists have of human prehistory would become clear. Unfortunately, because we don't have enough pieces of the puzzle yet, the picture we have of prehistory is still largely incomplete. What this chapter is really focused on is the various pictures or trends in world prehistory that archaeologists suggest they have seen.

In the opening chapter I also argued that one important reason for archaeology to remain part of anthropology is because it offers access to "the big question"—What does it mean to be human? I said I would try to answer that question at the end of the book. Well, I was not entirely honest. There is no widely accepted answer to the big question, but I think the various images scholars have seen in the puzzle that is prehistory may provide at least a glimpse of an answer.

## PROGRESS

One of the images that scholars have most widely suggested they see in the fragments of prehistory is that of human progress. As the nineteenth-century anthropologist Lewis Henry Morgan put it, "The history of the human race is one in source, one in experience, and one in progress" (1877:xxx). But we must be careful here, for Morgan meant what he said. Morgan, and other early scholars of cultural evolution, firmly believed in what anthropologists call **universal evolution**, the idea that all cultures evolve in exactly the same way. Morgan explains

> As it is undeniable that portions of the human family have existed in a state of savagery, other portions in a state of barbarism, and still other portions in a state of civilization, it seems equally so that these three distinct conditions are connected with each other in a natural as well as necessary sequence of progress (1877:3).

No archaeologist today would say such a universal "sequence of progress" is "undeniable." In fact, today archaeologists strongly deny such ideas. However, it is clear that some trends do appear to be nearly universal, such as population growth.

Rather than talk about universal evolution, archaeologists today tend to talk about **unilinear evolution**, trends in world prehistory that appear to occur all over the world, although not necessarily in exactly the same ways. Population growth appears to be one such trend, as does the development of technology. Do we call such unilinear trends progress? That's a matter of definition. For nineteenth-century anthropologists like Morgan, progress meant improvement—improvement in living standards, morality, art and literature, and the like. The yardstick for measuring improvement was Western European society, and in that sense the idea of progress was a highly Eurocentric one. However, progress does not have to be measured against Europe. Progress can also refer to increased efficiency, diversity, scale, or the like, and in those ways there do seem to be progressive unilinear trends in world prehistory.

**Universal evolution:** the idea that all cultures evolve in exactly the same way.

**Unilinear evolution:** trends in world prehistory that appear to occur all over the world, although not necessarily in the exact same ways.

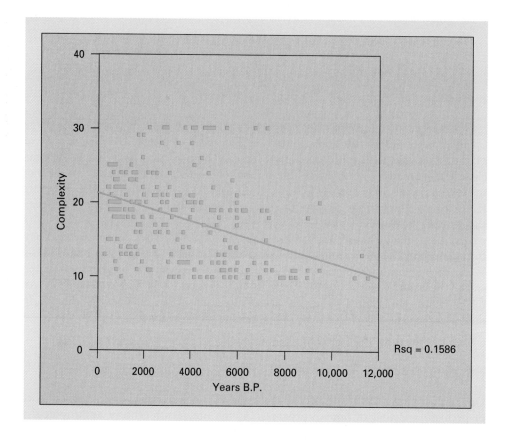

We can see evidence of progress, if that is what we want to call it, in the data from the archaeological traditions I described in Chapters 8 through 15. Figure 18.1, for example, presents cultural complexity plotted against time in years before present. Cultural complexity is measured by summing the scores on the 10 items in the Cultural Complexity Scale given in Appendix I. The variables we have looked at previously, like Density of Population and Social Stratification, are all items in this scale. The scale was developed by anthropologists George Peter Murdock and Catherine Provost in order to compare societies in terms of their relative complexity, but they make clear that their scale is only one way to look at complexity. Like progress, complexity can mean many things. Here the focus is on societal scale, integration, and technology.

Each point plotted in Figure 18.1 represents a single archaeological tradition. The tradition's horizontal position reflects the midpoint of the time period in which it existed, and the tradition's vertical position reflects the sum of its scores on the 10-item Cultural Complexity Scale. The line running through the plot shows where the middle of all the cases is located and reflects the overall trend (if any) in the data. It is usually referred to as a **regression line,** although I prefer to call it a **prediction line.** Looking at Figure 18.1 we see that cultural complexity, as measured by this scale (and, again, this is only one of a potentially infinite number of ways to define and measure complexity) has generally increased over time (from 12,000 years ago at the far right to the present at the far left of the plot). It is important to note that this trend is highly unlikely to be due to chance (statistics suggest it would occur less than one time in 1,000 by chance), and thus reflects a "real" trend in world prehistory. Measured by this scale, human cultures have tended to become more complex over time.

Note that not all societies have followed the overall trend toward increased complexity. Throughout world prehistory there have been some traditions that score lower on the Cultural Complexity Scale than the trend would predict (one can use

**Regression line:** see prediction line.

**Prediction line:** runs through the middle of a group of plotted points and shows the overall trend in the plotted data.

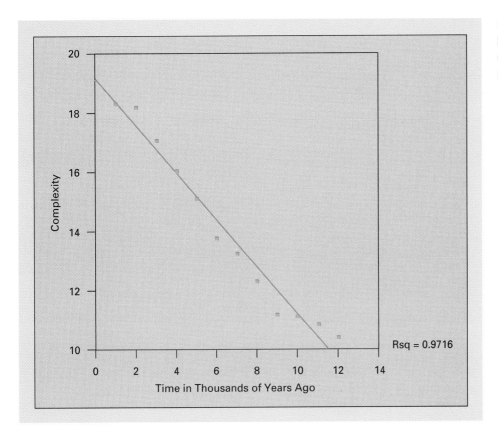

FIGURE **18.2**
Scatterplot of average
Cultural Complexity by Time
in years B.P.

the line running through the plot to suggest predicted values at any given point in time, which is why I like to call it a prediction line), and some that score higher. In other words, not all societies change in exactly the same way over time, so the idea that there is some universal evolutionary process going on does not seem to be supported. However, there is clearly a unilineal evolutionary trend toward greater cultural complexity, one that we can see more clearly in Figure 18.2.

Figure 18.2 shows a plot of the average score on the Cultural Complexity Scale plotted against time in years before present in 1,000-year intervals for the last 12,000 years. The average score for each time is based on the cultural complexity scores for all the archaeological traditions in existence at that time. An archaeological tradition that existed for two or three thousand years was counted in each of the two or three time periods for which an average was calculated. The unilineal evolutionary trend toward greater cultural complexity is dramatically illustrated here; indeed, the trend is so strong that given a cultural complexity value for one point in time you can predict the value for the next point in time with 97 percent accuracy (that's what the number to the right of the plot means).

## Population Growth

But what accounts for this image of "progress" in cultural complexity? One answer, widely accepted among archaeologists, is population growth. By most estimates, human population has been growing steadily for at least the last 30,000 years. Thirty thousand years ago there were only about two million people on earth. By 15,000 years ago there were more than six million people on earth, and by 10,000 years ago there were nearly nine million people on earth. Today the earth houses a staggering six billion people (although a large proportion of those people—fully one half—have been born during my lifetime). Clearly there has been an overall

FIGURE **18.3**

Scatterplot of Population
sub-scale by Time in years B.P.

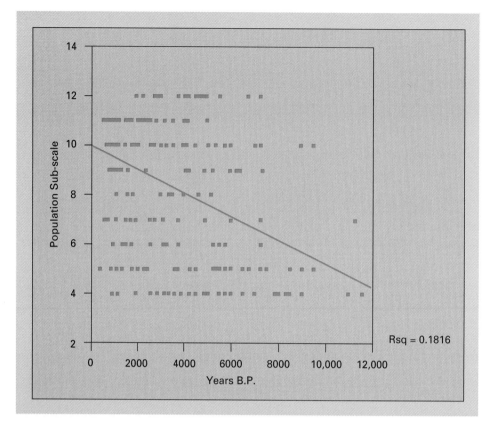

trend toward higher population, and we know from our examination of the evolution of food production and the rise of states that population growth seems to be an
important variable to understanding those fundamental transformations in human
culture.

Figure 18.3 provides evidence to back up the idea that there has been a significant trend toward population growth over the past 12,000 years. This figure is
based on an analysis of the Cultural Complexity Scale done by anthropologist Gary
Chick. He found that the scale appears to conflate two distinct subscales, one which
relates to population, and another which relates to technology. Plotted here are the
sum of those items that Chick argued formed a population scale (see Appendix I for
a more complete discussion). What we see in Figure 18.3 is a unilineal trend toward
increased population over the past 12,000 years. Indeed, statistically this relationship is stronger than the one for overall cultural complexity.

We can simplify Figure 18.3 by taking averages at 1,000-year intervals as we
did for cultural complexity in Figure 18.2. The results of doing so are shown in Figure 18.4. Here again we can see a clear growth trend in population over the past
12,000 years. We can see a similar trend if we look simply at the variable Density
of Population, which we have used several times in the preceding chapters. Figure 18.5 shows the average score on Density of Population at 1,000-year intervals
and, again, a strong trend is apparent. Does this mean that population growth
caused cultural complexity to increase? Many archaeologists would say yes, but
these data alone do not allow us to make such a conclusion. All we can say is that
"progress" in both cultural complexity and population are clearly evident in world
prehistory. (There are more sophisticated statistical techniques that might allow us
to examine causal relationships, but those go far beyond the scope of this text, and
perhaps beyond the reliability of the data.)

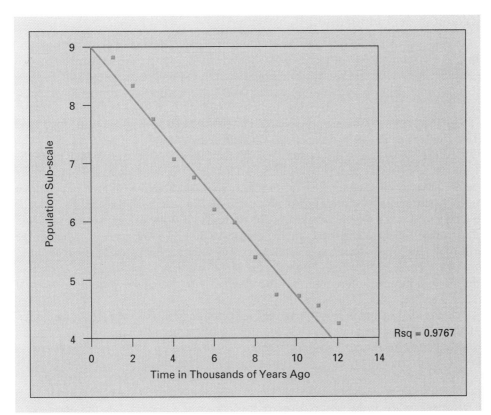

FIGURE **18.4**
Scatterplot of average
Population sub-scale by
Time in years B.P.

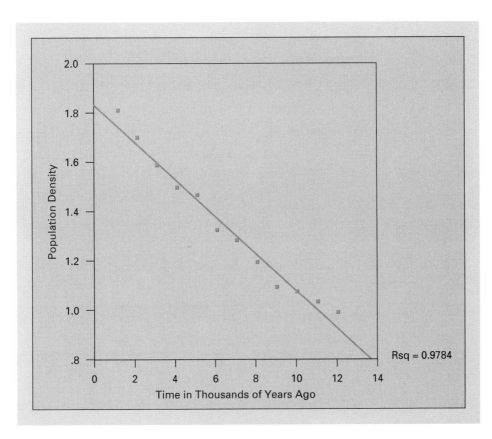

FIGURE **18.5**
Scatterplot of average
Population Density by
Time in years B.P.

## Technological Innovation

A second answer to the question of what might account for the image of "progress" in cultural complexity is technological innovation. As archaeologist V. Gordon Childe (whose work is described in more detail in the box feature) put it, "Technological progress is of course conspicuous. In the one direction of control over external nature men have been extending their capacities for half a million years" (1956:160). Support for Childe's statement can be seen in Figures 18.6, 18.7, and 18.8. Let's take a look at each of these figures individually.

Figure 18.6 shows the technology subscale that Chick identified within the Cultural Complexity Scale (see Appendix I for more details) plotted against years before present. Once again we can see a clear trend, although with an interesting set of high-scoring cases that may warrant additional research. Figure 18.7 shows the average score on the technology subscale plotted at 1,000-year intervals, and again illustrating an obvious trend. Finally, Figure 18.8 shows the average score on the Technological Specialization variable (see Appendix I) plotted in 1,000-year intervals for the last 12,000 years. As with the other two figures, we can see clearly that technology, however measured, has increased at a fairly regular pace over the past 12,000 years.

What might explain this "progress" in technology, and how might it be associated with cultural complexity? Childe, following earlier scholars such as Morgan and Friedrich Engels, argued that

> If the whole long process disclosed in the archaeological and literary records be surveyed, a single directional trend is most obvious in the economic sphere in the methods whereby the most progressive societies secure a livelihood. In this domain it will be possible to recognize radical and indeed revolutionary innovations . . . (1942:14–15).

FIGURE **18.6**

Scatterplot of Technology sub-scale by Time in years B.P.

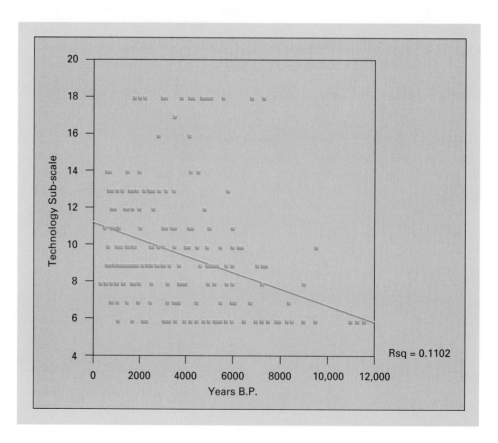

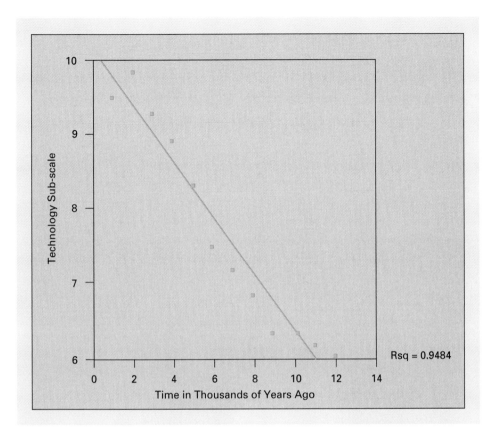

FIGURE **18.7**
Scatterplot of average
Technology sub-scale by
Time in years B.P.

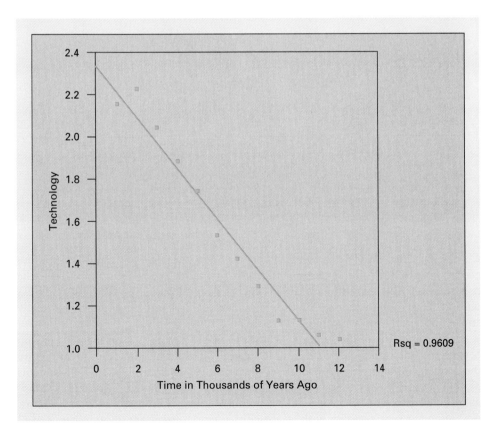

FIGURE **18.8**
Scatterplot of average Level
of Technology by Time in
years B.P.

# Vere Gordon Childe

Vere Gordon Childe has been called the "great synthesizer," for he is the person associated with the most important general overviews of Old World prehistory. His first major work, *The Dawn of European Civilization* (1925) synthesized the prehistory of Europe and also demonstrated the diffusion of traits from Southwest Asia and the Aegean northward into Europe. This was an important statement, for it demonstrated that archaeologists had to look beyond their specific region of interest if they wanted to fully understand cultural evolution within that region. Other important regional syntheses by Childe include *The Aryans* (1926), which attempted to trace the origins and spread of the Indo-Europeans, and *New Light on the Most Ancient East* (1934), which focused on the region from Egypt to

FIGURE **18.9**
Vere Gordon Childe.

Childe identified four such revolutions in human prehistory and history: the neolithic revolution (the evolution of food production); the urban revolution (the rise of states); the revolution in human knowledge (writing); and the industrial revolution. With each such "revolution," human groups became larger, more politically and economically sophisticated, and more culturally complex.

Anthropologist Leslie White took a somewhat different tack on the relationship between technology and complexity. He suggested that technological innovation and the growth of cultural complexity were products of an overall process of humans obtaining more energy from their environment. As he explained, "cultural development is the process of increasing the amount of energy harnessed and put to work per capita per year, together with all the consequences attendant upon this increase"

Pakistan and illustrated that features of civilization often attributed to the Greeks had actually emerged earlier in Egypt and Southwest Asia. Childe was a voluminous author: He also wrote *The Danube in Prehistory* (1929), *The Prehistory of Scotland* (1935), *Prehistoric Communities of the British Isles* (1947), and *Prehistoric Migrations of Europe* (1950), among many other works.

In addition to his synthetic works, Childe made important contributions to the study of cultural evolution. As Childe himself wrote "The most original and useful contributions that I may have made to prehistory are . . . interpretive concepts and methods of explanation" (1957:69). In *Man Makes Himself* (1935), Childe argued that human culture had evolved primarily through several great leaps, which he called revolutions. The main prehistoric ones were the neolithic (or agricultural) and urban revolutions. The idea that the origins of agriculture and cities were important milestones in cultural evolution remains strong in archaeology. In *What Happened in History* (1942), Childe introduced a broader vision of cultural evolution, one that combined his notions of revolutions with important technological innovations such as the use of bronze and the use of iron. In this way he took his very punctuated vision of cultural evolution and provided a more gradual mechanism for the period between revolutions. Finally, in *Social Evolution* (1951), Childe offered both a critique of many of the ideas of universal, punctuated evolution that he had put forward in *Man Makes Himself* and *What Happened in History* and a model for how the study of cultural evolution might be scientifically undertaken. The fact that Childe's ideas developed over time and that he provided many of his own critiques illustrates his scholarly integrity and insight.

Childe was not only a scholar, but also had a diverse academic career. He served as the librarian for the Royal Anthropological Institute (1925–1927); as professor of prehistoric archaeology at the University of Edinburgh (1927–1946); and as director of the Institute of Archaeology at the University College London (1946–1956). As scholar and teacher, Childe is remembered as a figure who transformed our understanding of European prehistory and cultural evolution in general.

SOURCES: Childe, V. Gordon, 1958, "Retrospect," *Antiquity* 32: 69–74; Rouse, Irving, 1958, "Vere Gordon Childe: 1892–1957," *American Antiquity* 24: 82–84.

(1959:42). The "consequences attendant upon" mechanisms, usually technological, that allowed for increased energy capture included population growth, political centralization, economic specialization, and other aspects of what we have called cultural complexity.

For both Childe and White, the link between technology and complexity exists because

> The social organization of the use of tools and machines is an important aspect of the technological process. Such things as division of labor, specialization, cooperation, systematization, and rationalization may affect the operation of the technological process very considerably (White 1959:55).

In other words, the way in which technology is integrated into the existing culture is just as important as the technology itself. Perhaps more significantly, culture strongly affects the ways in which technology might be used. As White explains

> Technologies exist and function within social systems and are consequently conditioned by them. A social system may stimulate the technology it embraces, encourage full and free exercise of its functions, and promote its growth and development. Or it may restrict free technological exercise and expression and impose curbs upon its growth (1959:27).

Technological innovation and cultural complexity are linked, therefore, because the two continually affect one another—technology shapes culture and culture conditions the manner in which innovations are employed.

## INTERDEPENDENCE

A second image that some archaeologists have seen in the puzzle of the past is one of increasing interdependence, both between and among human populations. One aspect of increasing interdependence that we experience every day is globalization. For example, I was recently in China where there seemed to be a Kentucky Fried Chicken franchise on every corner. When I returned to my home in Appleton, Wisconsin, I found to my surprise that my community has no less than eight Chinese restaurants. But sharing tastes in food is not the only aspect of globalization we regularly experience. In the United States we are well aware of our dependence on oil from other nations, while in China the people are well aware of their dependence on manufacturing goods for export to other nations. As Kwame Appiah and Henry Louis Gates put it, "we all participate, albeit from different cultural positions, in a global system of culture" (1997:xi).

This "global system of culture" was not always present. We might envision something like a common culture among humans until the Upper Paleolithic era, when human groups began to move into more diverse environments and develop local adaptations. But for the last 40,000 years at least, human cultures appear to have been primarily diverging, rather than becoming more interdependent. Is globalization only a recent phenomenon, or do our data suggest that growing interdependence has been a trend for some time? Let's find out.

Figure 18.10 shows the average score on the Political Integration variable, which we looked at in the last chapter, at 1,000-year intervals for the last 12,000 years. As with the other variables we have considered, there is a strong linear relationship. Average Political Integration has been steadily increasing for 12 millennia. Since the Political Integration variable essentially measures the number of communities that are unified within a single polity, we can see that over time autonomous communities have tended to become part of higher order political units, and this suggests that over time interdependence among local populations has increased. What does this mean for our understanding of global interdependence? It appears to suggest that what we are experiencing today is the outcome of at least 12,000 years of growing interdependence among populations.

It is interesting to note that, in theory at least, we should be able to follow the prediction line on the graph upwards and predict that in 1,000 years global integration will have increased by about 10 percent. Unfortunately, integration seems to have increased far more than that in only the past few decades. Today, as I noted earlier, all humans live in state societies, so that all societies should be coded with a value of 3 on the Political Integration variable on the X-axis (which represents today). It would seem that political integration has seen a dramatic leap in the past two or three centuries. So while the globalization we experience today is the outcome of 12,000 years of growing interdependence, it is also the outcome of what appears to be a unique period of extremely rapid growth. The same can be

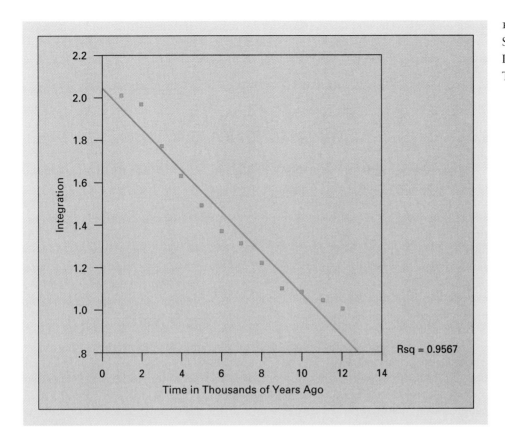

FIGURE **18.10**
Scatterplot of average
Political Integration by
Time in years B.P.

said for population, which has been growing with astounding speed for the past 200 years. Technology, too, seems to be far outpacing the prediction line that the last 12,000 years would suggest.

Recognizing the unusual speed of current globalization, population growth, and technological innovation is important, for it shows us the uniqueness of our current situation, and clearly illustrates how important it is for us to understand our past. Without knowledge of our past we would not be able to perceive the current conditions of rapid growth, to understand the exceptional, and perhaps dangerous, situation our world is in, nor to use that understanding to help shape our future. For me, this is one of the answers to the "big question" of what it means to be human. Today, at least, it means living in a time of unprecedented change—change that follows a general pattern established in prehistory, but accelerated to a pace that seems impossible to sustain. To explain what I mean by that, and to provide a better overall answer to the "big question," let me step back to the puzzle of prehistory and offer my own interpretation of the picture it presents.

## THE BIG PICTURE

The image I see when I look at the fragmentary puzzle of prehistory is one of increasing human control over the natural world. Each of the last two chapters has focused on what I have called a human event—a major transformation that, while taking place independently across the globe and over a long period of time, affected the entire human species. In the first part of the book we considered another human event, the evolution of culture. What ties these human events together? My answer is control of nature.

Here's how the story goes: About two million years ago humans developed culture and began to manipulate the environment with culture. At first these manipulations were simple extensions of human capabilities—stone and bone tools to augment teeth and hands. Later, perhaps 1.5 million years ago, humans began to create artificial environments for themselves by using shelter, clothing, and fire. The cultural extension of human capabilities continued through the development of more diverse and sophisticated tools. At some point during the Upper Paleolithic, humans developed a secondary world—the world of the imagination, a world that encompassed the past and future, the natural and the supernatural, a world that allowed humans to conceive of dramatically new ways to control the world in which they lived.

Beginning perhaps 12,000 years ago, humans began to actively manipulate the plants and animals upon which they subsisted and developed food production. In this development humans made a radical leap from using the natural world to actively shaping the natural world to better suit their own needs. Over time, questions about how the environment would be used, and issues surrounding sustainability of soils, animal herds, and other resources became focused in the hands of small groups of individuals. Initially, decisions were in the hands of descent groups or perhaps communities, but over time they were given over to (or taken over by) elites, chiefs, and, later, kings. Thus, within a few thousand years after implementing food production, humans developed states and created specialists who controlled environmental manipulation.

I am not alone in seeing human control over the natural world as the image emerging from the puzzle of prehistory. Indeed, this is essentially the image that both Childe and White saw. However, Childe and White envisioned the increased human control over the natural world as a universal phenomenon, one in which all peoples in all cultures played a role, if not at the same time, at least in the same manner. I view it much more as a unilineal rather than a universal process, with control directed by an increasingly attenuated group of people. Among neolithic societies, descent groups and perhaps whole communities made decisions about how the natural world would be shaped (through agricultural fields, irrigation systems, and the like). In early states the government decided. Today single organizations like the World Bank, the International Monetary Fund, and the World Trade Organization make decisions about the natural world that affect millions of people. These organizations, whose membership is made up primarily of European and North American elites, exert vast power over the earth. Far from being a universal trend, most people today are largely disenfranchised from decisions about how we shape the world around us.

If the picture I see in the puzzle of prehistory is increasing human control over nature, then what is my answer to the "big question" of what it means to be human? Well, humans are animals that use culture to shape the natural world to suit their needs. To be human means to be at once dependent upon the natural world and continually shaping its characteristics. The important lesson in this answer, one that becomes more pressing when we consider the explosive increase in the rate of cultural change in recent centuries, is that we must be careful to shape the world in ways that are sustainable, both in terms of natural resources and in terms of culture itself. We all know that natural resources are inherently limited, and while culture may not have any limits in quantity, there do seem to be limits in terms of scale and conflict. We need to be mindful not to exceed them.

Is the image I see really the one portrayed in the puzzle of prehistory? At this point no one can say. The puzzle is too fragmentary, and we simply do not have enough pieces to make an informed argument. Archaeologists all over the world are working to add pieces to the puzzle of prehistory, and each day we learn more. Perhaps you will add a piece to the puzzle, and not necessarily by becoming an archaeologist. All humans share prehistory, and we need to work together as a human community to preserve and record those precious pieces of the past that have been left to us. Every human has the ability to help by supporting preservation and research. Governments need to know that we are concerned about our human past, and that we support efforts to recover what we can. Funding is necessary to carry out research, and local support of archaeological efforts, from landowners to state agencies, is absolutely necessary for preservation and research to be accomplished. In the end, I think, the words William Shakespeare wrote some four centuries ago still convey a powerful message: "What's past is prologue." If we let our past slip away because we are too busy focusing on the present, we may well lose our future.

## ⬡ SUMMARY

Archaeologists know the past incompletely. The past is a puzzle for which we have only a few pieces. Despite the fragmentary picture, many archaeologists have proposed images that they see in the record of the past. One of the most common is the image of progress over time, and human cultures seems to have become more complex during the course of world prehistory. Looked at in more detail, progress can been seen in terms of human population growth and technological diversity and sophistication. Whether the growth in population and technological diversity and sophistication should be called progress is a matter of debate, but the fact of their presence can be readily demonstrated through the archaeological record.

Other archaeologists argue that the image in the puzzle of prehistory is one of increasing interdependence among human populations, that the globalization we experience today is the end result of a long trend toward increasing interdependence. While archaeological data do support this position, interdependence seems to have increased dramatically within the past few centuries, as have population growth and technology. Perhaps the most interesting image in the puzzle of prehistory is the dramatic changes that have occurred in recent history.

My own view is that prehistory presents a picture showing humans exercising increasing control over nature. Not only are humans shaping the natural world to a greater degree than ever before, but fewer humans are involved in the decisions about how the natural world will be impacted. This, to me, is a troubling picture, and one we should be mindful of as we move into the future.

## ⬡ DISCUSSION QUESTIONS

1. What "images" do you see in the puzzle of prehistory?
2. Which of the three "images" discussed in this chapter seems to be the clearest or most accurate?
3. Will more data help to clarify our understanding of world prehistory? How?

## ⬡ ESSAY QUESTIONS

1. Critique the idea of progress presented in this chapter. Is it accurate to speak of progress in world prehistory?
2. Critique the quantitative approach to examining world prehistory used in this chapter. Can the past be appropriately examined or understood in terms of numeric data?
3. Sociologist Robert Nisbet argued that, in terms of trends in world prehistory such as those presented in this chapter, "long-run directionality tends to be in the beholder's eye, not in the material themselves" (1969:284). Use the evidence in this chapter and any other information you can find to either support or refute Nisbet's statement.

## ✐ RESEARCH PROJECT

The eHRAF Collection of Archaeology (see www.yale.edu/hraf) provides categorized and searchable primary sources on many of the archaeological traditions discussed in this book. If your library subscribes to the eHRAF Collection of Archaeology, select ten archaeological traditions and code a set of variables of interest to you concerning some question in world prehistory. Analyze your data and report your results. (If your library does not subscribe the eHRAF Collection of Archaeology, you can also do this project using standard library and Internet resources.)

## ✸ KEY SOURCES

Chick, 1997; Childe, 1936, 1956; Engels, 1884; Morgan, 1877; Murdock and Provost, 1973; Nisbet, 1969; Peregrine, 2001; Sahlins and Service, 1960; Sanderson, 1990; Service, 1975; White, 1959.

# WHAT DOES AN ARCHAEOLOGIST DO?

Archaeologists only know prehistory by finding, recovering, and interpreting objects that ancient people discarded or lost. Archaeology and anthropology are comparative disciplines, with the archaeologist or anthropologist being a specialist in one or more areas. These scientists must compare their findings to other findings from different areas and specialties to determine how they fit into our existing knowledge of prehistory. Archaeology, as a branch of anthropology, attempts to answer the big question: "What does it mean to be human?" While we still do not have the answer, we are afforded glimpses through our research.

The Media Lab can be found in Chapter 18 on the Companion Website™ http://www.prenhall.com/peregrine

## WEB ACTIVITY

Progress and interdependence are elements of the "big picture." Scholars have alluded to some form of human progress since the nineteenth century. While our understanding of the form this progress has taken has changed, the outside world shows us that our societies have changed and are changing. The interdependence that we archaeologists see between and among human populations is another piece of the puzzle. In today's world, globalization is an example of this process. Political integration is another. Finally, the "big picture" may be explained by an increase in human control over nature. The control of nature seems to indicate the evolution of culture. In this activity, you will view a video of an archaeologist describing the many comparative aspects of archaeology.

## Activity

1. View the video. How is archaeology a comparative discipline? What do archaeologists do, besides excavate sites?

2. Why does understanding the question "What does it mean to be human" matter? What are we without this question?

3. How do we reach the "big picture" as described in the last chapter of this book?

# Appendix
# Codebook Used for Statistical Analyses

To create the data used in the crosstabulations and scatterplots presented in Chapters 16, 17, and 18, each archaeological tradition was rated on each of the following variables.

The scores on these 10 variables were summed for each tradition to create a score for Cultural Complexity, as used in Chapter 18. Also in Chapter 18 two subscales were used. The first subscale relates to Technology, and is the sum of Variables 1, 5, 6, 7, 9, and 10. The second subscale relates to Population and is the sum of Variables 2, 3, 4, and 8.

Variable 1:  Writing and Records
    1 = None
    2 = Mnemonic or nonwritten records
    3 = True writing

Variable 2:  Fixity of Residence
    1 = Nomadic
    2 = Seminomadic
    3 = Sedentary

Variable 3:  Agriculture
    1 = None
    2 = 10% or more, but secondary
    3 = Primary

Variable 4:  Urbanization (size of the largest settlement)
    1 = Fewer than 100 persons
    2 = 100–399 persons
    3 = 400+ persons

Variable 5:  Technological Specialization
    1 = None
    2 = Pottery
    3 = Metalwork (alloys, forging, casting)

Variable 6:  Land Transport
    1 = Human only
    2 = Pack or draft animals
    3 = Vehicles

Variable 7:  Money
    1 = None
    2 = Domestically usable articles
    3 = Currency

Variable 8:  Density of Population
    1 = Less than 1 person/square mile
    2 = 1–25 persons/square mile
    3 = 26+ persons/square mile

Variable 9:  Political Integration
    1 = Autonomous local communities
    2 = 1 or 2 levels above community
    3 = 3 or more levels above community

Variable 10: Social Stratification
    1 = Egalitarian
    2 = 2 social classes
    3 = 3 or more social classes or castes

# Glossary

**Absolute dating** techniques that provide absolute dates in years before the present.

**Age sets** groups of people who were born during the same period of time. Individuals in the same age set share social roles and go through important life events together.

**Age/area concept** a way to organize prehistory into temporal units, called ages, usually defined by technology, and located in a particular area. European Bronze Age or Southeastern European Chalcolithic are examples of age/area designations.

**Agricultural** societies that rely primarily on domesticates and use land intensively.

**Ahu** a low platform, usually faced with stone, used for religious rituals throughout Polynesia.

**Altiplano** another name used for the *puna*, a high-altitude plateau in the Andes that lies between roughly 2500 and 4500 meters above sea level.

**Anthropology** the comparative and evolutionary study of humans and their cultures.

**Antiquarians** eighteenth- and nineteenth-century scholars who were the first to systematically record and describe ancient monuments and objects.

**Archaeological site** a location where artifacts, ecofacts, fossils, and features are found in context.

**Archaeological tradition** a group of populations sharing similar subsistence practices, technology, and forms of sociopolitical organization, which are spatially contiguous over a relatively large area and which endure temporally for a relatively long period.

**Archaeologists** scholars who practice archaeology.

**Archaeology** a method or set of techniques for collecting and analyzing ancient objects and their contexts.

**Ardipithecus ramidus** perhaps the first hominid, dating to some 4.4 million years ago. Its dentition combines ape-like and australopithecine-like features, and its skeleton suggest it was bipedal.

**Artifact** any object of human manufacture.

**Australopithecine** a general term referring to members of the genus *Australopithecus.*

**Australopithecus** the genus associated with the first well-established bipedal hominids.

**Australopithecus afarensis** an australopithecine that lived 4 to 3 million years ago in East Africa and was definitely bipedal.

**Australopithecus africanus** an australopithecine that lived between about 3 and 2 million years ago, and is known primarily from southern Africa.

**Australopithecus anamensis** an australopithecine that lived perhaps 4.2 million years ago.

**Australopithecus bahrelghazali** an australopithecine that lived in what is today Chad about 3 million years ago. It is the first early hominid found outside of the African Rift Valley system.

**Australopithecus garhi** an australopithecine from East Africa dating from about 2.5 million years ago.

**Ayllus** individual descent groups that resided in a single village and formed an important organizing element in Andean polities.

**Ball courts** long rectangular or I-shaped areas, often with sloping sides, used to play the Mesoamerican ball game—a game something like a combination of soccer and basketball.

**Bands** groups of fifteen to thirty people who live and work together as a single social and economic unit.

**Beringia** a landmass, located in what today is the Bering Sea, that linked Asia and North America during the last ice age.

**Bifacial tool** a tool worked or flaked on two sides.

**Biodistance** studies which use genetic markers to determine the biological relationships among populations.

**Bipedal** locomotion in which an animal walks on its two hind legs.

**Blades** thin stone flakes whose lengths are usually more than twice their widths.

**Bolas** a hunting tool consisting of three stones connected by three strings tied together. When thrown around the legs of an animal, the strings wrap around the legs and prevent the animal from running away.

**Boreal forests** dense subarctic conifer forests located south of tundra zones.

**Bullae** clay containers made during the Uruk tradition that served as bills of lading for goods.

**Castes** social groups that are defined by occupation and are ascribed to a person at birth.

**Ceramic** an artifact made from clay (paste) that has been heated (fired) to give it strength.

**Chiefs** political leaders who base authority on high status rather than on the use of force.

**Chiefdom** a polity having a central political figure whose authority rests on status rather than force.

**Clan** a descent group that traces ancestry back to mythical founders of the society.

**Classical archaeology** archaeology focused on the "classical" civilizations of Greece and Rome.

**Codebook** provides definitions used to assign values to cases on specific variables.

**Conservation** the process of treating artifacts, ecofacts, fossils, and in some cases features, to stop decay and, if possible, even reverse the deterioration process.

**Context** the relationships between and among ancient objects.

**Cro-Magnon** modern humans who lived in western Europe about 35,000 years ago.

**Cross-tabulation** shows the number of cases that have a particular value on two variables.

**Cultural evolution** changes in the scale, complexity, or integration of cultural behaviors among a group of people.

**Culture** the learned behaviors shared by a group of people that aid them in the ongoing process of survival.

**Culture history** a descriptive chronology of the cultures that inhabited a given location.

**Cylinder seals** cylinders with carved designs in them that are rolled across wet clay in order to mark and seal shipments.

**Deciduous forests** forests comprised of trees that lose their leaves in the winter.

**Dendrochronology** an absolute dating method that uses the annual growth rings of trees to determine the year in which a tree died.

**Descent group** a group of people who share descent from a common ancestor.

**Descriptive questions** ask about the nature of the archaeological record and can be thought of as questions that start with who, what, when, or where.

**Domestication** process through which humans manipulate plant or animals species to enhance desirable features and eliminate undesirable ones.

**Earth lodge** semisubterranean structure constructed with wattle and daub or sod walls and a thatched or sod roof.

**Ecofact** a natural object that has been used or modified by humans.

**Ecological theories** posit that human culture is an adaptation to the environment, and thus culture functions to maintain humans and the environment in a sustainable balance.

**Empires** incorporate a number of independent polities within an overarching political structure, usually through military conquest.

**Ethnographers** scholars who record the behaviors, beliefs, and traditions of living peoples.

**Excavation** the recovery of buried archaeological data in context.

**Falaj irrigation** a type of irrigation in which water from mountain aquifers is transported through subterranean channels to lower-lying agricultural fields.

**Feature** human creations and disturbances that have become intrinsic parts of archaeological sites.

**Fossil** the remains of an ancient plant or animal that has turned to stone through a complex process of mineralization.

**Four-field approach** refers to anthropology's combined use of four distinct subdisciplines—ethnography, linguistic anthropology, archaeology, and biological anthropology—to address questions about human behavior and culture.

**Genus** a group of related species.

**Geoglyphs** designs incised in rock.

**Hard hammer** a technique of stone tool manufacture where one stone is used to knock flakes from another stone. Flakes produced through hard hammer percussion are usually large and crude.

**High arctic** arctic lands largely barren of vegetation and covered in snow or ice much of the year.

**Historians** scholars who use texts to describe and understand the past.

**Historical particularism** the theoretical framework that viewed each culture as the product of a particular set of historical circumstances and not as the product of a universal evolutionary process.

**Hominids** the group of primates consisting of humans and their direct ancestors, the australopithecines and the paranthropoids.

**Homo** the genus to which modern humans and their ancestors belong.

**Homo erectus** the first hominid species to be widely distributed in the Old World. The earliest finds are possibly 1.8 million years old. The brain (averaging 895–1040 cc) was larger than that found in any of the australopithecines or *H. habilis* but smaller than the average brain of a modern human.

**Homo habilis** an early species belonging to our genus, *Homo*, found in East Africa, and dating from about 2 million years ago.

**Homo heidelbergensis** a transitional species between *Homo erectus* and *Homo sapiens*.

**Homo neandertalensis** the technical name for the Neandertals, a group of robust and otherwise anatomically distict hominids that are close relatives of modern humans.

**Homo rudophensis** an early species belonging to our genus, *Homo*, that is similar enough to *Homo habilis* that some paleoanthropologists make no distinction between the two.

**Homo sapiens** the technical name for modern humans.

**Hunting and gathering** a way of life where subsistence is based exclusively on wild foods.

**Indicator fossil** any artifact, ecofact, fossil, or feature that is unique to a particular time period and by its presence can be used to indicate the date of an archaeological deposit.

**Indirect percussion** a method of working stone using a punch of antler or wood, which is struck with a hammer to produce stone blades from a core.

**Kenyanthropus platyops** a newly discovered hominid from East Africa dating to about 3.5 million years ago. Many scholars believe it to be a new species of australopithecine and not a new genus as currently designated.

**Kiva** a round, semisubterranean structure used primarily for public gatherings and rituals.

**Kurgans** large conical burial mounds built by the peoples of the Eurasian steppe.

**Labret** an ornamental lip plug.

**Levallois method** a method of making stone tools that allowed flake tools of a predetermined size to be produced from a shaped core.

**Lithic** a stone tool made or used by humans.

**Lower Paleolithic** the time period encompassing the Oldowan and Acheulean traditions.

*Marae* a religious structure found throughout Polynesia.

**Materialist theories** posit that the way humans organize labor and technology to get resources out of the material world is the primary force shaping culture.

**Matrilineal** descent traced through mothers.

**Microliths** small, razorlike blade fragments that were attached to wooden or bone handles to form cutting tools and projectile points.

**Mauryan Empire** an empire located in the Ganges River valley, dating to roughly 2300 B.P.

*M'ita* a system of labor mobilization in the Inca empire in which each *ayllu* was expected to supply a set number of people each year to work on imperial projects.

*Moai* massive stone figures in human form found on Easter Island.

**Moas** flightless birds indigenous to New Zealand that went extinct soon after human colonization.

**Neandertals** a group of robust and otherwise anatomically distict hominids that are close relatives of modern humans.

**Occipital torus** a ridge of bone running horizontally across the back of the skull in apes and some hominids.

**Oracle bones** turtle shell or cattle scapula that were cracked by heat and then "read" by a diviner to predict the future.

**Paleoanthropologist** a scholar who studies ancient humans and human evolution.

**Palisade** a defensive wall built of vertical posts.

**Paranthropoids** members of the genus *Paranthropus*.

*Paranthropus* a genus of early hominids with extremely large faces and teeth.

*Paranthropus aethiopicus* the earliest paranthropoid, dating to about 2.5 million years ago, and found in East Africa.

*Paranthropus boisei* the largest of the paranthropoids, this East African species dates from about 2.2 to 1.3 million years ago.

*Paranthropus robustus* a paranthropoid found in South Africa dating from about 1.8 to 1 million years ago.

**Pastoralism** subsistence based on domesticated animals.

**Patrilineal** descent traced through fathers.

**Pedestrian survey** a method of finding archaeological sites by walking along while scanning the ground surface for artifacts.

**Percussion flaking** a toolmaking technique in which one stone is struck with a stone or other object to remove a flake.

**Pit houses** round, semisubterranean dwellings, often covered with a thatch or sod roof.

**Pleistocene megafauna** giant species of animals that lived during the last ice age.

**Potlatch** an event among Northwest Coast peoples in which chiefs gave away vast amounts of wealth in order to demonstrate power and embarrass other chiefs.

**Prediction line** runs through the middle of a group of plotted points and shows the overall trend in the plotted data.

**Prehistory** the time in the past before written documents allow a good picture of life.

**Pressure flaking** a stone-working technique whereby small flakes are struck off by pressing against the core with a bone, antler, or wood tool.

**Processual questions** ask how and why the archaeological record takes the form it does, and about the processes of cultural stability and change over time.

**Prognathic** a physical feature that is sticking out or pushed forward, such as the jaws in apes and some hominid species.

**Publishing** an important part of archaeological research, since archaeologists are required to disseminate the results of their research to others.

**Pueblos** blocks of mud-brick or adobe rooms built together to form a single, large structure.

*Puna* a high-altitude plateau in the Andes that lies between roughly 2500 and 4500 meters above sea level.

**Rachis** the seed-bearing part of a plant stem.

**Radiocarbon dating** a method of absolute dating that uses the decay of carbon-14 to assign a date to an object.

**Ramada** a roofed courtyard.

**Regression line** see prediction line.

**Relative dating** techniques used to assign a date to an object or deposit based on its relative context with other objects or deposits.

**Remote sensing** a variety of techniques that provide the ability to locate archaeological deposits below the ground without digging.

**Sagittal crest** a ridge of bone running along the top of the skull in apes and early hominids.

**Sagittal keel** an inverted v-shaped ridge running along the top of the skull in *Homo erectus*.

**Sampling** the process of selecting a small number of representative cases from a larger group of cases.

**Seriation** a method of relative dating that uses the percentages of particular artifact styles to assign relative dates.

**Seals** pieces of carved ceramic or stone used to make impressions in wet clay used to seal the contents of materials being shipped. Typically seals identify the owner of a shipment.

**Semisubterranean** a structure built partially below ground.

**Sexually dimorphic** marked differences in size and appearance between males and females of a species.

**Slash-and-burn** a way of preparing agricultural fields by cutting brush and trees, letting them dry, and burning the debris.

**Soft hammer** a technique of stone tool manufacture in which a bone or wood hammer is used to strike flakes from a stone.

**Spear-thrower** a stick or board used to help propel a spear, giving the thrower greater force and accuracy.

**States** polities in which leaders govern by force.

**Stratified** archaeological sites that have clear separation between deposits dating to different times.

**Stratigraphy** the analysis and interpretation of stratified deposits.

**Swidden** a form of agriculture where fields shift from location to location every few years. The slash-and-burn method is often used to prepare swidden fields.

**Tablets** rectangular pieces of clay that were written upon using a stylus. Tablets were dried or baked to form a permanent written record of a transaction or event.

**Tamped earth** a method of making walls in China, where earth is pounded into a mould made by two parallel boards that are raised as the walls grow higher.

**Taphonomy** the study of site formation and disturbance.

**Taurodontism** having teeth with an enlarged pulp cavity.

**Teosinte** a tall, wild grass that grows widely in Mexico and is thought to be ancestral to maize.

**Test excavation** small excavations used to test whether important archaeological deposits are located in a given area.

**Tholoi** a circular, domed structure.

**Tsetse** a fly that causes sleeping sickness among domesticated cattle.

**Tundra** arctic lands where lichens, mosses, and grasses grow.

**Typology** a set of categories (or types) that represent the range of known variation in a given object.

**Torcs** thick metal neck-rings, often of gold or bronze and highly decorated, which were thought to provide good fortune to the wearer.

**Unifacial tool** a tool worked or flaked on one side only.

**Unilinear evolution** trends in world prehistory that appear to occur all over the world, although not necessarily in the exact same ways

**Universal evolution** the idea that all cultures evolve in exactly the same way.

**Universal evolutionary theory** posits that there is an underlying, universal path along which all cultures progress.

**Venus figurines** small sculptures of women with exaggerated hips and breasts, made by Upper Paleolithic peoples.

**Wattle-and-daub** building using mat walls covered with mud to form a solid and relatively substantial structure.

**Wigwam** a structure constructed of poles bent to form a dome and covered with bark or woven reeds.

**Younger Dryas** a cold and arid period at the end of the last ice age, about 11,000 B.P. to 10,000 B.P.

**Yurt** a large domed tent constructed by covering a wooden framework with thick felt mats.

**Zebu** a type of cattle domesticated in South Asia with a distinctive hump and dewlap.

# Bibliography

Ackerman, Robert E. 1982. "The Neolithic-Bronze Age Cultures of Asia and the Norton Phase of Alaskan Prehistory." *Arctic Anthropology* 19(2):11–38.

———. 1992. "Earliest Stone Industries of the North Pacific Coast of North America." *Arctic Anthropology* 29(2):18–27.

———. 2001a. "Late Tundra." In *Encyclopedia of Prehistory*, Vol. 2: *Arctic and Subarctic*, ed. P.N. Peregrine and M. Ember. New York: Kluwer/Plenum, 111–115.

———. 2001b. "Thule." In *Encyclopedia of Prehistory*, Vol. 2: *Arctic and Subarctic*, ed. P.N. Peregrine and M. Ember. New York: Kluwer/Plenum, 208–212.

Adams, Barbara. 1988. *Predynastic Egypt*. Aylesbury: Shire Publications.

Adams, Richard E.W. 1977. *The Origins of Maya Civilization*. Albuquerque: University of New Mexico Press.

Adams, Robert M. 1981. *The Heartland of Cities*. Chicago: University of Chicago Press.

Adams, Robert M., and Hans Nissen. 1972. *The Uruk Countryside*. Chicago: University of Chicago Press.

Adler, Michael. 1996. *The Prehistoric Pueblo World, A.D. 1150–1350*. Tucson: University of Arizona Press.

———. 2001. "Late Anasazi." In *Encyclopedia of Prehistory*, Vol. 6: *North America*, ed. P.N. Peregrine and M. Ember. New York: Kluwer/Plenum, 223–240.

Agrawal, D.P. 1982. *The Archaeology of India*. London: Crzon Press.

Aiello, Leslie, and Christopher Dean. 1990. *An Introduction to Human Evolutionary Anatomy*. London: Academic Press.

Aikens, C. Melvin. 1993. *Archaeology of Oregon*. Portland: US Department of the Interior, Bureau of Land Management.

Aikens, C. Melvin, and Takayasu Higuchi. 1982. *Prehistory of Japan*. New York: Academic Press.

Aitken, Martin J. 1961. *Physics and Archaeology*. New York, Interscience Publishers.

———. 1990. *Science-Based Dating in Archaeology*. New York: Longman.

Akazawa, Takeru, and Melvin Aikens. 1986. *Prehistoric Hunter-Gatherers in Japan*. Tokyo: University of Tokyo Museum, Bulletin 27.

Akkermans, P. M. M.G. 1993. *Villages in the Steppe: Latter Neolithic Settlement and Subsistence in the Balikh Valley, Northern Syria*. Ann Arbor, MI: International Monographs in Prehistory.

Aldenderfer, Mark. 1989. "The Archaic Period in the South-Central Andes." *Journal of World Prehistory* 3:117–158.

———. 1993. *Domestic Architecture, Ethnicity, and Complementarity in the South Central Andes*. Iowa City: University of Iowa Press.

———. 1998. *Montane Foragers: Asana and the South-Central Andean Archaic*. Iowa City: University of Iowa Press.

———. 2002. "Late Andean Hunting-Collecting." In *Encyclopedia of Prehistory*, Vol. 7: *South America*, ed. P.N. Peregrine and M. Ember. New York: Kluwer/Plenum, 200–216.

Alexander, John. 1972. *Yugoslavia before the Roman Conquest*. London: Thames and Hudson.

Algaze, Guillermo. 1989. "The Uruk Expansion: Cross-cultural Exchange in the Early Mesopotamian Civilization." *Current Anthropology* 30(5):571–608.

———. 1993. *The Uruk World System: The Dynamics of Expansion of Early Mesopotamian Civilization*. Chicago: University of Chicago Press.

Alkire, W.H. 1977. *An Introduction to the Peoples and Cultures of Micronesia*. 2nd ed. Menlo Park, CA: Cummings.

Allchin, Bridget, and Raymond Allchin. 1982. *The Rise of Civilization in India and Pakistan*. Cambridge: Cambridge University Press.

Allchin, Raymond. 1990. "Patterns of City Formation in Early South Asia." *South Asian Studies* 6:163–174.

Allchin, Raymond, and Bridget Allchin. 1997. *Origins of a Civilization: The Prehistory and Early Archaeology of South Asia*. Delhi: Viking.

Allen, Jim, and Chris Gosden. 1991. *Report of the Lapita Homeland Project*. Canberra: Dept. of Prehistory, Australian National University.

Allison, Penelope. 1999. *The Archaeology of Household Activities*. London: Routledge.

Alvarez Palma, Anna Maria. 1990. *Huatabampo: Consideractiones Sobre una Communidad Agricola Prehispanica en el Sur de Sonora*. Hermosillo: Centro Regional Sonora, INAH.

Ambrose, Stanley H. 1997. "The Ceramic Late Stone Age." In *Encyclopedia of Precolonial Africa*, ed. J.O. Vogel. Walnut Creek, CA: Alta Mira, 381–385.

———. 2001. "East African Neolithic." In *Encyclopedia of Prehistory*, Vol. 1: *Africa*, ed. P.N. Peregrine and M. Ember. New York: Kluwer/Plenum, 97–109.

Ames, Kenneth M. 1994. "The Northwest Coast: Complex Hunter-Gatherers, Ecology, and Social Evolution." *Annual Review of Anthropology* 23:209–229.

Ames, Kenneth, Don Dumond, Jerry Galm, and Rick Minor. 1998. "Prehistory of the Southern Plateau." In *Handbook of North American Indians*, vol. 12, ed. D. Walker. Washington, DC: Smithsonian Institution Press, 103–119.

Ames, Kenneth, and Herbert Maschner. 1999. *Peoples of the Northwest Coast: Their Archaeology and Prehistory*. New York: Thames and Hudson.

Anati, E. 1963. *Palestine before the Hebrews*. London: Jonathan Cape.

Anderson, David G. 1994. *The Savannah River Chiefdoms*. Tuscaloosa: University of Alabama Press.

Anderson, David G., and Kenneth E. Sassaman. 1996. *The Paleoindian and Early Archaic Southeast*. Tuscaloosa: University of Alabama Press.

Anderson, Douglas D. 1968. "A Stone Age Campsite at the Gateway to America." *Scientific American* 218(6):24–33.

———. 1970. *Akmak: An Early Archaeological Assemblage from Onion Portage, Northwest Alaska*. Copenhagen: Acta Arctica 16.

———. 1988. "Onion Portage: The Archaeology of a Stratified Site from the Kobuk River." *Anthropological Papers of the University of Alaksa* 22(1–2).

Andrews, Anthony P. 1993. "Late Postclassic Lowland Maya Archaeology." *Journal of World Prehistory* 7:35–69.

Arnold, Bettina. 2001. "West-Central European Early Iron Age." In *Encyclopedia of Prehistory*, Vol. 4: *Europe*, ed. P.N. Peregrine and M. Ember. New York: Kluwer/Plenum, 383–398.

Arnold, Bettina, and D. Blair Gibson. 1995. *Celtic Chiefdom, Celtic State*. Cambridge: Cambridge University Press.

Arnold, Jeanne. 2001. *Origins of a Pacific Coast Chiefdom: The Chumash of the Channel Islands*. Salt Lake City: University of Utah Press.

Arnold, Philip J. 1994. "An Overview of Southern Veracruz Archaeology." *Ancient Mesoamerica* 5:215–221.

Arsenault, Daniel. 2002. "Moche." In *Encyclopedia of Prehistory*, Vol. 7: *South America*, ed. P.N. Peregrine and M. Ember. New York: Kluwer/Plenum, 272–279.

Askarov, A., V. Volkov, and N. Ser-Odjav. 1992. "Pastoral and Nomadic Tribes at the Beginning of the First Millennium B.C." In *History of Civilizations of Central Asia*, Vol. 1, ed. A.H. Dani and V.M. Masson. Paris: UNESCO Publishing, 459–472.

Aveni, Anthony. 1990. *The Lines of Nazca*. Philadelphia: American Philosophical Society.

Ayala, Francisco J. 1995. "The Myth of Eve: Molecular Biology and Human Origins." *Science* (December 22):1930–1936.

Bagley, Robert. 1999. "Shang Archaeology." In *The Cambridge History of Ancient China*, ed. M. Lowe and E.L. Shaughnessy. Cambridge: Cambridge University Press, 124–231.

Bahn, Paul. 1996. *The Cambridge Illustrated History of Archaeology*. Cambridge: Cambridge University Press.

———. 1998. "Neanderthals Emancipated." *Nature* 394:719–720.

Bailey, Douglas, and Ivan Panayotov. 1995. *Prehistoric Bulgaria*. Madison, WI: Prehistory Press.

Baillie, M.G.L. 1995. *A Slice Through Time: Dendrochronology and Precision Dating*. London: Batsford.

Balter, Michael, and Ann Gibbons. 2000. "A Glimpse of Humans' First Journey out of Africa," *Science* 288:948–950.

Banerjee, N.R. 1965. *The Iron Age in India*. Mysore: Munshiram Manoharlal.

Banning, Edward B. 1998. "The Neolithic Period: Triumphs of Architecture, Agriculture and Art." *Near Eastern Archaeology* 61:188–237.

———. 2000. *The Archaeologist's Laboratory: The Analysis of Archaeological Data*. New York: Kluwer/Plenum.

———. 2002a. "Aceramic Neolithic." In *Encyclopedia of Prehistory*, Vol. 8: *South and Southwest Asia*, ed. P.N. Peregrine and M. Ember. New York: Kluwer/Plenum, 1–20.

———. 2002b. "Ceramic Neolithic." In *Encyclopedia of Prehistory*, Vol. 8: *South and Southwest Asia*, ed. P.N. Peregrine and M. Ember. New York: Kluwer/Plenum, 40–55.

Bard, Kathryn. 1994. *From Farmers to Pharaohs: Mortuary Evidence for the Rise of Complex Society in Egypt*. Sheffield: Sheffield Academic Press.

Barich, Barbara E. 1987. *Archaeology and Environment in the Libyan Sahara*. Oxford: British Archaeological Reports, International Series 368.

Barker, Graham. 1985. *Prehistoric Farming in Europe*. Cambridge: Cambridge University Press.

Barker, Philip A. 1993. *Techniques of Archaeological Excavation*. New York: Routledge.

Barnes, Gina L. 1990. *Hoabinhian, Jomon, Yayoi, Early Korean States*. Oxford: Oxbow Books.

———. 1993. *China, Korea, and Japan: The Rise of Civilization in East Asia*. New York: Thames and Hudson.

———. 1999. *The Rise of Civilization in East Asia*. London: Thames and Hudson.

Barnett, William. 2001. "Impressed Ware." In *Encyclopedia of Prehistory*, Vol. 4: *Europe*, ed. P.N. Peregrine and M. Ember. New York: Kluwer/Plenum, 185–188.

Barton, R., E. Nicholas, A.J. Roberts, and D.A. Roes. 1991. *The Late Glacial of Northwest Europe*. London: Council for British Archaeology, Research Reports 77.

Barut, Sibel. 1994. "Middle and Later Stone Age Lithic Technology and Land Use in East African Savannas." *African Archaeological Review* 12:44–70.

Bar-Yosef, Ofer. 1980. "Prehistory of the Levant." *Annual Review of Anthropology* 9:101–133.

———. 1995. "Earliest Food Producers—Pre-Pottery Neolithic (8000–5500)." In *The Archaeology of Society in the Holy Land*, ed. T.E. Levy. New York: Facts on File, 190–204.

Basilov, Vladimir. 1989. *Nomads of Eurasia*. Seattle: University of Washington Press.

Bauer, Brian. 1997. *The Development of the Inca State*. Austin: University of Texas Press.

Bawden, G. 1996. *The Moche*. Oxford: Blackwell.

Beierle, John. 2002. "Iranian Bronze Age." In *Encyclopedia of Prehistory*, Vol. 8: *South and Southwest Asia*, ed. P.N. Peregrine and M. Ember. New York: Kluwer/Plenum, 156–159.

Bell, James A. 1994. *Reconstructing Prehistory: Scientific Method in Archaeology*. Philadelphia: Temple University Press.

Bell, Robert E. 1984. *Prehistory of Oklahoma*. Orlando, FL: Academic Press.

Bellwood, Peter. 1987. "The Prehistory of Island Southeast Asia." *Journal of World Prehistory* 1:171–224.

———. 1992. "Southeast Asia Before History." In *Cambridge History of Southeast Asia*, Vol. 1, ed. N. Tarling. Cambridge: Cambridge University Press, pp. 55–136.

———. 1997. *Prehistory of the Indo-Malaysian Archipelago*. Honolulu: University of Hawaii Press.

———. 2001. "Southeast Asia Neolithic and Early Bronze." In *Encyclopedia of Prehistory*, Vol. 4: *Europe*, ed. P.N. Peregrine and M. Ember. New York: Kluwer/Plenum, 287–306.

Bender, Barbara. 1978. "Gatherer-Hunter to Farmer: A Social Perspective." *World Archaeology* 10:361–392.

———. 1985. "Prehistoric Developments in the American Midcontinent and in Brittany, Northwest France." In *Prehistoric Hunter-Gatherers*, ed. T. Douglas Price and James Brown. New York: Academic, 21–57.

Bender, Susan, and George Smith. 2000. *Teaching Archaeology*. Washington, DC: Society for American Archaeology.

Benson, Elizabeth P. 1981. *The Olmec and their Neighbors*. Washington, DC: Dumbarton Oaks.

Benson, Elizabeth P., and Jill Guthrie. 1996. *The Olmec World: Ritual and Rulership*. Princeton: Princeton Art Museum.

Bentley, G.C. 1986. "Indigenous States of Southeast Asia." *Annual Review of Anthropology* 15:275–305.

Ben-Tor, A. 1992. *The Archaeology of Ancient Israel*. New Haven: Yale University Press.

Berdan, Frances F. 1982. *The Aztecs of Central Mexico: An Imperial Society*. New York: Holt, Rinehart, Winston.

Bermann, M. 1994. *Lukurmata: Household Archaeology in Prehispanic Bolivia*. Princeton: Princeton University Press.

Berry, Sarah, and Leon Doyon. 2001. "Huatabampo." In *Encyclopedia of Prehistory*, Vol. 5: *Middle America*, ed. P.N. Peregrine and M. Ember. New York: Kluwer/Plenum, 218–220.

Biagi, Paolo, W. Torke, M. Tosi, and H. Uerpmann. 1984. "Qurum: A Case Study of Coastal Archaeology in Northern Oman." *World Archaeology* 16(1):43–61.

Bibby, T.G. 1969. *Looking for Dilmun*. New York: Praeger.

Binford, Lewis R. 1964. "A Consideration of Archaeological Research Design," *American Antiquity* 29:425–441.

———. 1971. "Post-Pleistocene Adaptations." In *Prehistoric Agriculture*, ed. Stuart Struever. Garden City, NY: Natural History Press.

———. 1977. *For Theory Building in Archaeology*. New York: Academic Press.

———. 1983. *Working at Archaeology*. New York: Academic Press.

———. 1984. *Faunal Remains from Klasies River Mouth*. Orlando, FL: Academic Press.

Binford, Lewis R., and Chuan Kun Ho. 1985. "Taphonomy at a Distance: Zhoukoudian, 'The Cave Home of Beijing Man'?" *Current Anthropology* 26:413–442.

Binford, Sally, and Lewis Binford. 1968. *New Perspectives in Archaeology*. Chicago: Aldine.

———. 1969. "Stone Tools and Human Behavior." *Scientific American* (April): 70–84.

Binghua, Wang. 1996. "A Preliminary Analysis of the Archaeological Cultures of the Bronze Age in the Region of Xinjiang." *Anthropology and Archaeology of Eurasia* 34(4):67–86.

Bird, Junius. 1988. *Travels and Archaeology in South Chile*. Iowa City: University of Iowa Press.

Blanton, Richard E. 2001. "Southern Mexican Highlands Classic." In *Encyclopedia of Prehistory*, Vol. 5: *Middle America*, ed. P.N. Peregrine and M. Ember. New York: Kluwer/Plenum, 381–392.

Blanton, Richard E., Gary Feinman, Stephen Kowalewski, and Linda Nicholas. 1999. *Ancient Oaxaca*. Cambridge: Cambridge University Press.

Blanton, Richard E., Stephen Kowalewski, Gary Feinman, and Laura Finsten. 1993. *Ancient Mesoamerica: A Comparison of Change in Three Regions*. Cambridge: Cambridge University Press.

Blitz, J.H. 1993. *Ancient Chiefdoms of the Tombigbee*. Tuscaloosa: University of Alabama Press.

Bloch, Marc. 1953. *The Historian's Craft*. New York: Vintage.

Blumler, Mark A., and Roger Byrne. 1991. "The Ecological Genetics of Domestication and the Origins of Agriculture," *Current Anthropology* 32:23–35.

Boardman, J. 1999. *The Greeks Overseas* (4th ed.). London: Thames and Hudson.

Bockstoce, John. 1979. *Archaeology of Cape Nome, Alaska*. Philadelphia: University Museum Monographs 38.

Bogucki, Peter. 1988. *Forest Farmers and Stockherders: Early Agriculture and Its Consequences in North-Central Europe*. Cambridge: Cambridge University Press.

Bordaz, Jacques. 1970. *Tools of the Old and New Stone Age*. Garden City, NY: Natural History Press.

Borden, Charles. 1975. *Origins and Development of Early Northwest Coast Culture to about 3000 B.C.* Ottawa: National Museum of Man, Mercury Series 45.

Bordes, François. 1961. "Mousterian Cultures in France." *Science* (September 22): 803–810.

Borrero, Luis, and Nora Franco. 1997. "Early Patagonian Hunter-Gatherers: Subsistence and Technology." *Journal of Anthropological Research* 53:219–239.

Braidwood, Linda S., and Robert J. Braidwood. 1986. "Prelude to the Appearance of Village-Farming Communities in Southwestern Asia." In *Ancient Anatolia: Aspects of Change and Cultural Development. Essays in Honor of Machteld J. Mellink*, ed. J.V. Vorys Canby, E. Porada, B.S. Ridgway, and T. Stech. Madison: University of Wisconsin Press, 3–11.

Braidwood, Robert. 1960. "The Agricultural Revolution." *Scientific American* 203(3): 130–152.

Braidwood, Robert, and Linda Braidwood. 1969. "Current Thoughts on the Beginnings of Food Production in Southwestern Asia" *Mélanges de l'Université Saint-Joseph* 45(8):149–155.

Braidwood, Robert, and Bruce Howe. 1960. "Prehistoric Investigations in Iraqi Kurdistan." *Studies in Ancient Oriental Civilization 31*. Chicago: University of Chicago Press.

Braidwood, Robert J., and Gordon R. Willey. 1962. "Conclusions and Afterthoughts." In *Courses toward Urban Life: Archeological Considerations of Some Cultural Alternatives*, ed. Robert J. Braidwood and Gordon R. Willey. Viking Fund Publications in Anthropology No. 32. Chicago: Aldine.

Branigan, Keith. 1988. *Archaeology Explained*. London: Duckworth.

Braudel, Fernand. 1980. *On History*. Chicago: University of Chicago Press.

Bräuer, Günter. 1984. "A Craniological Approach to the Origin of Anatomically Modern *Homo sapiens* in Africa and Implications for the Appearance of Modern Europeans." In Fred Smith and Frank Spencer, eds, *The Origins of Modern Humans*. New York: A.R. Liss, 327–410.

Bray, Tamara. 2002. "Inca." In *Encyclopedia of Prehistory*, Vol. 7: *South America*, ed. P.N. Peregrine and M. Ember. New York: Kluwer/Plenum, 150–194.

Brennan, Louis A. 1973. *Beginner's Guide to Archaeology; The Modern Digger's Step-by-step Introduction to the Expert Ways of Unearthing the Past*. Harrisburg, PA: Stackpole Books.

Briard, J. 1979. *The Bronze Age in Barbarian Europe*. London: Routledge.

Brochado, Jose P. 2002. "Tupi." In *Encyclopedia of Prehistory*, Vol. 7: *South America*, ed. P.N. Peregrine and M. Ember. New York: Kluwer/Plenum, 343–354.

Broom, Robert. 1950. *Finding the Missing Link*. London: Watts.

Brose, David, and N'omi Greber. 1979. *Hopewell Archaeology*. Kent, OH: Kent State University Press.

Brothwell, Don R. 1981. *Digging Up Bones: The Excavation, Treatment and Study of Human Skeletal Remains*. Ithaca, NY: Cornell University Press.

Brothwell, Don R., and A. Mark Pollard. 2001. *Handbook of Archaeological Science*. New York: John Wiley.

Browman, David. 2002a. "Andean Regional Development." In *Encyclopedia of Prehistory*, Vol. 7: *South America*, ed. P.N. Peregrine and M. Ember. New York: Kluwer/Plenum, 1–17.

———. 2002b. "Highland Andean Formative." In *Encyclopedia of Prehistory*, Vol. 7: *South America*, ed. P.N. Peregrine and M. Ember. New York: Kluwer/Plenum, 123–137.

Brown, James A. 1991. *Aboriginal Culture Adaptations in the Midwestern Prairies*. New York: Garland.

Brown, James A., and Patricia O'Brien. 1990. *At the Edge of Prehistory*. Kampsville, IL: Center for American Archaeology.

Bruhns, Karen O. 1994. *Ancient South America*. Cambridge: Cambridge University Press.

Brumfiel, Elizabeth M. 1983. "Aztec State Making: Ecology, Structure, and the Origin of the State," *American Anthropologist* 85:261–84.

Bryan, Alan, and Ruth Gruhn. 1993. *Brazilian Studies*. Corvalis, OR: Oregon State University, Center for the Study of the First Americans.

Bulbeck, David. 2001. "Island Southeast Asia Late Prehistoric." In *Encyclopedia of Prehistory*, Vol. 4: *Europe*, ed. P.N. Peregrine and M. Ember. New York: Kluwer/Plenum, 82–116.

Bulmer, Susan. 1975. "Settlement and Economy in Prehistoric Papua New Guinea: A Review of the Archaeological Evidence." *Journal de la Societe des Oceanistes* 31:7–75.

Burger, Richard L. 1984. *The Prehistoric Occupation of Chavin de Huantar, Peru*. Berkeley: University of California Press.

———. 1992. *Chavin and the Development of Andean Civilization*. London: Thames and Hudson.

Burley, David B. 1998. "Tongan Archaeology and the Tongan Past, 2850—150 B.P." *Journal of World Prehistory* 12:337–392.

Byrd, Brian F., and C.M. Monahan. 1995. "Death, Mortuary Ritual, and Natufian Social Structure." *Journal of Anthropological Archaeology* 14:251–287.

Byrne, Roger. 1987. "Climatic Change and the Origins of Agriculture." In *Studies in the Neolithic and Urban Revolutions*, ed. Linda Manzanilla. British Archaeological Reports International Series 349.

Caldwell, Joseph, and Robert Hall. 1964. *Hopewellian Studies*. Springfield, IL: Illinois State Museum.

Campbell, Sarah K. 1985. *Summary of Results: The Chief Joseph Dam Cultural Resources Project*. Seattle: University of Washington, Office of Public Archaeology.

Caneva, I. 1988. *El Geili: The History of a Middle Nile Environment, 7000 B.C.–A.D. 1500*. Oxford: British Archaeological Reports, International Series 424.

Cann, Rebecca. 1988. "DNA and Human Origins." *Annual Review of Anthropology* 17:127–143.

Cann, Rebecca, M. Stoneking, and A.C. Wilson. 1987. "Mitochondrial DNA and Human Evolution." *Nature* 325:31–36.

Carlson, Roy, and L.D. Bona. 1996. *Early Human Occupation in British Columbia*. Vancouver: University of British Columbia Press.

Carneiro, Robert L. 1970. "A Theory of the Origin of the State," *Science*, August 21:733–38.

———. 1988. "The Circumscription Theory: Challenge and Response," *American Behavioral Scientist* 31:506–508.

Carstens, Kenneth C., and Patty Jo Watson, eds. 1996. *Of Caves and Shell Mounds*. Tuscaloosa: University of Alabama Press.

Carter, Elizabeth, and Matthew Stolper. 1984. *Elam: Surveys of Political History and Archaeology.* Berkeley: University of California Press.

Chadwick, John. 1970. *The Mycenaean World.* Cambridge: Cambridge University Press.

Champion, Timothy, Clive Gamble, Stephen Shennan, and Alasdair Whittle. 1984. *Prehistoric Europe.* London: Academic Press.

Chang, Kwang-Chih. 1980. *Shang Civilization.* New Haven: Yale University Press.

———. 1986. *Archaeology of Ancient China.* New Haven: Yale University Press.

———. 1999. "China on the Eve of the Historical Period." In *The Cambridge History of Ancient China*, ed. M. Lowe and E.L. Shaughnessy. Cambridge: Cambridge University Press, 37–73.

Chapman, Carl H. 1975. *The Archaeology of Missouri I.* Columbia: University of Missouri Press.

Chapman, Jefferson. 1985. *Tellico Archaeology.* Knoxville: University of Tennessee Press.

Charnais, Peter. 1953. "Economic Factors in the Decline of the Roman Empire," *Journal of Economic History* 13: 412–424.

Charoenwongsa, Pisit, and Bennet Bronson. 1988. *Prehistoric Studies: The Stone and Metal Ages in Thailand.* Bangkok: Amarin.

Chartkoff, Joseph, and Kerry Chartkoff. 1984. *The Archaeology of California.* Stanford: Stanford University Press.

Chase, Arlen, and Prudence Rice. 1985. *The Lowland Maya Postclassic.* Austin: University of Texas Press.

Chatters, James C. 1986. *The Wells Reservoir Archaeological Project.* Elllengsburg: Central Washington University Archaeological Report 86-6.

Chattopadhyaya, Indrani. 2002. "South Asian Microlithic." In *Encyclopedia of Prehistory, Vol. 8: South and Southwest Asia*, ed. P.N. Peregrine and M. Ember. New York: Kluwer/Plenum, 309–323.

Chattopadhyaya, Umesh. 2002a. "Ganges Neolithic." In *Encyclopedia of Prehistory*, Vol. 8: *South and Southwest Asia*, ed. P.N. Peregrine and M. Ember. New York: Kluwer/Plenum, 127–132.

———. 2002b. "Gangetic India." In *Encyclopedia of Prehistory*, Vol. 8: *South and Southwest Asia*, ed. P.N. Peregrine and M. Ember. New York: Kluwer/Plenum, 133–137.

Chen, K.T., and F. Hiebert. 1995. "The Late Prehistory of Xinjiang in Relation to Its Neighbors." *Journal of World Prehistory* 9(2):243–300.

Cheng, Te-k'un. 1957. *Archaeological Studies in Szechwan.* Cambridge: Cambridge University Press.

———. 1966. *New Light on Prehistoric China.* Toronto: University of Toronto Press.

Chernetsov, V.N., and W. Moszynska. 1974. *Prehistory of Western Siberia.* Montreal: Arctic Institute of North America, McGill-Queen's University Press.

Chernykh, E.N. 1992. *Ancient Metallurgy in the USSR.* Cambridge: Cambridge University Press.

Chick, Garry. 1997. "Cultural Complexity: The Concept and Measurement." *Cross-Cultural Research* 31:275–307.

Childe, V. Gordon. 1936. *Man Make Himself.* New York: Mentor Books.

———. 1956. *Piecing Together the Past.* New York: Praeger.

Christiansen, George. 2001. "Late Eastern Woodland." In *Encyclopedia of Prehistory*, Vol. 6: *North America*, ed. P.N. Peregrine and M. Ember. New York: Kluwer/Plenum, 248–268.

Christenson, Andrew. 1989. *Tracing Archaeology's Past: The Historiography of Archaeology.* Carbondale: Southern Illinois University Press.

Chun-Tong, Yeung, and Brenda Li Wai-ling. 1995. *Archaeology in Southeast Asia.* Hong Kong: University of Hong Kong Museum and Art Gallery.

Church, Warren. 2002. "Chavín." In *Encyclopedia of Prehistory*, Vol. 7: *South America*, ed. P.N. Peregrine and M. Ember. New York: Kluwer/Plenum, 38–58.

Claessen, Henri J.M., and Pieter van de Velde. 1991. *Early State Economics.* New Brunswick: Transaction Publishers.

Clark, Anthony. 1996. *Seeing Beneath the Soil: Prospecting Methods in Archaeology.* London: Batsford.

Clark, J. Desmond. 1970. *The Prehistory of Africa.* New York: Praeger.

Clark, Donald W. 1979. *Ocean Bay: An Early North Pacific Maritime Culture.* Ottawa: National Museum of Man, Mercury Series 86.

———. 1991. *Western Subarctic Prehistory.* Hull: National Museum of Civilization.

———. 1992. "Archaeology on Kodiak: The Quest for Prehistory and Its Implications for North Pacific Prehistory." *Anthropological Papers of the University of Alaska* 24(1–2):109–126.

———. 1997. *The Early Kachemak Phase on Kodiak Island.* Hull: Canadian Museum of Civilization, Mercury Series 155.

———. 2001a. "Kodiak." In *Encyclopedia of Prehistory*, Vol. 2: *Arctic and Subarctic*, ed. P.N. Peregrine and M. Ember. New York: Kluwer/Plenum, 71–86.

———. 2001b. "Northwest Microblade." In *Encyclopedia of Prehistory*, Vol. 2: *Arctic and Subarctic*, ed. P.N. Peregrine and M. Ember. New York: Kluwer/Plenum, 129–134.

———. 2001c. "Ocean Bay." In *Encyclopedia of Prehistory*, Vol. 2: *Arctic and Subarctic*, ed. P.N. Peregrine and M. Ember. New York: Kluwer/Plenum, 152–164.

Clark, J. Desmond. 1959. *The Prehistory of Southern Africa.* London: Penguin.

———. 1982. "The Cultures of the Middle Palaeolithic/Middle Stone Age." In *Cambridge History of Africa*, Vol. 1: *From Earliest Times to c. 500 B.C.*, ed. J. Desmond Clark. Cambridge: Cambridge University Press, 248–341.

Clark, J. Desmond. 1993. "The Aterian of the Central Sahara." In *Environmental Change and Human Culture in the Nile Basin and Northern Africa until the Second Millennium B.C.*, ed. L. Krsysaniak. Poznan: Poznan Archaeological Museum, 49–67.

Clark, J. Desmond, and S.A. Brandt. 1984. *From Hunters to Farmers: The Causes and Consequences of Food Production in Africa.* Berkeley: University of California Press.

Clark, Gerald H. 1977. *Archaeology on the Alaska Peninsula: The Coast of Shelikof Strait 1963–1965.* Eugene: University of Oregon Anthropological Papers 13.

Clarke, David L. 1972. *Models in Archaeology.* London, Methuen.

———. 1978. *Analytical archaeology.* New York: Columbia University Press.

Clist, Bernard. 1989. "Archaeology in Gabon, 1886–1988," *African Archaeological Review* 7:59–95.

Close, Angela. 1987. *Prehistory of Arid North Africa.* Dallas, TX: Southern Methodist University Press.

Coe, Michael, and Richard Diehl. 1980. *In the Land of the Olmec.* Austin: University of Texas Press.

Cohen, Mark N. 1977. *The Food Crisis in Prehistory: Overpopulation and the Origins of Agriculture.* New Haven: Yale University Press.

———. 1987. "The Significance of Long-term Changes in Human Diet and Food Economy." In *Food and Evolution: Toward a Theory of Human Food Habits*, ed. Marvin Harris and Eric B. Ross. Philadelphia: Temple University Press, 269–73.

———. 1989. *Health and the Rise of Civilization.* New Haven: Yale University Press.

———. 2002. "Were Early Agriculturalists Less Healthy Than Food Collectors?" In *Archaeology: Original Readings in Method and Practice*, ed. P.N. Peregrine, C. R. Ember, and M. Ember. Upper Saddle River, NJ: Prentice Hall.

Cohen, Mark N., and George J. Armelagos. 1984. *Paleopathology at the Origins of Agriculture.* Orlando, FL: Academic Press.

Cohen, Ronald, and Elman R. Service. 1978. *Origins of the State: The Anthropology of*

*Political Evolution.* Philadelphia: Institute for the Study of Human Issues.

Cohen, Ronald, and Judith Toland. 1988. *State Formation and Political Legitimacy.* New Brunswick: Transaction Publishers.

COHMAP Personnel. 1988. "Climatic Changes of the Last 18,000 Years." *Science* 241:1043–1052.

Coles, John, and Anthony Harding. 1979. *The Bronze Age in Europe.* New York: St. Martins Press.

Collins, John. 1997. *The European Iron Age.* London: Routledge.

Connah, Graham. 1981. *Three Thousand Years in Africa: Man and His Environment in the Lake Chad Region of Nigeria.* Cambridge: Cambridge University Press.

———. 1987. *African Civilizations.* Cambridge: Cambridge University Press.

Conroy, Glenn C. 1990. *Primate Evolution.* New York: Norton.

Cooke, Richard. 2001. "Gran Coclé." In *Encyclopedia of Prehistory,* Vol. 5: *Middle America,* ed. P.N. Peregrine and M. Ember. New York: Kluwer/Plenum, 197–203.

Cordell, Linda S. 1994. *Ancient Pueblo Peoples.* Washington, DC: Smithsonian Institution Press.

———. 1997. *Archaeology of the Southwest.* San Diego: Academic Press.

Cordell, Linda S., and George Gumerman. 1989. *The Dynamics of Southwestern Prehistory.* Washington, DC: Smithsonian Institution Press.

Cordy, Ross H. 1981. *A Study of Prehistoric Change: The Development of Complex Societies in the Hawaiian Islands.* New York: Academic Press.

———. 1993. *The Lelu Stone Ruins.* Honolulu: University of Hawaii Press, Asian and Pacific Archaeology Series, Number 10.

Corrales Ulloa, Francisco. 2001. "Chiriquí." In *Encyclopedia of Prehistory,* Vol. 5: *Middle America,* ed. P.N. Peregrine and M. Ember. New York: Kluwer/Plenum, 54–68.

Coupland, Gary G. 1998. "Maritime Adaptation and Evolution of the Developed Northwest Coast Pattern on the Central Northwest Coast." *Arctic Anthropology* 35:36–56.

———. 2001. "Middle Northwest Coast." In *Encyclopedia of Prehistory,* Vol. 2: *Arctic and Subarctic,* ed. P.N. Peregrine and M. Ember. New York: Kluwer/Plenum, 116–126.

Cowan, C. Wesley. 1987. *First Farmers of the Middle Ohio Valley: Fort Ancient Societies, A.D. 1000–1670.* Cincinnati: Museum of Natural History.

Cowan, C. Wesley, and Patty Jo Watson. 1992. *The Origins of Agriculture: An International Perspective.* Washington, DC: Smithsonian Institution Press.

Cowgill, George L. 1997. "State and Society at Teotihuacan, Mexico." *Annual Review of Anthropology* 26:129–161.

———. 2001. "Central Mexico Classic." In *Encyclopedia of Prehistory,* Vol. 5: *Middle America,* ed. P.N. Peregrine and M. Ember. New York: Kluwer/Plenum, 12–21.

Crabtree, Pam, and Douglas Campana. 2001. *Archaeology and Prehistory.* Boston: McGraw-Hill.

Craib, John. 1983. "Micronesian Prehistory: An Archeological Overview." *Science* 219:922–927

Crawford, Harriet. 1991. *Sumer and the Sumerians.* Cambridge: Cambridge University Press.

———. 1998. *Dilmun and Its Gulf Neighbours.* Cambridge: Cambridge University Press.

Cronyn, J.M. 1990. *The Elements of Archaeological Conservation.* New York: Routledge.

Crown, Patricia, and W. James Judge. 1991. *Chaco and Hohokam: Prehistoric Regional Systems in the American Southwest.* Santa Fe, NM: School of American Research Press.

Culbert, T. Patrick. 1991. *Classic Maya Political History.* Cambridge: Cambridge University Press.

Cullen, T. 1995. "Mesolithic Mortuary Ritual at Franchthi Cave, Greece." *Antiquity* 69:270–289.

Cunliffe, Barry. 1994. "Iron Age Societies in Western Europe and Beyond, 800–140 B.C." In *Oxford Illustrated Prehistory of Europe,* ed. B. Cunliffe. Oxford: Oxford University Press, 336–372.

———. 1997. *The Ancient Celts.* Oxford: Oxford University Press.

D'Altroy, Terrence N. 1992. *Provincial Power in the Inka Empire.* Washington, DC: Smithsonian Institution Press.

Dancy, W.S., and P. Pacheco. 1997. *Ohio Hopewell Community Organization.* Kent, OH: Kent State University Press.

Daniel, Glyn. 1950. *A Hundred Years of Archaeology.* London: Duckworth.

———. 1981. *A Short History of Archaeology.* London: Thames and Hudson.

Daniel, I. Randolph. 2001. "Early Eastern Archaic." In *Encyclopedia of Prehistory,* Vol. 6: *North America,* ed. P.N. Peregrine and M. Ember. New York: Kluwer/Plenum, 55–80.

Dart, Raymond. 1925. "Australopithecus africanus: The Man-Ape of South Africa," *Nature,* 115:195.

David, Nicholas, and Jonathan Driver. 1989. *The Next Archaeology Workbook.* Philadelphia: University of Pennsylvania Press.

Davidson, Janet. 1984. *Prehistory of New Zealand.* Auckland: Longman Paul.

———. 2001. "Maori." In *Encyclopedia of Prehistory,* Vol. 4: *Europe,* ed.

P.N. Peregrine and M. Ember. New York: Kluwer/Plenum, 222–242.

Davies, Jack. 1992. "Review of Aegean Prehistory I: The Islands of the Aegean." *American Journal of Archaeology* 96: 699–756.

Davies, Simon. 1987. *The Archaeology of Animals.* New Haven, Yale University Press.

Davis, Loren. 2001. "Cascade." In *Encyclopedia of Prehistory,* Vol. 6: *North America,* ed. P.N. Peregrine and M. Ember. New York: Kluwer/Plenum, 27–29.

Dawson, Alistar. 1992. *Ice Age Earth.* London: Routledge.

Day, Michael. 1986. *Guide to Fossil Man.* Chicago: University of Chicago Press.

Deacon, Hillary J. 1976. *Where Hunters Gathered: A Study of Holocene Stone Age Peoples in the Eastern Cape.* Cape Town: South African Archaeological Society.

Deacon, Janette. 1984. "Later Stone Age People and Their Descendents in Southern Africa." In *Southern African Prehistory and Paleoenvironments,* ed. R. Klein. Rotterdam: Balkema, 221–328.

Deacon, Terrence. 1997. *The Symbolic Species: The Co-Evolution of Language and the Brain.* New York: W.W. Norton.

Deagan, Kathleen. 1988. "The Archaeology of the Spanish Contact Period in the Caribbean." *Journal of World Prehistory* 2:187–231.

Dean, Patricia. 2001. "Fremont." In *Encyclopedia of Prehistory,* Vol. 6: *North America,* ed. P.N. Peregrine and M. Ember. New York: Kluwer/Plenum, 195–212.

Debono, Fernand, and Bodil Mortensen. 1988. *The Predynastic Cemetery at Heliopolis.* Mainz: Phillip von Zabern.

DeCorse, Christopher, and Sam Spiers. 2001a. "West African Iron Age." In *Encyclopedia of Prehistory,* Vol. 1: *Africa,* ed. P.N. Peregrine and M. Ember. New York: Kluwer/Plenum, 313–318.

———. 2001b. "West African Regional Development." In *Encyclopedia of Prehistory,* Vol. 1: *Africa,* ed. P.N. Peregrine and M. Ember. New York: Kluwer/Plenum, 339–345.

DeLaguna, Frederica. 1975. *The Archaeology of Cook Inlet, Alaska.* Anchorage: Alaska Historical Society.

Delougaz, P., and H. Kantor. 1996. *Choga Mish,* Volume I: *The First Five Seasons.* Chicago: Oriental Institute.

de Lumley, Henry. 1969. "A Paleolithic Camp at Nice." *Scientific American* (May):42–50.

Demarest, Arthur, and Geoffrey Conrad. 1992. *Ideology and Pre-Columbian Civilizations.* Santa Fe: School of American Research Press.

de Maret, Pierre. 1985. "Recent Archaeological Research and Dates from Central

Africa." *Journal of African History* 26: 129–148.

Denbow, James. 1990. "Congo to Kalihari: Data and Hypotheses about the Political Economy of the Western Stream of the Early Iron Age." *African Archaeological Review* 8:139–176.

Dent, Richard. 1995. *Chesapeake Prehistory.* New York: Plenum.

Deo, S.B. 1982. *Recent Researches on the Chalcolithic and Megalithic Cultures of the Deccan.* Madras: University of Madras.

Derevianko, A.P. 1990. *Paleolithic of North Asia and the Problem of Ancient Migrations.* Novosibirsk: Academy of Sciences of the USSR.

———. 1998. *The Paleolithic of Siberia: New Discoveries and Interpretations.* Urbana: University of Illinois Press.

Derevyanko, A.P., and Lu Zun-E. 1992. "Upper Paleolithic Cultures." In *History of Civilizations of Central Asia,* Vol. 1, ed. A.H. Dani and V.M. Masson. Paris: UNESCO Publishing, 89–126.

Dever, William. 1987. "Middle Bronze Age: The Zenith of the Urban Canaanite Era." *Biblical Archaeologist* 50:149–177.

Dhavalikar, M.K. 1988. *First Farmers of the Deccan.* Pune: Ravish.

Diakonoff, I.M. 1985a. "Elam." In *The Cambridge History of Iran,* Vol. 2: *The Median and Archaemenian Periods,* ed. I. Gerschevitch. Cambridge: Cambridge University Press, 1–24.

———. 1985b. "Media." In *The Cambridge History of Iran,* Vol. 2: *The Median and Archaemenian Periods,* ed. I. Gerschevitch. Cambridge: Cambridge University Press, 36–148.

Dickinson, Oliver. 1994. *The Aegean Bronze Age.* Cambridge: Cambridge University Press.

Dickson, D. Bruce. 1990. *The Dawn of Belief.* Tucson: University of Arizona Press.

———. 2001. "Western European Mesolithic." In *Encyclopedia of Prehistory,* Vol. 4: *Europe,* ed. P.N. Peregrine and M. Ember. New York: Kluwer/ Plenum, 436–454.

Diehl, Richard A. 1983. *Tula: The Toltec Capital of Ancient Mexico.* New York: Thames and Hudson.

Diehl, Richard, and Catherine Berlo. 1989. *Mesoamerica after the Decline of Teotihuacan, A.D. 700–900.* Washington, DC: Dumbarton Oaks.

Dillehay, Thomas D. 1989. *Monte Verde: A Late Pleistocene Settlement in Chile,* Vol. 1: *Paleoenvironmental and Site Context.* Washington, DC: Smithsonian Institution Press.

———. 1997. *Monte Verde: a Late Pleistocene Settlement in Chile,* Vol. 2: *The Archaeological Context.* Washington, DC: Smithsonian Institution Press.

———. 2000. *The Settlement of the Americas: A New Prehistory.* New York: Basic Books.

———. 2002. "Old South American Hunting-Collecting." In *Encyclopedia of Prehistory,* Vol. 7: *South America,* ed. P.N. Peregrine and M. Ember. New York: Kluwer/Plenum, 293–303.

Dillehay, Thomas D., G. Ardila, G. Politis, and M. Beltrão. 1992. "Earliest Hunter-Gatherers of South America." *Journal of World Prehistory* 6:145–204.

Dillon, Brian D. 1993. *Practical Archaeology: Field and Laboratory Techniques and Archaeological Logistics.* Los Angeles: Institute of Archaeology, University of California, Los Angeles.

Dobres, Marcia-Anne. 1998. "Venus Figurines." In Brian Fagan, ed., *Oxford Companion to Archaeology.* Oxford: Oxford University Press, 740–741.

Dobzhansky, Theodosius. 1962. *Mankind Evolving: The Evolution of the Human Species.* New Haven, CT: Yale University Press.

Dolukhanov, P.M. 1986. "Foragers and Farmers in West-Central Asia." In *Hunters in Transition,* ed. M. Zvelebil. Cambridge: Cambridge University Press, 121–123.

Donnan, Christopher. 1985. *Early Ceremonial Architecture in the Andes.* Washington, DC: Dumbarton Oaks.

Downum, Christian E., Paul R. Fish, and Suzanne K. Fish. 1994. "Refining the Role of Cerros de Trincheras in Southern Arizona." *The Kiva* 59:27–38.

Doyel, David. 2001. "Late Hohokam." In *Encyclopedia of Prehistory,* Vol. 6: *North America,* ed. P.N. Peregrine and M. Ember. New York: Kluwer/Plenum, 278–290.

Dragoo, Don. 1963. *Mounds for the Dead: An Analysis of the Adena Culture.* Pittsburgh: Carnegie Museum.

Duarte, Cidalia, J. Mauricio, P.B. Pettitt, P. Souto, E. Trinkaus, H. van der Plicht, and J. Zilhao. 1999. "The Early Upper Paleolithic Human Skeleton from the Abrigo do Lagar Velho (Portugal) and Modern Human Emergence in Iberia." *Proceedings of the National Academy of Sciences of the United States* 96: 7604–7609.

Dumond, Don E. 1981. *Archaeology on the Alaska Peninsula: The Naknek Region 1960–1975.* University of Oregon Anthropological Papers 21.

———. 1987. *Eskimos and Aleuts.* New York: Thames and Hudson.

———. 2001a. "Norton." In *Encyclopedia of Prehistory,* Vol. 2: *Arctic and Subarctic,* ed. P.N. Peregrine and M. Ember. New York: Kluwer/Plenum, 135–151.

———. 2001b. "Western Arctic Small Tool." In *Encyclopedia of Prehistory,* Vol. 2: *Arctic and Subarctic,* ed. P.N. Peregrine

and M. Ember. New York: Kluwer/ Plenum, 213–224.

Dye, D.H., and C.A. Cox, eds. 1990. *Towns and Temples Along the Mississippi.* Tuscaloosa: University of Alabama Press.

Earle, Timothy. 1978. *Economic and Social Organization of a Complex Chiefdom: The Halele'a District, Kaua'i, Hawaii.* Ann Arbor: University of Michigan, Museum of Anthropology, Anthropological Papers 63.

———. 2002. "Andean Regional States." In *Encyclopedia of Prehistory,* Vol. 7: *South America,* ed. P.N. Peregrine and M. Ember. New York: Kluwer/Plenum, 18–33.

Edens, Christopher, and Wilkinson, T.J. 1998. "Southwest Arabia During the Holocene: Recent Archaeological Developments." *Journal of World Prehistory* 12:55–119.

Eggert, Manfred K.H. 1992. "The Central African Rain Forest: Historical Speculation and Archaeological Facts." *World Archaeology* 24:1–24.

———. 1997. "Equatorial Africa Iron Age." In *Encyclopedia of Precolonial Africa,* ed. J.O. Vogel. Walnut Creek, CA: Altamira, 429–435.

Ehrenreich, Robert. 1991. *Metals in Society.* Philadelphia: The University Museum, University of Pennsylvania.

Eldredge, Niles. 1991. *Fossils: The Evolution and Extinction of Species.* New York: H.N. Abrams.

Ellis, Chris J., and Neal Ferris. 1990. *The Archaeology of Southern Ontario to A.D. 1650.* London: Ontario Archaeological Society.

Emerson, T.E. 1997. *Cahokia and the Archaeology of Power.* Tuscaloosa: University of Alabama Press.

Emerson, T.E., and R.B. Lewis. 1991. *Cahokia and the Hinterlands: Middle Mississippian Cultures of the Midwest.* Urbana: University of Illinois Press.

Emory, Kenneth P. 1933. *Stone Remains in the Society Islands.* Honolulu: Bernice P. Bishop Museum, Bulletin 116.

Engels, Friedrich. 1884. *Origin of the Family, Private Property, and the State.* New York: International Publishers.

Englert, Sebastian. 1970. *The Island at the Center of the World: New Light on Easter Island.* New York: Scribners.

Engwall, Evan. 2001a. "Early Northwest South American Littoral." In *Encyclopedia of Prehistory,* Vol. 5: *Middle America,* ed. P.N. Peregrine and M. Ember. New York: Kluwer/Plenum, 147–154.

———. 2001b. "Late Northwest South American Littoral." In *Encyclopedia of Prehistory,* Vol. 5: *Middle America,* ed. P.N. Peregrine and M. Ember. New York: Kluwer/Plenum, 268–291.

Enloe, James. 2001. "Magdelenian." In *Encyclopedia of Prehistory,* Vol. 4:

*Europe,* ed. P.N. Peregrine and M. Ember. New York: Kluwer/Plenum, 198–209.

Epstein, C. 1977. "The Chalcolithic Culture of the Golan." *Biblical Archeologist* 40: 57–62.

———. 1998. *The Chalcolithic Culture of the Golan.* Jerusalem: Israel Antiquities Authority.

Erdosy, George. 1987. "Early Historic Cities in India." *South Asian Studies* 3:1–23.

Erlandson, Jon, Mark Tveskov, and Scott Byram. 1998. "The Development of Maritime Adaptations on the Southern Northwest Coast of North America." *Arctic Anthropology* 35:6–22.

Esse, D. 1991. *Subsistence, Trade and Social Change in Early Bronze Age Palestine.* Chicago: University of Chicago Press.

Fagan, Brian. 1995. *Time Detectives: How Archaeologists Use Technology to Recapture the Past.* New York: Simon & Schuster.

———. 2000. *In the Beginning: An Introduction to Archaeology.* Upper Saddle River, NJ: Prentice Hall.

———. 2001. *People of the Earth.* Upper Saddle River, NJ: Prentice Hall.

Falk, Dean. 1980. "Hominid Brain Evolution: The Approach from Paleoneurology." *Yearbook of Physical Anthropology.* 23:93–108.

———. 1983. "Cerebral Cortices of East African Early Hominids." *Science* 221:1072–1074.

Farnsworth, Kenneth, and Thomas Emerson. 1986. *Early Woodland Archaeology.* Kampsville, IL: Center for American Archaeology.

Fattovich, R. et al. 1984. "The Archaeology of the Eastern Sahel, Sudan: Preliminary Results." *African Archaeology Review* 2:173–188.

Feder, Kenneth L. 1998. *Lessons from the Past: An Introductory Reader in Archaeology.* Mountain View, CA: Mayfield.

Feil, D.K. 1987. "Papua New Guinea Highlands Prehistory: A Social Anthropologist's View." In *The Evolution of Highland Papua New Guinea Societies,* ed. D.K. Feil. Cambridge: Cambridge University Press, 12–37.

Feinman, Gary. 2001. "Postclassic Southern Mexican Highlands." In *Encyclopedia of Prehistory,* Vol. 5: *Middle America,* ed. P.N. Peregrine and M. Ember. New York: Kluwer/Plenum, 361–377.

Feinman, Gary M., Stephen A. Kowalewski, Laura Finsten, Richard E. Blanton, and Linda Nicholas. 1985. "Long-Term Demographic Change: A Perspective from the Valley of Oaxaca, Mexico," *Journal of Field Archaeology* 12:333–362.

Feinman, Gary M., and Joyce Marcus. 1998. *Archaic States.* Santa Fe, NM: School of American Research.

Fernandez Castro, M.C. 1995. *Iberia in Prehistory.* Oxford: Blackwell.

Finkbeiner, Uwe, and Wolfgang Röllig. 1986. *Gamdat Nasr: Period or Regional Style?* Wiesbaden: Beihefte zum Tübinger Atlas des Vorderen Orients, Reihe B.

Finsten, Laura. 2001. "Late Highland Mesoamerican Preclassic." In *Encyclopedia of Prehistory,* Vol. 5: *Middle America,* ed. P.N. Peregrine and M. Ember. New York: Kluwer/Plenum, 257–267.

Fish, Paul R. 1981. "Beyond Tools: Middle Paleolithic Debitage Analysis and Cultural Inference." *Journal of Anthropological Research* 37:374–386.

———. 2001. "Trincheras." In *Encyclopedia of Prehistory,* Vol. 5: *Middle America,* ed. P.N. Peregrine and M. Ember. New York: Kluwer/Plenum, 393–396.

Fitting, James E. 1972. "The Schultz Site at Green Point: A Stratified Occupation in the Saginaw Valley of Michigan." *Memoirs of the Museum of Anthropology* 4. Ann Arbor: University of Michigan.

Fitzhugh, William W., and Aron Crowell. 1988. *Crossroads of the Continents: Cultures of Siberia and Alaska.* Washington, DC: Smithsonian Institution Press.

Fladmark, Knut. 1990. *Prehistory of British Columbia.* Ottawa: National Museum of Man.

Flannery, Kent V. 1965. "The Ecology of Early Food Production in Mesopotamia," *Science,* March 12, 1252.

———. 1969. "The Origins and Ecological Effects of Early Domestication in Iran and the Near East." In *The Domestication and Exploitation of Plants and Animals,* ed. Peter J. Ucko and G. W. Dimbleby. Chicago: Aldine.

———. 1972. "The Cultural Evolution of Civilizations," *Annual Review of Ecology and Systematics* 3:399–426.

———. 1973. "The Origins of Agriculture," *Annual Review of Anthropology* 2:274.

———. 1976. *The Early Mesoamerican Village.* New York: Academic Press.

———. 1986. *Guila Naquitz: Archaic Foraging and Early Agriculture in Oaxaca, Mexico.* New York: Academic Press.

Fleagle, John G. 1999. *Primate Adaptation and Evolution.* San Diego: Academic Press.

Fleming, Stuart. 1976. *Dating in Archaeology.* New York: St. Martin's Press.

Fortey, Richard. 1991. *Fossils: The Key to the Past.* Cambridge: Harvard University Press.

Foster, Michael, and Shirley Gorenstein. 2000. *Greater Mesoamerica: The Archaeology of West and Northwest Mexico.* Salt Lake City: University of Utah Press.

Foster, Michael, and Phil Weigand. 1985. *Archaeology of West and Northwest Mesoamerica.* Boulder, CO: Westview Press.

Fowler, William R. 1991. *Formation of Complex Society in Southeastern Mesoamerica.* Boca Raton, FL: CRC Press.

Fox, John. 1987. *Maya Postclassic State Formation.* Cambridge: Cambridge University Press.

Frank, Susan. 1982. *Glass and Archaeology.* New York: Academic Press.

Frayer, David, M. Wolpoff, A. Thorne, F. Smith, and G. Pope. 1993. "Theories of Modern Human Origins: The Paleontological Test." *American Anthropologist* 95:14–50.

Freeman, Leslie G. 1994. "Torralba and Ambrona: A Review of Discoveries." In Robert Corruccini and Russell Ciochon, eds, *Integrative Paths to the Past.* Upper Saddle River, NJ: Prentice Hall, 597–637.

Frere, Shepherd. 1987. *Britannia: A History of Roman Britain.* 3rd ed. London: Routledge & Kegan Paul.

Frison, George C. 1991. *Prehistoric Hunters of the High Plains.* San Diego: Academic Press.

Frumkin, Gregoire. 1970. *Archaeology in Soviet Central Asia.* Leiden: E.J. Brill.

Fry, Robert. 2001. "Postclassic Maya." In *Encyclopedia of Prehistory,* Vol. 5: *Middle America,* ed. P.N. Peregrine and M. Ember. New York: Kluwer/Plenum, 353–360.

Gabunia, Leo, A. Vekua, D. Lordkipanidze, et al. 2000. "Earliest Pleistocene Hominid Cranial Remains from Dmanisi, Republic of Georgia: Taxonomy, Geological Setting, and Age." *Science* 288:1019–1025.

Galaty, Michael. 2001. "Southeastern European Bronze Age." In *Encyclopedia of Prehistory,* Vol. 4: *Europe,* ed. P.N. Peregrine and M. Ember. New York: Kluwer/Plenum, 351–355.

Gamble, Clive. 1986. *The Paleolithic Settlement of Europe.* Cambridge: Cambridge University Press.

Gao, Q., and Y.K. Lee. 1993. "A Biological Perspective on Yangshao Kinship." *Journal of Anthropological Archaeology* 12:266–298.

Garanger, Jose. 1967. "Archaeology and the Society Islands." In *Polynesian Culture History: Essays in Honor of Kenneth P. Emory,* ed. Genevieve Highland. Honolulu: Bernice P. Bishop Museum, 215–240.

———. 1982. *Archaeology of the New Hebrides: Contribution to Knowledge of the Central Islands.* Sydney: University of Sydney.

Gheorghiu, Dragos. 2001a. "Southeastern European Early Chalcolithic." In *Encyclopedia of Prehistory,* Vol. 4: *Europe,* ed. P.N. Peregrine and M. Ember. New York: Kluwer/Plenum, 356–366.

———. 2001b. "Southeastern European Late Chalcolithic." In *Encyclopedia of Prehistory,* Vol. 4: *Europe,* ed. P.N. Peregrine and M. Ember. New York: Kluwer/Plenum, 367–380.

Ghosh, Amalananda. 1973. *The City in Early Historical India.* Shimla: Indian Institute of Advanced Study.

———. 1990. *An Encyclopedia of Indian Archaeology,* 2 vols. Leiden: E.J. Brill.

Gibbons, Ann. 1995. "First Americans: Not Mammoth Hunters, but Forest Dwellers?" *Science* (April 19):346–347.

Gibbon, Guy. 1984. *Anthropological Archaeology.* New York: Columbia University Press.

———. 1989. *Explanation in Archaeology.* Oxford: Basil Blackwell.

———. 2001. "Oneota." In *Encyclopedia of Prehistory,* Vol. 6: *North America,* ed. P.N. Peregrine and M. Ember. New York: Kluwer/Plenum, 389–407.

Giddings, James L. 1964. *The Archaeology of Cape Denbigh.* Providence, RI: Brown University Press.

Giddings, James L., and Douglas D. Anderson. 1986. *Beach Ridge Archaeology of Cape Krusenstern.* Washington, DC: National Park Service, Publications in Archaeology 20.

Gifford, Edward W. 1951. *Archaeological Excavations in Fiji.* Berkeley: University of California Press.

Gilead, I. 1988. "The Chalcolithic Period in the Levant." *Journal of World Prehistory* 2:398–443.

Gilman, Antonio. 1974. "Neolithic of Northwest Africa." *Antiquity* 48:273–282.

———. 1975. *Prehistory of Tangier, Morocco.* Cambridge, MA: Peabody Museum of Archaeology and Ethnology.

Glover, Ian. 1977. "The Hoabinhian: Hunter-Gatherers of Early Agriculturalists in Southeast Asia?" In *Hunters, Gatherers, and First Farmers Beyond Europe,* ed. J.V.S. Megaw. Leicester: Leicester University Press, 145–166.

Glover, Ian, and B. Syme. 1993. "The Bronze Age in Southeast Asia." *Man and Environment* 16:41–74.

Glumac, Petar. 1991. *Recent Trends in Archaeometallurgical Research.* Philadelphia: The University Museum, University of Pennsylvania.

Goebel, Ted. 2001a. "Siberian Early Upper Paleolithic." In *Encyclopedia of Prehistory,* Vol. 2: *Arctic and Subarctic,* ed. P.N. Peregrine and M. Ember. New York: Kluwer/Plenum, 181–185.

———. 2001b. "Siberian Late Upper Paleolithic." In *Encyclopedia of Prehistory,* Vol. 2: *Arctic and Subarctic,* ed. P.N. Peregrine and M. Ember. New York: Kluwer/Plenum, 186–191.

———. 2001c. "Siberian Middle Upper Paleolithic." In *Encyclopedia of Prehistory,* Vol. 2: *Arctic and Subarctic,* ed. P.N. Peregrine and M. Ember. New York: Kluwer/Plenum, 192–196.

———. 2001d. "Siberian Mousterian." In *Encyclopedia of Prehistory,* Vol. 2: *Arctic and Subarctic,* ed. P.N. Peregrine and M. Ember. New York: Kluwer/Plenum, 197–200.

Goebel, Ted, and Peter Peregrine. 2001. "Siberian Neolithic and Bronze Age." In *Encyclopedia of Prehistory,* Vol. 2: *Arctic and Subarctic,* ed. P.N. Peregrine and M. Ember. New York: Kluwer/Plenum, 201–202.

Goldberg, Paul, D. Nash, and M. Petraglia. 1993. *Formation Processes in Archaeological Context.* Madison, WI: Prehistory Press.

Golden, Jonathan. 2002a. "Early Bronze Age." In *Encyclopedia of Prehistory,* Vol. 8: *South and Southwest Asia,* ed. P.N. Peregrine and M. Ember. New York: Kluwer/Plenum, 86–111.

———. 2002b. "Middle Bronze Age." In *Encyclopedia of Prehistory,* Vol. 8: *South and Southwest Asia,* ed. P.N. Peregrine and M. Ember. New York: Kluwer/Plenum, 291–303.

Goldstein, Paul. 2002. "Tiwanaku." In *Encyclopedia of Prehistory,* Vol. 7: *South America,* ed. P.N. Peregrine and M. Ember. New York: Kluwer/Plenum, 319–342.

Golson, Jack. 1977. "No Room at the Top: Agricultural Intensification in the New Guinea Highlands." In *Sunda and Sahul: Prehistoric Studies in Southeast Asia, Melanesia and Australia,* ed. J Allen, J. Golson, and R. Jones. London: Academic Press, 601–638.

———. 1989. "The Origins and Development of New Guinea Agriculture." In *Foraging and Farming: The Evolution of Plant Exploitation,* ed. David R. Harris and Gordon C. Hillman. London: Unwin Hyman, 678–687.

Golson, Jack, and D.S. Gardiner. 1990. "Agriculture and Sociopolitical Organization in New Guinea Highlands Prehistory." *Annual Review of Anthropology* 19:395–417.

Goodman, Alan H., and George J. Armelagos. 1985. "Disease and Death at Dr. Dickson's Mounds," *Natural History,* September 18.

Gopher, A., and Gophna, R. 1993. "Cultures of the Eighth and Seventh Millennia BP in the Southern Levant: A Review of the 1990s." *Journal of World Prehistory* 7: 297–353.

Goring-Morris, Nigel. 2002a. Epipaleolithic. In *Encyclopedia of Prehistory,* Vol. 8: *South and Southwest Asia,* ed. P.N. Peregrine and M. Ember. New York: Kluwer/Plenum, 122–126.

———. 2002b. Natufian. In *Encyclopedia of Prehistory,* Vol. 8: *South and Southwest Asia,* ed. P.N. Peregrine and M. Ember. New York: Kluwer/Plenum, 304–308.

Gorman, Chester. 1971. "The Hoabinhian and After: Subsistence Patterns in Southeast Asia during the Late Pleistocene and Early Recent Periods." *World Archaeology* 2:300–320.

Gosden, Christopher. 1989. "Lapita Sites of the Bismark Archipelago." *Antiquity* 63:561–586.

———. 1999. *Anthropology and Archaeology: A Changing Relationship.* New York: Routledge.

Graves, Michael W. 1986. "Organization and Differentiation within Late Prehistoric Ranked Social Units, Mariana Islands, Western Pacific." *Journal of Field Archaeology* 13:139–154.

Graves, Michael, and R.C. Green. 1993. *The Evolution and Organization of Prehistoric Society in Polynesia.* Auckland: New Zealand Archaeological Monograph 19.

Grayson, Donald K. 1993. *The Desert's Past: A Natural Prehistory of the Great Basin.* Washington, DC: Smithsonian Institution Press.

Green, Miranda. 1995. *The Celtic World.* London: Routledge.

Green, Roger C. 1996. "Settlement Patterns and Complex Society in the Windward Society Islands." In *Mémoire de Pierre, Mémoire d'Homme. Hommage à José Garanger,* eds. Michèle Julien, M. Orliac, C. Orliac. Paris: Publications de la Sorbonne, 209–227.

Green, Roger C., and J.N. Davidson. 1969. *Archaeology in Western Samoa.* Auckland: Auckland Institute and Museum, Bulletin, Number 6.

Green, Roger C., K. Green, R. Rappaport, A. Rappaport, and J.M. Davidson. 1967. *Archaeology on the Island of Mo'orea, French Polynesia.* New York: American Museum of Natural History, Anthropological Papers 51, Part 2.

Green, William. 1995. *Oneota Archaeology: Past, Present, and Future.* Iowa City: University of Iowa, Office of the State Archaeologist.

Greenberg, Joseph H., and Merritt Ruhlen. 1992. "Linguistic Origins of Native Americans." *Scientific American* (November): 94–99.

Greenfield, Haskell. 2001. "European Early Bronze Age." In *Encyclopedia of Prehistory,* Vol. 4: *Europe,* ed. P.N. Peregrine and M. Ember. New York: Kluwer/Plenum, 139–156.

Greengo, Robert E. 1986. *Prehistory of the Priest Rapids-Wanapum Region, Columbia River, Washington.* Oxford: British Archaeological Reports, International Series 290.

Gregg, Michael, Robert Bozell, and Susan Vehik. 2001. "Plains Woodland." In *Encyclopedia of Prehistory,* Vol. 6: *North America,* ed. P.N. Peregrine and M. Ember. New York: Kluwer/Plenum, 432–452.

Gregg, S.A. 1988. *Foragers and Farmers: Population Interaction and Agricultural*

*Expansion in Prehistoric Europe.* Chicago: University of Chicago Press.

Gremillion, Kristen. 1997. *People, Plants, and Landscapes: Studies in Paleoethnobotany.* Tuscaloosa: University of Alabama Press.

Grine, Frederick E. 1986. "Dental Evidence for Dietary Differences in Australopithecus and Paranthropus: A Quantitative Analysis of Permanent Molar Microwear," *Journal of Human Evolution* 15:783–822.

——. 1988. *Evolutionary History of the "Robust" Australopithecines.* New York: Aldine de Gruyter.

——. 1993. "Australopithecine Taxonomy and Phylogeny: Historical Background and Recent Interpretation." In *The Human Evolution Source Book,* ed. R.L. Ciochon and J.G. Fleagle. Engelwood Cliffs, NJ: Prentice Hall.

Grove, David C. 1997. "Olmec Archaeology: A Half Century of Research and Its Accomplishments." *Journal of World Prehistory* 11:51–101.

Gumerman, George. 1991. *Exploring the Hohokam.* Albuquerque: University of New Mexico Press.

——. 1994. *Themes in Southwest Prehistory.* Santa Fe: School of American Research Press.

Gururaja Rao, S.P. 1972. *Megalithic Culture in South India.* Mysore: University of Mysore.

Haaland, R. 1987. *Socio-Economic Differentiation in the Neolithic Sudan.* Oxford: British Archaeological Reports, International Series 350.

Haas, Jonathan. 1982. *The Evolution of the Prehistoric State.* New York: Columbia University Press.

——. 2001. "Early Anasazi." In *Encyclopedia of Prehistory,* Vol. 6: *North America,* ed. P.N. Peregrine and M. Ember. New York: Kluwer/Plenum, 34–42.

Haas, Jonathan, Shelia Pozorski, and Thomas Pozorski. 1987. *The Origins and Development of Andean States.* Cambridge: Cambridge University Press.

Haeussler, Alice M. 1996. *The Dental Anthropology of Russia, Ukraine, Georgia: Evaluation of Five Hypotheses for Paleo-Indian Origins.* Ann Arbor: UMI.

——. 2001. "Eastern European Mesolithic." In *Encyclopedia of Prehistory,* Vol. 4: *Europe,* ed. P.N. Peregrine and M. Ember. New York: Kluwer/Plenum, 91–123.

Hall, K.R. 1985. *Maritime Trade and State Development in Early Southeast Asia.* Sydney: George Allen and Unwin.

Harding, A.F. 1983. "The Bronze Age in Central and Eastern Europe: Advances and Prospects." In *Advances in World Archaeology,* Vol. 2, ed. F. Wendorf and A. Close. New York: Academic, 1–50.

——. 1994. "Reformation in Barbarian Europe, 1300–600 B.C." In *The Oxford Illustrated Prehistory of Europe,* ed. B. Cunliffe. Oxford: Oxford University Press, 304–355.

Harris, Edward. 1989. *Principles of Archaeological Stratigraphy.* London: Academic Press.

Harris, Marvin. 1979. *Cultural Materialism: The Struggle for a Science of Culture.* New York: Random House.

Hasenstab, Robert J. 2001. "Proto-Iroquois." In *Encyclopedia of Prehistory,* Vol. 6: *North America,* ed. P.N. Peregrine and M. Ember. New York: Kluwer/Plenum, 453–465.

Hassan, Fekri A. 1981. *Demographic Archaeology.* New York: Academic Press.

——. 1988. "The Predynastic of Egypt." *Journal of World Prehistory* 2:135–185.

Hastorf, Christine. 1993. *Agriculture and the Onset of Political Inequality before the Inka.* Cambridge: Cambridge University Press.

Hastorf, Christine, and Virginia Popper. 1988. *Current Paleoethnobotany: Analytical Methods and Cultural Interpretations of Archaeological Plant Remains.* Chicago: University of Chicago Press.

Haury, Emil. 1985. *The Mogollon Culture of the Forestdale Valley, East-Central Arizona.* Tucson: University of Arizona Press.

Hawkins, Alicia, and Maxine Kleindeinst. 2001. "Aterian." In *Encyclopedia of Prehistory,* Vol. 1: *Africa,* ed. P.N. Peregrine and M. Ember. New York: Kluwer/Plenum, 23–46.

Hays, Christopher. 2001. "Adena." In *Encyclopedia of Prehistory,* Vol. 6: *North America,* ed. P.N. Peregrine and M. Ember. New York: Kluwer/Plenum, 1–13.

Healan, Dan M. 1989. *Tula of the Toltecs.* Iowa City: University of Iowa Press.

Hedeager, Lotte. 1992. *Iron Age Societies: From Tribe to State in Northern Europe, 500 B.C. to A.D. 700.* Oxford: Blackwell.

Heizer, Robert Fleming. 1958. *A Guide to Archaeological Field Methods.* Palo Alto, CA: National Press.

——. 1959. *The Archaeologist at Work: A Source Book in Archaeological Method and Interpretation.* New York, Harper.

Helmer, J.W., S. VanDyke, and F.J. Kense. 1977. *Problems in the Prehistory of the North American Subarctic: The Athapaskan Question.* Calgary: Archaeological Association of the University of Calgary.

Helms, Mary W. 1979. *Ancient Panama: Chiefs in Search of Power.* Austin: University of Texas Press.

Henderson, A. Gwynn. 1992. *Fort Ancient Cultural Dynamics in the Middle Ohio Valley.* Madison, WI: Prehistory Press.

Henderson, A. Gwynn, and David Pollack. 2001. "Fort Ancient." In *Encyclopedia of Prehistory,* Vol. 6: *North America,* ed. P.N. Peregrine and M. Ember. New York: Kluwer/Plenum, 174–194.

Henderson, Julian. 2000. *The Science and Archaeology of Materials: An Investigation of Inorganic Materials.* New York: Routledge.

Henn, W. 1978. *Archaeology on the Alaska Peninsula: The Ugashik Drainage, 1973–1975.* University of Oregon Anthropological Papers 4.

Henry, Donald O. 1986. "The Prehistory and Paleoenvironments of Jordan: An Overview." *Paléorient* 12:5–26.

——. 1989. *From Foraging to Agriculture: The Levant at the End of the Ice Age.* Philadelphia: University of Pennsylvania Press.

Herrera, R. Sergio. 2001. "Olmec." In *Encyclopedia of Prehistory,* Vol. 5: *Middle America,* ed. P.N. Peregrine and M. Ember. New York: Kluwer/Plenum, 346–350.

Hershkovitz, I., O. Bar-Yosef, and B. Arensburg. 1994. "The Pre-Pottery Neolithic Populations of South Sinai and Their Relations to Other Circum-Mediterranean Groups: An Anthropological Study." *Paléorient* 20:59–84.

Hesse, Brian. 1985. *Animal Bone Archaeology: From Objectives to Analysis.* Washington, DC: Tarazacum.

Hester, Thomas R., Harry J. Shafer, and Kenneth L. Feder. 1997. *Field Methods in Archaeology.* Mountain View, CA: Mayfield.

Hewes, Gordon W. 1961. "Food Transport and the Origin of Hominid Bipedalism," *American Anthropologist,* 63:687–710.

Heyerdahl, Thor, and Edwin Ferdon. 1961. *Reports of the Norwegian Archaeological Expedition to Easter Island and the East Pacific,* Vol. 1: *Archaeology of Easter Island.* Santa Fe: School of American Research.

Higham, Charles. 1989. *The Archaeology of Mainland Southeast Asia from 10,000 B.C. to the Fall of Angkor.* Cambridge: Cambridge University Press.

——. 1996a. *The Bronze Age of Southeast Asia.* Cambridge: Cambridge University Press.

——. 1996b. "Review of Archaeology in Mainland Southeast Asia." *Journal of Archaeological Research* 4:3–50.

Higham, Charles, and Tracey L.-D. Lu. 1998. "The Origins and Dispersal of Rice Cultivation." *Antiquity* 72:867–877.

Higham, Charles, and Rachanie Thosarat. 1998. *Prehistoric Thailand.* Cambridge: Cambridge University Press.

Hijjara, Ismail H. 1997. *The Halaf Period in Northern Mesopotamia.* London: Nabu.

Hiscock, Peter. 2001a. "Early Australian." In *Encyclopedia of Prehistory, Vol. 3: East Asia and Oceania,* ed. P.N. Peregrine and M. Ember. New York: Kluwer/Plenum, 18–22.

———. 2001b. "Late Australian." In *Encyclopedia of Prehistory, Vol. 3: East Asia and Oceania,* ed. P.N. Peregrine and M. Ember. New York: Kluwer/Plenum, 132–149.

Hodder, Ian. 1990. *The Domestication of Europe: Structure and Contingency in Neolithic Societies.* Oxford: Basil Blackwell.

———. 1991. *Reading the Past: Current Approaches to Interpretation in Archaeology.* Cambridge: Cambridge University Press.

———. 1999. *The Archaeological Process: An Introduction.* Oxford: Blackwell.

Hodder, Ian, and Clive Orton. 1976. *Spatial Analysis in Archaeology.* Cambridge: Cambridge University Press.

Hoddinott, R. 1981. *The Thracians.* London: Thames and Hudson.

Hoffecker, John F., W. Rogers Powers, and Ted Geobel. 1993. "The Colonization of Beringia and the Peopling of the New World." *Science* (January 1):51.

Hoffmann, J.L. 1996. *Archaeology and Paleoecology of the Central Great Plains.* Fayetteville: Arkansas Archaeological Survey.

Hoffman, Michael A. 1979. *Egypt before the Pharaohs: The Prehistoric Foundations of Egyptian Civilization.* New York: Knopf.

Holder, Preston. 1970. *Hoe and Horse on the Great Plains.* Lincoln: University of Nebraska Press.

Hole, Frank. 1987. *Archaeology of Western Iran: Settlement and Society from Prehistory to the Islamic Conquest.* Washington, DC: Smithsonian Institution Press.

———. 1994. "Environmental Shock and Urban Origins." In *Chiefdoms and Early States in the Near East: The Organizational Dynamics of Complexity,* ed. Gil Stein and Mitchell S. Rothman. Madison, WI: Prehistory Press, 121–152.

Hole, Frank, and Kent V. Flannery. 1967. "The Prehistory of Southwestern Iran: A Preliminary Report." *Proceedings of the Prehistoric Society* 33:147–206.

Hole, Frank, Kent V. Flannery, and James A. Neely. 1969. "Prehistory and Human Ecology of the Deh Luran Plain." *Memoirs of the Museum of Anthropology No. 1.* Ann Arbor: University of Michigan.

Holliday, Vance. 1992. *Soils in Archaeology: Landscape Evolution and Human Occupation.* Washington, DC: Smithsonian Institution Press.

Hoopes, John W. 2001a. "Early Chibcha." In *Encyclopedia of Prehistory, Vol. 5: Middle America,* ed. P.N. Peregrine and M. Ember. New York: Kluwer/Plenum, 100–115.

———. 2001b. "Late Chibcha." In *Encyclopedia of Prehistory, Vol. 5: Middle America,* ed. P.N. Peregrine and M. Ember. New York: Kluwer/Plenum, 239–256.

Hosler, Dorothy. 1994. *The Sounds and Color of Power: The Sacred Metallurgical Technology of Ancient West Mexico.* Cambridge, MA: MIT Press.

Howell, J.M. 1983. *Settlement and Economy in Neolithic Northern France.* Oxford: British Archaeological Reports, International Series 157.

Huckell, Bruce. 1996. "The Archaic Prehistory of the American Southwest." *Journal of World Prehistory* 10:305–373.

Huffman, T.N. 1989. *Iron Age Migrations.* Johannesburg: Witwatersrand University Press.

Hunter, Andrea A. 2001. "Early Eastern Woodland." In *Encyclopedia of Prehistory, Vol. 6: North America,* ed. P.N. Peregrine and M. Ember. New York: Kluwer/Plenum, 81–97.

Hurt, Wesley. 1974. *The Interrelationships between the Natural Environment and Four Sambaquis, Coast of Santa Catarina, Brazil.* Bloomington: Indiana University Press.

———. 1998. *Explorations into American Archaeology: Essays in Honor of Wesley R. Hurt.* Lanham, MD: University Press of America.

———. 2002a. "Early East Brazilian Uplands." In *Encyclopedia of Prehistory, Vol. 7: South America,* ed. P.N. Peregrine and M. Ember. New York: Kluwer/Plenum, 98–107.

———. 2002b. "Late East Brazilian Uplands." In *Encyclopedia of Prehistory, Vol. 7: South America,* ed. P.N. Peregrine and M. Ember. New York: Kluwer/Plenum, 228–234.

———. 2002c. "Sambaqui." In *Encyclopedia of Prehistory, Vol. 7: South America,* ed. P.N. Peregrine and M. Ember. New York: Kluwer/Plenum, 304–316.

Hyslop, John. 1990. *Inka Settlement Planning.* Austin: University of Texas Press.

Iceland, Harry, and Thomas Hester. 2001. "Lowland Mesoamerican Archaic." In *Encyclopedia of Prehistory, Vol. 5: Middle America,* ed. P.N. Peregrine and M. Ember. New York: Kluwer/Plenum, 292–302.

Ingersoll, Daniel, John E. Yellen, and William Macdonald. 1977. *Experimental Archeology.* New York: Columbia University Press.

Isaac, Glynn. 1971. "The Diet of Early Man: Aspects of Archaeological Evidence from Lower and Middle Pleistocene Sites in Africa." *World Archaeology* 2:278–299.

———. 1984. "The Archaeology of Human Origins: Studies of the Pleistocene in East Africa, 1971–1981." In Fred Wendorf and Angela E. Close, eds, *Advances in World Archaeology 3.* Orlando, FL: Academic Press.

Isbell, William H. 1997. *Mummies and Mortuary Monuments: A Postprocessual Prehistory of Central Andean Social Organization.* Austin: University of Texas Press.

Isbell, William H., and G.F. McEwan. 1991. *Huari Political Organization: Prehistoric Monumental Architecture and State Government.* Washington, DC: Dumbarton Oaks.

Jarrige, J.-F. 1991. "Mehrgarh: Its Place in the Development of Ancient Cultures in Pakistan." In *Forgotten Cities on the Indus,* ed. M. Jansen, M. Mulloy, and G. Urban. Mainz am Rhein: Phillip von Zabern, 34–49.

———. 1993. "The Early Architectural Traditions of Greater Indus as Seen from Mehrgarh, Baluchistan." In *Urban Form and Meaning in South Asia: The Shaping of Cities from Prehistoric to Precolonial Times,* ed. H. Spodek and D.M. Srinivasan. Washington, DC: National Gallery of Art, 25–34.

Jarrige, C., J.-F. Jarrige, R.H. Meadow, and G. Quivron, eds. 1995. *Mehrgarh Field Reports 1975 to 1985—From the Neolithic to the Indus Civilization.* Karachi: Department of Culture and Tourism, Government of Sindh and the French Foreign Ministry.

Jayaswal, Vidula. 2002. "South Asian Upper Paleolithic." In *Encyclopedia of Prehistory, Vol. 8: South and Southwest Asia,* ed. P.N. Peregrine and M. Ember. New York: Kluwer/Plenum, 324–341.

Jennings, Jesse D. 1978. *Prehistory of Utah and the Eastern Great Basin.* Salt Lake City: University of Utah Anthropological Papers 98.

———. 1979. *Prehistory of Polynesia.* Cambridge: Harvard University Press.

Jennings, Jesse D., and Richard Holmer. 1980. *Archaeological Excavations in Western Samoa.* Honolulu: Bernice P. Bishop Museum, Pacific Anthropological Records, Number 32.

Jennings, Jesse D., R.N. Holmer, J.C. Janetski, and H.L. Smith. 1976. *Excavations on Upolu, Western Samoa.* Honolulu: Bernice P. Bishop Museum, Pacific Anthropological Records, Number 25.

Joffe, A.H. 1993. *Settlement and Society in the Early Bronze I & II Southern Levant.* Sheffield: Sheffield Academic Press.

Johanson, Donald C., and Tim D. White. 1979. "A Systematic Assessment of Early African Hominids," *Science,* January 26, 321.

Johnson, Alfred E. 1963. "The Trincheras Culture of Northwestern Sonora." *American Antiquity* 29:174–186.

Johnson, Allen, and Timothy Earle. 1987. *The Evolution of Human Societies.* Stanford: Stanford University Press.

Johnson, Gregory A. 1973. *Local Exchange and Early State Development in Southwestern Iran.* Papers of the Museum of Anthropology 51. Ann Arbor: University of Michigan.

———. 1987. "The Changing Organization of Uruk Administration on the Susiana Plain." In *Archaeology of Western Iran,* ed. Frank Hole. Washington, DC: Smithsonian Institution Press, 107–139.

Johnson, Jay K. 2001. "Middle Eastern Woodland." In *Encyclopedia of Prehistory,* Vol. 6: *North America,* ed. P.N. Peregrine and M. Ember. New York: Kluwer/Plenum, 322–334.

Johnson, John R., and Sarah Berry. 2001. "Late Southern California." In *Encyclopedia of Prehistory,* Vol. 6: *North America,* ed. P.N. Peregrine and M. Ember. New York: Kluwer/Plenum, 297–305.

Jones, Steve, Robert Martin, and David Pilbeam. 1992. *The Cambridge Encyclopedia of Human Evolution.* Cambridge: Cambridge University Press.

Jolly, Clifford. 1970. "The Seed-Eaters: A New Model of Hominid Differentiation Based on a Baboon Analogy," *Man* 5:5–28.

Judge, W. James, and Jerry Dawson. 1972. "Paleo-Indian Settlement Technology in New Mexico." *Science* (June 16): 1210–1216.

Kan, Michael, Clement Meighan, and H.B. Nicholson. 1989. *Sculpture of Ancient West Mexico: Nayarit, Jalisco, Colima.* Los Angeles: Los Angeles County Museum.

Keall, E. 1998. "Encountering Megaliths on the Tihamah Plain of Yemen." *Proceedings of the Seminar for Arabian Studies* 28:139–147.

Keatinge, Richard W. 1988. *Peruvian Prehistory: An Overview of Pre-Inca and Inca Society.* Cambridge: Cambridge University Press.

Keegan, William F. 1992. *The People Who Discovered Columbus: The Prehistory of the Bahamas.* Gainesville: University Press of Florida.

———. 1994. "West Indian Archaeology I: Overview and Foragers." *Journal of Archaeological Research* 2:255–284.

———. 2001. "Early Caribbean." In *Encyclopedia of Prehistory,* Vol. 5: *Middle America,* ed. P.N. Peregrine and M. Ember. New York: Kluwer/Plenum, 85–99.

Keeley, Lawrence. 1980. *Experimental Determination of Stone Tool Uses.* Chicago: University of Chicago Press.

Keightly, David. 1999. "The Shang: China's First Historical Dynasty." In *The Cambridge History of Ancient China,* ed. M. Lowe and E.L. Shaughnessy. Cambridge: Cambridge University Press, 232–291.

Keiji, Imamura. 1996. *Prehistoric Japan.* London: University College of London Press.

Kemp, Barry J. 1989. *Ancient Egypt.* London: Routledge.

Kenoyer, Jonathan M. 1998. *Ancient Cities of the Indus Valley Civilization.* Karachi: Oxford University Press.

———. 2000. "Wealth and Socio-Economic Hierarchies of the Indus Valley Civilization." In *Order, Legitimacy and Wealth in Early States,* ed. J. Richards and M. Van Buren. Cambridge: Cambridge University Press, 90–112.

———. 2002a. "Indus Neolithic." In *Encyclopedia of Prehistory,* Vol. 8: *South and Southwest Asia,* ed. P.N. Peregrine and M. Ember. New York: Kluwer/Plenum, 151–155.

———. 2002b. "Early Indus." In *Encyclopedia of Prehistory,* Vol. 8: *South and Southwest Asia,* ed. P.N. Peregrine and M. Ember. New York: Kluwer/Plenum, 116–121.

———. 2002c. "Mature Indus." In *Encyclopedia of Prehistory,* Vol. 8: *South and Southwest Asia,* ed. P.N. Peregrine and M. Ember. New York: Kluwer/Plenum, 269–281.

Kenrick, Douglas. 1995. *Jomon of Japan: The World's Oldest Pottery.* London: Keagan Paul.

Kent, Susan. 1991. *Domestic Architecture and the Use of Space.* Cambridge: Cambridge University Press.

Kerr, Richard A. 1998. "Sea-Floor Dust Shows Drought Felled Akkadian Empire," *Science,* January 16:325–26.

Kiguradze, Tamaz. 2001a. "Caucasian Chalcolithic." In *Encyclopedia of Prehistory,* Vol. 4: *Europe,* ed. P.N. Peregrine and M. Ember. New York: Kluwer/Plenum, 38–54.

———. 2001b. "Caucasian Neolithic." In *Encyclopedia of Prehistory,* Vol. 4: *Europe,* ed. P.N. Peregrine and M. Ember. New York: Kluwer/Plenum, 55–76.

Kim, Chong-Hak. 1978. *The Prehistory of Korea.* Honolulu: University of Hawaii Press.

Kim, Won-Yong. 1986. *Introduction to Korean Archaeology.* Seoul: Ilchisa.

King, Chester. 1990. *Evolution of Chumash Society: A Comparative Study of the Artifacts Used in Social System Maintenance in the Santa Barbara Channel Region before A.D. 1804.* New York: Garland.

King, Chester. 2001. "Early Southern California." In *Encyclopedia of Prehistory,* Vol. 6: *North America,* ed. P.N. Peregrine and M. Ember. New York: Kluwer/Plenum, 144–157.

Kirch, Patrick V. 1985. *Feathered Gods and Fishhooks.* Honolulu: University of Hawaii Press.

———. 1988. *Niuatoputapu: The Prehistory of a Polynesian Chiefdom.* Seattle: Burke Museum, Monograph 5.

———. 1990. "The Evolution of Sociopolitical Complexity in Prehistoric Hawaii." *Journal of World Prehistory* 4:311–345.

———. 1997. *The Lapita Peoples: Ancestors of the Oceanic World.* Oxford: Blackwell.

———. 2001. "Lapita." In *Encyclopedia of Prehistory,* Vol. 4: *Europe,* ed. P.N. Peregrine and M. Ember. New York: Kluwer/Plenum, 150–155.

Kirch, Patrick V., and Terry L. Hunt. 1993. *The To'aga Site: Three Millennia of Polynesian Occupation in the Manu'a Islands, American Samoa.* Berkeley: Archaeological Research Facility, Contributions, Number 52.

Kirkbride, Diana. 1968. "Beidha: Early Neolithic Life South of the Dead Sea." *Antiquity* 42:263–274.

Kislev, M.E. 1984. "Emergence of Wheat Agriculture." *Paléorient* 10:61–70.

Kislev, M.E., and Bar-Yosef, O. 1988. "The Legumes: The Earliest Domesticated Plants in the Near East?" *Current Anthropology* 29:175–178.

Kitchen, K.A. 1993. "The Land of Punt." In *The Archaeology of Africa,* ed. T. Shaw, P. Sinclair, B. Andah, and A. Okpoko. London: Routledge, 587–608.

Klein, Richard G. 1974. "Ice-Age Hunters of the Ukraine." *Scientific American* (June):96–105.

———. 1977. "The Ecology of Early Man in Southern Africa." *Science,* July 8, 120.

———. 1983. "The Stone Age Prehistory of Southern Africa." *Annual Review of Anthropology* 12:38–39.

———. 1989. *The Human Career: Human Biological and Cultural Origins.* Chicago: University of Chicago Press.

———. 1994. "Southern Africa before the Iron Age." In *Integrative Paths to the Past,* ed. R.S. Corruccini and R.L. Ciochon. Englewood Cliffs, NJ: Prentice Hall, 471–519.

Knapp, A. Bernard. 1992. "Independence and Imperialism: Politico-economic Structures in the Bronze Age Levant Archaeology." In *Annales, and Ethnohistory,* ed. B. Knapp. Cambridge: Cambridge University Press, 83–98.

Knecht, Heidi. 1997. *Projectile Technology.* New York: Plenum.

Knecht, H., A. Pike-Tay, and R. White. 1993. *Before Lascaux: The Complex Record of the Early Upper Paleolithic.* Boca Raton, FL: CRC Press.

Knobloch, Patricia. 2002. "Huari." In *Encyclopedia of Prehistory,* Vol. 7: *South America,* ed. P.N. Peregrine and M. Ember. New York: Kluwer/Plenum, 138–149.

Kohl, Philip L. 1978. "The Balance of Trade in Southwestern Asia in the Mid-Third Millennium B.C." *Current Anthropology* 19(3):463–492.

———. 2001. "Caucasian Bronze Age." In *Encyclopedia of Prehistory*, Vol. 4: *Europe*, ed. P.N. Peregrine and M. Ember. New York: Kluwer/Plenum, 32–37.

Köhler, Christiana. 2001. "Lower Egypt Predynastic." In *Encyclopedia of Prehistory*, Vol. 1: *Africa*, ed. P.N. Peregrine and M. Ember. New York: Kluwer/Plenum, 150–160.

Kohler-Rollefson, I. 1992. "A Model for the Development of Nomadic Pastoralism on the Transjordanian Plateau." In *Pastoralism in the Levant: Archaeological Materials in Anthropological Perspectives*, ed. O. Bar-Yosef and A. Khazanov. Madison, WI: Prehistory Press, 11–18.

Kolata, Alan. 1993. *The Tiwanaku: Portrait of an Andean Civilization*. Cambridge, MA: Basil Blackwell.

———. 1996. *Tiwanaku and Its Hinterland: Archaeology and Paleoecology of an Andean Civilization*. Washington, DC: Smithsonian Institution Press.

Kolb, Michael J. 1994. "Monumentality and the Rise of Religious Authority in Precontact Hawaii." *Current Anthropology* 35:521–547.

———. 2001. "Hawaiian." In *Encyclopedia of Prehistory*, Vol. 4: *Europe*, ed. P.N. Peregrine and M. Ember. New York: Kluwer/Plenum, 66–70.

Konner, Melvin, and Carol Worthman. 1980. "Nursing Frequency, Gonadal Function, and Birth Spacing among !Kung Hunter-Gatherers." *Science*, February 15, 788–91.

Kooyman, Brian P. 2000. *Understanding Stone Tools and Archaeological Sites*. Albuquerque: University of New Mexico Press.

Kovács, Tibor. 1977. *The Bronze Age in Hungary*. Budapest: Corvina.

Kowalewski, Stephen. 1990. "The Evolution of Complexity in the Valley of Oaxaca." *Annual Review of Anthropology* 19: 39–58.

Kramer, Andrew. 2002. "Natural History and Evolutionary Fate of *Homo erectus*." In P.N. Peregrine, C.R. Ember, and M. Ember, eds, *Physical Anthropology: Original Readings in Method and Practice*. Upper Saddle River, NJ: Prentice Hall, 140–154.

Kramer, Carol. 1982. *Village Ethnoarchaeology—Rural Iran in Archaeological Perspective*. New York: Academic Press.

Krings, Matthias, A. Stone, R.W. Schmitz, H. Krainitzki, M. Stoneking, and S. Paabo. 1997. "Neandertal DNA Sequences and the Origin of Modern Humans." *Cell* 90:19–30.

Kristiansen, Kristian. 1984. *Settlement and Economy in Later Scandinavian Prehistory*. Oxford: British Archaeological Reports, International Series 603.

———. 1987. "Centre and Periphery in Bronze Age Scandinavia." In *Centre and Periphery in the Ancient World*, ed. M. Rowlands and K. Kristiansen. Cambridge: Cambridge University Press, 74–85.

———. 1998. *Europe Before History*. Cambridge: Cambridge University Press.

Kubba, Isamil. 1987. *Mesopotamian Architecture and Town Planning*. Ankara: BAR International Series.

Kushnareva, Karine. 1997. *The Southern Caucasus in Prehistory*. Philadelphia: University Musuem Monograph 39.

Kuzmina, Elena. 2001. "Andronovo." In *Encyclopedia of Prehistory*, Vol. 4: *Europe*, ed. P.N. Peregrine and M. Ember. New York: Kluwer/Plenum, 1–21.

Kuznar, Lawrence. 2002. "Late Highland Andean Archaic." In *Encyclopedia of Prehistory*, Vol. 7: *South America*, ed. P.N. Peregrine and M. Ember. New York: Kluwer/Plenum, 235–252.

Labbe, Armand J. 1986. *Colombia before Columbus*. New York: Rizzoli.

Lamberg-Karlovsky, C.C. 1971. "The Proto-Elamite Settlement of Tepe Yahya." *Iran* (9):87–96.

Lamberg-Karlovsky, C.C., and Thomas W. Beale. 1986. *Excavations at Tepe Yahya, Iran: The Early Periods*. American School of Prehistoric Research Bulletin 38. Cambridge: The Peabody Museum of Archaeology and Ethnology, Harvard University.

Lamberg-Karlovsky, C.C., and Jeremy Sabloff. 1979. *Ancient Civilizations*. Menlo Park, CA: Cummings.

Lambert, Joseph B. 1997. *Traces of the Past: Unraveling the Secrets of Archaeology through Chemistry*. Reading, MA: Addison-Wesley.

Lange, Frederick W. 1988. *Costa Rican Art and Archaeology*. Boulder: University of Colorado Press.

———. 1992. *Wealth and Hierarchy in the Intermediate Area*. Washington, DC: Dumbarton Oaks.

———. 1996. *Paths to Central American Prehistory*. Niwot: University Press of Colorado.

———. 2001. "Nicoya." In *Encyclopedia of Prehistory*, Vol. 5: *Middle America*, ed. P.N. Peregrine and M. Ember. New York: Kluwer/Plenum, 328–345.

Lange, Frederick W., and Doris Stone. 1984. *The Archaeology of Lower Central America*. Albuquerque: School of American Research Press.

Lange, Frederick W., Payson Sheets, Anibal Martinez, and Suzanne Abel-Vidor. 1992. *Archaeology of Pacific Nicaragua*. Albuquerque: University of New Mexico Press.

Larichev, V.E., U. Khol'ushkin, and I. Laricheva. 1988. "The Upper Paleolithic of Northern Asia: Achievements, Problems, and Perspectives I: Western Siberia." *Journal of World Prehistory* 2:359–396.

———. 1990. "The Upper Paleolithic of Northern Asia: Achievements, Problems, and Perspectives II: Central and Eastern Siberia." *Journal of World Prehistory* 4:347–385.

Larson, Mary Lou. 2001. "Late High Plains Archaic." In *Encyclopedia of Prehistory*, Vol. 6: *North America*, ed. P.N. Peregrine and M. Ember. New York: Kluwer/Plenum, 209–277.

Lathrap, Donald W., Jorge Marcos, and James Zeidler. 1977. "Real Alto: An Ancient Ceremonial Center." *Archaeology* 30(1):2–13.

Laughlin, William. 1980. *Aleuts: Survivors of the Bering Land Bridge*. New York: Holt, Rinehart, Winston.

Laville, H., J.-P. Rigaud, and J. Sacket. 1980. *Rock Shelters of the Perigord*. New York: Academic Press.

Layton, Robert. 1998. *An Introduction to Theory in Anthropology*. Cambridge: Cambridge University Press.

Leakey, Louis S.B. 1960. "Finding the World's Earliest Man," *National Geographic* (September):420–435.

Leakey, Mary. 1971. *Olduvai Gorge: Excavations in Beds I and II*. Cambridge: Cambridge University Press.

———. 1979. *Olduvai Gorge: My Search for Early Man*. London: Collins.

Leakey, Meave, C.S. Feibel, I. McDougall, and A. Walker. 1995. "New Four-Million-Year-Old Hominid Species from Kanapoi and Allia Bay, Kenya," *Nature* 376:565–571.

Lee, Yun Kuen. 2001. "Yangshao." In *Encyclopedia of Prehistory*, Vol. 4: *Europe*, ed. P.N. Peregrine and M. Ember. New York: Kluwer/Plenum, 333–349.

Lehmer, Donald J. 1971. *Introduction to Middle Missouri Archaeology*. Washington, DC: National Park Service.

Lekson, Stephen. 2001. "Early Mogollon." In *Encyclopedia of Prehistory*, Vol. 6: *North America*, ed. P.N. Peregrine and M. Ember. New York: Kluwer/Plenum, 115–129.

Levy, Thomas E. 1983. "The Emergence of Specialized Pastoralism in the Southern Levant." *World Archaeology* 15:15–36.

———. 1998. *The Archaeology of Society in the Holy Land*, 2nd ed. London: Leicester University Press.

———. 2002. "Chalcolithic." In *Encyclopedia of Prehistory*, Vol. 8: *South and Southwest Asia*, ed. P.N. Peregrine and M. Ember. New York: Kluwer/Plenum, 56–74.

Lieberman, Daniel E. 1995. "Testing Hypotheses about Recent Human Evolution from Skulls: Integrating Morphology, Function, Development, and Phylogeny." *Current Anthropology* 36:159–197.

Lieberman, Philip. 1991. *Uniquely Human: The Evolution of Speech, Thought, and Selfless Behavior.* Cambridge, MA: Harvard University Press.

Lillios, Katina. 2001. "European Megalithic." In *Encyclopedia of Prehistory,* Vol. 4: *Europe,* ed. P.N. Peregrine and M. Ember. New York: Kluwer/Plenum, 157–184.

Linares, Olga. 1968. *Cultural Chronology of the Gulf of Chiriqui, Panama.* Washington, DC: Smithsonian Institution Press.

Linares, Olga, and A.J. Ranere. 1980. *Adaptive Radiation in Prehistoric Panama.* Cambridge, MA: Harvard University, Peabody Museum Monographs 5.

Link, David, and Andrzej Weber. 2001. "Cis-Baikal Neolithic and Bronze Age." In *Encyclopedia of Prehistory,* Vol. 2: *Arctic and Subarctic,* ed. P.N. Peregrine and M. Ember. New York: Kluwer/Plenum, 18–22.

Linname, U. 1975. *The Dorset Culture: A Comparative Study in Newfoundland and the Arctic.* St. John's: Newfoundland Museum.

Linton, Ralph. 1925. *Archaeology of the Marquesas Islands.* Honolulu: Bernice P. Bishop Museum Bulletin 23.

Liu, Li. 1996. "Settlement Patterns, Chiefdom Variability, and the Development of States in North China." *Journal of Anthropological Archaeology* 15:237–288.

Logan, Brad, and Lauren Ritterbush. 2001. "Plains Archaic." In *Encyclopedia of Prehistory,* Vol. 6: *North America,* ed. P.N. Peregrine and M. Ember. New York: Kluwer/Plenum, 410–431.

Lourandos, H. 1996. *Continent of Hunter-Gatherers: New Perspectives in Australian Prehistory.* Cambridge: Cambridge University Press.

Lovejoy, C. Owen. 1988. "Evolution of Human Walking," *Scientific American* 259:82–89.

Lubell, David. 1984. "Paleoenvironments and Epipaleolithic Economies in the Maghreb (ca. 20,000 to 5000 B.P.)." In *From Hunters to Farmers,* ed. J.D. Clark and S. Brandt. Berkeley: University of California Press, 41–56.

———. 2001. "Late Pleistocene-Early Holocene Maghreb." In *Encyclopedia of Prehistory,* Vol. 1: *Africa,* ed. P.N. Peregrine and M. Ember. New York: Kluwer/Plenum, 129–150.

Lubell, David, P. Sheppard, and M. Jackes. 1984. "Continuity in the Epipaleolithic of Northern Africa with Emphasis on the Maghreb." *Advances in World Archaeology* 3:141–191.

Lumbreras, Luis G. 1974. *Peoples and Cultures of Ancient Peru.* Washington, DC: Smithsonian Institution Press.

Lyman, R. Lee. 1991. *Prehistory of the Oregon Coast.* San Diego: Academic Press.

———. 1994. *Vertebrate Taphonomy.* Cambridge: Cambridge University Press.

Lynch, Thomas F. 1980. *Guitarrero Cave: Early Man in the Andes.* New York: Academic Press.

MacDonald, K.C., and P. Allsworth-Jones. 1997. "The Late Stone Age and Neolithic Cultures of West Africa and the Sahara." In *Encyclopedia of Precolonial Africa,* ed. J.O. Vogel. Walnut Creek, CA: Altamira, 394–398.

MacGregor, Arthur. 1985. *Bone, Antler, Ivory, and Horn: The Technology of Skeletal Materials since the Roman Period.* Totowa, NJ: Croom Helm.

Mack, Joanne. 2001. "Late Sierra Nevada." In *Encyclopedia of Prehistory,* Vol. 6: *North America,* ed. P.N. Peregrine and M. Ember. New York: Kluwer/Plenum, 293–296.

MacNeish, Richard S. 1991. *The Origins of Agriculture and Settled Life.* Norman: University of Oklahoma Press.

———. 2001. "Early Mesoamerican Archaic." In *Encyclopedia of Prehistory,* Vol. 5: *Middle America,* ed. P.N. Peregrine and M. Ember. New York: Kluwer/Plenum, 116–128.

MacNeish, Richard S., and A. Nelken-Terner. 1983. "The Preceramic of Mesoamerica." *Journal of Field Archaeology* 10: 71–84.

MacNeish, Richard S., Thomas Patterson, and David Browman. 1975. *The Central Peruvian Prehistoric Interaction Sphere.* Andover, MA: Papers of the R.S. Peabody Foundation for Archaeology.

MacNeish, Richard S., A. Garcia Cook, L. G. Lumbreras, R.K. Vierra, and A. Nelken-Terner. 1981. *Prehistory of the Ayacucho Basin, Peru,* Vol. 2: *Excavations and Chronology.* Ann Arbor: University of Michigan Press.

MacNeish, Richard S., R.K. Vierra, A. Nelken-Terner, R. Lurie, and A. Garcia Cook. 1983. *Prehistory of the Ayacucho Basin, Peru,* Vol. 4: *The Preceramic Way of Life.* Ann Arbor: University of Michigan Press.

Magalhaes, Marcos. 1994. *Archaeology of Carajas: The Prehispanic Presence of Man in Amazonia.* Rio de Janeiro: Companhia Valle do Rio Doce.

Magee, Peter. 1996a. "The Chronology of the Southeast Arabian Iron Age." *Arabian Archaeology and Epigraphy* 7:240–252.

———. 1996b. "Excavations at Muweilah. Preliminary Report on the First Two Seasons of Excavations." *Arabian Archaeology and Epigraphy* 7:195–213.

———. 2002. "Late Arabian Littoral." In *Encyclopedia of Prehistory,* Vol. 8: *South and Southwest Asia,* ed. P.N. Peregrine and M. Ember. New York: Kluwer/Plenum, 247–260.

Magee, Peter, and R. Carter. 1999. "Agglomeration and Regionalism: Southeastern Arabia between 1400 and 1100 B.C." *Arabian Archaeology and Epigraphy* 10:161–179.

Maisels, C.K. 1993. *The Near East: Archaeology in the "Cradle of Civilization."* London: Routledge.

Mallory, J.P. 1989. In *Search of the Indo-Europeans.* London: Thames and Hudson.

Mantu, C.M., G. Dumitroaia, and A. Tsaravopoulos. 1997. *Cucuteni: The Last Great Chalcolithic Civilization of Europe.* Bucharest: Athena.

Marcus, Joyce, and Kent Flannery. 1996. *Zapotec Civilization: How Urban Society Evolved in Mexico's Oaxaca Valley.* New York: Thames and Hudson.

Marean, C.W. 1992. "Hunter to Herder: Large Mammal Remains from the Hunter-Gatherer Occupation at Ekanpune ya Muto Rock Shelter, Central Rift, Kenya." *African Archaeological Review* 10:65–127.

Marinescu-Bilcu, Silvia. 1981. *Tirpesti: From Prehistory to History in Eastern Romania.* Oxford: British Archaeological Reports, International Series.

Marks, Anthony E., and A. Mohammed-Ali. 1991. *The Late Prehistory of the Eastern Sahel.* Dallas: Southern Methodist University Press.

Marshack, Alexander. 1972. *The Roots of Civilization.* New York: McGraw-Hill.

Martin, Paul S., and H.E. Wright. 1967. *Pleistocene Extinctions: The Search for a Cause.* New Haven: Yale University Press.

Martindale, Andrew R.C. 2001. "Late Northwest Coast." In *Encyclopedia of Prehistory,* Vol. 2: *Arctic and Subarctic,* ed. P.N. Peregrine and M. Ember. New York: Kluwer/Plenum, 87–110.

Marx, Karl. 1913. *The Eighteenth Brumaire of Louis Bonaparte.* Chicago: H.C. Kerr.

Masden, David B. 1989. *Exploring the Fremont.* Salt Lake City: University of Utah Occasional Papers 8.

Mason, Ronald J. 1981. *Great Lakes Archaeology.* New York: Academic Press.

———. 2001. "Initial Shield Woodland." In *Encyclopedia of Prehistory,* Vol. 2: *Arctic and Subarctic,* ed. P.N. Peregrine and M. Ember. New York: Kluwer/Plenum, 59–68.

Masuda, Shozo, Izumi Shimada, and Craig Morris. 1985. *Andean Ecology and Civilization.* Tokyo: University of Tokyo Press.

Matson, Robert G. 1991. *The Origins of Southwestern Agriculture.* Tucson: University of Arizona Press.

Matson, Robert G., and Gary Coupland. 1995. *Prehistory of the Northwest Coast.* San Diego: Academic Press.

Matsui, Akira. 2001. "Jomon." In *Encyclopedia of Prehistory*, Vol. 4: *Europe*, ed. P.N. Peregrine and M. Ember. New York: Kluwer/Plenum, 119–126.

Matthews, Roger J. 1992a. "Defining the Style of the Period: Jemdet Nasr, 1926–28." *Iraq* 54:1–34.

———. 1992b. "Jemdet Nasr: The Site and the Period." *Biblical Archaeologist* 55:196–203.

———. 1999. *The Early Prehistory of Mesopotamia, 500,000 to 4,500 B.C.* Turnhout: Brepols.

———. 2002. "Halafian." In *Encyclopedia of Prehistory*, Vol. 8: *South and Southwest Asia*, ed. P.N. Peregrine and M. Ember. New York: Kluwer/Plenum, 138–150

Matyushin, G. 1986. "The Mesolithic and Neolithic in the Southern Urals and Central Asia." In *Hunters in Transition*, ed. M. Zvelebil. Cambridge: Cambridge University Press, 133–150.

Maxwell, Moreau S. 1976. *Eastern Arctic Prehistory: Paleoeskimo Problems.* Washington, DC: Society for American Archaeology, Memoir 31.

———. 1985. *Prehistory of the Eastern Arctic.* Orlando: Academic Press.

Mazar, A. 1990. *Archaeology of the Land of the Bible, 10,000–586 B.C.E.* New York: Doubleday.

McBurney, Charles. 1967. *Haua Fteah (Cyrenaica) and the Stone Age of the South East Mediterranean.* Cambridge: Cambridge University Press.

McCartney, Allen, and Douglas Veltre. 2001. "Aleutian." In *Encyclopedia of Prehistory*, Vol. 2: *Arctic and Subarctic*, ed. P.N. Peregrine and M. Ember. New York: Kluwer/Plenum, 1–13.

McCorriston, Joy, and Frank Hole. 1991. "The Ecology of Seasonal Stress and the Origins of Agriculture in the Near East," *American Anthropologist* 93:46–69.

McDermott, LeRoy. 1996. "Self-representation in Female Figurines." *Current Anthropology* 37:227–275.

McDonald, Kim A. 1998. "New Evidence Challenges Traditional Model of How the New World Was Settled." *Chronicle of Higher Education* (March 13):A22.

McDowell-Loudan, Ellis E. 2001. *Archaeology: Introductory Guide for Classroom and Field.* Upper Saddle River: Prentice Hall.

McGhee, Robert. 1990. *Canadian Arctic Prehistory.* Hull: Canadian Museum of Civilization.

———. 1996. *Ancient People of the Arctic.* Vancouver: University of British Columbia Press.

McGuire, Randall. 1992. *A Marxist Archaeology.* San Diego: Academic Press.

McHenry, Henry. 1982. "The Pattern of Human Evolution: Studies on Bipedalism, Mastication, and Encephalization." *Annual Review of Anthropology* 11:151–173.

McIntosh, Susan K. 1999. *Beyond Chiefdoms: Pathways to Complexity in Africa.* Cambridge: Cambridge University Press.

———. 2001a. "West African Late Stone Age." In *Encyclopedia of Prehistory*, Vol. 1: *Africa*, ed. P.N. Peregrine and M. Ember. New York: Kluwer/Plenum, 319–322.

———. 2001b. "West African Neolithic." In *Encyclopedia of Prehistory*, Vol. 1: *Africa*, ed. P.N. Peregrine and M. Ember. New York: Kluwer/Plenum, 323–338.

McIntosh, Susan K., and Roderick McIntosh. 1983. "Current Directions in West African Prehistory." *Annual Review of Anthropology* 12:215–258.

———. 1988. "From Stone to Metal: New Perspectives on the Later Prehistory of West Africa." *Journal of World Prehistory* 2:89–133.

McKern, Will C. 1929. *Archaeology of Tonga.* Honolulu: Bernice P. Bishop Museum, Bulletin 60.

McNett, Charles W. 1985. *Shawnee-Minisink: A Stratified Paleoindian-Archaic Site in the Upper Delaware Valley of Pennsylvania.* Orlando: Academic Press.

Meacham, William. 1978. *Sham Wan, Lamma Island: An Archaeological Site Study.* Hong Kong: Hong Kong Archaeological Society, Monograph 3.

———. 1983. "Origins and Development of the Yueh Coastal Neolithic: A Microcosm of Culture Change on the Mainland of East Asia." In *The Origins of Chinese Civilization*, ed. David N. Keightley. Berkeley: University of California Press, 147–176.

Meadow, Richard H. 1991. *Harappa Excavations 1986–1990.* Madison: Prehistory Press.

Meggers, Betty J. 1966. *Ecuador.* London: Thames and Hudson.

———. 1971. *Amazonia: Man and Nature in a Conterfeit Paradise.* Chicago: Aldine.

———. 1988. "Prehistory of Amazonia." In *People of the Tropical Forest*, ed. J.S. Denslow and C. Padoch. Berkeley: University of California Press.

Mellaart, J. 1975. *The Neolithic of the Near East.* London: Thames and Hudson.

Mellars, Paul. 1989. "Major Issues in the Emergence of Modern Humans." *Current Anthropology* 30:349–385.

———. 1994. "The Upper Paleolithic Revolution." In Barry Cunliffe, ed., *The Oxford Illustrated Prehistory of Europe.* Oxford: Oxford University Press, 42–78.

———. 1996. *The Neanderthal Legacy.* Princeton: Princeton University Press.

———. 1998. "The Fate of the Neanderthals." *Nature* 395:539–540.

Mellars, Paul, and Christopher Stringer. 1989. *The Human Revolution.* Princeton: Princeton University Press.

Meltzer, David, Don Fowler, and Jeremy Sabloff. 1986. *American Archaeology: Past and Future.* Washington: Smithsonian Institution Press.

Melyukova, A.I. 1990. "The Scythians and Sarmatians." In *The Cambridge History of Early Inner Asia*, ed. D. Sinor. Cambridge: Cambridge University Press, 97–117.

Milanich, Jerald T. 1994. *Archaeology of Precolumbian Florida.* Gainesville: University Press of Florida.

Milisauskas, Sarunas. 1978. *European Prehistory.* New York: Academic Press.

———. 2001. "Linear Pottery." In *Encyclopedia of Prehistory*, Vol. 4: *Europe*, ed. P.N. Peregrine and M. Ember. New York: Kluwer/Plenum, 191–197.

Milisauskas, Sarunas, and J. Kruk. 1989. "Neolithic Economy in Central Europe." *Journal of World Prehistory* 3:403–446.

Miller, Sheryl. 2001a. "Nachikufan." In *Encyclopedia of Prehistory*, Vol. 1: *Africa*, ed. P.N. Peregrine and M. Ember. New York: Kluwer/Plenum, 190–196.

———. 2001b. "Tshitolian." In *Encyclopedia of Prehistory*, Vol. 1: *Africa*, ed. P.N. Peregrine and M. Ember. New York: Kluwer/Plenum, 278–286.

Miller-Antonio, Sari. 2001. "Ordosian." In *Encyclopedia of Prehistory*, Vol. 3: *East Asia and Oceania*, ed. P.N. Peregrine and M. Ember. New York: Kluwer/Plenum, 274–282.

Milliken, Sarah. 2001. "Northern Mediterranean Mesolithic." In *Encyclopedia of Prehistory*, Vol. 4: *Europe*, ed. P.N. Peregrine and M. Ember. New York: Kluwer/Plenum, 224–235.

Millon, Rene. 1981. "Teotihuacan: City, State, and Civilization." In J.A. Sabloff, ed., *Supplement to the Handbook of Middle American Indians*, Vol. 1: *Archaeology.* Austin: University of Texas Press, 198–243.

Ming, Wang Hai. 2001. "Majiabang." In *Encyclopedia of Prehistory*, Vol. 4: *Europe*, ed. P.N. Peregrine and M. Ember. New York: Kluwer/Plenum, 206–221.

Minor, Rick. 2001a. "Archaic Oregon Coast." In *Encyclopedia of Prehistory*, Vol. 6: *North America*, ed. P.N. Peregrine and M. Ember. New York: Kluwer/Plenum, 14–20.

———. 2001b. "Formative Oregon Coast." In *Encyclopedia of Prehistory*, Vol. 6: *North America*, ed. P.N. Peregrine and M. Ember. New York: Kluwer/Plenum, 158–173.

Minor, Rick, and Kathryn Anne Toepel. 1986. *The Archaeology of the Tahkenitch Landing Site: Early Prehistoric Occupation on the Oregon Coast.* Eugene, OR: Heritage Research Associates Report 46.

Mitchell, Peter. 1997. "Holocene Stone Age Hunter-Gatherers South of the Limpopo River, ca. 10,000–2000 B.P." *Journal of World Prehistory* 11:359–424.

Mochanov, Yuri. 1969. "Early Neolithic of the Aldan." *Arctic Anthropology* 6(1): 95–118.

Mohammed-Ali, A. 1982. *The Neolithic Period in the Sudan, C. 6000–2500 B.C.* Oxford: British Archaeological Reports, International Series 139.

Mohen, Jean-Pierre. 1990. *The World of the Megaliths.* New York: Facts on File.

Moore, Andrew M.T. 1985. "The Development of Neolithic Societies in the Near East." *Advances in World Archaeology* 4:1–69.

Moore, Jerry. 1996. *Architecture and Power in the Prehispanic Andes: The Archaeology of Public Buildings.* Cambridge: Cambridge University Press.

_____. 2002. "Chimu." In *Encyclopedia of Prehistory*, Vol. 7: *South America*, ed. P.N. Peregrine and M. Ember. New York: Kluwer/Plenum, 58–72.

Moratto, Michael. 1984. *California Archaeology.* New York: Academic Press.

Morell, Virginia. 1995. "The Earliest Art Becomes Older—and More Common." *Science* (March 31):1908–1909.

Morgan, Lewis Henry. 1877. *Ancient Society.* New York: Henry Holt.

Morgan, William N. 1988. *Prehistoric Architecture in Micronesia.* Austin: University of Texas Press.

Moseley, Michael E. 1992. *The Incas and Their Ancestors: The Archaeology of Peru.* London: Thames and Hudson.

Moseley, Michael, and Alana Cordy-Collins. 1990. *The Northern Dynasties: Kingship and Statecraft in Chimor.* Washington, DC: Dumbarton Oaks.

Moseley, Michael, and Kent Day. 1982. *Chan Chan: Andean Desert City.* Albuquerque: University of New Mexico Press.

Moss, Madonna, and Jon Erlandson. 1998. "Reflections on North American Pacific Coast Prehistory." *Journal of World Prehistory* 9:1–45.

Muller, John. 1997. *Mississippian Political Economy.* New York: Plenum.

Mulvaney, D.J. 1975. *Prehistory of Australia.* Sydney: Penguin.

Murdock, George Peter, and Catherine Provost. 1973. "Measurement of Cultural Complexity." *Ethnology* 12:379–392.

Murowchick, Robert. 1994. *China: Ancient Culture, Modern Land.* Norman: University of Oklahoma Press.

Murra, John V. 1980. *Economic Organization of the Inka State.* Greenwich: JAI Press.

Murray, Matthew. 2001. "Western European Late Bronze Age." In *Encyclopedia of Prehistory*, Vol. 4: *Europe*, ed. P.N. Peregrine and M. Ember. New York: Kluwer/Plenum, 415–435.

Murray, T. 1998. *Archaeology of Aboriginal Australia.* Sydney: Allen and Unwin.

Myers, Thomas P. 2001. "Ecuadorian Highlands." In *Encyclopedia of Prehistory*, Vol. 5: *Middle America*, ed. P.N. Peregrine and M. Ember. New York: Kluwer/Plenum, 155–196.

Nami, Hugo G. 1995. "Archaeological Research in the Argentinean Rio Chico Basin." *Current Anthropology* 36:661–664.

Narain, L.A. 1979. "The Neolithic Cultures of Eastern India." In *Essays in Indian Protohistory*, ed. D.P. Agrawal and D.K. Chakrabarti, Delhi: B.R. Publishing, 301–309.

Narayan, B. 1996. *Prehistoric Archaeology of Bihar.* Patna: K.P. Jayswal Research Institute.

Nelson, Sarah. 1993. *The Archaeology of Korea.* Cambridge: Cambridge University Press.

_____. 1995. *The Archaeology of Northeast China.* London: Routledge.

_____. 1996. "Ideology and the Formation of an Early State in Northeast China." In *Ideology and the Early State*, ed. H.J.M. Claessen and J.G. Oosten. Leiden, E.J. Brill.

_____. 2001a. "Chulum." In *Encyclopedia of Prehistory*, Vol. 3: *East Asia and Oceania*, ed. P.N. Peregrine and M. Ember. New York: Kluwer/Plenum, 1–11.

_____. 2001b. "Hongshan." In *Encyclopedia of Prehistory*, Vol. 3: *East Asia and Oceania*, ed. P.N. Peregrine and M. Ember. New York: Kluwer/Plenum, 77–81.

Neumann, Thomas William, and Robert M. Sanford. 2001a. *Cultural Resources Archaeology: An Introduction.* Walnut Creek, CA: AltaMira.

_____. 2001b. *Practicing Archaeology: A Training Manual for Cultural Resources Archaeology.* Walnut Creek, CA: AltaMira.

Newton, L., and Zarins, J. 2000. "Aspects of Bronze Age Art of Southern Arabia: The Pictorial Landscape and Its Relation to Economic and Socio-Political Status." *Arabian Archaeology and Epigraphy.* 11:154–179.

Nichols, Deborah, and Thomas Charlton. 2001. "Central Mexico Classic." In *Encyclopedia of Prehistory,* Vol. 5: *Middle America*, ed. P.N. Peregrine and M. Ember. New York: Kluwer/Plenum, 22–53.

Nihon, Kokogahu. 1949. *Toro* (2 vols.). Tokyo: Mainichi Shinbunsha.

Nisbet, Robert. 1969. *Social Change and History: Aspects of the Western Theory of Development.* New York: Oxford University Press.

Nissen, Hans. 1988. *The Early History of the Ancient Near East, 9000–2000 B.C.* Chicago: University of Chicago Press.

_____. 1993. "The Early Uruk Period, A Sketch." In Frangipane, M. et al., eds. *Between the Rivers and Over the Mountains.* Rome: Università di Roma, 123–132.

Noble, William, and Ian Davidson. 1996. *Human Evolution, Language, and Mind.* Cambridge: Cambridge University Press.

Noël Hume, Ivor. 1969. *Historical Archaeology.* New York, Knopf.

Noelli, Francisco. 1998. "The Tupi: Explaining Origin and Expansions in Terms of Archaeology and of Historical Linguistics." *Antiquity* 72:648–663.

Nuñez, A.L. 1983. "Paleoindian and Archaic Cultural Periods in the Arid and Semiarid Regions of Northern Chile." *Advances in World Archaeology* 2:161–203.

O'Connell, J.F., and J. Allen. 1998. "When Did Humans First Arrive in Australia and Why Is It Important to Know?" *Evolutionary Anthropology* 6:132–146.

O'Connor, Terrence P. 2000. *The Archaeology of Animal Bones.* College Station: Texas A&M University Press.

Odell, George. 1996. *Stone Tools: Theoretical Insights into Human Prehistory.* New York: Plenum.

Ohnersorgon, Michael, and Mark Varien. 1996. "Formal Architecture and Settlement Organization in Ancient West Mexico." *Ancient Mesoamerica* 7:103–120.

Okladnikov, A.P. 1959. *Ancient Populations of Siberia and Its Cultures.* Cambridge, MA: Peabody Museum, Harvard University.

_____. 1965. *The Soviet Far East in Antiquity.* Toronto: University of Toronto Press.

_____. 1970. *Yakutia before Its Incorporation into the Russian State.* Montreal: McGill-Queen's Press.

_____. 1990. "Inner Asia at the Dawn of History." In *Cambridge History of Early Inner Asia*, ed. D. Sinor. Cambridge: Cambridge University Press, 41–96.

Oliver, Douglas. 1974. *Ancient Tahitian Society* (3 vols.). Honolulu: University of Hawaii Press.

Orquera, Luis Abel. 1987. "Advances in the Archaeology of the Pampa and Patagonia." *Journal of World Prehistory* 1:333–413.

Orton, Clive, Paul Tyers, and Alan Vince. 1993. *Pottery in Archaeology.* Cambridge: Cambridge University Press.

Park, Robert. 2001. "Eastern Arctic Small Tool." In *Encyclopedia of Prehistory*, Vol. 2: *Arctic and Subarctic*, ed. P.N. Peregrine and M. Ember. New York: Kluwer/Plenum, 27–45.

Parkes, Penelope A. 1987. *Current Scientific Techniques in Archaeology.* New York: St. Martin's.

Parry, J.T. 1984. "Air Photo Interpretation of Fortified Sites: Ring-ditch Fortifications in Southern Viti Levu, Fiji." *New Zealand Journal of Archaeology* 6:71–93.

Parry, William J. 2002. "When and How Did Humans Populate the New World?" In P.N. Peregrine, C. Ember, and M. Ember, eds, *Archaeology: Original Readings in Method and Practice.* Upper Saddle River, NJ: Prentice Hall, 167–179.

Pasztory, Esther. 1997. *Teotihuacan: An Experiment in Living.* Norman: University of Oklahoma Press.

Pauketat, Timothy J. 1994. *The Ascent of Chiefs.* Tuscaloosa: University of Alabama Press.

Pauketat, Timothy J., and T.E. Emerson. 1997. *Cahokia: Domination and Ideology in the Mississippian World.* Lincoln: University of Nebraska Press.

Pearsall, Deborah. 1989. *Paleoethnobotany: A Handbook of Procedures.* San Diego: Academic Press.

Pearson, Richard. 1992. *Ancient Japan.* New York: George Braziller.

Pearson, Richard, Gina L. Barnes, and Karl L. Hutterer. 1986. *Windows on the Japanese Past: Studies in Archaeology and Prehistory.* Ann Arbor: Center for Japanese Studies, University of Michigan.

Peasnall, Brian L. 2002a. "Iranian Chalcolithic." In *Encyclopedia of Prehistory,* Vol. 8: *South and Southwest Asia,* ed. P.N. Peregrine and M. Ember. New York: Kluwer/Plenum, 163–198.

———. 2002b. "Iranian Mesolithic." In *Encyclopedia of Prehistory,* Vol. 8: *South and Southwest Asia,* ed. P.N. Peregrine and M. Ember. New York: Kluwer/ Plenum, 211–227.

———. 2002c. "Iranian Neolithic." In *Encyclopedia of Prehistory,* Vol. 8: *South and Southwest Asia,* ed. P.N. Peregrine and M. Ember. New York: Kluwer/Plenum, 228–246.

———. 2002d. "Ubaid." In *Encyclopedia of Prehistory,* Vol. 8: *South and Southwest Asia,* ed. P.N. Peregrine and M. Ember. New York: Kluwer/Plenum, 370–388.

Peltenburg, E. 1989. *Early Society in Cyprus.* Edinburgh: Edinburgh University Press.

Peregrine, Peter N. 2001. *Archaeological Research: A Brief Introduction.* Upper Saddle River, NJ: Prentice Hall.

———. 2001. "Cross-Cultural Comparative Approaches in Archaeology." *Annual Review of Anthropology* 30:1–18.

———. 2001. "Amur Neolithic and Bronze Age." In *Encyclopedia of Prehistory,* Vol. 2: *Arctic and Subarctic,* ed. P.N. Peregrine and M. Ember. New York: Kluwer/Plenum, 16–17.

———. 2001. "Aurignacian." In *Encyclopedia of Prehistory,* Vol. 4: *Europe,* ed. P.N. Peregrine and M. Ember. New York: Kluwer/Plenum, 22–23.

———. 2001. "Central Plains Village." In *Encyclopedia of Prehistory,* Vol. 6: *North America,* ed. P.N. Peregrine and M. Ember. New York: Kluwer/Plenum, 30–31.

———. 2001. "Corded Ware." In *Encyclopedia of Prehistory,* Vol. 4: *Europe,* ed. P.N. Peregrine and M. Ember. New York: Kluwer/Plenum, 77–78.

———. 2001. "Cosumnes." In *Encyclopedia of Prehistory,* Vol. 6: *North America,* ed.

P.N. Peregrine and M. Ember. New York: Kluwer/Plenum, 32–33.

———. 2001. "Daxi." In *Encyclopedia of Prehistory,* Vol. 3: *East Asia and Oceania,* ed. P.N. Peregrine and M. Ember. New York: Kluwer/Plenum, 16–17.

———. 2001. "Dorset." In *Encyclopedia of Prehistory,* Vol. 2: *Arctic and Subarctic,* ed. P.N. Peregrine and M. Ember. New York: Kluwer/Plenum, 23–24.

———. 2001. "Early and Middle High Plains Archaic." In *Encyclopedia of Prehistory,* Vol. 6: *North America,* ed. P.N. Peregrine and M. Ember. New York: Kluwer/ Plenum, 43–44.

———. 2001. "Early Nomad." In *Encyclopedia of Prehistory,* Vol. 3: *East Asia and Oceania,* ed. P.N. Peregrine and M. Ember. New York: Kluwer/Plenum, 23–24.

———. 2001. "Early Northwest Coast." In *Encyclopedia of Prehistory,* Vol. 2: *Arctic and Subarctic,* ed. P.N. Peregrine and M. Ember. New York: Kluwer/Plenum, 25–26.

———. 2001. "Early Sierra Nevada." In *Encyclopedia of Prehistory,* Vol. 6: *North America,* ed. P.N. Peregrine and M. Ember. New York: Kluwer/Plenum, 142–143.

———. 2001. "East African Microlithic." In *Encyclopedia of Prehistory,* Vol. 1: *Africa,* ed. P.N. Peregrine and M. Ember. New York: Kluwer/Plenum, 95–96.

———. 2001. "Eastern Central Asia Neolithic and Bronze Age." In *Encyclopedia of Prehistory,* Vol. 3: *East Asia and Oceania,* ed. P.N. Peregrine and M. Ember. New York: Kluwer/Plenum, 60–61.

———. 2001. "Fijian." In *Encyclopedia of Prehistory,* Vol. 3: *East Asia and Oceania,* ed. P.N. Peregrine and M. Ember. New York: Kluwer/Plenum, 64–65.

———. 2001. "Harder." In *Encyclopedia of Prehistory,* Vol. 6: *North America,* ed. P.N. Peregrine and M. Ember. New York: Kluwer/Plenum, 213–214.

———. 2001. "High Plains Late Prehistoric." In *Encyclopedia of Prehistory,* Vol. 6: *North America,* ed. P.N. Peregrine and M. Ember. New York: Kluwer/Plenum, 215–216.

———. 2001. "Highland Mesoamerican Archaic." In *Encyclopedia of Prehistory,* Vol. 5: *Middle America,* ed. P.N. Peregrine and M. Ember. New York: Kluwer/ Plenum, 216–217.

———. 2001. "Hopewell." In *Encyclopedia of Prehistory,* Vol. 6: *North America,* ed. P.N. Peregrine and M. Ember. New York: Kluwer/Plenum, 217–220.

———. 2001. "Hotchkiss." In *Encyclopedia of Prehistory,* Vol. 6: *North America,* ed. P.N. Peregrine and M. Ember. New York: Kluwer/Plenum, 221–222.

———. 2001. "Kelteminar." In *Encyclopedia of Prehistory,* Vol. 4, *Europe,* ed.

P.N. Peregrine and M. Ember. New York: Kluwer/Plenum, 189–190.

———. 2001. "Late Desert Archaic." In *Encyclopedia of Prehistory,* Vol. 6: *North America,* ed. P.N. Peregrine and M. Ember. New York: Kluwer/Plenum, 241–242.

———. 2001. "Late Paleoindian." In *Encyclopedia of Prehistory,* Vol. 6: *North America,* ed. P.N. Peregrine and M. Ember. New York: Kluwer/Plenum, 291–292.

———. 2001. "Melanesian." In *Encyclopedia of Prehistory,* Vol. 3: *East Asia and Oceania,* ed. P.N. Peregrine and M. Ember. New York: Kluwer/Plenum, 252–253.

———. 2001. "Micronesian." In *Encyclopedia of Prehistory,* Vol. 3: *East Asia and Oceania,* ed. P.N. Peregrine and M. Ember. New York: Kluwer/Plenum, 254–255.

———. 2001. "Mississippian" In *Encyclopedia of Prehistory,* Vol. 6: *North America,* ed. P.N. Peregrine and M. Ember. New York: Kluwer/Plenum, 335–338.

———. 2001. "New Guinea Neolithic." In *Encyclopedia of Prehistory,* Vol. 3: *East Asia and Oceania,* ed. P.N. Peregrine and M. Ember. New York: Kluwer/Plenum, 272–273.

———. 2001. "Northeastern European Bronze Age." In *Encyclopedia of Prehistory,* Vol. 4: *Europe,* ed. P.N. Peregrine and M. Ember. New York: Kluwer/ Plenum, 222–223.

———. 2001. "Northern Archaic." In *Encyclopedia of Prehistory,* Vol. 2: *Arctic and Subarctic,* ed. P.N. Peregrine and M. Ember. New York: Kluwer/Plenum, 131–132.

———. 2001. "Paleo-Arctic." In *Encyclopedia of Prehistory,* Vol. 2: *Arctic and Subarctic,* ed. P.N. Peregrine and M. Ember. New York: Kluwer/Plenum, 169–170.

———. 2001. "Patayan." In *Encyclopedia of Prehistory,* Vol. 6: *North America,* ed. P.N. Peregrine and M. Ember. New York: Kluwer/Plenum, 408–409.

———. 2001. "Paya." In *Encyclopedia of Prehistory,* Vol. 5: *Middle America,* ed. P.N. Peregrine and M. Ember. New York: Kluwer/Plenum, 351–352.

———. 2001. "Peiligang." In *Encyclopedia of Prehistory,* Vol. 3: *East Asia and Oceania,* ed. P.N. Peregrine and M. Ember. New York: Kluwer/Plenum, 283–284.

———. 2001. "Preclassic Maya." In *Encyclopedia of Prehistory,* Vol. 5: *Middle America,* ed. P.N. Peregrine and M. Ember. New York: Kluwer/Plenum, 378–380.

———. 2001. "Samoan." In *Encyclopedia of Prehistory,* Vol. 3: *East Asia and Oceania,* ed. P.N. Peregrine and M. Ember. New York: Kluwer/Plenum, 285–286.

———. 2001. "San Dieguito." In *Encyclopedia of Prehistory*, Vol. 6: *North America*, ed. P.N. Peregrine and M. Ember. New York: Kluwer/Plenum, 466–467.

———. 2001. "Scandinavian Iron Age." In *Encyclopedia of Prehistory*, Vol. 4: *Europe*, ed. P.N. Peregrine and M. Ember. New York: Kluwer/Plenum, 315–317.

———. 2001. "Scythian." In *Encyclopedia of Prehistory*, Vol. 4: *Europe*, ed. P.N. Peregrine and M. Ember. New York: Kluwer/Plenum, 324–327.

———. 2001. "Shield Archaic." In *Encyclopedia of Prehistory*, Vol. 2: *Arctic and Subarctic*, ed. P.N. Peregrine and M. Ember. New York: Kluwer/Plenum, 181–182.

———. 2001. "Siberian Protohistoric." In *Encyclopedia of Prehistory*, Vol. 2: *Arctic and Subarctic*, ed. P.N. Peregrine and M. Ember. New York: Kluwer/Plenum, 205–206.

———. 2001. "Southeast China Early Neolithic." In *Encyclopedia of Prehistory*, Vol. 3: *East Asia and Oceania*, ed. P.N. Peregrine and M. Ember. New York: Kluwer/Plenum, 310–311.

———. 2001. "Southeastern European Neolithic." In *Encyclopedia of Prehistory*, Vol. 4: *Europe*, ed. P.N. Peregrine and M. Ember. New York: Kluwer/Plenum, 381–382.

———. 2001. "Southern and Eastern Africa Later Stone Age." In *Encyclopedia of Prehistory*, Vol. 1: *Africa*, ed. P.N. Peregrine and M. Ember. New York: Kluwer/Plenum, 257–259.

———. 2001. "Southern and Eastern Africa Middle Stone Age." In *Encyclopedia of Prehistory*, Vol. 1: *Africa*, ed. P.N. Peregrine and M. Ember. New York: Kluwer/Plenum, 260–261.

———. 2001. "Southern Mediterranean Neolithic." In *Encyclopedia of Prehistory*, Vol. 1: *Africa*, ed. P.N. Peregrine and M. Ember with Antonio Gilman. New York: Kluwer/Plenum, 262–263.

———. 2001. "Tahitian." In *Encyclopedia of Prehistory*, Vol. 3: *East Asia and Oceania*, ed. P.N. Peregrine and M. Ember. New York: Kluwer/Plenum, 329–330.

———. 2001. "Tongan." In *Encyclopedia of Prehistory*, Vol. 3: *East Asia and Oceania*, ed. P.N. Peregrine and M. Ember. New York: Kluwer/Plenum, 331–332.

———. 2001. "Tucannon." In *Encyclopedia of Prehistory*, Vol. 6: *North America*, ed. P.N. Peregrine and M. Ember. New York: Kluwer/Plenum, 468–469.

———. 2001. "West-Central European Late Iron Age." In *Encyclopedia of Prehistory*, Vol. 4: *Europe*, ed. P.N. Peregrine and M. Ember with Ralph Rowlett. New York: Kluwer/Plenum, 399–411.

———. 2001. "Western European Earlier Bronze Age." In *Encyclopedia of Prehistory*, Vol. 4: *Europe*, ed. P.N. Peregrine and M. Ember. New York: Kluwer/Plenum, 412–414.

———. 2001. "Windmiller." In *Encyclopedia of Prehistory*, Vol. 6: *North America*, ed. P.N. Peregrine and M. Ember. New York: Kluwer/Plenum, 470–471.

———. 2001. "Yayoi." In *Encyclopedia of Prehistory*, Vol. 3: *East Asia and Oceania*, ed. P.N. Peregrine and M. Ember. New York: Kluwer/Plenum, 349–350.

———. 2002. "Arabian Upper Paleolithic." In P.N. Peregrine and M. Ember, eds, *Encyclopedia of Prehistory*, Vol. 8: *South and Southwest Asia*. New York: Kluwer/Plenum, 24–25.

———. 2002. "South Asia Upper Paleolithic." In P.N. Peregrine and M. Ember, eds, *Encyclopedia of Prehistory*, Vol. 8: *South and Southwest Asia*. New York: Kluwer/Plenum, 368–369.

Peregrine, Peter, and Peter Bellwood. 2001. "Southeast Asia Upper Paleolithic." In *Encyclopedia of Prehistory*, Vol. 3: *East Asia and Oceania*, ed. P.N. Peregrine and M. Ember. New York: Kluwer/Plenum, 307–309.

Peregrine, Peter N., Carol R. Ember, and Melvin Ember. 2002. *Archaeology: Original Readings in Method and Practice*. Upper Saddle River, NJ: Prentice Hall

Peterkin, Gail L., H.M. Bricker, and P. Mellars. 1993. *Hunting and Animal Exploitation in the Later Paleolithic and Mesolithic of Eurasia*. Washington, DC: American Anthropological Association, Archaeological Papers 4.

Phillips, James L., and James Brown. 1983. *Archaic Hunter-Gatherers in the American Midwest*. New York: Academic Press.

Phillipson, David W. 1977. *The Later Prehistory of Eastern and Southern Africa*. New York: Africana.

———. 1993. *African Archaeology*. Cambridge: Cambridge University Press.

Piana, Ernesto L. 2002. "Magellan-Fuegan." In *Encyclopedia of Prehistory*, Vol. 7: *South America*, ed. P.N. Peregrine and M. Ember. New York: Kluwer/Plenum, 255–271.

Pigott, Vincent C. 1999. The *Archaeometallurgy of the Asian Old World*. Philadelphia: The University Museum, University of Pennsylvania.

Pike-Tay, Anne. 2001. "Perigordian." In *Encyclopedia of Prehistory*, Vol. 4: *Europe*, ed. P.N. Peregrine and M. Ember. New York: Kluwer/Plenum, 236–263.

Piperno, Dolores, and Deborah Pearsall. 1998. *The Origin of Agriculture in the Lowland Neotropics*. New York: Academic Press.

Pittman, Holly. 1993. "Pictures of an Administration: The Late Uruk Scribe at Work." In M. Frangipane et al., eds., *Between the Rivers and Over the Mountains*, Rome: Università di Roma La Sapienza, 235–246.

Pitul'ko, Vladimir V. 1993. "An Early Holocene Site in the Siberian High Arctic." *Arctic Anthropology* 30(1):13–21.

———. 2001. "Holocene Stone Age of Northeast Asia." In *Encyclopedia of Prehistory*, Vol. 2: *Arctic and Subarctic*, ed. P.N. Peregrine and M. Ember. New York: Kluwer/Plenum, 46–58.

Pitul'ko, Vladimir, and A.K. Kasparov. 1996. "Ancient Arctic Hunters: Material Culture and Survival Strategy." *Arctic Anthropology* 33(1):1–31.

Plog, Stephen. 1997. *Ancient Peoples of the American Southwest*. London: Thames and Hudson.

Pollard, A. Mark, and Carl Heron. 1996. *Archaeological Chemistry*. Cambridge: Royal Society of Chemistry.

Pollard, Helen. 1993. *Tariacuri's Legacy: The Prehispanic Tarascan State*. Norman: University of Oklahoma Press.

———. 1997. "Recent Research in West Mexican Archaeology." *Journal of Archaeological Research* 5:345–384.

———. 2001. "West Mexico Postclassic." In *Encyclopedia of Prehistory*, Vol. 5: *Middle America*, ed. P.N. Peregrine and M. Ember. New York: Kluwer/Plenum, 397–415.

Pollock, Susan. 1999. *Ancient Mesopotamia*. Cambridge: Cambridge University Press.

———. 2000. *Mesopotamia: The Eden That Never Was*. Cambridge: Cambridge University Press.

Pool, Christopher. 2001. "Gulf Coast Classic." In *Encyclopedia of Prehistory*, Vol. 5: *Middle America*, ed. P.N. Peregrine and M. Ember. New York: Kluwer/Plenum, 204–217.

Possehl, Gregory L. 1993. *Harappan Civilization: A Recent Perspective*. New Delhi: Oxford.

———. 1999. *Indus Age: The Beginnings*. New Delhi, Oxford and IBH.

Possehl, Gregory L., and Michael Witzel. 2002. "Vedic." In *Encyclopedia of Prehistory*, Vol. 8: *South and Southwest Asia*, ed. P.N. Peregrine and M. Ember. New York: Kluwer/Plenum, 389–395.

Postgate, J. Nicholas. 1992. *Early Mesopotamia: Society and Economy at the Dawn of History*. London: Routledge.

Potts, Daniel T. 1980. *Tradition and Transformation: Tepe Yahya and the Iranian Plateau during the Third Millennium, B.C.* Cambridge: Harvard University.

———. 1990. *The Arabian Gulf in Antiquity*. Oxford: Clarendon.

———. 1999. *The Archaeology of Elam*. Cambridge: Cambridge University Press.

Potts, Richard. 1988. *Early Hominid Activities at Olduvai*. New York: Aldine de Gruyter.

Poulsen, Jens. 1968. "Archaeological Excavations on Tongatapu." In *Prehistoric*

*Culture in Oceania,* ed. I. Yawata and Y. Sinoto. Honolulu: Bernice P. Bishop Museum, 85–92.

———. 1977. "Archaeology and Prehistory." In *Friendly Islands: A History of Tonga,* ed. N. Rutherford. Oxford: Oxford University Press, 4–26

Powers, William R. 1973. "Paleolithic Man in Northeast Asia." *Arctic Anthropology* 10(2):1–106.

Pozorsky, Shelia, and Thomas Pozorsky. 1987. *Early Settlement and Subsistence in the Casma Valley, Peru.* Iowa City: University of Iowa Press.

———. 2002a. "Early Coastal Andean Formative." In *Encyclopedia of Prehistory,* Vol. 7: *South America,* ed. P.N. Peregrine and M. Ember. New York: Kluwer/Plenum, 78–97.

———. 2002b. "Late Coastal Andean Formative." In *Encyclopedia of Prehistory,* Vol. 7: *South America,* ed. P.N. Peregrine and M. Ember. New York: Kluwer/Plenum, 217–227.

Praetzellis, Adrian. 2000. *Death by Theory: A Tale of Mystery and Archaeological Theory.* Mountain View, CA: Altamira.

Prescott, Christopher. 2001. "Scandinavian Neolithic." In *Encyclopedia of Prehistory,* Vol. 4: *Europe,* ed. P.N. Peregrine and M. Ember. New York: Kluwer/Plenum, 318–323.

Preucel, Robert. 1991. *Processual and Postprocessual Archaeologies: Multiple Ways of Knowing the Past.* Carbondale: Southern Illinois University Press.

Price, T. Douglas. 2000. *Europe's First Farmers.* Cambridge: Cambridge University Press.

Price, T. Douglas, and Gary Feinman. 2001. *Images of the Past.* Mountain View, CA: Mayfield.

Price, T. Douglas, and A.B. Gebauer. 1995. *Last Hunters, First Farmers: New Perspectives on the Prehistoric Transition to Agriculture.* Santa Fe, NM: School of American Research Press.

Pringle, Heather. 1998. "The Slow Birth of Agriculture." *Science* 282:1446–1450.

Proulx, Donald. 2002. "Nasca." In *Encyclopedia of Prehistory,* Vol. 7: *South America,* ed. P.N. Peregrine and M. Ember. New York: Kluwer/Plenum, 280–288.

Proussakov, Dmitry. 2001. "Early Dynastic Egypt." In *Encyclopedia of Prehistory,* Vol. 1: *Africa,* ed. P.N. Peregrine and M. Ember. New York: Kluwer/Plenum, 77–85.

Purdy, Barbara A. 1996. *How to Do Archaeology the Right Way.* Gainesville: University Press of Florida.

Ragir, Sonia R. 1972. *The Early Horizon in Central California Prehistory.* Berkeley: University of California, Contributions of the University of California Archaeological Research Facility 15.

Ramenofsky, Anne F., and Anastasia Steffen. 1998. *Unit Issues in Archaeology: Measuring Time, Space, and Material.* Salt Lake City: University of Utah Press.

Rapp, George Robert, and Christopher L. Hill. 1998. *Geoarchaeology: The Earth-science Approach to Archaeological Interpretation.* New Haven: Yale University Press.

Rawson, Jessica. 1996. *Mysteries of Ancient China: New Discoveries from the Early Dynasties.* New York: George Brazilier.

Ray, R. 1987. *Ancient Settlement Patterns of Eastern India: Prehistoric Period.* Calcutta: Pearl.

Redman, Charles L. 1978. *The Rise of Civilization: From Early Farmers to Urban Society in the Ancient Near East.* San Francisco: Freeman.

Reed, Charles A. 1977. *Origins of Agriculture.* The Hague: Mouton.

Reid, J. Jefferson. 2001. "Late Mogollon." In *Encyclopedia of Prehistory,* Vol. 6: *North America,* ed. P.N. Peregrine and M. Ember. New York: Kluwer/Plenum, 287–290.

Reid, J. Jefferson, and Stephanie Whittlesey. 1997. *The Archaeology of Ancient Arizona.* Tucson: University of Arizona Press.

———. 1999. *Grasshopper Pueblo: A Story of Archaeology and Ancient Life.* Tucson: University of Arizona Press.

Renfrew, Colin. 1983. *The Megalithic Monuments of Western Europe.* London: Thames and Hudson.

Renfrew, Colin. 1997. *The Emergence of Civilization: The Cyclades and the Aegean in the Third Millennium B.C.* London: Methuen.

Renfrew, Colin, and Paul Bahn. 1996. *Archaeology: Theories, Methods, and Practice.* New York: Thames and Hudson.

Rhee, Song-Nai. 2001. "Mumun." In *Encyclopedia of Prehistory,* Vol. 4: *Europe,* ed. P.N. Peregrine and M. Ember. New York: Kluwer/Plenum, 256–271.

Rhee, Song-Nai, and Mong-Lyong Choi. 1992. "Emergence of Complex Society in Prehistoric Korea." *Journal of World Prehistory* 6:51–95.

Rice, Michael. 1990. *Egypt's Making: The Origins of Ancient Egypt 5000–2000 B.C.* London: Routledge.

———. 1994. *Archaeology of the Arabian Gulf.* London: Routledge.

Rice, Patricia C., and Ann L. Paterson. 1985. "Cave Art and Bones: Exploring the Interrelationships." *American Anthropologist* 87:94–100.

———. 1986. "Validating the Cave Art-Archeofaunal Relationship in Cantabrian Spain." *American Anthropologist* 88: 658–667.

Rice, Prudence. 1987. *Pottery Analysis: A Sourcebook.* Chicago: University of Chicago Press.

Rice, Tamara. 1961. *The Scythians.* 3rd ed. London: Thames and Hudson.

Richie, William A. 1980. *Archaeology of New York State.* Harrison, NY: Harbor Hill Books.

Rick, John W. 1980. *Prehistoric Hunters of the High Andes.* New York: Academic Press.

———. 2002. "Early Highland Andean Archaic." In *Encyclopedia of Prehistory,* Vol. 7: *South America,* ed. P.N. Peregrine and M. Ember. New York: Kluwer/Plenum, 108–120.

Rightmire, G. Philip. 1990. *The Evolution of Homo erectus: Comparative Anatomical Studies of an Extinct Human Species.* Cambridge: Cambridge University Press.

———. 1997. "Human Evolution in the Middle Pleistocene: The Role of *Homo heidelbergensis.*" *Evolutionary Anthropology* 6:281–227.

———. 2000. "*Homo erectus.*" In Eric Delson, Ian Tattersall, John van Couvering, and Alison Brooks, eds, *Encyclopedia of Human Evolution and Prehistory.* New York: Garland, 322–326.

Rivera, M. 1991. "The Prehistory of Northern Chile: A Synthesis." *Journal of World Prehistory* 5:1–47.

Rizkana, Ibrahim, and Jürgen Seeher. 1987–1990. *Maadi,* Parts I–IV. Mainz: Phillip von Zabern.

Roaf, Michael. 1990. *Cultural Atlas of Mesopotamia.* New York: Facts on File.

Robbins, L.H. 1984. "Late Prehistoric Aquatic and Pastoral Adaptations West of Lake Turkana, Kenya." In *From Hunters to Farmers: The Causes and Consequences of Food Production in Africa,* ed. J.D. Clark and S.A. Brandt. Berkeley: University of California Press, 206–211.

———. 1998. "Eastern African Advanced Foragers." In *Encyclopedia of Precolonial Africa,* ed. J.O. Vogel. Walnut Creek: Altamira, 335–341.

Robertshaw, P. 1989. "The Development of Pastoralism in East Africa." In *The Walking Larder: Patterns of Domestication, Pastoralism, and Predation,* ed. J. Clutton-Brock. London: Unwin Hyman, 207–214.

———. 1993. "The Beginnings of Food Production in Southwestern Kenya." In *The Archaeology of Africa,* ed. T. Shaw, P. Sinclair, B. Andah, and A. Okpoko. London: Routledge, 358–371.

Robertson, John H. 2001. "South African Iron Age." In *Encyclopedia of Prehistory,* Vol. 1: *Africa,* ed. P.N. Peregrine and M. Ember. New York: Kluwer/Plenum, 260–271.

Rogers, J.D., and B.D. Smith. 1995. *Mississippian Communities and Households.* Tuscaloosa: University of Alabama Press.

Rogers, Malcolm. 1966. *Ancient Hunters of the Far West.* San Diego: Union-Tribune.

Rolett, Barry. 1993. "Marquesan Prehistory and the Origins of East Polynesia

Culture." *Journal de la Société des Océanistes* 96:29–47.

———. 1998. *Hanamiai: Prehistoric Colonization and Cultural Change in the Marquesas Islands.* New Haven: Yale Publications in Anthropology 81.

———. 2001. "Marquesan." In *Encyclopedia of Prehistory,* Vol. 4: *Europe,* ed. P.N. Peregrine and M. Ember. New York: Kluwer/Plenum, 243–251.

Rolle, Renate. 1980. *The World of the Scythians.* Berkeley: University of California Press.

Roosevelt, Anna C. 1980. *Parmana: Prehistoric Maize and Manioc Subsistence along the Amazon and Orinoco.* New York: Academic Press.

———. 1991. *Moundbuilders of the Amazon: Geophysical Archaeology on Marajo Island, Brazil.* San Diego: Academic Press.

———. 1995. "Early Pottery in the Amazon: Twenty Years of Scholarly Obscurity." In *The Emergence of Pottery,* ed. W. Barnett and J. Hoopes. Washington, DC: Smithsonian Institution Press, 115–131.

———. 1998a. "Paleoindian and Archaic Occupation in the Lower Amazon: A Summary and Comparison." In *Explorations in American Archaeology: Essays in Honor of Wesley R. Hurt,* ed. Mark G. Plew. Lanham, MD: University Press of America, 165–191.

———. 1998b. "Amazonian Hunter-Gatherers." In *Advances in Historical Ecology,* ed. W. Balee. New York: Columbia University Press, 120–212.

———. 1998c. "Paleoindian and Archaic Occupations in the Lower Amazon: A Summary and Comparison." In *Explorations in American Archaeology: Essays in Honor of Wesley R. Hurt,* ed. Mark G. Plew. Lanham, MD: University Press of America, 165–191.

———. 1999a. "The Maritime-Highland-Forest Dynamic and the Origins of Complex Society." In *History of the Native Peoples of the Americas: South America,* ed. F. Salomon and S. Schwartz. Cambridge: Cambridge University Press, 264–349.

———. 1999b. "Ancient Hunter-Gatherers of South America." In *Cambridge Encyclopedia of Hunter-Gatherers,* ed. R. Lee and R. Daly. Cambridge: Cambridge University Press, 86–92.

———. 2002a. "Early Amazonian." In *Encyclopedia of Prehistory,* Vol. 7: *South America,* ed. P.N. Peregrine and M. Ember. New York: Kluwer/Plenum, 75–77.

———. 2002b. "Late Amazonian." In *Encyclopedia of Prehistory,* Vol. 7: *South America,* ed. P.N. Peregrine and M. Ember. New York: Kluwer/Plenum, 195–199.

———. 2002c. "Old Amazonian Collecting-Hunting." In *Encyclopedia of Prehistory,* Vol. 7: *South America,* ed. P.N. Peregrine and M. Ember. New York: Kluwer/Plenum, 293–303.

Roosevelt, Anna C. et al. 1996. "Paleoindian Cave Dwellers in the Americas: The Peopling of the Americas." *Science* 272:373–384.

Rose, M.D. 1984. "Food Acquisition and the Evolution of Positional Behaviour: The Case of Bipedalism." In *Food Acquisition and Processing in Primates,* ed. David J. Chivers, Bernard A. Wood, and Alan Bilsborough. New York: Plenum, 509–524.

Ross, Richard E. 1990. "Prehistory of the Oregon Coast." In *Handbook of North American Indians,* Vol. 7, ed. W. Suttles. Washington, DC: Smithsonian Institution Press, 554–559.

Roth, Barbara. 2001. "Early Desert Archaic." In *Encyclopedia of Prehistory,* Vol. 6: *North America,* ed. P.N. Peregrine and M. Ember. New York: Kluwer/Plenum, 45–54.

Rothman, Mitchell. 1989. "Out of the Heartland: The Evolution of Complexity in Peripheral Mesopotamia During the Uruk Period: Workshop Summary." *Paléorient* 15/1:279–290.

———. 2000. *Uruk Mesopotamia and Its Neighbors: Cross-cultural Interactions and the Consequences in the Era of State Formation.* Santa Fe: SAR.

———. 2002. "Late Chalcolithic Mesopotamia." In *Encyclopedia of Prehistory,* Vol. 8: *South and Southwest Asia,* ed. P.N. Peregrine and M. Ember. New York: Kluwer/Plenum, 201–210.

Roubet, Collette. 2001. "Neolithic of Capsian." in *Encyclopedia of Prehistory,* Vol. 1: *Africa,* ed. P.N. Peregrine and M. Ember. New York: Kluwer/Plenum, 197–219.

Rouse, Irving. 1992. *The Tainos: Rise and Decline of the People Who Greeted Columbus.* New Haven: Yale University Press.

Roy, Tribhuvan Nath. 1983. *The Ganges Civilization: A Critical Study of the Painted Grey Ware and Northern Black Polished Ware Periods of the Ganga Plains of India.* New Delhi: Ramanand Vidya Bhawan.

Runnels, Curtis. 1995. "Review of Aegean Prehistory IV: The Stone Age of Greece from the Palaeolithic to the Advent of the Neolithic." *American Journal of Archaeology* 99:699–728.

Rutter, Jeremy. 1993. "Review of Aegean Prehistory II: The Prepalatial Bronze Age of the Southern and Central Greek Mainland." *American Journal of Archaeology* 97:745–797.

Sabloff, Jeremy A. 1990. *The New Archaeology and the Ancient Maya.* New York: W.H. Freeman.

Sabloff, Jeremy A., and E. Wyllys Andrews. 1986. *Late Lowland Maya Civilization.*

Albuquerque: University of New Mexico Press.

Sahlins, Marshall, and Elman Service. 1960. *Evolution and Culture.* Ann Arbor: University of Michigan Press.

Salomon, Frank. 1986. *Native Lords of Quito in the Age of the Incas: The Political Economy of North Andean Chiefdoms.* Cambridge: Cambridge University Press.

Sampson, C. Garth. 1974. *The Stone Age Archaeology of Southern Africa.* New York: Academic Press.

Sampson, Ross. 1990. *Social Archaeology of Houses.* Edinburgh: Edinburgh University Press.

Sanders, William T. 1968. "Hydraulic Agriculture, Economic Symbiosis, and the Evolution of States in Central Mexico." In *Anthropological Archaeology in the Americas,* ed. Betty J. Meggers. Washington, DC: Anthropological Society of Washington.

Sanders, William T, Jeffrey Parsons, and Robert Stantley. 1979. *The Basin of Mexico: Ecological Processes in the Evolution of a Civilization.* New York: Academic Press.

Sanders, William T., and Barbara J. Price. 1968. *Mesoamerica.* New York: Random House.

Sanderson, Stephen. 1990. *Social Evolutionism: A Critical History.* Oxford: Basil Blackwell.

Sankalia, H.D. 1974. *Prehistory and Protohistory of India and Pakistan.* 2nd ed. Poona: Deccan College Research Institute.

Sant, U. 1991. *Neolithic Settlement Pattern of North-eastern and Northern India.* Delhi: Sarita Book House.

Sassaman, Kenneth E. 2001a. "Late Eastern Archaic." In *Encyclopedia of Prehistory,* Vol. 6: *North America,* ed. P.N. Peregrine and M. Ember. New York: Kluwer/Plenum, 243–247.

———. 2001b. "Middle Eastern Archaic." In *Encyclopedia of Prehistory,* Vol. 6: *North America,* ed. P.N. Peregrine and M. Ember. New York: Kluwer/Plenum, 318–321.

Sassaman, Kenneth, and David G. Anderson. 1996. *Archaeology of the Mid-Holocene Southeast.* Gainesville: University Press of Florida.

Savage, Stephen H. 2001. "Upper Egypt Predynastic." In *Encyclopedia of Prehistory,* Vol. 1: *Africa,* ed. P.N. Peregrine and M. Ember. New York: Kluwer/Plenum, 287–312.

Savage-Rubaugh, E.S. 1992. "Language Training of Apes." In Steve Jones, Robert Martin, and David Pilbeam, eds, *The Cambridge Encyclopedia of Human Evolution.* Cambridge: Cambridge University Press, 138–142.

Scarre, Christopher. 1983. *Ancient France, 6000–2000 B.C.* Edinburgh: Edinburgh University Press.

Scarry, John F. 1996. *Political Structure and Change in the Prehistoric Southeastern United States.* Gainesville: University Press of Florida.

Scarry, C. Margaret. 1993. *Foraging and Farming in the Eastern Woodlands.* Gainesville: University Press of Florida.

Schele, Linda, and David Freidel. 1990. *A Forest of Kings.* New York: William Morrow.

Schick, Kathy, and Nicholas Toth. 1993. *Making Silent Stones Speak.* New York: Simon & Schuster.

Schiffer, Michael B. 1976. *Behavioral Archeology.* New York: Academic Press.

———. 1987. *Formation Processes of the Archaeological Record.* Albuquerque: University of New Mexico Press.

———. 2001. *Social Theory in Archaeology.* Salt Lake City: University of Utah Press.

Schledermann, P. 1990. *Crossroads to Greenland: 3000 Years of Prehistory in the Eastern High Arctic.* Calgary: Arctic Institute of North America.

Schlesier, K.H. 1994. *Plains Indians, A.D. 500–1500.* Norman: University of Oklahoma Press.

Schmidt, Peter R. 1996. *The Culture and Technology of African Iron Production.* Gainesville: University Press of Florida.

Schwartz, Glenn M. 1994. "Before Ebla: Models of Pre-State Political Organization in Syria and Northern Mesopotamia." In *Chiefdoms and Early States in the Near East: The Organizational Dynamics of Complexity,* ed. G. Stein and M. Rothman. Madison: Prehistory Press, 153–174.

Scott, Raymond J. 1998. "Beginnings of Sedentism in the Lowlands of Northwestern South America." In *Recent Advances in the Archaeology of the Northern Andes,* ed. A. Oyuela-Caycedo and J.S. Raymond. Los Angeles: Institute of Archaeology, University of California, Los Angeles, Monograph 39, 11–19.

Sease, Catherine. 1994. *A Conservation Manual for the Field Archaeologist.* Los Angeles: Institute of Archaeology, University of California.

Sebastian, Lynne. 1992. *The Chaco Anasazi: Sociopolitical Evolution in the Prehistoric Southwest.* Cambridge: Cambridge University Press.

Semenov, S.A. 1970. *Prehistoric Technology.* Bath, UK: Adams & Dart.

Service, Elman R. 1975. *Origins of the State and Civilization: The Process of Cultural Evolution.* New York: Norton.

Shanks, Michael, and Christopher Tilley. 1992. *Re-constructing Archaeology: Theory and Practice.* London: Routledge.

Sharer, Robert J. 1994. *The Ancient Maya.* Stanford: Stanford University Press.

———. 2001. "Classic Maya." In *Encyclopedia of Prehistory,* Vol. 5: *Middle America,* ed. P.N. Peregrine and M. Ember. New York: Kluwer/Plenum, 69–81.

Sharer, Robert J., and David Grove. 1989. *Regional Perspectives on the Olmec.* Cambridge: Cambridge University Press.

Sharma, G.R. 1980. *History to Prehistory: Archaeology of the Ganga Valley and the Vindhyas.* Allahabad: Department of Ancient History, Culture, and Archaeology, University of Allahabad.

Sharma, G.R., V.D. Misra, D. Mandal, B.B. Misra, and J.N. Pal. 1980. *Beginnings of Agriculture: From Hunting and Food Gathering to Domestication of Plants and Animals.* Allahabad: Abinash Prakashan.

Shaw, C.T. 1977. "Hunters, Gatherers, and First Farmers in West Africa." In *Hunters, Gatherers and First Farmers Beyond Europe,* ed. J.V.S. Megaw. Leicester: Leicester University Press, 69–126.

———. 1978. *Nigeria: Its Archaeology and Early History.* London: Thames and Hudson.

Shelach, Gideon. 1998. "Settlement Pattern Study in Northeast China: Results and Insights on Potential Contributions of Western Theory to Chinese Archaeology." *Antiquity* 72:114–127.

———. 1999. *Leadership Strategies, Economic Activity, and Interregional Interaction: Social Complexity in Northeast China.* New York: Kluwer/Plenum.

———. 2001a. "Early Xiajiadian." In *Encyclopedia of Prehistory,* Vol. 4: *Europe,* ed. P.N. Peregrine and M. Ember. New York: Kluwer/Plenum, 25–31.

———. 2001b. "Late Xiajiadian." In *Encyclopedia of Prehistory,* Vol. 4: *Europe,* ed. P.N. Peregrine and M. Ember. New York: Kluwer/Plenum, 127–131.

Shelmerdine, Cynthia. 1997. "Review of Aegean Prehistory IV: The Palatial Bronze Age of the Southern and Central Greek Mainland." *American Journal of Archaeology* 101:537–585.

Shennan, Stephen. 1993. "Settlement and Social Change in Central Europe, 3500–1500 B.C." *Journal of World Prehistory* 7:121–162.

Shepard, Anna. 1963. *Ceramics for the Archaeologist.* Washington, DC: Carnegie Institute of Washington.

Sherratt, Andrew. 1994. "The Transformation of Early Agrarian Europe: The Later Neolithic and Copper Ages, 4500–2500 B.C." In *Oxford Illustrated Prehistory of Europe,* ed. B. Cunliffe. Oxford: Oxford University Press, 167–201.

———. 1997. *Economy and Society in Prehistoric Europe: Changing Perspectives.* Princeton: Princeton University Press.

Shinde, Vasant. 1989. "New Light on the Origin, Settlement System and Decline of the Jorwe Culture of the Deccan, India." *South Asian Studies* 5:60–72.

———. 1990. "The Malwa Culture in Maharashtra: A Study of Settlement and Subsistence Patterns." *Man and Environment* XV(2):53–60.

———. 1991. "Craft Specialization and Social Organization in the Chalcolithic Deccan, India." *Antiquity* 65(249): 796–807.

———. 1994. "The Deccan Chalcolithic: A Recent Perspective." *Man and Environment* XIX(2):169–178.

———. 2002a. "Central Indian Chalcolithic." In *Encyclopedia of Prehistory,* Vol. 8: *South and Southwest Asia,* ed. P.N. Peregrine and M. Ember. New York: Kluwer/Plenum, 34–39.

———. 2002b. "South Indian Chalcolithic." In *Encyclopedia of Prehistory,* Vol. 8: *South and Southwest Asia,* ed. P.N. Peregrine and M. Ember. New York: Kluwer/Plenum, 342–358.

Shipman, Pat. 1986. "Scavenging or Hunting in Early Hominids: Theoretical Framework and Tests." *American Anthropologist* 88:27–43.

Shishlina, Natalia. 2001. "Eurasian Steppe Nomad." In *Encyclopedia of Prehistory,* Vol. 4: *Europe,* ed. P.N. Peregrine and M. Ember. New York: Kluwer/Plenum, 124–139.

Shoocongdej, Rasmi. 2001. "Hoabinhian." In *Encyclopedia of Prehistory,* Vol. 4: *Europe,* ed. P.N. Peregrine and M. Ember. New York: Kluwer/Plenum, 71–76.

Silva, R. Jane. 1997. *An Introduction to the Study and Analysis of Flaked Stone Artifacts and Lithic Technology.* Tucson: Center for Desert Archaeology.

Silverman, Helaine. 1993. *Cahuachi in the Ancient Nasca World.* Iowa City: University of Iowa Press.

Simpson, Scott W. 2002. "Australopithecus afarensis and Human Evolution." In *Physical Anthropology: Original Readings in Method and Practice,* ed. P.N. Peregrine, C.R. Ember, and M. Ember. Upper Saddle River, NJ: Prentice Hall, 103–123.

Sinha, H.P. 1994. *Archaeological and Cultural History of North Bihar, With Special Reference to Neolithic Chirand.* New Delhi: Ramanand Vidya Bhawan.

Sinopoli, Carla M. 1991. *Approaches to Archaeological Ceramics.* New York: Plenum.

Sinopoli, Carla. 2002a. "Central India Neolithic." In *Encyclopedia of Prehistory,* Vol. 8: *South and Southwest Asia,* ed. P.N. Peregrine and M. Ember. New York: Kluwer/Plenum, 21–33.

———. 2002b. "South Indian Iron Age." In *Encyclopedia of Prehistory,* Vol. 8: *South and Southwest Asia,* ed. P.N. Peregrine and M. Ember. New York: Kluwer/Plenum, 359–367.

Slobodin, Sergi B. 1999. "Northeast Asia in the Late Pleistocene and Early Holocene." *World Archaeology* 30(3):484–502.

———. 2001a. "Kamchatka Meoslithic." In *Encyclopedia of Prehistory,* Vol. 2: *Arctic and Subarctic,* ed. P.N. Peregrine and M. Ember. New York: Kluwer/Plenum, 69–70.

———. 2001b. "Old Itel'men." In Encyclopedia of Prehistory, Vol. 2: *Arctic and Subarctic,* ed. P.N. Peregrine and M. Ember. New York: Kluwer/Plenum, 165–166.

———. 2001c. "Tarya Neolithic." In *Encyclopedia of Prehistory,* Vol. 2: *Arctic and Subarctic,* ed. P.N. Peregrine and M. Ember. New York: Kluwer/Plenum, 205–207.

Smiley, Francis E. 2001. "Basketmaker." In *Encyclopedia of Prehistory,* Vol. 6: *North America,* ed. P.N. Peregrine and M. Ember. New York: Kluwer/Plenum, 21–26.

Smith, Andrew B. 1986. "Cattle Domestication in North Africa." *African Archaeological Review* 4:197–203.

———. 1992a. *Pastoralism in Africa.* Athens: Ohio University Press.

———. 1992b. "Origins and Spread of Pastoralism in Africa." *Annual Review of Anthropology,* 21:125–141.

———. 2001. "Saharo-Sudanese Neolithic." In *Encyclopedia of Prehistory,* Vol. 1: *Africa,* ed. P.N. Peregrine and M. Ember. New York: Kluwer/Plenum, 245–259.

Smith, Bruce D. 1976. *Prehistoric Patterns of Human Behavior: A Case Study in the Mississippi Valley.* New York: Academic Press.

———. 1990. *The Mississippian Emergence.* Washington, DC: Smithsonian Institution Press.

———. 1992. *Rivers of Change.* Washington, DC: Smithsonian Institution Press.

———. 1995. *The Emergence of Agriculture.* New York: Scientific American Library.

Smith, David. 2001. "Northeast Middle Woodland." In *Encyclopedia of Prehistory,* Vol. 6: *North America,* ed. P.N. Peregrine and M. Ember. New York: Kluwer/Plenum, 358–376.

Smith, Fred H. 1984. "Fossil Hominids from the Upper Pleistocene of Central Europe and the Origin of Modern Humans." In Fred Smith and Frank Spencer, eds, *The Origins of Modern Humans.* New York: A.R. Liss, 51–136.

Smith, M.A, M. Spriggs, and B. Fankhauser. 1993. *Sahul in Review: Pleistocene Archaeology in Australia, New Guinea, and Island Melanesia.* Canberra: Department of Prehistory, Australian National University.

Smith, Michael E. 1996. *The Aztecs.* Cambridge: Blackwell.

Smith, Philip E.L. 1986. *Paleolithic Archaeology in Iran.* Philadelphia: The University Museum, University of Pennsylvania.

Snow, Dean R. 1980. *The Archaeology of New England.* New York: Academic Press.

———. 2001. "Northeast Late Woodland." In *Encyclopedia of Prehistory,* Vol. 6:

*North America,* ed. P.N. Peregrine and M. Ember. New York: Kluwer/Plenum, 339–357.

Soffer, Olga. 1987. *The Pleistocene Old World.* New York: Plenum.

Soffer, Olga, and N.D. Praslov. 1993. *From Kostenki to Clovis.* New York: Plenum.

Solecki, Rose L. 1981. *An Early Village Site at Zawi Chemi Shanidar.* Malibu: Undena.

Sorensen, M.L.S., and R. Thomas. 1989. *The Bronze Age–Iron Age Transition in Europe.* Oxford: British Archaeological Reports, International Series 483.

South, Stanley A. 1977. *Method and Theory in Historical Archeology.* New York: Academic Press.

Spencer, Allan J. 1993. *Early Egypt: The Rise of Civilization in the Nile Valley.* London: British Museum Press.

Spencer, Frank. 1984. "The Neandertals and Their Evolutionary Significance: A Brief Historical Survey." In Fred Smith and Frank Spencer, eds, *The Origins of Modern Humans.* New York: A.R. Liss, 1–50.

Spores, Ronald. 1984. *The Mixtecs in Ancient and Colonial Times.* Norman: University of Oklahoma Press.

Spriggs, Matthew. 1997. *The Island Melanesians.* Oxford: Blackwell.

Stanish, Charles. 1992. *Ancient Andean Political Economy.* Austin: University of Texas Press.

———. 2002. "Aymara Kingdoms." In *Encyclopedia of Prehistory,* Vol. 7: *South America,* ed. P.N. Peregrine and M. Ember. New York: Kluwer/Plenum, 34–37.

Stark, Barbara, and Philip J. Arnold. 1997. *Olmec to Aztec: Settlement Patterns in the Ancient Gulf Lowlands.* Tucson: University of Arizona Press.

Stark, Miriam T. 1998. "The Transition to History in the Mekong Delta: A View from Cambodia." *International Journal of Historical Archaeology* 2:175–204.

———. 2001. "Mainland Southeast Asia Late Prehistoric." In *Encyclopedia of Prehistory,* Vol. 4: *Europe,* ed. P.N. Peregrine and M. Ember. New York: Kluwer/ Plenum, 160–205.

Stein, Gil. 1989. *Rites, Riches, and Rulers: Economic Differentiation and Ceremonial Elaboration in Pre-State Societies of Mesopotamia.* Washington, DC: American Anthropological Association.

Stein, Gil, and M. S. Rothman. 1994. *Chiefdoms and Early States in the Near East: The Organizational Dynamics of Complexity.* Madison, WI: Prehistory Press.

Storey, Rebecca. 1992. *Life and Death in the Ancient City of Teotihuacan.* Tuscaloosa: University of Alabama Press.

Stoltman, James B. 1973. *The Laurel Culture in Minnesota.* St. Paul: Minnesota Historical Society, Prehistoric Archaeology Series 8.

———. 1991. *New Perspectives on Cahokia.* Madison, WI: Prehistory Press.

Stothert, Karen. 1985. "The Preceramic Las Vegas Culture of Coastal Ecuador." *American Antiquity* 50:613–637.

———. 2001. "Manteño." In *Encyclopedia of Prehistory,* Vol. 5: *Middle America,* ed. P.N. Peregrine and M. Ember. New York: Kluwer/Plenum, 303–327.

Strauss, Lawrence Guy. 1989. "On Early Hominid Use of Fire." *Current Anthropology* 30:488–491.

———. 2001. "Solutrean." In *Encyclopedia of Prehistory,* Vol. 4: *Europe,* ed. P.N. Peregrine and M. Ember. New York: Kluwer/Plenum, 328–350.

Stringer, Christopher B. 1985. "Evolution of a Species." *Geographical Magazine,* 57:601–607.

———. 2000. "Neandertals." In Eric Delson, Ian Tattersall, John van Couvering, and Alison Brooks, eds, *Encyclopedia of Human Evolution and Prehistory.* New York: Garland, 469–474.

Stringer, Christopher B., J.J. Hublin, and B. Vandermeersch. 1985. "The Origin of Anatomically Modern Humans in Western Europe." In Fred Smith and Frank Spencer, eds, *The Origins of Modern Humans.* New York: A.R. Liss, 137–201.

Sulimurski, Tadeusz. 1968. *Corded Ware and Globular Amphorae Northeast of the Carpathians.* London: Athlone.

———. 1970. *Prehistoric Russia: An Outline.* London: John Baker.

Sullivan, M.E., P.J. Hughes, and J. Golson. 1987. "Prehistoric garden terraces in the eastern highlands of Papua New Guinea." *Tools & Tillage* 5:199–213, 260.

Susman, Randall. 1994. "Fossil Evidence for Early Hominid Tool Use," *Science* (September 9):1570–1573.

Sutton, John E. 1996. "The Growth of Farming Communities in Africa from the Equator Southwards." *Azania* 29–30.

Sutton, Mark, and Brooke Arkush. 1996. *Archaeological Laboratory Methods: An Introduction.* Dubuque, IA: Kendall/ Hunt.

Swisher, C.C., G.H. Curtis, T. Jacob, A.G. Getty, A. Suprijo, and N. Widiasmoro. 1994. "Age of the Earliest Known Hominids in Java, Indonesia." *Science* (February 25):1118–1121.

Szathmary, Emöke J.E. 1993. "Genetics of Aboriginal North Americans." *Evolutionary Anthropology* 1:202–220.

Tainter, Joseph. 1988. *The Collapse of Complex Societies.* Cambridge: Cambridge University Press.

Tankersley, Kenneth B. 2001. "Early Paleoindian." In *Encyclopedia of Prehistory,* Vol. 6: *North America,* ed. P.N. Peregrine and M. Ember. New York: Kluwer/ Plenum, 130–141.

Tankersley, K.B., and B.L. Issac. 1990. "Early Paleoindian Economies of Eastern North America." *Research in Economic*

*Anthropology, Supplement 5.* Greenwich, CT: JAI Press.

Tattersall, Ian. 1999. *The Last Neanderthal.* Boulder, CO: Westview.

Taylor, R.E., and M.J. Aitken. 1997. *Chronometric Dating in Archaeology.* New York: Plenum.

Taylor, Timothy. 1994. "Thracians, Scythians, and Dacians." In *The Oxford Illustrated Prehistory of Europe,* ed B. Cunliffe. Oxford: Oxford University Press, 547–590.

———. 2001a. "East-Central European Iron Age." In *Encyclopedia of Prehistory,* Vol. 4: *Europe,* ed. P.N. Peregrine and M. Ember. New York: Kluwer/Plenum, 79–90.

———. 2001b. "Northeast European Iron Age." In *Encyclopedia of Prehistory,* Vol. 4: *Europe,* ed. P.N. Peregrine and M. Ember. New York: Kluwer/Plenum, 210–221.

Taylor, Walter W. 1948. *A Study of Archaeology.* Carbondale, Southern Illinois University Press.

———. 1988. *Contributions to Coahuila Archaeology.* Carbondale: Southern Illinois University Press.

Templeton, Alan. 1993. "The 'Eve' Hypotheses: A Genetic Critique and Reanalysis." *American Anthropologist* 95:51–72.

———. 1996. "Gene Lineages and Human Evolution." *Science* (May 31):1363.

Terberger, Thomas. 1992. "Les structures de l'habitat de Gonnersdorf." In *Le Peuplement Magdelenian: Paleogeographie Physique et Humaine,* ed. J.-P. Rigaud, H. Laville, and B. Vandermeersch. Paris: Editions du Comite des Travauz Historiques et Scientifiques, 431–441.

Thomas, Julian. 2001. *Interpretive Archaeology: A Reader.* Leicester: Leicester University Press.

Thomas, Nicholas. 1990. *Marquesan Societies: Inequality and Political Transformation in Eastern Polynesia.* Oxford: Clarendon.

Thompson, Laura. 1940. *Southern Lau, Fiji: An Ethnography.* Honolulu: Bernice P. Bishop Museum, Bulletin 162.

Thrane, Henrik. 2001. "Scandinavian Bronze Age." In *Encyclopedia of Prehistory,* Vol. 4: *Europe,* ed. P.N. Peregrine and M. Ember. New York: Kluwer/Plenum, 299–314.

Todd, Malcolm. 1992. *The Early Germans.* Oxford: Blackwell.

Tosi, Maurizio. 1986. "The Emerging Picture of Prehistoric Arabia." *Annual Review of Anthropology* 15:461–490.

Townshend, Richard F. 1998. *Ancient West Mexico.* London: Thames and Hudson.

Treistman, Judith. 1974. *Early Cultures of Szechwan and Yunnan.* Ithaca: Cornell University Press, East Asia Papers, Number 3.

Trigger, Bruce G. 1989. *A History of Archaeological Thought.* Cambridge: Cambridge University Press.

Trigger, Bruce G., B. Kemp, D. O'Connor, and A. Lloyd. 1983. *Ancient Egypt: A Social History.* Cambridge: Cambridge University Press.

Trinkaus, Erik. 1984. "Western Asia." In Fred Smith and Frank Spencer, eds, *The Origins of Modern Humans.* New York: A.R. Liss, 251–294.

———. 1985. "Pathology and the Posture of the La Chapelle-aux-Saints Neandertal." *American Journal of Physical Anthropology* 67:19–41.

———. 1986. "The Neandertals and Modern Human Origins." *Annual Review of Anthropology* 15:193–218.

Trinkaus, Erik, and W.W. Howells. 1979. "The Neanderthals." *Scientific American* (December):118–133.

Trinkaus, Erik, and Pat Shipman. 1993. "Neandertals: Images of Ourselves," *Evolutionary Anthropology* 1:194–201.

Turner, Christy G. 1989. "Teeth and Prehistory in Asia." *Scientific American* (February):88–96.

Turpin, Solveig. 2001. "Coahuilan." In *Encyclopedia of Prehistory,* Vol. 5: *Middle America,* ed. P.N. Peregrine and M. Ember. New York: Kluwer/Plenum, 82–84.

Ubelaker, Douglas H. 1989. *Human Skeletal Remains: Excavation, Analysis, Interpretation.* Washington, DC: Taraxacum.

Ucko, Peter. 1995. *Theory in Archaeology: A World Perspective.* London: Routledge.

Ucko, Peter J., and Andrée Rosenfeld. 1967. *Paleolithic Cave Art.* New York: McGraw-Hill.

Uerpmann, M. 1992. "Structuring the Late Stone Age of Southeastern Arabia." *Arabian Archaeology And Epigraphy* 3(2):65–109.

Underhill, Anne. 1994. "Variation in Settlements During the Longshan Period in Northern China." *Asian Perspectives* 33: 197–228.

———. 1997. "Current Issues in Chinese Neolithic Archaeology." *Journal of World Prehistory* 11:103–160.

———. 2001a. "Dawenkou." In *Encyclopedia of Prehistory,* Vol. 4: *Europe,* ed. P.N. Peregrine and M. Ember. New York: Kluwer/Plenum, 12–15.

———. 2001b. "Longshan." In *Encyclopedia of Prehistory,* Vol. 4: *Europe,* ed. P.N. Peregrine and M. Ember. New York: Kluwer/Plenum, 156–160.

Unger, Achim, Arno Schniewind, and Wibke Unger. 2001. *Conservation of Wood Artifacts: A Handbook.* New York: Springer.

Upham, Steadman. 1990. *The Evolution of Political Systems.* Cambridge: Cambridge University Press.

Valladas, H., J.L. Joron, G. Valladas, O. Bar-Yosef, and B. Vandermeersch. 1988. "Thermoluminescence Dating of Mousterian 'Proto-Cro-Magnon' Remains from Israel and the Origin of Modern Man." *Nature* (February 18):614–616.

van Andel, Tjeerd, and Susan Sutton. 1987. *Landscape and People of the Franchthi Region: Excavations at Franchthi Cave, Greece, 2.* Bloomington: Indiana University Press.

van den Brink, Edwin. 1988. *Archaeology of the Nile Delta.* Amsterdam: Netherlands Foundation for Archaeological Research in Egypt.

———. 1992. *The Nile Delta in Transition: 4th–3rd Millennium B.C.* Jerusalem: van den Brink.

Van Heekeren, H.R. 1958. *The Bronze–Iron Age in Indonesia.* The Hague: Martinus Nijhoff.

Van Noten, Francis. 1982. *The Archaeology of Central Africa.* Graz: Akademische Druck- und Verlangsanstalt.

van Rossum, Peter. 2001. "Early Highland Mesoamerican Preclassic." In *Encyclopedia of Prehistory,* Vol. 5: *Middle America,* ed. P.N. Peregrine and M. Ember. New York: Kluwer/Plenum, 129–146.

Vansina, Jan. 1990. *Paths in the Rain Forests: Toward a History of Political Tradition in Equatorial Africa.* London: James Currey.

Van Tilburg, Jo Anne. 1994. *Easter Island Archaeology, Ecology, and Culture.* Washington, DC: Smithsonian Institution Press.

———. 2001. "Easter Island." In *Encyclopedia of Prehistory,* Vol. 4: *Europe,* ed. P.N. Peregrine and M. Ember. New York: Kluwer/Plenum, 45–59.

Vasil'ev, S.A. 1993. "The Upper Paleolithic of Northern Asia." *Current Anthropology* 34:82–92.

Verma, A.K. 1988. *Neolithic Culture of Eastern India.* New Delhi: Ramanand Vidya Bhawan.

Vierra, Brad J. 1994. *Archaic Hunter-Gatherer Archaeology in the American Southwest.* Portales, NM: Eastern New Mexico University Contributions to Anthropology.

Vigilant, Linda, M. Stoneking, H. Harpending, K. Hawkes, and A. Wilson. 1991. "African Populations and the Evolution of Human Mitochondrial DNA." *Science* 253:1503–1507.

Vita-Finzi, Claudio. 1978. *Archaeological Sites in their Setting.* London: Thames and Hudson.

Vivian, R. Gwinn. 1990. *The Chacoan Prehistory of the San Juan Basin.* San Diego: Academic Press.

Voigt, Mary M. 1983. *Hajji Firuz Tepe, Iran: The Neolithic Settlement.* Philadelphia:

The University Museum, University of Pennsylvania.

Wadley, Lyn. 1987. *Later Stone Age Hunters and Gatherers of the Southern Transvaal.* Oxford: Cambridge Monographs in African Archaeology 25.

———. 1993. "The Pleistocene Later Stone Age South of the Limpopo River." *Journal of World Prehistory* 7:243–296.

———. 2001. "Wilton." In *Encyclopedia of Prehistory*, Vol. 1: *Africa*, ed. P.N. Peregrine and M. Ember. New York: Kluwer/Plenum, 346–354.

Wallerstein, Immanuel. 1974. *The Modern World-System I.* New York: Academic Press.

Washburn, Sherwood. 1960. "Tools and Human Evolution," *Scientific American,* September, 63.

Watkins, T. 1992. "The Beginning of the Neolithic: Searching for Meaning in Material Culture Change," *Paléorient* 18:63–75.

Watson, Patty Jo, Steven A. LeBlanc, Charles L. Redman. 1984. *Archeological Explanation: The Scientific Method in Archeology.* New York: Columbia University Press.

Wheat, Joe Ben. 1967. "A Paleo-Indian Bison Kill." *Scientific American* (January): 44–47.

Weaver, Muriel Porter. 1993. *The Aztecs, Maya, and Their Predecessors.* San Diego: Academic Press.

Weber, Andrzej. 1994. "Social Evolution among Neolithic and Early Bronze Age Foragers in the Lake Baikal Region: New Light on Old Models." *Arctic Anthropology* 31(2):1–15.

———. 1995. "The Neolithic and Early Bronze Age of the Lake Baikal Region: A Review of Recent Research." *Journal of World Prehistory* 9:99–165.

Webster, Graham. 1974. *Practical Archaeology: An Introduction to Archaeological Field-work and Excavation.* New York: St. Martin's Press.

Wedel, Waldo. 1986. *Central Plains Prehistory.* Lincoln: University of Nebraska Press.

Weeks, John M. 2001. "Late Caribbean." In *Encyclopedia of Prehistory*, Vol. 5: *Middle America,* ed. P.N. Peregrine and M. Ember. New York: Kluwer/Plenum, 221–238.

Weigand, Phil C. 2001. "West Mexico Classic." In *Encyclopedia of Prehistory*, Vol. 5: *Middle America,* ed. P.N. Peregrine and M. Ember. New York: Kluwer/Plenum, 397–415.

Weiss, Harvey, M.A. Courty, W. Wetterstrom, F. Guichard, L. Senior, R. Meadow, and A. Curnow. 1993. "The Genesis and Collapse of Third Millennium North Mesopotamian Civilization," *Science* 261:995–1004.

Wells, Peter. 1980. *Culture Contact and Culture Change: Early Iron Age Central Europe and the Mediterranean World.* Cambridge: Cambridge University Press.

———. 1981. *The Emergence of Iron Age Economy.* Cambridge, MA: Harvard University Press.

———. 1984. *Farms, Villages, and Cites: Commerce and Urban Origins in Late Prehistoric Europe.* Ithaca, NY: Cornell University Press.

Wendorf, Fred. 1968. *Prehistory of Nubia.* Dallas: Southern Methodist University Press.

———. 2001. "Late Paleolithic Egypt." In *Encyclopedia of Prehistory*, Vol. 1: *Africa,* ed. P.N. Peregrine and M. Ember. New York: Kluwer/Plenum, 116–128.

Wendorf, Fred, and R. Schild. 1976. *Prehistory of the Nile Valley.* New York: Academic Press.

———. 1980. *Prehistory of the Eastern Sahara.* New York: Academic Press.

Wendorf, Fred, R. Schild, and A. Close. 1984. *Cattle-Keepers of the Eastern Sahara.* New Delhi: Pauls Press.

———. 1989. *Prehistory of the Wadi Kubbaniya* (3 vols). Dallas: Southern Methodist University Press.

Wenke, Robert J. 1989. "Egypt: Origins of Complex Societies." *Annual Review of Anthropology* 18:129–155.

———. 1991. "The Evolution of Early Egyptian Civilization: Issue and Evidence." *Journal of World Prehistory* 5: 279–329.

———. 1999. *Patterns in Prehistory.* New York: Oxford University Press.

West, F.H. 1981. *Archaeology of Beringia.* New York: Columbia University Press.

———. 1996. *American Beginnings: The Prehistory and Palaeoecology of Beringia.* Chicago: University of Chicago Press.

Wetterstrom, Wilma. 1993. "Foraging and Farming in Egypt: The Transition from Hunting and Gathering to Horticulture in the Nile Valley." In *The Archaeology of Africa: Food, Metals, and Towns,* ed. T. Shaw, B. Andah, P. Sinclair, and A. Okapo. London: Unwin Hyman, 154–226.

Wheeler, Peter. 1984. "The Evolution of Bipedality and Loss of Functional Body Hair in Hominids," *Journal of Human Evolution* 13:91–98.

———. 1991. "The Influence of Bipedalism in the Energy and Water Budgets of Early Hominids," *Journal of Human Evolution* 23:379–388.

Wheeler, R. E. Mortimer. 1968. *The Indus Civilization.* 2nd ed. Cambridge: Cambridge University Press.

White, Devon, and Stephen Lekson. 2001. "Early Hohokam." In *Encyclopedia of Prehistory*, Vol. 6: *North America,* ed. P.N. Peregrine and M. Ember. New York: Kluwer/Plenum, 98–114.

White, J.P. 1972. *Ol Tumbuna: Archaeological Excavations in the Eastern Central Highlands, Papua New Guinea.* Canberra: Australian National University, Department of Prehistory, Terra Australis 2.

———. 1995. "Modeling the Development of Early Rice Agriculture." *Asian Perspectives* 34:37–68.

White, J.P., and J.F. O'Connell. 1982. *Prehistory of Australia, New Guinea, and Sahul.* New York: Academic Press.

White, Leslie A. 1959. *The Evolution of Culture.* New York: McGraw-Hill.

White, Randall. 1982. "Rethinking the Middle/Upper Paleolithic Transition." *Current Anthropology* 23:169–175.

White, Timothy D., G. Suwa, and B. Asfaw. 1994. "Australopithecus ramidus, a New Species of Early Hominid from Aramis, Ethiopia," *Nature* 371:306–333.

———. 1995. "Corrigendum: Australopithecus ramidus, a New Species of Early Hominid from Aramis, Ethiopia," *Nature* 375:88.

Whitley, David S. 1998. *Reader in Archaeological Theory: Post-processual and Cognitive Approaches.* New York: Routledge.

Whittaker, John. 1994. *Flintknapping: Making and Understanding Stone Tools.* Austin: University of Texas Press.

Whittle, Alasdair. 1985. *Neolithic Europe: A Survey.* Cambridge: Cambridge University Press.

———. 1996. *Europe in the Neolithic: The Creation of New Worlds.* Cambridge: Cambridge University Press.

Wilford, John Noble. 1997. "Ancient German Spears Tell of Mighty Hunters of Stone Age." *New York Times* (March 4):C6.

Wilkinson, Robert L. 1995. "Yellow Fever: Ecology, Epidemiology, and Role in the Collapse of the Classic Lowland Maya Civilization," *Medical Anthropology* 16: 269–294.

Wilkinson, T.J. 1990. "Soil Development and Early Land Use in the Jazira Region, Upper Mesopotamia." *World Archaeology* 22:87–103.

Wilkinson, Toby. 1999. *Early Dynastic Egypt.* London: Routledge.

Willey, Gordon, and Jeremy Sabloff. 1980. *A History of American Archaeology.* San Francisco: W.H. Freeman.

Williams, M.A.J., and H. Faure. 1982. *The Sahara and the Nile: Quarternary Environments and Prehistoric Occupation in Northern Africa.* Rotterdam: A.A. Balkema.

Williams, Mark, and Daniel Elliott. 1998. *A World Engraved: Archaeology of the Swift Creek Culture.* Tuscaloosa: University of Alabama Press.

Williams, Mark, and G. Shapiro. 1990. *Lamar Archaeology: Mississippian Chiefdoms in the Deep South.* Tuscaloosa: University of Alabama Press.

Wills, Wirt H. 2001. "Middle Desert Archaic." In *Encyclopedia of Prehistory,* Vol. 6: *North America,* ed. P.N. Peregrine and M. Ember. New York: Kluwer/ Plenum, 306–317.

Wills, Wirt H., and Robert D. Leonard. 1994. *The Ancient Southwestern Community.* Albuquerque: University of New Mexico Press.

Wilson, David A. 1988. *Prehistoric Settlement Patterns in the Lower Santa Valley, Peru.* Washington, DC: Smithsonian Institution Press.

Wilson, John. 1987. *From the Beginning: The Archaeology of the Maori.* Auckland: Penguin.

Wilson, S.M. 1997. *The Indigenous Peoples of the Caribbean.* Gainesville: University Press of Florida.

Winchell, Frank. 2001a. "Early Khartoum." In *Encyclopedia of Prehistory,* Vol. 1: *Africa,* ed. P.N. Peregrine and M. Ember. New York: Kluwer/Plenum, 86–94.

———. 2001b. "Khartoum Neolithic." In *Encyclopedia of Prehistory,* Vol. 1: *Africa,* ed. P.N. Peregrine and M. Ember. New York: Kluwer/Plenum, 110–115.

Windes, Thomas C. 1993. *The Spadefoot Toad Site* (2 vols.). Santa Fe: National Park Service, Reports of the Chaco Center 12.

Wiseman, James. 1998. "Reforming Academia." *Archaeology* 51 (September/ October): 27–30.

———. 2001. "Declaration of Independence." *Archaeology* 54 (July/August): 10–12.

Wittfogel, Karl. 1957. *Oriental Despotism: A Comparative Study of Total Power.* New Haven: Yale University Press.

Wolpoff, Milford. 1999. *Paleoanthropology.* Boston: McGraw-Hill.

Wolpoff, Milford H., and Abel Nkini. 1985. "Early and Early Middle Pleistocene Hominids from Asia and Africa." In Eric Delson, ed., *Ancestors: The Hard Evidence.* New York: A.R. Liss, 202–204.

Wood, Bernard A. 1992. "Evolution of Australopithecines." In *The Cambridge Encyclopedia of Human Evolution,* ed. Steve Jones, Robert Martin, and David Pilbeam. New York: Cambridge University Press.

Wood, W. Raymond. 1998. *Archaeology on the Great Plains.* Lawrence: University Press of Kansas.

Workman, William E. 1992. "The Kachemak Tradition Occupation of Kachemak Bay: Site Inventory Similarities, Variation and the Question of Settlement Systems." *Anthropological Papers of the University of Alaska* 24(1–2):205–227.

Wotzka, Hans-Peter. 2001a. "Central African Neolithic." In *Encyclopedia of Prehistory,* Vol. 1: *Africa,* ed. P.N. Peregrine and M. Ember. New York: Kluwer/Plenum, 46–58.

———. 2001b. "Central African Iron Age." In *Encyclopedia of Prehistory,* Vol. 1: *Africa,* ed. P.N. Peregrine and M. Ember. New York: Kluwer/Plenum, 59–76.

Wright, Gary A. 1971. "Origins of Food Production in Southwestern Asia: A Survey of Ideas." *Current Anthropology* 12.

Wright, Henry T. 1986. "The Evolution of Civilizations." In *American Archaeology Past and Future,* ed. David J. Meltzer, Don D. Fowler, and Jeremy A. Sabloff. Washington, DC: Smithsonian Institution Press, 323–365.

Wright, Henry T., and Gregory A. Johnson. 1975. "Population, Exchange, and Early State Formation in Southwestern Iran." *American Anthropologist* 77:267.

Wright, James V. 1967. *The Laurel Tradition and the Middle Woodland Period.* Ottawa: National Museum of Canada, Bulletin 217.

———. 1972a. *The Shield Archaic.* Ottawa: National Museum of Man, Publications in Archaeology 3.

———. 1972b. *Ontario Prehistory: An Eleven Thousand Year Archaeological Outline.* Ottawa: National Museum of Man.

———. 1995. *A History of the Native People of Canada,* Vol. 1: *10,000–1000 B.C.* Hull: Canadian Museum of Civilization, Mercury Series 152.

Wright, James V., and James E. Anderson. 1963. *The Donaldson Site.* Ottawa: National Museum of Canada, Bulletin 184.

Wright, M. 1985. "Contacts between Egypt and Syro-Palestine during the Protodynastic Period." *Biblical Archaeologist* 48:240–253.

Wu Rukang, and John Olsen. 1985. *Paleoanthropology and Paleolithic Archaeology in the People's Republic of China.* Orlando: Academic Press.

Wyroll, Thomas. 2001. "North African Protohistoric." In *Encyclopedia of Prehistory,* Vol. 1: *Africa,* ed. P.N. Peregrine and M. Ember. New York: Kluwer/Plenum, 220–238.

Yamei, Hou, R. Potts, and Y. Baoyin, et al. 2000. "Mid-Pleistocene Acheulean-like Stone Technology of the Bose Basin, South China." *Science* 287:1622–1626.

Yamanaka, Ichiro, and Peter N. Peregrine. 2001. "Japanese Upper Paleolithic." In *Encyclopedia of Prehistory,* Vol. 3: *East Asia and Oceania,* ed. P.N. Peregrine and M. Ember. New York: Kluwer/Plenum, 117–118.

Yerkes, R.W. 1988. "The Woodland and Mississippian Traditions in the Prehistory of Midwestern North America." *Journal of World Prehistory* 2:307–358.

Yoffee, Norman. 1995. "Political Economy in Early Mesopotamian States." *Annual Review of Anthropology* 24:281–311.

Yoffee, N., and J. J. Clark. 1993. *Early Stages in the Evolution of Mesopotamian Civilization.* Tucson: University of Arizona Press.

Yoffee, Norman, and George Cowgill. 1988. *The Collapse of Ancient States and Civilizations.* Tucson, AZ: University of Arizona Press.

Yoffee, Norman, and Andrew Sherratt. 1993. *Archaeological Theory: Who Sets the Agenda?* New York: Cambridge University Press.

Yun, Mu-Byong. 1987. *Bronze Age of Korea.* Seoul: Yekyong.

Zarins, Juris. 1989. "Pastoralism in Southwest Asia: The Second Millennium B.C." In *The Walking Larder,* ed. J. Clutton-Brock. London: Unwin Hyman, 127–155.

———. 2002a. "Early Arabian Pastoral." In *Encyclopedia of Prehistory,* Vol. 8: *South and Southwest Asia,* ed. P.N. Peregrine and M. Ember. New York: Kluwer/ Plenum, 77–85.

———. 2002b. "Middle Arabian Pastoral." In *Encyclopedia of Prehistory,* Vol. 8: *South and Southwest Asia,* ed. P.N. Peregrine and M. Ember. New York: Kluwer/Plenum, 284–290.

———. 2002c. "Late Arabian Pastoral." In *Encyclopedia of Prehistory,* Vol. 8: *South and Southwest Asia,* ed. P.N. Peregrine and M. Ember. New York: Kluwer/ Plenum, 261–268.

Zeidler, James A. 2001. "Central Coast Regional Chiefdoms." In *Encyclopedia of Prehistory,* Vol. 5: *Middle America,* ed. P.N. Peregrine and M. Ember. New York: Kluwer/Plenum, 1–11.

Zeitlin, Robert N. 1984. "Summary Report on Three Seasons of Field Investigations into the Archaic Period Prehistory of Lowland Belize." *American Anthropologist* 86:358–368.

Zettler, Richard, and Lee Horne. 1998. *Treasures from the Royal Tombs of Ur.* Philadelphia: University of Pennsylvania Museum.

Zhimin, An. 1988. "Archaeological Research on Neolithic China." *Current Anthropology* 29:753–759.

———. 1992a. "Neolithic Communities in Eastern Parts of Central Asia." In *History of Civilizations of Central Asia,* Vol. 1, ed. A.H. Dani and V.M. Masson. Paris: UNESCO, 153–189.

———. 1992b. "The Bronze Age in Eastern Parts of Central Asia." In *History of Civilizations of Central Asia*, Vol. 1: ed. A.H. Dani and V.M. Masson. Paris: UNESCO, 319–336.

Zihlman, Adrienne L. 1992. "The Emergence of Human Locomotion: The Evolutionary Background and Environmental Context." In *Topics in Primatology*, Vol. 1: *Human Origins*, ed. Toshisada Nishida, William C. McGrew, Peter Marler, Martin Pickford, and Frans B. M. de Waal. Tokyo: University of Tokyo Press, 409–422.

Zimmerman, Larry J. 1985. *Peoples of Prehistoric South Dakota*. Lincoln: University of Nebraska Press.

———. 2001. "Northern Plains Village." In *Encyclopedia of Prehistory*, Vol. 6: *North America*, ed. P.N. Peregrine and M. Ember. New York: Kluwer/Plenum, 377–388.

Zohary, Daniel. 1969. "The Progenitors of Wheat and Barley in Relation to Domestication and Agricultural Dispersal in the Old World." In *The Domestication and Exploitation of Plants and Animals*, ed. Ucko and Dimbleby. Chicago: Aldine.

Zvelevbil, M. 1986. *Hunters in Transition: Mesolithic Societies of Temperate Eurasia and Their Transition to Farming*. Cambridge: Cambridge University Press.

# Photo Credits

**CHAPTER 1** AP/Wide World Photos: 3; Lowell Georgia: 4; Clark Erickson: 8; Naturhistorisches Museum, Vienna, Austria/Erich Lessing/Art Resource, N.Y.: 10; John Egan, Irish-American, 1810–1882. c. 1850. "Panorama of the Monumental Grandeur of the Mississippi Valley." Tempera on lightweight fabric, 90 x 4176 in. (228.6 x 10607.1 cm). The Saint Louis Art Museum. Eliza McMillan Fund: 11.

**CHAPTER 2** Peter N. Peregrine: 18 (top and bottom); Peter N. Peregrine: 19; Peter N. Peregrine: 20; Courtesy Frank H. McClung Museum, The University of Tennessee, Knoxville: 21 (top); Amos, James L./Photo Researchers, Inc.: 21 (bottom); Peter N. Peregrine: 24.

**CHAPTER 3** Peter N. Peregrine: 46; Peter N. Peregrine: 47; Peter N. Peregrine: 49; Dean Conger/Corbis: 51; Courtesy Frank H. McClung Museum, The University of Tennessee, Knoxville: 52; Dr. Roger Grace: 53; Bettmann/Corbis: 55; Peter N. Peregrine: 56.

**CHAPTER 4** © Christian Jegou/Photo Researchers, Inc.: 67; Glen Wexler/TimePix: 71; © John Reader/Photo Researchers, Inc.: 77; R.I.M. Campbell © Bob Campbell: 82; Kenneth Garrett Photography: 83.

**CHAPTER 5** NGS Image Collection/Gordon Gahan/National Geographic Society: 92; The Natural History Museum, London: 96; National Museums of Kenya, Nairobi. © David L. Brill. David L. Brill/Brill Atlanta: 100 (bottom); NGS Image Collection/Eli Richman/National Geographic Society: 103; Peter N. Peregrine: 110 (top).

**CHAPTER 6** Chris Hellier/Corbis: 118; The Natural History Museum, London: 127; Philippe Pailly/Eurelios Photographic Press Agency: 132.

**CHAPTER 7** Roger De La Harpe/Corbis: 143; Pictures of Record, Inc.: 145; NGS Image Collection/Jack Unruh/National Geographic Society: 146; © Archivo Iconografico, S.A./Corbis: 150; Peter N. Peregrine: 156; University of Colorado Museum-Boulder, Joe Ben Wheat Photo: 157; NGS Image Collection/Kenneth Garrett/National Geographic Society: 158.

**CHAPTER 8** Wolfgang Kaehler/Corbis: 168; Kennan Ward/Corbis: 174; Dan Guravich/Corbis: 176; Tom Brakefield/Corbis: 179; NGS Image Collection/Edward S. Curtis/National Geographic Society: 180; Richard Maynard/Corbis: 182.

**CHAPTER 9** Corbis: 192; Peter N. Peregrine: 194; Pictures of Record, Inc.: 196; Peter N. Peregrine: 197; Cahokia Mounds State Historic Site: 199; Picture Desk, Inc./Kobal Collection: 202; Peter N. Peregrine: 203; National Museum of American Art/Art Resource, N.Y.: 204; William Henry Jackson/Corbis: 206; Werner Forman Archive, Utah Museum of Natural History/Art Resource, N.Y.: 208; Donald Hiser/City of Phoenix/Pueblo Grande Museum and Archaeological Park: 211; Henry Groskinsky/TimePix: 213; Andrew T. Kelley/Corbis: 216; Alfred L. Kroeber/Phoebe Hearst Museum of Anthropology: 218.

**CHAPTER 10** Corbis: 233; Chris Fox/Corbis: 235; Discovered by Dr. Joyce Marcus and Kent Flannery/Drawing by Marc Orsen. Courtesy of Joyce Marcus: 236 (top); Pictures of Record, Inc.: 236 (bottom); Pictures of Record, Inc.: 237; Pictures of Record, Inc.: 242;

Harry Shafer: 244; Pictures of Record, Inc.: 245; Pictures of Record, Inc.: 248 (top and bottom); Pictures of Record, Inc.: 250; Gianni Dagli Orti/Corbis: 251; Rudolf Schirimpff/Art Resource, N.Y.: 253; University of Pennsylvania Museum, Philadelphia (Neg.# S4-140668)/University of Pennsylvania Museum of Archaeology and Anthropology: 255; D.K. Bonatti, Christopher Columbus reaching New World. © Historical Picture Archive/Corbis: 257.

**CHAPTER 11** Werner Forman Archive/Courtesy Entwistle Gallery, London/Art Resource, N.Y.: 270; Marilyn Bridges/Corbis: 271; Marilyn Bridges/Corbis: 272; Brian A. Vikander/Corbis: 273; Marilyn Bridges/Corbis: 274; Picture Desk, Inc./Kobal Collection: 275; Teresa Cristina de Borges Franco: 282.

**CHAPTER 12** Wolfgang Kaehler/Corbis: 289 (bottom); Courtesy Fred Wendorf/Southern Methodist University: 292; Roger Wood/Corbis: 295; Robert Holmes/Corbis: 303; Werner Forman Archive/Courtesy Entwistle Gallery, London/Art Resource, N.Y.: 309.

**CHAPTER 13** Archivo Iconografico, S.A./Corbis: 320; Picture Desk, Inc./Kobal Collection: 321; Jason Hawkes/Corbis: 324; National Museum of Denmark: 325; Picture Desk, Inc./Kobal Collection: 326; NGS Image Collection/Godan Gahan/National Geographic Society: 330; Picture Desk, Inc./Kobal Collection: 332; Picture Desk, Inc./Kobal Collection: 336; Paul Almasy/Corbis: 337; Eric Lessing/Art Resource, N.Y.: 339 (top and bottom); Galen Rowell/Corbis: 341; Jeannine Kavis-Kimball/AERI: 342; Archivo Iconografico, S.A./Corbis: 343.

**CHAPTER 14** Scala/Art Resource, N.Y.: 352; Roger Ressmeyer/Corbis: 354; Lowell Georgia/Corbis: 357; Sakamoto Photo Research Laboratory/Corbis: 361; Asian Art & Archaeology, Inc./Corbis: 366; Lowell Georgia/Corbis: 367; Adrian Arbib/Corbis: 369; Courtesy © Dr. Glenn R. Summerhayes: 370; Hulton-Deutsch/Corbis: 371; © The Natural History Museum, London: 374.

**CHAPTER 15** Kevin Schafer/Corbis: 386; Shanti Pappu, Ph.D. © Deccan College, Post-graduate and Research Institute, Pune: 390; NGS Image Collection/Randy Olson/National Geographic Society: 393 (top and bottom); Paul Almasy/Corbis: 396; Scala/Art Resources, N.Y.: 397; Archivo Iconografico, S.A./Corbis: 399; Christie's Images/Corbis: 402; NGS Image Collection/Steve Raymer/National Geographic Society: 406 (top); Pictures of Record, Inc.: 409; Pictures of Record, Inc.: 410; NGS Image Collection/Kenneth Garrett/National Geographic Society: 412; Hanan Isachar/Corbis: 413; Franck Raux/Art Resource, N.Y.: 416; Archivo Iconografico, S.A./Corbis: 420 (bottom); Nik Wheeler/Corbis: 422; Art Resource, N.Y.: 424.

**CHAPTER 16** Musee des Antiquites Nationales, St.-Germain-en-Laye, France/Erich Lessing/Art Resource, N.Y.: 436 (top); Courtesy of Joyce Marcus and Kent Flannery, University of Michigan: 441; © Robert S. Peabody Museum of Archaeology, Phillips Academy, Andover, Massachusetts. All Rights Reserved/Peabody Museum of Archaeology and Ethnology: 446; Pictures of Record, Inc.: 448; Swiss National Museum, Zurich. Inventory number: A-432. Neg. number 143463/Schweizerisches Landesmuseum: 449.

**CHAPTER 17** Robert Holmes/Corbis: 456; Courtesy of Museum of Anthropology, University of Michigan: 457 (top); Associated

# Name Index

# Subject Index